WH S

Revision

AS and A Level

mathematics

First published 2000
exclusively for WHSmith by

Hodder and Stoughton Educational
338 Euston Road
LONDON NW1 3BH

A CIP record for this book is available from the British Library

Text: Linda Bostock, Sue Chandler, Philip Hooper
Mind Maps: The Buzan Centres

ISBN 0-340-74329-8

10 9 8 7 6 5 4 3 2 1

Year 2005 2004 2003 2002 2001 2000

Typeset by Tech-Set Ltd, Gateshead, Tyne and Wear.

Printed and bound in Great Britain for Hodder & Stoughton Educational by
Redwood Books, Trowbridge, Wilts.

Contents

Revision for A level success iv
Introduction vii

Pure Mathematics **1**

- **1** Mathematical language 5
- **2** Coordinate geometry and problem solving 9
- **3** Algebra 12
- **4** Functions 17
- **5** Sequences and series 22
- **6** Radians, arcs and sectors 25
- **7** Exponential, logarithmic and modulus functions 28
- **8** Trigonometry 32
- **9** Differentiation 37
- **10** Integration 41
- **11** Proof 45
- **12** Algebra 2 47
- **13** Coordinate geometry 2 51
- **14** Trigonometry 2 56
- **15** Differentiation 2 61
- **16** Integration 2 66
- **17** Differential equations 73
- **18** The binomial theorem 76
- **19** Iteration 79
- **20** Vectors 81

Mechanics **87**

- **1** Force 90
- **2** Working with forces 94
- **3** Constant acceleration and force 100
- **4** Work, energy and power 107
- **5** Impulse and momentum 112
- **6** Projectiles 116
- **7** Parallel forces, moment 120
- **8** Centre of gravity 125
- **9** Equilibrium in a plane 130
- **10** Newton's Law of Restitution 135
- **11** Motion in a horizontal circle 140
- **12** Motion in a vertical circle 145
- **13** Hooke's Law and elastic strings 151
- **14** Variable motion in a plane 155
- **15** Simple harmonic motion 160
- **16** Centre of mass of a rigid body 166

Statistics **171**

- **1** Collecting and defining data 172
- **2** Representing data 174
- **3** Methods for summarising sample data 180
- **4** Probability 187
- **5** Random variables 196
- **6** Correlation and regression 202
- **7** The binomial and Poisson distributions 209
- **8** The normal distribution 216
- **9** Estimation and confidence intervals 223
- **10** Hypothesis testing 230
- **11** The χ^2 significance test 239

Index **249**

You are now in the most important educational stage of your life and are soon to take exams that may have a major impact on your future career and goals. As one A Level student put it: 'It's crunch time!'

At this crucial stage of your life, the thing you need even more than subject knowledge is the knowledge of **how** to remember, **how** to read faster, **how** to comprehend, **how** to study, **how** to take notes and **how** to organise your thoughts. You need to know how to **think**; you need a basic introduction on how to use that super computer inside your head – your brain.

The next few pages contain a goldmine of information on how you can achieve success, both at school and in your A Level exams, as well as in your professional or university career. These pages will give you information on memory, thinking skills, speed reading and study that will enable you to be successful in all your academic pursuits. You will learn:

1 How to remember more *while* you are learning.
2 How to remember more *after* you have finished a class or a study period.
3 How to use special techniques to improve your memory.
4 How to use a revolutionary note-taking technique called Mind Maps that will double your memory and help you to write essays and answer exam questions.
5 How to read everything faster, while at the same time improving comprehension and concentration.
6 How to zap your revision.

How to understand, improve and master your memory

Your memory really is like a muscle. Don't exercise it and it will grow weaker; do exercise it and it will grow incredibly more powerful. There are really only four main things you need to understand about your memory in order to increase its power dramatically:

1 Recall during learning – you must take breaks!

When you are studying, your memory can concentrate, understand and remember well for between 20 and 45 minutes at a time. Then it needs a break. If you carry on for longer than this without one, your memory starts to break down. If you study for hours non-stop, you will remember only a fraction of what you have been trying to learn and you will have wasted valuable revision time.

So, ideally, *study for less than an hour*, then take a five- to ten-minute break. During this break, listen to music, go for a walk, do some exercise or just daydream. (Daydreaming is a necessary brainpower booster – geniuses do it regularly.)

During the break your brain will be sorting out what it has been learning and you will go back to your study with the new information safely stored and organised in your memory banks.

Make sure you take breaks at regular intervals as you work through your *Revise AS and A Level* book.

2 Recall after learning – surfing the waves of your memory

What do you think begins to happen to your memory straight after you have finished learning something? Does it immediately start forgetting? No! Your brain actually *increases* its power and carries on remembering. For a short time after your study session, your brain integrates the information making a more complete picture of everything it has just learnt. Only then does the rapid decline in memory begin, and as much as 80% of what you have learnt can be forgotten in a day.

However, if you catch the top of the wave of your memory, and briefly review back what you have been revising at the correct time, the memory is stamped in far more strongly and stays at the crest of the wave for much longer. To maximise your brain's power to remember, take a few minutes and use a Mind Map to review what you have learnt at the end of a day. Then review it at the end of a week, again at the end of a month and, finally, a week before the exams. That way you'll surf-ride your memory wave all the way to your exam, success, and beyond!

3 The memory principle of association

The muscle of your memory becomes stronger when it can **associate** – when it can link things together.

Think about your best friend and all the things your mind automatically links with that person. Think about your favourite hobby and all the associations your mind has when you think about (remember) that hobby.

When you are studying, use this memory principle to make associations between the elements in your subjects and to thus improve both your memory and your chances of success.

4 The memory principle of imagination

The muscle of your memory will improve significantly if you can produce big **images** in your mind. Rather than just memorising the name of an historical character, **imagine** that character as if you were a video producer filming that person's life.

Your new success formula: Mind Maps®

You have noticed that when people go on holidays or travels they take maps. Why? To give them a general picture of where they are going, to help them locate places of special interest and importance, to help them find things more easily and to help them remember distances, locations and so on.

It is exactly the same with your mind and with study.

If you have a 'map of the territory' of what you have to learn, then everything is easier. In learning and study, the Mind Map is that special tool.

As well as helping you with all areas of study, the Mind Map actually *mirrors the way your brain works.* Your Mind Maps can be used for taking notes from your study books, taking notes in class, preparing your homework, presenting your homework, reviewing your tests, checking your and your friends' knowledge in any subject, and for *helping you understand anything you learn.*

As you will see, Mind Maps use, throughout, Imagination and Association. As such, they automatically strengthen your memory muscle every time you use them. Throughout this *Revise AS and A Level* book you will find Mind Maps that summarise the most important areas of the subject you are studying. Study them, add some colour, personalise them, and then have a go at drawing your own – you will remember them far better! Put them on your walls and in your files for a quick and easy review of the topic.

How to draw a Mind Map

1 Start in the middle of the page with the paper turned sideways. This gives your brain more radiant freedom for its thoughts.

2 Always start by drawing a picture or symbol. Why? because **a picture is worth a thousand words to your brain**. Try to use at least three colours, as colour helps your memory even more.

3 Let your thoughts flow, and write or draw your ideas on coloured branching lines connected to your central image. These key symbols and words are the headings for your topic.

4 Next, add facts and ideas by drawing more, smaller, branches on to the appropriate main branches, just like a tree.

5 Always print each word clearly on its line. Use only one word per line.

6 To link ideas and thoughts on different branches, use arrows, colours, underlining and boxes.

How to read a Mind Map

1 Begin in the centre, the focus of your topic.

2 The words/images attached to the centre are like chapter headings; read them next.

3 Always read out from the centre, in every direction (even on the left-hand side, where you will have to read from right to left; instead of the usual left to right).

Using Mind Maps

Mind Maps are a versatile tool – use them for taking notes in class or from books, for solving problems, for brainstorming with friends, and for reviewing and revising for exams – their uses are infinite! You will find them invaluable for planning essays for coursework and exams. Number your main branches in the order in which you want to use them and off you go – the main headings for your essay are done *and* all your ideas are logically organised.

Super speed reading and study

What happens to your comprehension as your reading speed rises? 'It goes down.' Wrong! It seems incredible, but it has been proved that the faster you read, the more you comprehend and remember.

So here are some tips to help you to practise reading faster – you'll cover the ground much more quickly, remember more *and* have more time for revision and leisure activities.

How to make study easy for your brain

When you are going somewhere, is it easier to know beforehand where you are going, or not? Obviously it is easier if you do know. It is the same for your brain and a book. When you get a new book, there are seven things you can do to help your brain get to 'know the territory' faster.

1 Scan through the whole book in less than 20 minutes, as you would do if you were in a shop thinking whether or not to buy it. This gives your brain control.

2 Think about what you already know about the subject. You'll often find out it's a lot more than you thought. A good way of doing this is to draw a quick Mind Map on everything you know after you have skimmed through it.

3 Ask who, what, why, where, when and how questions about what is in the book. Questions help your brain 'fish' the knowledge out.

4 Ask your friends what they know about the subject. This helps them review the knowledge in their own brains and helps your brain get new knowledge about what you are studying.

5 Have another quick speed through the book, this time looking for any diagrams, pictures and illustrations, and also at the beginnings and ends of chapters. Most information is contained in the beginnings and ends.

6 Build up a Mind Map as you study the book. This helps your brain organise and hold (remember) information as you study.

7 If you come across any difficult parts in your book, mark them and move on. Your brain *will* be able to solve the problems when you come back to them a little bit later, much like saving the difficult bits of a jigsaw puzzle for later. When you have finished the book, quickly review it one more time and then discuss it with friends. This will lodge it permanently in your memory banks.

Super speed reading

1 First read the whole text (whether it's a lengthy book or an exam paper) very quickly, to give your brain an overall idea of what's ahead and get it working. (It's like sending out a scout to look at the territory you have to cover – it's much easier when you know what to expect.) Then read the text again for more detailed information.

2 Have the text a reasonable distance away from your eyes. In this way your eye/brain system will be able to see more at a glance and will naturally begin to read faster.

3 Take in groups of words at a time. Rather than reading 'slowly and carefully', read faster, more enthusiastically. Your comprehension will rocket!

4 Take in phrases rather than single words while you read.

5 Use a guide. Your eyes are designed to follow movement, so a thin pencil underneath the lines you are reading, moved smoothly along, will 'pull' your eyes to faster speeds.

Helpful hints for exam revision

To avoid exam panic, cram at the start of your course, not the end. It takes the same amount of time, so you may as well use it where it is best placed!

Use Mind Maps throughout your course and build a Master Mind Map for each subject – a giant Mind Map that summarises everything you know about the subject.

Use memory techniques, such as mnemonics (verses or systems for remembering things like dates and events or lists).

Get together with one or two friends to revise, compare Mind Maps and discuss topics.

And finally ...

- *Have fun while you learn* – studies show that those people who enjoy what they are doing understand and remember it more and generally do better.
- *Use your teachers* as resource centres. Ask them for help with specific topics and with more general advice on how you can improve your all-round performance.
- *Personalise your* ***Revise AS and A Level*** book by underlining and highlighting, by adding notes and pictures. Allow your brain to have a conversation with it!

Your amazing brain and its amazing cells

Your brain is like a super computer. The world's best computers have only a few thousand or hundred thousand computer chips. Your brain has 'computer chips' too; they are called brain cells. Unlike the computer, you do not have only a few thousand computer chips – the number of brain cells in your head is a *million million*! This means you are a genius just waiting to discover yourself! All you have to do is learn how to get those brain cells working together, and you'll not only become more smart, you'll have more free time to pursue your other fun activities.

The more you understand your amazing brain, the more it will repay and amaze you!

Introduction

This is a revision guide – it is not intended to replace a text book or course notes but to be used as an extra resource.

The material in this book concentrates on how to use the facts. If you do not understand where these facts come from or what they mean, use your notes and text books. There are many books on A level mathematics – if you cannot follow an explanation in one book, find others and try them. You do not need to buy other books – use libraries.

There are often several ways of answering questions on particular topics and, in this book, we may have given a method that is not familiar to you. Use your own methods when you are happy with them and understand them.

There are questions for you to try but only enough to give you some confidence that you know what you are doing. For more practice on a topic that you feel you need to reinforce, use your own, and other, textbooks. In addition to the questions included in this book you should work questions from as many recent past examination papers as you can get your hands on.

This is your book, so use it. Write on it, draw on it, use a highlighter to mark anything you particularly want to remember. In other words use it as you would use your own notes. Also it is a good idea to make your own mind maps for topics, including on them those facts and techniques that YOU think are important.

You must consult the subject specifications for the examination you will be taking. There are two reasons why this is essential: the topics in this book cover the majority of the content specified for AS and A Level Mathematics but not every topic in every specification from every examination board is covered and a few topics that are covered may not be required for your examination. Pure Mathematics is needed by everyone but you will be combining this with either Mechanics or Statistics or some of each. You should also use your subject specifications to make sure that you know as much as possible about each paper that you will be taking: in particular, you should know what topics are to be examined, which formulae you are expected to know and what kind of calculator will be allowed.

In this revision guide

⚠ means take note of this

ℹ means that this is important information that you should learn and remember.

Pure Mathematics

1 **Mathematical language**. Glossary. Fractions. Quadratic equations. Simultaneous equations. Quadratic and cubic graphs. Mathematical reasoning.

2 **Coordinate geometry and problem solving**. Gradient of a line. Equation of a line. Parallel and perpendicular lines.

3 **Algebra**. Completing the square. Expanding brackets. Factor theorem and factorisation. Laws of logs.

4 **Functions**. Definition of a function. Inverse function. Transformations of curves.

5 **Sequences and series**. AP's and GP's.

6 **Radians, arcs and sectors**.

7 **Exponential, logarithmic and modulus functions**.

8 **Trigonometry**. Trigonometric functions and identities. Solving trig equations.

9 **Differentiation**. Differentiation of polynomials, e^x, $\ln x$. Second order derivatives. Equations of tangents and normals. Stationary values.

10 **Integration**. Definite integration. Area under a curve.

11 **Proof**. Direct proof. Proof by contradiction. Use of counter-examples.

12 **Algebra 2**. Rational functions. Algebraic division. Remainder theorem. Partial fractions.

13 **Coordinate geometry 2**. The equation of a circle. Parametric equations.

14 **Trigonometry 2**. Inverse and reciprocal trig functions. Pythagorean identities. Compound and double angle identities. Expressing $a\cos\theta + b\sin\theta$ as $r\cos(\theta+\alpha)$ and equivalent forms. Solving trig equations.

15 **Differentiation 2**. Differentiation of trig functions. Product, quotient and chain rules. Implicit and parametric differentiation.

16 **Integration 2**. Standard integrals. Integration by substitution and by parts. Integrating fractions and trig functions. Volumes of revolution. Trapezium rule.

17 **Differential equations**. Forming and solving differential equations with separable variables. Exponential growth and decay.

18 **The binomial theorem**.

19 **Iteration**. Location of roots of an equation using change of sign. Iteration using $x = g(x)$.

20 **Vectors**. Vectors in 3 dimensions. Position vectors. Distance between two points. Scalar product. Vector equation of a line. Angle between two lines. Parallel, intersecting and skew lines.

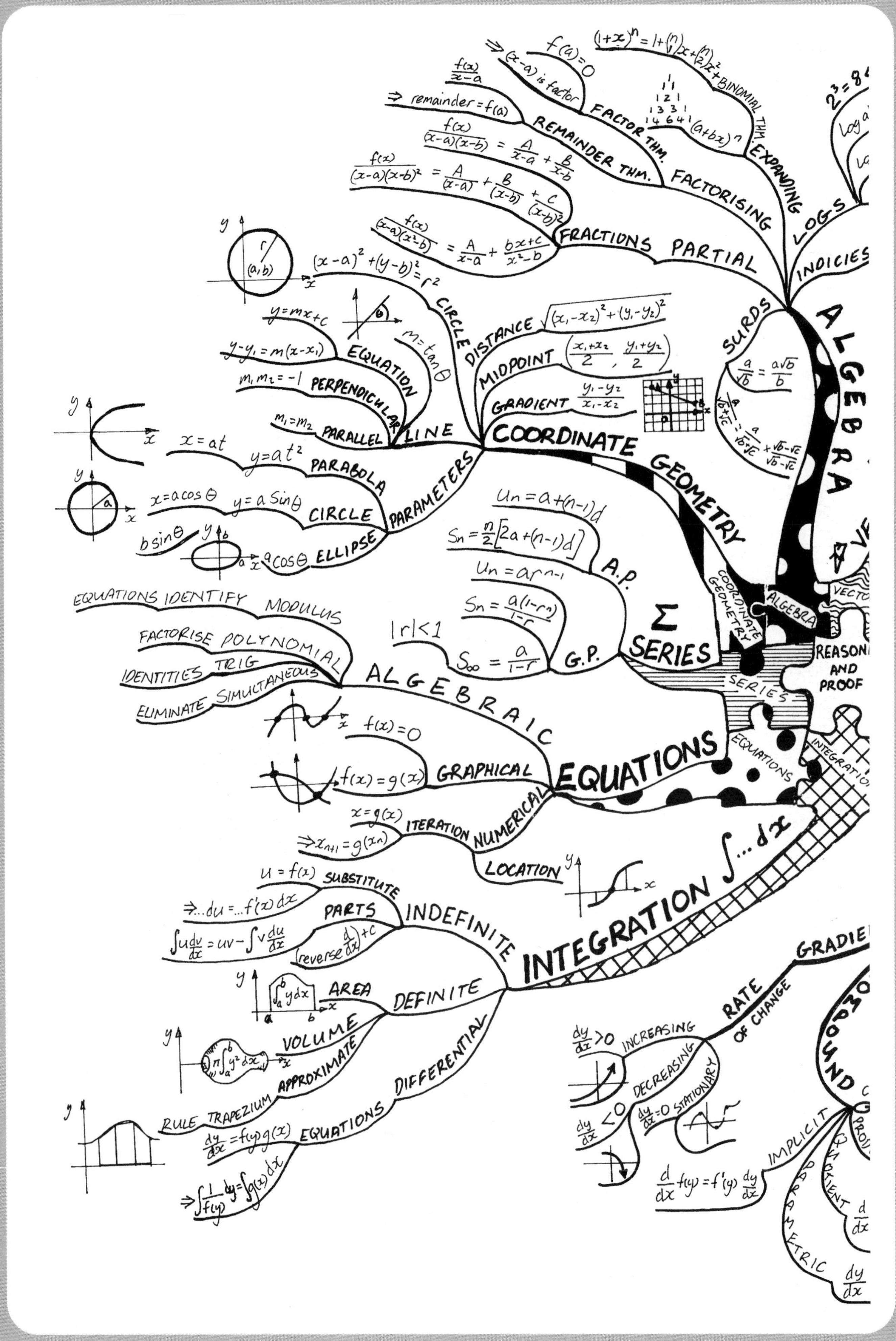
ALGEBRA
FACTOR THM.
REMAINDER THM.
FACTORISING
EXPANDING
BINOMIAL THM.
LOGS
INDICIES
SURDS
FRACTIONS PARTIAL
COORDINATE GEOMETRY
CIRCLE
EQUATION
PERPENDICULAR
PARALLEL
LINE
DISTANCE
MIDPOINT
GRADIENT
PARAMETERS
PARABOLA
CIRCLE
ELLIPSE
SERIES
A.P.
G.P.
ALGEBRAIC
EQUATIONS IDENTIFY
MODULUS
FACTORISE POLYNOMIAL
IDENTITIES TRIG
ELIMINATE SIMULTANEOUS
GRAPHICAL
EQUATIONS
NUMERICAL
ITERATION
LOCATION
INTEGRATION
INDEFINITE
SUBSTITUTE
PARTS
DEFINITE
AREA
VOLUME
APPROXIMATE
RULE TRAPEZIUM
DIFFERENTIAL EQUATIONS
RATE OF CHANGE
INCREASING
DECREASING
STATIONARY
IMPLICIT
PARAMETRIC
COMPOUND
REASONING AND PROOF

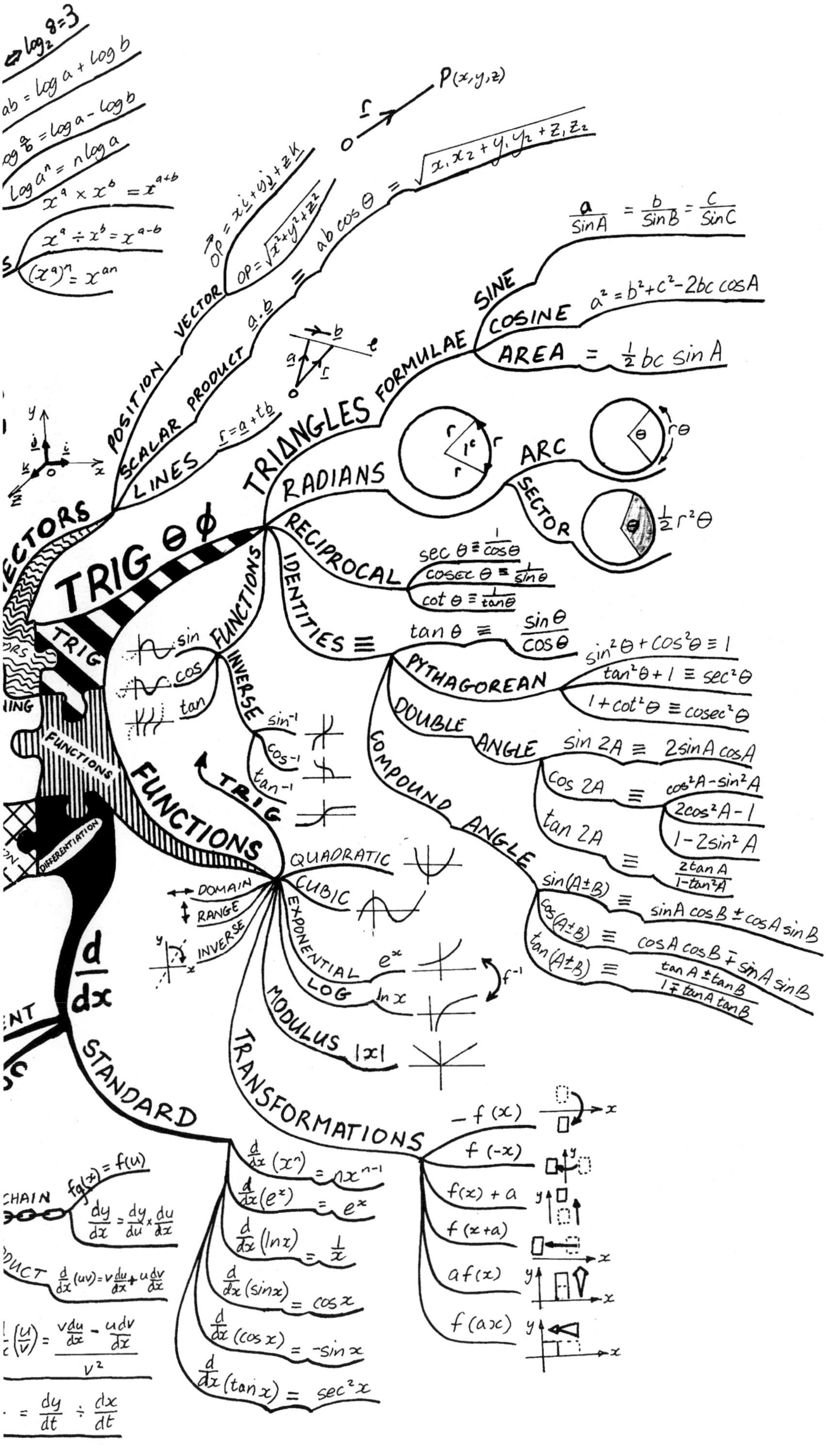

⇔ log₂ 8 = 3
log ab = log a + log b
log a/b = log a − log b
log aⁿ = n log a
x^a × x^b = x^(a+b)
x^a ÷ x^b = x^(a−b)
(x^a)ⁿ = x^(an)
P(x, y, z)
r
O
OP = xi + yj + zk
OP = √(x² + y² + z²)
= ab cos θ = √(x₁x₂ + y₁y₂ + z₁z₂)
POSITION VECTOR
SCALAR PRODUCT a.b
LINES r = a + tb
VECTORS
TRIG θ φ
TRIANGLES FORMULAE
SINE a/sin A = b/sin B = c/sin C
COSINE a² = b² + c² − 2bc cos A
AREA = ½ bc sin A
RADIANS
ARC rθ
SECTOR ½r²θ
RECIPROCAL
sec θ ≡ 1/cos θ
cosec θ ≡ 1/sin θ
cot θ ≡ 1/tan θ
IDENTITIES ≡
tan θ ≡ sin θ/cos θ
PYTHAGOREAN
sin²θ + cos²θ ≡ 1
tan²θ + 1 ≡ sec²θ
1 + cot²θ ≡ cosec²θ
DOUBLE ANGLE
sin 2A ≡ 2sin A cos A
cos 2A ≡ cos²A − sin²A
2cos²A − 1
1 − 2sin²A
tan 2A ≡ 2tan A/(1 − tan²A)
COMPOUND ANGLE
sin(A±B) ≡ sin A cos B ± cos A sin B
cos(A±B) ≡ cos A cos B ∓ sin A sin B
tan(A±B) ≡ (tan A ± tan B)/(1 ∓ tan A tan B)
TRIG FUNCTIONS
sin
cos
tan
INVERSE
sin⁻¹
cos⁻¹
tan⁻¹
TRIG
FUNCTIONS
QUADRATIC
CUBIC
EXPONENTIAL eˣ
LOG ln x
f⁻¹
MODULUS |x|
DOMAIN
RANGE
INVERSE
TRANSFORMATIONS
−f(x)
f(−x)
f(x) + a
f(x + a)
af(x)
f(ax)
DIFFERENTIATION
d/dx
STANDARD
d/dx (xⁿ) = nxⁿ⁻¹
d/dx (eˣ) = eˣ
d/dx (ln x) = 1/x
d/dx (sin x) = cos x
d/dx (cos x) = −sin x
d/dx (tan x) = sec²x
CHAIN fg(x) = f(u)
dy/dx = dy/du × du/dx
d/dx (uv) = v du/dx + u dv/dx
(u/v) = (v du/dx − u dv/dx)/v²
= dy/dt ÷ dx/dt

Glossary

This is a glossary of words, symbols and formulae that are used in the Pure Maths section. It is not comprehensive. If you are unsure of the meaning of mathematical words you find, use a mathematics dictionary.

Asymptote – a line that a curve approaches but never meets.

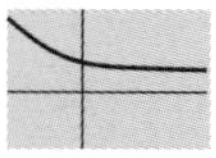

Coefficient – the number in front of a term in an expression, including its sign.
Complementary angles add up to 90°.
Cubic A cubic expression is $ax^3 + bx^2 + cx + d$ where a, b, c and d are constants (i.e. numbers).
Difference between two squares
$a^2 - b^2 \equiv (a + b)(a - b)$
Discriminant – the section of the formula for solving quadratic equations that is under the square root,

i.e. $b^2 - 4ac$. $\quad \dfrac{-b \pm \sqrt{b^2 - 4ac}}{2a}$

Dividend – The expression being divided by another. (See quotient.)
Divisor – The expression that is divided into another. (See quotient.)
Equations are valid for some, but not all, values of the variables, e.g. $x + 3 = 5$ is true only when x is 2.
Exponent is another word for power or index
Formula for solving a quadratic equation is

$$\frac{-b \pm \sqrt{b^2 - 4ac}}{2a}$$

Identities. An identity is the equivalence of two versions of the same expression,
e.g. $(x + 1)^2 \equiv x^2 + 2x + 1$.
An identity is true for all values of the variables.
Integer – A whole number, positive or negative.
Irrational number – A number that cannot be written as a fraction with integer numerator and denominator, e.g. $\sqrt{2}, \pi$.
Linear A linear expression has the form $ax + b$ where a and b are constants.
Ordinate – The y-coordinate of a point.
Polynomials. A polynomial is the sum of terms containing integer powers of the variables. The highest power gives the order of the polynomial, e.g. $3x^4 - 2x + 1$ is a polynomial in x of order 4.
Quadratic – A quadratic expression has the form $ax^2 + bx + c$ where a, b and c are constants (i.e. numbers).
Quotient The result (not including the remainder) of a division of one expression (the dividend) by another (the divisor), e.g.
27 (dividend) ÷ 8 (divisor) = 3 (quotient), remainder 4.
Rational number – Any number that can be written as a fraction with integer numerator and denominator.
Roots – the values that satisfy an equation.
Squaring a bracket
$(a + b)^2 \equiv a^2 + 2ab + b^2$
$(a - b)^2 \equiv a^2 - 2ab + b^2$

Subject of a formula – the quantity isolated on one side of the = sign, e.g. A is the subject of the formula $A = \frac{1}{2}bc$.
Subtend an angle – an angle at a point whose arms are drawn to the endpoints of a given line or curve is subtended by the line or curve.

The angle θ is subtended at P by the arc AB.

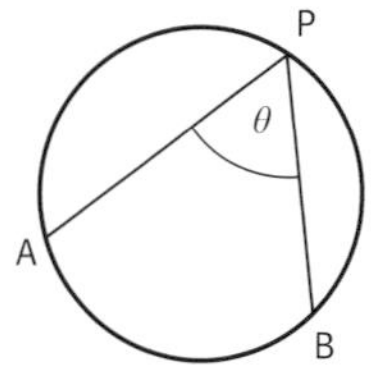

Supplementary angles add up to 180°.
Trig ratios – the name given to the sine, cosine and tangent of an angle.

Symbols

∞ infinity

$\sum$ means sum, e.g. $\sum_{r=1}^{6} r^2$ means sum the values of r^2 for $r = 1, 2, 3, 4, 5, 6$
i.e. $1^2 + 2^2 + 3^2 + 4^2 + 5^2 + 6^2$.

$\mathbb{R}$ means the real numbers, i.e. all numbers that can be represented on a number line.

$\in$ means included in (a member of), e.g. $x \in \mathbb{R}$ means x is a real number.

$f : x \mapsto f(x)$ means the function f that changes a value of x to the value $f(x)$.

Before you start you should

- know that algebra is part of the basic language of mathematics; it underpins most of mathematics beyond GCSE.

You need to know the following facts and techniques and be confident when using them.

Further facts and techniques are given at the start of some sections.

Algebraic fractions

These obey the same rules as arithmetic fractions.

- Fractions can be cancelled but only by quantities that are factors of both the *complete* numerator and the *complete* denominator,

  e.g. $\dfrac{2x + 4y}{6xy}$ can be cancelled by 2 because 2 is a factor of both the complete numerator and the denominator.

⚠ You cannot cancel x (or y) because neither are factors of the numerator.

- Fractions must have the same denominator before they can be added or subtracted,
  e.g. $\frac{x}{y} + \frac{3z}{2y}$ must be written as $\frac{2x}{2y} + \frac{3z}{2y}$ before adding the numerators $\Rightarrow \frac{2x + 3z}{2y}$
- A fraction with two (or more) terms in the numerator can be expressed as the sum (or difference) of separate fractions,
  e.g. $\frac{2x + 3z}{2y} \equiv \frac{2x}{2y} + \frac{3z}{2y} \equiv \frac{x}{y} + \frac{3z}{2y}$
- Fractions can be written in different ways,
  e.g. $2.5x \equiv 2\frac{1}{2}x \equiv \frac{5}{2}x \equiv \frac{5x}{2} \equiv 5x \div 2$.
  $\frac{-a - b}{2a - b} \equiv \frac{b + a}{b - 2a}$, $-\frac{x - y}{x + y} \equiv \frac{y - x}{x + y}$ and so on.

⚠ Do not assume that you have a wrong answer if yours is not the same as the given answer – check whether it is given in a different form.

Quadratic equations

A quadratic equation has (or can be arranged in) the form $ax^2 + bx + c = 0$;
it has either 2 distinct roots or 1 repeated root or no real roots.

- You can find the nature of the roots, without having to solve the equation, by looking at the discriminant:
  $b^2 - 4ac > 0 \Rightarrow$ 2 distinct roots
  $b^2 - 4ac = 0 \Rightarrow$ 1 repeated root
  $b^2 - 4ac < 0 \Rightarrow$ no real roots

If the roots are α and β, the equation can be written as $(x - \alpha)(x - \beta) = 0$.

Solving a pair of simultaneous equations by substitution

One way to solve a pair of simultaneous equations is by addition or subtraction to get rid of one of the letters. This is not always possible; you cannot eliminate a letter from this pair by adding or subtracting:

$$x - y = 4 \qquad [1]$$
$$x^2 - 2y^2 = 7 \qquad [2]$$

But you can rearrange [1] to $x = y + 4$ and *substitute* $y + 4$ for x in [2] to give an equation with just one letter,

i.e. $(y + 4)^2 - 2y^2 = 7$
$\Rightarrow$ $y^2 - 8y - 9 = 0$
$\Rightarrow$ $(y - 9)(y + 1) = 0$
$\Rightarrow$ $y = 9$ and (from [1],) $x = 13$
or $y = -1$ and $x = 3$.

Quadratic graphs

An equation of the form $y = ax^2 + bx + c$ gives a curve whose shape is called a parabola.

When a is positive, the curve is "∪" shaped.

When a is negative, the curve is "∩" shaped.

The curve has a line of symmetry – this is halfway between the points where the curve cuts the x-axis.

This, for example, is the graph of a quadratic function.

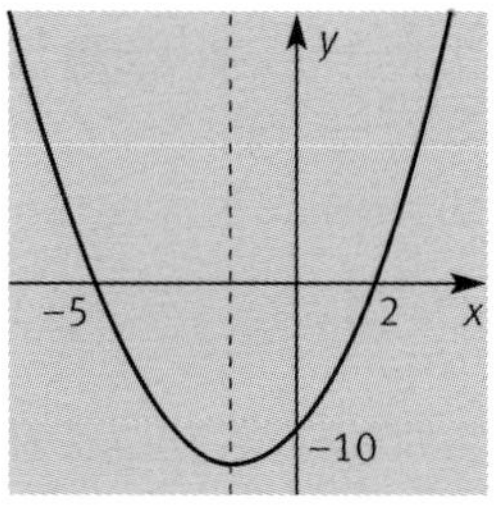

You can use this graph to

- find the equation of the curve:
  the curve cuts the x-axis where $y = 0$, i.e. where $x = 2$ and $x = -5$. These are the solutions of the equation $(x - 2)(x + 5) = 0$
  $\Rightarrow$ the equation of the curve is
  $y = k(x - 2)(x + 5)$.
  Also $y = -10$ when $x = 0$
  $\Rightarrow$ $k = 1$
- write down the value of x where y is a minimum and use it to find this minimum value of y:
  the line of symmetry is half way between $x = 2$ and $x = -5$, i.e. at $x = -1.5$.
  When $x = -1.5$,
  $y = (-1.5 - 2)(-1.5 + 5) = -12.25$

If the curve $y = ax^2 + bx + c$ does not cross the x-axis, the equation $ax^2 + bx + c = 0$ has no real roots.

If the curve touches the x-axis, the equation $ax^2 + bx + c = 0$ has a repeated root, i.e. two equal roots.

Cubic graphs

An equation of the form $y = ax^3 + bx^2 + cx + d$ gives a cubic curve which usually has two turning points, although these turning points may coalesce to give one point of inflexion,

i.e , when $a > 0$

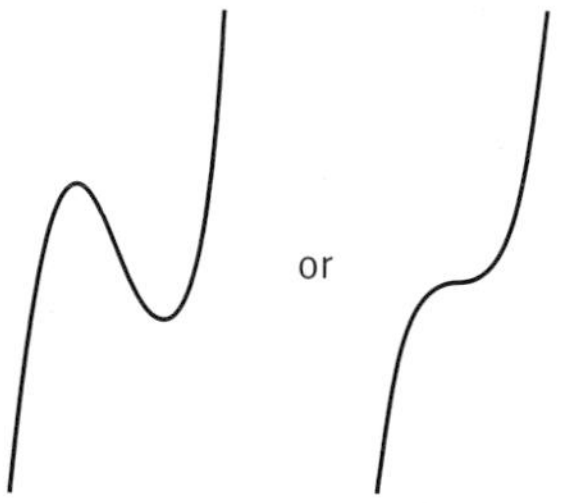

When a is negative, the curves are the other way up.

When you know where the curve crosses the x-axis, you can write down one or more roots of the equation $ax^3 + bx^2 + cx + d = 0$, depending on the number of times that the curve cuts the x-axis.

You can also write down the equation of the curve, given enough information on its graph.

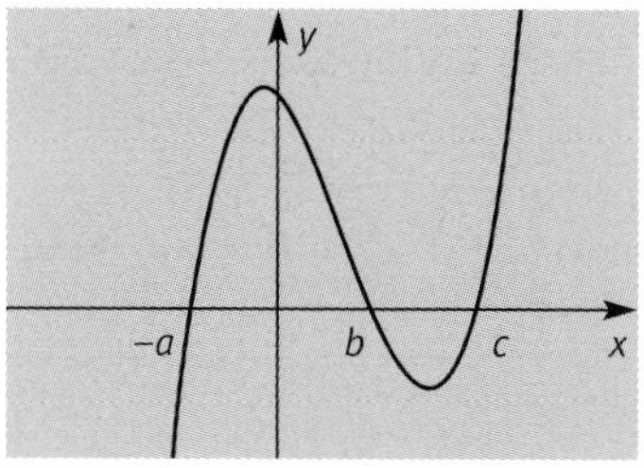

The equation of this curve, for example, is $y = k(x + a)(x - b)(x - c)$,

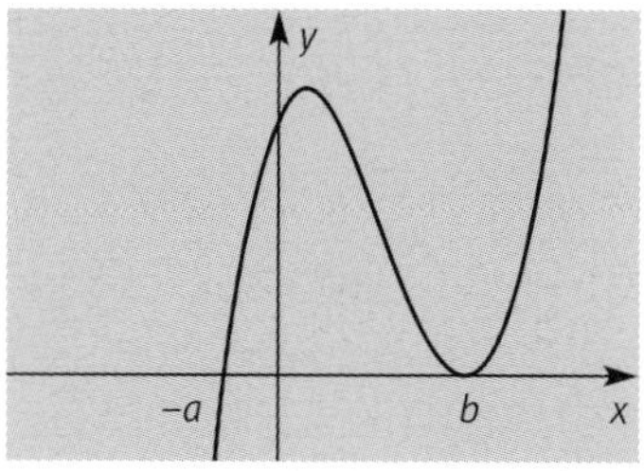

whereas the equation of this curve is $y = k(x + a)(x - b)^2$.

(The curve touches the x-axis at $x = b$, so $(x - b)$ is a repeated factor.)

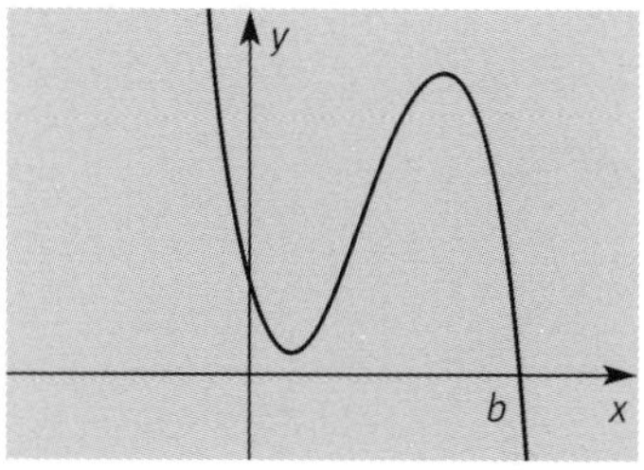

This curve crosses the x-axis only once, so without more information you cannot give its equation. You can deduce that the x^3 term is negative, and that the equation $ax^3 + bx^2 + cx + d = 0$ has only one root.

Questions

If you get more than one wrong answer ☛ GCSE or an A level text book for information and practice.

1 Express as the simplest possible fraction

a $\dfrac{2x - 6x}{3x^2}$ **b** $\dfrac{x}{2} + \dfrac{2}{x}$

c $\dfrac{2a^2 - 4ab}{4a}$ **d** $\left(\frac{1}{2}x^3\right)\left(\dfrac{1}{x}\right)$.

2 Solve the simultaneous equations $x - 3y + 4 = 0$ and $x^2 - xy = 0$

3 Without solving the equations, show that $x^2 - x + 1 = 0$ has no roots whereas $x^2 - x - 1 = 0$ has two distinct roots.

4

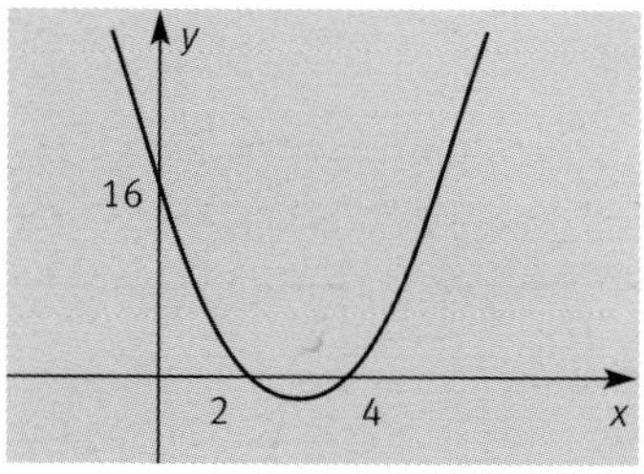

The equation of the graph is $y = ax^2 + bx + c$. Find the values of a, b and c.

Answers

1a $-\dfrac{4}{3x}$ **b** $\dfrac{x^2 + 4}{2x}$ **c** $\dfrac{a - 2b}{2}$ **d** $\dfrac{x^2}{2}$

2 $x = 0$ and $y = \frac{4}{3}$ or $x = 2$ and $y = 2$

3 For $x^2 - x + 1 = 0$, $b^2 - 4ac = -3$ so no roots.
For $x^2 - x - 1 = 0$, $b^2 - 4ac = 5$ so 2 distinct roots.

4 $y = 2(x - 2)(x - 4) = 2x^2 - 12x + 16$, so $a = 2$, $b = -12$ and $c = 16$.

Reasoning

Mathematical reasoning involves correctly linking statements. It is important that other people can follow your reasoning so explain your steps and link them when possible.

Links are made using words or symbols.
The symbols used are
$\Rightarrow$ which means 'implies' or 'gives' or 'therefore'
$\Leftarrow$ which means 'is implied by' or 'if'
$\Leftrightarrow$ which means 'implies and is implied by' or 'if and only if'

These symbols (or the equivalent words) must be used correctly.

For example, $k = 2 \Rightarrow k^2 = 4$ is true
but $k^2 = 4 \Rightarrow k = 2$ is not,
because $k = -2$ is also implied.

However, it is true that

$$k^2 = 4 \Leftarrow k = 2$$

i.e. $\quad k^2 = 4$ if $k = 2$

You can use the symbol $\Leftrightarrow$ to combine two statements when the first implies the second and vice-versa, e.g.

both $\quad k = \pm 2 \Rightarrow k^2 = 4$

and $\quad k = \pm 2 \Leftarrow k^2 = 4 \quad$ are true,

so you can write

$$k = \pm 2 \Leftrightarrow k^2 = 4$$

or $\quad k = \pm 2$ if and only if $k^2 = 4$.

Example

Find the conditions that p must satisfy for the equation $4x^2 - px + 1 = 0$ to have two distinct real roots.

Solution

Using the formula, the roots of $4x^2 - px + 1 = 0$ are given by $x = \dfrac{p \pm \sqrt{p^2 - 16}}{8}$.

x has two real distinct values if and only if

$$p^2 - 16 > 0$$
$$\Rightarrow (p - 4)(p + 4) > 0$$
$$\Rightarrow p < -4 \text{ or } p > 4$$

Showing a statement is correct

When you are asked to show or to prove that a statement is true, start from the given information (or from known facts) and correctly reason your way to the statement.

For example, to show that eliminating x from the pair of equations $x - 4y = 2$ and $x^2 - y^2 = 2$ gives the equation $15y^2 + 16y + 2 = 0$, start with the pair of given equations and number them so that they can be referred to.

$x - 4y = 2 \quad [1] \quad$ and $\quad x^2 - y^2 = 2 \quad [2]$

$[1] \Rightarrow x = 2 + 4y$

Substituting $2 + 4y$ for x in [2] gives

$$(2 + 4y)^2 - y^2 = 2 \Rightarrow 4 + 16y + 16y^2 - y^2 = 2$$
$$\Rightarrow 15y^2 + 16y + 2 = 0$$

Questions

1 Are the following links correct? If they are not, which symbol should be used?

a x is an even number $\Rightarrow x^2$ is an even number.

b the interior angles of a polygon are equal $\Rightarrow$ the polygon is regular.

c the equation of a curve is $y = 3(x + 1)^2$ $\Leftrightarrow$ the curve touches the x-axis at $x = -1$.

2 Show that the equation $x^2 - 6x = p$ has equal roots if and only if $p = -9$.

3 Given that $\dfrac{1}{x} = \dfrac{2x - 1}{n}$, find the conditions that the values of n must satisfy in order that x is a real number.

Answers

1a yes

b no, $\Leftarrow$ as the sides also need to be equal

c no, $\Rightarrow$ the equation could have other factors.

2 $x^2 - 6x = p \Leftrightarrow x^2 - 6x - p = 0$ which has equal roots $\Leftrightarrow 36 + 4p = 0 \Leftrightarrow p = -9$

3 $\dfrac{1}{x} = \dfrac{2x - 1}{n} \Rightarrow n = 2x^2 - x \Rightarrow 2x^2 - x - n = 0$; x is a real number $\Leftrightarrow 2x^2 - x - n = 0$ has real roots $\Rightarrow 1 + 8n \geqslant 0 \Rightarrow n \geqslant -\frac{1}{8}, n \neq 0$ because $\dfrac{2x - 1}{n}$ must be defined.

Take a break

PREVIEW

By the end of this topic you will have revised:

- ✔ **how to find the coordinates of the midpoint of a line joining two given points,**
- ✔ **how to find the equation of a straight line,**
- ✔ **what the conditions are for two straight lines to be parallel or perpendicular,**
- ✔ **strategies for solving problems.**

Before you start you should:

- know how to find the distance between two points whose coordinates are known,
- know how to find the gradient of the line through two points whose coordinates are known,
- know that the equation of any straight line can be written in the form $y = mx + c$ and the meaning of m and c,
- know that the midpoint of the line joining (x_1, y_1) to (x_2, y_2) is $\left(\dfrac{x_1 + x_2}{2}, \dfrac{y_1 + y_2}{2}\right)$.

TEST YOURSELF

If you get more than one wrong answer go to GCSE Higher or A level text book for information and practice.

1 **Find the distance between the points**
a) (4, 3) and (2, 7) b) (−1, 5) and (−4, −1).

2 **Find the gradient of the line through each of the pairs of points in question 1.**

3 **Write down the gradient and the coordinates of the points where the line cuts the x- and y-axes when the equation is**
a) $y = 5x - 4$ b) $2y + x = 4$

4 **Find the midpoint of the line joining**
a) (5, −2) & (−1, −4) b) (2t, t + 1) & (4t, 4)

Answers

1 **a)** $2\sqrt{5}$ **b)** $3\sqrt{5}$
2 **a)** −2 **b)** 2
3 **a)** 5, $(\frac{4}{5}, 0)$, (0, −4) **b)** $-\frac{1}{2}$, (4, 0), (0, 2)
4 **a)** (2, −3) **b)** $(3t, \frac{1}{2}t + 2\frac{1}{2})$

The equation of a straight line

To find the equation of a line you need to know *either* the coordinates of two points on the line *or* the gradient and the coordinates of one point on the line.

Given the coordinates of two points, you can work out the gradient of the line so, in either case, you can find the equation of the line using

$$y - y_1 = m(x - x_1)$$

where (x_1, y_1) is a point on the line and m is its gradient.

It is usual to simplify the resulting equation so that it does not contain fractions, and to give it in a form similar to $ax + by + c = 0$ where a, b and c are integers.

Gradient

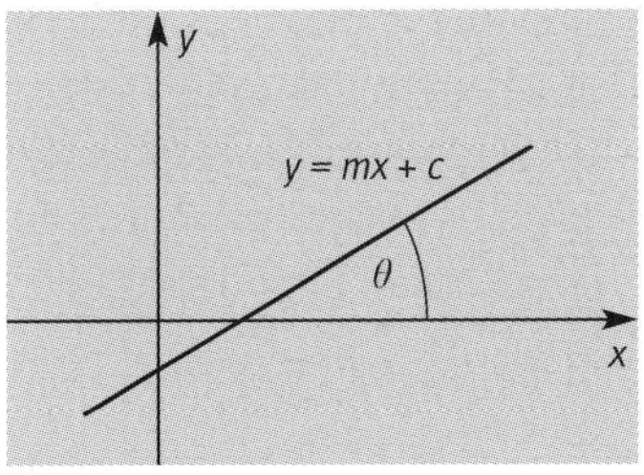

The line $y = mx + c$ makes an angle θ with the x-axis where $m = \tan\theta$

Parallel and perpendicular lines

Two lines are parallel when they have the same gradient.

Two lines are perpendicular when the product of their gradients is −1.

You can use these facts to:

- see whether lines whose equations are known are parallel or perpendicular. You can usually do this mentally by rearranging the equations in the form $y = mx + c$.
- find the equation of a line that is perpendicular (or parallel) to a given line. For example, to find the line through (5, 2) perpendicular to the line $2x - 3y + 5 = 0$, first find the gradient of the given line:
  $2x - 3y + 5 = 0 \Rightarrow y = \frac{2}{3}x + \frac{5}{3} \Rightarrow$ gradient $= \frac{2}{3}$.
  The gradient of a perpendicular line is $-\frac{3}{2}$.
  (Check: $-\frac{3}{2} \times \frac{2}{3} = -1$)
  $\therefore$ its equation is $y - 2 = -\frac{3}{2}(x - 5)$
  $\Rightarrow 2y - 4 = -3x + 15 \Rightarrow 3x + 2y - 19 = 0$.

Solving problems

In questions where steps needed to find the answer are not given explicitly, you have to puzzle out what to do yourself. There are strategies that may help. These are illustrated on a coordinate geometry problem, but they apply to all problems.

- When appropriate (and it is for any geometry problem) draw a diagram (a sketch is good enough, don't waste time making it look beautiful): put on it all the information known *and* what has to be found.
- How many unknown quantities are involved in what you have to find? This gives the number of equations you need.
- Look for facts that you know, including those that aren't spelt out in the question. Look for further facts that follow from these facts.
- Look for relationships between those facts. Express any that you find algebraically.

⚠ Don't always expect to 'see' your way through to the end of a problem at the start. Try following a line of argument and, if it leads to a dead end, try another (except under examination conditions – cut your losses and return to the problem only if you have time at the end.)

Example

The points A(1, 4), B(2, 7) and C(5, −1) lie on the circumference of a circle.

Find the coordinates of the centre of the circle.

Solution

There are two unknowns: the *x*- and *y*-coordinates of the centre D; so you want two equations.

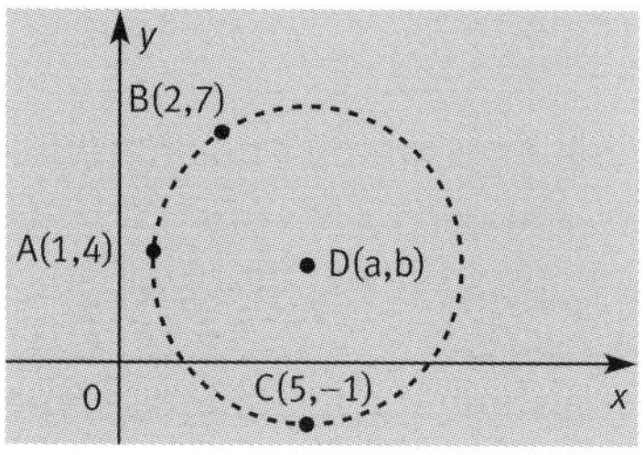

For this problem you may notice that DB, DA and DC are radii (fact ⇐ given information), so DB = DA = DC (relationships); these can be turned into equations because each length can be expressed in terms of *a*, *b* and the coordinates of the other end of the line.

$$DB^2 = (a-2)^2 + (b-7)^2,$$
$$DA^2 = (a-1)^2 + (b-4)^2,$$
$$DC^2 = (a-5)^2 + (b+1)^2.$$

$$\therefore \quad (a-2)^2 + (b-7)^2 = (a-1)^2 + (b-4)^2 \qquad [1]$$

$$\text{and } (a-1)^2 + (b-4)^2 = (a-5)^2 + (b+1)^2 \qquad [2]$$

This gives a pair of equations that can be solved simultaneously for *a* and *b*. (They are not as daunting as they appear – solve them.) Alternatively, you should know that the centre of a circle lies on the perpendicular bisector of a chord: the equation of the perpendicular bisector of any of the three chords can be found, but two are enough. D lies on both perpendicular bisectors so D is their point of intersection.

Midpoint of AC is $(3, \frac{3}{2})$.

Gradient of AC $= -\frac{5}{4} \Rightarrow$ gradient of $\perp = \frac{4}{5}$

Equation of perpendicular bisector of AC is

$$y - \tfrac{3}{2} = \tfrac{4}{5}(x-3) \Rightarrow 10y - 8x + 9 = 0 \qquad [1]$$

Similarly the equation of the perpendicular bisector of AB is

$$6y + 2x - 36 = 0 \qquad [2]$$

These equations can be solved simultaneously to find their point of intersection. Solve them and check that they give the same answer as the first pair.

Questions

1 The equation of a line *l* is $2x + 3y - 7 = 0$.

a Find the equation of the line through $(3, -2)$ that is perpendicular to *l*.

b Find the point where these two lines intersect.

2 The vertices of triangle ABC are A(−3, 3), B(4, 4) and C(5, −3).

a Prove that angle ABC is a right-angle.

b Find the area of triangle ABC.

3 The line passing through the points A(*p*, 4) and B(3, −1) has gradient $\frac{1}{2}$. Find the value of *p*.

4 The points A(3, 5), B(2, 9) and C(−3, 2) are three vertices of the parallelogram ABCD. Find the equations of the sides CD and AD.

Answers:

1a $3x - 2y - 13 = 0$ **b** $(\frac{53}{13}, -\frac{5}{13})$

2a gradient AB $= \frac{1}{7}$, gradient BC $= -7$; $\frac{1}{7} \times -7 = -1$, ∴ AB⊥BC

b area = 25 sq units

3 13

4 CD: $4x + y + 10 = 0$, AD: $7x - 5y + 4 = 0$

Take a break

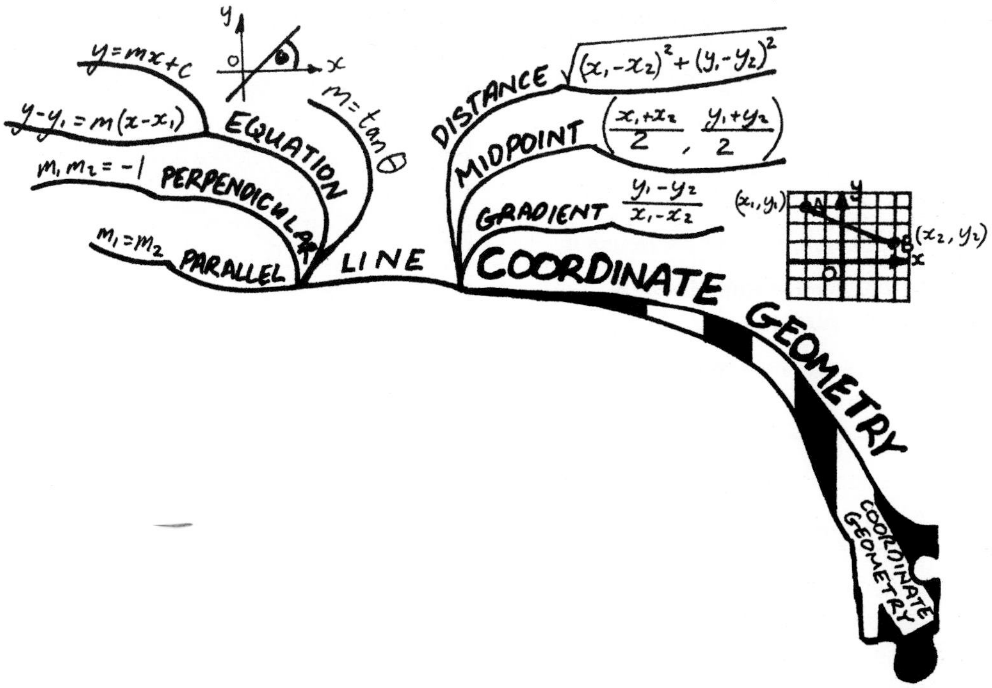

Review topics 1 and 2

1 Sketch the curve whose equation is $y = (2x - 3)(x + 1)$ and write down the value of x where the curve turns.

2 Describe the nature of the roots of the equation $x^2 - 4x + 3 = 0$.

3 What are the necessary and sufficient conditions that a must satisfy for the curve $y = ax^2 + 2x + 1$ to touch the x-axis?

4 Express $\dfrac{2x - 3y}{4}$ as the sum of two separate fractions.

5 Find the point of intersection of the line $4x - 3y + 5 = 0$ with the line that passes through the origin and is perpendicular to the given line.

Answers

1 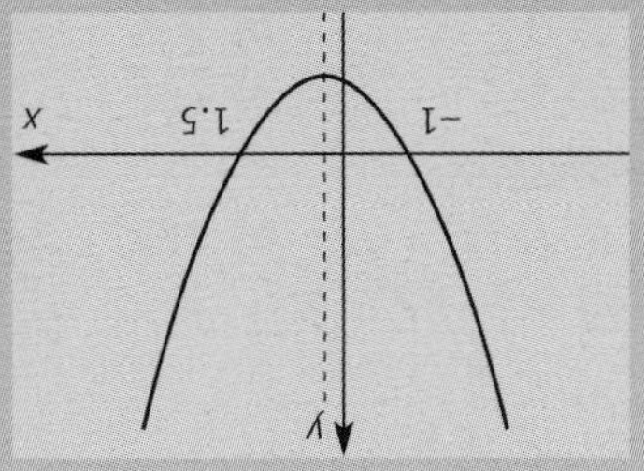

; 0.25

2 $b^2 - 4ac = 16 - 12 > 0$, so the equation has 2 distinct roots.

3 If the curve touches the x-axis, the equation $ax^2 + 2x + 1 = 0$ must have equal roots, i.e. $b^2 - 4ac = 0 \Rightarrow 4 - 4a = 0 \Rightarrow a = 1$.

4 $\dfrac{x}{2} - \dfrac{3y}{4}$

5 $\left(-\frac{4}{5}, \frac{3}{5}\right)$

Take a break

PREVIEW

By the end of this topic you will have revised:

- ✔ **how to complete the square,**
- ✔ **how to expand an expression to get rid of brackets,**
- ✔ **what the factor theorem is and how to use it,**
- ✔ **how to rationalise the denominator of a fraction containing surds,**
- ✔ **what a logarithm is and how to use the laws of logarithms.**

Before you start you should:

- know how to expand a pair of brackets such as $(x - 2y)(3x + 2y)$ to get $3x^2 - 4xy - 4y^2$,
- be able to factorise quadratic expressions,
- know the meaning of positive, negative, zero and fractional indices,
- know and be able to use the laws of indices,
- know what a surd is and be able to simplify simple expressions containing surds.

TEST YOURSELF

Less than 4 parts of a question correct see GCSE (Higher) or A level text book for information and practice.

1 Expand

a) $(x + 3)(x + 5)$
b) $(3s - 2t)(5s - 4t)$
c) $(x^2 - 7)(x^2 + 8)$ **d)** $(a^2 - b)(a^2 + b)$
e) $(3p - 2q)^2$

2 Factorise

a) $x^2 - 3x + 2$ **b)** $9x^2 - 1$
c) $3x^2 - 6x + 3$ **d)** $20 + 6x - 2x^2$
e) $6a^2b - 3ab^2 - 3b^3$

3 Evaluate

a) 5^3 **b)** 3^{-2} **c)** $(\frac{4}{9})^{\frac{1}{2}}$
d) $8^{-\frac{2}{3}}$ **e)** $(\frac{3}{2})^0$

4 Simplify

a) $(x^5)^3$ **b)** $12a^7 \div 3a^4$
c) $x^2 \times xy^3 \div y^4$ **d)** $t^{\frac{1}{2}} \times t^{\frac{3}{4}} \times t^{-1}$
e) $\dfrac{b^3}{b^2 \times b^5}$

5 Simplify

a) $\sqrt{2}(3 - 4\sqrt{2})$
b) $(1 + \sqrt{3})(1 - \sqrt{3})$
c) $\dfrac{5}{\sqrt{5}}$ **d)** $\dfrac{1}{\sqrt{2}} + \dfrac{3}{2\sqrt{2}}$
e) $(2\sqrt{3} - 1)(3 + \sqrt{2})$

Answers

1 a) $x^2 + 8x + 15$ **b)** $15s^2 - 22st + 8t^2$ **c)** $x^4 + x^2 - 56$
d) $a^4 - b^2$ **e)** $9p^2 - 12pq + 4q^2$
2 a) $(x - 2)(x - 1)$ **b)** $(3x - 1)(3x + 1)$ **c)** $3(x - 1)^2$
d) $2(5 - x)(2 + x)$ **e)** $3b(2a - b)(a + b)$
3 a) 125 **b)** $\frac{1}{9}$ **c)** $\frac{2}{3}$ **d)** $\frac{1}{4}$ **e)** 1
4 a) x^{15} **b)** $4a^3$ **c)** $\frac{x^3}{y}$ **d)** $t^{\frac{1}{4}}$ **e)** $\frac{1}{b^4}$
5 a) $3\sqrt{2} - 8$ **b)** -2 **c)** $\sqrt{5}$ **d)** $\frac{5\sqrt{2}}{4}$
e) $6\sqrt{3} - \sqrt{2} - 3 + 2\sqrt{6}$

Completing the square

The process of expressing a quadratic in the form $a(x + b)^2 + c$ is called completing the square.

You can do this by writing the given quadratic as identical to $a(x + b)^2 + c$,

e.g. $$2x^2 - 5x + 1 \equiv a(x + b)^2 + c$$

then fully expand the RHS

$$2x^2 - 5x + 1 \equiv ax^2 + 2abx + ab^2 + c$$

Now you can use the fact that, because this is an identity, the coefficient of x^2 on both sides is the same, so $a = 2$; the coefficient of x on both sides is the same, so $-5 = 2ab \Rightarrow b = -\frac{5}{4}$; the constant on each side is the same, so $1 = ab^2 + c \Rightarrow c = -\frac{17}{8}$.

(This process is called comparing coefficients.)

$$\therefore \quad 2x^2 - 5x + 1 \equiv 2(x - \tfrac{5}{4})^2 - \tfrac{17}{8}$$

When the coefficient of x^2 is 1, you can complete the square mentally, e.g.

$$x^2 + 5x - 1 = (x + \tfrac{5}{2})^2 - 1 - \tfrac{25}{4} = (x + \tfrac{5}{2})^2 - \tfrac{29}{4}$$

i.e. take the coefficient of x on the left hand side and halve it; add this to x and square, then subtract the square of half the coefficient of x from the number term.

You can use the completed square form:

- to solve quadratic equations,
  e.g. $2x^2 - 5x + 1 = 0 \Rightarrow 2(x - \frac{5}{4})^2 - \frac{17}{8} = 0$
  $\Rightarrow (x - \frac{5}{4})^2 = \frac{17}{16} \Rightarrow x - \frac{5}{4} = \pm\frac{\sqrt{17}}{4}$
  i.e. $x = \frac{5+\sqrt{17}}{4}$ or $\frac{5-\sqrt{17}}{4}$
- to find the maximum or minimum value of a quadratic function and the value of x at which it occurs,
  e.g. $f(x) = 2x^2 - 5x + 1 \equiv 2(x - \frac{5}{4})^2 - \frac{17}{8}$
  Because $(x - \frac{5}{4})^2 \geqslant 0$ for all values of x and is equal to 0 when $x = \frac{5}{4}$, $f(x)$ has a least value of $-\frac{17}{8}$ when $x = \frac{5}{4}$.

Expanding brackets

Be systematic when you need to expand an expression such as $(3x - 5)(4x^2 - 5x + 6)$; multiply each term in the quadratic by $3x$ and then multiply each term in the quadratic by -5:

$$\begin{array}{rr} & 12x^3 - 15x^2 + 18x \\ & -20x^2 + 25x - 30 \\ \hline \text{lastly add the results:} & 12x^3 - 35x^2 + 43x - 30 \end{array}$$

To expand three linear brackets, start by expanding two brackets to give a quadratic, then multiply this by the remaining linear factor, e.g.

$$(x-1)(x-2)(x+3) = (x-1)(x^2+x-6)$$
$$= x^3 - 7x + 6$$

Pascal's triangle

This array of numbers is called Pascal's Triangle.

```
        1
      1   1
    1   2   1
  1   3   3   1
1   4   6   4   1
```

You can use the numbers in a row to help expand a power of a linear expression.

For example, to expand $(x + y)^4$, start with x^4, then reduce the power of x by 1 and increase the power of y by 1 until you get to y^4. Now use the numbers in the row beginning 1 4 . . . as the coefficients of these terms,

i.e. $(x + y)^4 = x^4 + 4x^3y + 6x^2y^2 + 4xy^3 + y^4$

and to expand $(2x - 3)^3$, replace x by $2x$ and y by -3 and use the numbers in the row 1, 3, . . . $\Rightarrow$

$$(2x-3)^3 = (2x)^3 + 3(2x)^2(-3) + 3(2x)(-3)^2 + (-3)^3$$
$$= 8x^3 - 36x^2 + 54x - 27.$$

Questions

1 Express $x^2 - 5x + 2$ in completed square form. Hence give the exact solutions of the equation $x^2 - 5x + 2 = 0$.

2 Given that $2x^2 - 4x - 7 \equiv p(x - q)^2 + r$, find the values of p, q and r. Hence give the minimum value of $2x^2 - 4x - 7$.

3 Expand $(x^2 - 1)(x^3 - 3x + 5)$ giving your answer in descending powers of x.

4 Expand $(3x - 1)^3$.

Answers

1 $(x - \frac{5}{2})^2 - \frac{17}{4}$; $\dfrac{5 + \sqrt{17}}{2}$, $\dfrac{5 - \sqrt{17}}{2}$

2 $p = 2, q = 1, r = -9$; -9

3 $x^5 - 4x^3 + 5x^2 + 3x - 5$

4 $27x^3 - 27x^2 + 9x - 1$.

The factor theorem

The FACTOR THEOREM states that when $f(x)$ is a polynomial

$f(a) = 0 \Leftrightarrow (x - a)$ is a factor of $f(x)$.

Note that a is the value of x for which the factor is equal to 0.

You can use the factor theorem:

- to show, for example, that $3x - 4$ is a factor of $3x^3 - 10x^2 + 17x - 12$.
  You can do this by substituting $\frac{4}{3}$ (the value of x for which $3x - 4 = 0$) for x in $3x^3 - 10x^2 + 17x - 12$, and showing that the result is zero,
  i.e. $3(\frac{4}{3})^3 - 10(\frac{4}{3})^2 + 17(\frac{4}{3}) - 12$
  $= \frac{64}{9} - \frac{160}{9} + \frac{68}{3} - 12 = 0$
  $\Rightarrow 3x - 4$ is a factor of $3x^3 - 10x^2 + 17x - 12$.
- to find linear factors, and hence to solve polynomial equations.
  For example, to find the factors of $2x^3 - 3x^2 - 3x + 2$, start by identifying possible factors:
  the factors must start with $2x$ or x to give $2x^3$ and the factors must end with ± 1 or ± 2 to give $+2$, so possible factors are
  $(x \pm 1), (x \pm 2), (2x \pm 1)$.

Now try these in turn:
$f(1) = 2 - 3 - 3 + 2 \neq 0$
so $(x - 1)$ is not a factor of $f(x)$.

$f(-1) = -2 - 3 + 3 + 2 = 0$
so $(x + 1)$ is a factor of $f(x)$.

$f(2) = 16 - 12 - 6 + 2 = 0$
so $(x - 2)$ is a factor of $f(x)$.

A cubic has at most three linear factors; having identified two of them, the third factor is obvious because you know what the product of the three is;

i.e $\quad (x + 1)(x - 2)(? \pm ?) \equiv 2x^3 - 3x^2 - 3x + 2$

so the third bracket must start with $2x$ (to give $2x^3$) and end with -1 (to give $+2$)

$\Rightarrow \quad (x + 1)(x - 2)(2x - 1) \equiv 2x^3 - 3x^2 - 3x + 2$

You can use these factors to solve the equation

$$2x^3 - 3x^2 - 3x + 2 = 0$$

i.e. $(x + 1)(x - 2)(2x - 1) = 0 \Rightarrow x = -1, 2 \text{ or } \frac{1}{2}$

The method above works only when the cubic has three linear factors, but not all cubics have three linear factors.

You can use the factor theorem to find just one linear factor; the remaining factor is a quadratic which can be found and which may or may not factorise. This method can be used to factorise any cubic.

For example, $3x^3 - 5x^2 + 6x - 4$ has a linear factor: $x - 1$.

You can find the quadratic factor by writing
$3x^3 - 5x^2 + 6x - 4 \equiv (x - 1)(ax^2 + bx + c)$
then expanding the RHS gives
$3x^3 - 5x^2 + 6x - 4 \equiv ax^3 + (b - a)x^2 + (c - b)x - c$.
Then comparing coefficients:

$a = 3$; $b - 3 = -5$ so $b = -2$; $c = 4$
$\therefore \quad 3x^3 - 5x^2 + 6x - 4 \equiv (x - 1)(3x^2 - 2x + 4)$
(There is no need to write this down – you can do the comparisons mentally.)

Questions

1 Solve the equation $6x^3 + 13x^2 + 4x - 3 = 0$.

2 Given that $(x - 2)$ is a factor of $2x^3 + x^2 + px + 6$, find the value of p.

Answers

1 $-1, -\frac{3}{2}, \frac{1}{3}$ 2 -13.

Rationalising the denominator

When a fraction contains a surd in the denominator, the denominator is an irrational number.

To turn the denominator into a rational number (i.e. to rationalise it) means getting rid of any surds.

When the denominator has a single term, multiplying top and bottom of the fraction by the surd will get rid of it, e.g.

$$\frac{2 + 3\sqrt{3}}{5\sqrt{2}} = \frac{2 + 3\sqrt{3}}{5\sqrt{2}} \times \frac{\sqrt{2}}{\sqrt{2}} = \frac{2\sqrt{2} + 3\sqrt{6}}{10}$$

When the denominator has two terms, multiply top and bottom by the two terms but with the opposite sign between them,
e.g. to rationalise the denominator of
$\frac{1 - \sqrt{3}}{1 + 2\sqrt{3}}$, multiply top and bottom by $1 - 2\sqrt{3}$,

i.e. $\frac{1 - \sqrt{3}}{1 + 2\sqrt{3}} \times \frac{1 - 2\sqrt{3}}{1 - 2\sqrt{3}} = \frac{7 - 3\sqrt{3}}{-11} = \frac{3\sqrt{3} - 7}{11}$

Questions

Express each of the following fractions in the form $a + b\sqrt{5}$

1 $\frac{2}{\sqrt{5} - 1}$ 2 $\frac{3 + 2\sqrt{5}}{5 - 2\sqrt{5}}$

Answers

1 $\frac{1}{2} + \frac{1}{2}\sqrt{5}$ 2 $7 + \frac{16}{5}\sqrt{5}$

Logarithms

The LOGARITHM of a given number is the power to which a fixed number, called the BASE, must be raised to be equal to the given number.

So the logarithm of 8 with a base of 2 (written $\log_2 8$) is 3 because $2^3 = 8$.

In general $\log_a b = c \Leftrightarrow a^c = b$

In particular, $\log_a 1 = 0$ for any value of a except zero, since $a^0 \equiv 1$

When the base is the natural number e, $\log_e$ is written as ln, so $\ln x$ means the power to which e must be raised to give x,

i.e. $\ln x = y \Leftrightarrow e^y = x$

- You can use these definitions to remove the log term from an equation, e.g. if $\log_3 x = y$, then $x = 3^y$.

The LAWS OF LOGARITHMS show how logarithms can be combined. They are

$$\log_a x + \log_a y = \log_a xy$$

$$\log_a x - \log_a y = \log_a \frac{x}{y}$$

$$\log_a x^n = n \log_a x$$

$\log_a (x + y)$ is NOT equal to $\log_a x + \log_a y$
$\log_a xy$ is NOT equal to $\log_a x \times \log_a y$
(These are common mistakes – avoid them.)

You can use the laws of logs to

- write an expression containing the sums and differences of logarithms as a single logarithm, provided that all the logarithms have the same base,

  e.g. $\log_3 5 - 2\log_3 4 = \log_3 5 - \log_3 16 = \log_3 \frac{5}{16}$

⚠ You cannot express $\log_2 5 + \log_3 6$ as a single logarithm because the bases are different.

- solve equations containing logarithms by first expressing any sums and differences of logarithms as a single logarithm, then removing the logarithm,

  e.g. to solve the equation

  $$2 + 2\log_3 x = \log_3 (x-5)^2$$

  collect the log terms on one side:

  $$2 = \log_3 (x-5)^2 - 2\log_3 x$$

  express those log terms as a single log:

  $$\log_3 (x-5)^2 - \log_3 x^2 = \log_3 \frac{(x-5)^2}{x^2}$$

  $$\therefore \quad 2 = \log_3 \frac{(x-5)^2}{x^2} \quad \text{so } 3^2 = \frac{(x-5)^2}{x^2}$$

This is an algebraic equation that simplifies to $8x^2 + 10x - 25 = 0$ and so can be solved.

Questions

1 Evaluate

a $\log_3 9$ **b** $\log_3 \frac{1}{27}$ **c** $\log_a a^4$

2 Express without logarithms

a $\log_2 x = y$ **b** $\log_x 2 = y$

c $\ln x = y$ **d** $2\log_x (2y - x) = 0$

3 Express as a single logarithm

a $\ln x - 2\ln y$ **b** $2\log_b 3 + \log_b 5 - \log_b 15$

4 Solve the equations

a $\log_2 x - 2\log_2 (x-1) = 1$

b $2\ln x + \ln(2x - 1) = 0$.

Answers

1a 2 **b** −3 **c** 4

2a $x = 2^y$ **b** $2 = x^y$ **c** $x = e^y$ **d** $(2y - x)^2 = 1$

3a $\ln \frac{x}{y^2}$ **b** $\log_b 3$

4a $\frac{1}{2}, 2$ **b** 1.

Take a break

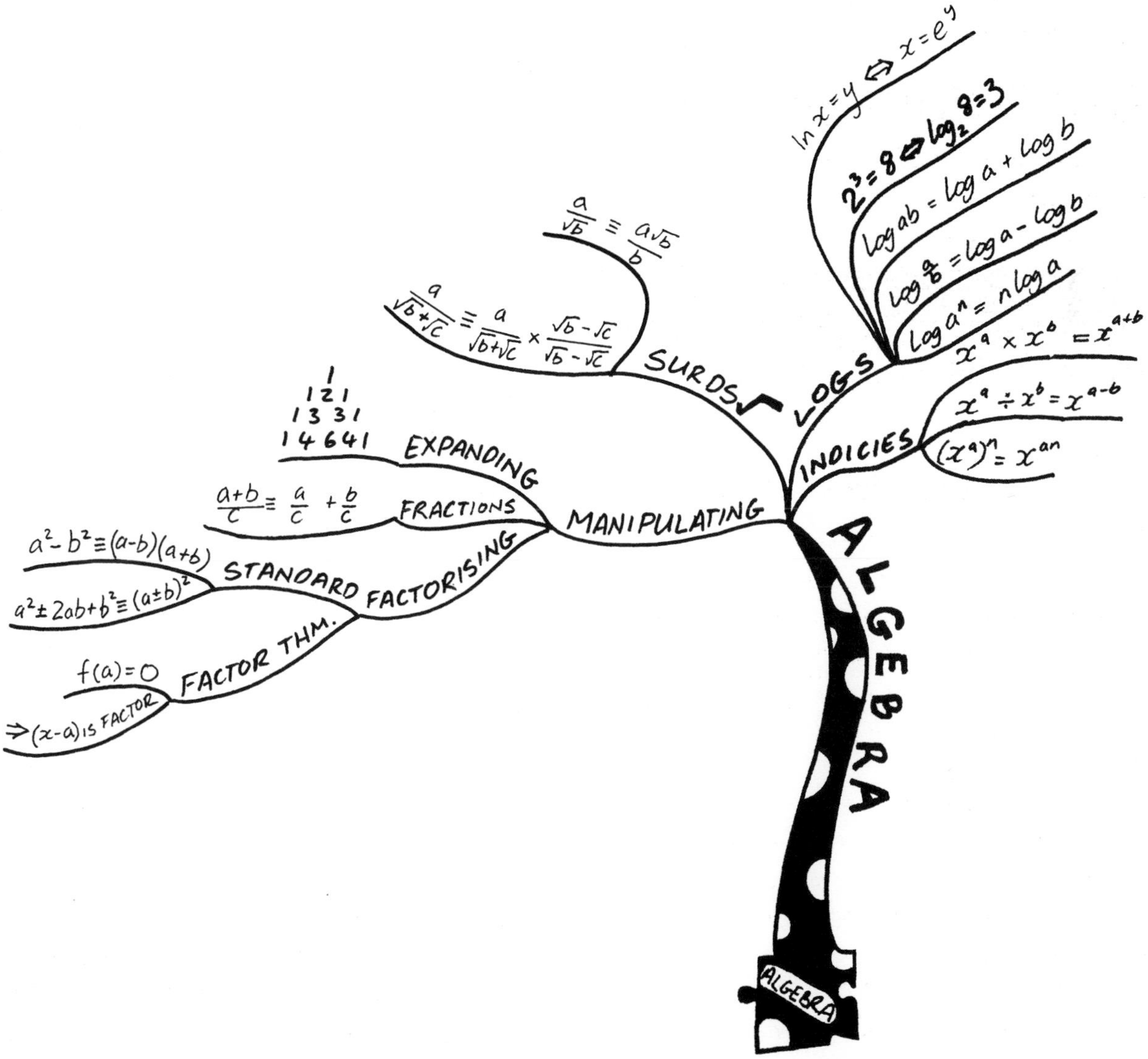

Review

1a What are the necessary and sufficient conditions for the line l to be the perpendicular bisector of the line joining A(1, 3), B(−2, 4)?

b Find the equation of the perpendicular bisector of the line joining A and B.

2 Show that $x + 2$ is a factor of $x^3 + x^2 + 2x + 8$.
Hence prove that the equation $x^3 + x^2 + 2x + 8 = 0$ has only one real root.

3 Write $x^2 - 7x + 4$ in completed square form.

4a Find the value of $\log_{10} 1000$ **b** Given that $\ln(2x + 1) = y$, express x in terms of y.

5 Solve the equation $2 \log_5 15 - \log_5 75 - \log_5 x = 2$

Answers

1a l must pass through the midpoint of AB, i.e. through $(-\frac{1}{2}, \frac{7}{2})$ **and** l must be perpendicular to AB, i.e. l must have a gradient of 3.

b $y = 3x + 5$

2 $f(-2) = -8 + 4 - 4 + 8 = 0$, $\therefore$ $x + 2$ is a factor of f(x); $x^3 + x^2 + 2x + 8 = (x + 2)(x^2 - x + 4) = 0$
$\Rightarrow x = -2$ or $x^2 - x + 4 = 0$ which has no real solutions because "$b^2 - 4ac$" $= -15 < 0$

3 $(x - \frac{7}{2})^2 - \frac{33}{4}$

4a 3 **b** $2x + 1 = e^y \Rightarrow x = \frac{1}{2}(e^y - 1)$

5 $\frac{3}{25}$

Take a break

PREVIEW

By the end of this topic you will have revised:

- ✔ **the meaning of a function,**
- ✔ **what domain and range of a function mean,**
- ✔ **how to find a function of a function,**
- ✔ **what the inverse of a function is and how to find it,**
- ✔ **how to transform curves.**

Before you start you should:

- understand the transformations 'reflection in a line' and 'translation',
- know what a compound transformation is.

TEST YOURSELF

If you get the answer wrong see GCSE text book for information and practice

Describe the transformation that gives the black triangle from the grey triangle.

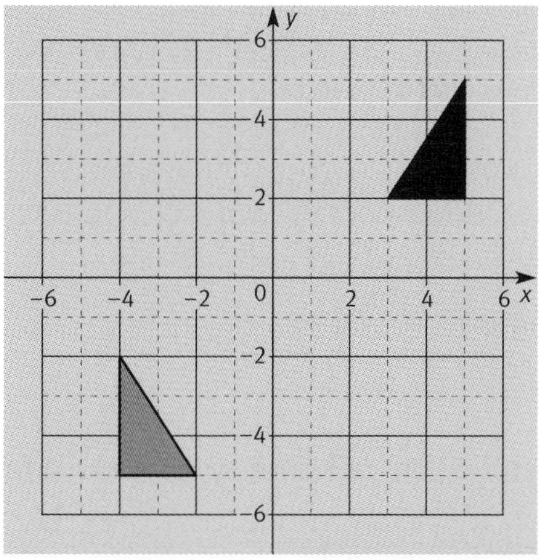

Answer

Reflect in y-axis then translate by $\begin{pmatrix}1\\7\end{pmatrix}$, or translate by $\begin{pmatrix}-1\\7\end{pmatrix}$ then reflect in the y-axis, etc.

Function

A rule that changes a single number to another single number is a function, so the rule 'halve and add 1' is a function as it transforms 0.8 to 1.4 and only to 1.4.

⚠ A rule that changes one number to two or more numbers is NOT a function, so the rule 'take the square root' is not a function as it changes 4 to the two numbers 2 and −2.

A function f changes a number x to the number $f(x)$, e.g. when f is 'halve and add 1',

$$f(6) = \tfrac{1}{2}(6) + 1 = 4.$$

and, for any number x, $f(x) = \tfrac{1}{2}x + 1$.

Plotting values of $f(x)$ against values of x gives the graph of the function: the equation of the graph is $y = f(x)$.

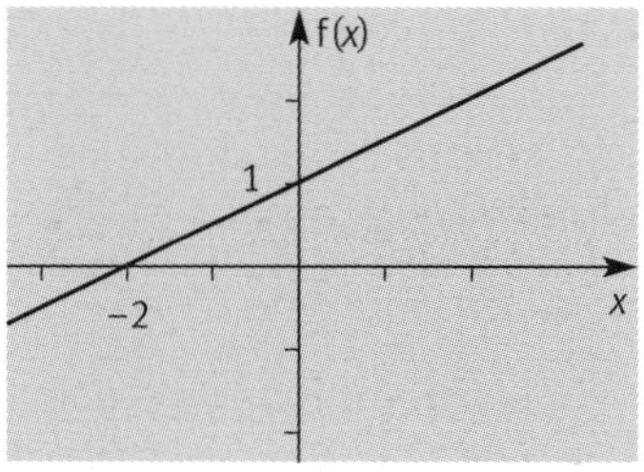

Domain and range

The domain of a function is the set of numbers that the rule operates on, i.e. the set of values that x can take.

This set can contain any numbers, provided that each of them gives one and only one value for $f(x)$,

e.g., when $f(x) = \dfrac{1}{x}$, one possible domain is $x = -2, -1, 1, 1.5$; the only value that can never be included in the domain is $x = 0$ because $\frac{1}{0}$ is meaningless.

The range of a function is the set of values of the corresponding changed numbers, i.e. the values of $f(x)$.

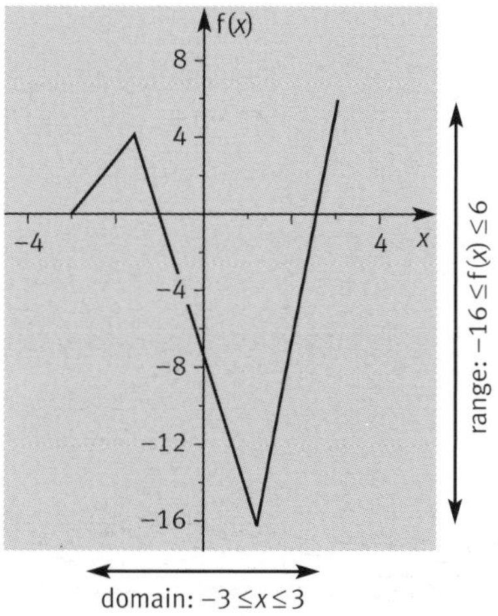

Function of a function

Given two functions, f and g, fg means the function f applied to the function g, and fg is a function of a function,

e.g. when $f(x) = \dfrac{1}{3x - 1}$ and $g(x) = x^2 + 3$,

$$fg(x) = f[g(x)] = \frac{1}{3g(x) - 1} = \frac{1}{3(x^2 + 3) - 1} = \frac{1}{3x^2 + 8}.$$

Inverse function

In general, what is done to change numbers to other numbers can be undone.

A rule that undoes a function, i.e. that changes values of f(x) back to values of x, is the inverse rule. When this rule takes one value of f(x) back to one and only one value of x, it is a function in its own right; it is called the inverse of the function f and is written as f^{-1}.

Not all functions have an inverse function. You can tell if f^{-1} exists from a sketch of the graph of $y = f(x)$:

For $f(x) = x^3$, one value of f(x) gives one and only one value of x so f^{-1} exists.

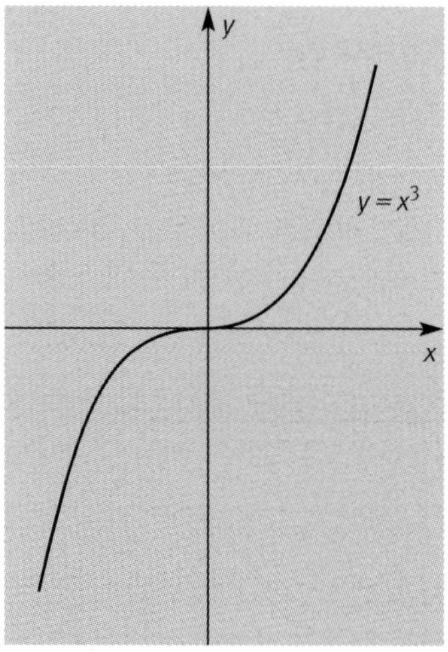

For $f(x) = x^2 - 1$, $x \in \mathbb{R}$, one value of f(x) gives two values of x, so f^{-1} does not exist. However f^{-1} does exist if the domain of f is restricted to $x \geqslant 0$.

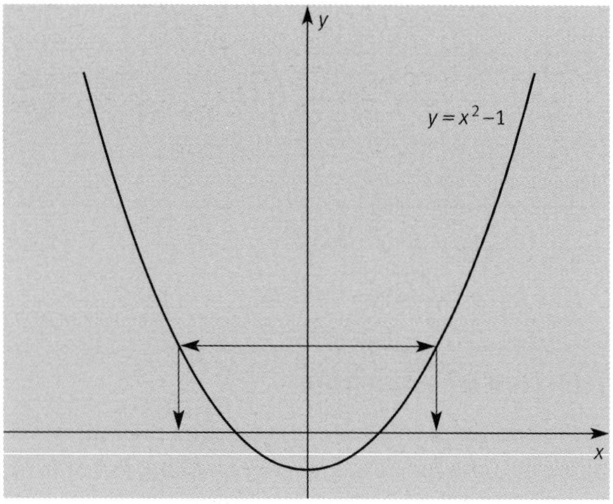

To find $f^{-1}(x)$, use the equation $y = f(x)$; replace x by y and y by x, then solve for y; the result is $f^{-1}(x)$,

e.g. when $f(x) = \frac{1}{2}x + 1$, $f^{-1}(x)$ is found from $y = \frac{1}{2}x + 1$ as follows:

interchange x and y: $x = \frac{1}{2}y + 1$

solve for y: $2x = y + 2$

$\Rightarrow$ $y = 2x - 2$,

i.e. $f^{-1}(x) = 2x - 2$

To draw the graph of $y = f^{-1}(x)$, reflect the graph of $y = f(x)$ in the line $y = x$.

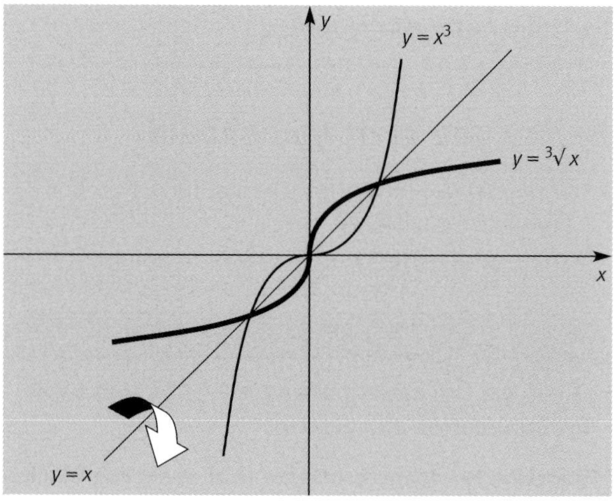

The domain of a function is the range of its inverse and the range of a function is the domain of its inverse.

Questions

1 The functions f and g are defined by

$f(x) = x^2 - 3$ and $g(x) = \dfrac{1}{x-2}$

Find **a** $g(-2)$ **b** $gf(x)$ **c** $g^{-1}(x)$ **d** $ff(x)$.

2 The function f is defined by $f(x) = x^2 - 1$ for $0 \leqslant x \leqslant 4$.

a Give the range of f.

b Explain why f^{-1} exists.

c Sketch the graph of $y = f^{-1}(x)$.

Answers

1a $-\frac{1}{4}$ **b** $\dfrac{1}{x^2-5}$ **c** $\dfrac{1+2x}{x}$ **d** $x^4 - 6x^2 + 6$

2a $-1 \leqslant f(x) \leqslant 15$

b For the domain given, one value of f(x) gives only one value of x.

c

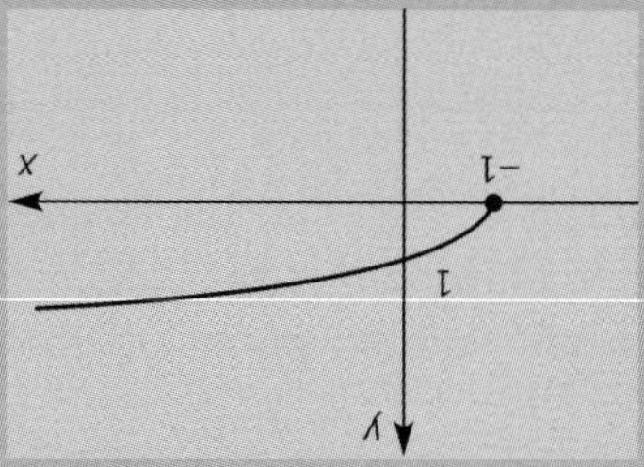

Transformations of curves

The curve $y = -f(x)$ is the reflection in the x-axis of the curve $y = f(x)$.

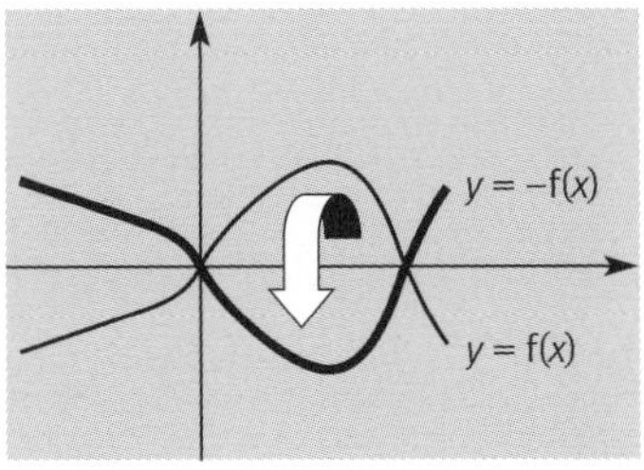

The curve $y = f(-x)$ is the reflection in the y-axis of the curve $y = f(x)$.

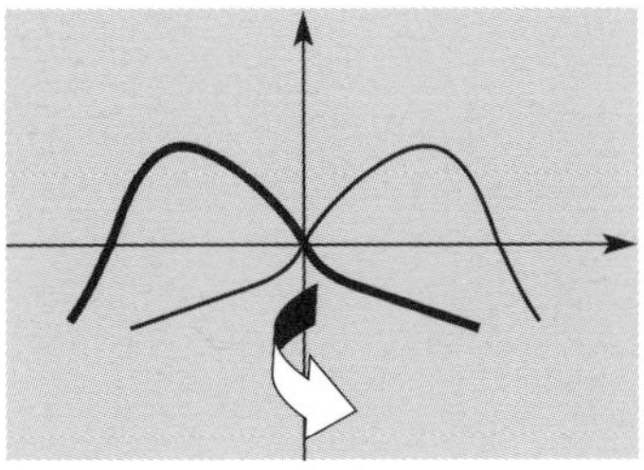

The curve $y = f(x) + a$ is the translation of the curve $y = f(x)$ by a units up the y-axis. If a is negative the curve moves down.

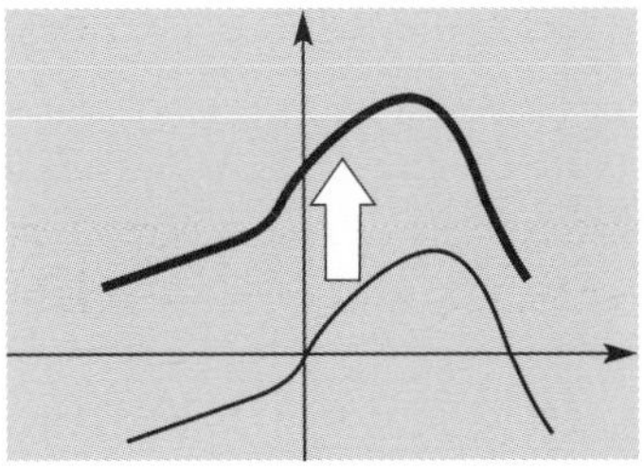

The curve $y = f(x + a)$ is the translation of the curve $y = f(x)$ by a units back along the x-axis. If a is negative, the curve moves forward along the x-axis.

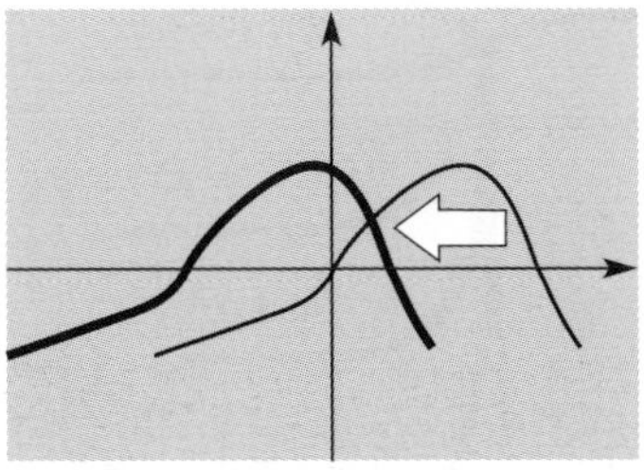

The curve $y = af(x)$ is a one-way stretch of the curve $y = f(x)$ by a units parallel to the y-axis. When $a < 1$, the curve shrinks parallel to the y-axis.

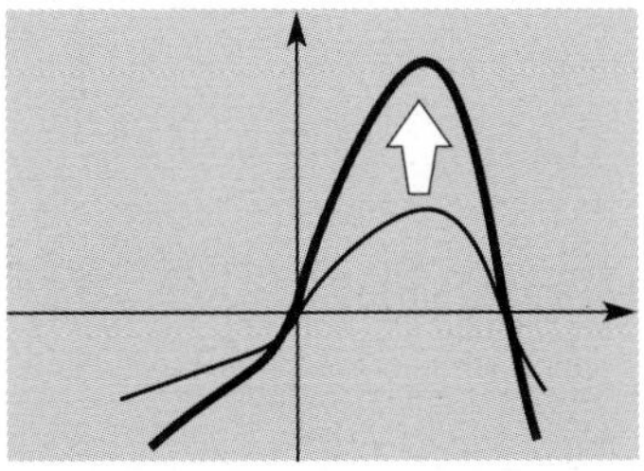

The curve $y = f(ax)$ is a one-way reduction of the curve $y = f(x)$ by a units parallel to the x-axis. When $a < 1$, the curve expands parallel to the x-axis.

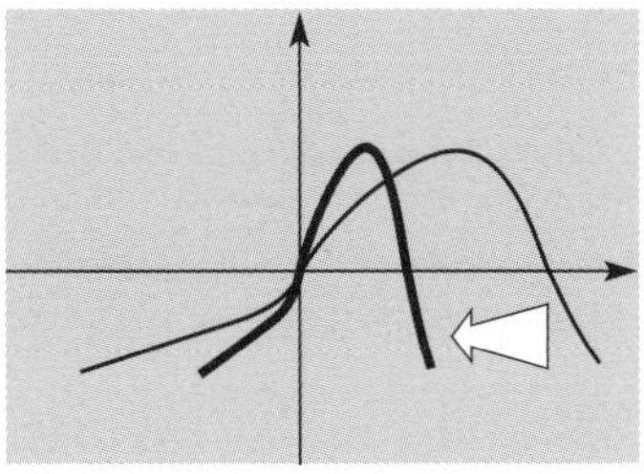

Compound transformations

To sketch a compound transformation of a curve $y = f(x)$, start with a sketch of $y = f(x)$, then identify the order of the transformations and apply them to the given curve in that order,

e.g. to sketch the curve $y = 2 - f(x)$

you need to recognise that $y = 2 - f(x)$ is the compound transformation 'reflect $y = f(x)$ in the x-axis then translate it two units up the y-axis'. Start by sketching $y = f(x)$, reflect it in the x-axis to give $y = -f(x)$, then lift this 2 units.

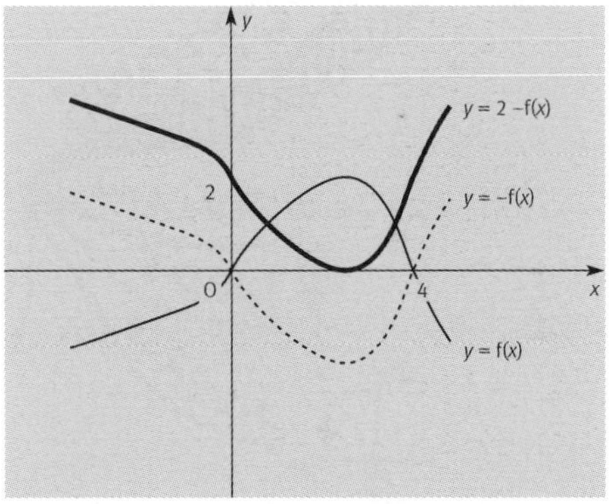

Question

The diagram shows a sketch of $y = f(x)$.
Sketch the curve

a $y = f(x + 2)$ **b** $y = \frac{1}{3}f(x)$ **c** $f(3x) - 2$

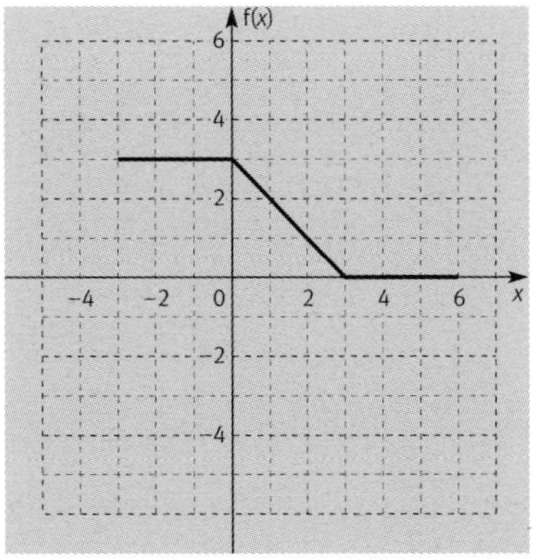

Answer

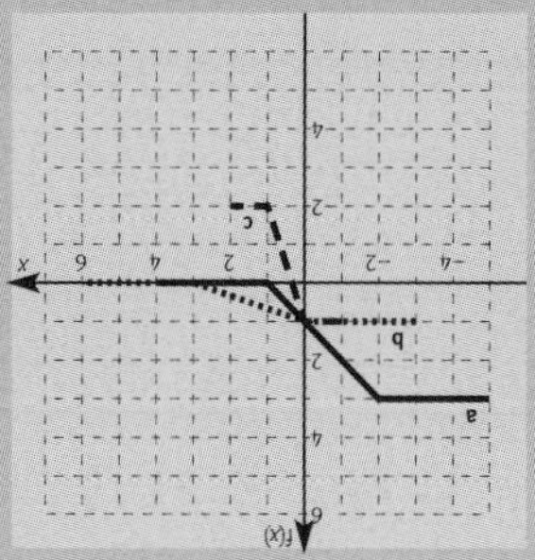

Take a break

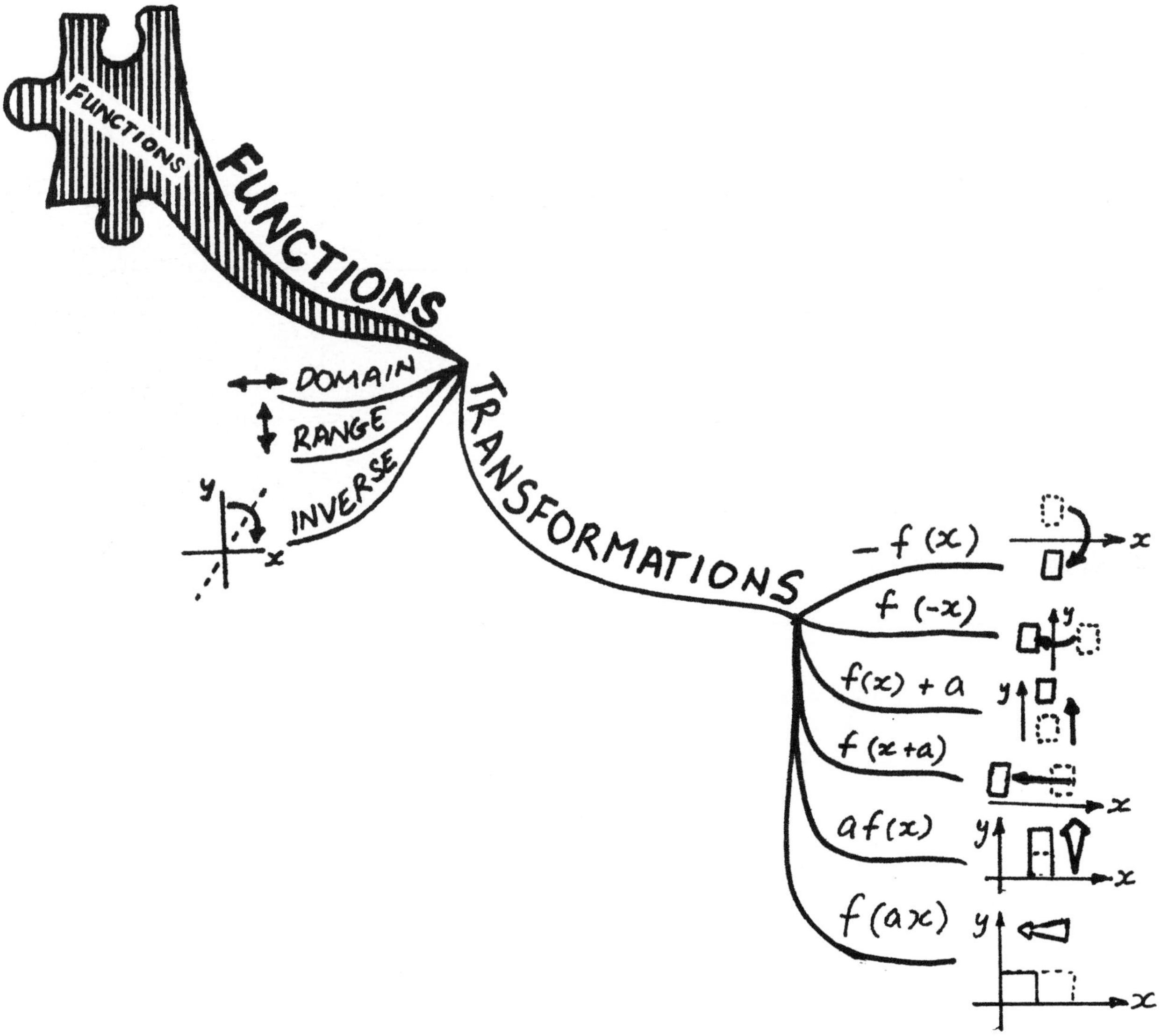

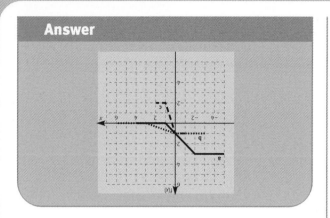

Review

1 Show that $(x + 2)$ is a factor of $x^3 - 2x^2 + 16$.

2 C is the midpoint of the line joining A$(-1, 5)$ and B$(2, -7)$.

a Find the length of AB and the coordinates of C.

b Find the equation of the line through A and C.

c Prove that the line with equation $2x - 8y - 9 = 0$ is the perpendicular bisector of AB.

3 The sketch shows the graph of $y = f(x)$ where $f(x) = \sqrt{x - 2}$.

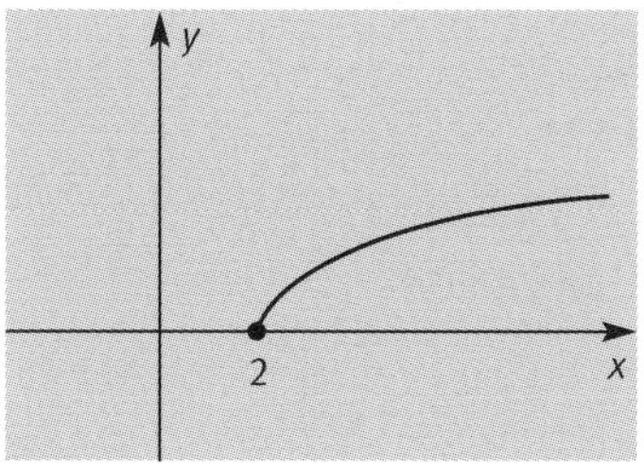

a Give the domain and range of f. **b** Define $f^{-1}(x)$ and give its range.

4 Simplify

a $\dfrac{1}{\sqrt{2} + 6}$ **b** $\dfrac{\sqrt{2} - 3}{\sqrt{3} - 2}$

5a Express $\ln x - 2 \ln xy + \ln (x + y)$ as a single logarithm. **b** Write down the value of $\ln e$.

Answers

1 $f(-2) = (-2)^3 - 2(-2)^2 + 16 = -8 - 8 + 16 = 0 \Rightarrow (x + 2)$ is a factor of $f(x)$.

2a $\sqrt{153}$ **b** $(\frac{1}{2}, -1)$ **c** $4x + y - 1 = 0$

d any convincing argument: e.g. gradient of AB is -4; gradient of given line is $-\frac{1}{4}$, therefore lines are perpendicular. C$(\frac{1}{2}, -1)$ lies on given line as $2(\frac{1}{2}) - 8(-1) - 9 = 0$ so $2x - 8y - 9 = 0$ is the perpendicular bisector of AB.

3a $x \geqslant 2$, $f(x) \geqslant 0$ **b** $f^{-1}(x) = x^2 + 2$ for $x \geqslant 0$, $f^{-1}(x) \geqslant 2$

4a $\dfrac{6 - \sqrt{2}}{34}$ **b** $6 - \sqrt{6} + 3\sqrt{3} - 2\sqrt{2}$

5a $\ln\left(\dfrac{x + y}{xy^2}\right)$ **b** 1

Take a break

PREVIEW

By the end of this topic you will have revised:

- ✔ **the meaning of a sequence and of a series,**
- ✔ **what an arithmetic progression (AP) is and how to find any term and the sum of a given number of terms,**
- ✔ **what a geometric progression (GP) is and how to find any term and the sum of a given number of terms of a GP,**
- ✔ **what the sum to infinity of a GP means,**
- ✔ **how to tackle problems about APs and GPs.**

Before you start you should:

- understand the meaning of 'the nth term' of a sequence and notation used for sequences,
- know how to find a given term of a sequence from the nth term.

TEST YOURSELF

Any wrong answers, see GCSE Higher or A level text book for information and practice.

1 **The nth term of a sequence is $\frac{n+1}{2n}$.**

Find the first term and the 11th term.

2 **The first term of a sequence is $\frac{1}{4}$.**

The nth term is given by $x_n = \dfrac{1}{x_{n-1}+1}$

Find the 2nd and 3rd terms of this sequence.

Answers

1 $1, \frac{6}{11}$ **2** $\frac{4}{5}, \frac{5}{9}$

Sequences and series

A sequence is a progression of numbers formed by a rule.

A series is the sum of the terms of a sequence.

When u_n is the nth term of the sequence $u_1, u_2, \ldots,$

$\sum_{n=1}^{20} u_n$ means the series $u_1 + u_2 + u_3 + \ldots + u_{20}$.

Arithmetic progression (AP)

An arithmetic progression is a sequence of numbers where the difference between consecutive terms (called the common difference) is always the same,

e.g. $1, 4, 7, 10, 13, \ldots$

When the first term is a and the common difference is d, the first few terms of an AP are

$$a,\ a+d,\ a+2d,\ a+3d, \ldots$$

The nth term is $a + (n-1)d$.

The sum of the first n terms of any sequence is S_n,

i.e. $S_n = \sum_{r=1}^{n} u_r$.

For an AP,
$S_4 = (a) + (a+d) + (a+2d) + (a+3d)$

and $S_n = \frac{n}{2}(2a + (n-1)d)$

or $S_n = \frac{n}{2}(a + l)$ where l is the last term.

The first n natural numbers, $1, 2, 3, \ldots, n$, form an AP with $a = 1$ and $d = 1$.

Their sum, i.e. $1 + 2 + \ldots + n$, is $\frac{1}{2}n(n+1)$.

Geometric progression (GP)

A geometric progression is a sequence of numbers where the ratio between consecutive terms (called the common ratio) is always the same; e.g. 3, 6, 12, 24, 48, ...

When the first term is a and the common ratio is r, the first few terms of a GP are

$$a,\ ar,\ ar^2,\ ar^3, \ldots$$

The nth term is ar^{n-1}.

The sum of the first n terms is given by

$$S_n = \frac{a(1-r^n)}{1-r}.$$

When $-1 < r < 1$,

as $n \to \infty$, $r^n \to 0$, and $S_n \to \dfrac{a}{1-r}$.

This value is called 'the sum to infinity' and is denoted by S, or by S_∞,

i.e. $$S = \frac{a}{1-r}$$

Problems involving APs and GPs

Questions about APs and GPs come in two types.

1 Questions that state the sequence you have to deal with: these give some information about the terms and ask for other facts to be found.

Express the given information in terms of a, d (or r as appropriate) and n, then use the resulting equations to find their values; when you know a, d or r, you can answer any question asked about the series.

Example

The 10th term of an AP is 25 and the 20th term is 20. Find the sum of the first 100 terms.

Solution

The 10th term of an AP is $a + 9d$,

$$\therefore \quad a + 9d = 25 \qquad [1]$$

The 20th term of an AP is $a + 19d$,

$$\therefore \quad a + 19d = 20 \qquad [2]$$

Solving [1] and [2] simultaneously gives

$$d = -\tfrac{1}{2} \text{ and } a = 29\tfrac{1}{2}.$$

Using $S_n = \dfrac{n}{2}(2a + (n-1)d)$ gives

$$S_{100} = 50(59 - 99 \times \tfrac{1}{2}) = 475.$$

2 Questions where a situation leads to a sequence that you have to recognise. These involve repeated changes over equal time spans.

This type of question must be tackled systematically; start at the beginning of the time span and write down the value of the quantity after the first change.

Remove any brackets but *do no other calculations.* Repeat for the next few changes until you see the pattern of the sequence forming.

Example

Martin takes out a loan of £6000 which he agrees to repay at the rate of £100 at the end of each calendar month.

Interest of 1% of the balance at the beginning of the month is charged at the end of each month.

Find the amount that Martin owes after 24 repayments.

Solution

Owed:

after any one month:

balance at the start of the month
+1% of that balance − £100

at the start: £6000

after 1 month:

$$£6000 + 1\% \text{ of } £6000 - £100$$
$$= £(6000 \times 1.01 - 100)$$

after 2 months:

$$£(6000 \times 1.01 - 100) \times 1.01 - £100$$
$$= £(6000 \times 1.01^2 - 100 \times 1.01 - 100)$$

after 3 months:

$$£(6000 \times 1.01^2 - 100 \times 1.01 - 100) \times 1.01 - £100$$
$$= £(6000 \times 1.01^3 \underline{- 100 \times 1.01^2 - 100 \times 1.01 - 100)}$$

The pattern is now clear; this involves a GP with $a = 100$ and $r = 1.01$.
The amount outstanding after 24 months is

$$£6000 \times 1.01^{24} - £(100 + 100 \times 1.01 + 100 \times 1.10^2) \ldots + 100 \times 1.10^{23})$$
$$= £6000 \times 1.01^{24} - £\frac{100(1 - 1.01^{24})}{1 - 1.01}$$
$$= £4921.06 \text{ to the nearest penny.}$$

Questions

1 The first term of a GP is 8 and the eighth term is $\frac{1}{16}$. Find

a the common ratio,

b the sum of the first ten terms,

c the sum to infinity.

2 The first term of an AP is 100 and the second term is 90.
Find the values of n for which the sum of the first n terms is 450 and explain why there are two values.

3 Jane pays £50 into a regular savings scheme on the first day of each calendar month. Interest is added to her savings on the last day of each calendar month at the rate of 0.3% of the amount in the scheme at the start of that month. Find, to the nearest £10, the amount in Jane's scheme at the end of 10 years.

Answers

1a $\frac{1}{2}$ **b** $\frac{1023}{64}$ **c** 16

2 6, 15; the terms become negative after the 10th term so the sum decreases for $n > 10$.

3 £7230

Take a break

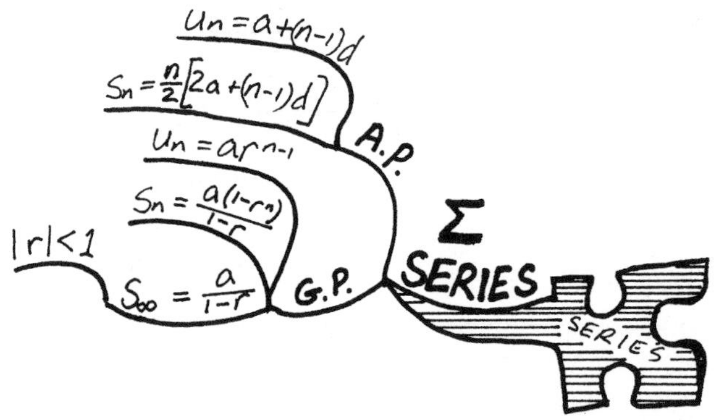

Review

1 A student is asked to show that the line l with equation $4y + x - 19 = 0$ is the perpendicular bisector of the line joining the points A(3, −1) and B(5, 7). The student produced the following argument:

The gradient of l is $-\frac{1}{4}$.
The gradient of AB is 4
$\therefore$ l is perpendicular to AB, so l is the perpendicular bisector of AB.

Explain why the student has not shown that l is the perpendicular bisector of AB.

2a Factorise $2x^3 - 3x^2 - 8x - 3$.

b i Express $\log_a 12 - 2\log_a 3 - \log_a 4$ as $\log_a k$, and give the value of k.
ii Given that $\log_a 12 - 2\log_a 3 - \log_a 4 = \frac{1}{2}$, find the value of a.

3 The functions f and g are given by $f(x) = x^2 - 2x$, $x \in \mathbb{R}$, and $g(x) = \sqrt{x}$, $x > 0$.

a Sketch the curves

$y = f(x)$ and $y = f(x + 2)$.

b Explain why $f^{-1}(x)$ does not exist but that $fg(x)$ does exist.

4a What is the condition for the value of $\sum_{n=1}^{\infty} ar^{n-1}$ to be finite?

b An AP has first term a and common difference d.

Write down in terms of a, d and n
i the sum of the first n terms
ii the sum of the first $2n$ terms.

Hence show that the sum of the second n terms is given by $\frac{n}{2}(2a + (3n - 1)d)$

Answers

1 The student has shown only that l is ⊥ to AB. It must also be shown that the midpoint of AB lies on l.

2a $(x + 1)(x - 3)(2x + 1)$ **b i** $\log_a \frac{1}{3}$ **ii** $\frac{1}{9}$

3a

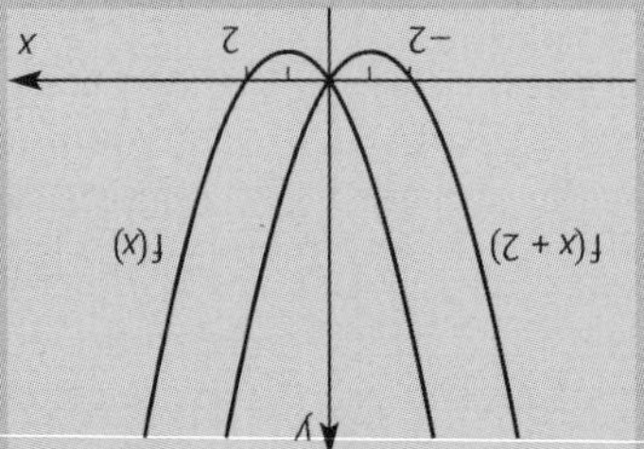

b one value f(x) gives 2 values of x so the inverse mapping is not one to one, $fg(x) = x - 2\sqrt{x}$ and this has one value for all values of $x > 0$.

4a $-1 < r < 1$ **b i** $\frac{n}{2}(2a + (n - 1)d)$ **ii** $n(2a + (2n - 1)d)$

Take a break

PREVIEW

By the end of this topic you will have revised:

- ✔ **what a radian is and how to convert between radians and degrees,**
- ✔ **how to use radians to find the length of an arc and the area of a sector of a circle.**

Before you start you should:

- know that, in any triangle ABC,

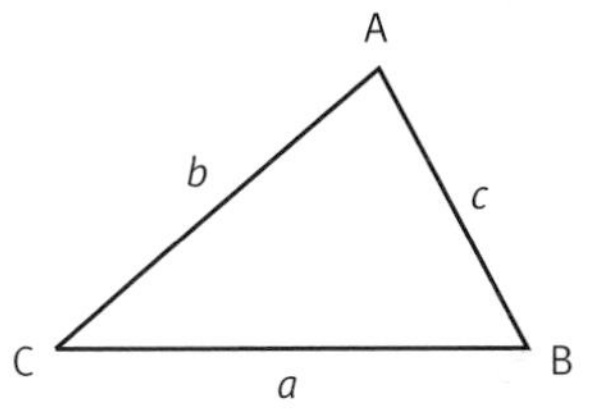

$\frac{\sin A}{a} = \frac{\sin B}{b} = \frac{\sin C}{c}$,
$a^2 = b^2 + c^2 - 2bc \cos A$,
Area $= \frac{1}{2}ab \sin C$,
- know the properties of tangents to circles and angles in circles,
- know

$\sin 30° = \frac{1}{2}$, $\cos 30° = \frac{\sqrt{3}}{2}$, $\tan 30° = \frac{1}{\sqrt{3}}$

$\sin 45° = \cos 45° = \frac{1}{\sqrt{2}}$, $\tan 45° = 1$

$\sin 60° = \frac{\sqrt{3}}{2}$, $\cos 60° = \frac{1}{2}$, $\tan 60° = \sqrt{3}$.

TEST YOURSELF

More than one wrong answer, see GCSE Higher or A level text book for information and practice.

1. **In ΔPQR, $r = 5$ cm, $q = 3.5$ cm and angle QPR = 150°. Find QR and the area of △PQR.**
2. **AB is the diameter of a circle, O is its centre and C is a point on the circumference where angle CAB = 30°. The radius of the circle is r and the tangent at C meets AB produced at D. Find**
   a) the angles of △OCD
   b) the area of △OCD in terms of r.

Answers

1 8.22 cm, 4.375 cm²
2 a) ∠C = 90°, ∠O = 60°, ∠D = 30° b) $\frac{\sqrt{3}}{2}r^2$

Radians

The radian is a unit in which angles are measured. 1 radian (1 rad) is the size of the angle subtended at the centre of a circle by an arc equal in length to the radius of the circle.

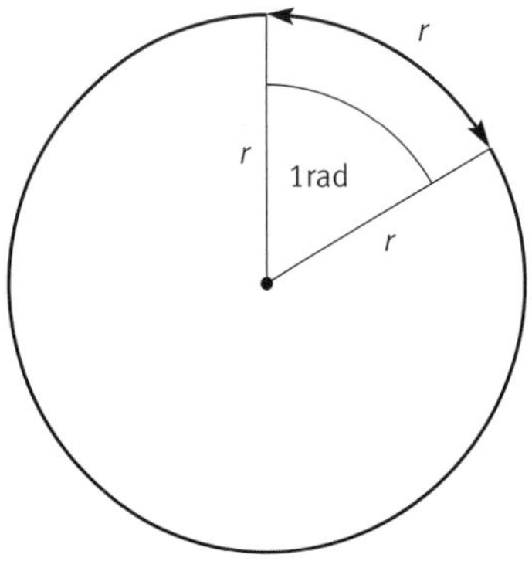

You can change from degrees to radians by multiplying the number of degrees by $\frac{\pi}{180}$.
You can change from radians to degrees by multiplying the number of radians by $\frac{180}{\pi}$.

$360° = 2\pi$, $180° = \pi$, $90° = \frac{\pi}{2}$, $45° = \frac{\pi}{4}$,

$60° = \frac{\pi}{3}$, $30° = \frac{\pi}{6}$

Arc length and area of sector

When an arc subtends an angle of θ radians at the centre of a circle of radius r,

the length of the arc is $r\theta$,
the area of the sector is $\frac{1}{2}r^2\theta$.

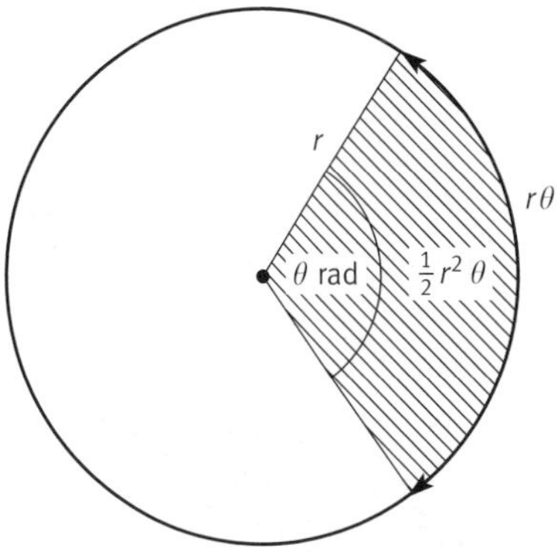

Problems

Remember to look for facts, including those that are not spelt out in the question. Express those facts in mathematical terms and look for relationships between facts.

Example

In the diagram, O is the centre of a circle of radius r cm. AT and BT are tangents to the circle and angle AOB $= \frac{2\pi}{3}$ rad. Show that the area of the shaded region is $\frac{1}{3}r^2(3\sqrt{2} - \pi)$.

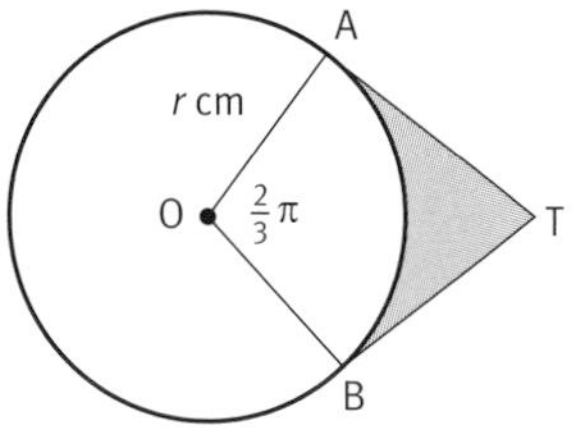

Solution

The area of the shaded region cannot be found directly but it can be found by combining areas that can be calculated: e.g.
(area of kite OATB) − (area of sector AOB).

The area of sector AOB is $\frac{1}{2} \times r^2 \times \frac{2\pi}{3} = \frac{\pi r^2}{3}$

The kite is symmetrical about OT, so $\angle AOT = \frac{\pi}{3}$, and $\angle A = \angle B = \frac{\pi}{2}$
(mark these facts on the diagram).

You can find the area of the kite by doubling the area of $\triangle$AOT but you first need to find the length of another side of $\triangle$AOT. You can do this by using trigonometry:

$$\tan\frac{\pi}{3} = \frac{AT}{r} \Rightarrow AT = r\tan\frac{\pi}{3} \Rightarrow AT = r\sqrt{3}$$

$\therefore$ area $\triangle AOT = (\frac{1}{2})r \times r\sqrt{3} = (\frac{1}{2})r^2\sqrt{3}$

so area of kite OATB $= r^2\sqrt{3}$

$\therefore$ area shaded is $r^2\sqrt{3} - \frac{\pi r^2}{3} = \frac{1}{3}r^2(3\sqrt{3} - \pi)$.

Question

AB is a diameter of a circle, centre O and radius r. P is a point on the circumference of the circle such that angle PBO $= \theta$ radians.

a Find, in terms of r and θ,
  i the length of the arc AP and the length of the chord AP,
  ii the area enclosed by the line AP and the arc AP.

b Given that the area of triangle APO is equal to the area enclosed by the line AP and the arc AP, show that $\theta = \sin 2\theta$

Answers

a $2r\theta, 2r\sin\theta$ **b** $r^2(\theta - \frac{1}{2}\sin 2\theta)$

Take a break

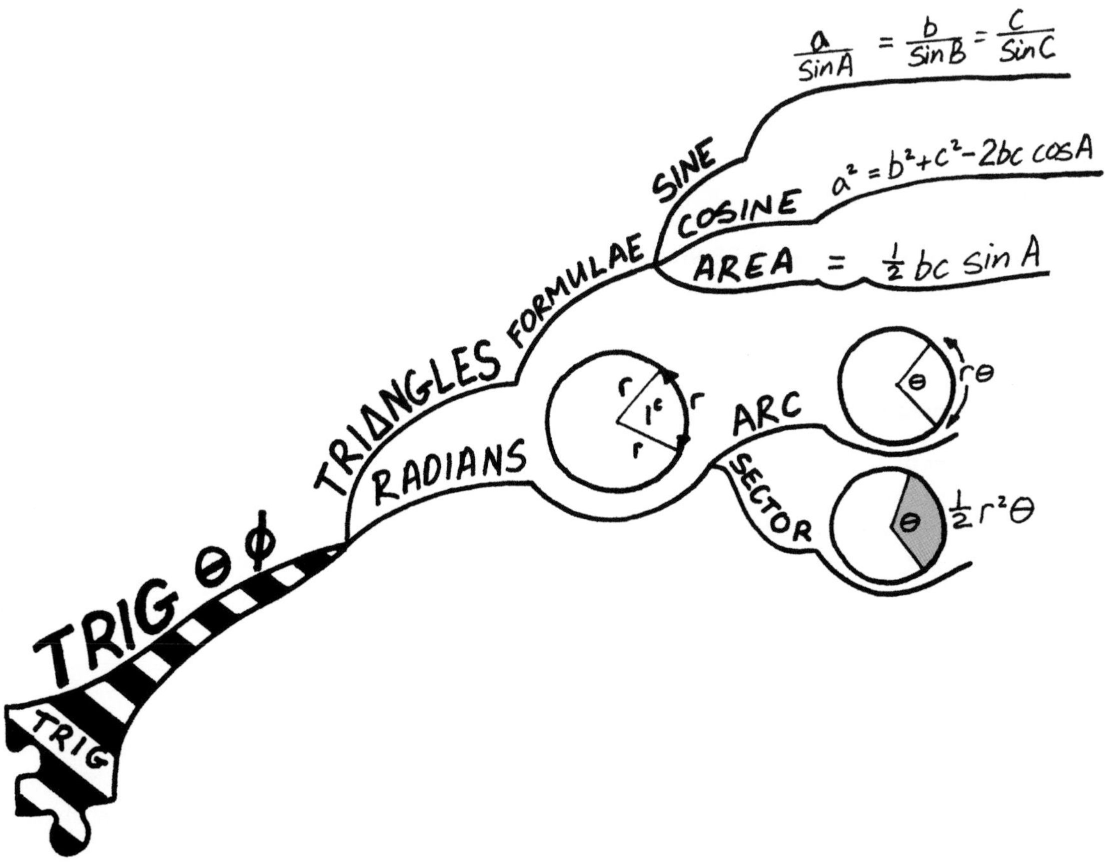

Review

1 Give the conditions that a must satisfy for $(x + a)$ to be a factor of $2x^3 - x + 1$.

2 The first term of an AP is a and d is the common difference. Write down, in terms of a and d, the 10th term and the sum of the first 10 terms of the AP.

3 A and B are two points on the circumference of a circle whose radius is r. AB subtends an angle of $\frac{\pi}{4}$ radians at the centre of a circle.
Show that the area enclosed by the arc AB and the chord AB is equal to $\frac{1}{8}r^2(\pi - 2\sqrt{2})$.

4 Find the value of
a $\log_3 81$ **b** $3\log_a a^{\frac{1}{2}}$ **c** $\log_2 16 - \log_4 64$.

5 $f(x) = 1 + 2x$ and $g(x) = 4x^2$ for all values of x.
Find $fg(x)$ and explain why $fg(x)$ does not have an inverse function.

6 The points A(1, 2), B(3, 4) and C(1, 6) lie on the circumference of a circle.
Show that AB is perpendicular to BC and hence find the coordinates of the centre of the circle.

Answers

1 $-2a^3 + a + 1 = 0$

2 $a + 9d, 10a + 45d$

4a 4 **b** $1\frac{1}{2}$ **c** 1

5 $fg(x) = 1 + 8x^2$; any value of $fg(x) > 1$ gives two values of x so $fg(x)$ does not have an inverse.

6 grad AB = 1, grad BC = −1, $(1) \times (-1) = -1$,
$\therefore$ AB $\perp$ BC, (1, 4)

Take a break

PREVIEW

By the end of this topic you will have revised:

- ✔ **what a modulus function is and how to sketch graphs of modulus functions,**
- ✔ **what logarithmic and exponential functions are and the shape of their graphs,**
- ✔ **how to solve equations and inequalities involving these functions.**

Before you start you should:

- know how to solve simultaneous equations in two unknowns algebraically,
- be aware that equations can be solved graphically by finding the coordinates of points of intersection,
- be confident about using logs.

TEST YOURSELF

Any wrong answer, see GCSE Higher or A level text book for information and practice.

1 **Solve the equations** $3y + 2x = 7$, $4y = 5 - 3x$

2 **Find the value of x for which**
$x^2 - 2xy + y^2 = 9$ **and** $2x - y = 7$.

3 **By sketching appropriate graphs, show that the equation $x^3 = x + 1$ has a root between $x = 0$ and $x = 2$.**

Answers

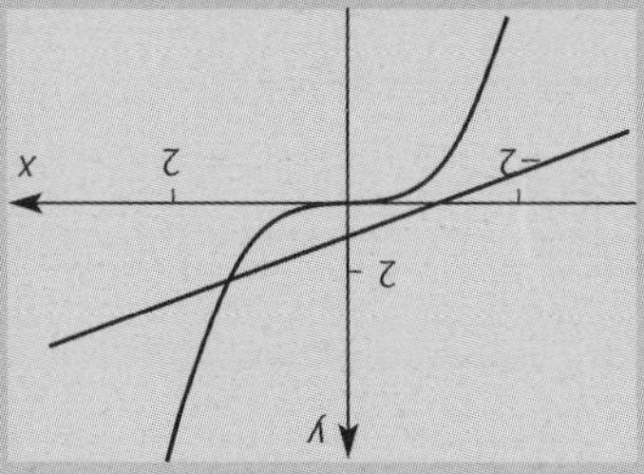

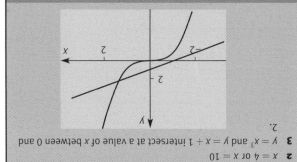

1 $x = -13, y = 11$
2 $x = 4$ or $x = 10$
3 $y = x^3$ and $y = x + 1$ intersect at a value of x between 0 and 2.

Exponential and logarithmic functions

The exponential function f is given by $f(x) = e^x$ where e is the irrational number 2.71828....

The diagram shows the graph of $f(x) = e^x$.

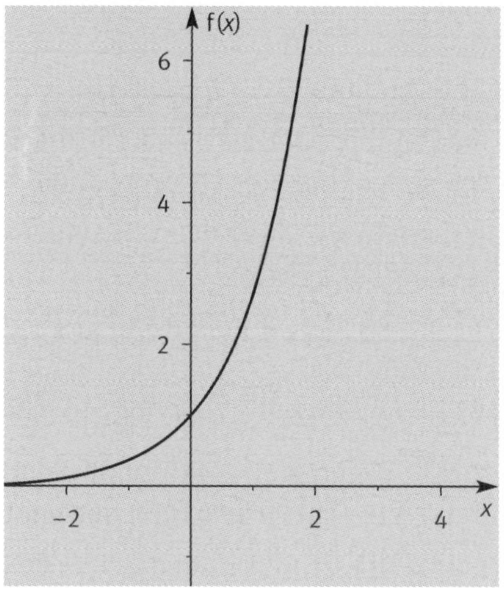

The curve passes through (0, 1) and the negative x-axis is an asymptote.

The inverse of the exponential function is found from $y = e^x$ by interchanging x and y and then solving for y i.e. $x = e^y \Rightarrow y = \ln x$, so $f^{-1}(x) = \ln x$

The function g given by $g(x) = \ln x$ is called the logarithmic function and it is the inverse of the exponential function.

The diagram shows the curve $y = \ln x$. The curve passes through (1, 0) and the negative y-axis is an asymptote; $\ln x$ exists only for positive values of x.

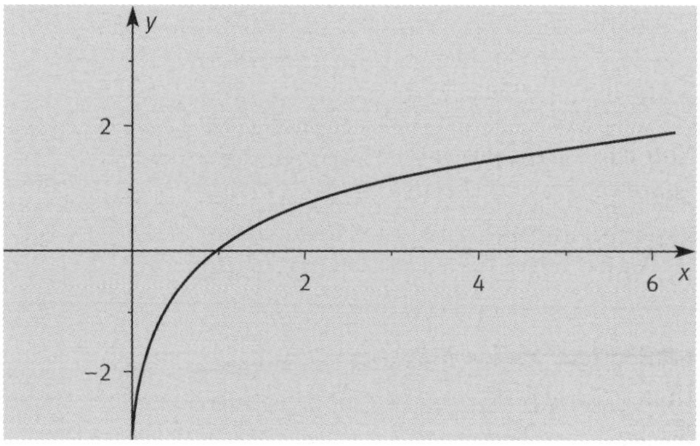

Modulus functions

$|x|$ is called the modulus of x (or mod x) and it means 'whatever the value of x is, make it positive', e.g. $|3| = 3$ and $|-3| = 3$

Similarly, $|2x - 3|$ means that whatever the value of $2x - 3$ is, you make it positive, e.g. when $x = 1$, $|2x - 3| = |-1| = 1$

To draw the curve $y = |f(x)|$, first draw the curve $y = f(x)$ then reflect in the x-axis the parts of $y = f(x)$ that are below the x-axis,

e.g. this is the curve $y = |x^2 - 2x|$

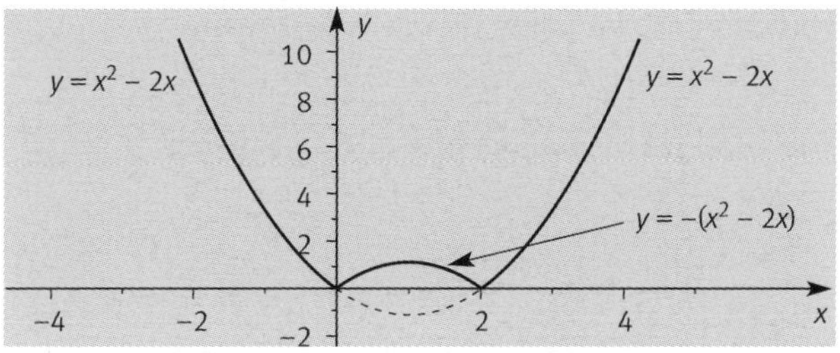

The equation of the parts of the curve that have not been reflected is $y = f(x)$ and the equation of the parts of the curve that have been reflected is $y = -f(x)$.

When $y = f(|x|)$, then

$y = f(x)$ for positive values of x

and $y = f(-x)$ for negative values of x,

e.g. $|3|^3 = 27$ and $|-3|^3 = |3|^3 = 27$.

You can draw the curve $y = f(|x|)$ by drawing $y = f(x)$ for $x \geqslant 0$ and the reflection of $y = f(x)$ in the y-axis for $x < 0$.

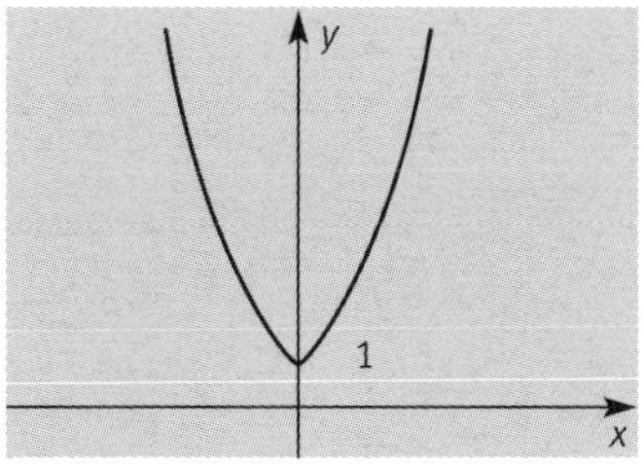

The diagram shows the curve $y = e^{|x|}$.

Curve sketching

You can use the transformations in Pure 4 to help sketch curves whose equations involve modulus or exponential functions, e.g.
to sketch the curve whose equation is

$y = 3 - |2x - 1|$,

start with $y = |2x - 1|$,
then reflect this in the x-axis to give $y = -|2x - 1|$,
finally move $y = -|2x - 1|$ by 3 units up the y-axis to give $y = -|2x - 1| + 3$.

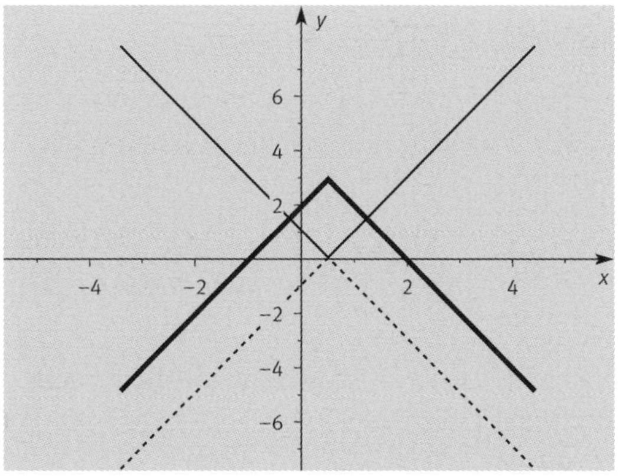

To sketch the curve $y = e^{1-x}$, you can write the equation as $y = e \times e^{-x}$
so start with $y = e^x$,
then reflect this in the y-axis to give $y = e^{-x}$
finally stretch $y = e^{-x}$ by e units parallel to the y-axis to give $y = e^{1-x}$

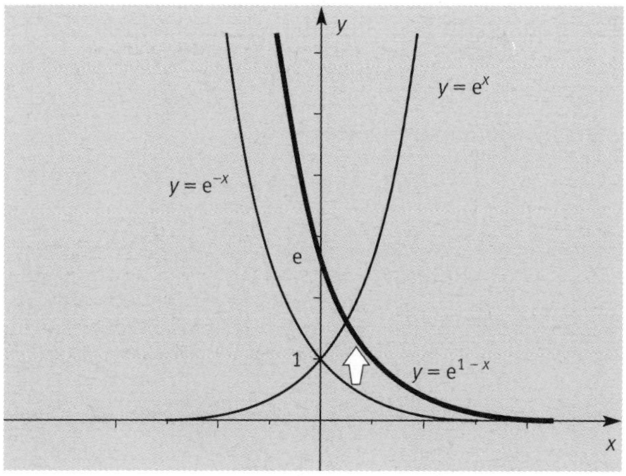

When you sketch a graph, you do not have to scale the axes, but you should mark intercepts on the axes.

Questions

1 On the same set of axes, sketch the graph of $y = e^{-2x}$ and $y = 2 - 3x$. How many roots does the equation $2 - 3x = e^{-2x}$ have?

2 Given that $f(x) = e^{3x}$

a find $f^{-1}(x)$

b sketch the graph of $y = 3f^{-1}(x) + 1$.

3 On the same set of axes, sketch the curves

$y = |x - 3| + 1$ and $y = |x^2 - 4|$.

How many points of intersection are there?

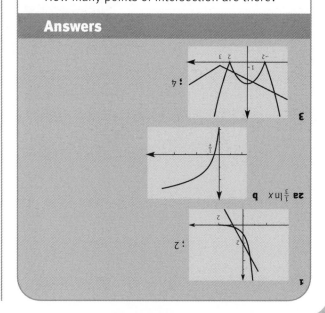

Answers

1 : 2

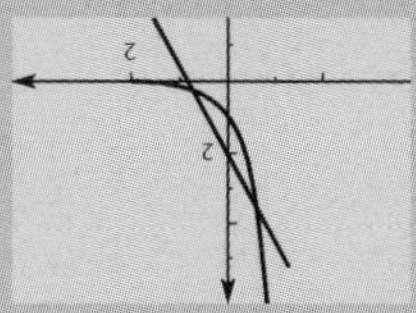

2a $\frac{1}{3}\ln x$ **b**

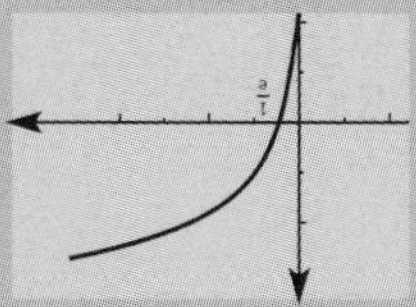

3 : 4

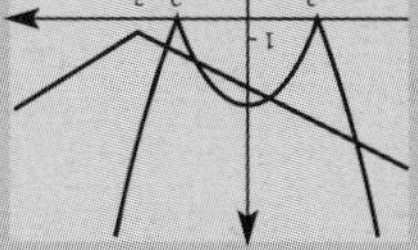

Solving equations and inequalities

You can use sketches of curves to help with the solution of equations and inequalities; this gives a 'picture' that indicates the number of solutions and, when modulus functions are involved, shows which equations you need to solve.

For example, to find the values of x for which

$$|2x - 3| < \tfrac{1}{2}(x + 4)$$

start by sketching the graphs of

$$y = |2x - 3| \text{ and } y = \tfrac{1}{2}(x + 4)$$

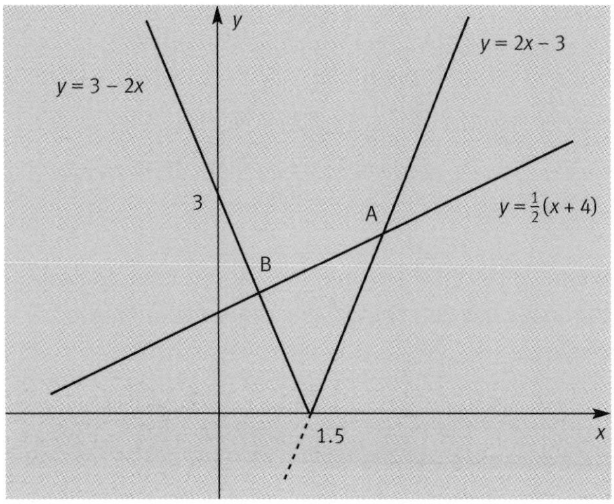

$|2x - 3| < \frac{1}{2}(x + 4)$ between A and B.

You can find the value of x at A by solving
$2x - 3 = \frac{1}{2}(x + 4) \quad \Rightarrow \quad x = \frac{10}{3}$

You can find the values of x at B by solving
$3 - 2x = \frac{1}{2}(x + 4) \quad \Rightarrow \quad x = \frac{2}{5}$

$\therefore\ |2x - 3| < \frac{1}{2}(x + 4) \quad \text{for} \quad \frac{2}{5} < x < 3\frac{1}{3}$.

Questions

1 Find the values of x for which $|x^2 - 1| = x$.

2 Find, in terms of natural logarithms, the range of values of x for which $|4 - e^x| < e^x$.

Answers

1 $\frac{1}{2}(1 + \sqrt{5}), \frac{1}{2}(-1 + \sqrt{5})$ **2** $x > \ln 2$

Take a break

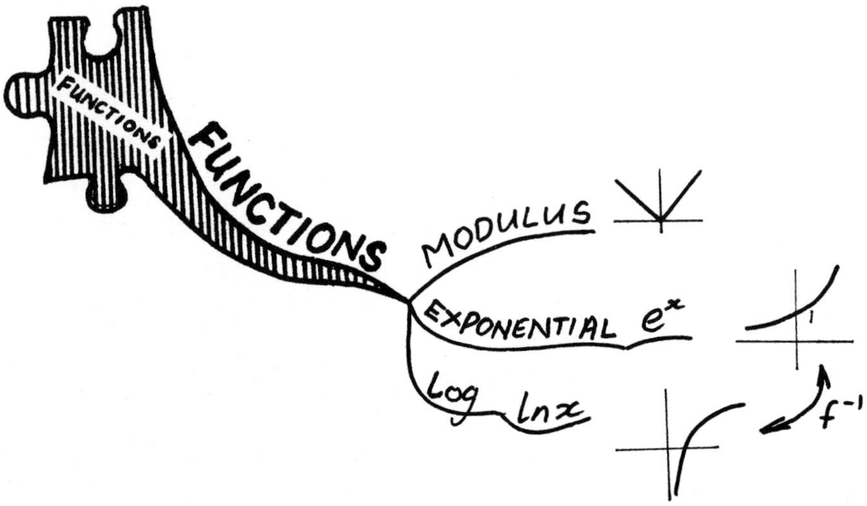

Review

1 Find the discriminant of the expression

$$2x^2 - px + 2.$$

What are the conditions that p must satisfy for the equation $2x^2 - px + 2 = 0$ to have two real and distinct roots?

2 Find the equation of the line that passes through (1, 5) and that is perpendicular to the line with equation $2y - 5x = 1$.

3 Solve the equations

a $2\ln x - \ln(x+2) = 0$

b $x^3 - 2x^2 - 2x - 3 = 0$

4 What are the conditions that a function f must satisfy for f^{-1} to exist?

5 The 2nd term of a geometric progression is 4 and the 5th term is $-\frac{1}{2}$. Find the 8th term and the sum to infinity.

6 A and B are two points on the circumference of a circle whose centre is O and whose radius is a. The smaller of the two angles AOB is β radians. Find, in terms of a and β, the area of the larger segment cut off by the chord AB.

7 Sketch the graph of

a $y = |\ln x|$

b $y = \ln|x|$.

Answers

1 $p^2 - 16$, $p < -4$ or $p > 4$ **2** $2x + 5y - 27 = 0$

3a 2 (−1 is not a solution because ln (−1) does not exist).

b 3

4 f must be such that all values of f(x) come from one and only one value of x.

5b $\frac{1}{16}$, $-\frac{16}{3}$ **6** $\frac{1}{2}a^2(2\pi - \beta) + \frac{1}{2}a^2\sin\beta$

7a

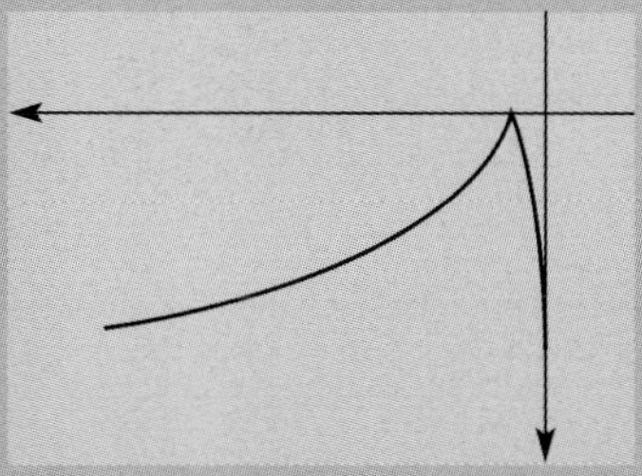

b

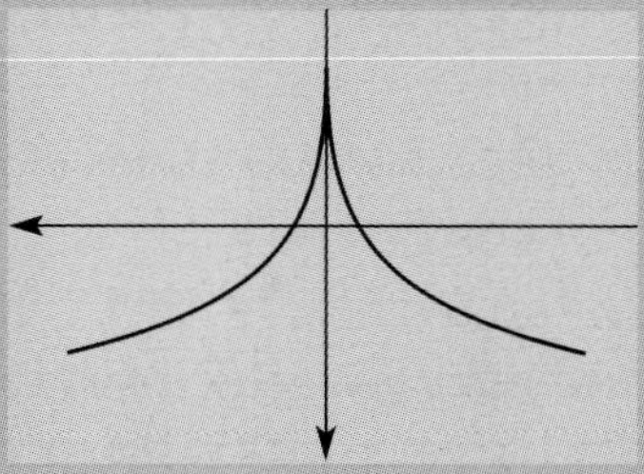

Take a break

PREVIEW

By the end of this topic you will have revised:

- ✔ **how to sketch graphs of trigonometric functions,**
- ✔ **relationships between trigonometric functions,**
- ✔ **how to solve trigonometric equations.**

Before you start you should:

- know the shapes of the graphs of $y = \sin x$, $y = \cos x$, $y = \tan x$ and their properties,
- know that $-1 \leqslant \sin x \leqslant 1$, $-1 \leqslant \cos x \leqslant 1$ and that $\tan x$ can have any value,
- remember the values of sine, cosine and tangent of 45°, 30° and 60°,
- be confident about using radians.

TEST YOURSELF

Any wrong answers, see GCSE higher or A level text book for information and practice.

1 a) Sketch the graph of
i) $y = \sin x$ ii) $y = \cos x$ iii) $y = \tan x$ for $-\pi \leqslant x \leqslant 4\pi$

b) Write down the values of x within this range for which
i) $\sin x = 0$ ii) $\cos x = 0$ iii) $\tan x = 1$

2 Describe a geometric transformation that maps the curve $y = \sin x$ to the curve $y = \cos x$.

Answers

1a i

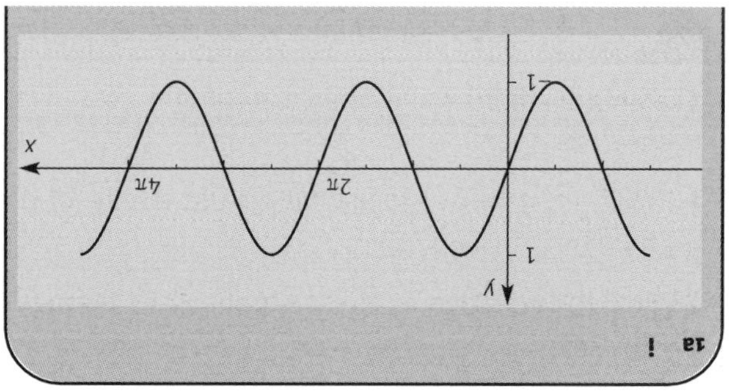

ii

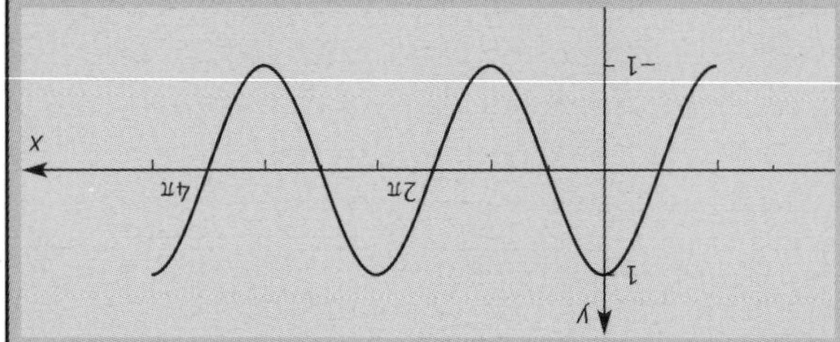

iii

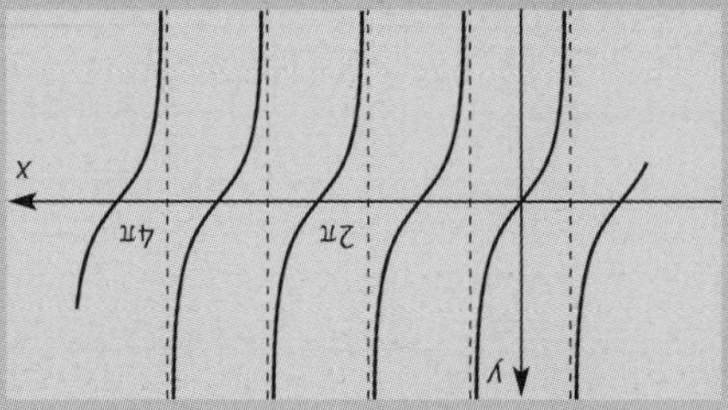

b i $-\pi, 0, \pi, 2\pi, 3\pi, 4\pi$

ii $-\frac{1}{2}\pi, \frac{1}{2}\pi, \frac{3}{2}\pi, \frac{5}{2}\pi, \frac{7}{2}\pi$

iii $-\frac{3}{4}\pi, \frac{1}{4}\pi, \frac{5}{4}\pi, \frac{9}{4}\pi, \frac{13}{4}\pi$

2 a translation of $\pi/2$ units to the left along the x-axis.

Curve sketching

The shape of the graph of $f(x) = \sin x$ is called a sine wave; the pattern repeats every interval of 2π. The graph of $f(x) = \cos x$ is also a sine wave, translated by $\frac{1}{2}\pi$ radians to the left.

You can use the transformations $y = f(ax)$ and $y = af(x)$ to sketch the graphs of, for example, $y = \sin 2x$, $y = 2 \sin x$, $y = \cos 3x$, and so on.

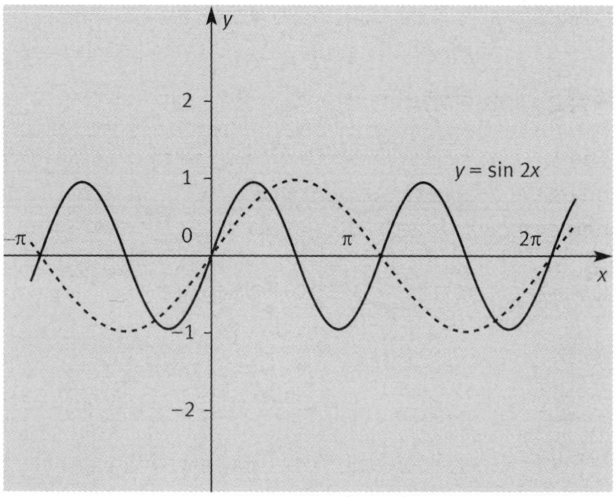

The basic pattern of the curve $y = \sin 2x$ repeats twice in every interval of 2π.

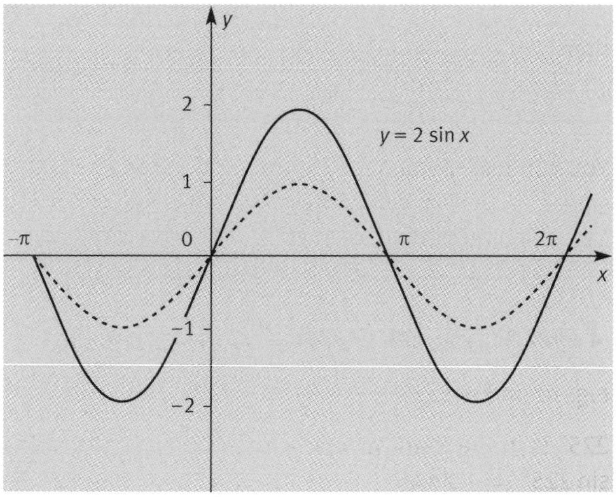

The basic pattern of $y = \sin ax$ and of $y = \cos ax$ repeats a times in each interval of 2π.

Questions

Sketch the graphs of the curves in the interval $0 \leqslant x \leqslant 2\pi$.

1 $y = 3\cos x$ **2** $y = 1 - \sin x$

3 $y = \cos 3x$ **4** $y = |\sin x|$.

Answers

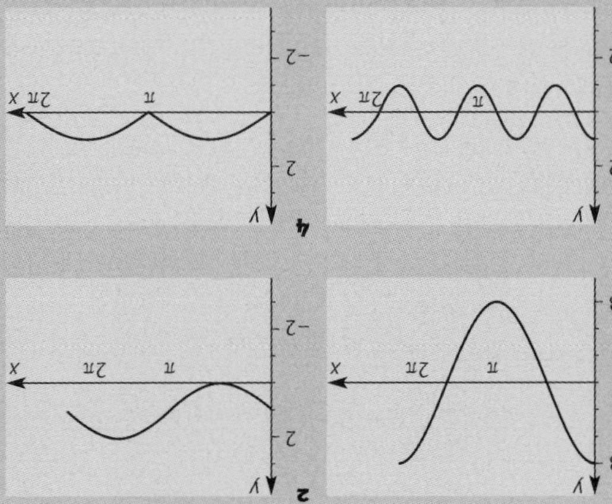

Trigonometric functions

The trigonometric functions are defined using a quadrant diagram; for any value of θ, draw the perpendicular from P to the x-axis,

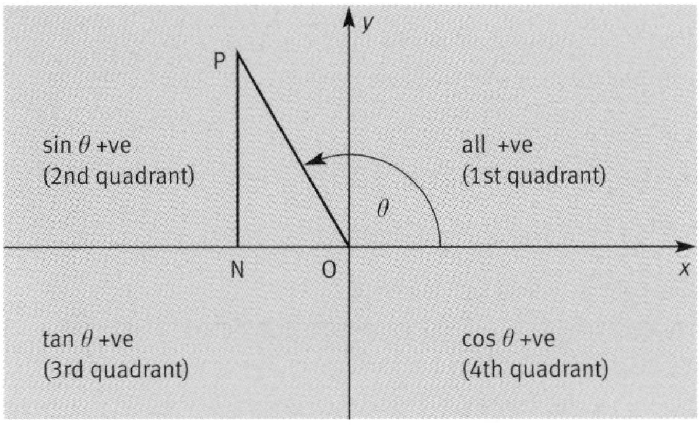

then

$$\sin\theta = \frac{NP}{OP}, \ \cos\theta = \frac{ON}{OP}, \ \tan\theta = \frac{NP}{ON}.$$

You can use the quadrant diagram to write down the sine, cosine or tangent of an angle in terms of the trig ratio of an acute angle.

Draw the angle in a quadrant diagram and draw the perpendicular to the x-axis (⚠ not to the y-axis):

e.g. to find $\sin 225°$,

225° is in the third quadrant, so $\sin 225°$ is negative,

$$\sin 225° = -\sin 45°$$
$$= -\frac{1}{\sqrt{2}}$$

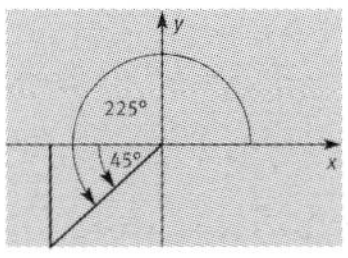

and to find $\cos(-30°)$, (a negative angle is a clockwise rotation from Ox)

$-30°$ is in the fourth quadrant and $\cos(-30°)$ is positive:

$$\cos(-30°) = \cos 30°$$
$$= \frac{\sqrt{3}}{2}$$

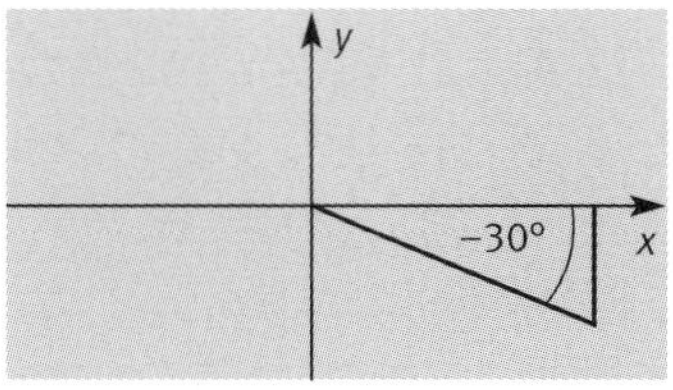

Trigonometric identities

The definitions above lead directly to these relationships:

1 $\sin\theta \equiv \cos(90° - \theta)$, $\cos\theta \equiv \sin(90° - \theta)$,

$$\tan\theta \equiv \frac{1}{\tan(90° - \theta)}$$

2 $\tan\theta \equiv \dfrac{\sin\theta}{\cos\theta}$

3 $\sin^2\theta + \cos^2\theta \equiv 1$

You can use these identities

- to find the other trig ratios of an angle when you know one of them,

  e.g. given $\sin\theta = \dfrac{\sqrt{3}}{3}$ and that θ is obtuse, you can find $\cos\theta$ using

  $$\cos^2\theta \equiv 1 - \sin^2\theta \Rightarrow \cos^2\theta = 1 - \left(\frac{\sqrt{3}}{3}\right)^2 = \tfrac{2}{3},$$

  $$\therefore \cos\theta = -\sqrt{\frac{2}{3}} = -\frac{\sqrt{6}}{3}.$$

  ($\cos\theta$ is negative as θ is obtuse, i.e. θ is in the second quadrant.)
  You can now find $\tan\theta$.

- to give an expression containing a mixture of trig ratios in terms of just one ratio, e.g. to express $\tan^2\theta + \cos\theta$ in terms of $\cos\theta$, you can use identity 2 followed by identity 3 to give

  $$\tan^2\theta + \cos\theta \equiv \frac{\sin^2\theta}{\cos^2\theta} + \cos\theta$$
  $$\equiv \frac{1 - \cos^2\theta}{\cos^2\theta} + \cos\theta.$$

Questions

1 Write down the exact value of

a $\sin 120^\circ$ **b** $\sin \frac{11\pi}{4}$ **c** $\tan 225^\circ$

d $\cos \frac{3\pi}{2}$ **e** $\tan 135^\circ$.

2 Given that $\sin\alpha = \frac{\sqrt{2}}{3}$ and that α is an obtuse angle, find $\cos\alpha$.

3 Given that $\tan\frac{\pi}{8} = \sqrt{2} - 1$, find in surd form, the value of $\tan\frac{3\pi}{8}$.

4 Express in terms of $\sin x$

a $\cos^2 x - 2\sin x$ **b** $\tan^2 x + 1$.

Answers

1a $\sqrt{3}/2$ **b** $1/\sqrt{2}$ **c** 1 **d** 0 **e** -1

2 $-\frac{\sqrt{7}}{3}$ **3** $\sqrt{2} + 1$ $\left(\frac{\pi}{8} \text{ and } \frac{3\pi}{8} \text{ add to } \frac{\pi}{2}\right)$

4a $1 - \sin^2 x - 2\sin x$ **b** $\frac{1}{1 - \sin^2 x}$

Solving trig equations

You can solve very simple trig equations with the help of a sketch graph of the basic trig function,

e.g. to solve $\cos x = -\frac{1}{2}$ for $0^\circ \leqslant x \leqslant 360^\circ$, sketch $y = \cos x$ for $0^\circ \leqslant x \leqslant 360^\circ$.

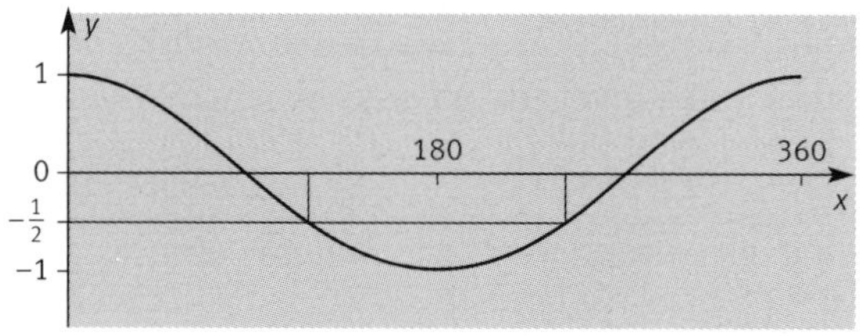

This shows that there are two solutions, symmetrical about 180°.

The acute angle whose cosine is $\frac{1}{2}$ is 60°,

$\therefore$ the solutions are $180^\circ - 60^\circ$ and $180^\circ + 60^\circ$, i.e. $x = 120^\circ$ and 240°.

When the angle is not a simple x, you can still use a standard graph but change the range,

e.g to solve $\sin 2x = 1$ for $-180^\circ \leqslant x \leqslant 180^\circ$, sketch the sine function for $-360^\circ \leqslant 2x \leqslant 360^\circ$ (doubling the range because the angle is $2 \times x$).

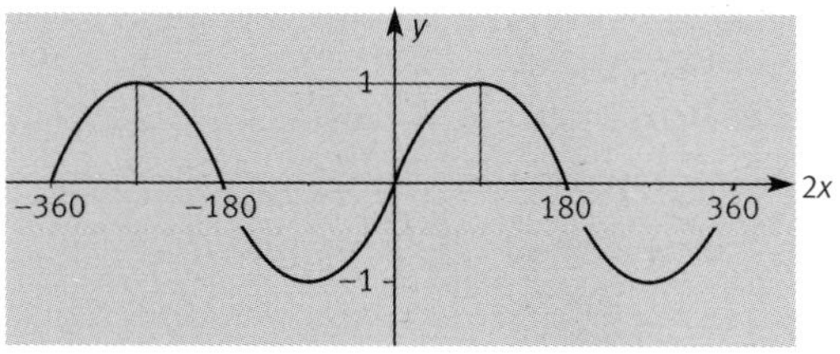

This shows that there are two values of $2x$ in this range,

i.e. $2x = 90^\circ$ or $2x = -270^\circ$

$\therefore$ $x = 45^\circ$ or $x = -135^\circ$.

The equation $\cos(x - 30^\circ) = -\frac{1}{2}$ involves the trig ratio of the compound angle $(x - 30^\circ)$. To solve this for values of x in the range $-180^\circ \leqslant x \leqslant 180^\circ$, start with a sketch of the standard cosine function for $-210^\circ \leqslant x - 30^\circ \leqslant 150^\circ$ (shifting the range by -30° because the angle is shifted by -30°).

This shows that $x - 30^\circ = 120^\circ$ or -120° so $x = 150^\circ$ or -90°.

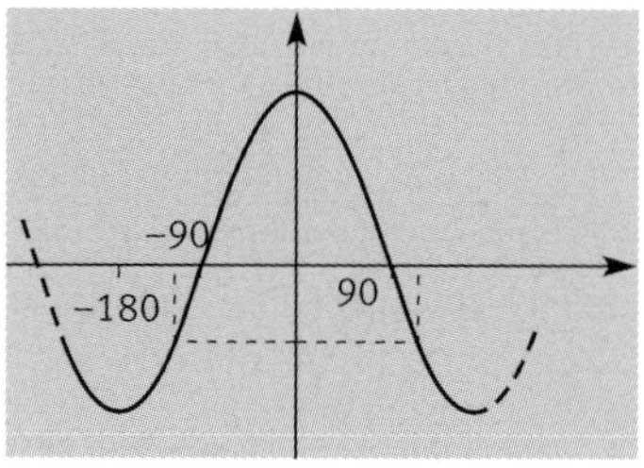

To solve any trig equation, you should aim to reduce it to simple equations similar to those above and you can use the trig identities to do this.

For example, to solve

$$\sin^2 x + 2\cos x = 0 \quad \text{for} \quad 0 \leqslant x \leqslant 2\pi$$

you can use the identity $\sin^2 x + \cos^2 x \equiv 1$ to express $\sin^2 x$ in terms of $\cos^2 x$,

i.e. $\sin^2 x + 2\cos x = 0$

$\Rightarrow 1 - \cos^2 x + 2\cos x = 0$

which is a quadratic equation in $\cos x$.

So $\cos^2 x - 2\cos x - 1 = 0$

$\Rightarrow \cos x = 1 + \sqrt{2}$ (>1 so not possible)

or $\cos x = 1 - \sqrt{2}$.

Using a calculator, $\cos x = 1 - \sqrt{2}$

$\Rightarrow x = 1.998$ rad.

From a sketch you can see that there is another solution,

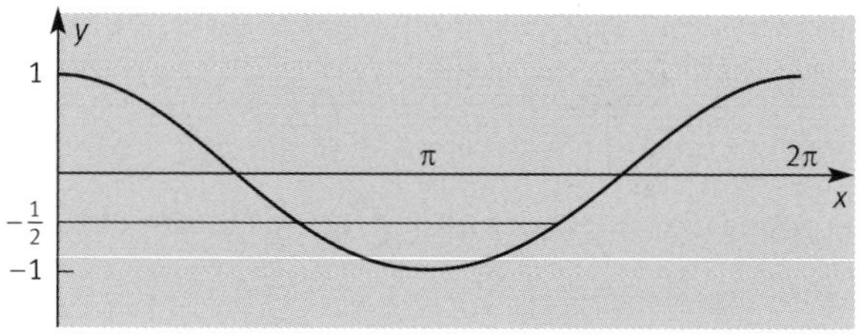

$x = (2\pi - 1.998)$ rad $= 4.285$ rad,

i.e. $x = 2.00$ rad or 4.29 rad (correct to 3 s.f.).

Do's and don'ts when solving equations

(trig or otherwise)

✔ Give your answers in the same unit as is given in the problem. (If you use your calculator to find angles check the angle mode.)

✘ Do not divide an equation by an expression containing the unknown. If you do, you may lose solutions,
e.g. if the equation $2\cos^2 x - \cos x = 0$ is divided by $\cos x$ to give $2\cos x - 1 = 0$ you lose the solutions for which $\cos x = 0$. Always factorise in this situation;
i.e. $2\cos^2 x - \cos x = 0$
$\Rightarrow \cos x(2\cos x - 1) = 0$
$\Rightarrow \cos x = 0 \quad \text{or} \quad 2\cos x - 1 = 0.$

✔ If you multiply an equation by an expression containing the unknown, you must exclude from your solution the possibility that the expression is equal to zero,
e.g. to solve $\tan x - \sin x = 0$,
replacing $\tan x$ by $\dfrac{\sin x}{\cos x}$ gives

$$\frac{\sin x}{\cos x} - \sin x = 0.$$

Multiplying by $\cos x$ gives

$$\sin x - \sin x \cos x = 0 \text{ provided } \cos x \neq 0.$$

Questions

Answers that are not exact should be given correct to 2 decimal places.

1 Solve the equation

$$\cos 3x = 1$$

for $0° \leqslant x \leqslant 180°$.

2 Solve the equation $\sin(x + 45)° = 1$ for values of x between 0° and 360°.

3 Find the values of θ in the range $0 \leqslant \theta \leqslant 2\pi$ for which $2\sin^2\theta + 3\cos\theta - 3 = 0$.

4 Find the solutions of the equation

$$3\cos\theta = 4\tan\theta$$

in the range $0° \leqslant \theta \leqslant 360°$.

Answers

1 0°, 120°
2 45°
3 $0, \frac{\pi}{3}, \frac{5\pi}{3}, 2\pi$
4 32.36°, 147.64°.

Take a break

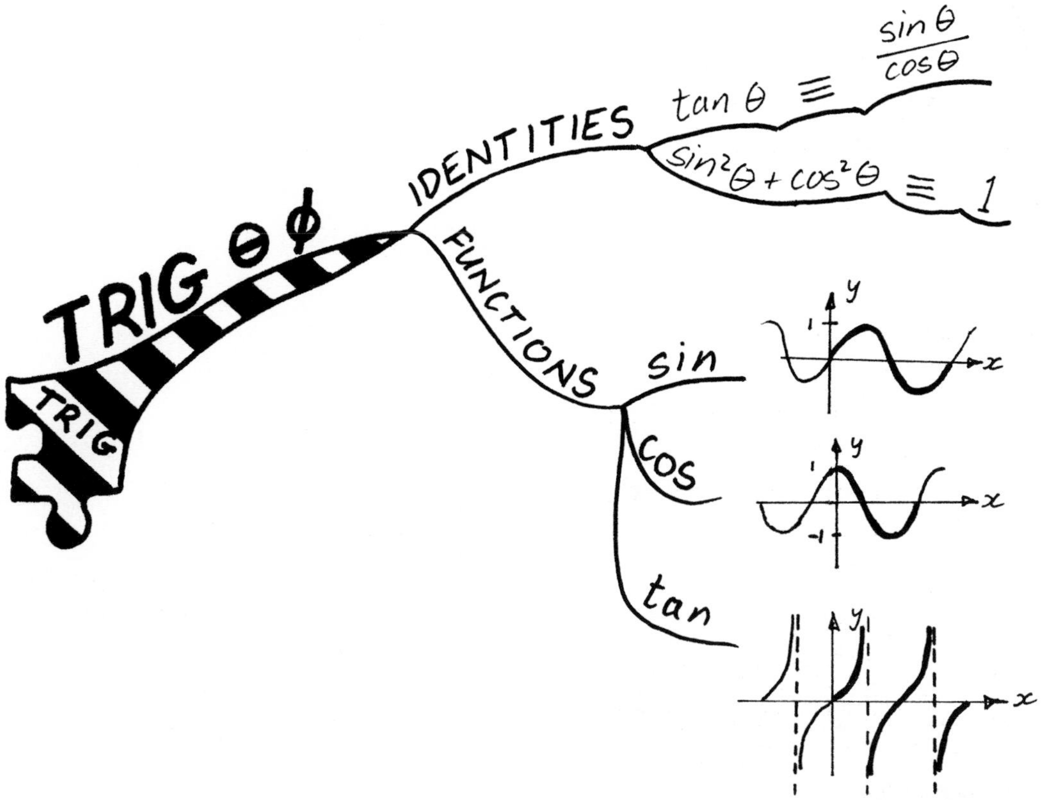

Review

1 Write down the equation of the line that is parallel to the line $ax + 2ay + 4 = 0$ and passes through $(a, 2a)$.

2a Express $3x^2 - 5x - 5$ in the form $a(x + b)^2 + c$, giving the values of a, b, and c. Hence find the exact solutions of the equation $3x^2 - 5x - 5 = 0$.

b Given that $x = a^b$ and $y = a^c$, express a^{2b-c} in terms of x and y only.

3a The diagram shows the graph of $y = \mathrm{f}(x)$.
Draw the graphs of

i $y = \frac{1}{2}\mathrm{f}(x)$
ii $y = 1 + \mathrm{f}(-x)$
iii $y = -\mathrm{f}(2x)$
iv Give the domain and range of the function f.

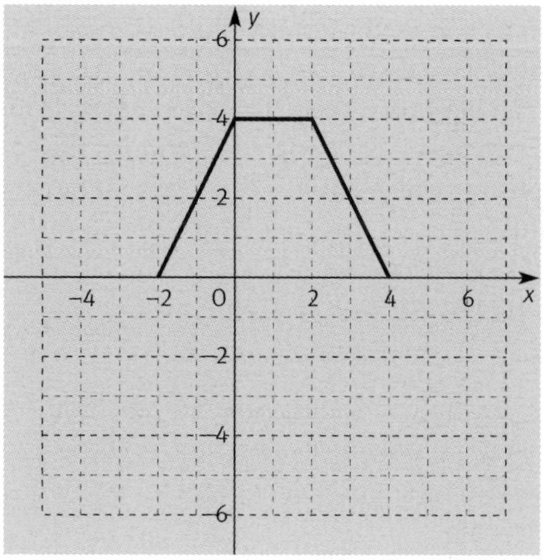

b Write down $\mathrm{fg}(x)$ where $\mathrm{f}(x) = \mathrm{e}^x$ and $\mathrm{g}(x) = 2x + 1$.

4 The first term of a GP is a and the common ratio is r. Give, in terms of a and r,

a the 10th term, **b** the sum of the first 10 terms.

5 The diagram shows two arcs of circles. Angle AOB $= \dfrac{\pi}{2}$ radians.

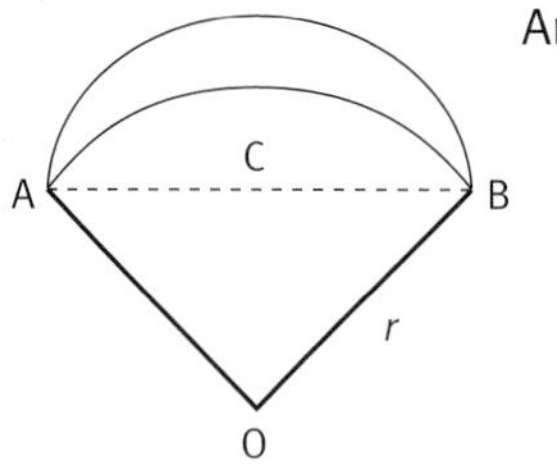

The smaller arc is of a circle, centre O, radius r. The larger arc is of a circle, centre C where C is the midpoint of AB. Find, in terms of r and π, the perimeter of the crescent enclosed by the arcs.

6 Solve the equation $|3x + 1| = 2 - x$.

7 Find the values of θ for $0 \leqslant \theta \leqslant 2\pi$ for which **a** $\sin\left(\theta - \dfrac{\pi}{4}\right) = 0$ **b** $\cos^2\theta - 2\sin^2\theta = 7\cos\theta$.

Answers

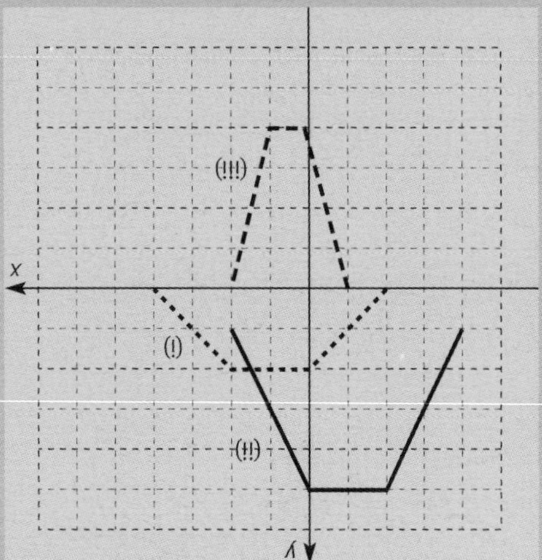

1 $x + 2y - 5a = 0$ **2a** $3(x - \frac{5}{6})^2 - \frac{85}{12}$, $\dfrac{5 \pm \sqrt{85}}{6}$ **b** $\dfrac{x^2}{y}$

3a i to **iii** see graph
iv $-2 < x < 4$, $0 < \mathrm{f}(x) \leqslant 4$ **b** e^{2x+1}

4a ar^9 **b** $\dfrac{a(1 - r^{10})}{1 - r}$

5 $\frac{1}{2}\pi r(1 + \sqrt{2})$

6 $\frac{1}{4}$, $-\frac{3}{2}$

7a $\dfrac{\pi}{4}$, $\dfrac{5\pi}{4}$ **b** 1.83 rad, 4.45 rad.

Take a break

PREVIEW

By the end of this topic you will have revised:

- ✔ **the meaning of $\frac{dy}{dx}$,**
- ✔ **how to differentiate powers of *x*,**
- ✔ **how to differentiate exponential and log functions,**
- ✔ **what stationary points are, how to find them and distinguish between them,**
- ✔ **how to find equations of tangents and normals to curves.**

Before you start you should:

- realise that the gradient of a curve at a point P on the curve is equal to the gradient of the tangent to the curve at that point,
- be confident about using indices.

The meaning of $\frac{dy}{dx}$

When $y = f(x)$, the derivative of y with respect to x $\left(\text{i.e. } \frac{dy}{dx}\right)$, is the rate at which y is increasing with respect to x.

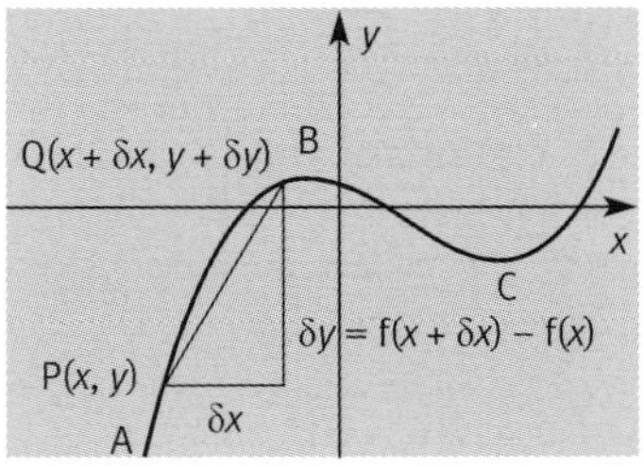

At a general point $P(x, y)$ on the curve $y = f(x)$,

$$\frac{dy}{dx} = \lim_{\delta x \to 0} \frac{\delta y}{\delta x} = \lim_{\delta x \to 0} \frac{f(x + \delta x) - f(x)}{\delta x}$$

$= \text{gradient of the curve at P}$

$= f'(x)$

E.g. when $y = x^3$, $\frac{dy}{dx} = \lim_{\delta x \to 0} \frac{(x - \delta x)^3 - x^3}{\delta x}$

$$= \lim_{\delta x \to 0} \frac{3x^2\delta x + 3x(\delta x)^2 + (\delta x)^3}{\delta x}$$

$$= \lim_{\delta x \to 0} (3x^2 + 3x\delta x + (\delta x)^2) = 3x^2.$$

Between A and B, y is increasing,

i.e. $\frac{dy}{dx}$ is positive, and f is an increasing function.

Between B and C, y is decreasing,

i.e. $\frac{dy}{dx}$ is negative, and f is a decreasing function.

Finding $\frac{dy}{dx}$

You need to know the derivatives of these standard functions.

$y =$	$\frac{dy}{dx} =$
k	0
x^n	nx^{n-1}
e^x	e^x
e^{ax}	ae^{ax}
$\ln x$	$\frac{1}{x}$
$\ln ax$	$\frac{1}{x}$

When $f(x)$ is multiplied by a constant, $f'(x)$ is multiplied by the same constant,

e.g. $y = 3e^{2x} \Rightarrow \frac{dy}{dx} = 3(2e^{2x}) = 6e^{2x}$.

You can differentiate a sum or difference of functions by adding the derivatives of all of the terms,
e.g. when $y = 4x^{\frac{1}{2}} + \ln x + 2$,

$$\frac{dy}{dx} = (4)(\tfrac{1}{2}x^{-\frac{1}{2}}) + \frac{1}{x} + 0 = 2x^{-\frac{1}{2}} + \frac{1}{x}.$$

⚠ You cannot differentiate a product or a quotient of functions in the same way,

e.g. $\frac{d}{dx}(x^2)(1 - x)$ is NOT $\frac{d}{dx}(x^2) \times \frac{d}{dx}(x + 1)$.

A product must be expanded and a quotient must be divided out to give separate terms before differentiation (unless you know the product and quotient rules, in which case you can use them),
e.g. to differentiate $f(x) = x^2(1 + \sqrt{x})$, multiply out the bracket and write $\sqrt{x}$ in index form,
i.e. $f(x) = x^2 + x^2 \times x^{\frac{1}{2}} = x^2 + x^{\frac{5}{2}}$,
so $f'(x) = 2x + \frac{5}{2}x^{\frac{3}{2}}$.

And to differentiate $f(x) = \frac{1 + \sqrt{x}}{x^2}$, write the fraction as two separate fractions, and express each fraction in the form x^n, i.e. $f(x) = \frac{1}{x^2} + \frac{\sqrt{x}}{x^2} = x^{-2} + x^{-\frac{3}{2}}$
so $f'(x) = -2x^{-3} - \frac{3}{2}x^{-\frac{5}{2}}$.

Second order derivatives

$\frac{dy}{dx}$ $(= f'(x))$ is a first order derivative (it is the first derivative of y).

The derivative of $\frac{dy}{dx}$ w.r.t. x is a second order derivative.

It gives the rate of increase of $\frac{dy}{dx}$ w.r.t. x and is written as $\frac{d^2y}{dx^2}$ or $f''(x)$ $\left(\text{or } \frac{d}{dx}\left(\frac{dy}{dx}\right)\right)$,

e.g. when $y = x^3 - 2x$, $\frac{dy}{dx} = 3x^2 - 2$ and $\frac{d^2y}{dx^2} = 6x$.

Questions

1 Find $f'(x)$ when $f(x)$ is

a $x^3 - 6x^2$ **b** $e^x - 2x$ **c** $4 \ln 3x$

d $(x - 3)(x + 1)$ **e** $\frac{1 - x}{\sqrt{x}}$

2 Given that $f(x) = x^3$, explain why f is an increasing function for all values of x except $x = 0$.

3 $f(x) = e^x(e^x + 1)$. Find $f''(x)$.

4 Find the gradient of the curve whose equation is $y = x^2 + \ln 2x$ at the point on the curve where $x = 2$.
Hence find the equation of the tangent to the curve at this point.

5 The value, £P, of an antique chair t years after purchase is assumed to be given by $P = 800e^{0.04t}$.

Find the value of $\frac{dP}{dt}$ when $t = 3$ and explain what it means.

Answers

1a $3x^2 - 12x$ **b** $e^x - 2$ **c** $\frac{4}{x}$ $\left(\text{NOT } \frac{4}{3x}\right)$ **d** $2x - 2$

e $-\frac{1}{2}x^{-\frac{3}{2}} - \frac{1}{2}x^{-\frac{1}{2}}$

2 $f'(x) = 3x^2$ and $3x^2 > 0$ for all x except 0

3 $4e^{2x} + e^x$ **4** 4.5, $9x - 2y - 10 + 2\ln 4 = 0$

5 36.08 (4 s.f.); after 3 years the chair is increasing in value at the rate of £36.08 a year.

Tangents and normals

A tangent to a curve touches the curve at the point of contact. The normal to a curve passes through the point of contact and is perpendicular to the tangent.

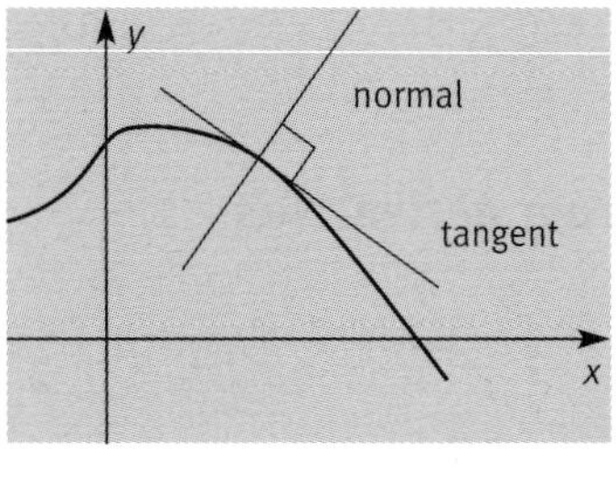

To find the equation of a tangent or a normal to a curve at a given point on the curve, start by finding the gradient, i.e. the value of $\frac{dy}{dx}$, at that point.

For example, to find the equation of the normal to the curve $y = x^3 - 5x$ at the point where $x = 1$, you need the coordinates of a point on the normal and its gradient.

From the equation of the curve, the normal goes through $(1, -4)$.

Next find the value of $\frac{dy}{dx}$ where $x = 1$.

$\frac{dy}{dx} = 3x^2 - 5$, so when $x = 1$, $\frac{dy}{dx} = -2$, so the gradient of the normal is $\frac{1}{2}$.

$\therefore$ the equation of the normal is

$y + 4 = \frac{1}{2}(x - 1) \Rightarrow x - 2y - 9 = 0$.

Question

Find the equation of the tangent and the normal to the curve $y = 2 - x - e^x$ where $x = 0$.

Answer

$2x + y - 1 = 0$, $x - 2y + 2 = 0$.

Stationary values

At the points A, B and C, y is neither increasing nor decreasing; f is stationary and $\frac{dy}{dx} = 0$.

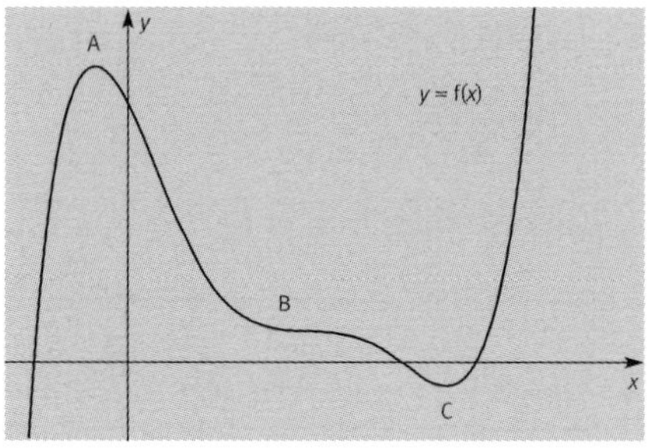

You can find the stationary values of $f(x)$ by finding the values of x for which $\frac{dy}{dx} = 0$, and then use them to find the corresponding values of $f(x)$.

Points like A and C are turning points. At A, the value of y is a (local) maximum. At C, the value of y is a (local) minimum.
Points like B are points of inflexion; the curve does not turn at a point of inflexion.

You can distinguish between maximum and minimum turning points by finding the sign of $\frac{d^2y}{dx^2}$ at the point.

When $\frac{d^2y}{dx^2} = 0$, the point may be a maximum or a minimum or a point of inflexion. In this case you can find out which it is by finding the sign of $\frac{dy}{dx}$ on each side of the point: this tells you which way the curve slopes on either side of that point. (You can, if you prefer, use this in all cases.)

$\frac{d^2y}{dx^2}$	+ve	−ve	zero
y	min	max	not known

x	left of point	at point	right of point
$\frac{dy}{dx}$	−ve \	–	/ +ve
	+ve /	–	\ −ve
	+ve / −ve \	– –	/ +ve \ −ve

For example, to find the stationary points on $y = x^4 - 2x^3$ and their nature, first find $\frac{dy}{dx}$ and the values of x for which it is zero.

$$\frac{dy}{dx} = 4x^3 - 6x^2,$$

so $\frac{dy}{dx} = 0$ when $4x^3 - 6x^2 = 0 \quad \Rightarrow \quad x = 0$ or $\frac{3}{2}$.

When $x = 0$, $y = 0$ and when $x = \frac{3}{2}$, $y = -\frac{27}{16}$,

$\therefore$ the stationary values of y are 0 and $-\frac{27}{16}$.

To find their nature, use the second derivative:

$\frac{d^2y}{dx^2} = 12x^2 - 12x$ so when $x = \frac{3}{2}$, $\frac{d^2y}{dx^2} > 0$,

i.e. $(\frac{3}{2}, -\frac{27}{16})$ is a minimum point on the curve.

When $x = 0$, $\frac{d^2y}{dx^2} = 0$ so use the sign of $\frac{dy}{dx}$:

x	−1	0	1
$\frac{dy}{dx}$	−ve \	0 –	−ve \

This shows that (0, 0) is a point of inflexion on the curve.

Questions

1 Find the stationary point on the curve whose equation is $y = x - \ln x$.
Determine, by calculation, the nature of this point.

2 The equation of a curve is $y = 2e^{2x} - 4x$.

a Show that the curve has just one stationary point and prove that y is a minimum here.

b Sketch the curve.

3 The area of card, A m^2, used for a packing vases of different heights is given by $A = 3x^3 - x + 3$ where x m is the height of the vase.
Find the value of x for which A is least.

Answers

1 (1, 1), minimum

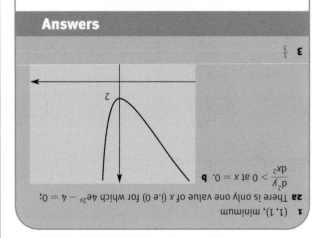

2a There is only one value of x (i.e 0) for which $4e^{2x} - 4 = 0$; $\frac{d^2y}{dx^2} > 0$ at $x = 0$. **b**

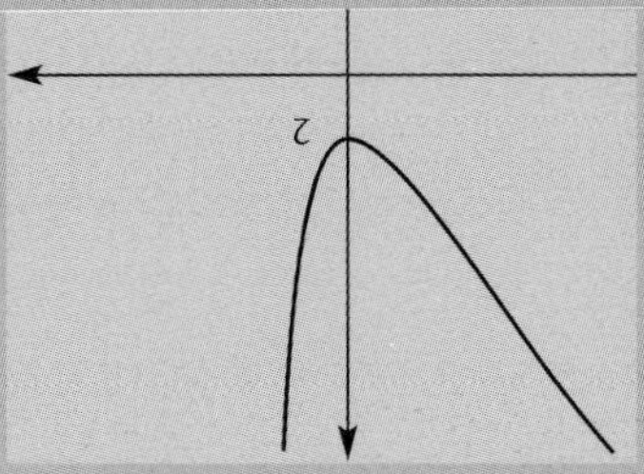

3 $\frac{1}{3}$

Take a break

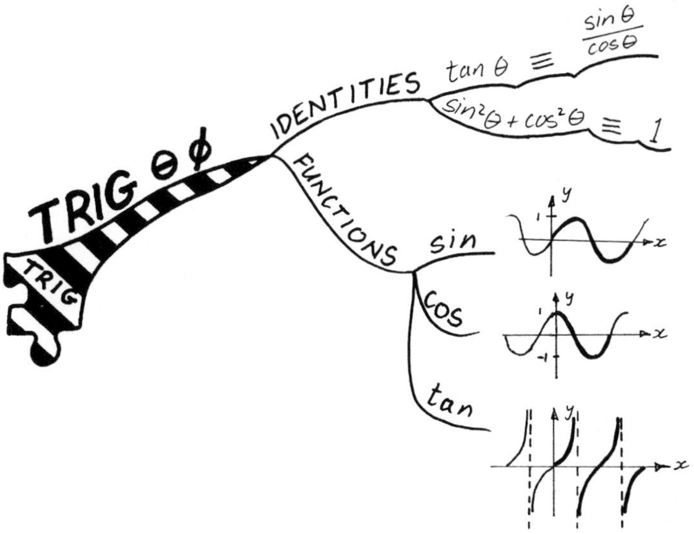

Review

1 $f(x) = |x|$ and $g(x) = \cos 2x$.
Find $fg(x)$ and sketch the graph of $y = fg(x)$ for $0° \leqslant x \leqslant 180°$.
Hence, or otherwise, find the values of x in this range for which $fg(x) = \frac{1}{2}$.

2 The diagram shows two circles, each of radius r, whose centres, A and B, are r units apart.

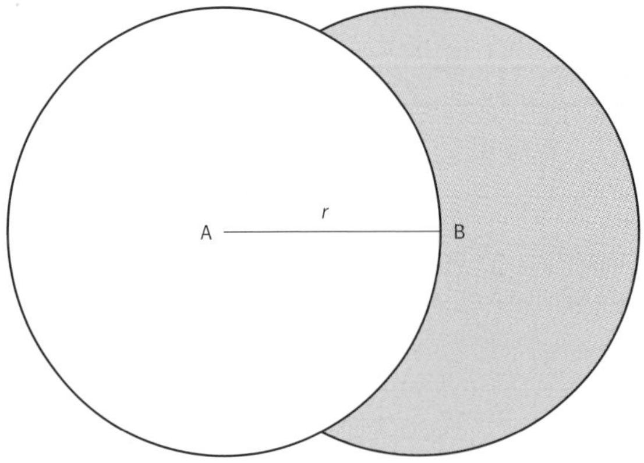

Find the area of the shaded region, giving your answer in term of π.

3 The equation of a curve is $y = x^3 - 3x^2$.
Find the value of $\frac{d^2y}{dx^2}$ at the point on the curve where $x = 1$.
Why does this value not imply that y has a stationary value at $x = 1$.

4 A tap drips water onto a solid floor at the rate of 5 cm^3 per hour. At the end of each hour, 10% of the volume of water that was on the floor at the beginning of that hour has evaporated. How much water is on the floor 24 hours after the tap starts dripping?

5 Given that $f(x) = x^4 + 2x^3 - 2x$, show that f has a stationary value where $x = -1$.

6 Given that $2 \log_3 x + \log_3 y = 2$, express y in terms of x.

Answers

1 $|\cos 2x|$,

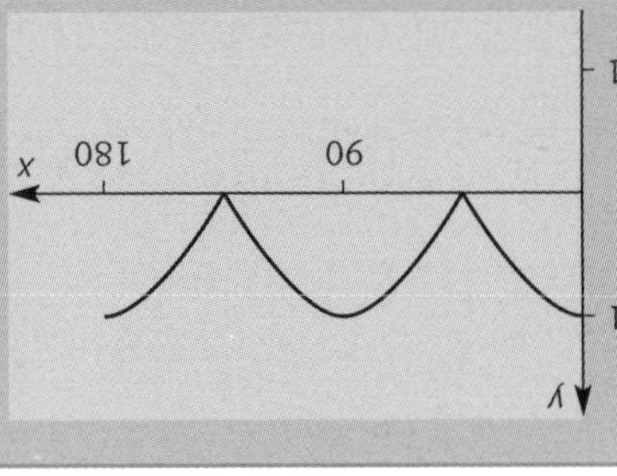

$30°, 60°, 120°, 150°$

2 $\frac{r^2}{6}(2\pi + 3\sqrt{3})$ **3** 0; $\frac{dy}{dx} \neq 0$ where $x = 1$

4 46.0 cm^3

5 $f'(x) = 4x^3 + 6x^2 - 2$ and $f'(-1) = 0$ **6** $y = \frac{9}{x^2}$.

Take a break

PREVIEW

By the end of this topic you will have revised:

- ✔ **how to integrate powers of x and the exponential function,**
- ✔ **the difference between definite and indefinite integrals,**
- ✔ **how to use integration to find areas.**

Integration

The process of integration reverses differentiation, e.g. the integral of x^2 w.r.t. x $\left(\text{i.e. } \int x^2 dx\right)$ means the function whose derivative is x^2. You can work this out each time but it is easier to remember these standard integrals.

$\mathbf{f}(x) =$	$\int \mathbf{f}(x)\mathbf{d}x =$
a	ax
x^n	$\frac{1}{n+1}x^{n+1}$
e^x	e^x
e^{ax}	$\frac{1}{a}e^{ax}$
$\frac{1}{x}$	$\ln\lvert x\rvert$
0	k

You can check your answers by differentiating them; you have made a mistake if you do not get the function you were asked to integrate.

You can integrate across the sum or difference of functions, e.g.

$$\int (x^{\frac{1}{2}} + 2)dx = \int x^{\frac{1}{2}}dx + \int 2dx + \int 0dx$$

(0 can be added to any function)

$$= \frac{1}{\frac{3}{2}}x^{\frac{3}{2}} + 2x + k = \tfrac{2}{3}x^{\frac{3}{2}} + 2x + k$$

A constant, k, must be added to any integrated function (including those in the table above); the value of k cannot be found unless you have more information about the function.

When f(x) is multiplied by a constant, $\int f(x)dx$ is multiplied by the same constant,

e.g. $\int 3e^{2x}dx = 3\int e^{2x}dx = 3(\tfrac{1}{2}e^{2x}) + k$

⚠ You cannot integrate a product or a quotient in the same way,

e.g. $\int \frac{x+1}{x^2}dx$ is NOT equal to $\dfrac{\int (x+1)dx}{\int x^2 dx}$.

A product must be expanded and a quotient must be divided out to give separate terms before integration (unless you know how to integrate by parts, in which case you can use it),

e.g. to find $\int x^2(1+\sqrt{x})dx$, multiply out the bracket and write $\sqrt{x}$ in index form,

$$\int x^2(1+\sqrt{x})dx$$
$$= \int (x^2 + x^2 \times x^{\frac{1}{2}})dx = \int (x^2 + x^{\frac{5}{2}})dx$$
$$= \tfrac{1}{3}x^3 + \tfrac{2}{7}x^{\frac{7}{2}} + k$$

and to find $\int \frac{1+\sqrt{x}}{x}dx$, write the fraction as two separate fractions, and express each fraction in the form x^n,

i.e. $\int \frac{1+\sqrt{x}}{x}dx = \int \left(\frac{1}{x} + \frac{x^{\frac{1}{2}}}{x}\right)dx$

$$= \int (x^{-1} + x^{-\frac{1}{2}})dx = \ln\lvert x\rvert + \frac{1}{\frac{1}{2}}x^{\frac{1}{2}} + k$$
$$= \ln\lvert x\rvert + 2x^{\frac{1}{2}} + k$$

⚠ A common mistake is to muddle integration with differentiation especially with powers of x. It may help you remember that to **in**tegrate you **in**crease the power.

Questions

Find

1 $\int (x^3 - 2x)dx$ **2** $\int (3x^3 + 4e^{2x})dx$

3 $\int (2x+1)(3x-2)dx$ **4** $\int \frac{x+1}{x}dx$

5 $\int \frac{1+x}{\sqrt{x}}dx$ **6** $\int \left(1+\frac{1}{x}\right)^2 dx$

Answers

1 $\frac{1}{4}x^4 - x^2 + k$ **2** $\frac{3}{4}x^4 + 2e^{2x} + k$

3 $2x^3 - \frac{1}{2}x^2 - 2x + k$ **4** $x + \ln\lvert x\rvert + k$

5 $2x^{\frac{1}{2}} + \frac{2}{3}x^{\frac{3}{2}} + k$ **6** $x + 2\ln\lvert x\rvert - \frac{1}{x} + k$

Definite integration

$\int 4x\,dx$ is an indefinite integral; the result is a function $\left(\int 4x\,dx = 2x^2 + k\right)$.

$\int_2^4 4x\,dx$ is a definite integral; the result is a number.

If $\int f(x)\,dx = g(x)$ then

$$\int_a^b f(x)\,dx = \Big[g(x)\Big]_a^b = \Big[g(b)\Big] - \Big[g(a)\Big]$$

e.g. $\int_2^4 4x\,dx = \Big[2x^2\Big]_2^4 = (2 \times 4^2) - (2 \times 2^2) = 24.$

⚠ There is no need to add k because it cancels. Do not try to do too much calculation mentally; it is easy to make errors especially when negative signs are involved.

Questions

Evaluate

1 $\int_2^6 (3x - 2)\,dx$ **2** $\int_1^4 \frac{1}{x}\,dx$

3 $\int_0^2 (1 - 2e^{-x})\,dx$ **4** $\int_1^4 (1 + e^x)^2\,dx.$

Answers

1 40 **2** $\ln 4$ **3** $2e^{-2}$

4 $\frac{1}{2}(e^8 + 4e^4 - e^2 - 4e + 6).$

Finding areas by integration

The definite integral $\int_a^b f(x)\,dx$ gives the shaded area in the diagram.

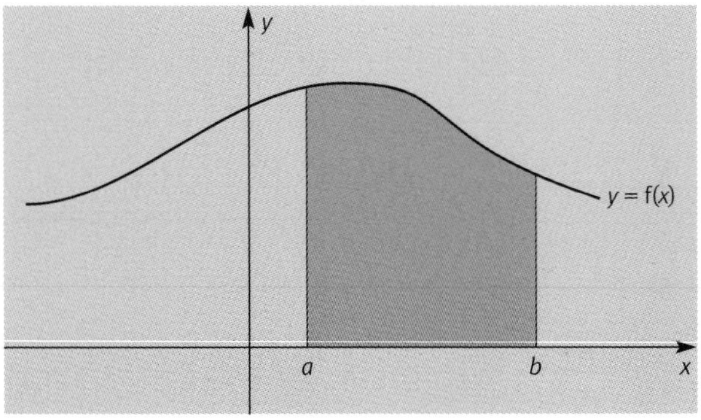

This area is below the curve $y = f(x)$ between $x = a$ and $x = b$, i.e. it is the region bounded by the curve, the x-axis and the lines $x = a$ and $x = b$.

To find an area bounded partly by a curve, start by drawing a diagram.

Identify all the lines that bound the area asked for and remember that when the region is above the x-axis, the answer is positive, when the region is below the x-axis, the answer is negative.

To find an area bounded by a curve that is partly above and partly below the x-axis, you must use integration to find each area separately.

For example, the area enclosed by $y = (x + 1)(x - 1)(x - 3)$ and the x- and y-axes, is partly above and partly below the x-axis.

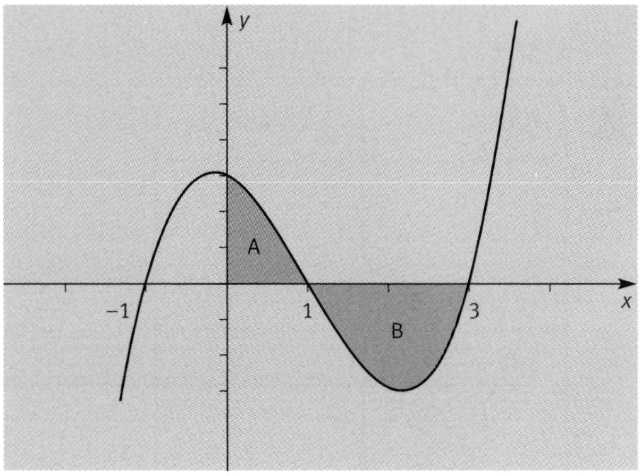

To find A, use $\int_0^1 (x + 1)(x - 1)(x - 3)\,dx$

$$= \int_0^1 (x^3 - 3x^2 - x + 3)\,dx$$

$$= \Big[\tfrac{1}{4}x^4 - x^3 - \tfrac{1}{2}x^2 + 3x\Big]_0^1 = \tfrac{7}{4}.$$

To find B, use $\int_1^3 (x + 1)(x - 1)(x - 3)\,dx$

$$= \Big[\tfrac{1}{4}x^4 - x^3 - \tfrac{1}{2}x^2 + 3x\Big]_1^3 = -4$$

so the area of B is 4 square units,

$\therefore$ the area enclosed by the curve and the x- and y-axes is $\frac{7}{4} + 4 = 5\frac{3}{4}$.

⚠ You cannot find the area in one step by using $\int_0^3 (x + 1)(x - 1)(x - 3)\,dx$; this gives the difference between the areas of A and B.

When an area is not completely between a curve and the x-axis, you can find it by considering the required area as the sum or difference of areas you can find.

For example, this area

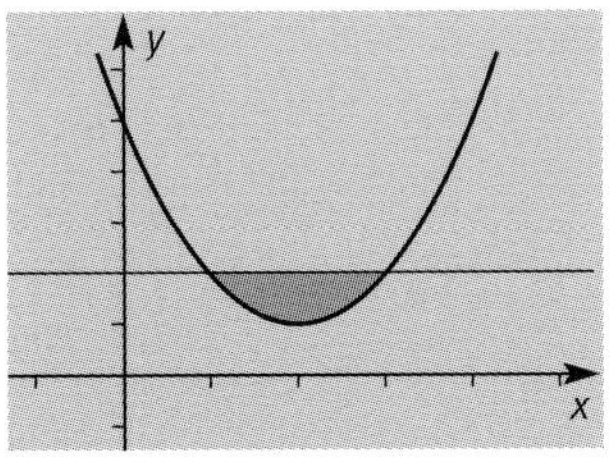

can be found from
area rectangle ABCD – area below curve between x at C and x at D.

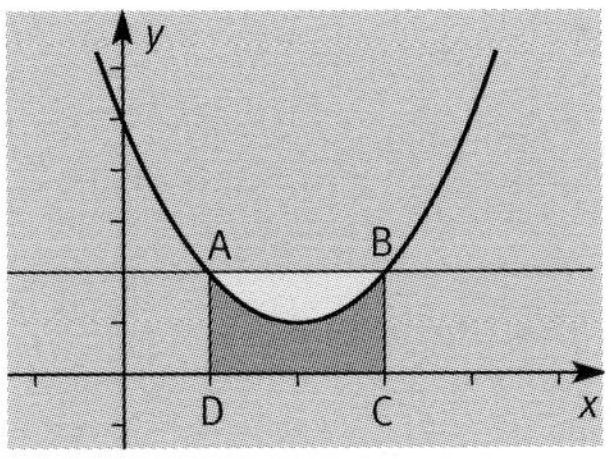

Similarly the area bounded by the curve, the tangent to the curve and the x-axis, can be found from (area under the curve between the values of x at A and at D) – (area of triangle BCD).

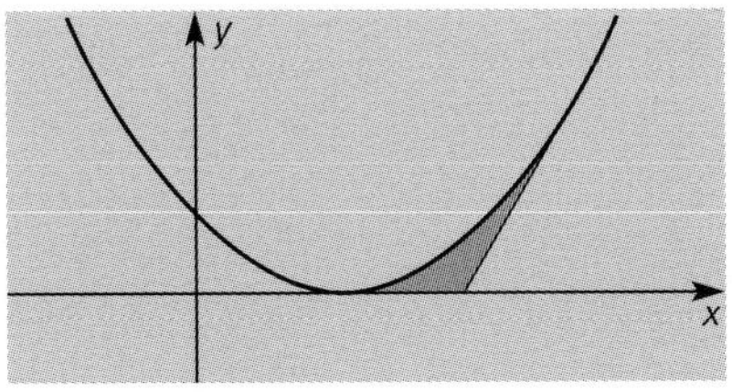

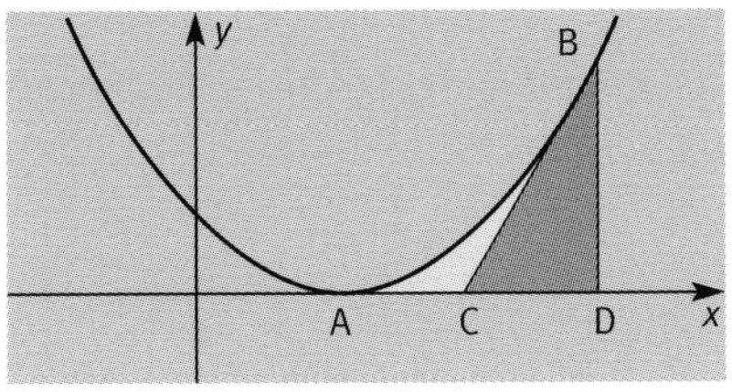

You do not need to use integration to find areas bounded by straight lines.

Questions

1 Find the area enclosed by the curve $y = x(x - 2)$ and the x-axis.

2 Find, in terms of e, the area enclosed by the axes, the curve $y = e^x$ and the line $x = 2$.

3a Sketch the curve $y = x^2 + 1$ and the line $y = x + 3$.

b Find the coordinates of the points of intersection of the curve and the line.

c Find the area enclosed by the curve and the line.

Answers

1 $1\frac{1}{3}$ **2** $e^2 - 1$

3a

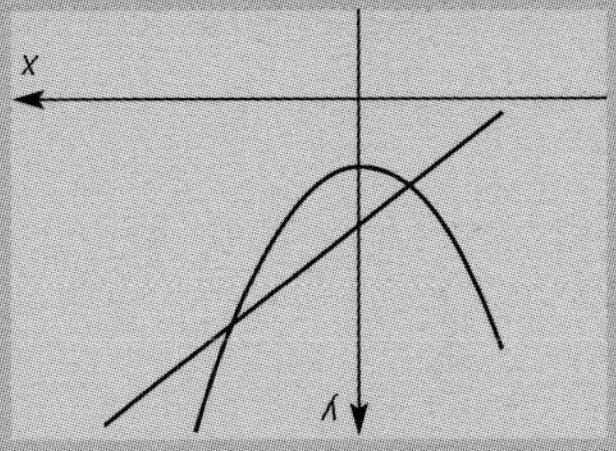

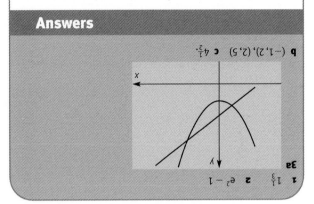

b $(-1, 2), (2, 5)$ **c** $4\frac{1}{2}$.

Take a break

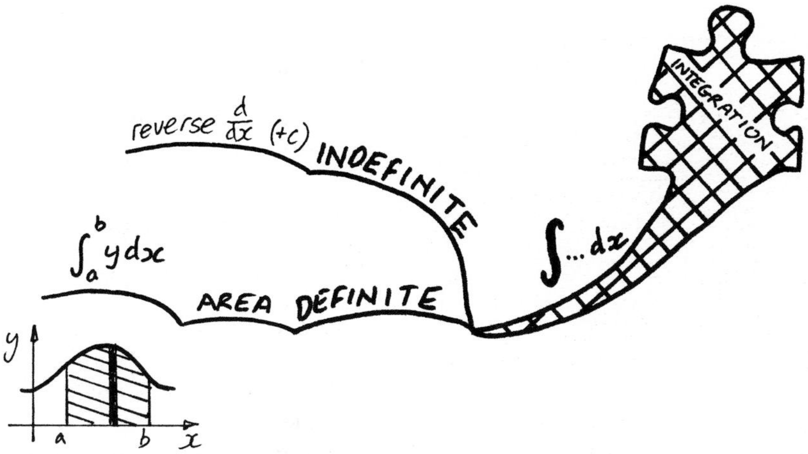

Review

1 Factorise $x^3 + 4x^2 - 3x - 18$.
Hence sketch the curve $y = x^3 + 4x^2 - 3x - 18$.

2 Solve the inequality $|2 - x| < \frac{1}{2}x$.

3 The diagram shows a circle, centre O and radius r.

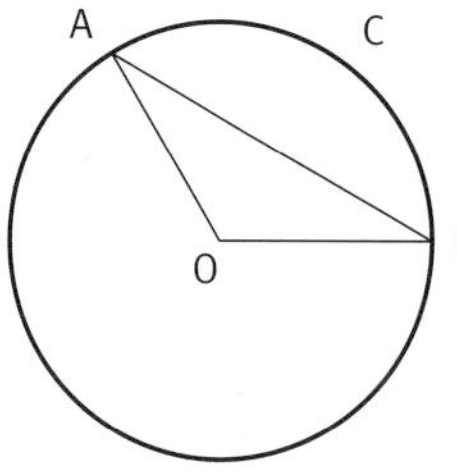

The angle AOB $= \theta$ radians and the area of triangle AOB is equal to the area of the segment ABC.
Show that $\theta = 2\sin\theta$.

4 The diagram shows the curve whose equation is $y = 1 + 4x - x^2$ and the line $y + x - 5 = 0$.

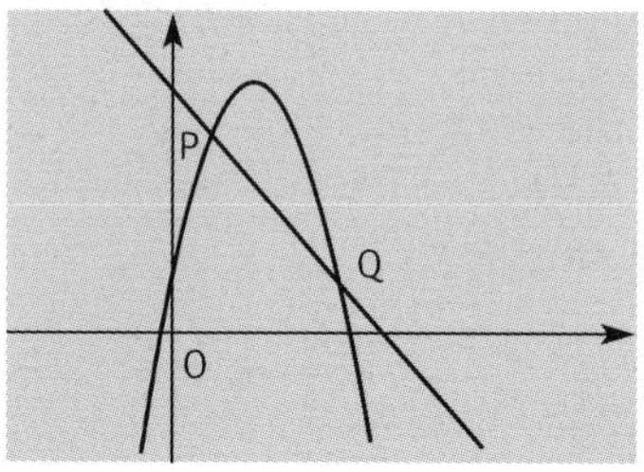

a Find the coordinates of P and Q.
b Write $1 + 4x - x^2$ in the form $a - (x - b)^2$.
Hence write down the coordinates of the stationary point on the curve.
c Find the area enclosed by the curve and the line.

5 Solve the equation $2\sin^2 x = 5\cos x$ for $0 \leqslant x \leqslant 360°$.

6 A ball is dropped from a height h m and bounces repeatedly until it comes to rest. After each bounce the ball reaches a height a times the height it reached on the previous bounce. Write down an expression for the total distance covered by the ball

a just before the second bounce, **b** just before the third bounce, **c** just before it comes to rest.

7 Given that $y = 50 - 15e^{-2x}$, find

a the value of y when $x = 0$, **b** the value that y approaches as x gets larger,
c how y is changing when $y = 20$.

Answers

1 $(x - 2)(x + 3)^2$

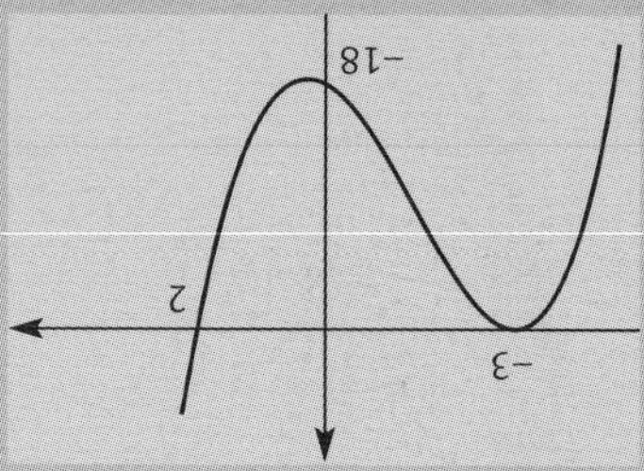

2 $\frac{4}{3} < x < 4$

4a P(1, 4) Q(4, 1) **b** $5 - (x - 2)^2$, (2, 5) **c** $4\frac{1}{2}$

5 69.5°, 290.5°

6a $h + 2ah$ **b** $h + 2ah + 2a^2h$ **c** $\frac{h(1 + a)}{1 - a}$

7a 35 **b** 50 **c** increasing at 60 units w.r.t. x.

Take a break

PREVIEW

By the end of this topic you will have revised:

- ✔ **the difference between a demonstration and a proof,**
- ✔ **the meaning of a direct proof,**
- ✔ **how to use contradiction to prove that a statement is true,**
- ✔ **the use of a counter example to show that a statement is false.**

Before you start you should:

- know that the proofs of mathematical results you use at A level are in text books.

Demonstration

A demonstration shows that a statement is true in a particular case. For example, $2 \times 4 = 8$ shows that the product of 2 and 4 is an even number; it does not show that the product of *any* two even numbers is itself even.

Proof

A mathematical proof deals with a general case and so covers all possibilities; to prove that the product of two even numbers is always even, you can start with any two even numbers, a and b, and argue from there:

i.e. a is an even number
$\Rightarrow \quad a = 2x$ where x is a positive integer
and b is an even number
$\Rightarrow \quad b = 2y$ where y is a positive integer.
$\therefore \quad ab = 4xy.$
$4xy$ is an even number $\Rightarrow$ ab is an even number.

The proof given above is direct. A direct proof starts from known and previously proved mathematical facts and then argues by direct deduction to the required statement,
i.e. to prove that statement B is true, start with known fact A, then

$$\text{A} \Rightarrow \ldots \Rightarrow \text{B}.$$

Example

Prove that, for all values of a, b and c,

$$\log_a bc = \log_a b + \log_a c$$

Solution

Start with these facts:

if $\log_a b = x$ then $b = a^x$
and if $\log_a c = y$ then $c = a^y$
then multiply b by c $\quad \Rightarrow bc = (a^x)(a^y).$
From the laws of indices $\quad \Rightarrow bc = a^{x+y}$
then, using the definition of a logarithm again,
this gives $\quad \log_a bc = x + y$
$\therefore \quad \log_a bc = \log_a b + \log_a c$

Questions

1 Prove that the square of an odd integer is itself odd. (The general form of an odd integer is $2n + 1$ where n is any integer.)

2 Prove that $\log_a \dfrac{b}{c} = \log_a b - \log_a c$.

Answers

1 $(2n+1)^2 = 4n^2 + 4n + 1 = 2(2n^2 + 2n) + 1$ which is an odd number.

2 $\log_a b = x$ and $\log_a c = y \Rightarrow b = a^x$ and $c = a^y$
$\Rightarrow \dfrac{b}{c} = \dfrac{a^x}{a^y} = a^{x-y} \Rightarrow \log_a \dfrac{b}{c} = x - y = \log_a b - \log_a c.$

Proof by contradiction

A proof by contradiction starts with the assumption that the statement you are trying to show to be true is, in fact, false. You then reason your way to a position that contradicts the assumption. This means that the assumption is wrong, so the statement is true.

Example

Prove by contradiction that the square root of any prime number is irrational.

Solution

Start with the assumption that there is a prime number whose square root is not irrational, i.e. assume that there is a prime number, p, such that $\sqrt{p} = \dfrac{a}{b}$ where a and b are integers,

$\Rightarrow \quad p = \dfrac{a^2}{b^2} \quad \Rightarrow \quad b^2 = 1$ as p is an integer

$\therefore p = a^2 \quad \Rightarrow \quad p$ is not a prime number as a^2 is not prime.

This contradicts the assumption, therefore the square root of any prime number is irrational.

Questions

Prove by contradiction that

1 the product of any two odd integers is odd

2 if the square of an integer is even, the integer itself is even.

Answers

1 Assume that $(2a + 1)(2b + 1)$ is even.
$(2a + 1)(2b + 1) = 4ab + 2(a + b) + 1 = 2(2ab + a + b) + 1$
which is odd so contradicts the assumption,
$\therefore (2a + 1)(2b + 1)$ is odd.

2 Assume that if n^2 is even, then n is odd
$\Rightarrow n = 2k + 1 \Rightarrow n^2 = 4k^2 + 4k + 1$ which is odd.
This contradicts the assumption $\therefore n$ is even.

Counter examples

To show that a statement is not true, you need to find just one instance that shows it to be false, i.e. a counter example.

To show that it is not true that the product of two irrational numbers is itself irrational, you can use $\sqrt{2}$ and $\sqrt{8}$, both of which are irrational, to show that $(\sqrt{2})(\sqrt{8}) = \sqrt{16} = 4$ which is rational.

Questions

Find a counter example to show that each of the following statements is not true.

1 $\sin(x + y) = \sin x + \sin y$

2 $\ln(x + y) = \ln x + \ln y$

3 $\frac{3x + y}{2x} = \frac{3 + y}{2}$.

Answers

(Each is one of many possible counter examples.)

1 $\sin(30° + 60°)[=1] \neq \sin 30° + \sin 60° \left[= \frac{1}{2} + \frac{\sqrt{3}}{2}\right]$

2 $\ln(1 + e)[=1.3\ldots] \neq \ln 1 + \ln e[=1]$

3 $\frac{3(2) + 1}{2(2)} = \frac{7}{4} \neq \frac{3 + 1}{2} = 2$ (using $x = 2$, $y = 1$)

Take a break

Review

1 Express $\frac{2}{x - 1} + \frac{5}{x + 1} + \frac{3}{2x - 1}$ as a fraction in its simplest form.

2 Show that $(x - 2)$ is a factor of $3x^3 - 5x^2 - x - 2$ and find the other factor.

3 Express $2 \ln x - \ln(x + 1)$ as a single logarithm.

4 Find $\frac{d}{dx}(x(2x - 1))$.

5 Express $5x^2 - 3x + 2$ in the form $a(x + b)^2 + c$ giving the values of a, b and c.

6 Prove that $2\cos^2\theta - \sin^2\theta + 1 \equiv 3\cos^2\theta$.

Answers

1 $\frac{x(17x - 13)}{(x^2 - 1)(2x - 1)}$ 2 $(3x^2 + x + 1)$ 3 $\ln \frac{x^2}{x + 1}$ 4 $4x - 1$ 5 $5(x - \frac{3}{10})^2 + \frac{31}{20}$.

Take a break

PREVIEW

By the end of this topic you will have revised:

- ✔ **the meaning of a rational function and when such a function is proper,**
- ✔ **how to divide one polynomial by another,**
- ✔ **how to use the remainder theorem,**
- ✔ **how to express a rational function as a sum or difference of simpler rational functions.**

Before you start you should:

- be able to divide simple algebraic expressions mentally,
- recognise quickly when expressions can be factorised and be able to factorise them,
- know how to add and subtract algebraic fractions, and simplify the result,
- know what the order of a polynomial means.

TEST YOURSELF

If you get more than one wrong answer, see GCSE Higher or A level text book for information and practise

1 **Find a)** $x^2 \div x$ **b)** $3y^4 \div y^2$ **c)** $-5a^2 \div a^2$.

2 **Factorise where possible**
a) $4x^2 - 16$ **b)** $x^3 - 1$ **c)** $2x^2 + 9$.

3 **Express as a single fraction in its lowest terms.**
a) $\dfrac{1}{x-1} + \dfrac{2}{x+1}$ **b)** $\dfrac{x}{x^2-1} + \dfrac{2}{x+1}$
c) $\dfrac{2}{x+1} + \dfrac{3}{(x+1)^2} - \dfrac{1}{x-1}$.

Answers

1 a) x **b)** $3y^2$ **c)** -5
2 a) $4(x-2)(x+2)$ **b)** $(x-1)(x^2+x+1)$ **c)** not pos.
3 a) $\dfrac{3x-1}{(x-1)(x+1)}$ **b)** $\dfrac{3x-2}{(x-1)(x+1)}$
c) $\dfrac{(x+3)(x-2)}{(x+1)^2(x-1)}$ (do not expand denominators)

Rational functions

A rational function is a fraction where the numerator and the denominator are both polynomials,

e.g. $\dfrac{x^2+x-1}{x^3-2x}$.

A rational function is PROPER when the order of the numerator is *less* than the order of the denominator,

e.g. $\dfrac{x}{x^2+2}$ is proper but $\dfrac{x^2}{x^2+2}$ is not.

Algebraic division

When $\dfrac{f(x)}{g(x)}$ is improper, you can divide $f(x)$ by $g(x)$ to find the quotient and remainder.
(Similarly $290 \div 56$ gives 5, remainder 10.)
Start by writing the calculation in long division format, filling in any missing powers of x with zeroes, then proceed by dividing the highest power term of $f(x)$ by the highest power term of $g(x)$, e.g. to divide $2x^3 - 5x^2 + 7$ by $x^2 - 3$, start by dividing $2x^3$ by x^2 then follow the steps below.

[1] $(2x^3 \div x^2)$ $(-5x^2 \div x^2)$ [4]

$$
\begin{array}{rll}
 & 2x - 5 & \\
x^2 - 3 \,\big)\!\! & 2x^3 - 5x^2 + 0x + 7 & \\
 & 2x^3 + 0x - 6x & \text{(multiply } x^2 - 3 \text{ by } 2x) \quad [2] \\
 & -5x^2 + 6x + 7 & \text{(subtract)} \quad [3] \\
 & -5x^2 + 0x + 15 & \text{(multiply } x^2 - 3 \text{ by } 5) \quad [5] \\
 & +6x - 8 & \text{(subtract)} \quad [6]
\end{array}
$$

$6x \div x^2$ does not give a positive integer power of x, so this is the remainder.

i.e. $(2x^3 - 5x^2 + 7) \div (x^2 - 3)$
$= 2x - 5$, remainder $6x - 8$.

- You can use this to express an improper fraction as a mixed fraction,

  e.g. $\dfrac{2x^3 - 5x^2 + 7}{x^2 - 3} = 2x - 5 + \dfrac{6x - 8}{x^2 - 3}$

  (In the same way as $\frac{290}{56} = 5 + \frac{10}{56}$.)

⚠ You do not always need to use division. The example below shows another method that is quick and easy when the highest power term on the top is the same as the highest power term on the bottom.

By writing $\dfrac{x^2}{x^2+2}$ as

$$\frac{x^2+2-2}{x^2+2} = \frac{x^2+2}{x^2+2} - \frac{2}{x^2+2}$$

(add 2 to the top to get an expression divisible by the bottom and then subtract 2 to leave the value of the fraction unaltered) you can express $\dfrac{x^2}{x^2+2}$ as the mixed fraction $1 - \dfrac{2}{x^2+2}$.

Questions

1 Find the quotient and the remainder when $4x^3 - 7x^2 + 2x - 1$ is divided by $x - 2$.

2 Express as mixed fractions

a $\dfrac{x+4}{x-2}$ **b** $\dfrac{x^2+4x}{x^2-2}$ **c** $\dfrac{2x^3-4x^2}{x+3}$

Answers

1 quotient: $4x^2 + x + 4$, remainder 7

2a $1 + \dfrac{6}{x-2}$ **b** $1 + \dfrac{4x+2}{x^2-2}$ **c** $2x^2 - 10x + 30 - \dfrac{90}{x+3}$

The remainder theorem

The REMAINDER THEOREM states that

> when a polynomial $f(x)$ is divided by $(x - a)$, the remainder is $f(a)$

because, in general, $\dfrac{f(x)}{(x-a)} = q(x) + \dfrac{R}{(x-a)}$

$\Rightarrow \quad f(x) = q(x)(x-a) + R$

and when $x = a$, $f(a) = R$.

The FACTOR THEOREM is a special case of the remainder theorem because, when $(x - a)$ is a factor of $f(x)$, there is no remainder
so $R = 0 \Rightarrow f(a) = 0$.

- You can use the remainder theorem for problems where a polynomial is divided by a linear function and you are interested in the remainder ONLY.

For example, given that
$f(x) = x^3 - 5x^2 + ax - 8$ has a remainder of 4 when divided by $x - 2$, you can use the fact that $f(2) = 4$ to find the value of a,
i.e. $2^3 - 5(2)^2 + 2a - 8 = 4 \quad \Rightarrow \quad a = 12$.

Questions

1 Find the remainder when $x^4 - 2x^3 + 6x$ is divided by $(2x - 1)$.

2 $2x^3 + ax^2 - 3x + 5$ leaves a remainder of 1 when divided by $x - 1$. Find the value of a.

3 $ax^3 - x^2 + x + b$ has a factor $(x + 2)$ and leaves a remainder of 20 when divided by$(x - 2)$. Find the values of a and b.

Answers

1 $\frac{45}{16}$ **2** -3

3 $f(-2) = 0$ & $f(2) = 20 \Rightarrow a = 1, b = 14$

Partial fractions

Two fractions such as $\dfrac{2}{x-3} - \dfrac{1}{2x+1}$ can be expressed as the single fraction $\dfrac{3x+5}{(x-3)(2x+1)}$.

This process can be reversed; any fraction whose denominator is a polynomial with factors, can be expressed as the sum or difference of two or more simpler fractions, called partial fractions.

You can do this by following these steps.

- Check that the fraction is proper – if it isn't, express it as a mixed fraction.
- Write down the partial fractions using letters for unknown constants: their denominators are the factors of the denominator of the original fraction and the number of partial fractions is equal to the number of these factors. These examples illustrate the forms of the numerators of the partial fractions:

$$\frac{2x}{(x-1)(2x+1)} \equiv \frac{A}{x-1} + \frac{B}{2x+1} \qquad [1]$$

$$\frac{2x}{(x+1)(2x^2+1)} \equiv \frac{A}{x+1} + \frac{Bx+C}{2x^2+1} \qquad [2]$$

$$\frac{2x}{(x+2)(x+1)^2} \equiv \frac{A}{x+2} + \frac{B}{x+1} + \frac{C}{(x+1)^2} \qquad [3]$$

i.e.

- linear denominator $\rightarrow$ top is constant,
- quadratic denominator (that doesn't factorise) $\rightarrow$ top is linear (i.e. $Bx + C$)
- repeated denominator $\rightarrow$ two partial fractions, one with single denominator, the other with repeated denominator, both tops are constants.

- Use the following steps to find the constants.

Express the RHS as a single fraction, then use the fact that the denominators are identical:
In [3] for example,

$2x \equiv A(x+1)^2 + B(x+2)(x+1) + C(x+2)$
$x = -1 \quad \Rightarrow \quad -2 = C$
$x = -2 \quad \Rightarrow \quad -4 = A$
Comparing x^2 terms: $A + B = 0 \quad \Rightarrow \quad B = 4$

$$\therefore \quad \frac{2x}{(x+2)(x+1)^2} \equiv -\frac{4}{x+2} + \frac{4}{x+1} - \frac{2}{(x+1)^2}.$$

This method can always be used to find all the unknown constants but, as the example above shows, you may have to solve three (or more) equations simultaneously.

There is a short cut (the COVERUP METHOD) that can be used to find the denominators of the partial fractions with linear denominators that are NOT repeated (A and B in [1], A in [2], A in [3]). If the coverup method is new to you, it is worth learning as it is quick, easy and in most cases can be done mentally.

- The coverup method works by using the RHS, covering up the factor that is the denominator of the partial fraction concerned, then substituting the value of x that makes that factor zero, into the remaining terms.

In [1], for example,

$$\frac{2(1)}{\cancel{(x-1)}(2(1)+1)} = A \quad \Rightarrow \quad A = \tfrac{2}{3}$$

and
$$\frac{2(-\frac{1}{2})}{(-\frac{1}{2}-1)\cancel{(2x+1)}} = B$$
$$\Rightarrow \quad B = \tfrac{2}{3}$$

$$\therefore \quad \frac{2x}{(x-1)(2x+1)} \equiv \frac{\frac{2}{3}}{x-1} + \frac{\frac{2}{3}}{2x+1}$$
$$\equiv \frac{2}{3(x-1)} + \frac{2}{3(2x+1)}.$$

In [2] for example you can use a combination of the methods, i.e. $A = -\frac{2}{3}$ (coverup method)

$$\Rightarrow \quad 2x \equiv -\tfrac{2}{3}(2x^2+1) + (Bx + C)(x+1)$$

Comparing constants: $0 = -\frac{2}{3} + C \quad \Rightarrow \quad C = \frac{2}{3}$

Comparing x^2 terms: $0 = -\frac{4}{3} + B \quad \Rightarrow \quad B = \frac{4}{3}$

$$\therefore \quad \frac{2x}{(x-1)(2x^2+1)} \equiv \frac{-\frac{2}{3}}{x+1} + \frac{\frac{4}{3}x + \frac{2}{3}}{2x^2+1}$$
$$\equiv \frac{4x+2}{3(2x^2+1)} - \frac{2}{3(x+1)}.$$

You can use partial fractions to simplify:

- differentiation (Pure 15)
- integration (Pure 16)
- expansions using the binomial theorem (Pure 18).

Questions

Express in partial fractions

1 $\dfrac{3x-1}{(x-1)(x+3)}$ **2** $\dfrac{x^2+1}{(2x-1)(x^2+5)}$

3 $\dfrac{5}{(2x-1)(x+2)^2}$ **4** $\dfrac{8x^2-2}{(x+1)(4x-1)}$

Answers

1 $\dfrac{1}{2(x-1)} + \dfrac{5}{2(x+3)}$ **2** $\dfrac{5}{21(2x-1)} + \dfrac{8x+4}{21(x^2+5)}$

3 $\dfrac{4}{5(2x-1)} - \dfrac{2}{5(x+2)} - \dfrac{1}{(x+2)^2}$

4 $2 - \dfrac{6}{5(x+1)} - \dfrac{6}{5(4x-1)}$

Take a break

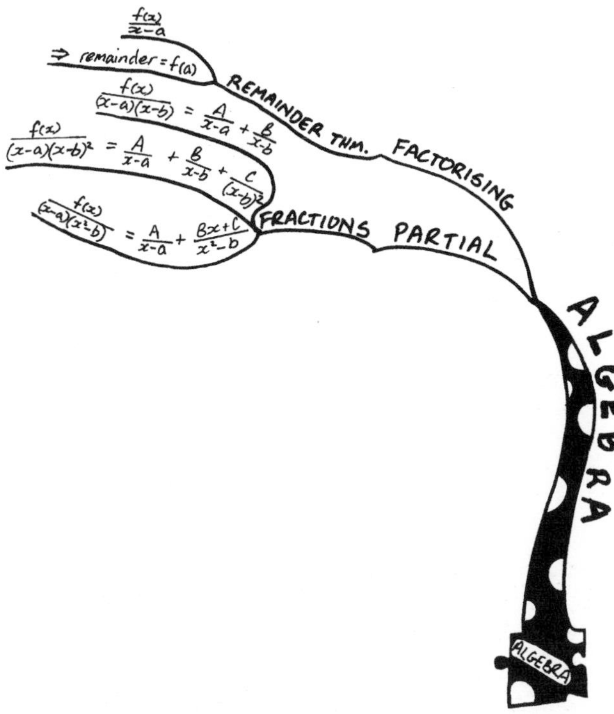

Review

1 Sketch the curve $y = (x-2)^2(2x+1)$.

2 Express $\tan^2\theta$ in terms of $\sin\theta$.

3 Express $2x^2 - 5x$ in the form $a(x+b)^2 + c$, giving the values of a, b and c.

4 Given that $\ln y + \ln k = x$, express y in terms of x.

5 Solve the equation $\sqrt{2}\cos\left(x - \frac{\pi}{3}\right) = 1$ for values of x between 0 and 2π giving your answer in terms of π.

6 Express $\dfrac{2}{(x-1)(x^2+1)}$ in partial fractions.

Answers

1

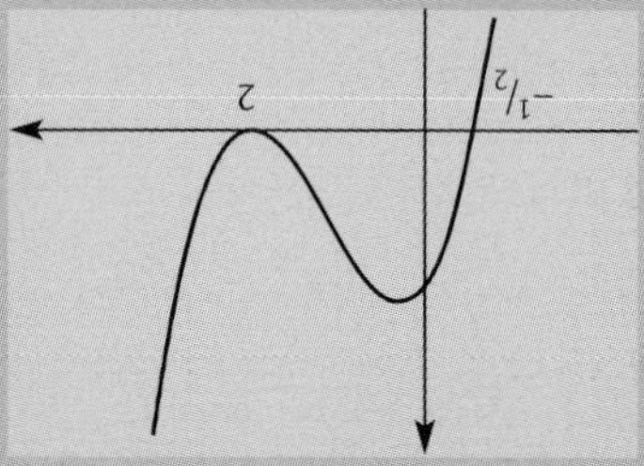

2 $\dfrac{\sin^2\theta}{1-\sin^2\theta}$

3 $2(x-\frac{5}{4})^2 - \frac{25}{8}$ 4 $y = \frac{1}{k}e^x$

5 $\frac{\pi}{12}, \frac{7\pi}{12}$ 6 $\dfrac{1}{x-1} - \dfrac{x+1}{x^2+1}$.

Take a break

PREVIEW

By the end of this topic you will have revised:

- ✔ **how to recognise the equation of a circle and use it to find the centre and radius,**
- ✔ **what parameters are and how they are used to give equations of a curve,**
- ✔ **how to sketch a curve from its parametric equations.**

Before you start you should:

- be able to 'complete the square',
- know the properties of circles,
- know the properties of tangents to circles,
- know the trig identities from Pure 8.

TEST YOURSELF

If you get more than one wrong answer, go to GCSE Higher or A level text book for information and practice.

1 **Express $x^2 - 6x$ in the form $(x - a)^2 + b$.**

2 **Express $x^2 + 7x$ in the form $(x + a)^2 + b$.**

3 **The points $(-4, 7)$ and $(2, -9)$ are the ends of a diameter of a circle. Find the coordinates of the centre of the circle and its radius.**

4 **AT and BT are tangents to the circle whose centre is C. Write down the sizes of angles TAC and ATC and find the lengths of AT and BT.**

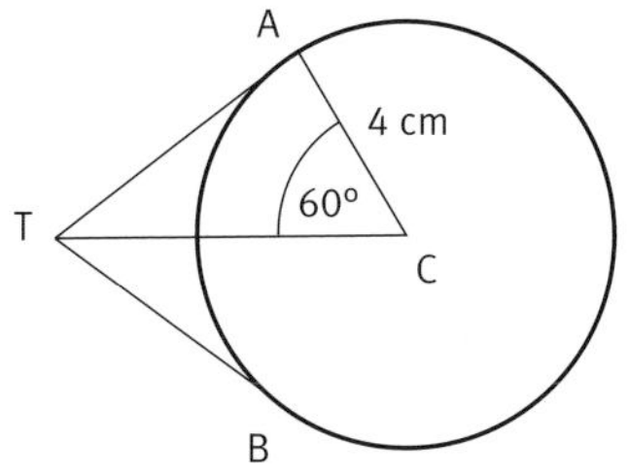

5 **Given that $\cos\theta = 3a$ and $\sin\theta = 2a$, show that $13a^2 = 1$.**

Answers

1 $(x - 3)^2 - 9$ 2 $(x + \frac{7}{2})^2 - \frac{49}{4}$ 3 $(-1, -1)$, $\sqrt{73}$

4 $90°$, $30°$, $AT = BT = 4\sqrt{3}$. 5 Use $\cos^2\theta + \sin^2\theta \equiv 1$

The equation of a circle

The equation of a circle of radius r whose centre is at the point (a, b) is

$$(x - a)^2 + (y - b)^2 = r^2$$

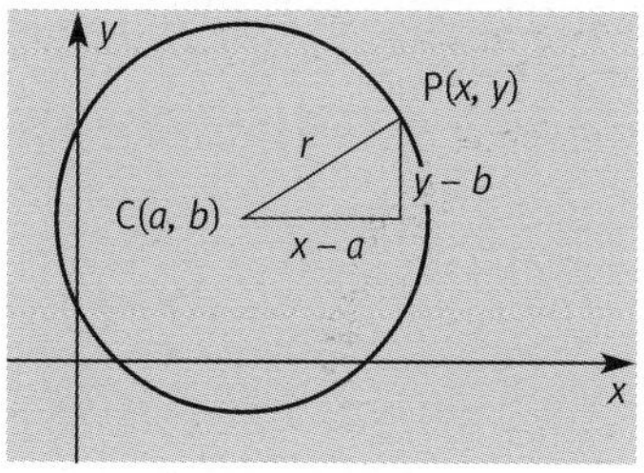

A point P(x, y) is on this circle if and only if $CP^2 = r^2 \Rightarrow (x - a)^2 + (y - b)^2 = r^2$.

- You can use this to write down the equation of a circle when you know the coordinates of its centre and its radius.
  For example, the circle with centre $(2, -1)$ and radius 4 has equation
  $$(x - 2)^2 + (y + 1)^2 = 16$$

When the brackets in the equation

$$(x - a)^2 + (y - b)^2 = r^2$$

are expanded, it becomes

$$x^2 + y^2 - 2ax - 2by + a^2 + b^2 - r^2 = 0$$

so any equation of the form

$$x^2 + y^2 + 2fx + 2gy + c = 0$$

where $c = f^2 + g^2 - r^2$, is the equation of a circle with centre $(-f, -g)$ provided that the value of c gives a positive value for r^2. (Any two of f, g and c may be zero.)

For example, $2x^2 + 2y^2 + 5x + 2 = 0$ may be the equation of a circle. You can find out by dividing the equation by 2,

$$\Rightarrow \quad x^2 + y^2 + \tfrac{5}{2}x + 1 = 0$$

Then use $c = f^2 + g^2 - r^2$ to find r^2 and check that it is positive: $r^2 = \frac{25}{16} - 1 = \frac{9}{16}$

Therefore $2x^2 + 2y^2 + 5x + 2 = 0$ is the equation of a circle with centre $(-\frac{5}{4}, 0)$ and radius $\frac{3}{4}$.

But $x^2 + 2y^2 + 5x + 2 = 0$ cannot be the equation of a circle because the coefficients of x^2 and y^2 are different.

Questions

Determine which of these equations give circles. For those that do, write down the coordinates of the centre and the radius.

1 $x^2 - y^2 = 3$

2 $x^2 + y^2 = 2y$

3 $x^2 + 2xy + y^2 = 6$

4 $y^2 + 5 = 4x - x^2$

5 $x^2 + y^2 = 4$

6 The points $(1, -1)$ and $(4, 1)$ are the ends of a diameter of a circle. Show that the equation of the circle is $x^2 + y^2 - 5x + 3 = 0$.

Answers

1 no (coefficients of x^2 and y^2 are not equal)

2 yes $(x^2 + y^2 = 2y \Rightarrow x^2 + y^2 - 2y = 0$
$\Rightarrow x^2 + (y-1)^2 = 1)$, centre (0, 1), radius 1.

3 no (contains an xy term)

4 no because $y^2 + 5 = 4x - x^2 \Rightarrow x^2 - 4x + y^2 + 5 = 0$
$\Rightarrow r^2 = -1$.

5 yes, centre the origin and radius 2.

Solving problems

⚠ An instinctive response when asked for the equation of a tangent to a curve with a cartesian equation is to differentiate.

But many coordinate geometry problems involving circles and lines can be solved simply by using the properties of circles and tangents; in particular you can find the gradient at a point on the circumference by using the fact that a tangent to a circle is perpendicular to the radius at the point of contact.

Use calculus as a last resort in any circle problem.

To solve any problem, remember to look for facts that are not spelt out in the question and then for relationships between facts.

You may be able to jog your memory for relevant facts by working back from what you are asked to find.

For example:

The point A(2, 1) is on the circle with equation

$$x^2 + y^2 - 2x + 8y - 9 = 0$$

Find the equation of the tangent to the circle at A.

To solve this problem start by sketching a diagram (a 2p coin is useful for circles); this is easier if you know the centre of the circle:

$x^2 + y^2 - 2x + 8y - 9 = 0 \Rightarrow (x-1)^2 + (y+4)^2 = 26$
$\Rightarrow$ centre is $(1, -4)$

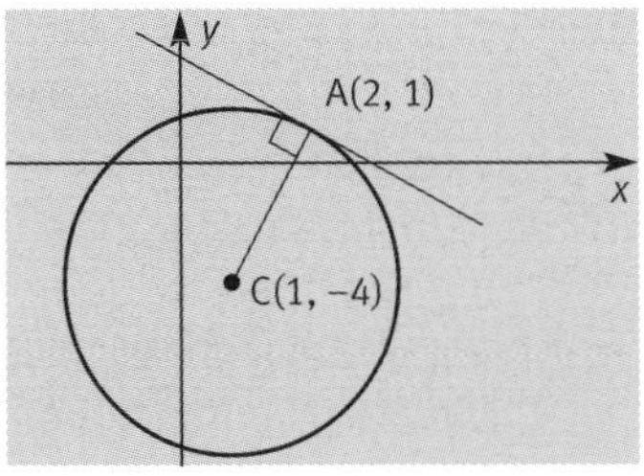

To find the equation of a line you need a point on the line (known, (2, 1)) and the gradient of the line (not known). So you need to find the gradient of the tangent at A.

You know that AC is $\perp$ to the tangent at A and the gradient of AC = 5,

$\therefore$ gradient of the tangent at A is $-\frac{1}{5}$.

Hence the equation of the tangent at A is

$$y - 1 = -\tfrac{1}{5}(x - 2) \Rightarrow x + 5y - 7 = 0.$$

Example

The tangents from the point T(5, 0) touch the circle

$$x^2 + y^2 = 9$$

at the points A and B. Find the area shaded in the diagram.

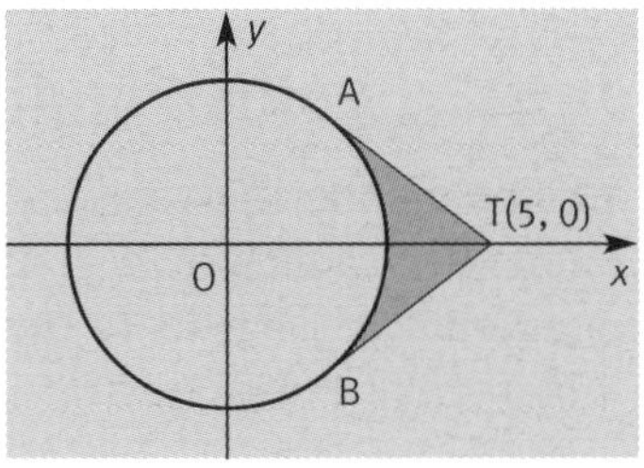

Solution

(Start by sketching a working diagram.)

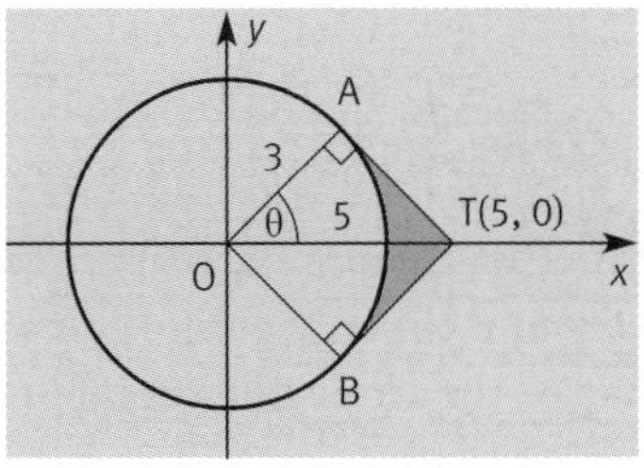

Shaded area = area OATB – area sector OAB

OATB consists of two congruent right-angled triangles since $O\hat{A}T = O\hat{B}T = 90°$,

$OA = OB = 3$ (radii of circle $x^2 + y^2 = 9$),

and $OT = 5$, so $AT = TB = 4$ (Pythagoras' thm). (Mark this on the diagram.)

$\therefore$ area OATB = 2 × area △OAT = 12 square units.

Area sector OAB $= \frac{1}{2}(3)^2(2\theta)$

From △OAT, $\sin\theta = \frac{4}{5} \Rightarrow \theta = 0.927\ldots$ rad

$\therefore$ area sector OAB = 8.345 . . . sq units

$\therefore$ shaded area = 3.65 sq units (3 sf).

Questions

1 Find the length of the tangents from the point (2, 5) to the circle $(x+3)^2 + y^2 - 1 = 0$.

2 Is the point (1, 1) on, inside or outside the circle $x^2 + y^2 - 2y - 3 = 0$?
Find the equation of the tangent to the circle at the point on the circle where $x = 2$.

3 The line $y = x + c$ is a tangent to the circle $x^2 + y^2 - 4y + 1 = 0$.
Find the possible values of c.

Answers

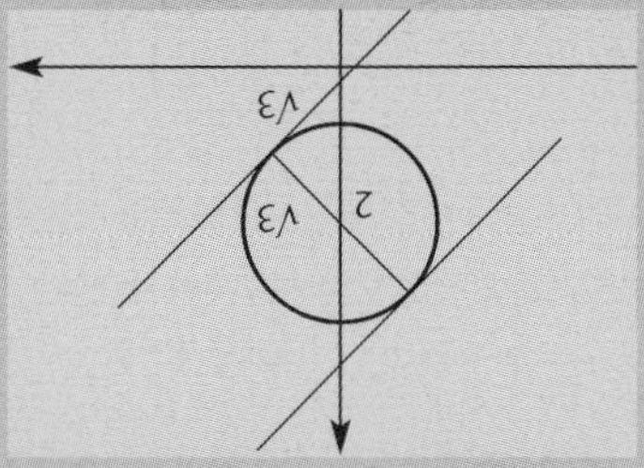

1 7

2 inside (from (1, 1) to the centre < radius); $x = 2$

3 $2 \pm \sqrt{6}$

(the radius is $\sqrt{3}$, the line is at 45° to the x-axis, then use Pythag. thm.). (OR if $y = x + c$ touches $x^2 + y^2 - 4y + 1 = 0$, when these equations are solved simultaneously, they must have equal roots, i.e. '$b^2 - 4ac$' = 0, which gives a quadratic equation in c that can be solved to find the values of c.)

Take a break

Parametric equations

The equation of a curve may be given as a direct relationship between x and y, called the Cartesian equation, e.g. $x^2 = y^3$, or as parametric equations where x and y are each expressed in terms of a third variable, called a parameter, e.g. $x = t^3$, $y = t^2$.

You can use parametric equations to:

- find the gradient function in terms of the parameter – see Pure 15,
- find the Cartesian equation by eliminating the parameter,
  e.g. when $x = t^3$ and $y = t^2$
  then $x^2 = t^6$ and $y^3 = t^6 \Rightarrow x^2 = y^3$.
  Similarly, when $x = 2\cos\theta$ and $y = 3\sin\theta$
  then $\frac{x}{2} = \cos\theta$ and $\frac{y}{3} = \sin\theta$
  and using the identity $\cos^2\theta + \sin^2\theta \equiv 1$
  $\Rightarrow \left(\frac{x}{2}\right)^2 + \left(\frac{y}{3}\right)^2 = 1 \quad \Rightarrow \quad 9x^2 + 4y^2 = 36$,
- sketch a curve directly from its parametric equations. You can do this by giving the parameter arbitrary values to find corresponding values of x and y,
  e.g. for $x = t^3$ and $y = t^2$:

t	-2	-1	$-\frac{1}{2}$	0	$\frac{1}{2}$	1	2
x	-8	-1	$-\frac{1}{8}$	0	$\frac{1}{8}$	1	8
y	4	1	$\frac{1}{4}$	0	$\frac{1}{4}$	1	4

Plotting these points gives this sketch:

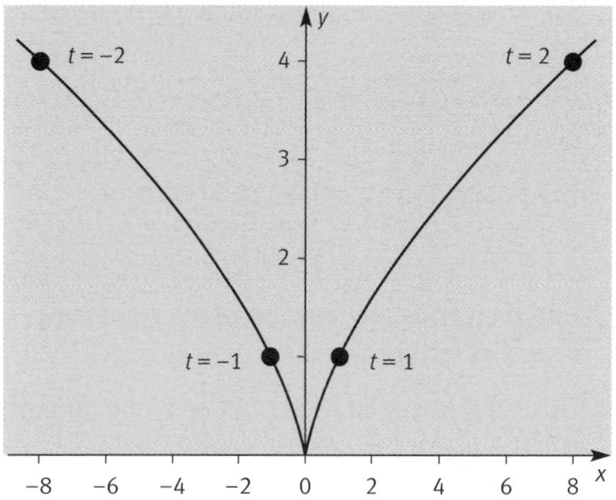

Do not make assumptions about the shape of a curve. You may be tempted to assume that this curve has a minimum turning point at O: always investigate. See what happens to x and to y as the parameter approaches its value at that point. For this curve, as $|t| \to 0$, $x \to 0$ faster than $y \to 0$, so the curve gets steeper. Alternatively, look at the gradient function of the curve at and around that point.

These are some curves that you should recognise from their parametric equations.

- $x = r\cos\theta$, $y = r\sin\theta$ give a circle, centre O, radius r:

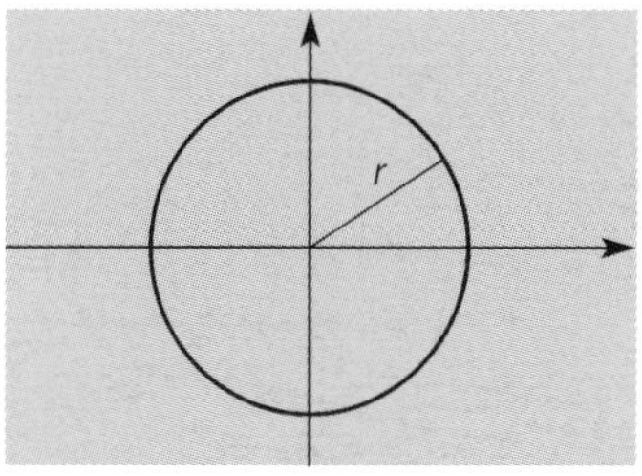

- $x = a\cos\theta$, $y = b\sin\theta$ give an ellipse, centre O:

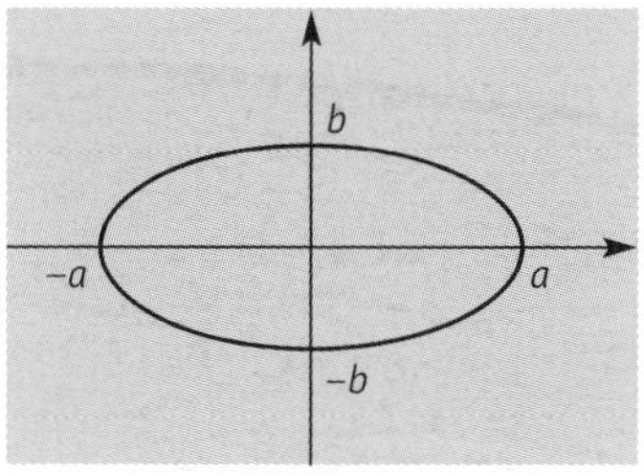

- $x = \frac{a}{t}$, $y = at$ give this hyperbola:

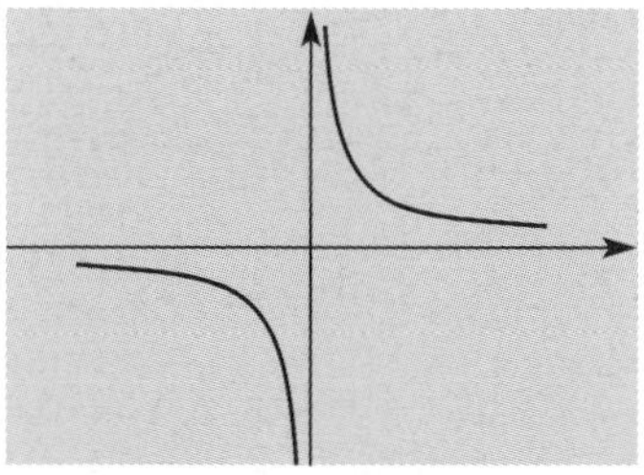

Questions

1 Sketch the curve whose parametric equations are

a $x = 5\cos\theta,\ y = 5\sin\theta$

b $x = 5\cos\theta,\ y = 2\sin\theta$

2 The parametric equations of a curve are

$$x = \frac{1}{t},\ y = 2 + t.$$

Find the cartesian equation of the curve and draw a sketch of the curve.

3 This curve is called an astroid and its parametric equations are $x = \cos^3\theta,\ y = \sin^3\theta$.

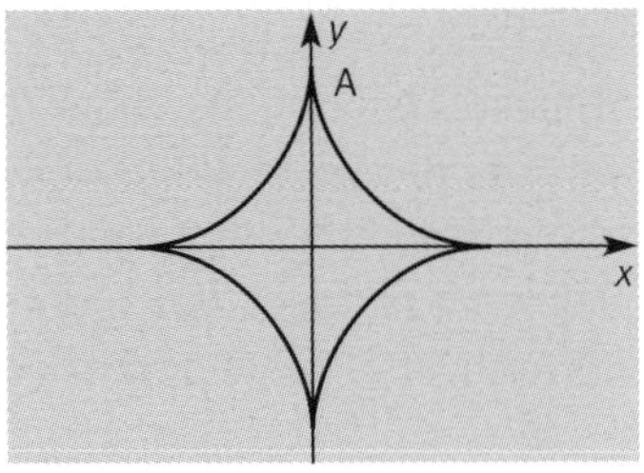

Find

a the value of θ at A and the coordinates of A,

b the cartesian equation of the curve.

Answers

1

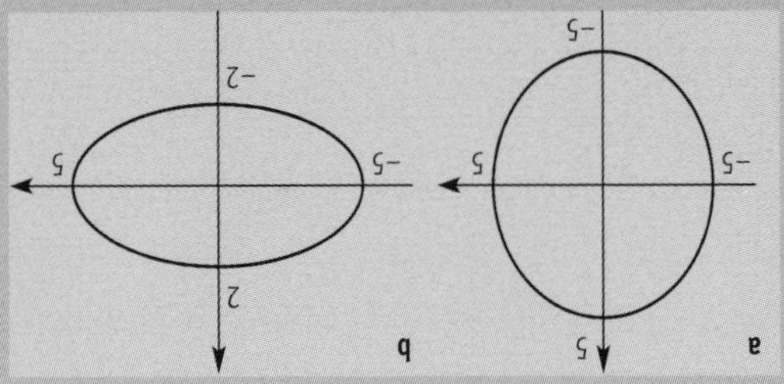

2 $y = 2 + \frac{1}{x}$;

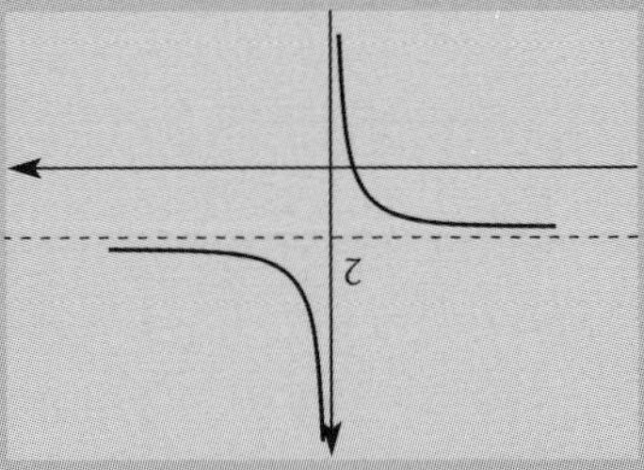

3a $\frac{\pi}{2}$, (0, 1)

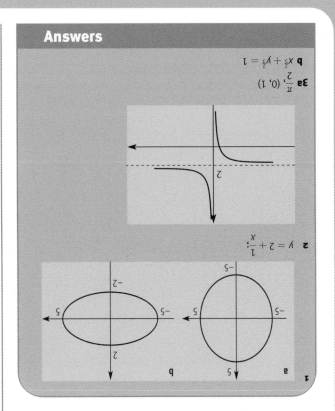

b $x^{\frac{2}{3}} + y^{\frac{2}{3}} = 1$

Take a break

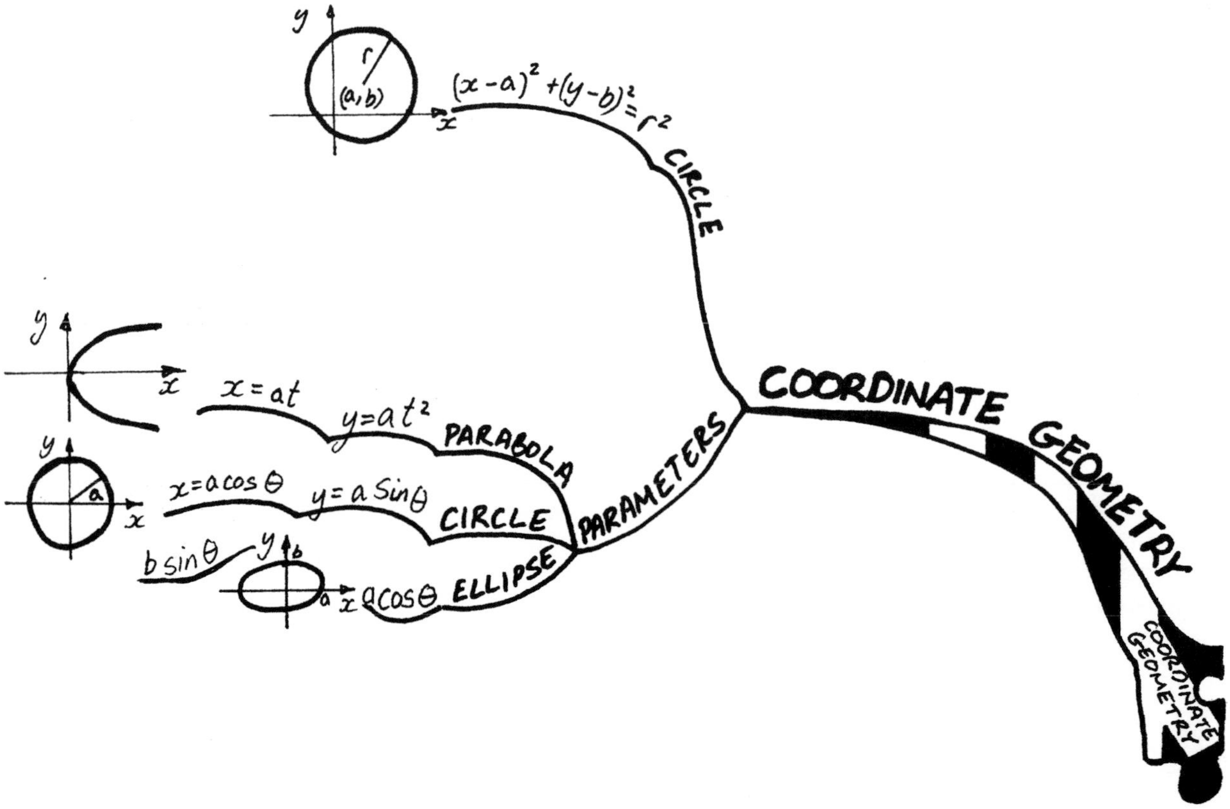

Review

1 $f(x) = \dfrac{1}{x+1}$, $0 \leqslant x \leqslant 1$

a Find $f^{-1}(x)$ and state its domain and range.

b On the same set of axes sketch the curves $y = f(x)$ and $y = f^{-1}(x)$.

2 Solve the equation $\tan\theta = 2\sin\theta$ for $0 \leqslant \theta \leqslant \pi$, giving answers in terms of π.

3 Find the remainder when $4x^3 - 2x^2 + 5$ is divided by $2x^2 - 1$.

4 Express $\dfrac{3x}{(x+2)(x-1)^2}$ in partial fractions.

5 Find the stationary point on the curve $y = 3x - e^{3x}$ and determine its nature.

Answers

1a $f^{-1}(x) = \dfrac{1-x}{x}$; domain $\frac{1}{2} \leqslant x \leqslant 1$, range $0 \leqslant f^{-1}(x) \leqslant 1$.

b

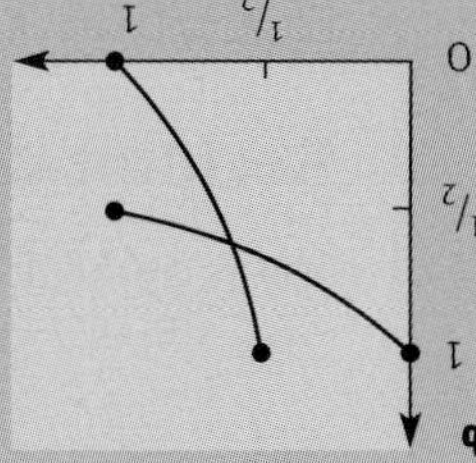

2 $0, \dfrac{\pi}{3}, \pi$ **3** $2x + 4$ **4** $-\dfrac{2}{3(x+2)} + \dfrac{2}{3(x-1)} + \dfrac{1}{(x-1)^2}$ **5** $(0, -1)$, max.

PREVIEW

By the end of this topic you will have revised:

- ✔ **reciprocal and inverse trig functions,**
- ✔ **compound and double angle identities,**
- ✔ **techniques for solving trig equations.**

Before you start you need to:

- remember the work on functions in Pure 4,
- know and instantly recognise the trig identities in Pure 8,
- remember the techniques for solving trig equations in Pure 8.

Inverse trig functions

The function $f(x) = \sin x$, $x \in \mathbb{R}$, does not have an inverse because one value of $\sin x$ maps to many values of x.

But when $f(x) = \sin x$ for $-\frac{\pi}{2} \leqslant x \leqslant \frac{\pi}{2}$, there is an inverse denoted by $f^{-1}(x) = \sin^{-1} x$ (or sometimes arcsin x) where $\sin^{-1} x$ means "the angle whose sine is x".

The diagram shows the graph of $y = \sin^{-1} x$

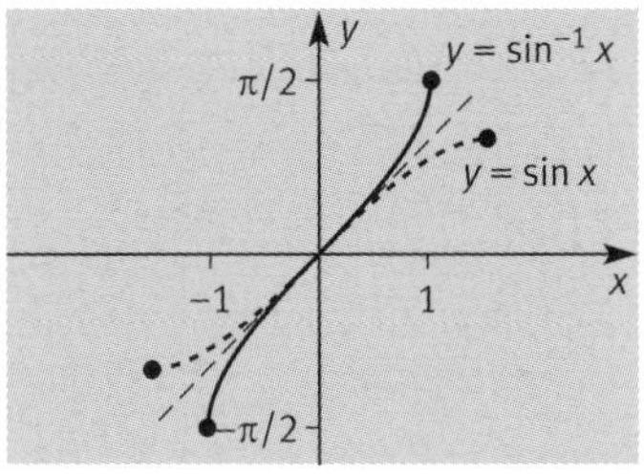

The curve stops at the points $\left(1, \frac{\pi}{2}\right)$ and $\left(-1, -\frac{\pi}{2}\right)$,

i.e. $f(x) = \sin^{-1} x$ has range $-\frac{\pi}{2}$ to $\frac{\pi}{2}$ and domain $-1 \leqslant x \leqslant 1$.

Likewise the function $f(x) = \cos x$, $x \in \mathbb{R}$, does not have an inverse, but $f(x) = \cos x$, $0 \leqslant x \leqslant \pi$ does; it is denoted by $f^{-1}(x) = \cos^{-1} x$.

The diagram shows the curve $y = \cos^{-1} x$.

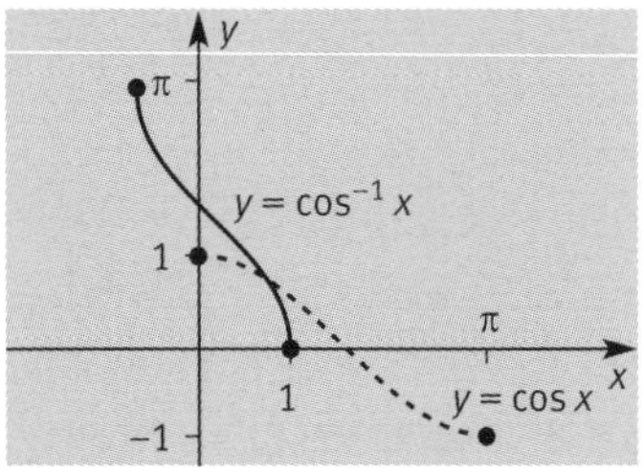

$f(x) = \cos^{-1} x$ has domain $-1 \leqslant x \leqslant 1$ and range 0 to π.

The function $f(x) = \tan x$, $-\frac{\pi}{2} \leqslant x \leqslant \frac{\pi}{2}$, has an inverse denoted by $f^{-1}(x) = \tan^{-1} x$.

This is the graph of $y = \tan^{-1} x$.

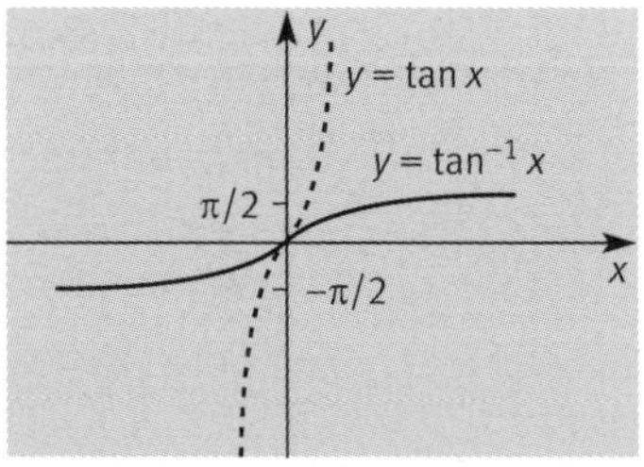

The domain of $f(x) = \tan^{-1} x$ is all values of x and the range is $-\frac{\pi}{2} < f(x) < \frac{\pi}{2}$.

Reciprocal trig functions

The reciprocal trig functions are $\sec x$, $\operatorname{cosec} x$ and $\cot x$ where

i $\quad$ se**c** $x \equiv \frac{1}{\textbf{c}\text{os}\, x}$, co**s**ec $x \equiv \frac{1}{\textbf{s}\text{in}\, x}$, co**t** $x \equiv \frac{1}{\textbf{t}\text{an}\, x}$

(sec is short for secant, cosec is short for cosecant and cot is short for cotangent).

Memory aid: use the third letter.

Their graphs are:

$f(x) = \sec x$

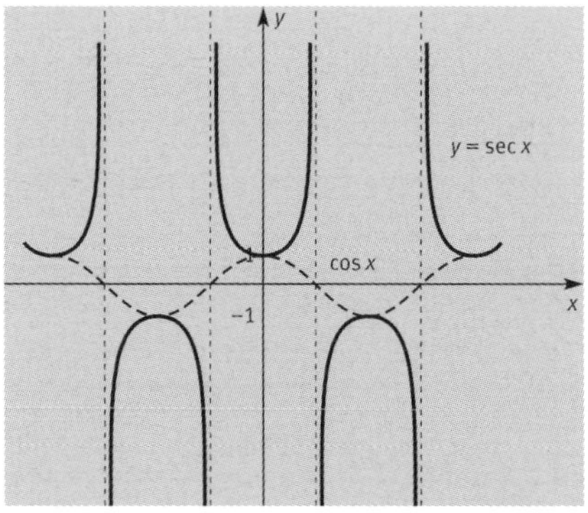

$f(x) = \operatorname{cosec} x$

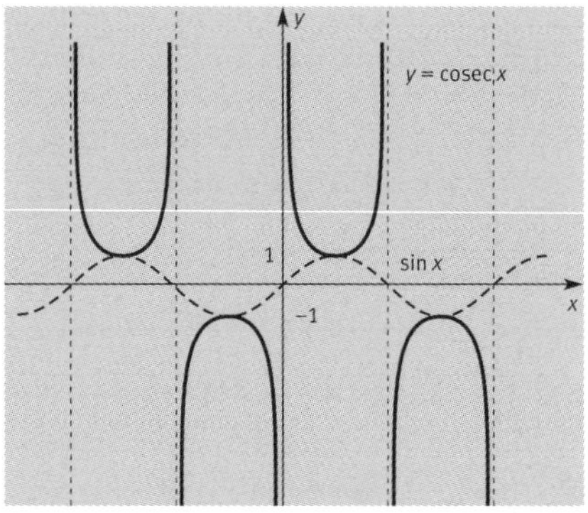

The graphs of sec x and cosec x:

- have a pattern that repeats every 2π,
- have no values of y between -1 and 1; i.e. for any value of x,

$$|\sec x| \geqslant 1 \text{ and } |\text{cosec}\, x| \geqslant 1$$

$y = \cot x$

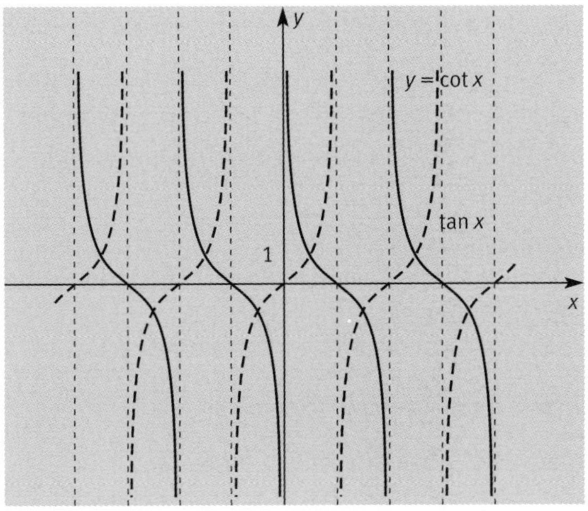

The graph of cot x:

- has a pattern that repeats every interval of π,
- shows that cot x takes all values.

Trig identities

Pythagorean Identities

$$\sin^2 x + \cos^2 x \equiv 1$$
$$\tan^2 x + 1 \equiv \sec^2 x$$
$$1 + \cot^2 x \equiv \text{cosec}^2 x$$

The second and third identities are alternative forms of the first. The second is obtained by dividing the first by $\cos^2 x$, i.e.

$$\frac{\sin^2 x}{\cos^2 x} + 1 \equiv \frac{1}{\cos^2 x} \Rightarrow \tan^2 x + 1 \equiv \sec^2 x$$

and the third comes from dividing the first by $\sin^2 x$.

Compound Angle Identities

For any two angles, A and B,

$$\sin(A \pm B) \equiv \sin A \cos B \pm \cos A \sin B$$
$$\cos(A \pm B) \equiv \cos A \cos B \mp \sin A \sin B$$
$$\tan(A \pm B) \equiv \frac{\tan A \pm \tan B}{1 \mp \tan A \tan B}.$$

⚠ Be careful with the signs, particularly in $\cos(A \pm B)$ and in $\tan(A \pm B)$: read the top signs on both sides and vice-versa.

Double Angle Identities

Replacing A and B with x in the compound angle identities gives

$$\sin 2x \equiv 2 \sin x \cos x$$

$$\cos 2x \equiv \begin{cases} \cos^2 x - \sin^2 x \\ 2\cos^2 x - 1 \\ 1 - 2\sin^2 x \end{cases}$$

$$\tan 2x \equiv \frac{2 \tan x}{1 - \tan^2 x}.$$

You can use these identities to write trig expressions in different forms.

You will need to do this to:

- solve some trig equations,
- differentiate and integrate some trig functions – see Pure 15 and 16.

⚠ You need to know all these identities so well that you can recall then instantly AND be able to recognise the RHS of an identity,

e.g. given $\sin 2\theta \cos\theta + \cos 2\theta \sin\theta$, bells should ring in your head telling you that this is the expansion of $\sin(A + B)$ with 2θ replacing A and θ replacing B, i.e.

$$\sin 2\theta \cos\theta + \cos 2\theta \sin\theta \equiv \sin(2\theta + \theta) \equiv \sin 3\theta$$

⚠ These are common mistakes – avoid them.

$\sin A + \sin B$ is NOT equal to $\sin(A + B)$,
$\cos(\theta + \alpha)$ is NOT equal to $\cos\theta + \cos\alpha$,
$\tan 2x$ is NOT equal to $2 \tan x$, and so on.

Do's and don'ts when you have to prove that one form of a trig expression is identical to another form.

- ✔ It is easiest to work with sin and cos, so express any other trig ratio in terms of sin and/or cos.
- ✘ Do not try to work with both sides of an identity at the same time. Start with the more complicated side unless multiple angles are involved. If they are you may find it profitable (time-wise) to break down the trig ratio of a multiple angle into trig ratios of the single angle, e.g. to break down $\cos 3x$, express it as $\cos(2x + x)$ then use the compound angle identity followed by the double angle identity.
- ✔ If you cannot see where to go next with the side you are working on, work on the other side and see if you can make them meet in the middle.

Example

Prove that $\sin^2\theta \equiv \frac{1}{2}(1-\cos 2\theta)$

Solution

Start with the RHS. As the LHS involves $\sin\theta$, use the version of double angle formula for $\cos 2\theta$ in terms of $\sin\theta$.

$$\begin{aligned}\text{RHS} &= \tfrac{1}{2}(1-\cos 2\theta)\\ &= \tfrac{1}{2}(1-(1-2\sin^2\theta))\\ &= \tfrac{1}{2}(1-1+2\sin^2\theta) = \sin^2\theta = \text{LHS}\end{aligned}$$

Questions

1 Prove that $\cos^2\theta \equiv \frac{1}{2}(\cos 2\theta + 1)$.

2 Show that $\tan x + \cot x \equiv 2\operatorname{cosec} 2x$.
Sketch the graph of $y = 2\operatorname{cosec} 2x$ and hence find the values of x between 0 and $\pi/2$ for which $\tan x + \cot x < 4$.

3 Prove that $\cos 3x \sec x \equiv 1 - 4\sin^2 x$.

Answers

2 (Start with LHS $= \frac{\sin x}{\cos x} + \frac{\cos x}{\sin x}$ and express as a single fraction.) $\frac{\pi}{12} < x < \frac{5\pi}{12}$

Take a break

Expressing $a\cos\theta + b\sin\theta$ as $R\cos(\theta \pm \alpha)$ or $R\sin(\theta \pm \alpha)$

The expression $a\cos\theta + b\sin\theta$, where a and b are numbers can be expressed in any of the four forms $R\cos(\theta \pm \alpha)$ or $R\sin(\theta \pm \alpha)$, where $R > 0$ and α is acute.

For example, to express $3\cos\theta + 4\sin\theta$ as $R\cos(\theta - \alpha)$, follow these steps.

1 Start with $3\cos\theta + 4\sin\theta \equiv R\cos(\theta - \alpha)$.

2 Use the appropriate compound angle identity to expand the RHS, i.e.
$3\cos\theta + 4\sin\theta \equiv R\cos\theta\cos\alpha + R\sin\theta\sin\alpha$.

3 As this is an identity, you can compare coefficients of $\cos\theta$ and of $\sin\theta$. This gives two equations, i.e.
$3 = R\cos\alpha$ [1] and $4 = R\sin\alpha$ [2].

4 Find R by squaring [1] and [2] then adding to eliminate α, i.e.

$$\begin{aligned}9+16 &= R^2\cos^2\alpha + R^2\sin^2\alpha\\ &= R^2(\cos^2\alpha + \sin^2\alpha) = R^2\\ \Rightarrow \quad R &= 5\end{aligned}$$

5 Divide [2] by [1] to eliminate R, i.e.

$$\frac{4}{3} = \frac{\sin\alpha}{\cos\alpha} = \tan\alpha \Rightarrow \alpha = \tan^{-1}\left(\frac{4}{3}\right)$$

$\alpha = 0.93$ rad (2dp)

$\therefore \quad 3\cos\theta + 4\sin\theta \equiv 5\cos(\theta - 0.93)$.

⚠ You can leave out step 4 because, for all four forms, $R = \sqrt{a^2+b^2}$.

Don't leave out steps 2, 3 and 5 – it is easy to get signs wrong and to get the value of $\tan\alpha$ upside down.

Exam questions usually give the form to use, but if you have to choose, match the first trig ratio to the alternative form, i.e.

$a\,\mathbf{cos}\,\theta \pm b\sin\theta \equiv R\,\mathbf{cos}\,(\theta \mp \alpha)$ (watch signs)
$a\,\mathbf{sin}\,\theta \pm b\cos\theta \equiv R\,\mathbf{sin}\,(\theta \pm \alpha)$.

You can use these alternative forms to:

- find turning points on $y = a\cos\theta + b\sin\theta$,
- sketch the graph of $y = a\cos\theta + b\sin\theta$,
- solve equations of the form $a\cos\theta + b\sin\theta = c$ where $c \neq 0$.

For example, $3\cos\theta + 4\sin\theta \equiv 5\cos(\theta - 0.93)$.

To find the maximum and minimum values of

$$y = 3\cos\theta + 4\sin\theta$$

use $y = 5\cos(\theta - 0.93)$, which has a maximum value of 5 and a minimum value of -5. (They occur where $\cos(\theta - 0.93) = \pm 1$.)

To sketch the graph of $y = 3\cos\theta + 4\sin\theta$, you can use $y = 5\cos(\theta - 0.93)$ which is the cosine curve stretched by 5 units parallel to the y-axis and translated 0.93 units in the +ve direction of the x-axis, i.e.

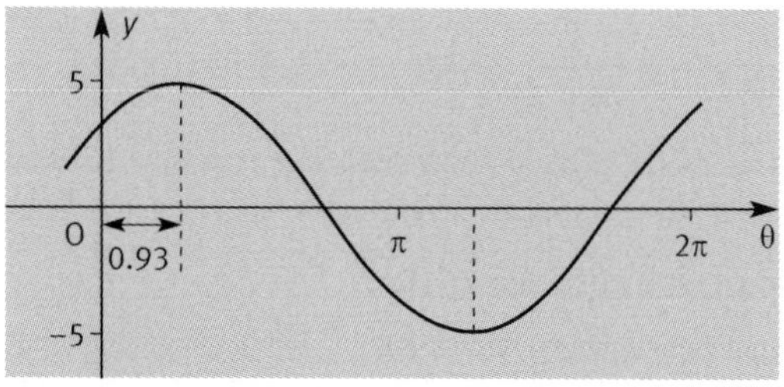

To solve the equation

$$3\cos\theta + 4\sin\theta = 1 \text{ for } 0 \leqslant \theta \leqslant 2\pi$$

you can write $5\cos(\theta - 0.93) = 1$
$\Rightarrow \quad \cos(\theta - 0.93) = \frac{1}{5}$

This is now in one of the forms in Pure 8:

$\Rightarrow \quad \theta - 0.93 = 1.37$ or $2\pi - 1.37$
$\Rightarrow \quad \theta = 2.30$ rad or 5.84 rad (2 dp).

⚠ You do not need to use these alternative forms to solve the equation $a\cos\theta + b\sin\theta = 0$, (i.e. $c = 0$) since dividing by $\cos\theta$ reduces the equation to $\tan\theta = -\frac{a}{b}$.
(Remember to add $\cos\theta \neq 0$.)

Questions

1 Prove that, when $a\cos\theta + b\sin\theta$ is written in the form $R\cos(\theta - \alpha)$, $R = \sqrt{a^2 + b^2}$.

2 Express $5\cos x + 12\sin x$ in the form $R\sin(x + \alpha)$ giving the values of α in degrees correct to 1 decimal place.
Hence find

a the values of x between 0 and 360° for which $5\cos x + 12\sin x = 13$,

b the maximum and minimum values of

$$\frac{1}{5\cos x + 12\sin x + 1}$$

and the smallest values of x at which they occur.

Answers

1 $a\cos\theta + b\sin\theta \equiv R\cos(\theta - \alpha)$
$\equiv R\cos\theta\cos\alpha + R\sin\theta\sin\alpha$
$\Rightarrow \quad a = R\cos\theta$ and $b = R\sin\theta$
$\Rightarrow \quad a^2 + b^2 = R^2(\cos^2\theta + \sin^2\theta) = R^2$

2 $13\sin(x + 22.6°)$

a $67.4°$

b max $-\frac{1}{12}$ when $x + 22.6° = 270° \Rightarrow x = 247.4°$, min $\frac{1}{14}$ when $x + 22.6° = 90° \Rightarrow x = 67.4°$
$\left(\frac{1}{5\cos x + 12\sin x + 1} \equiv \frac{1}{13\sin(x + 22.6°) + 1}\right.$ is maximum when the denominator is minimum $\Rightarrow$ when $13\sin(x + 22.6°)$ is minimum and vice-versa.$\Big)$

Solving trig equations

Trig equations may involve different multiples of the unknown angle and/or a mixture of trig ratios.

Watch out for equations of the form $a\cos\theta + b\sin\theta = c$; questions asking for solutions of this form of equation do not always start with the hint of asking you to express $a\cos\theta + b\sin\theta$ as $R\cos(\theta - \alpha)$.

For other forms of equations use the trig identities to express

i different multiples of the angle in terms of one multiple of that angle,

ii different ratios in terms of just one ratio.

⚠ Look for factors after every step. If you miss a factor at an early stage, the solution is likely to be more complicated.

Example

Solve the equation $\sin 4x + \cos 2x = 0$ for $0° \leqslant x \leqslant 180°$.

Solution

This equation contains $4x$ and $2x$ so start by using the double angle identity to express $\sin 4x$ in terms of the angle $2x$.

$\sin 4x + \cos 2x = 0$
$\Rightarrow \quad 2\sin 2x\cos 2x + \cos 2x = 0$

$\cos 2x$ is a factor:
$\Rightarrow \quad \cos 2x(2\sin 2x + 1) = 0$

$\therefore \quad \cos 2x = 0 \Rightarrow 2x = 90°, 270°$
or $\quad \sin 2x = -\frac{1}{2} \Rightarrow 2x = 210°, 330°$
$\therefore \quad x = 45°, 105°, 135°, 165°.$

Example

Solve the equation $\cos 2x + \sin x = 0$ for $-\pi \leqslant x \leqslant \pi$.

Solution

Use the identity for $\cos 2x$; there are three forms of this identity, and as the other term is $\sin x$, use the form that involves $\sin x$.

$$\cos 2x + \sin x = 0$$
$\Rightarrow \quad 1 - 2\sin^2 x + \sin x = 0$

There are no obvious factors, but it is quadratic in $\sin x$.

$\Rightarrow \quad 2\sin^2 x - \sin x - 1 = 0$
$\Rightarrow \quad (2\sin x + 1)(\sin x - 1) = 0$
$\Rightarrow \quad \sin x = -\frac{1}{2}$ so $x = -\frac{\pi}{6}$ or $-\frac{5\pi}{6}$
or $\quad \sin x = 1$ so $x = \frac{\pi}{2}$

Questions

Solve these equations for the range shown.

1 $\sec x = 1 + \tan^2 x$, $0 \leqslant x \leqslant \pi$

2 $\cos x = \sin\frac{1}{2}x - 2$, $-2\pi \leqslant x \leqslant 2\pi$

3 $1 - 2\sin^2\theta = \sin 2\theta$, $0° \leqslant \theta \leqslant 360°$

Answers

1 (Use $1 + \tan^2 x \equiv \sec^2 x \Rightarrow \sec x = 0$ (no values of x), or $\sec x = 1$); 0

2 (Use $\cos x \equiv 1 - 2\sin^2\frac{1}{2}x$); π

3 (Recognise $1 - 2\sin^2\theta \equiv \cos 2\theta \Rightarrow \tan 2\theta = 1$); $22.5°, 112.5°, 202.5°, 292.5°$.

Take a break

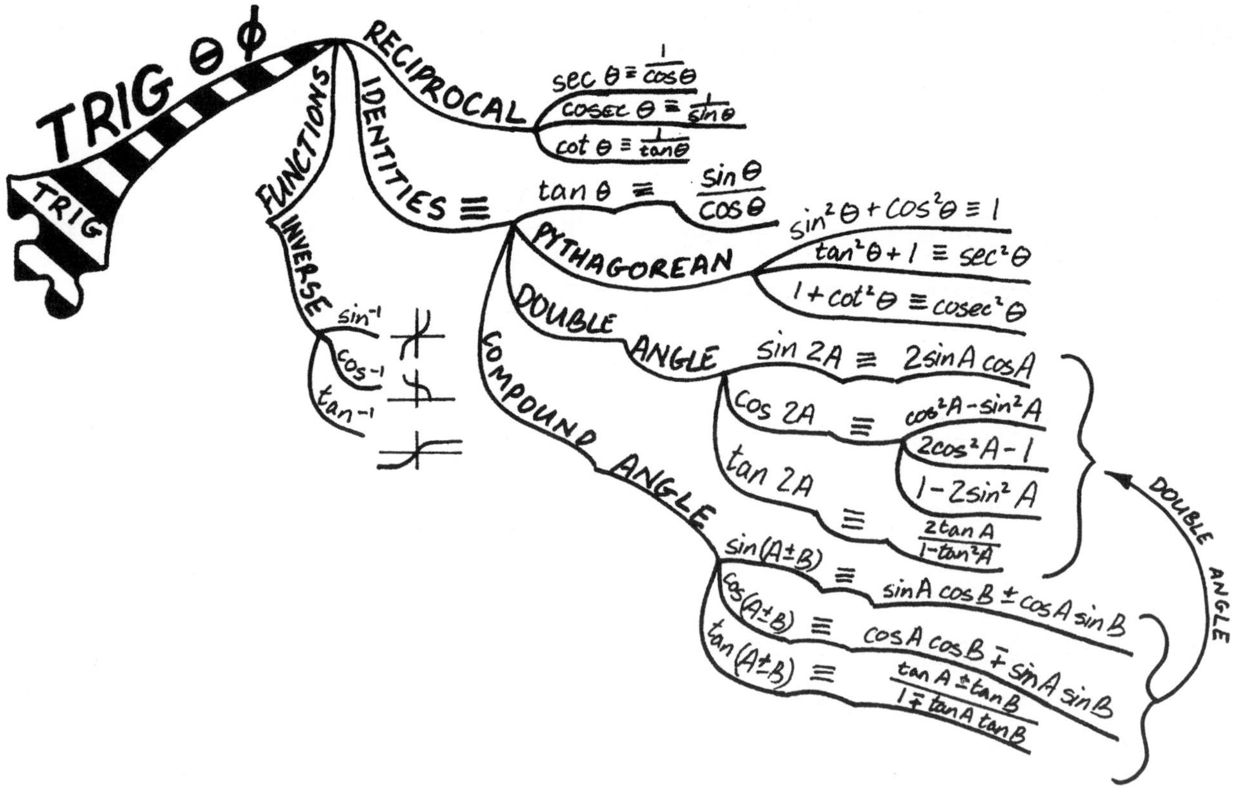

Review

1 Find $\dfrac{d^2y}{dx^2}$ when $y = 2\ln x + \dfrac{1}{x}$.

2 The parametric equations of a curve are

$$x = \sin\theta,\ y = 1 + \cos 2\theta$$

Find the cartesian equation of this curve.

3 Express $\dfrac{1}{(x-2)(x+1)}$ in partial fractions.

4 Find exact solutions to the equation

$$2\log_2 x - \log_2(1 + x) = 3.$$

5 Find the length of the tangents from the point $(-4, 1)$ to the circle

$x^2 + y^2 - 8x - 2y + 5 = 0.$

Hence find the gradients of these tangents.

Answers

1 $\dfrac{2-2x}{x^3}$ **2** $y = 2 - 2x^2$ **3** $\dfrac{1}{3(x-2)} - \dfrac{1}{3(x+1)}$

4 $4 \pm 2\sqrt{6}$

5 $2\sqrt{13}$, $\pm\sqrt{\dfrac{3}{13}}$ (use gradient of a line = tangent of angle made with x-axis)

Take a break

PREVIEW

By the end of this topic you will have revised:

- ✔ **the derivatives of trig functions,**
- ✔ **the chain rule,**
- ✔ **how to differentiate products and quotients of functions,**
- ✔ **how to differentiate functions given parametrically and implicitly.**

Before you start you need to:

- know the derivatives of the standard functions from Pure 9,
- remember how to find equations of tangents and normals.

TEST YOURSELF

If you get any wrong answers, go to Pure 9.

1 **Find $\frac{dy}{dx}$ where y is**

a) $3x^2$ **b)** $2\ln x$ **c)** $\frac{1}{x}$ **d)** $1+\sqrt{x}$

e) $3e^x$.

2 **Find the equation of the normal to the curve $y = x^3 - 6x$ at the point where $x = 1$.**

Answers

1 **a)** $6x$ **b)** $\frac{2}{x}$ **c)** $-\frac{1}{x^2}$ **d)** $\frac{1}{2\sqrt{x}}$ **e)** $3e^x$

2 $x - 3y - 16 = 0$.

Derivatives of sin *x*, cos *x* and tan *x*

When $y = \sin x$, $\frac{dy}{dx} = \cos x$,

when $y = \cos x$, $\frac{dy}{dx} = -\sin x$,

when $y = \tan x$, $\frac{dy}{dx} = \sec^2 x$.

provided that x is in radians.

⚠ Be careful with the signs: it is, for example, easy to mistake $\frac{d}{dx}(\cos x)$ which is $-\sin x$, for $\int \cos x \, dx$, which is $\sin x$.

The chain rule

When y is a function of a function, i.e. $y = f(u)$ where $u = g(x)$, then

$$\frac{dy}{dx} = \frac{dy}{du} \times \frac{du}{dx}.$$

- You can use the chain rule to differentiate any function of a function,

e.g. when $y = \sin 3x$,

$y = \sin u$ where $u = 3x$

$\Rightarrow \frac{dy}{du} = \cos u$ and $\frac{du}{dx} = 3$,

$\therefore \frac{dy}{dx} = (\cos u) \times 3 = 3\cos 3x$

and when $y = \ln(x^2 - 2)$,

$y = \ln u$ where $u = x^2 - 2$

$\Rightarrow \frac{dy}{du} = \frac{1}{u}$ and $\frac{du}{dx} = 2x$

$\therefore \frac{dy}{dx} = \left(\frac{1}{u}\right) \times 2x = \frac{2x}{x^2 - 2}$.

You should aim to go direct from $f(x)$ to $f'(x)$, i.e. to do the intermediate steps in your head.

The chain rule gives these results which you need to know.

f(*x*) =	**f′(*x*) =**
e^{ax}	ae^{ax}
$\ln ax$	$\frac{1}{x}$ ⚠ not $\frac{a}{x}$
$\ln g(x)$	$\frac{g'(x)}{g(x)}$
$(a+bx)^n$	$nb(a+bx)^{n-1}$
$\sin ax$	$a\cos ax$
$\cos ax$	$-a\sin ax$

Questions

Differentiate with respect to x

1 $\cos(2x - \pi)$ **2** $e^{(x^2-4)}$ **3** $\ln(x^2 - 3)$

4 $\sin^3 x$ **5** $(3x^2 - 2)^{-2}$ **6** $2e^{-4kx}$

7 $\ln\cos x$ **8** $\sqrt{x^3 + 1}$.

Answers

1 $-2\sin(2x - \pi)$ **2** $2xe^{(x^2-4)}$ **3** $\frac{2x}{x^2 - 3}$

4 $3\cos x \sin^2 x$ **5** $-12x(3x^2 - 2)^{-3}$ **6** $-8ke^{-4kx}$

7 $-\tan x$ **8** $(3x^2)(\frac{1}{2})(x^3 + 1)^{-\frac{1}{2}} = \frac{3x^2}{2\sqrt{x^3 + 1}}$.

Products and quotients

When $y = uv$ where $u = f(x)$ and $v = g(x)$,

$$\frac{dy}{dx} = v\frac{du}{dx} + u\frac{dv}{dx}.$$

You may find this formula easier to use if you place its component parts in a table,
e.g. when $y = 2x^2 \cos x$,

y is the product of $2x^2$ and $\cos x$

$u = 2x^2$	$\frac{du}{dx} = 4x$
$v = \cos x$	$\frac{dv}{dx} = -\sin x$

$$\Rightarrow \frac{dy}{dx} = (\cos x)(4x) + (2x^2)(-\sin x)$$
$$= 2x(2\cos x - x\sin x)$$

When $y = \frac{u}{v}$ where $u = f(x)$ and $v = g(x)$,

$$\frac{dy}{dx} = \frac{v\frac{du}{dx} - u\frac{dv}{dx}}{v^2}$$

e.g. when $y = \frac{2x}{3x^2 - 2}$,

$u = 2x$	$\frac{du}{dx} = 2$
$v = 3x^2 - 2$	$\frac{dv}{dx} = 6x$

$$\Rightarrow \frac{dy}{dx} = \frac{2(3x^2-2) - (2x)(6x)}{(3x^2-2)^2} = -\frac{2(3x^2+2)}{(3x^2-2)^2}.$$

Memory aid: each formula starts with VDU

In a product or a quotient, u and/or v may be a function of a function, so you may have to use the chain rule as well,

e.g. when $y = x(x^2-1)^5$,

$u = x$	$\frac{du}{dx} = 1$
$v = (x^2-1)^5$	$\frac{dv}{dx} = 10x(x^2-1)^4$

$$\Rightarrow \frac{d}{dx}(x(x^2-1)^5) = (x-1)^5 + (x)(10x)(x^2-1)^4$$
$$= (x^2-1)^4(x^2 - 1 + 10x^2)$$
$$= (x^2-1)^4(11x^2-1).$$

You do not always have to use one of these formulae; look for ways of rearranging an expression to a form that makes it easier to differentiate.

Ask yourself these questions.

i Can you easily multiply out a product to give separate terms?

ii Can you split a quotient into simpler fractions?

E.g. $\frac{x-1}{\sqrt{x}} = x^{\frac{1}{2}} - x^{-\frac{1}{2}}$ (splitting into two fractions and using indices),

and $\frac{2}{(x+1)(x-1)} = \frac{1}{x-1} - \frac{1}{x+1}$
$= (x-1)^{-1} - (x+1)^{-1}$
(using partial fractions and then indices).

Questions

Differentiate and simplify the result.

1 x^2e^x **2** $\frac{x^2}{e^x}$ **3** $3x\sin 4x$

4 $\frac{3x^3-1}{x^2+2}$ **5** $\frac{\sqrt{x^2+1}}{x}$ **6** $x\sqrt{x^2+1}$

7 $x\ln(1-x)$

Answers

1 $xe^x(x+2)$ **2** $\frac{x(2-x)}{e^x}$ **3** $3\sin 4x + 12x\cos 4x$

4 $\frac{x(3x^3+18x+2)}{(x^2+2)^2}$

5 $\frac{x^2(x^2+1)^{-\frac{1}{2}} - (x^2+1)^{\frac{1}{2}}}{x^2}$ then multiply top and bottom by $(x^2+1)^{\frac{1}{2}} \Rightarrow \frac{-1}{x^2\sqrt{x^2+1}}$

6 $\frac{2x^2+1}{\sqrt{x^2+1}}$ **7** $\ln(1-x) - \frac{x}{1-x}$

Differentiating parametric equations

When $y = f(t)$ and $x = g(t)$ you can find $\frac{dy}{dx}$ in terms of t by using the chain rule, $\frac{dy}{dx} = \frac{dy}{dt} \times \frac{dt}{dx}$, where $\frac{dt}{dx} = 1/\frac{dx}{dt}$,

i.e. $$\frac{dy}{dx} = \frac{dy}{dt} \div \frac{dx}{dt}$$

For example, when $x = t^3$ and $y = t^2$

$$\frac{dy}{dx} = \frac{d}{dt}(t^2) \div \frac{d}{dt}(t^3) = \frac{2t}{3t^2} = \frac{2}{3t}.$$

Example

Find the equation of the normal to the curve

$$x = \cos^2\theta,\ y = \sin 2\theta$$

at the point where $\theta = \frac{1}{3}\pi$.

Solution

The normal is perpendicular to the tangent at the point of contact, so first find the gradient of the tangent $\left(\text{i.e. } \frac{dy}{dx}\right)$ where $\theta = \frac{1}{3}\pi$.

$$\frac{dy}{dx} = \frac{dy}{d\theta} \times \frac{d\theta}{dx} = \frac{2\cos 2\theta}{-2\cos\theta\sin\theta} = -\frac{2\cos 2\theta}{\sin 2\theta}$$

When $\theta = \frac{1}{3}\pi$, $\frac{dy}{dx} = -\frac{2\cos\frac{2}{3}\pi}{\sin\frac{2}{3}\pi} = \frac{2}{\sqrt{3}}$

So the gradient of the normal is $-\frac{\sqrt{3}}{2}$.

Also, when $\theta = \frac{1}{3}\pi$, $x = \frac{1}{4}$ and $y = \frac{\sqrt{3}}{2}$

$\therefore$ the equation of the normal is

$$y - \frac{\sqrt{3}}{2} = -\frac{\sqrt{3}}{2}(x - \tfrac{1}{4}) \Rightarrow 4x\sqrt{3} + 8y - 5\sqrt{3} = 0.$$

Questions

1 The parametric equations of a curve are

$$x = \sin 2\theta,\ y = \cos\theta$$

Find the gradient of the curve at the point where $\theta = \frac{\pi}{6}$. Hence find the equation of the tangent to the curve at the point $\left(\frac{\sqrt{3}}{2}, \frac{\sqrt{3}}{2}\right)$.

2 The parametric equations of a curve are

$$x = t + \ln t,\ y = t^2.$$

Find $\frac{dy}{dx}$ in terms of t.

Answers

1 $-\frac{1}{2}$; $2x + 4y - 3\sqrt{3} = 0$ **2** $\frac{2t^2}{t+1}$.

Implicit differentiation

The equation $3x^2 - y^2 = 9$ cannot be expressed neatly in the form $y = f(x)$, but y is implicitly a function of x.

You can differentiate each term of this equation with respect to x,

i.e. $\frac{d}{dx}(3x^2) - \frac{d}{dx}(y^2) = \frac{d}{dx}(9)$.

Differentiating a function of x w.r.t. x is straight forward, e.g. $\frac{d}{dx}(3x^2) = 6x$.

You can differentiate a function of y w.r.t. x by using the chain rule, i.e. when $u = f(y)$,

$$\frac{du}{dx} = \frac{du}{dy} \times \frac{dy}{dx} = \frac{d[f(y)]}{dy} \times \frac{dy}{dx}$$

This means that the derivative of $f(y)$ w.r.t. x is given by differentiating $f(y)$ w.r.t. y and multiplying the result by $\frac{dy}{dx}$,

so when $f(y) = y^2$, $\frac{d}{dx}(y^2) = 2y\frac{dy}{dx}$.

$$\therefore \quad \frac{d}{dx}(3x^2) - \frac{d}{dx}(y^2) = \frac{d}{dx}(9) \Rightarrow 6x - 2y\frac{dy}{dx} = 0.$$

Example

The equation of a curve is $x^2 - 2xy + 3y^2 = 4$.

Find an expression for $\frac{dy}{dx}$ in terms of x and y.

Solution

$$\frac{d}{dx}(x^2) - \frac{d}{dx}(2xy) + \frac{d}{dx}(3y^2) = \frac{d}{dx}(4)$$

$$\Rightarrow \quad 2x - \frac{d}{dx}(2xy) + 6y\frac{dy}{dx} = 0.$$

$2xy$ is a product of $2x$ and y, so you can use the product rule to differentiate it, i.e

$$\frac{d}{dx}(2xy) = y\frac{d}{dx}(2x) + 2x\frac{d}{dx}(y) = 2y + 2x\frac{dy}{dx}$$

$$\therefore \quad 2x - \left(2y + 2x\frac{dy}{dx}\right) + 6y\frac{dy}{dx} = 0 \Rightarrow \frac{dy}{dx} = \frac{y - x}{3y - x}.$$

⚠ If you are asked to find a relationship involving $\frac{d^2y}{dx^2}$, do not isolate $\frac{dy}{dx}$ before differentiating again.

For example, given $3x^2 - y^2 = 9$,

to show that $2y\frac{d^2y}{dx^2} = 6 - 2\left(\frac{dy}{dx}\right)^2$

start by differentiating once $\Rightarrow 6x - 2y\frac{dy}{dx} = 0$

then differentiate this

$$\Rightarrow \quad 6 - \left(2\frac{dy}{dx}\right)\left(\frac{dy}{dx}\right) - 2y\frac{d^2y}{dx^2} = 0$$

$$\Rightarrow \quad 2y\frac{d^2y}{dx^2} = 6 - 2\left(\frac{dy}{dx}\right)^2.$$

Questions

1 The equation of a curve is $x^2y - y^3 = 3$.

Find $\frac{dy}{dx}$ in terms of x and y.

2 Given $y = xe^y$, show that $\frac{dy}{dx} = e^y + y\frac{dy}{dx}$.

Hence show that

$$(1 - y)\frac{d^2y}{dx^2} = e^y\frac{dy}{dx} + \left(\frac{dy}{dx}\right)^2.$$

Answer

1 $\frac{2xy}{3y^2 - x^2}$.

Using logarithms

To differentiate a function where x appears as an index, you can take logarithms to 'bring down' the index and then use implicit differentiation.

For example, when $f(x) = a^x$, start with $y = a^x$, then $\ln y = x\ln a$

$$\Rightarrow \quad \frac{1}{y}\frac{dy}{dx} = \ln a \quad \Rightarrow \quad \frac{dy}{dx} = y\ln a = a^x \ln a,$$

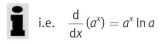

i.e. $\frac{d}{dx}(a^x) = a^x \ln a$

Questions

Find the derivative of

1 x^x **2** xa^x.

Answers

1 $(\ln x + 1)x^x$ **2** $a^x(1 + x\ln a)$.

Take a break

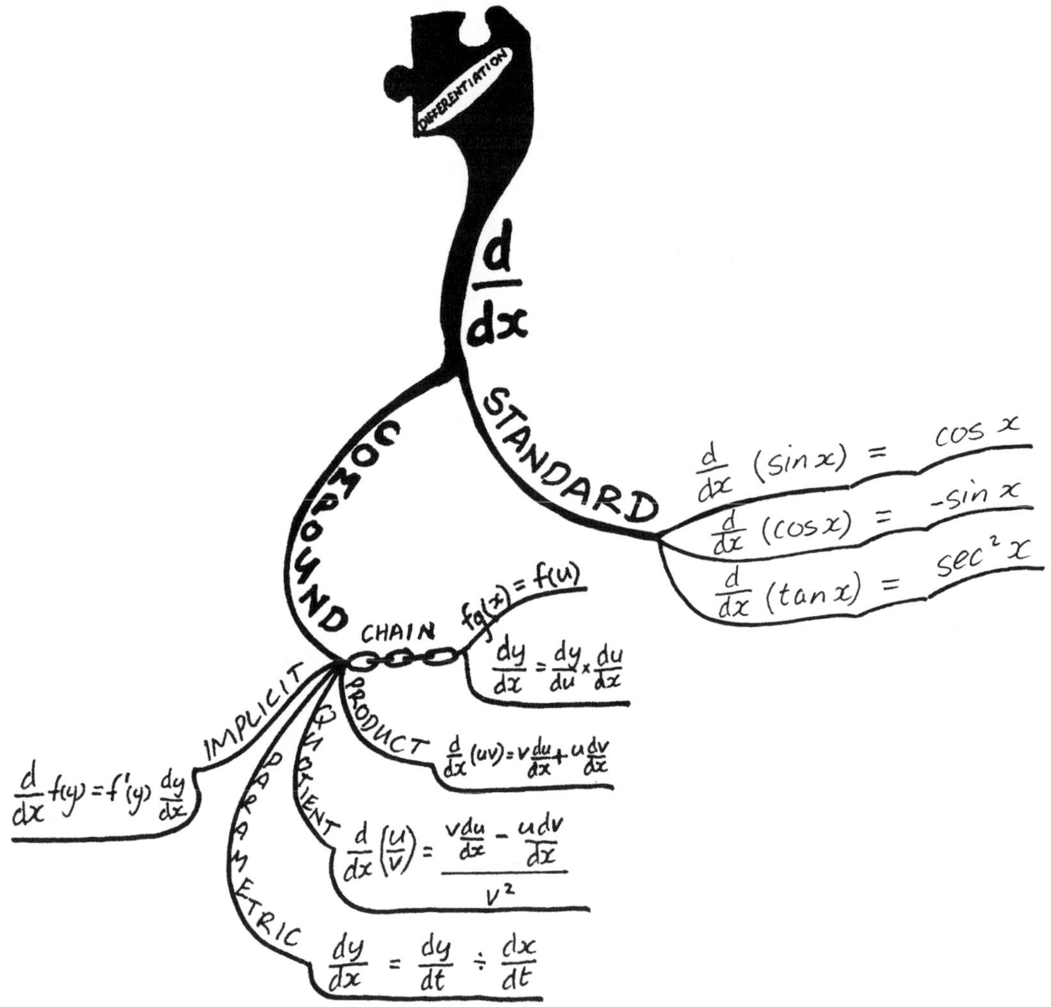

Review

1 Starting with $\cos(A + B) = \cos A \cos B - \sin A \sin B$, prove that $\cos 2x = 2\cos^2 x - 1$.

2 Prove that when $y = x^2$, $\frac{dy}{dx} = 2x$.

3 When $2x^3 - x^2 + ax - 2$ is divided by $(x - 1)$, the remainder is 3. Find the value of a.

4 Find the equations of the tangents from the origin to the circle $x^2 + y^2 - 4x + 3 = 0$.

5 Express $3\sin\theta + 2\cos\theta$ in the form $R\sin(\theta + \alpha)$ giving the exact values of R and α.

Answers

2 Use $\frac{dy}{dx} = \lim_{\delta x \to 0} \frac{f(x + \delta x) - f(x)}{\delta x}$ **3** 4 **4** $y\sqrt{3} = \pm x$ **5** $\theta = \sqrt{13}, \alpha = \tan^{-1}\frac{2}{3}$.

PREVIEW

By the end of this topic you will have revised:

- ✔ **the integrals of standard functions,**
- ✔ **how to use substitution and partial fractions to simplify an integral,**
- ✔ **how to use integration by parts,**
- ✔ **techniques for integrating trig functions,**
- ✔ **how to find a volume of revolution by integration,**
- ✔ **using the trapezium rule to find an approximate value for a definite integral.**

Before you start you need to:

- know how to find a definite integral,
- remember how to decompose a fraction into partial fractions,
- know the double angle identities.

TEST YOURSELF

If you get any answer wrong, go to Pure 10 or Pure 12.

1 **Find, in terms of e,** $\int_0^1 (3x^2 - 2e^x)\,dx$

2 **Express** $\dfrac{2}{(x+1)(2x-1)}$ **in partial fractions.**

3 **Express** $\cos^2 x$ **in terms of** $\cos 2x$**.**

Answers

1 $3 - 2e$

2 $\dfrac{4}{3(2x-1)} - \dfrac{2}{3(x+1)}$

3 $\frac{1}{2}(\cos 2x + 1)$.

Standard integrals

Remember that integration reverses differentiation, i.e $\int \cos x\,dx$ means find the function whose derivative w.r.t x is $\cos x$.

You can work this out each time but it is easier to remember these standard integrals.
Remember also that a constant of integration must be added to any indefinite integral.

$f(x) =$	$\int f(x)dx$
$\sin ax$	$-\frac{1}{a}\cos ax + k$
$\cos ax$	$\frac{1}{a}\sin ax + k$
$\sec^2 ax$	$\frac{1}{a}\tan ax + k$
$(a+bx)^n$	$\frac{1}{b(n+1)}(a+bx)^{n+1} + k$
e^{ax}	$\frac{1}{a}e^{ax} + k$
a^x	$\frac{1}{\ln a}a^x + k$
$\frac{g'(x)}{g(x)}$	$\ln\lvert g(x)\rvert + k$
$\tan x = \frac{\sin x}{\cos x}$	$-\ln\lvert\cos x\rvert$ or $\ln\lvert\sec x\rvert + k$

Remember that the integrals of trig functions are valid only when x is measured in radians.

Example

Find $\int (2-3x)^{-2}dx$.

Solution

Using $\int (a+bx)^n dx = \dfrac{1}{b(n+1)}(a+bx)^{n+1} + k$
with $a = 2$, $b = -3$ and $n = -2$ gives

$$\int (2-3x)^{-2}dx = \frac{1}{(-3)(-1)}(2-3x)^{-1} + k$$
$$= \tfrac{1}{3}(2-3x)^{-1} + k.$$

Example

Find $\int \dfrac{3x^2}{x^3-4}dx$.

Solution

The top of the fraction is the derivative of the bottom, so $\int \dfrac{3x^2}{x^3-4}dx = \ln\lvert x^3 - 4\rvert + k$

Remember that $\int af(x)dx = a\int f(x)dx$,

e.g. $\int 5(2x-1)^4dx = 5\int (2x-1)^4dx$

$$= 5 \times \frac{1}{2\times 5}(2x-1)^5 + k = \tfrac{1}{2}(2x-1)^5 + k.$$

Questions

Find

1 $\int 3\sin 2x\,dx$ **2** $\int (1+2x)^4\,dx$

3 $\int_0^{\frac{\pi}{4}} 2\cos 5x\,dx$ **4** $\int \frac{x}{x^2+1}\,dx.$

Answers

1 $-\frac{3}{2}\cos 2x + k$ **2** $\frac{1}{10}(1+2x)^5 + k$ **3** $-\frac{1}{5}\sqrt{2}$

4 $\frac{1}{2}\ln|x^2+1| + k.$

Integrating products

To integrate a product of functions, start by asking yourself "is one of the functions itself a function of a function?" When the answer is

- yes: use substitution
- no: use integration by parts.

Using substitution

When one of the factors in a product has the form $fg(x)$, use the substitution $u = g(x)$, i.e. substitute u for the 'inner' function.

In all but the most obvious cases, you will be given the substitution.

Example

Find $\int 2x(3x^2-5)^4\,dx$.

Solution

$(3x^2-5)^4$ is a function of $3x^2-5$ so use the substitution $u = 3x^2-5$.

When you substitute, all the variables must be expressed in terms of u, including $\int \ldots dx$ (which means integrate w.r.t x) which must be expressed as $\int \ldots du$ (i.e. integrate w.r.t to u).

You can do this by differentiating $u = 3x^2-5$

$\Rightarrow \ldots du = \ldots 6x\,dx \quad \Rightarrow \quad \ldots \frac{1}{6x}du = \ldots dx$

$$\text{Then } \int 2x(3x^2-5)^4\,dx = \int 2xu^4\,dx = \int (2xu^4)\frac{1}{6x}\,dx$$
$$= \frac{1}{3}\int u^4\,du = \frac{1}{15}u^5 + k$$
$$= \frac{1}{15}(3x^2-5)^5 + k.$$

When you use substitution to find an indefinite integral, you must give your answer in terms of the original variable, i.e. you must reverse the substitution.

But when you use substitution to find a definite integral, you do not have to reverse the substitution, instead you can change the limits, which are values of x, to the corresponding values of u,

e.g. to find $\int_1^2 2x(3x^2-5)^4\,dx$, use the substitution in the worked example to give $x = 1 \quad \Rightarrow \quad u = -2$ and $x = 2 \Rightarrow u = 7$, then $\int_1^2 2x(3x^2-5)^4\,dx$ becomes

$$\frac{1}{3}\int_{-2}^{7} u^4\,du = \left[\frac{1}{15}u^5\right]_{-2}^{7} = \frac{5613}{5}.$$

An alternative to an obvious substitution is to recognise the result of using the chain rule: if u is a function of x, the chain rule gives

$$\frac{d}{dx}f(u) = \frac{du}{dx}f'(u) \Rightarrow a\int\left(\frac{du}{dx}\right)f'(u)\,dx = af(u) + k$$

So, when one of the factors in a product is a function of a function and the other factor is a constant times the derivative of the 'inner' function, then you can integrate directly,

e.g. you can see that in $\int 2x(3x^2-5)^4\,dx$,

$\frac{d}{dx}(3x^2-5) = 6x$ and $2x = \frac{1}{3}(6x)$

$$\therefore \quad \int 2x(3x^2-5)^4\,dx = \frac{1}{3}\int 6x(3x^2-5)^4\,dx$$
$$= (\tfrac{1}{3})(\tfrac{1}{5})(3x^2-5)^5 + k$$

Using integration by parts

To integrate by parts, use the formula

$$\int u\frac{dv}{dx}\,dx = uv - \int v\frac{du}{dx}\,dx$$

You have to choose one factor as u $\left(\text{then the other is } \frac{dv}{dx} \text{ which must integrate}\right)$. If one factor will not integrate, choose it as u. When both can be integrated, chose as u the factor whose derivative is simpler (if one factor is a power of x, choose that as u).

For example, to find $\int x\ln x\,dx$, use $u = \ln x$ because $\int \ln x\,dx$ is not obvious, then $\frac{dv}{dx} = x$.

Write the component parts of the formula in a table:

$u = \ln x$	$\frac{du}{dx} = \frac{1}{x}$
$\frac{dv}{dx} = x$	$v = \frac{1}{2}x^2$

then $\int x \ln x \, dx = \frac{1}{2}x^2 \ln x - \int (\frac{1}{2}x^2)\left(\frac{1}{x}\right) dx$

$= \frac{1}{2}x^2 \ln x - \frac{1}{4}x^2 + k.$

To find $\int xe^x dx$, choose $u = x$ because $\frac{d}{dx}(x)$ is simpler than $\frac{d}{dx}(e^x)$.

Then $\int xe^x dx = xe^x - \int (1)(e^x) dx = xe^x - e^x + k.$

When using integration by parts to find a definite integral, remember that uv is fully integrated, so must be evaluated for the limits given,

e.g. $\int_1^2 x \ln x \, dx = \left[\frac{1}{2}x^2 \ln x\right]_1^2 - \int_1^2 \frac{1}{2}x \, dx$

You may have to use integration by parts twice to evaluate some integrals, e.g.

$$\int x^2 e^x dx = x^2 e^x - \int 2xe^x dx$$
$$= x^2e^x - 2(xe^x - e^x) + k$$
(integrating $2xe^x$ by parts)
$$= x^2e^x - 2xe^x + 2e^x + k.$$

⚠ Do not automatically try to use substitution or parts to integrate a product. Look first to see if the product can be easily expanded to give a sum or difference of functions,

e.g. $\int e^x(1 + e^x) dx = \int (e^x + e^{2x}) dx$

$= e^x + \frac{1}{2}e^{2x} + k.$

Questions

Find

1 $\int \cos x \sin^3 x \, dx$ **2** $\int x \sin 2x \, dx$

3 $\int_0^1 x^2 e^{-x} dx$

4 Use the substitution $u = x - 1$ to find

$$\int_1^2 x\sqrt{x-1} \, dx.$$

5 By writing $\int \ln x \, dx$ as $\int (1)(\ln x) dx$, use integration by parts to find $\int \ln x \, dx$.

Answers

1 $\frac{1}{4}\sin^4 x + k$ **2** $\frac{1}{4}\sin 2x - \frac{1}{2}x\cos 2x + k$

3 $2 - 5e^{-1}$ **4** $\frac{16}{15}$ **5** $x \ln x - x + k.$

Integrating fractions

To integrate a quotient of functions, ask yourself these questions.

- Can the fraction be easily split into two or more fractions, each of which can be integrated directly? For example, $\int \frac{e^x + 1}{e^x} dx$

  $= \int 1 + \frac{1}{e^x} dx = \int (1 + e^{-x}) dx = x - e^{-x} + k.$

- Is the top a constant times the derivative of the bottom? If it is, the integral is the constant times the log of the denominator,

  e.g. $\int \frac{x-1}{x^2 - 2x + 5} dx = \int \frac{\frac{1}{2}(2x-2)}{x^2 - 2x + 5} dx$

  $= \frac{1}{2}\ln|x^2 - 2x + 5| + k.$

- Is the denominator a polynomial that factorises? If it is, use partial fractions to give two (or more) separate fractions.

  e.g. $\int \frac{2}{(x-1)(x+1)} dx = \int \left(\frac{1}{x-1} - \frac{1}{x+1}\right) dx$

  $= \ln|x-1| - \ln|x+1| + k = \ln\left|\frac{x-1}{x+1}\right| + k.$

- Does the denominator contain a function of a function? If it does, substitute for the 'inner' function,

  e.g. to find $\int \frac{4}{\sqrt{1-x}} dx$, use $u = 1 - x$

  $\Rightarrow \ldots du = \ldots - dx,$

  $\therefore \int \frac{4}{\sqrt{1-x}} dx = \int \frac{-4}{\sqrt{u}} du = -\int 4u^{-\frac{1}{2}} du$

  $= -8u^{\frac{1}{2}} + k = -8\sqrt{1-x} + k.$

- Are you given a substitution? Questions are sometimes worded "Using the substitution …, or otherwise, find $\int \ldots dx$." Use the substitution; don't waste time looking for the 'otherwise'.

Questions

1 Find

a $\int \frac{1}{3x-2} dx$ **b** $\int \frac{2}{(2x-1)(x+1)} dx.$

2 Use the substitution $u = 2x + 1$ to find

$$\int \frac{2x}{(2x+1)^3} dx.$$

3 Use the substitution $x = 3\sin\theta$ to find

$$\int_0^3 \frac{1}{\sqrt{9 - x^2}} dx.$$

Answers

1a $\frac{1}{3}\ln|3x-2|+k$ **b** $\frac{2}{3}\ln\left|\frac{2x-1}{x+1}\right|+k$

2 $\frac{-4x-1}{4(2x+1)^2}+k$ **3** $\frac{\pi}{2}$.

Trig integrals

⚠ It is easy to use over-complicated methods to integrate trig functions; always check to see if it is a standard integral.

As well as the obvious standard integrals, you should recognise these:

$$\int \cos x \sin^n x\,dx = \frac{1}{n+1}\sin^{n+1} x + k$$

$$\int \sin x \cos^n x\,dx = -\frac{1}{n+1}\cos^{n+1} x + k$$

$$\int \sec^2 x \tan^n x\,dx = \frac{1}{n+1}\tan^{n+1} x + k.$$

For example, $\int \sin x \cos^2 x\,dx = -\frac{1}{3}\cos^3 x + k$

and $\int \cos x \sin x\,dx = \frac{1}{2}\sin^2 x + k$ (or $-\frac{1}{2}\cos^2 x$)

When the integral is not standard (or you do not recognise it as such), you can use trig identities to express the function in a form that you can integrate.

Even powers of sin *x* or cos *x*

You can use one of the identities $\sin^2\theta \equiv \frac{1}{2}(1-\cos 2\theta)$ or $\cos^2\theta \equiv \frac{1}{2}(1+\cos 2\theta)$ to double the angle and reduce the power,

e.g. $\int \cos^2 x\,dx = \int \frac{1}{2}(1+\cos 2x)\,dx$
$= \frac{1}{2}x + \frac{1}{4}\sin 2x + k.$

Odd powers

You can use the identity $\cos^2\theta + \sin^2\theta \equiv 1$ (or its equivalent) to express an odd power of a trig function in terms of $\cos x \sin^n x$ or the equivalent, e.g. $\sin^3 x = \sin x \sin^2 x = \sin x(1-\cos^2 x)$

$\therefore \quad \int \sin^3 dx = \int (\sin x - \sin x \cos^2 x)\,dx$
$= -\cos x + \frac{1}{3}\cos^3 x + k.$

Example

Find $\int \sin^2 4x\,dx$.

Solution

Using $\sin^2\theta \equiv \frac{1}{2}(1-\cos 2\theta)$, with $\theta = 4x$, gives

$\int \sin^2 4x\,dx = \int \frac{1}{2}(1-\cos 8x)\,dx = \frac{1}{2}(x - \frac{1}{8}\sin 8x) + k.$

Questions

1 Find

a $\int \sin^2 x\,dx$ **b** $\int \cos^5 x\,dx$.

2 Show that $\tan^4\theta \equiv \sec^2\theta\tan^2\theta - \sec^2\theta + 1$.

Hence find $\int \tan^4\theta\,d\theta$.

Answers

1a $\frac{1}{2}x - \frac{1}{4}\sin 2x + k$

b $\sin x - \frac{2}{3}\sin^3 x + \frac{1}{5}\sin^5 x + k$ $(\cos^5 x \equiv (\cos x)(1-\sin^2 x)^2)$

2 $\frac{1}{3}\tan^3\theta - \tan\theta + \theta + k$.

Take a break

Volumes of revolution

When the area between a section of a curve and the x-axis is rotated through 360° about the x-axis, you can find the volume formed from $\pi\int_a^b y^2\,dx$.

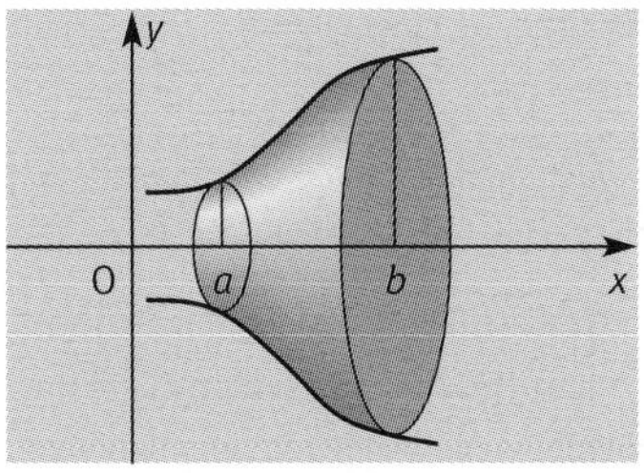

When the area between a section of a curve and the y-axis is rotated about the y-axis, you can find the volume formed from $\pi\int_a^b x^2\,dy$

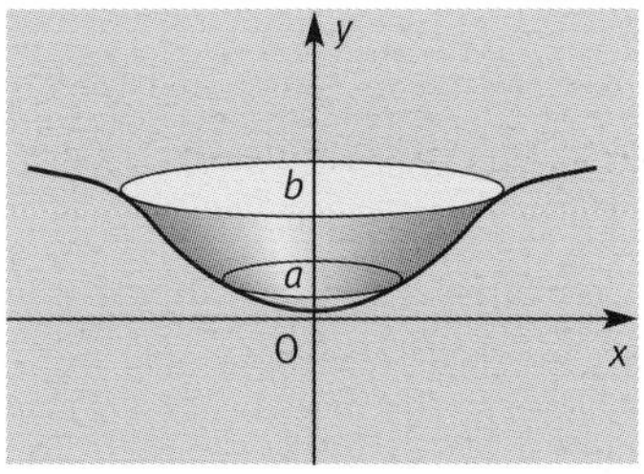

For example, the volume generated when the area under the section of the curve $y = 2x^2$ between $x = 0$ and $x = 2$ is rotated through 360° about $y = 0$ is given by

$$\pi\int_0^2 y^2\,dx = \pi\int_0^2 4x^4\,dx = \pi\left[\frac{4}{5}x^5\right]_0^2 = \frac{128}{5}\pi.$$

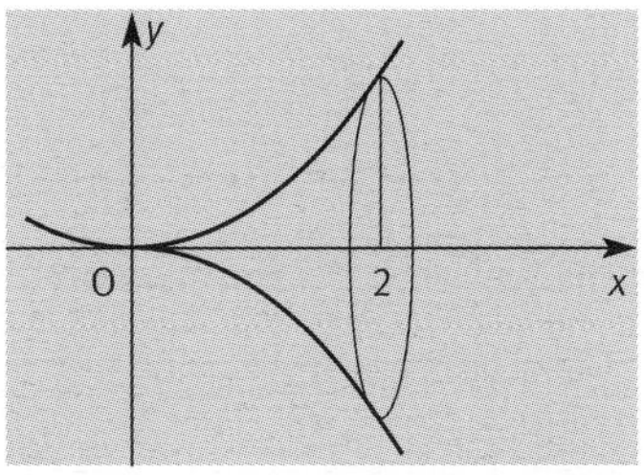

When a volume is generated by rotating an area that is not completely between a curve and the x-axis or the y-axis, you can find the volume by considering it as the sum or difference of two different volumes that you know that you can find.

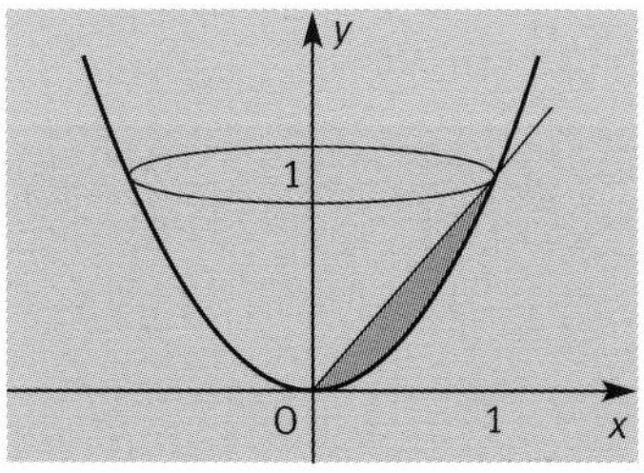

For example, the volume formed when the area enclosed by the curve $y = x^2$ and the line $y = x$ is rotated about the y-axis can be found from
(the volume formed when the area between $y = x^2$ and Oy is rotated about Oy)
– (the volume formed when the area between $y = x$ and Oy is rotated about Oy),

i.e. $\pi \int_0^1 x^2 \text{ (for the curve) } dy - \pi \int_0^1 x^2 \text{ (for the line) } dy$

$$= \pi \int_0^1 y\,dy - \pi \int_0^1 y^2\,dy.$$

(The volume generated from the line is a cone so you can use the formula for the volume of a cone instead of the integral.)

When a curve is defined parametrically, you can find an area or a volume of revolution by converting an integral with respect to x or to y to one with respect to t by using

$$x = f(t) \Rightarrow \ldots dx = \ldots f'(t)dt$$

or
$$y = g(t) \Rightarrow \ldots dy = \ldots g'(t)dt$$

⚠ When you find a definite integral you must make sure that the limits are
values of x for $\int \ldots dx$,
values of y for $\int \ldots dy$,
values of t for $\int \ldots dt$, and so on.

Example

A curve is defined parametrically by

$$x = 2\cos\theta \text{ and } y = 3\sin\theta.$$

Find the volume generated when the area between the section of the curve from $\theta = 0$ to $\theta = \dfrac{\pi}{2}$ is rotated about the y-axis.

Solution

The volume, V, is given by

$$\pi \int_{y \text{ when } \theta = 0}^{y \text{ when } \theta = \frac{\pi}{2}} x^2 dy$$

Using $x^2 = 4\cos^2\theta$ and $y = 3\sin\theta$
$\Rightarrow \ldots dy = \ldots 3\cos\theta d\theta$

$$V = \pi \int_0^{\frac{\pi}{2}} 12\cos^3\theta d\theta = \pi\Big[12\sin\theta - 4\sin^3\theta\Big]_0^{\frac{\pi}{2}} = 8\pi.$$

Questions

1 Find the volume formed when the area between the curve $y = \dfrac{1}{x}$, the x-axis and the lines $x = 1$ and $x = 2$ is rotated through 2π radians about the x-axis.

2 Find the volume formed when the area between the curve $y = x^2 - 1$, the x-axis and the lines $x = 1$ and $x = 2$ is rotated through 2π radians about the y-axis.

3 The parametric equations of a curve are

$$x = 2t \text{ and } y = t^2 - 1.$$

Find the volume generated when the area under the section of this curve between the points where $t = 0$ and $t = 3$ is rotated through 360° about Ox.

Answers

1 $\frac{1}{2}\pi$ **2** $\frac{9\pi}{2}$; $[12\pi - \pi\int_0^3 x^2 dy]$ **3** $\frac{336}{5}\pi$.

The trapezium rule

An approximate value for the area, A, between the curve $y = f(x)$, the x-axis and the lines $x = a$ and $x = b$ is found as follows.

Divide the area into n strips, each of width d, then calculate the sum of the areas of the trapeziums formed by joining the tops of the ordinates.

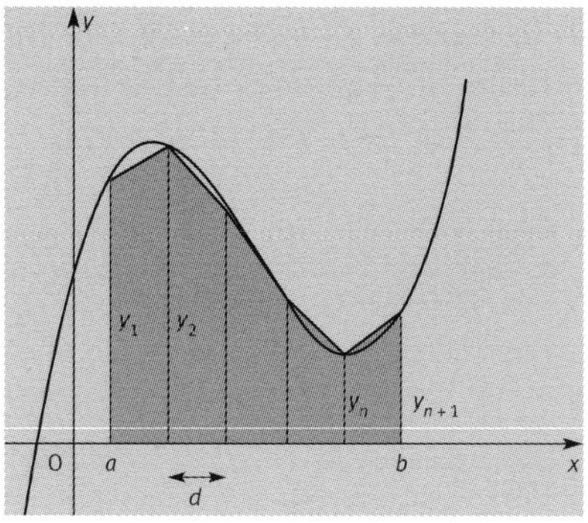

$A \approx \frac{1}{2}d(y_1 + 2y_2 + \ldots + 2y_n + y_{n+1})$

i.e. ($\frac{1}{2}$ width of the strips) × (the sum of the first and last ordinates + twice the sum of the other ordinates).

You can use the trapezium rule find an approximate value for $\int_a^b f(x)dx$ because this integral represents A.

Example

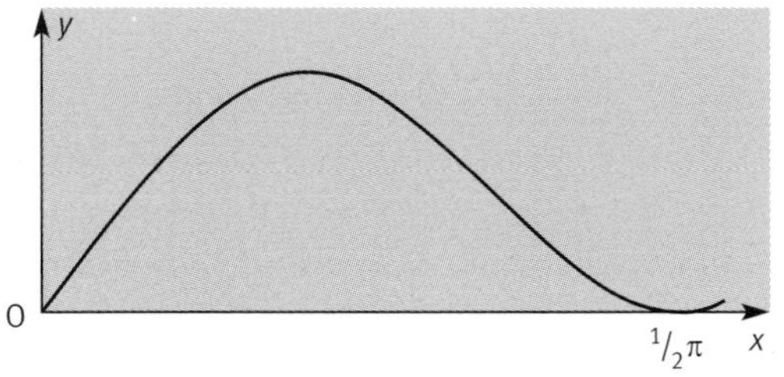

The diagram shows the section of the curve $y = x\cos^2 x$ from $x = 0$ to $\frac{1}{2}\pi$.

Use the trapezium rule with four strips to find an approximate value for $\int_0^{\frac{\pi}{2}} x\cos^2 x dx$, giving your answer correct to 3 significant figures.

Solution

Start by drawing a diagram showing the curve, the strips and the x-coordinate of the edge of each strip.

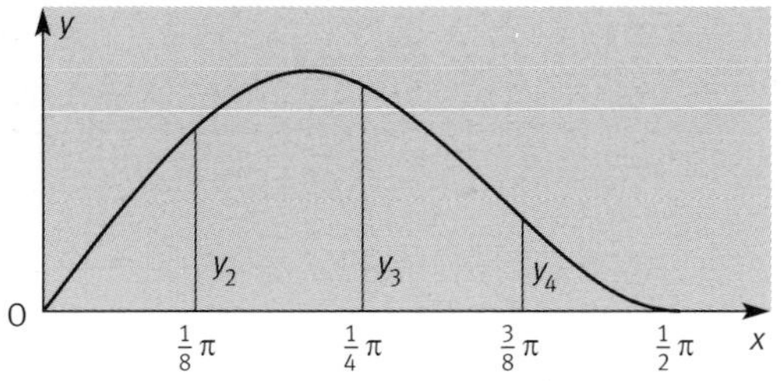

From the diagram you can see that

$d = \frac{1}{8}\pi$, $y_1 = 0$, $y_2 = \frac{\pi}{8}\cos^2\frac{\pi}{8}$,

$y_3 = \frac{\pi}{4}\cos^2\frac{\pi}{4}$, $y_4 = \frac{3\pi}{8}\cos^2\frac{3\pi}{8}$, and $y_5 = 0$.

$$\text{So } \int_0^{\frac{\pi}{2}} x\cos^2 x dx \approx \tfrac{1}{2}d(y_1 + 2y_2 + 2y_3 + 2y_4 + y_5)$$

$$= 0.354 \text{ to 3 s.f.}$$

Question

Use the trapezium rule with 3 strips to find an approximate value for $\int_0^{1.5} e^{x^2} dx$, giving your answer correct to two significant figures.

Answer

4.6

Take a break

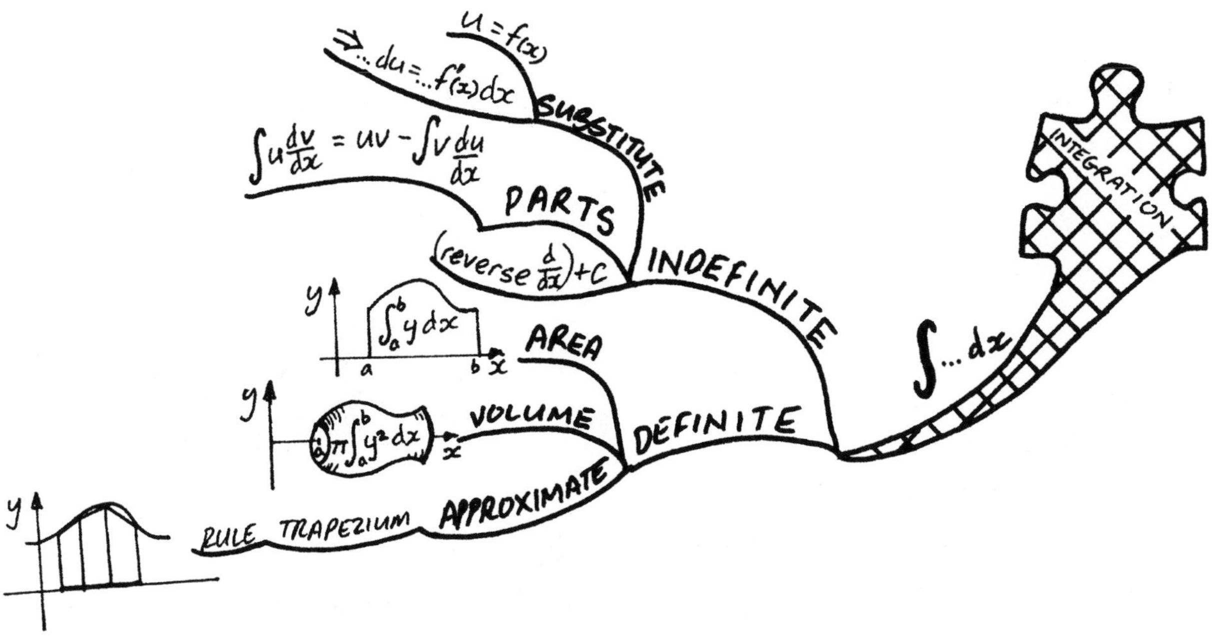

Review

1 Show that $\sin^4 x \equiv \frac{1}{8}(3 - 4\cos 2x + \cos 4x)$. Hence find $\int \sin^4 x dx$.

2 Find the area bounded by the curve whose parametric equations are $x = t^2$ and $y = 2t - 1$, the x-axis and the ordinates where $t = 2$ and $t = 3$.

3 Find $\frac{dy}{dx}$ when $y = (2x - 1)^4 e^x$.

4 Express $\frac{2x}{(1 - x)(1 + x)^2}$ in partial fractions.

5 The parametric equations of a curve are $x = \cos\theta, y = \sin^2\theta$.

a Find $\frac{dy}{dx}$ in terms of θ.

b Find the equation of the tangent to the curve at the point where $\theta = \frac{\pi}{4}$.

6 Given $y^2 - 2xy + 3x^2 = 0$, show that

$$\frac{dy}{dx} = \frac{y - 3x}{y - x}.$$

Answers

1 $\frac{1}{32}(12x - 8\sin 2x + \sin 4x)$ **2** $20\frac{1}{3}$

3 $(2x + 7)(2x - 1)^3 e^x$

4 $\frac{1}{2(1 + x)} - \frac{1}{(1 + x)^2} + \frac{1}{2(1 - x)}$

5a $-2\cos\theta$ **b** $2\sqrt{2}x + 2y - 3 = 0$.

Take a break

PREVIEW

By the end of this topic you will have revised:

- ✔ **how to form a differential equation,**
- ✔ **solving differential equations whose variables are separable,**
- ✔ **the meaning of exponential growth and decay.**

Before you start you should:

- know and be able to use the laws of logarithms,
- understand direct and inverse proportion (i.e. variation) and know how to find the constant of proportion,
- understand the meaning of $\frac{dy}{dx}$ in the context of how y is behaving with respect to x.

TEST YOURSELF

If you get any wrong answers, see GCSE higher or A level text book for information and practice.

1 a) Express $\ln(2x-1) - 3\ln(x+1) + \ln A$ as a single logarithm.
b) Express $\ln x = -2t$ without logarithms.

2 A quantity, v, is inversely proportional to the square of the quantity s. When $s = 2$, $v = 5$. Find v in terms of s.

3 Given that $\frac{dy}{dx} > 0$ for $x > 2$ and $\frac{dy}{dx} < 0$ for $x < 2$, describe the behaviour of y when
a) $x > 2$ b) $x < 2$.

Answers

1 a) $\ln \frac{A(2x-1)}{(x+1)^3}$ **b)** $x = e^{-2t}$

2 $v = \frac{20}{s^2}$

3 a) increasing **b)** decreasing.

Forming differential equations

A differential equation is a relationship between derivatives and variables,

e.g. $2t\frac{dv}{dt} = 3v^2 - 2v$.

A first order differential equation contains only the first derivative, a second order differential equation contains the second derivative (and maybe also the first derivative), and so on.

Differential equations arise from situations where one quantity is changing with respect to another and the rate at which that change occurs is known.

The rate at which a quantity y is changing with respect to a quantity x is $\frac{dy}{dx}$.

When the quantity y is increasing, $\frac{dy}{dx}$ is +ve.

When the quantity y is decreasing, $\frac{dy}{dx}$ is −ve.

To form a differential equation, look for the key words 'rate of' and 'increase' or 'rate of' and 'decrease': this is the derivative together with its sign. (Words equivalent to increase or decrease may be used, e.g. growth or decay.)

For example, a circular patch of water is evaporating. At time t, the area A of the patch is shrinking at a rate proportional to $\frac{1}{A}$.

This means that A is changing with respect to t, so the rate at which A is changing is $\frac{dA}{dt}$.

As A is shrinking, $\frac{dA}{dt}$ is −ve, $\therefore \frac{dA}{dt} = -\frac{k}{A}$.

Question

At any time t minutes, the rate at which the temperature of a pan of hot water falls is proportional to the temperature, T°C. Write down a differential equation relating T and t.

Answer

$\frac{dT}{dt} = -kT$.

Solving differential equations

Solving a differential equation means finding a direct relationship between the variables, i.e. a relationship that does not include derivatives, so integration is involved.

A straightforward differential equation, such as $\frac{dy}{dx} = 2x - 1$, has a solution $y = x^2 - x + k$, where k is a constant. This is called the general solution because it contains an unknown constant.

You need more information (i.e. a pair of corresponding values of x and y), to find a value for k. Given that $y = 2$ when $x = 3$ you can substitute these values into the general solution to give $k = -4$, so $y = x^2 - x - 4$. This is called a particular solution.

Variables separable

The differential equation $\frac{dy}{dx} = xy$ can be written as $\frac{1}{y}\frac{dy}{dx} = x$.

Integrating each side, i.e. $\int \frac{1}{y} dy = \int x\, dx$, gives the solution $\ln y = \frac{1}{2}x^2 + k$.

Any differential equation that can be arranged as $f(y)\frac{dy}{dx} = g(x)$ can be solved in same way,

i.e. $f(y)\frac{dy}{dx} = g(x) \Rightarrow \int f(y)dy = \int g(x)dx$

For example, the differential equation $\frac{dv}{dt} = \frac{1}{v}$ can be arranged as $v\frac{dv}{dt} = 1 \Rightarrow \int v\, dv = \int 1\, dt$

$\therefore$ the general solution is $\frac{1}{2}v^2 = t + k$.

⚠ Many differential equations involve two unknown constants, one of proportion and one of integration. You can use any letters you choose for these, but never use the same letter for both.

Examination questions usually ask you to form and then to solve a differential equation to give a general solution. This is often followed by asking for a particular solution.

Example

The rate of decay of the mass of a radioactive material is proportional to the mass, m kg, at time t years.

a Find a differential equation for m.

b Given that $m = 50$ when $t = 0$, show that $m = 50e^{-kt}$ where k is a positive constant.

c Given that the mass of this material halves every 5 years, find the value of k.

Solution

a The rate of change of m at time t is $\frac{dm}{dt}$. This is negative (the mass is decaying) and proportional to the mass,

$\therefore \quad \frac{dm}{dt} = -km.$

b $\frac{dm}{dt} = -km \Rightarrow \frac{1}{m}\frac{dm}{dt} = -k \Rightarrow \int \frac{1}{m} dm = \int -k\, dt$

$\therefore \quad \ln m = -kt + c.$

To give this in the form asked for, the relationship has to be expressed without logarithms,

i.e. $m = e^{-kt+c} \quad \Rightarrow \quad m = e^c \times e^{-kt}$

$\Rightarrow \quad m = Ae^{-kt}$ where $A = e^c$.

$m = 50$ when $t = 0 \quad \Rightarrow \quad 50 = Ae^0 = A$,

so $\quad m = 50e^{-kt}$.

c When $t = 0$, $m = 50$, so when $t = 5$, $m = 25$.

$\therefore \quad 25 = 50e^{-5k} \quad \Rightarrow \quad -5k = \ln\frac{1}{2}$

$\Rightarrow \quad k = \frac{1}{5}\ln 2.$

Exponential growth and decay

When the rate of change of a quantity is proportional to the quantity itself, i.e. $\frac{dy}{dx} \propto y$, the general solution is $y = Ae^{kx}$.

When k is +ve, y is growing exponentially and when k is −ve, y is decaying exponentially.

Many naturally occurring quantities behave in this way over time; this form of change is also called natural growth or decay; i.e. a quantity, Q, that is changing exponentially is related to time by

$\frac{dQ}{dt} = kQ \quad \Rightarrow \quad Q = Ae^{kt}$

when Q is growing

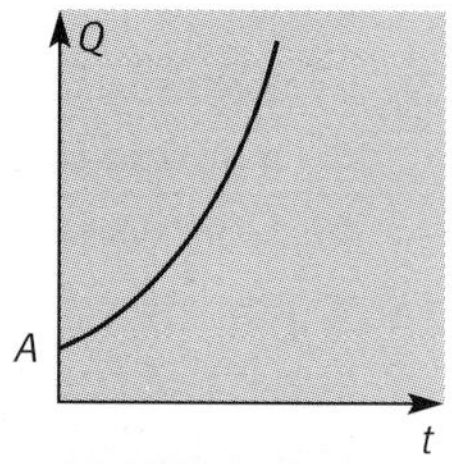

or $\frac{dQ}{dt} = -kQ \quad \Rightarrow \quad Q = Ae^{-kt}$

when Q is decaying

(k is a positive constant).

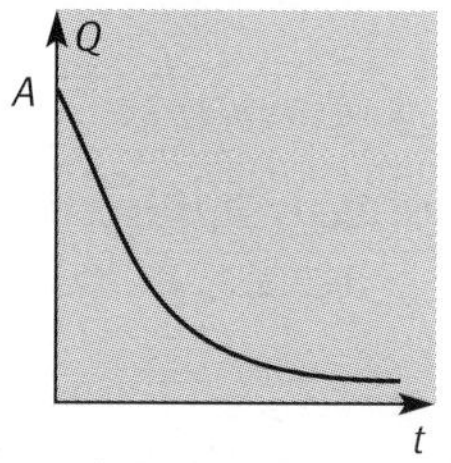

Questions

1 Find a general solution of the differential equation $\frac{dy}{dx} = y^2(2x + 1)$ giving y in terms of x.
Find a particular solution for which $y = 2$ when $x = 1$.

2 The rate at which water is leaking from a radiator is proportional to the volume of water in the radiator at that instant.
There are V litres of water in the radiator at time t hours.

a Form a differential equation and find a general solution for V in terms of t.
When the radiator is filled it holds 20 litres of water but 24 hours later, there are 18 litres of water in the radiator.

b How many litres of water are in radiator 72 hours after it is filled?

Answers

1 $y = \frac{1}{k - x - x^2}$; $y = \frac{2}{5 - 2x - 2x^2}$

2a $V = Ae^{-kt}$ **b** 14.58 litres

Take a break

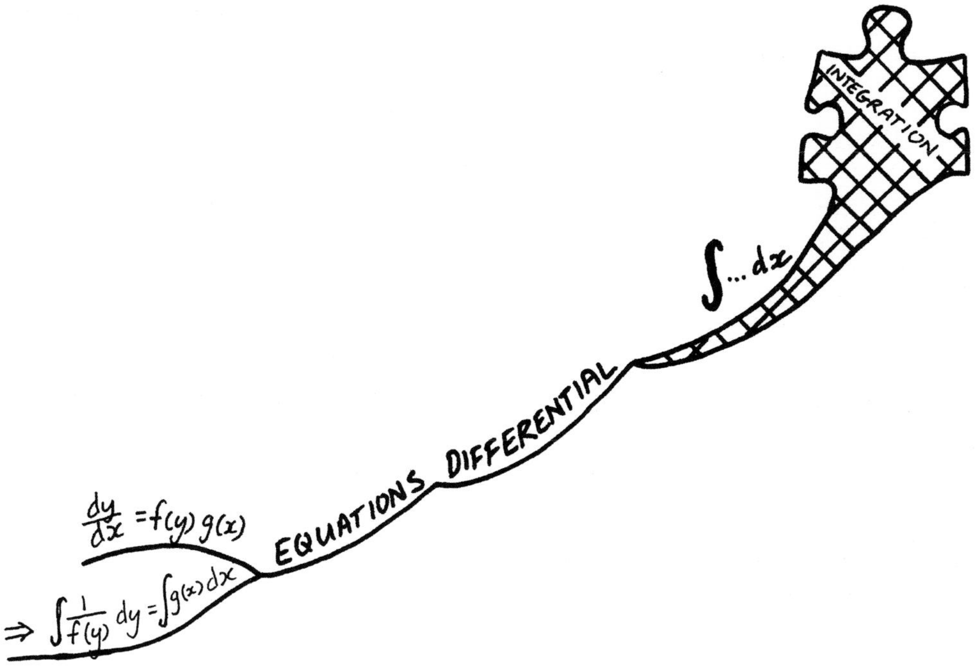

Review

1 Prove by contradiction that $\sqrt{2}$ is an irrational number.

2 Express $\frac{2}{(x-1)(x^2+2)}$ in partial fractions.

3 Find $\frac{dy}{dx}$ in terms of x and y if $x^2 + 2xy^2 = 4x$.

4 Express $\frac{2x^2 - 7x}{x^2 + 5x - 3}$ in the form $A + \frac{Bx + C}{x^2 + 5x - 3}$, giving the values of A, B and C.

5 The parametric equations of a curve are $x = 3\cos 2\theta$ and $y = 2\sin^2\theta$. Find the cartesian equation of the curve.

6 Find, to 1 d.p., the smallest positive value of θ for which $3\sin\theta - 4\cos\theta = 2$.

7 Use the substitution $u = \sin x$ to find $\int \sin^5 x \sin 2x\, dx$.

Answers

1 $\sqrt{2}$ is not irrational $\Rightarrow \sqrt{2} = a/b$ where a & b are integers with no common factors $\Rightarrow 2b^2 = a^2 \Rightarrow a$ even $\Rightarrow a = 2m \Rightarrow b^2 = 2m^2 \Rightarrow b$ even; a & b both even contradicts '$\sqrt{2} = a/b$ where a & b are integers with no common factors' etc.

2 $\frac{2}{3(x-1)} - \frac{2x+2}{3(x^2+2)}$ **3** $\frac{2 - x - y^2}{2xy}$ **4** $2 + \frac{-17x + 6}{x^2 + 5x - 3}$ **5** $3y + x - 3 = 0$ **6** 76.7° **7** $\frac{2}{7}\sin^7 x + k$.

Take a break

Pure 18 The binomial theorem

PREVIEW

By the end of this topic you will have revised:

- ✔ **the use of the binomial theorem to expand $(a + bx)^n$ as a series of ascending powers of x,**
- ✔ **how to find approximations.**

The binomial theorem

The binomial theorem states that, for any value of n,

$$(1+x)^n = 1 + \binom{n}{1}x + \binom{n}{2}x^2 + \binom{n}{3}x^3 + \ldots$$

where $\binom{n}{r} = \dfrac{n(n-1)(n-2)\ldots(n-r+1)}{r!}$

and $r!$ means the product of all the integers from r down to 1, e.g. $5! = 5 \times 4 \times 3 \times 2 \times 1$.

When n is a positive integer, the series terminates with the term x^n and is valid for all values of x.
For all other values of n, the series is infinite and is valid only for values of x in the range $-1 < x < 1$.

You may prefer to remember the binomial theorem in the form

$$(1+x)^n = 1 + nx + \frac{n(n-1)}{2!}x^2 + \frac{n(n-1)(n-2)}{3!}x^3 + \ldots$$

Two expansions that are worth remembering, both of which are valid for $|x| < 1$.

$$\frac{1}{1+x} = (1+x)^{-1} = 1 - x + x^2 - x^3 + x^4 - \ldots$$

$$\frac{1}{1-x} = (1-x)^{-1} = 1 + x + x^2 + x^3 + x^4 + \ldots$$

You can use the binomial theorem to expand expressions of the form $(a + bx)^n$ by taking a out of the bracket, i.e. writing

$(a+bx)^n = a^n\left(1 + \dfrac{bx}{a}\right)^n$ then replacing x by $\dfrac{bx}{a}$ in the standard expansion.

For example to expand $(3 - 2x)^4$, express it in the form $3^4\left(1 - \dfrac{2x}{3}\right)^4$. Then use the binomial theorem; replacing x by $-\dfrac{2x}{3}$ and n by 4 to give

$$3^4\left(1 + 4\left(-\frac{2x}{3}\right) + \frac{(4)(3)}{2}\left(-\frac{2x}{3}\right)^2 + \frac{(4)(3)(2)}{(3)(2)}\left(-\frac{2x}{3}\right)^3 + \left(-\frac{2x}{3}\right)^4\right)$$
$$= 81 - 216x + 216x^2 - 96x^3 + 16x^4.$$

This is valid for all values of x.
You can also use Pascal's Triangle – see Pure 3.

When the series is infinite, most examination questions ask for the first three or four terms of the expansion.

To find the first 4 terms in the expansion of $(1 - 2x)^{\frac{1}{2}}$, you can use the standard expansion replacing x with $-2x$ and n with $\frac{1}{2}$,

i.e. $(1 - 2x)^{\frac{1}{2}}$

$$= 1 + \tfrac{1}{2}(-2x) + \frac{(\frac{1}{2})(-\frac{1}{2})}{2}(-2x)^2 + \frac{(\frac{1}{2})(-\frac{1}{2})(-\frac{3}{2})}{(2)(3)}(-2x)^3 + \ldots$$

$\Rightarrow$ the first 4 terms are $1 - x - \frac{1}{2}x^2 - \frac{1}{2}x^3$.

This is valid for $|2x| < 1$, i.e. $|x| < \frac{1}{2}$.

When the series is infinite, you must give the range of values for which the expansion is valid.

Some expansions involve combining two simpler expansions.

For example, to expand $\dfrac{(3-2x)^4}{\sqrt{1-2x}}$ as far as the term in x^2, you can write this fraction as $(3-2x)^4(1-2x)^{-\frac{1}{2}}$ then expand each bracket as far as the term in x^2 and multiply the results,

i.e. $(3 - 2x)^4 = 81 - 216x + 216x^2 + \ldots$
and $(1 - 2x)^{-\frac{1}{2}} = 1 + x + \frac{3}{2}x^2 + \ldots$

$\therefore \quad (3-2x)^4(1-2x)^{-\frac{1}{2}} =$
$(81 - 216x + 216x^2 + \ldots)(1 + x + \frac{3}{2}x^2 + \ldots)$

$= 81 - 216x + 216x^2$ (1st bracket × 1)
$+ 81x - 216x^2 + \ldots$ (1st bracket × x)
$+ (81)(\frac{3}{2}x^2) + \ldots$

$= 81 - 135x + \frac{243}{2}x^2 + \ldots$

As you do not need the terms in x^3 and beyond, there is no need to take any part of this process further than the x^2 term.

Never try to divide by a series. Always bring the denominator up by using a negative index.

It is easier to add series than it is to multiply them. When the denominator factorises, you can use partial fractions to give a sum of two simpler fractions.

For example, to find the first three terms in the expansion of $\dfrac{4}{(x-1)(2x-1)}$, start by using partial fractions to write $\dfrac{4}{(x-1)(2x-1)} = \dfrac{4}{x-1} - \dfrac{8}{2x-1}$, then rearrange so that the x term is at the end of each bracket,

$$= -\frac{4}{1-x} + \frac{8}{1-2x}$$

then bring up the denominators,

$$= -4(1-x)^{-1} + 8(1-2x)^{-1}$$
$$= -4(1 + x + x^2 + \ldots) + 8(1 + 2x + 4x^2 + \ldots)$$
$$= 4 + 12x + 28x^2 + \ldots \text{ for } |x| < \tfrac{1}{2}.$$

Questions

1 Expand

a $(2-3x)^5$

b $\left(t - \dfrac{1}{t}\right)^4$

2 Write down the expansions of these expressions as far as the term containing x^4.

a $(2+x)^{-2}$ **b** $(1+3x)^{\frac{1}{3}}$ **c** $(1+x^2)^{-1}$.

3 Write down the expansions of these expressions as far as the term containing x^2.

a $\dfrac{1-2x}{(1+2x)^3}$ **b** $\dfrac{5}{(1-3x)(1+2x)}$.

Answers

1a $32 - 240x + 720x^2 - 1080x^3 + 810x^4 - 243x^5$

b $t^4\left(1 - \dfrac{1}{t^2}\right)^4 = t^4 - 4t^2 + 6 - \dfrac{4}{t^2} + \dfrac{1}{t^4}$

2a $\frac{1}{4} - \frac{1}{4}x + \frac{3}{16}x^2 - \frac{1}{8}x^3 + \frac{5}{64}x^4$, $|x| < 2$

b $1 + x - x^2 + \frac{5}{3}x^3 - \frac{10}{3}x^4$, $|x| < \frac{1}{3}$

c $1 - x^2 + x^4$, $|x| < 1$ (replacing x by x^2)

3a $1 - 8x + 36x^2$, $|x| < \frac{1}{2}$

b $5 + 5x + 35x^2$, $|x| < \frac{1}{3}$.

Numerical approximations

You can use the binomial expansion to find numerical approximations for numbers. For example you can use the expansion $(1-x)^{\frac{1}{2}} = 1 - \frac{1}{2}x - \frac{1}{8}x^2 - \frac{1}{16}x^3 - \ldots$ to find an approximate value for $\sqrt{11}$ by substituting $x = \frac{1}{100}$ (valid as $|x| < 1$)

$$\Rightarrow \quad (1-x)^{\frac{1}{2}} = \left(\tfrac{99}{100}\right)^{\frac{1}{2}} = \frac{3\sqrt{11}}{10}$$

$$\therefore \quad \frac{3\sqrt{11}}{10} \approx 1 - 0.005 - 0.000\,012\,5 - 0.000\,000\,062\,5 - \ldots$$

The terms in the expansion are rapidly getting smaller so you have enough here for a reasonable approximation.

$$\therefore \quad \frac{3\sqrt{11}}{10} \approx 1 - 0.005\,012\,562\,5$$

$$\Rightarrow \quad \sqrt{11} \approx 3.316\,624\,79\ldots$$

Algebraic approximations

You can use the first few terms of the binomial expansion to find a polynomial function that approximates to a given expression when x is small.

'x is small' means that the value of x is close to zero, so the values of the terms in the expansion rapidly become very small indeed. For example if x is small enough, the expansion of $(1-x)^{\frac{1}{2}}$ gives

$$(1-x)^{\frac{1}{2}} \approx 1 - \tfrac{1}{2}x$$

so $1 - \frac{1}{2}x$ is a linear approximation to $(1-x)^{\frac{1}{2}}$.

You can find a quadratic approximation by stopping at the x^2 term, and so on for cubic and higher order approximations.

Questions

1 Use the first three terms in the expansion of $(1-x)^{\frac{1}{2}}$ with $x = \frac{1}{50}$ to find an approximate value, to 4 d.p., for $\sqrt{2}$.

2 $\dfrac{(1-2x)^3}{\sqrt[3]{1+x}} \approx a + bx.$
Find the values of a and b.

Answers

1 $1.4142 \left(\left(\frac{49}{50}\right)^{\frac{1}{2}} = \dfrac{7}{5\sqrt{2}} = \dfrac{7\sqrt{2}}{10}\right)$

2 $a = 1, b = -\frac{19}{3}$.

Take a break

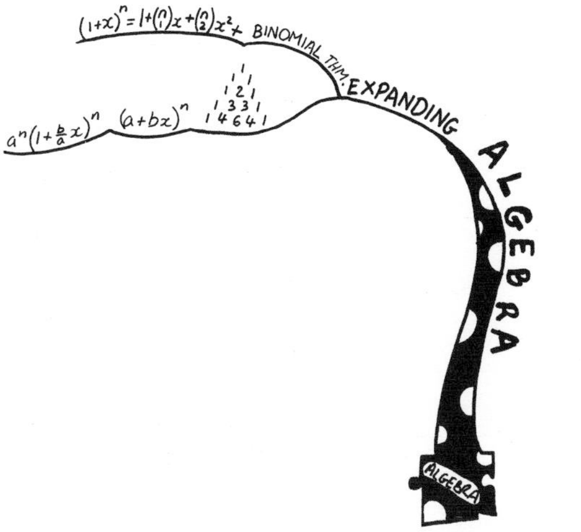

Review

1 $f(x) = \dfrac{4}{(x-1)(x+2)}$

Express f(x) in partial fractions. Hence find $\int f(x)\,dx$.

2a Expand $(1+x)^{-4}$ as a series of ascending powers of x as far as the term containing x^3.

b By substituting $x = n - 2n^2$, find the coefficient of n^3 in the expansion of $\dfrac{1}{(1+n-2n^2)^4}$ as a series of ascending powers of n.

3 Differentiate with respect to x

a x^3e^{3x} **b** $(2 + \sin 3x)^5$.

4 Solve the equation $2\cos 2\theta = \sin^2\theta$ for $0 \leqslant \theta \leqslant 360°$.

5 The points (2, −1) and (−5, 3) are the ends of a diameter of a circle. Find the equation of the circle.

6 The parametric equations of a curve are

$$x = \sin\theta,\ y = \theta\cos\theta.$$

The area between the x-axis and the section of this curve between the points where $\theta = 0$ and $\theta = \frac{1}{4}\pi$ is rotated about the x-axis.

a Show that volume generated is given by

$$\pi\int_0^{\frac{1}{4}\pi} \theta^2\cos^3\theta\,d\theta.$$

b Use the trapezium rule with 3 ordinates to find an approximate value for this integral.

7 At any time t seconds, the rate at which the mass Q grams of a substance is increasing is equal to $2Qt + Qe^t$.

Form a differential equation relating Q and t and solve it to find Q in terms of t, given that $Q = 5$ when $t = 0$.

Answers

1 $\dfrac{4}{3(x-1)} - \dfrac{4}{3(x+2)}$; $\dfrac{4}{3}\ln\left|\dfrac{x-1}{x+2}\right|$ **2a** $1 - 4x + 10x^2 - 20x^3$ **b** -60 **3a** $3x^2(x+1)e^{3x}$ **b** $15\cos 3x(2+\sin 3x)^4$

4 39.2°, 140.8°, 219.2°, 320.8° **5** $x^2 + y^2 + 3x - 2y - 13 = 0$ **6b** 0.285 **7** $\dfrac{dQ}{dt} = 2Qt + Qe^t$, $Q = 5e^{t^2-1+e^t}$

Take a break

PREVIEW

By the end of this topic you will have revised:

- ✔ **a way of locating a range in which a root of an equation lies,**
- ✔ **using iteration to find an approximate value for a root.**

Before you start you should:

- know what a convergent or a divergent sequence is,
- know how to generate a sequence from a recurrence relationship.

TEST YOURSELF

If you get more than one wrong answer, go to GCSE Higher or A level text book for information and practice.

Write down the first 3 terms of each sequence and determine whether the sequence converges or diverges.

1. $u_{n+1} = 2u_n - 4,\ u_1 = 0.5$

2. $u_{n+1} = \dfrac{u_n}{u_n + 1},\ u_1 = 0.5.$

Answers

1 0.5, −3, −10, diverges

2 0.5, 0.33, 0.25, converges

Locating a root

When $f(x) = 0$, the curve $y = f(x)$ crosses the x-axis. The values of x at these points are roots of the equation $f(x) = 0$.

If α is a root of $f(x) = 0$,
then on one side of $x = \alpha$, $f(x) > 0$
and on the other side, $f(x) < 0$,
i.e., if $f(x)$ changes sign in the interval $a < x < b$,
then $f(x) = 0$ has a root in the interval $a < x < b$.

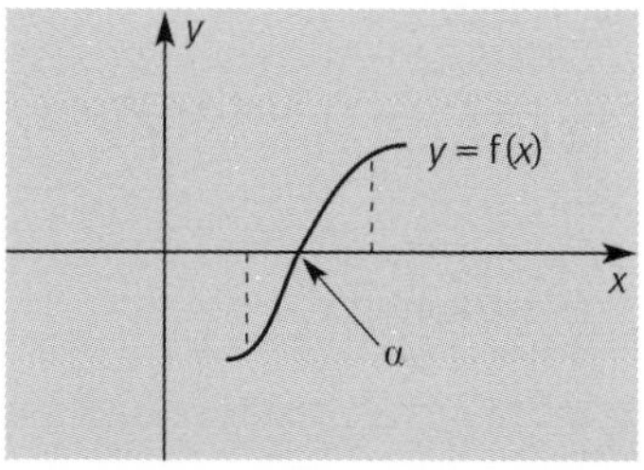

- You can use this fact to find a range of values in which a root of an equation lies. For example, to find, roughly, a root of the equation $x - \cos x = 0$, where x is measured in radians, start with a sketch.

You almost certainly do not know the shape of $y = x - \cos x$ but you should know the shapes of $y = x$ and $y = \cos x$; the roots of the equation $x - \cos x = 0$ are the values of x at the points of intersection of $y = x$ and $y = \cos x$.

This shows that there is a root, α, between 0 and $\frac{1}{2}\pi$; i.e. between 0 and 1.5 . . .

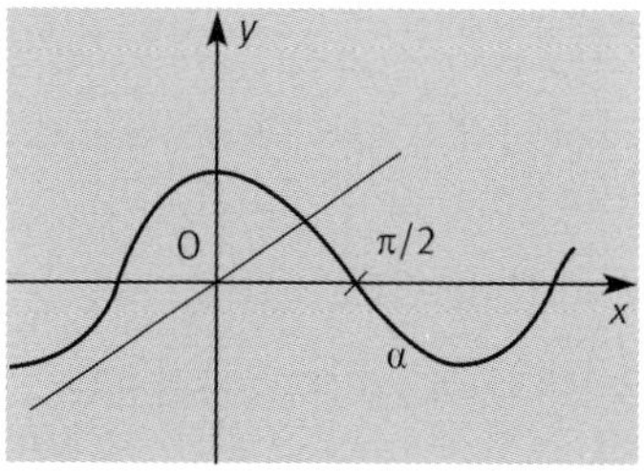

(It also shows that the equation $x - \cos x = 0$ has only one root as there is only one point of intersection.)

To narrow this range down, you can find

$$f(0.5) = 0.5 - \cos 0.5 = -0.3\ldots \qquad (-\text{ve})$$

and $$f(1) = 1 - \cos 1 = 0.4\ldots \qquad (+\text{ve})$$

$f(x)$ changes sign in the interval $0.5 < x < 1$,

$\therefore\ x - \cos x = 0$ has a root in this range.

⚠ Do not use the change of sign of $f(x)$ to locate a root in an interval in which the curve $y = f(x)$ has turning points or in which it has a break.

Question

Show that the equation $x \ln x - 2 = 0$ has a root between 2 and 2.5.

Answer

$f(x) = x \ln x - 2$; $f(2) = -0.6\ldots$, $f(2.5) = 0.2\ldots$

$\therefore\ x \ln x - 2 = 0$ has a root between 2 and 2.5.

Iteration

If the terms of the sequence generated by the iteration formula (i.e. recurrence relationship)

$$x_{n+1} = g(x_n)$$

converge to α, then α is a root of the equation

$$x = g(x).$$

- You can use this fact to find successively better approximations for a root of an equation.

You will also need:

- a starting value, i.e. a value for x_1; this is usually given but if it isn't you can find one using the change of sign test and then choosing any value within the interval,

- a rearrangement of the equation $f(x) = 0$ in the form $x = g(x)$ to give the iteration formula $x_{n+1} = g(x_n)$; this is also usually given. When it isn't, you can try different rearrangements, as there are usually several ways in which $f(x) = 0$ can be written as $x = g(x)$. Carry on until you find one that generates a sequence that converges.

For example, the equation $x - \cos x = 0$ has a root α between 0.5 and 1 and can be written as $x = \cos x$ which gives the iteration formula

$$x_{n+1} = \cos x_n$$

Taking $x_1 = 0.75$ (any value from 0.5 to 1 can be used)

gives $x_2 = \cos 0.75 = 0.731\ldots$
$x_3 = \cos 0.731\ldots = 0.744\ldots$
$x_4 = \cos 0.744\ldots = 0.735\ldots$

It looks as if $\alpha = 0.74$ correct to 2 d.p.

You can use the change of sign test to check whether or not this is correct:

if $\alpha = 0.74$ correct to 2 d.p. then $0.735 < \alpha < 0.745$

$f(0.735) = 0.735 - \cos 0.735 = -0.006\ldots$ (−ve)
$f(0.745) = 0.745 - \cos 0.745 = 0.009\ldots$ (+ve)
$\therefore \quad \alpha = 0.74$ correct to 2 d.p.

To find α correct to 3 d.p. you need to continue the iteration until the third decimal place stops changing. You then need to verify that the third decimal place is correct by using the change of sign test.

Question

The equation $x \ln 5x = 10$ has a root that is approximately equal to 3.5.

Use the iteration formula $x_{n+1} = \dfrac{10}{\ln 5x_n}$ to find this root correct to 3 decimal places.

Answer

3.495

Take a break

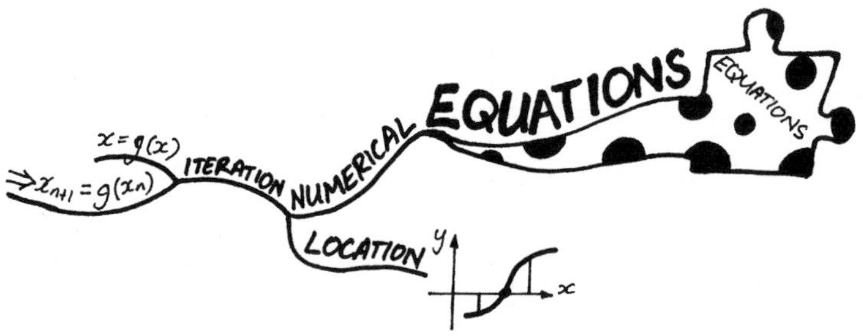

Review

1 $2x^3 + x^2 + ax + b$ has a factor $2x - 1$ and leaves a remainder $\frac{5}{2}$ when divided by $2x + 1$. Find the values of a and b.

2 Differentiate $x \sec x$ with respect to x.

3 Integrate with respect to x **a** $x \cos 2x$ **b** $\ln x$ **c** $\dfrac{1}{x(x-1)}$.

4 The expansion of $(1 - 3x)^n$ is an infinite series in which the coefficient of x^2 is 54. Find the value of n.

5 Is it true that, if n is a prime number, $n^2 + n + 1$ is also prime? Give a proof with your answer.

6 Find the values of x for which $f(x) = \sin^2 x + \cos 2x$ is stationary in the range $0 \leqslant x \leqslant \pi$.

7 Use the iteration formula with $x_{n+1} = \sqrt{x_n + \dfrac{3}{x_n}}$ with $x_1 = 2$ to find, to 4 s.f., x_2, x_3 and x_4. Write down the equation for which x_4 is an approximate root.

8 Find the solution of the differential equation $y\dfrac{dy}{dx} = y^2 - 1$ for which $y = 2$ when $x = 1$.

Answers

1 $a = -3, b = 1$ **2** $\sec x + x \sec x \tan x$ **3a** $\frac{1}{4}\cos 2x + \frac{1}{2}x \sin 2x + k$ **b** $x \ln x - x + k$ **c** $\ln\left|\dfrac{x-1}{x}\right| + k$

4 -3 **5** no: $7^2 + 7 + 1$ not prime. **6** $0, \dfrac{\pi}{2}, \pi$ **7** 1.871, 1.864, 1.864, $x^3 - x^2 - 3 = 0$ **8** $y^2 - 1 = 3e^{2x-2}$.

PREVIEW

By the end of this topic you will have revised:

- ✔ **vectors in 3 dimensions,**
- ✔ **the scalar product and how to use it to find the angle between two vectors,**
- ✔ **the equations of a line in 3 dimensions.**

Before you start you should:

- know the difference between a vector and a scalar and understand the common notation for vectors,
- know the meaning of $\mathbf{a} \pm \mathbf{b}$, $2\mathbf{a}$, $-3\mathbf{a}$, etc.

TEST YOURSELF

If you get more than one wrong answer, see GCSE Higher or A level text book for information and practice.

1 In the diagram,

a) is the length of BC a vector or a scalar?

b) Is the position of B relative to C a vector or a scalar?

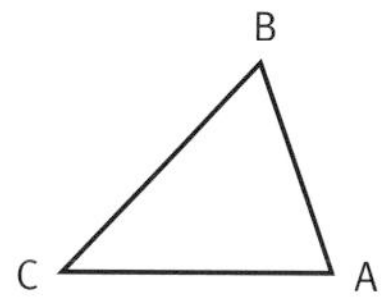

2 In the diagram, $\overrightarrow{CA} = \mathbf{a}$ and $\overrightarrow{CB} = \mathbf{b}$.

a) Express $\overrightarrow{BA}$ in terms of a and b.

b) D is the midpoint of AB. Find $\overrightarrow{CD}$ in terms of a and b.

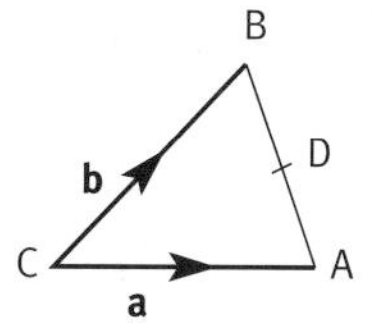

Answers

1 a) scalar **b)** vector

2 a) $\mathbf{a} - \mathbf{b}$ **b)** $\frac{1}{2}(\mathbf{a} + \mathbf{b})$.

Vectors in 3-D

$\mathbf{i}$, $\mathbf{j}$, and $\mathbf{k}$ are unit vectors in the directions Ox, Oy and Oz respectively.

$\mathbf{r} = \overrightarrow{OP}$ is the position vector of the point P(x, y, z), where $\mathbf{r} = x\mathbf{i} + y\mathbf{j} + z\mathbf{k}$.
$x\mathbf{i}$, $y\mathbf{j}$, $z\mathbf{k}$ are the Cartesian components of $\mathbf{r}$.

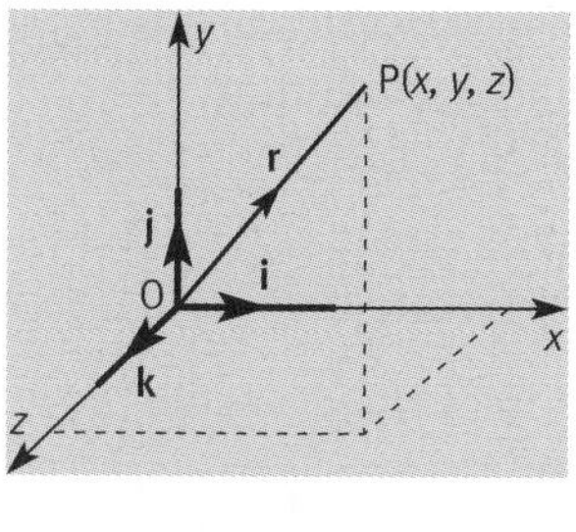

The magnitude of a vector is the length of the line that represents it.

The magnitude of $\mathbf{r}$ is written $|\mathbf{r}|$ or r,
so $|\mathbf{i}| = |\mathbf{j}| = |\mathbf{k}| = 1$

and $|\mathbf{r}| = \text{OP} = \sqrt{x^2 + y^2 + z^2}$.

You add or subtract vectors by adding or subtracting their Cartesian components.

You multiply a vector by a scalar by multiplying its components by that scalar.

For example,

when $\mathbf{a} = 3\mathbf{i} - 2\mathbf{j} + 5\mathbf{k}$ and $\mathbf{b} = 3\mathbf{j} - \mathbf{k}$,

$$\mathbf{a} + \mathbf{b} = (3 + 0)\mathbf{i} + (-2 + 3)\mathbf{j} + (5 - 1)\mathbf{k}$$
$$= 3\mathbf{i} + \mathbf{j} + 4\mathbf{k}$$

and $2\mathbf{b} - \mathbf{a} = (0 - 3)\mathbf{i} + (6 - (-2))\mathbf{j} + (-2 - 5)\mathbf{k}$

$$= -3\mathbf{i} + 8\mathbf{j} - 7\mathbf{k}.$$

⚠ When you draw a diagram to show points and lines in 3-D, mark a point O as the origin but do not draw the axes as they clutter up a diagram and do not usually help to make it clearer.

Example

$\mathbf{a}$ and $\mathbf{b}$ are the position vectors of the points A and B where $\mathbf{a} = 2\mathbf{i} - \mathbf{j}$ and $\mathbf{b} = \mathbf{j} + 5\mathbf{k}$.

Find the vectors $\overrightarrow{AB}$ and $\overrightarrow{OC}$ where C is the midpoint of AB.

Solution

$\overrightarrow{AB} = \mathbf{b} - \mathbf{a} = -2\mathbf{i} + 2\mathbf{j} + 5\mathbf{k}$

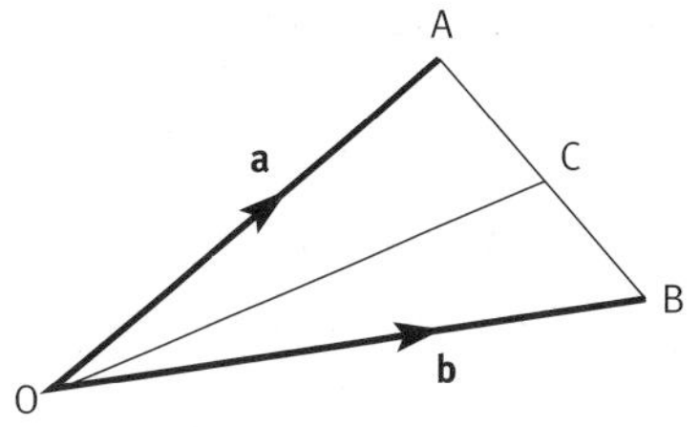

$$\overrightarrow{OC} = \mathbf{a} + \overrightarrow{AC} = \mathbf{a} + \tfrac{1}{2}\overrightarrow{AB}$$
$$= (2\mathbf{i} - \mathbf{j}) + (-\mathbf{i} + \mathbf{j} + 2\tfrac{1}{2}\mathbf{k})$$
$$= \mathbf{i} + 2\tfrac{1}{2}\mathbf{k}.$$

Questions

Given the points A(5, 0, 1) and B(2, −1, 0), find in terms of **i**, **j**, and **k**,

1 the position vector of A,

2 the vector $\overrightarrow{AB}$,

3 the position vector of the point C where C is the midpoint of AB.

Answers

1 $5\mathbf{i}+\mathbf{k}$ 2 $-3\mathbf{i}-\mathbf{j}-\mathbf{k}$ 3 $\frac{1}{2}(7\mathbf{i}-\mathbf{j}+\mathbf{k})$.

Scalar product

a.b is the scalar product of the vectors **a** and **b** and

$$\mathbf{a}.\mathbf{b} = |\mathbf{a}||\mathbf{b}|\cos\theta$$

where θ is the angle between **a** and **b**.

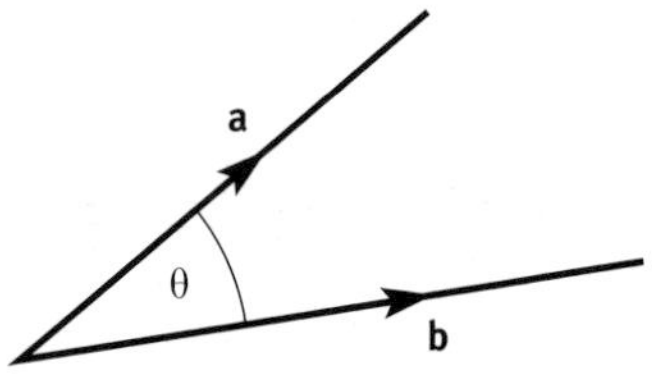

When

$\mathbf{a} = x_1\mathbf{i} + y_1\mathbf{j} + z_1\mathbf{k}$ and $\mathbf{b} = x_2\mathbf{i} + y_2\mathbf{j} + z_2\mathbf{k}$

$\mathbf{a}.\mathbf{b} = x_1x_2 + y_1y_2 + z_1z_2$

e.g. $(2\mathbf{i} - \mathbf{j} + 3\mathbf{k}).(\mathbf{i} - 3\mathbf{k})$

$= (2)(1) + (-1)(0) + (3)(-3)$

$= -7.$

When **a** and **b** are perpendicular, $\mathbf{a}.\mathbf{b} = 0$ since $\cos 90^\circ = 0$.

You can use the scalar product to:

- find the angle between two vectors, e.g. to find the angle between the vectors $2\mathbf{i} - \mathbf{j} + 3\mathbf{k}$ and $\mathbf{i} - 3\mathbf{k}$, start with
  $(2\mathbf{i} - \mathbf{j} + 3\mathbf{k}).(\mathbf{i} - 3\mathbf{k}) = |2\mathbf{i} - \mathbf{j} + 3\mathbf{k}||\mathbf{i} - 3\mathbf{k}|\cos\theta$
  $\Rightarrow \quad -7 = (\sqrt{14})(\sqrt{10})\cos\theta$
  $\therefore \quad \theta = 126.3^\circ$ (1 dp)
- show that two vectors are perpendicular. You can do this by showing that the scalar product of the two vectors is zero, (i.e. $\cos\theta = 0$).
  e.g. to show that $\mathbf{a} = 2\mathbf{i} + 5\mathbf{j} - \mathbf{k}$ is perpendicular to $\mathbf{b} = 6\mathbf{i} - \mathbf{j} + 7\mathbf{k}$,
  start with $\mathbf{a}.\mathbf{b} = (2\mathbf{i} + 5\mathbf{j} - \mathbf{k}).(6\mathbf{i} - \mathbf{j} + 7\mathbf{k})$
  $= 12 - 5 - 7 = 0.$

Question

Three points A, B and C have position vectors $\mathbf{a} = 2\mathbf{i} + 3\mathbf{j} + 2\mathbf{k}$, $\mathbf{b} = 6\mathbf{i} + 5\mathbf{j} - \mathbf{k}$ and $\mathbf{c} = 7\mathbf{i} + 11\mathbf{j} + \mathbf{k}$ respectively.

Find

a $\overrightarrow{AB}$ **b** $\overrightarrow{BC}$ **c** angle ABC.

Show that the vector $2\mathbf{i} - \mathbf{j} + 2\mathbf{k}$ is perpendicular to both $\overrightarrow{AB}$ and $\overrightarrow{BC}$.

Answer

a $\overrightarrow{AB} = 4\mathbf{i} + 2\mathbf{j} - 3\mathbf{k}$ **b** $\overrightarrow{BC} = \mathbf{i} + 6\mathbf{j} + 2\mathbf{k}$ **c** 73.1° (1 dp)

Equations of lines

The line l is parallel to the vector **b** and goes through the point A with position vector **a**.

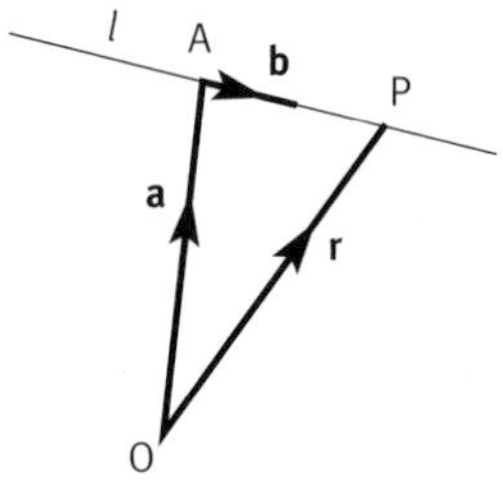

The vector equation of l gives the position vector of any point P on this line in terms of **a** and **b**.

For any point P on l, $\overrightarrow{AP}$ is a multiple of **b**, so $\overrightarrow{AP} = t\mathbf{b}$ where t is a parameter,

$\therefore$ the position vector of P, **r**, is given by

$$\mathbf{r} = \mathbf{a} + t\mathbf{b}.$$

There is no one 'right answer' for the vector equation of a given line:
a is only one of an infinite number of points on the line, and any multiple of **b** can replace **b**.

- From the vector equation of a line, you can 'read' a vector parallel to the line and a point on the line.

For example, given the line

$$\mathbf{r} = (2 - t)\mathbf{i} + (2 + 3t)\mathbf{j} - 5t\mathbf{k},$$

you can rearrange the equation in the form $\mathbf{r} = \mathbf{a} + t\mathbf{b}$, i.e. $\mathbf{r} = (2\mathbf{i} + 2\mathbf{j}) + t(-\mathbf{i} + 3\mathbf{j} - 5\mathbf{k})$ from which you can see that this line is parallel to $-\mathbf{i} + 3\mathbf{j} - 5\mathbf{k}$ and goes through the point with position vector $2\mathbf{i} + 2\mathbf{j}$.

You can find the position vector of other points on the line by giving t different values, e.g. when $t = 2$, $\mathbf{r} = 8\mathbf{j} - 10\mathbf{k}$, i.e. $8\mathbf{j} - 10\mathbf{k}$ is the position vector of a point on the line.

You can find a vector equation for a line if you know:

- the position vector of one point on the line and a vector parallel to the line,

e.g. a vector equation of the line through the point with position vector $2\mathbf{i} - \mathbf{j}$, that is parallel to the vector $3\mathbf{i} - \mathbf{j} + \mathbf{k}$, is

$$\mathbf{r} = 2\mathbf{i} - \mathbf{j} + t(3\mathbf{i} - \mathbf{j} + \mathbf{k})$$

- the position vectors of two points on the line,

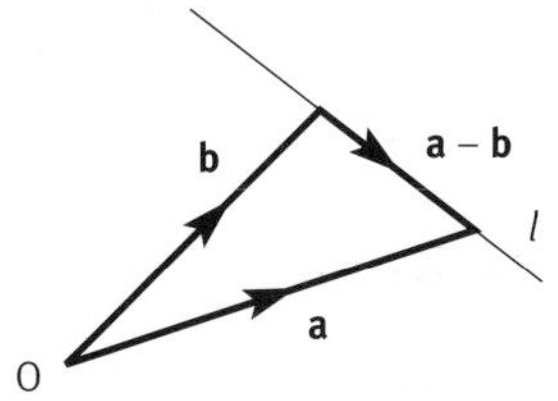

e.g. the line l through the points with position vectors $\mathbf{a} = \mathbf{i} - 3\mathbf{j} - \mathbf{k}$ and $\mathbf{b} = 4\mathbf{i} - \mathbf{k}$, is parallel to $\mathbf{a} - \mathbf{b}$, i.e. to $-3\mathbf{i} - 3\mathbf{j}$.
So a vector equation of l is

$$\mathbf{r} = \mathbf{i} - 3\mathbf{j} - \mathbf{k} + t(-3\mathbf{i} - 3\mathbf{j}).$$

Since $\mathbf{i} + \mathbf{j}$ is parallel to $-3\mathbf{i} - 3\mathbf{j}$, you can also use $\mathbf{r} = \mathbf{i} - 3\mathbf{j} - \mathbf{k} + t(\mathbf{i} + \mathbf{j})$ or, using $\mathbf{b}$ instead of $\mathbf{a}$, $\mathbf{r} = 4\mathbf{i} - \mathbf{k} + t(\mathbf{i} + \mathbf{j})$.

Example

A line l_1 passes through the points A(1, 0, 3) and B(−1, 2, 1).

a Find a vector equation for the line l_1.

b Write down a vector equation for the line l_2 that is parallel to AB and which passes through the point C(1, 1, 3).

c Find the angle between l_2 and the line through A and C.

Solution

a l_1 is parallel to $\overrightarrow{AB}$ and $\overrightarrow{AB} = \overrightarrow{OB} - \overrightarrow{OA}$
$= -2\mathbf{i} + 2\mathbf{j} - 2\mathbf{k}$.

As l_1 is parallel to any multiple of $\overrightarrow{AB}$, you can use $\frac{1}{2}\overrightarrow{AB}$, i.e. $-\mathbf{i} + \mathbf{j} - \mathbf{k}$, to give a simpler equation,
$\therefore$ using $\overrightarrow{OA}$ as the position vector of a point on l_1, a vector equation for l_1 is
$\mathbf{r} = \mathbf{i} + 3\mathbf{k} + t(-\mathbf{i} + \mathbf{j} - \mathbf{k})$.
(You can use $\overrightarrow{OB}$ instead of $\overrightarrow{OA}$.)

b l_2 is parallel to l_1, i.e. to $-\mathbf{i} + \mathbf{j} - \mathbf{k}$, so has a vector equation
$\mathbf{r} = \mathbf{i} + \mathbf{j} + 3\mathbf{k} + t(-\mathbf{i} + \mathbf{j} - \mathbf{k})$.

c You can find the angle, θ, between two lines by finding the angle between the vectors they are parallel to.
The line through A and C is parallel to $\overrightarrow{AC}$ and $\overrightarrow{AC} = \overrightarrow{OC} - \overrightarrow{OA} = \mathbf{j}$.
$\therefore$ θ is the angle between $\mathbf{j}$ and $-\mathbf{i} + \mathbf{j} - \mathbf{k}$.
Using the scalar product,
$\mathbf{j}.(-\mathbf{i} + \mathbf{j} - \mathbf{k}) = |\mathbf{j}| \times |-\mathbf{i} + \mathbf{j} - \mathbf{k}| \cos\theta$
$\Rightarrow \quad 1 = (1)(\sqrt{3}) \cos\theta$
$\Rightarrow \quad \theta = 54.7^\circ$ to 1 d.p.

Questions

1 Two points lie on a hill and have coordinates A(2, 6, 1) and B(2, −1, 4).
An overhead power cable is parallel to AB and passes through the point C(2, 8, 6). Find a vector equation for the line along which the cable lies.

2 An underground telephone line runs along a line whose vector equation is
$\mathbf{r} = (3 - 2t)\mathbf{i} + 5t\mathbf{j} + (t - 3)\mathbf{k}$ to a point A where $t = 2$ where it turns. The cable then runs to the point B(1, −3, 5). Find the angle through which the line turns at A.

Answers

1 $2\mathbf{i} + 8\mathbf{j} + 6\mathbf{k} + t(7\mathbf{j} - 3\mathbf{k})$ **2** 37.3° (1 dp)

Intersection of lines

In three dimensional space, two lines are either parallel, intersecting or skew.

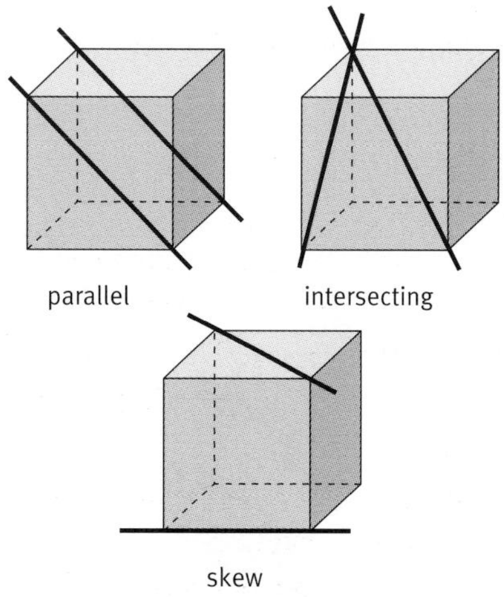

- You can find out whether they are parallel from their equations by arranging them, both if necessary, in the form $\mathbf{r} = \mathbf{a} + t\mathbf{b}$ and comparing the vectors parallel to each line.

For example, to find out if the lines

$\mathbf{r} = (2 - t)\mathbf{i} + (2 + 3t)\mathbf{j} - 5t\mathbf{k}$ [1]

and $\mathbf{r} = \mathbf{i} - s(2\mathbf{i} - \mathbf{j} + \mathbf{k})$ [2]

are parallel, first rearrange [1] as

$\mathbf{r} = 2\mathbf{i} + 2\mathbf{j} + t(-\mathbf{i} + 3\mathbf{j} - 5\mathbf{k})$.

Now you can see that
[1] is parallel to $-\mathbf{i} + 3\mathbf{j} - 5\mathbf{k}$,
[2] is parallel to $2\mathbf{i} - \mathbf{j} + \mathbf{k}$,
and as these are not parallel vectors, the lines are not parallel.

- You can find out if they intersect by finding the value of s and the value of t for which the $\mathbf{i}$ and $\mathbf{j}$ components of $\mathbf{r}$ are the same for both lines. Then use these values to find the $\mathbf{k}$ component of each line: if these are equal, the lines intersect but if they are not, the lines are either parallel or skew.

For example, to find out if the lines

$\mathbf{r} = (2 - t)\mathbf{i} + (2 + 3t)\mathbf{j} - 5t\mathbf{k}$ [1]

and $\mathbf{r} = \mathbf{i} - s(2\mathbf{i} - \mathbf{j} + \mathbf{k})$ [2]

intersect, start by equating the $\mathbf{i}$ components of [1] and [2]: this gives $2 - t = 1 - 2s$ [3]
then equate the $\mathbf{j}$ components of [1] and [2]: this gives $2 + 3t = s$ [4]

Solving [3] and [4] simultaneously gives $s = -1$ and $t = -1$.

Using $t = -1$ in [1] gives $\mathbf{r} = 3\mathbf{i} - \mathbf{j} + 5\mathbf{k}$.
Using $s = -1$ in [2] gives $\mathbf{r} = 3\mathbf{i} - \mathbf{j} + \mathbf{k}$.

The $\mathbf{k}$ components are not the same, so the lines do not intersect.

Lines intersect only when all three components of the two lines are the same, so to show that two lines intersect, you MUST show that the values found for the parameters give identical values for $\mathbf{r}$. This value of $\mathbf{r}$ is the position vector of the point of intersection of the lines.

Question

Show that the line $\mathbf{r} = 3\mathbf{i} - 4\mathbf{j} + 2\mathbf{k} + \lambda(\mathbf{i} - 2\mathbf{j})$ intersects the line through A(4, −3, 8) and B(2, −1, 4) and give the coordinates of the point of intersection.

Answer

(1, 0, 2) (where $\lambda = -2$)

Take a break

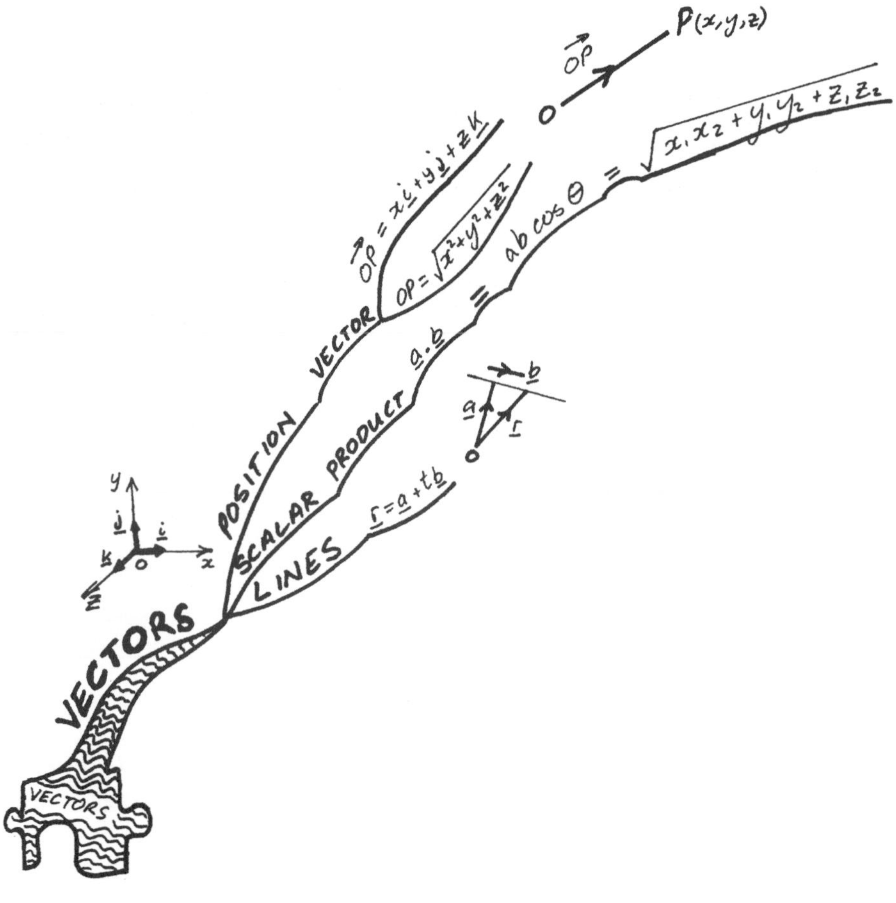

Review

1 Differentiate with respect to x

a $x\cos 2x$ **b** $(x^2-2)^6$ **c** $\dfrac{\cos x}{1-\sin x}$.

2 Integrate

a $(x-1)\ln x$ **b** $\cos x\sin^2 x$.

3 Evaluate $\displaystyle\int_0^3 x\sqrt{1+x}\,dx$ using the substitution $u^2 = 1 + x$.

4 Find the values of x in the range $0 \leqslant x \leqslant 360°$ for which

a $\cos 2x - \sin x = 1$ **b** $2\cos x - \sin x = 1$.

5 The equation of a circle is $x^2 + y^2 - 2x + 4y = 0$.

a Find the radius and coordinates of the centre.

b Find the equations of the tangents at the points on the circle where $x = 0$.

6 $f(x) = \dfrac{5}{(2-3x)(1+x)}$

a Express f(x) in partial fractions.

b Expand f(x) as a series of ascending powers of x as far as the term containing x^2.

c Find the area between the part of the curve $y = f(x)$ from $x = 2$ to $x = 3$ by

i integration

ii using the trapezium rule with two strips.

7 The equation of a curve is $xy^2 = 12$.
Find the equation of the tangent to the curve at the point where $y = 2$.

8 A fungal disease attacked a wood of beech trees. There were 500 trees in the wood before the fungus appeared and two years after this, 150 trees had died. It is assumed that t years after the fungus appeared, the rate at which trees are dying is proportional to the number, N, of trees still alive. Form a differential equation relating N and t and solve it to find the number of trees that are expected to have died after 5 years.

Answers

1a $\cos 2x - 2x\sin 2x$ **b** $12x(x^2-2)^5$ **c** $\dfrac{1}{1-\sin x}$ **2a** $(\frac{1}{2}x^2 - x)\ln x - \frac{1}{4}x^2 + x + k$ **b** $\frac{1}{3}\sin^3 x + k$ **3** $\frac{116}{15}$

4a 0°, 180°, 210°, 330°, 360° **b** 36.9°, 270° **5a** $\sqrt{5}$, $(1, -2)$ **b** $x - 2y = 0$, $x + 2y + 8 = 0$

6a $\dfrac{3}{2-3x} + \dfrac{1}{1+x}$ **b** $\frac{5}{2} + \frac{5}{4}x + \frac{35}{8}x^2$ **c i** $\ln\frac{21}{16}$ **ii** $\frac{515}{1848} = 0.279$ **7** $x + 3y = 9$ **8** $\dfrac{dN}{dt} = -kN$, 295.

Take a break

Mechanics

1 **Force**. Understanding Force. Modelling and drawing diagrams. Internal and external forces.

2 **Working with forces**. Resolving forces. Resultant of two forces and of coplanar forces. Use of **ij** notation. Equilibrium of concurrent forces. Friction. Coefficient of friction. Angle of friction. Review.

3 **Constant acceleration**. Motion with constant acceleration. Newton's Laws of Motion. Motion under gravity. Motion of connected bodies. Review.

4 **Work, power and energy**. Work. Mechanical energy. Kinetic and Potential energy. Relation between work done and mechanical energy. Solving problems. Conservation of mechanical energy. Power. Power of a moving vehicle. Power of a stationary engine. Review.

5 **Impulse and momentum**. Impulse. Momentum. Relation between impulse and momentum. Units. Instantaneous impulse. Conservation of momentum. Loss of energy at impact. Review.

6 **Projectiles**. Equations for velocity and displacement at time t. Derivation of formulae for time of flight, range, maximum range and greatest height. Equation of the path of a projectile (trajectory). Review.

7 **Parallel forces and moment**. Moment of a force. Resultant moment. Resultant of like and unlike parallel forces. Objects in equilibrium under the action of parallel forces. Review.

8 **Centre of gravity**. Centre of mass. Centre of gravity. C of G of simple plane figures and simple compound figures. Equilibrium of a lamina in a vertical plane with one side resting on a horizontal plane. Equilibrium of a lamina hanging freely from a point. Review.

9 **Equilibrium in a plane**. Equilibrium of three forces. Equilibrium of coplanar forces. Equilibrium of a lamina resting with one side on an inclined plane. Review.

10 **Newton's Law of Restitution**. Collision with a fixed surface. Two colliding objects. Newton's Law of Restitution. Review.

11 **Motion in a horizontal circle**. Acceleration of a body describing a circle. Circular motion on a horizontal plane. The conical pendulum. Banked tracks. Design speed. Review.

12 **Motion in a vertical circle**. Motion in a circle with non-constant speed. Tangential acceleration. Motion restricted to a vertical circle. Motion not restricted to a vertical circle. Review.

13 **Hooke's Law and elastic strings**. Elastic strings and springs. Hooke's Law. The energy in a stretched elastic string. Review.

14 **Variable motion in a plane**. Acceleration as a function of time. Using $F = ma$. Variable motion in two dimensions. Variable motion in three dimensions. Acceleration as a function of displacement. Review.

15 **Simple harmonic motion**. The basic equation for simple harmonic motion. The associated circular motion. The period. Horizontal oscillations of a particle on a spring or elastic string. Vertical oscillations. Review.

16 **Centre of mass of a rigid body**. Centre of mass of a uniform body made from uniform material. Centre of mass of a compound body. The centre of mass of a prism. Finding the centre of mass by integration. Equilibrium of a rigid body. Review.

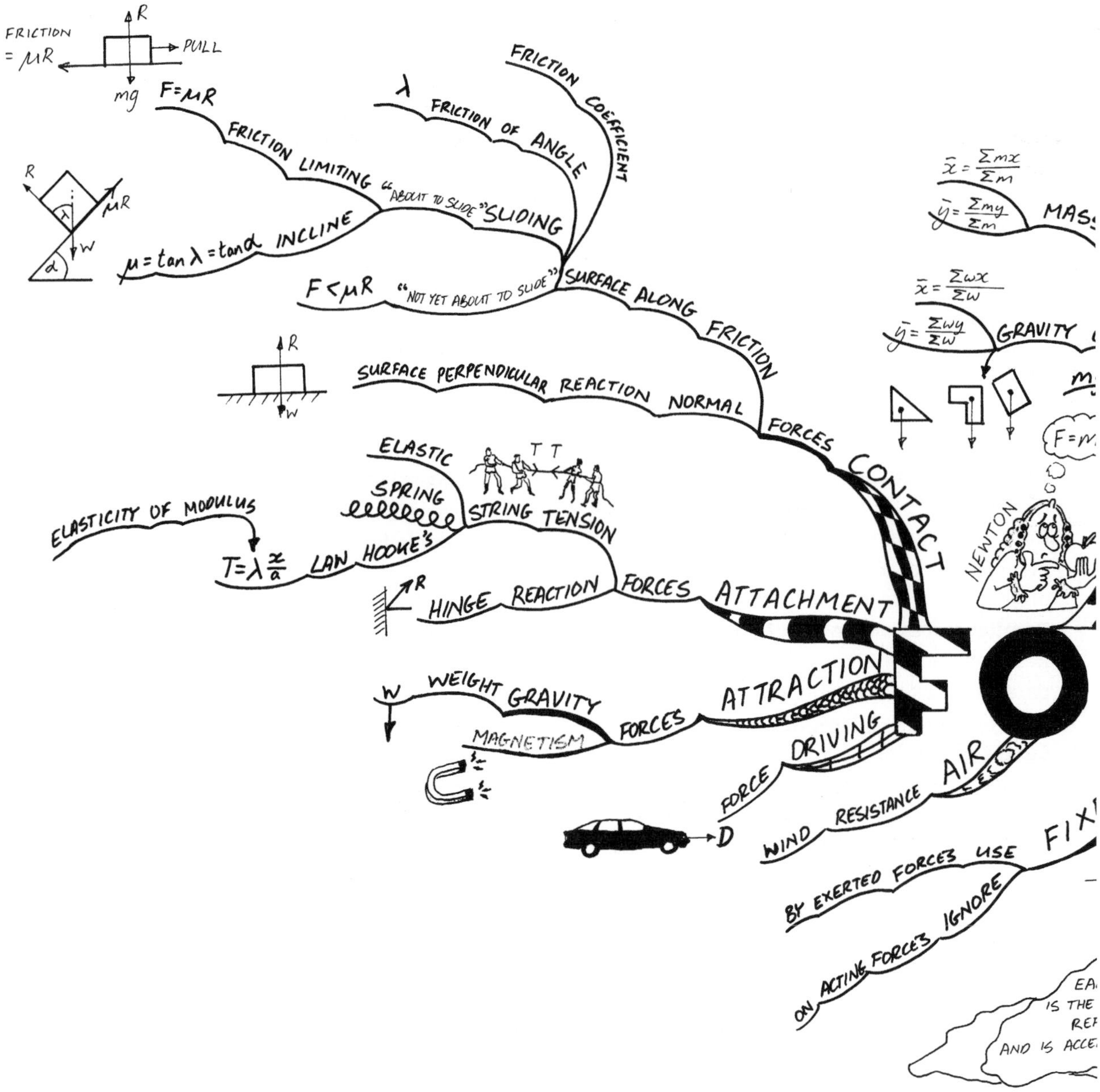
FRICTION = μR
R
PULL
mg
F=μR
FRICTION LIMITING
"ABOUT TO SLIDE" SLIDING
λ FRICTION OF ANGLE
FRICTION COEFFICIENT
R
μR
W
α
μ = tan λ = tan α INCLINE
F<μR "NOT YET ABOUT TO SLIDE"
SURFACE ALONG FRICTION
R
W
SURFACE PERPENDICULAR REACTION NORMAL
FORCES
CONTACT
ELASTIC
SPRING
T T
STRING TENSION
ELASTICITY OF MODULUS
T=λ x/a LAW HOOKE'S
R
HINGE REACTION
FORCES
ATTACHMENT
W
WEIGHT GRAVITY
MAGNETISM
FORCES
ATTRACTION
FORCE DRIVING
D
WIND RESISTANCE AIR
BY EXERTED FORCES USE
ON ACTING FORCES IGNORE
NEWTON
x̄ = Σmx/Σm
ȳ = Σmy/Σm
x̄ = Σwx/Σw
ȳ = Σwy/Σw
GRAVITY
IS THE
AND IS

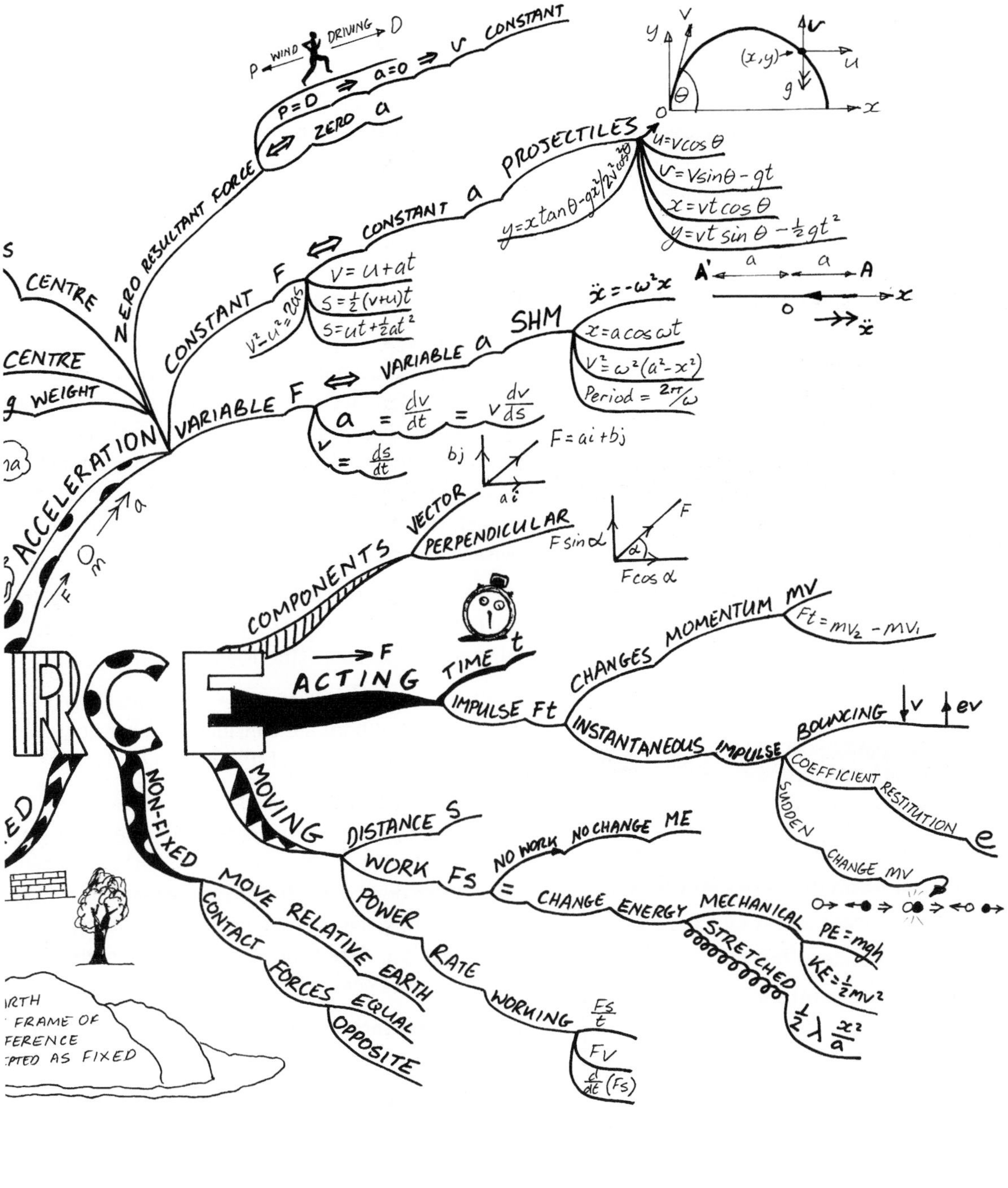

RCE
ACCELERATION
ZERO RESULTANT FORCE
P=D ⇒ a=0 ⇒ v CONSTANT
⇔ ZERO a
WIND
DRIVING
CONSTANT F ⇔ CONSTANT a
PROJECTILES
y=x tanθ - gx²/2V²cos²θ
u=Vcosθ
v=Vsinθ - gt
x=vt cosθ
y=vt sinθ - ½gt²
v=u+at
s=½(v+u)t
s=ut+½at²
v²-u²=2as
VARIABLE F ⇔ VARIABLE a
SHM
ẍ=-ω²x
x=a cos ωt
v²=ω²(a²-x²)
Period = 2π/ω
a = dv/dt = v dv/ds
v = ds/dt
F=ai+bj
COMPONENTS
VECTOR
PERPENDICULAR
F sin α
F cos α
ACTING TIME t
IMPULSE Ft
CHANGES MOMENTUM MV
Ft=mV₂ - mV₁
INSTANTANEOUS IMPULSE
BOUNCING
COEFFICIENT RESTITUTION e
SUDDEN CHANGE MV
MOVING
DISTANCE S
WORK Fs
NO WORK NO CHANGE ME
= CHANGE ENERGY MECHANICAL
PE=mgh
KE=½mv²
STRETCHED
½λx²/a
POWER
RATE
WORKING
Fs/t
Fv
d/dt(Fs)
NON-FIXED
MOVE RELATIVE EARTH
CONTACT FORCES EQUAL OPPOSITE
CENTRE
CENTRE
WEIGHT
FRAME OF
FERENCE
PTED AS FIXED

Introduction

The Mechanics section of this book aims at reminding you of the importance of the various types of force and the relationships between force and the properties of a moving, or a stationary, object.

The 'laws' of mechanics are only hypotheses based on experimental evidence and the situations in which we use them are often considerably simplified. Making assumptions to model a situation introduces approximations and it follows that the answers given are themselves only approximate. The appropriate degree of accuracy used depends on how reasonable the assumptions are. This affects the number of decimal places expected in an answer and also the value taken for g, the acceleration due to gravity.

Some Examining Boards specify this information in their rubric (often $g = 9.8$ and answers to 3 significant figures). If so you must follow this exactly. In this book these values are used in questions where the assumptions made are insignificant.

Other Boards however require 'an appropriate degree of accuracy' so you need to give this some thought. In many practical problems in this book, g is taken as 10 with answers to 2 significant figures. If in doubt use 9.8 and give answers to 3 sf.

Good luck with your revision.

PREVIEW

By the end of this topic you will have revised:

- ✔ **the importance of understanding what force is, what it does, where and which way it acts,**
- ✔ **where and how to mark forces on a diagram,**
- ✔ **the categories of common forces,**
- ✔ **the difference between internal and external forces,**
- ✔ **how to draw a simple diagram by modelling.**

Before you start you should:

- appreciate that the basis for solving most problems in mechanics is the drawing of a diagram with all forces correctly marked.

What is Force?

Force is the quantity that is capable of causing *change* in the motion of an object.

Change can mean:
that an object at rest begins to move,
or that an object already moving has its speed or direction, or both, altered,
or that a moving object comes to rest.

A force can act continuously, (e.g. gravity), or for a measurable time interval, or instantaneously (e.g. a blow).

⚠ Do not assume that because an object is moving there must be a force acting in the direction of motion. This is not necessarily so. When a hockey stick gives a blow to a puck on an ice rink, for example, the instantaneous force makes the puck *begin* to move but no further horizontal force acts on it as it continues to move on the smooth ice.

ℹ Forces act only when there is a physical reason for their presence. The main types of force are:

Contact forces – a pair of equal and opposite forces act between touching solid bodies, one acting on each body. Normal contact forces (normal reactions) are perpendicular to the surface of contact and act outwards from it. Frictional forces are also contact forces, acting in pairs; they act along the surface of contact. (The properties of frictional forces are revised in Mechanics 2.)

If one of the objects is fixed, disregard the force that acts *on* it but do consider the force exerted on a moveable object *by* the fixed one. (This is an *external* force.)

If both objects are able to move, the contact forces are *internal* and both are considered, separately, each acting on only one of the touching solids.

Forces of Attachment – similar to contact forces, these act in equal and opposite pairs and the force acting on a fixed object is disregarded. The commonest attachment is by a string or rope and the forces are tensions acting along the string, inwards at each end. Another type of attachment is a hinge or pivot; the direction of the force at a hinge is not generally known.

Gravitational force, or weight – attracts every object towards the centre of the earth.

Individual forces – commonest are air resistance, wind and driving force of a vehicle.

In any problem look for the type of force that is involved.

⚠ Do not look at the moving object and try to invent forces that are making it move.

Modelling and drawing diagrams

In questions you are often given a picture of a situation and it can be quite complicated.

Do not waste time in copying it; just sketch a simplified working diagram based on using models such as: a person is modelled as a particle (i.e. a point-sized mass) and objects even as large as a car can also be modelled as a particle as long as all the forces acting on it are concurrent. In a diagram a particle can be drawn as ○ or ● or □. An object which has forces acting at different points on it, can be modelled as a block or a rod. Do not worry too much about using a ruler to draw straight lines; on the other hand it does help if circles look right – a selection of coins is useful in an examination.

To model real life you can make some assumptions to simplify the situation. For instance you can assume that:

- if the weight of an object is small compared with other forces acting, it can be ignored and the object is called 'light'.
- the resistance to the motion of an object across a surface can be zero and the surface is called 'smooth'. Conversely, if there is a resistance to motion the surface is called rough. (Note that in both cases it is really the *contact,* rather than the surface, that is rough or smooth.).
- a taut string can have an unalterable length and is called inextensible.
- in general, air resistance to motion can be ignored.

You should be prepared to state the assumptions you make when solving a problem.

Now to return to drawing clear diagrams. If there is only one object, mark all the external forces and any individual forces. It helps to mark force arrows *away* from the object whenever possible, e.g. mark a driving force □→ not →□.

For clarity, when velocity and/or acceleration are to be marked as well as forces, use different arrowheads.

We use:

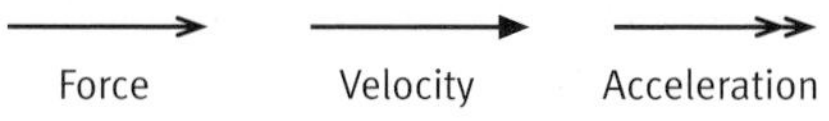

This example shows a vehicle, driving force (D), with acceleration a down a slope, against air resistance (R).

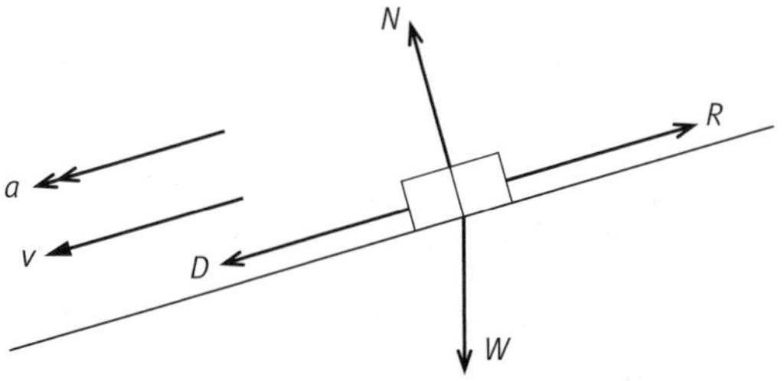

When more than one moveable object is involved, mark both internal and external forces. A separate diagram for each object is essential to show, individually, each one of a pair of internal forces acting on only one object.

It is not worth trying to get away with just one diagram. Make the diagrams big enough to hold all the marked information clearly. This example shows a boy sitting on a trailer that is being towed by a tractor (driving with force D). The first diagram is what might be given in an exam question; then we have three working diagrams, one each for the boy, the trailer and the tractor.

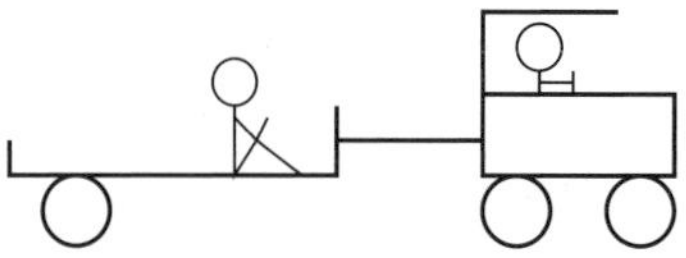

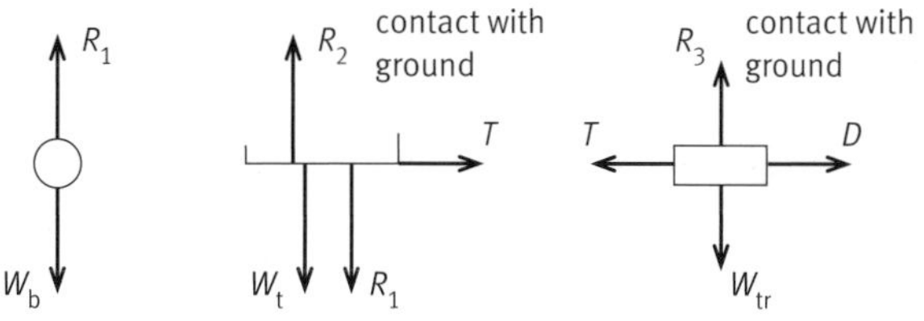

Boy Trailer Tractor

The internal forces are: the normal reactions between the trailer and the boy (R_1), and the tensions at the ends of the towbar (T). Internal forces appear twice, once on each of two separate diagrams.

Examples

In each case a diagram is drawn for each moveable object, showing all forces that act on that object. Velocities and accelerations are also marked where appropriate. These sketches indicate what is acceptable in an exam.

1 A plank of weight W rests against a fixed smooth rail at A, and with one end on rough ground. Note that it is the plank that provides the surface of contact, the rail provides only a *point* of contact, so the normal reaction is perpendicular to the plank. (The surface of contact can always be seen on a diagram as a line that does not end at the point of contact.)

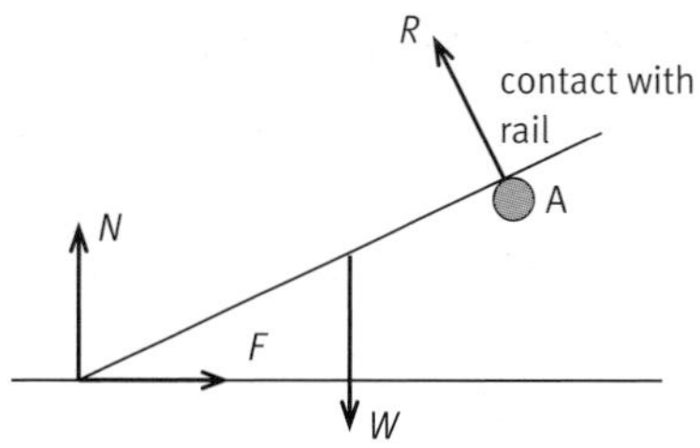

Only the plank is moveable so there are no internal forces.

2 Two identical blocks, A and B, with rough faces, are placed as shown on an inclined rough plane.

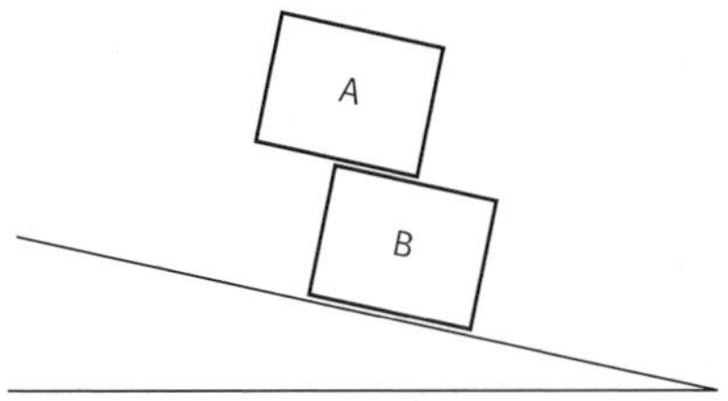

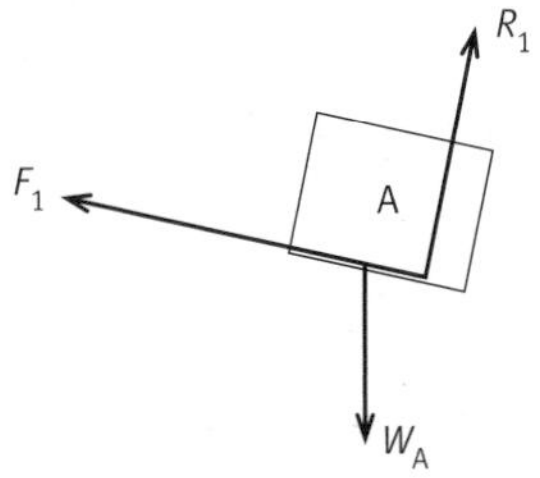

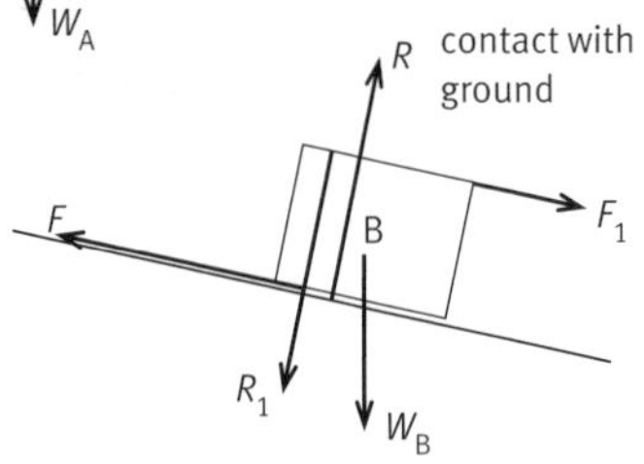

There are internal contact (R_1) and frictional (F_1) forces between the two blocks.

3 A conker is being whirled in a vertical circle. Mark the forces acting when the conker is

a at its lowest point

b halfway up to its highest point.

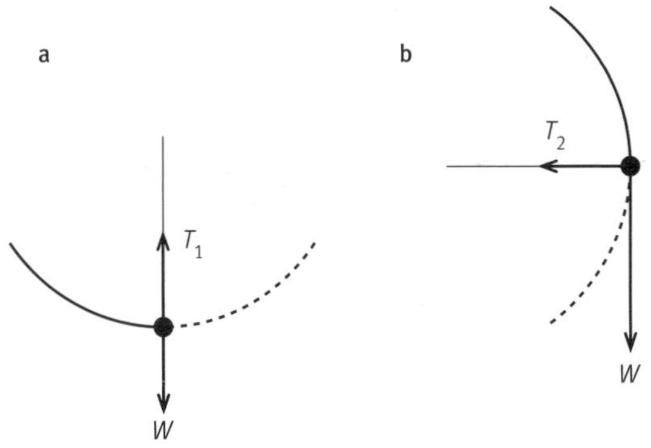

4 A platform, weight W_1, can be raised and lowered by a rope as shown. A man, weight W_2, stands on the platform carrying a briefcase, weight W_3, by means of a chain.

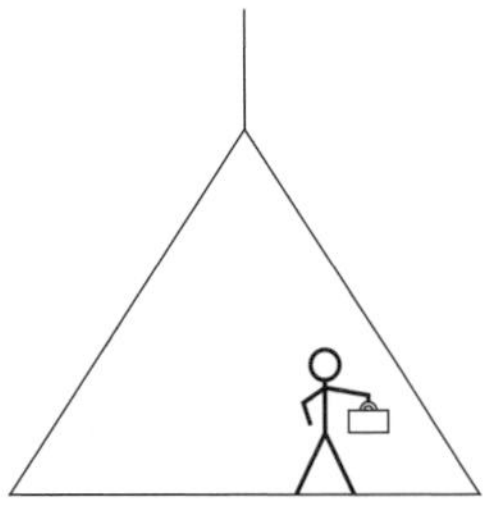

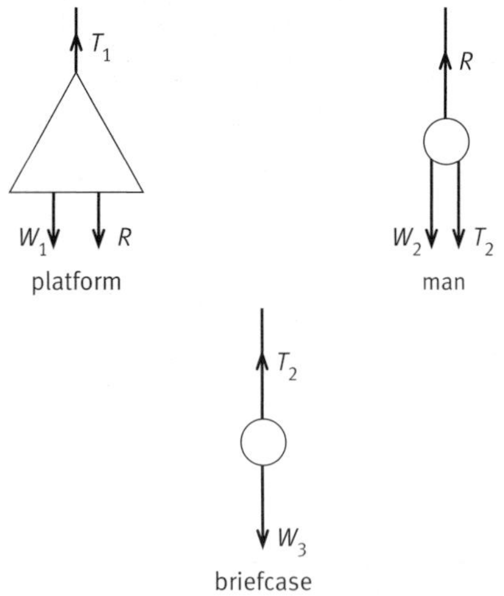

5 A beam is held, hinged to a wall at A and supported by a rope at B.

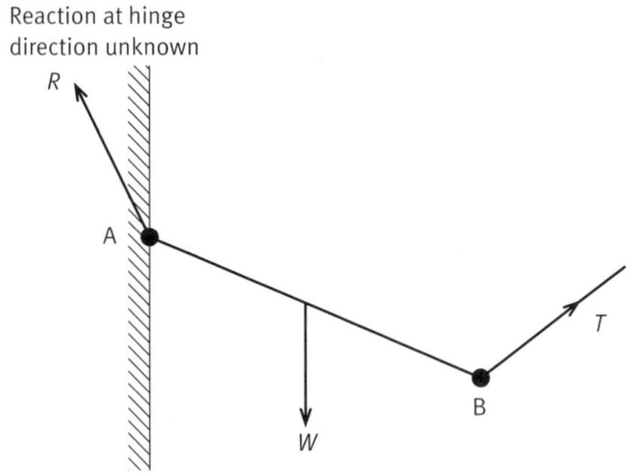

Questions

In each question a situation is described. Draw a working diagram for each moveable part of the system; mark velocity also where appropriate.

1 A vehicle is driving up an incline against a resisting force.

2 A cricket ball that was struck by the batsman, is now moving in the air towards the boundary.

3 A bead threaded onto a smooth wire in the shape of a vertical circle was dislodged from the highest point and is $\frac{3}{4}$ of the way to the lowest point.

4 A window cleaner is standing on the balcony of a flat and is lowering a bucket full of dirty water to the ground by a rope.

5 A sky-diver is falling freely.

6 A parachutist is falling, suspended from his parachute.

Answers

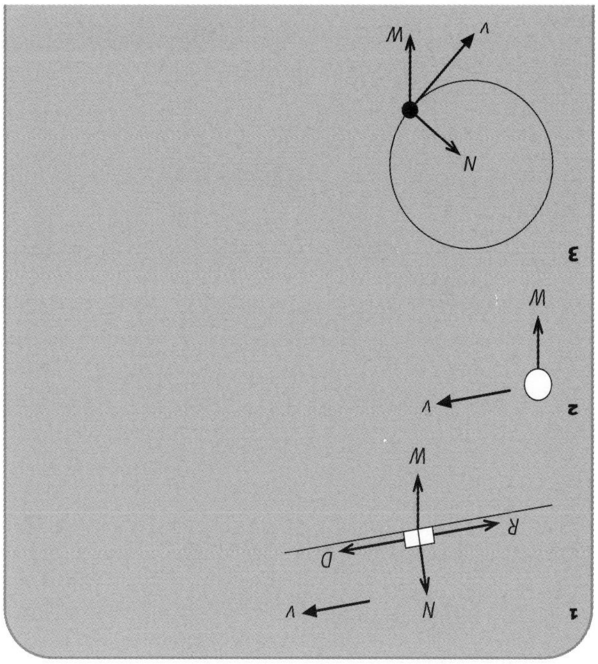

1
N
W
R
D
V
2
W
V
3
W
V
N

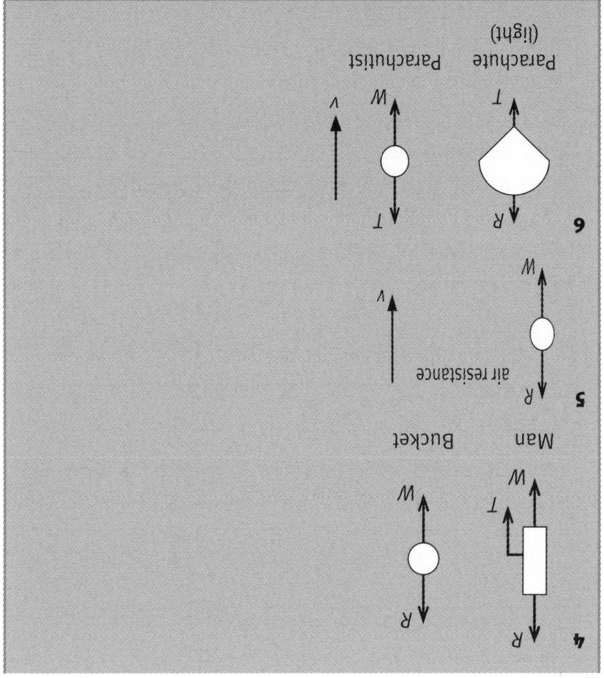

4
R
W
T
Man
R
W
Bucket
5
R
air resistance
W
V
6
R
T
Parachute
(light)
T
W
Parachutist
V

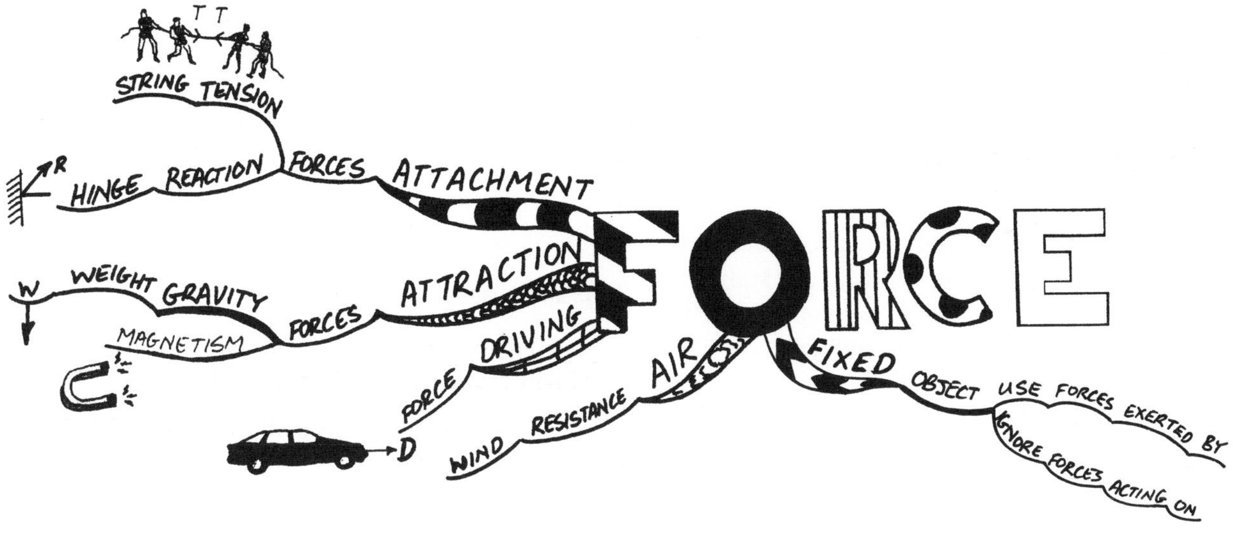

T T
STRING TENSION
R
HINGE REACTION
FORCES
ATTACHMENT
W
WEIGHT GRAVITY
MAGNETISM
FORCES
ATTRACTION
FORCE
FORCE DRIVING
D
WIND RESISTANCE AIR
FIXED OBJECT
USE FORCES EXERTED BY
IGNORE FORCES ACTING ON

PREVIEW

By the end of this topic you will have revised:

- ✔ **how to find the resultant of two perpendicular forces,**
- ✔ **how to resolve a force into two perpendicular components,**
- ✔ **how to find the resultant of a set of coplanar forces,**
- ✔ **how to deal with any vector in the form aj + bj and to find its magnitude and direction,**
- ✔ **how to find the resultant of a set of forces given in ij form,**
- ✔ **that a set of concurrent coplanar forces is in equilibrium if there is no overall force in each of two perpendicular directions,**
- ✔ **understanding when and where frictional forces act,**
- ✔ **the meaning of the coefficient of friction and the angle of friction and the relationship between them.**

Before you start you should:

- know that force is a vector,
- know that the resultant of a set of coplanar forces can be found by drawing the forces, to scale and in order. The line joining the starting point to the end point represents the resultant force in magnitude and direction,
- be able to write down the length of either side of a right-angled triangle *directly* in terms of the hypotenuse and cos or sin of an angle; and be accustomed to using the exact values of sin, cos and tan of 30°, 60°, and 45° and to recall these values from two right-angled triangles, i.e.

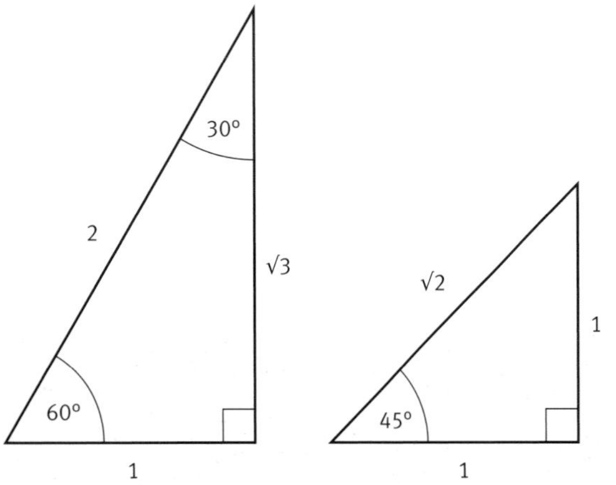

- know that a vector can be expressed in the form $a\mathbf{i} + b\mathbf{j}$ where $\mathbf{i}$ and $\mathbf{j}$ are unit vectors in the directions of Ox and Oy; a and b are the magnitudes of these vectors,
- be familiar with the symbols $\|$ and $\perp$ for parallel and perpendicular.
- know how to solve simultaneous equations.

Finding a resultant algebraically

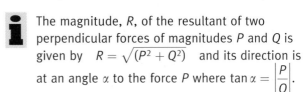

The magnitude, R, of the resultant of two perpendicular forces of magnitudes P and Q is given by $R = \sqrt{(P^2 + Q^2)}$ and its direction is at an angle α to the force P where $\tan\alpha = \left|\frac{P}{Q}\right|$.

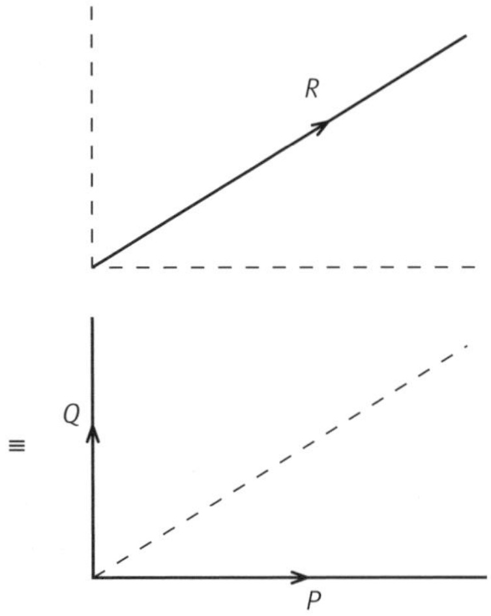

P and Q are the components of R.

The magnitude of a vector $a\mathbf{i} + b\mathbf{j}$ is $\sqrt{a^2 + b^2}$. $a\mathbf{i}$ and $b\mathbf{j}$ are the components of the vector.

For two vectors $a_1\mathbf{i} + b_1\mathbf{j}$ and $a_2\mathbf{i} + b_2\mathbf{j}$ the resultant is the vector $\boldsymbol{R}$ where $\boldsymbol{R} = (a_1 + a_2)\mathbf{i} + (b_1 + b_2)\mathbf{j}$, and $(a_1 + a_2)\mathbf{i}$ and $(b_1 + b_2)\mathbf{j}$ are the components of $\boldsymbol{R}$.

This work applies to any vector quantities, not just to forces.

Perpendicular components of a force

Given a force R at an angle α to the horizontal, the horizontal and vertical components of R are $R\cos\alpha$ and $R\sin\alpha$.

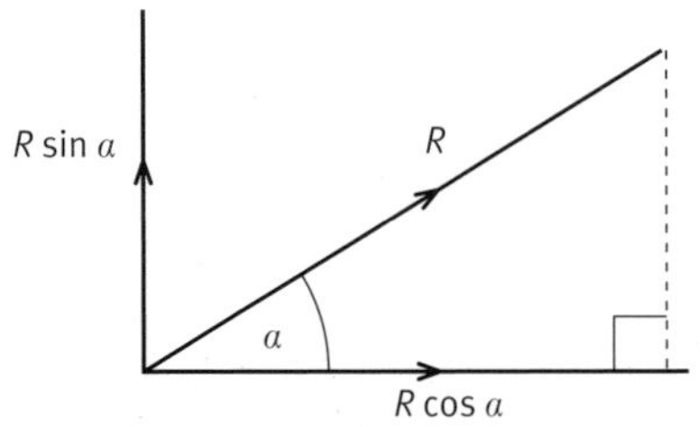

Forces can be resolved (i.e. split up into components) in other directions in the same way.

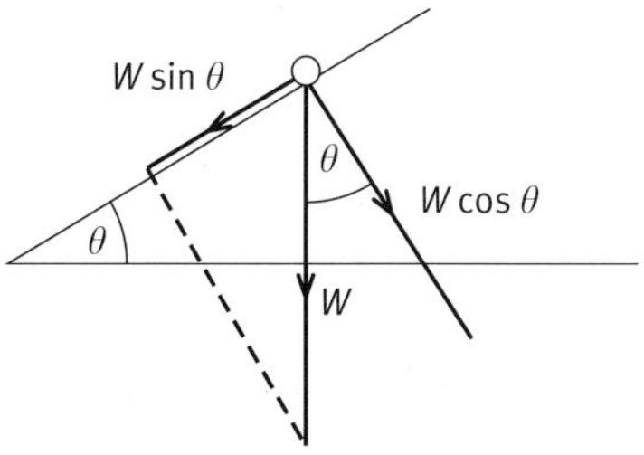

For example, if an object is placed on an inclined plane you could resolve its weight, parallel and perpendicular to the plane. In this example the components are marked on a diagram so their directions are clear. When you write down a component you can use an arrow on the diagram to indicate one direction as positive; then a component in the direction opposite to the arrow is negative.

You can speed up much of the work you do in mechanics if you can resolve forces quickly and accurately. So do practise, if you are not already at top speed.

Questions

1 Resolve each force horizontally and vertically.

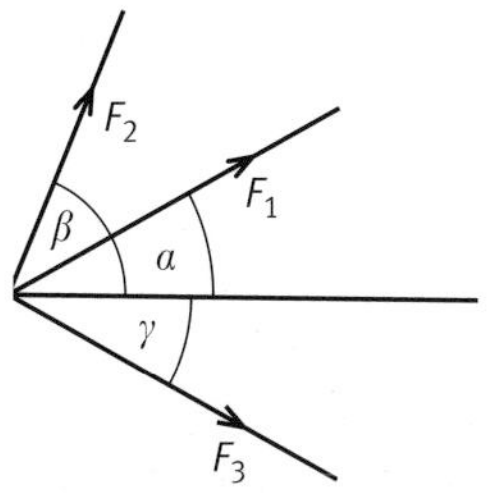

2 Resolve each force

a horizontally and vertically

b parallel and perpendicular to the plane.

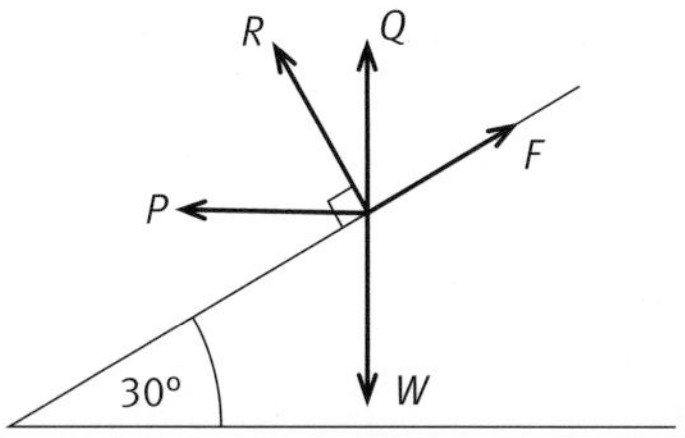

Answers

1 → $F_1 \cos\alpha$, $F_2 \cos\beta$, $F_3 \cos\gamma$; ↑ $F_1 \sin\alpha$, $F_2 \sin\beta$, $-F_3 \sin\gamma$

2a → $\frac{1}{2}\sqrt{3}F$, $-\frac{1}{2}R$, $-P$; ↑ $\frac{1}{2}F$, Q, $\frac{1}{2}\sqrt{3}R$, $-W$.

b ∥, F, $\frac{1}{2}Q$, $-\frac{1}{2}\sqrt{3}P$, $-\frac{1}{2}W$; ⊥, $\frac{1}{2}Q\sqrt{3}$, R, $\frac{1}{2}P$, $-\frac{1}{2}\sqrt{3}W$.

Finding the resultant of more than two coplanar forces

Resolve each force into a pair of perpendicular components in specified directions (often indicated by an arrow, e.g. →, ↑) and collect all the components in each of these two directions. This gives two perpendicular forces (usually denoted by X and Y) that are equivalent to the original set and their resultant is the resultant of the original set. Then the resultant force R is given by

$$R^2 = X^2 + Y^2 \quad \text{and} \quad \tan\alpha = \frac{Y}{X}$$

If expressed in **ij** form, the coefficients of **i** and **j** are the components of the given forces in the directions of the x and y axes, i.e. for a set of forces $a_n\mathbf{i} + b_n\mathbf{j}$ where $n = 1, 2, 3\ldots$, $X = \sum a_n$ and $Y = \sum b_n$.

Example

Find the resultant of the forces shown, giving its magnitude and its direction from the x-axis.

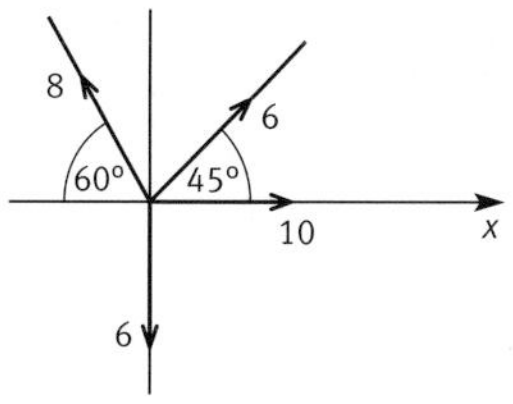

Solution

Resolving gives:

→ $X = 10 + 6\cos 45^\circ - 8\cos 60^\circ = 10.24\ldots$

↑ $Y = 6\sin 45^\circ + 8\sin 60^\circ - 6 = 5.17\ldots$

∴ $R = \sqrt{(10.24\ldots^2 + 5.17\ldots^2)} = 11.5$ (3 sf)

and $\tan\alpha = 5.17\ldots/10.24\ldots \Rightarrow \alpha = 26.8^\circ$ (3 sf)

Questions

In each question find the resultant of the given forces, giving the magnitude and the direction from the x-axis.

1 Forces represented by the vectors $4\mathbf{i} - 3\mathbf{j}$, $-7\mathbf{i} + 6\mathbf{j}$, $2\mathbf{i} + 9\mathbf{j}$ and $6\mathbf{i}$.

2

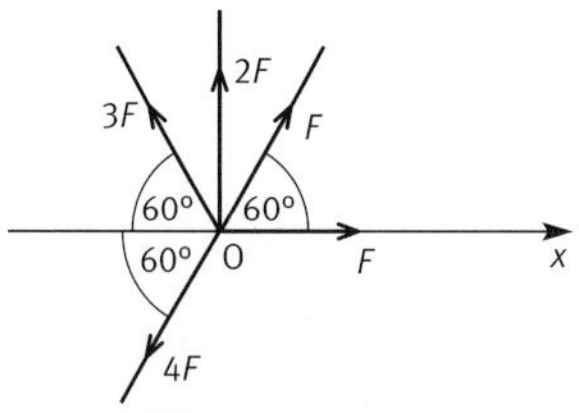

Answers

1 $5\mathbf{i} + 12\mathbf{j}$; 13N at 67.4° to Ox

2 $2\sqrt{2}F$ N at 135° to Ox.

Equilibrium of concurrent forces

A set of concurrent coplanar forces is *in equilibrium* when the resultant is zero.

- The resultant is zero if the sum of the components in each of two perpendicular directions is zero and you can use this fact to find the value of any unknown force in the set.
- If a set of forces $a_n\mathbf{i} + b_n\mathbf{j}$ where $n = 1, 2, 3, \ldots$ is in equilibrium, then $\sum a_n = 0$ and $\sum b_n = 0$.

Example

Forces of magnitudes 3 N, 2 N and 3 N act along AB, AC and DA respectively in a square ABCD. A fourth force, of magnitude F N, acts through A and the forces are in equilibrium. Find the magnitude and direction of the fourth force.

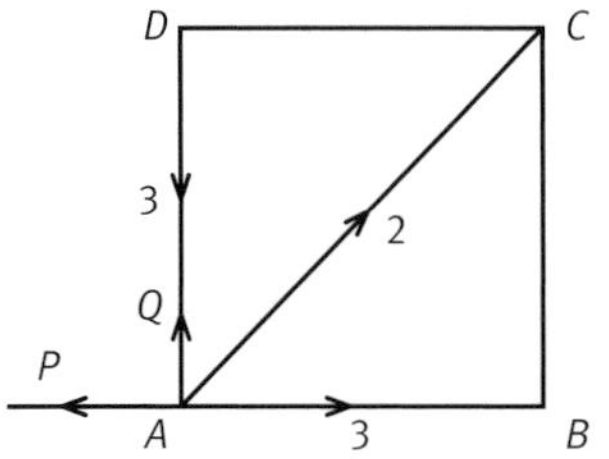

Solution

The direction of the fourth force is unknown so the easiest way to represent it is by its components P and Q as shown. Then F is the resultant of P and Q, in a direction making an angle θ with BA produced where $\tan\theta = \dfrac{Q}{P}$.

In equilibrium, $X = 0$ and $Y = 0$.

Resolving gives:

$\rightarrow \quad 3 + 2\cos 45^\circ - P = 0 \quad \Rightarrow \quad P = 4.41\ldots$

$\uparrow \quad 2\sin 45^\circ - 3 + Q = 0 \quad \Rightarrow \quad Q = 1.58\ldots$

$F = \sqrt{(4.41\ldots^2 + 1.58\ldots^2)}$

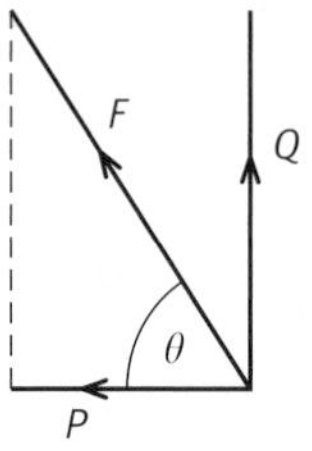

and $\tan\theta = \dfrac{1.58\ldots}{4.41\ldots}$

F is 4.69 N at 19.8° to BA produced (3 sf).

Questions

1 Find the magnitude of the resultant of this set of coplanar forces and the angle made by the resultant with the force of 7 N.

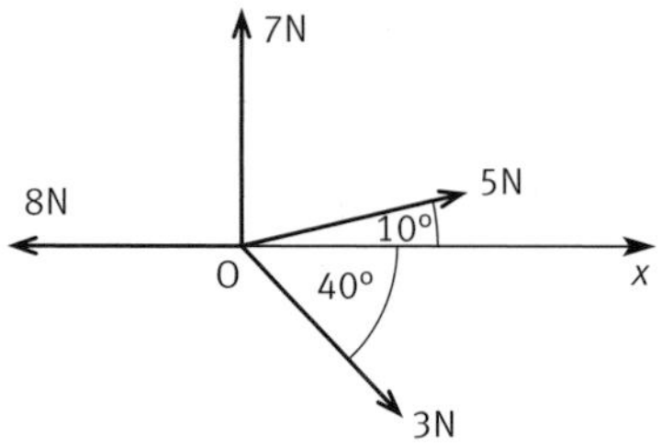

Hence state the magnitude and direction of the force P N that reduces the given set to equilibrium.

2 Three forces, measured in newtons, are represented by $2\mathbf{i} + 6\mathbf{j}$, $7\mathbf{i} - 8\mathbf{j}$ and $p\mathbf{i} + q\mathbf{j}$. Find p and q if

a the resultant of the three forces is $10\mathbf{i} + 2\mathbf{j}$.

b the resultant is parallel to the vector $\mathbf{i}$.

c the three forces are in equilibrium.

3 Forces act in a rectangle ABCD with sides $3a$ and $4a$, as shown. A fourth force, acting through A, reduces the system to equilibrium. Find the magnitude and the direction relative to AB of the fourth force.

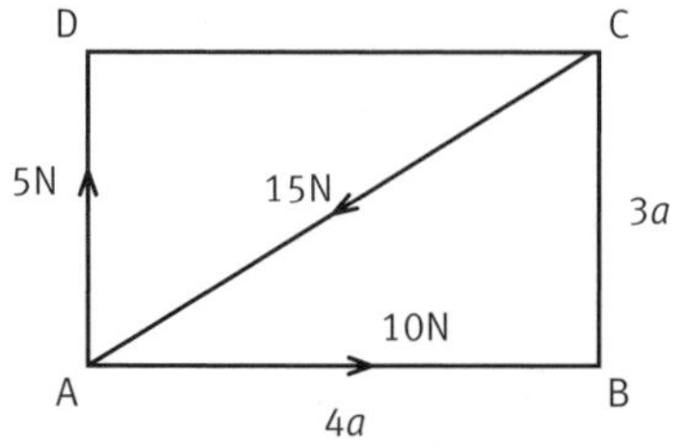

Answers

1 5.99 N at 7.5° to 7 N, on left, 5.99 N at 172.5° clockwise from 7 N.

2a $p = 1, q = 4$ **b** $q = 2$, p can have any value except -9.

c $p = -9, q = 2$

3 $2\sqrt{5}$ N at 63.4° to AB.

Friction

When two solid bodies are in contact there may be a tendency for one or both of them to move across the surface of the other, e.g. a block on an inclined plane. If they are in rough contact a pair of equal and opposite frictional forces act, resisting the motion between them. One frictional force acts on each surface, along the surface, in the direction to oppose motion (or the tendency to move). Frictional forces acting on fixed objects (external forces) are ignored.

This block A rests in rough contact with a fixed horizontal plane and is pulled by a force P.
The plane exerts a frictional force F on A, along the plane in the direction opposite to P.

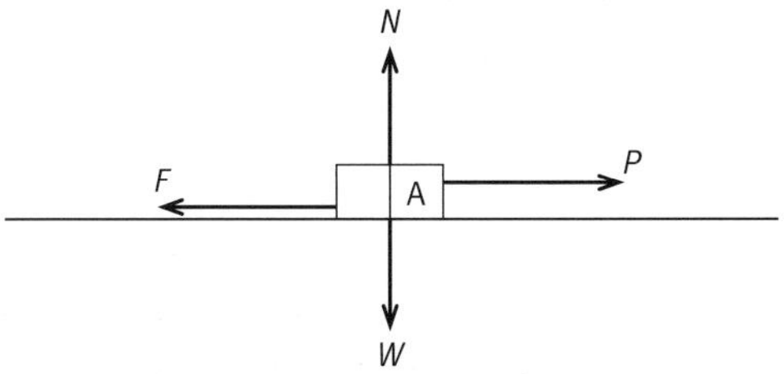

The value of a frictional force

The magnitude of a frictional force is equal and *opposite* to the force(s) in the direction of the tendency to move. Friction increases as these forces increase, up to a limiting value (limiting friction), when the body is just in equilibrium (i.e. just about to slide). If the resultant force tending to produce motion increases further, the body moves and, once it is moving, the frictional force maintains a constant value. (In fact, as you will know if you also study physics, this value is slightly lower than the limiting value when motion is just about to start but in A Level Mathematics we ignore this small difference.)

Coefficient of friction

The magnitude of the *limiting* frictional force is given by μR where μ is the coefficient of friction and R is the normal reaction between the objects. For two particular objects in contact, μ is constant.

$F = \mu R$ only when motion is on the point of starting, i.e. when equilibrium is limiting, or if motion is taking place.

A frictional force F is such that $0 \leqslant F \leqslant \mu R$. When friction is limiting, the resultant of F and R makes an angle λ with R where

λ is called the *angle of friction*

and $\tan \lambda = \mu$.

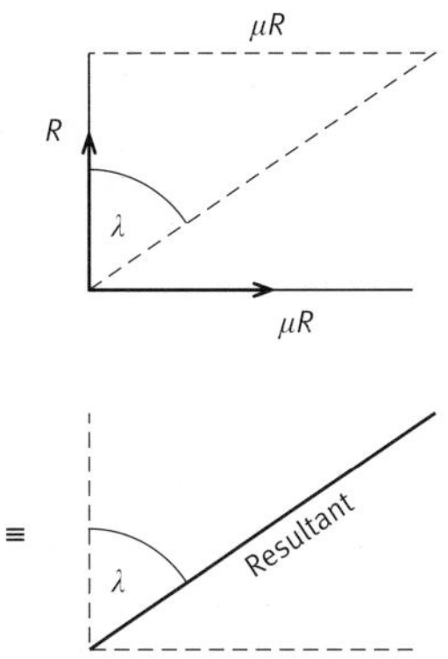

Example

A block of weight 17 N rests on a rough plane inclined at 20° to the horizontal and is just about to slip down.

a Find the coefficient of friction between the block and the plane.
b Explain the relationship between μ and the angle of inclination to the plane.

Solution

When an object is in equilibrium on a rough inclined plane it has a tendency to slip down the plane and friction opposes this tendency. Solving problems like this involves resolving forces in two perpendicular directions and it is usually best to choose the direction of the incline and the perpendicular to it.

a The block is about to slip downwards so friction is limiting (i.e. $F = \mu R$) and acts up the plane.

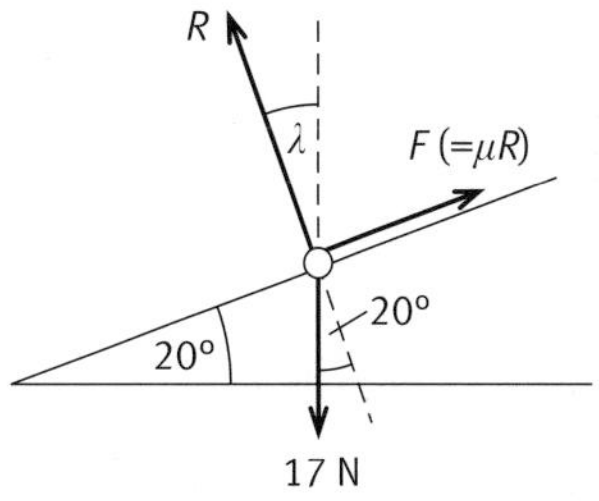

Resolving:

$\nearrow \quad \mu R - 17 \sin 20^\circ = 0$ [1]

$\nwarrow \quad R - 17 \cos 20^\circ = 0$ [2]

$$\frac{\mu R}{R} = \frac{17 \sin 20^\circ}{17 \cos 20^\circ}$$

$\Rightarrow \quad \mu = \tan 20^\circ = 0.36$ (2 sf)

b The angle between R and the vertical is λ and it is also equal to the angle of inclination of the plane. $\tan 20^\circ = \tan \lambda = \mu$.

This is true in general, i.e.

when a particle is in limiting equilibrium on a plane inclined at α to the horizontal, and no other external force is acting other than weight,

$$\mu = \tan \alpha$$

Questions

1 A crate of weight 120 N resting on a rough horizontal plane is pulled by a horizontal rope until it is just about to move. The tension in the rope is then 42 N; what is the coefficient of friction?

2 The diagram shows a block of weight 15 N, supported on a rough plane by a force P N acting up the plane. The plane is inclined at 30° to the horizontal and the coefficient of friction is 0.4.

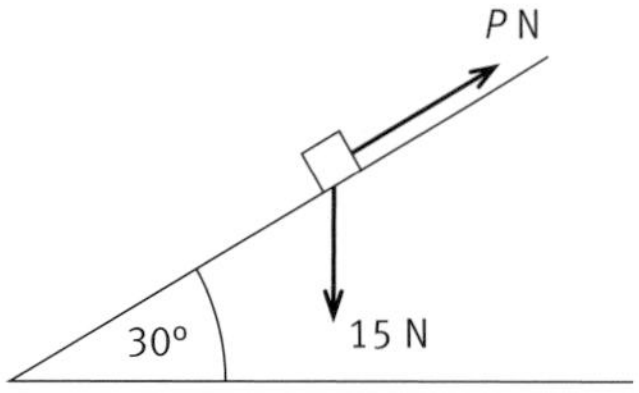

Find the value of P when the block is just about to slide

a down the plane **b** up the plane.

3 A book rests on the hinged lid of a desk and the lid is gradually opened. The coefficient of friction between the lid and the book is 0.35. Find the greatest angle through which the lid can be raised before the book slips.

4 A particle of weight W is placed on a ramp whose inclination to the horizontal is adjustable. When the surface is at 25° to the horizontal the particle is on the point of slipping down. If the angle is increased to 40° find the force needed to prevent the particle from slipping if the force is applied

a parallel to the surface of the ramp

b horizontally.

Answers

1 0.35 **2a** 2.30 **b** 12.7 **3** 19.3°
4a 0.29W **b** 0.27W.

Take a break

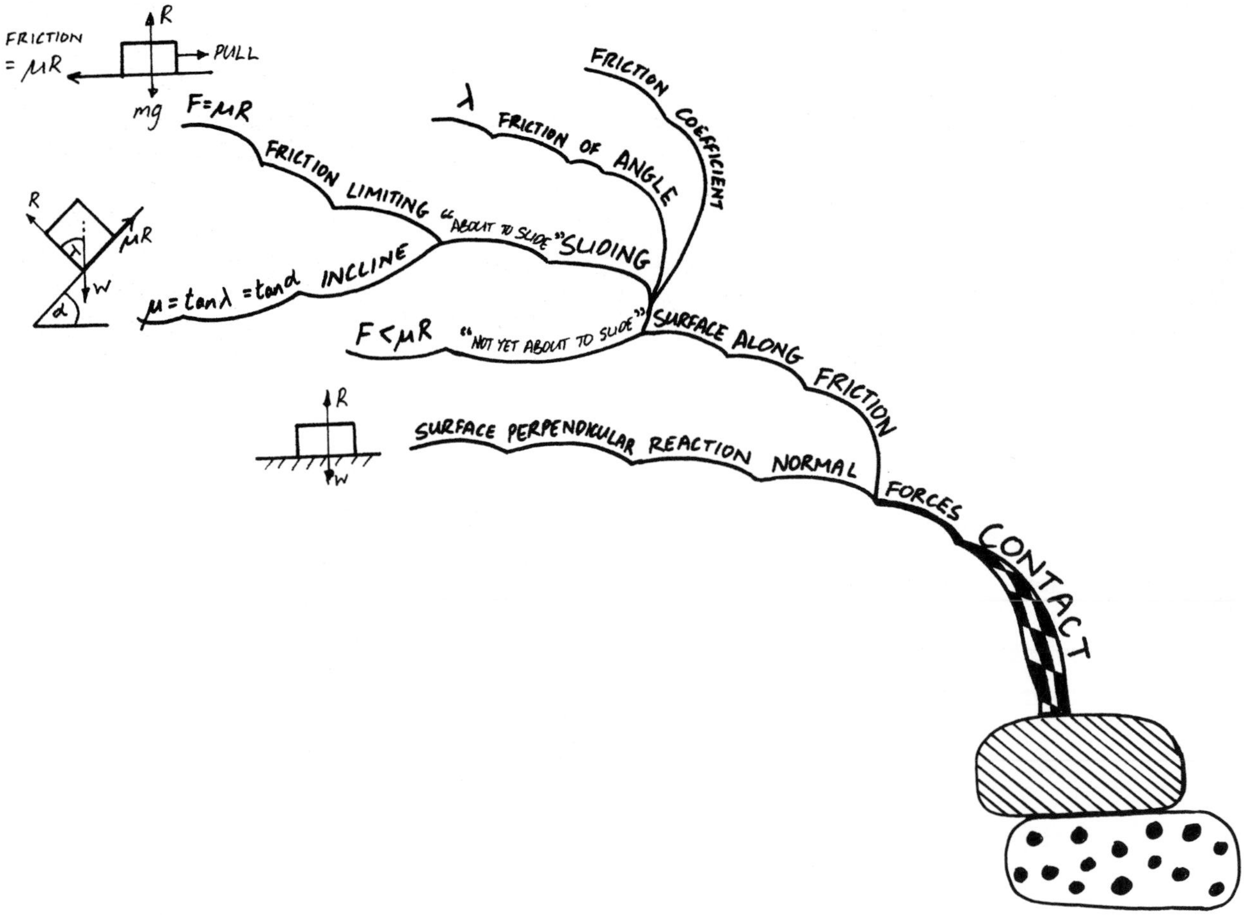

Review

1 The diagram shows a stone of weight W which was thrown into the air.

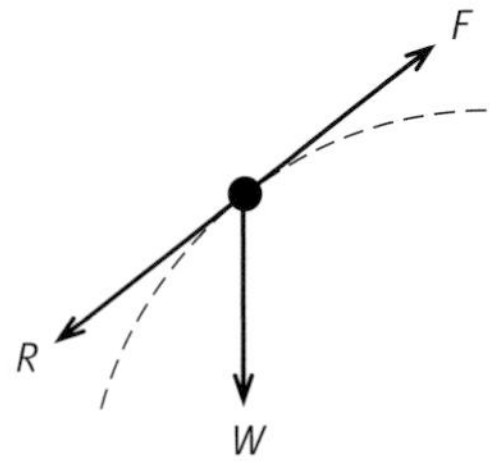

There is air resistance of magnitude R. One of the forces marked is incorrect.
State which one it is, giving a reason.

2 A load L of weight w is placed on the floor of a crate C weighing W that is being hauled up by a vertical rope. On separate diagrams mark all the forces that act on the load and on the crate.

3 A block B, of weight W, is placed on the surface of a rough plane inclined at an angle θ to the horizontal.
The coefficient of friction between block and plane is $\frac{1}{2}$.
If the block is on the point of slipping down the plane find $\tan\theta$.
If a force P is then applied to the block, up and parallel to the incline, find the value of P (in terms of W) if B is on the point of sliding up the plane.

Answers

1 F; there is nothing to cause a force in the direction of motion.

2

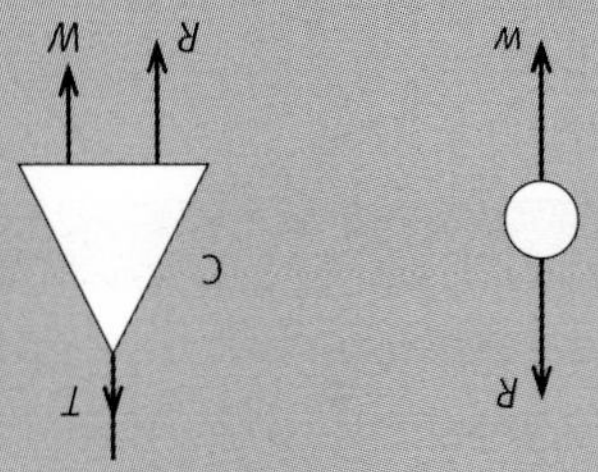

3 $\tan\theta = \frac{1}{2}$; $P = 0.89W$.

PREVIEW

By the end of this topic you will have revised:

- ✔ **the equations used for motion with constant acceleration,**
- ✔ **Newton's laws of motion and how to use them,**
- ✔ **how to tackle problems on a single object, or connected objects, when the acceleration is constant.**

Before you start you should:

- know that for a graph of displacement against time, the gradient represents velocity,
- know that for a graph of velocity against time, the gradient represents acceleration and the area under the graph represents the displacement at the end of the time interval,
- understand clearly the difference between the distance from A to B (the total ground covered) and displacement of B from A (the distance in a specified direction from A at any instant); displacement is a vector while distance is scalar.

TEST YOURSELF

If you have difficulty with any part of the following questions, refer to your early notes or a GCSE Higher text book.

1 A rail shuttle takes 3 minutes to travel from the Check-in Section to Terminal 2. The acceleration and retardation in the first and last sections of the journey are each approximately constant.
Here is the v/t graph for the whole journey.

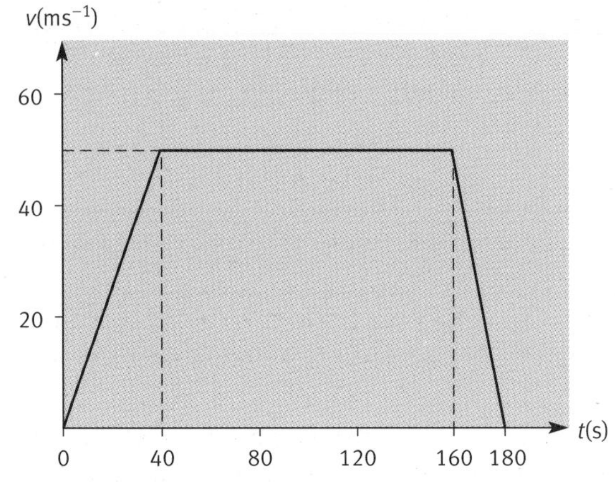

a) What is the acceleration during the first 40 seconds?

b) What is the retardation during the last 20 seconds?

c) How far does the shuttle travel while accelerating?

d) What happens between 40 s and 160 s from the start of the journey?

e) Find the total distance travelled.

2 When $t = 0$ a particle P passes through the origin O with speed $10\,\text{ms}^{-1}$ and travels along the x-axis with an acceleration of $-4\,\text{ms}^{-2}$. Sketch a v/t graph for the first 5 seconds of motion and use it to answer these questions.

a) What is P's speed after (i) 2 s (ii) 3 s?

b) What happens when $t = 2.5$ s?

c) What is the displacement of P from O after 5 seconds?

d) What distance does P travel in the first 5 seconds?

Answers

1a $1.25\,\text{ms}^{-2}$ **b** $2.5\,\text{ms}^{-2}$ **c** 1000 m
d travels at constant speed, $50\,\text{ms}^{-1}$ **e** 7.5 km.

2

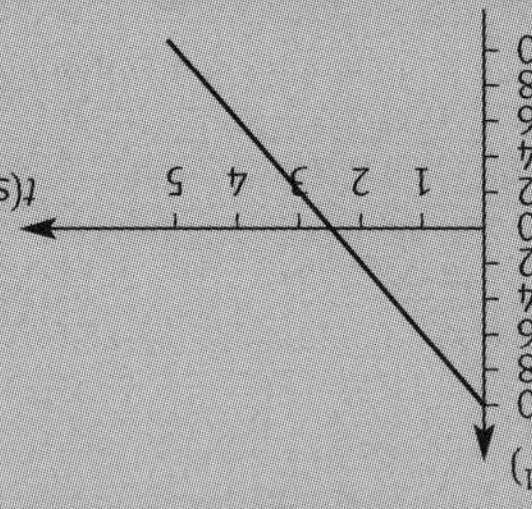

a i $2\,\text{ms}^{-1}$ **ii** $2\,\text{ms}^{-1}$ (opposite direction)
b the particle is instantaneously at rest and direction of motion reverses.
c zero
d 25 m (12.5 out and 12.5 back)

Motion in a straight line with constant acceleration

The usual symbols used for motion in a straight line with constant acceleration are:

initial velocity, u**, final velocity,** v
These are measured with respect to a specified positive direction.

acceleration, a or f
This is positive when velocity is increasing and negative when velocity is decreasing. Negative acceleration is also called retardation or deceleration. Note that the magnitude of an acceleration is also called acceleration.

displacement, s
This is the distance in a specified direction from a given starting point.

i The symbol t is used for a **length of time** measured from a given moment, i.e. t is a time interval.

The quantities above are related in several equations:

- $v = u + at$
- $s = \frac{1}{2}(u + v)t$
  (i.e. s = average speed × time)
- $s = ut + \frac{1}{2}at^2$ and $s = vt - \frac{1}{2}at^2$
- $v^2 = u^2 + 2as$

Remember that each formula contains only four symbols so, in simple problems, listing three given quantities plus the required one usually makes it easy to choose the right equation.

When problems involve several sections of motion, a graph can often help. If it is not possible to calculate the value of any unknown quantity directly from just one section, find expressions from two or more sections in terms of a common quantity.

Example

A monorail train takes 80 seconds to travel on a straight section of track from station P to station Q. It accelerates from P at $a\,\text{ms}^{-2}$ to a speed of $24\,\text{ms}^{-1}$ and maintains this speed for 40 seconds. It then decelerates uniformly to rest at Q at a rate of $2a\,\text{ms}^{-2}$. Find

a the value of a
b the distance from P to Q.

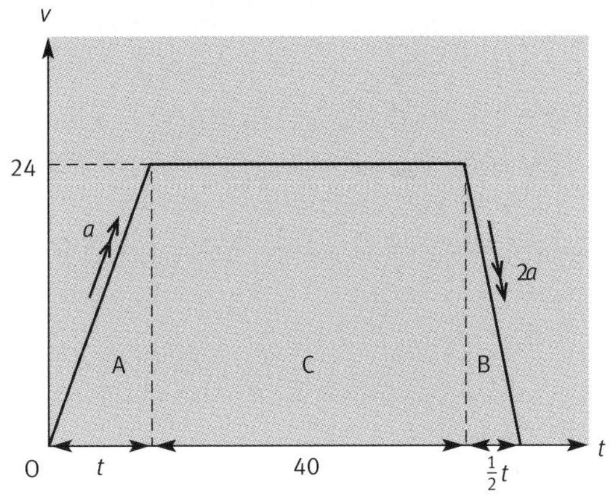

Solution

If s and t are the distance covered and time taken in section A, the distance and time in section B are $\frac{1}{2}s$ and $\frac{1}{2}t$ (because the gradient in A is twice the gradient in B and the height of the two triangles is the same).

In section A only u and v are known and this does not allow anything else to be evaluated. But the total time is known so use expressions for the time in each section.

a In A, $v = u + at$ gives $24 = 0 + at$
$\Rightarrow \quad t = 24/a$; hence the time in B is $12/a$.
Time in C is 40 and the total time is 80,
i.e. $24/a + 12/a + 40 = 80$
The acceleration is $0.9\,\text{ms}^{-2}$.

b In A, $v^2 = u^2 + 2as$ gives $24^2 = 2(0.9)s$
$\Rightarrow$ distance in A is 320 m
and distance in B is 160 m.
$\therefore \quad$ total distance $= (160 + 24 \times 40 + 320)$ m.
The distance from P to Q is 1440 m.

Questions

1 An athletic thief, running at $6\,\text{ms}^{-1}$, snatches a bag from a cyclist who has just stopped riding to speak to a friend. The thief hopes to reach a known hiding place 40 m further on. The cyclist immediately pedals after the thief, accelerating at $2.1\,\text{ms}^{-2}$. Will he catch the thief, and, if he does, after how long? (If he does, the thief and the cyclist will be in the same place at the same time.)

2 A motorcyclist tests his machine on a track where the times taken to cover successive distances can be recorded. He passes the first marker A when $t = 0$, three seconds later he passes B and after a further two seconds passes C. The distances between the markers are: AB = 50 m, BC = 80m. Assuming the acceleration a to be constant find the value of a and the speeds at B and C.
(Use one section from A to B and the other from A to C, using u for the speed at A in each case)

Answers

1 Yes, after 5.7 s
2 $\frac{28}{3}$ (9.33) ms^{-2}, $v_B = \frac{92}{3}$ (30.7) ms^{-1}, $v_C = \frac{148}{3}$ (49.3) ms^{-1}.

Motion under gravity

The acceleration due to gravity is constant and is denoted by $g\,\text{ms}^{-2}$. The value of g varies very slightly at different places on the earth's surface but 9.8 is the value generally used. The acceleration due to gravity is always vertically downwards so if the upward direction is taken as positive, the upward acceleration is $-g$. (This may happen in a problem where the initial motion is vertically upwards.) The description 'a body is falling freely under gravity' means that no force other than gravity is acting on the body.

Example

A ball is thrown vertically upwards from ground level, at 26 ms^{-1} and moves freely under gravity. Using $g = 9.8$ find, to 2 significant figures,

a the velocity after (i) 2 s (ii) 4 s,

b the time the ball takes to hit the ground and the distance it has travelled in this time.

Solution

a u, t and a are known and v is wanted.

i $v = u + at \quad \Rightarrow \quad v = 26 + (-9.8)2$

$\Rightarrow \quad v = 6.4$,

i.e. speed is 6.4 ms^{-1} upwards.

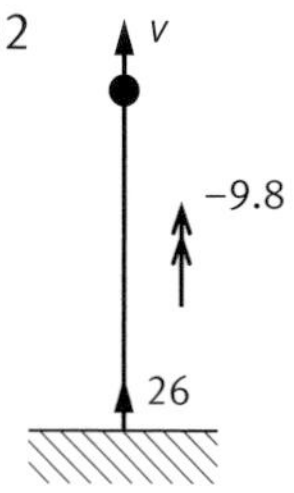

ii $v = -13.2$,

i.e. speed is 13 ms^{-1} downwards (2 sf).

b When it hits the ground $s = 0$

$s = ut + \frac{1}{2}at^2$ gives $0 = 26t + \frac{1}{2}(-9.8)t^2$

$t(26 - 4.9t) = 0 \quad \Rightarrow \quad t = 0$ (start) or 5.3...

The ball hits the ground after 5.3 s (2 sf).

At this time the displacement is zero but the distance travelled is twice the upward journey.

For the upward distance, $v^2 - u^2 = 2as$ gives

$0 - 26^2 = 2(-9.8)s \quad \Rightarrow \quad s = 34.48...$

Total distance travelled is 69 m (2 sf).

Questions

(Take $g = 10\ ms^{-2}$)

1 A ball is dropped from a height of 10 m. When it hits the ground it bounces but its speed is halved. Find the height to which it then rises.

2 A hovering helicopter drops a load P of mass 10 kg. Two seconds later it drops another load Q of mass 20 kg. Assuming no wind or air resistance, decide whether

a if the helicopter is high enough, Q lands before P

b P and Q land at the same time

c Q lands two seconds after P

d Q lands less than 2 seconds after P.

Answers

1 2.5 m

2a no, **b** no, **c** yes, **d** no

(The time for every drop is the same as it depends only on the height and g.)

Take a break

Newton's laws of motion

Before the days of Sir Isaac Newton, there was little understanding of the physical behaviour of everyday objects. In his Laws of Motion, Newton gave a simple, but revolutionary, explanation of forces, motion and the relationship between them.

The first law

A body will continue in its state of rest or uniform motion in a straight line unless a force acts on it.

This means that:

When an object is at rest, or its velocity is constant, there can be no resultant force acting on it and it is therefore in equilibrium. Conversely, if no resultant force acts on the body, the body is at rest or moving with uniform velocity.

If an object's motion is *changing* (either in speed or direction), a resultant force must be acting.

The second law

If a force acts on a body of constant mass, the acceleration produced is proportional to the force, i.e.

$F = ka$ where k is a constant of proportion.

When the unit of force (the newton, N) is defined as the amount of force needed to give a mass of 1 kg an acceleration of 1 ms^{-2}, the equation becomes

$F = ma$.

This is the *basic equation of motion*.

You can use the form $F = ma$ provided that the units are consistent, i.e. kg, ms^{-2} and N.

As F and a are both vector quantities, the force and the acceleration are always in the same direction.

All objects falling freely have the same acceleration, represented by $g\ ms^{-2}$ and this is caused by the weight of the object. Using $F = ma$, it follows that the weight of an object of mass m is mg.

The third law

This law states that forces between solid objects occur in equal and opposite pairs (i.e. action and reaction are equal and opposite). We used this property freely in Mechanics 1 and 2 as it is fundamental to the marking of forces on a diagram.

Newton's three laws are the basis for solving nearly all problems in mechanics. You use the third law to identify, and draw, the forces that are acting on each element of a system. When the resultant force has been found you apply the first law, either to a state of equilibrium or to motion in a straight line. Then, in the case of motion, the second law gives the link between that resultant force and the acceleration it produces. It also shows that, perpendicular to the direction of motion, the sum of the force components is zero.

Solving practical problems

The solution of most practical problems depends upon forming a mathematical model in which, unless it is otherwise stated:

- objects (masses, loads, people, vehicles, etc) are considered as particles
- there is no air resistance
- strings are light and inextensible
- there is no resistance from smooth surfaces, pulleys, etc.

Practical problems include approximations due to modelling and you can often take 10 as being an appropriate degree of accuracy for the value of g, and give answers to 2 significant figures, but

⚠ always check the instructions given by your Examining Board.

Example

A cyclist makes a trial run over a straight track of length 200 m. Starting from rest, he exerts a constant driving force of P N and his speed at the end of the track is 10 ms^{-1}. The combined mass of the cyclist and his bicycle is 80 kg and air resistance is negligible.

Solution

The driving force is constant so the acceleration is also constant. You cannot find P until you know the acceleration, which you find from the motion data.

$u = 0$, $v = 10$, $s = 200$ and a is wanted.
Using $v^2 = u^2 + 2as$ gives $a = \frac{1}{4}$,
i.e. the acceleration is $\frac{1}{4}$ ms^{-2}.

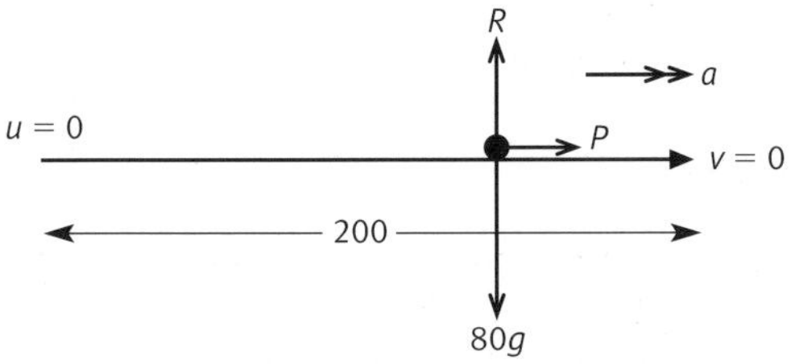

The using $F = ma$ $\rightarrow$ gives $P = 80 \times \frac{1}{4} = 20$.
The cyclist's driving force is 20 N.

Example

A car of mass 1250 kg is driving at maximum speed along a horizontal stretch of road against resisting forces totalling 1100 N. What is the driving force exerted by the car? The car then begins to descend an incline of gradient 1 in 20. Assuming that the resistance and the driving force are initially unchanged, find the acceleration just as the car begins to drive down the slope.

Solution

Model the car as a particle.

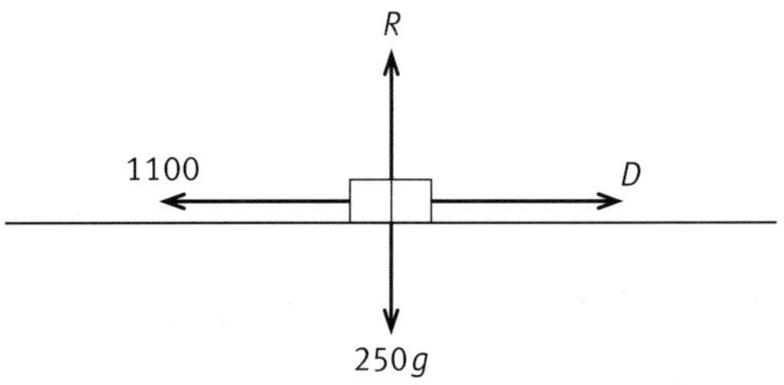

At maximum speed there is no acceleration, so the resultant force acting on the car is zero.
In the direction of motion $D - 1100 = 0$
$\Rightarrow$ the driving force is 1100 N.

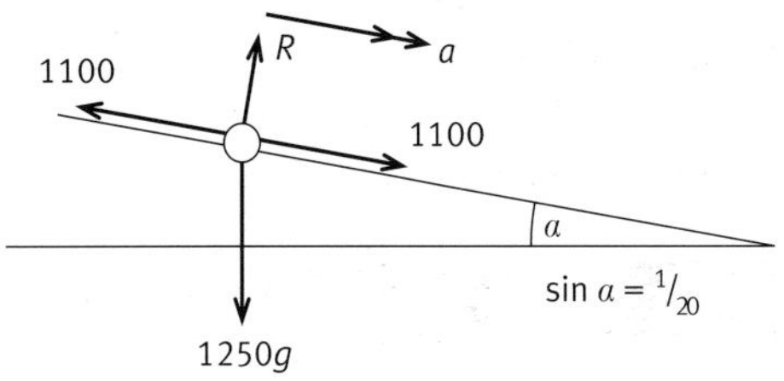

Using $F = ma$ down the slope gives
$1100 + 1250g \sin \alpha - 1100 = 1250a$
$\Rightarrow 1250\ (10)(\frac{1}{20}) = 1250a.$
So the acceleration is $\frac{1}{2}$ ms^{-2}.

⚠ Although units are not always inserted with the quantities on the diagrams and in the text, the correct unit must always be given in the answer.

Example

A girl is using a rope, held parallel to a slope, to pull her sledge up the slope which is inclined at 25° to the horizontal. The mass of the sledge is 15 kg and the coefficient of friction between the sledge and the snow-covered surface is 0.2. Find the tension in the rope to 2 sf, taking g as 10, if the sledge is pulled

a at a steady speed
b with an acceleration of 0.5 ms^{-2}.

Solution

a At a steady speed the acceleration is zero so the resultant force is zero.

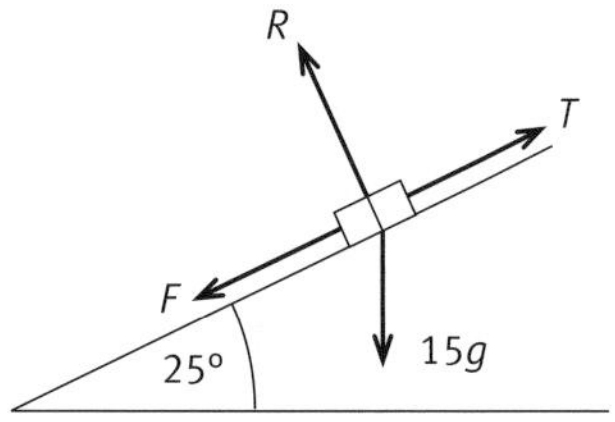

Resolving // to the plane ↗

$$T - F - 150\sin 25^\circ = 0 \qquad (g = 10)$$

⊥ to plane ↖

$$R = 150\cos 25^\circ = 0$$

$\Rightarrow \quad R = 135.9\ldots$

also $F = \mu R = 27.1\ldots$

$\therefore \quad T = 27.1\ldots + 150\sin 25^\circ = 90.6\ldots$

The tension is 91 N (2 sf).

b

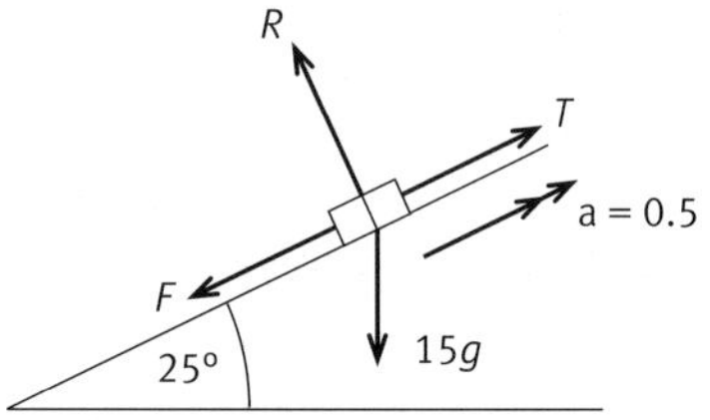

Resolving ⊥ to the plane ↖

$$R - 150\cos 25^\circ = 0 \quad \Rightarrow \quad R = 135.9\ldots$$

Using Newton's law up the plane

$$T - F - 150\sin 25^\circ = 150a = 150(0.5)$$

Again $\quad F = \mu R = 27.1$

$\Rightarrow \quad T - 27.1 - 63.4 = 75 \quad \Rightarrow \quad T = 165.5$

The tension is 170 N (2 sf).

Questions

1 A particle of mass 0.3 kg is moving down a rough plane inclined at 30° to the horizontal. Its speed at a point A is 1 ms^{-1} and A is 1.6 m from the foot B of the incline. If the coefficient of friction is $\frac{1}{4}$, find the speed of the particle at B and the time taken to go from A to B.

2 A girl, whose mass is 42 kg, is running at a steady speed of 4 ms^{-1} along a level road against a headwind of strength 11 N. When the road changes direction she finds that the wind has increased to 14 N. She carries on exerting the same force as before but after t seconds her speed has decreased to 2.8 ms^{-1}. Find the value of t and the distance the girl has covered in this time.

Answers

1 3.17 ms^{-1}, 0.77 s. **2** $t = 16.8$ s, $s = 57.1$ m

Take a break

Connected particles

You can use Newton's Laws to solve problems about bodies that are connected. The connection can be rigid, e.g. the tow-bar between a car and a caravan, or it can be flexible, e.g. a string or rope. The tow-bar exerts a tension inward at each end, acting on the object it is attached to at that end. A string connecting two particles may pass over a pulley. Each side of the string exerts a tension acting inward at each end, one tension acting on the particle and the other on the pulley. Further, if the pulley is smooth, the tensions on both sides of it are equal. The accelerations of the two particles are equal in magnitude.

Example

Two particles, A, mass 3 kg, and B, mass 8 kg, are linked by a light inextensible string hanging over a smooth pulley. If the system is released from rest find the acceleration of each particle and the tension in the string.

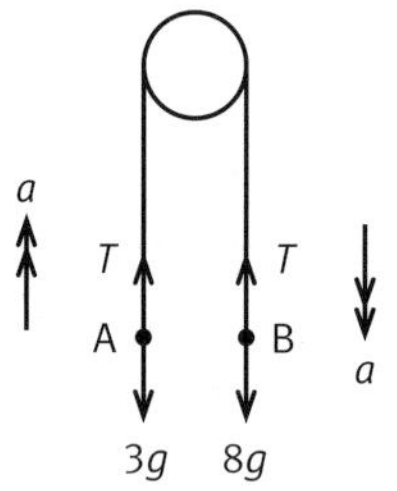

Solution

Using $F = ma$ for each particle separately gives

For A ↑	$T - 3g = 3a$	[1]
For B ↓	$8g - T = 8a$	[2]

Adding these equations gives $a = 5g/11$

Then $T = 3(a + g) = 48g/11$

The acceleration of each particle is $5g/11$ ms^{-2}

And the tension in the string is $48g/11$ N.

Note that the force exerted by the string on the pulley is $2T$, i.e. $96g/11$ N.

In some problems like the one above, one particle may be brought suddenly to rest when it hits the floor.

Example

Two small objects, A and B, each of mass m, are connected by a light inextensible string passing over a smooth pulley at the top of a smooth plane and are held as shown in the diagram.

They are released from rest and B hits the floor after 1 second. Find, in terms of g,

a the acceleration of the particles while they are both moving

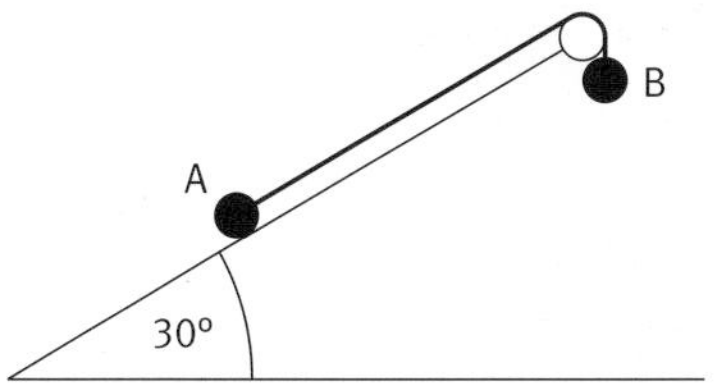

b B's speed when it hits the floor

c how much further up the slope A travels before coming to rest, assuming that it does not reach the pulley.

Solution

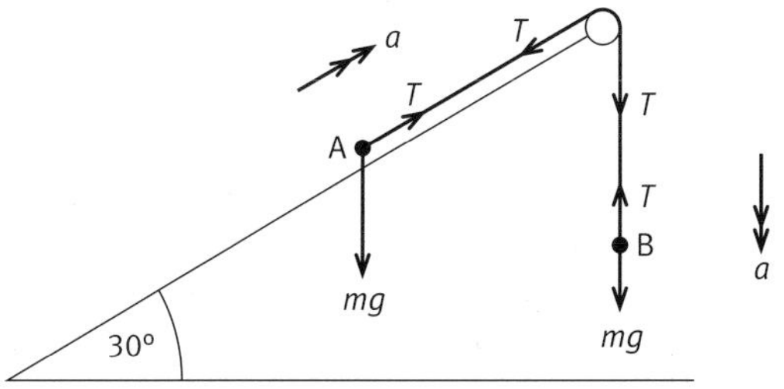

a Using $F = ma$ gives:

For A, // to the plane, $T - mg\sin 30^\circ = ma$

For B $\downarrow$, $mg - T = ma$

From these equations $a = \frac{1}{4}g$

The acceleration is $\frac{1}{4}g\,\text{ms}^{-2}$

b For the motion up to this instant,

$u = 0$, $a = \frac{1}{4}g$, $t = 1$ and v is wanted.

Using $v = u + at$ gives $v = 0 + \frac{1}{4}g$.

B's speed when it hits the floor is $\frac{1}{4}g\,\text{ms}^{-1}$.

(This is also A's speed.)

c When B hits the plane, the string goes slack and the tension in both portions of string disappears. The only force // to the plane now acting on A is the component of its weight down the plane and the acceleration is different.

So using $F = ma$ down the plane gives:

$$mg\sin 30^\circ = m(-f) \quad \Rightarrow \quad f = -\tfrac{1}{2}g$$

For A's further motion,

$u = \frac{1}{4}g$, $v = 0$, $f = -\frac{1}{2}g$ and s is wanted

$$v^2 - u^2 = 2fs \quad \Rightarrow \quad 0 - g^2/16 = -gs$$

$\therefore$ A travels a further $g/16$ m up the slope.

In **c** you could have marked the acceleration down the plane and used that as the positive direction.

Questions

1 The particles shown in the diagram are released from rest.

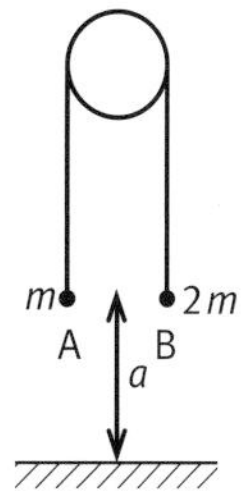

Find in terms of a and m,

a the acceleration of each particle and the tension in the string while both particles are moving, stating what assumptions you have made in your calculation

b how much higher A rises after B hits the plane.

2 A car of mass 700 kg is towing a trailer tent, whose mass is 100 kg, along a level road at a steady 24 ms^{-1}. The driving force exerted by the car is 2400 N.

a Write down the total resisting force.

The car then begins to accelerate at 0.2 ms^{-2}. Assuming that the resistance on the trailer tent is one quarter of the total resistance (which is unchanged) find

b the driving force required

c the tension in the tow-bar.

Answers

1a $g/3$, $\frac{4}{3}mg$; string is light and inextensible, pulley is smooth
b $a/3$

2a 2400 N **b** 2560 N **c** 620 N

Take a break

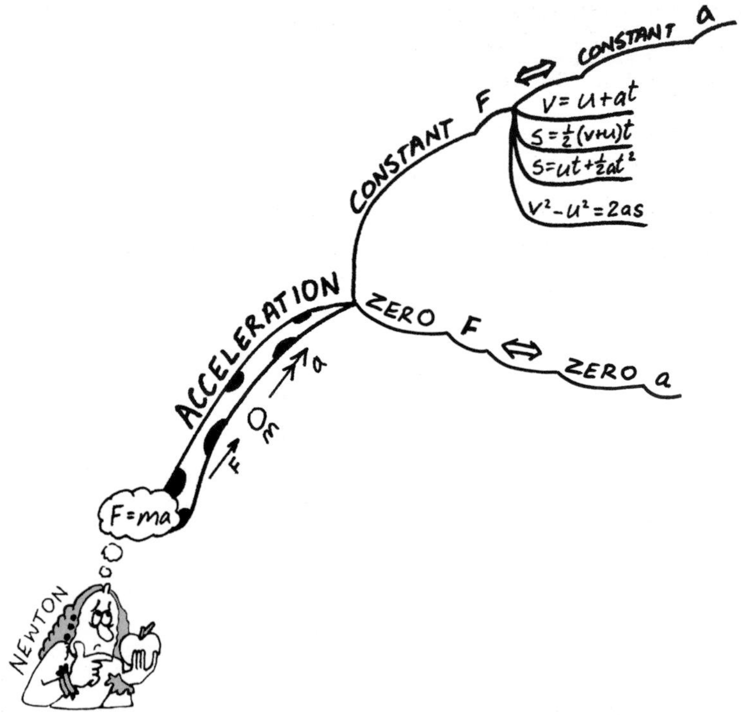

Review

1 Rob is asked to draw and mark up two diagrams of a conker being whirled round in a horizontal circle at the end of a light string. One is the view looking down on the whirling conker from above; the other is the view with his eye on a level with the conker. Here are his diagrams.

State which forces are correctly marked, which are wrong and why.

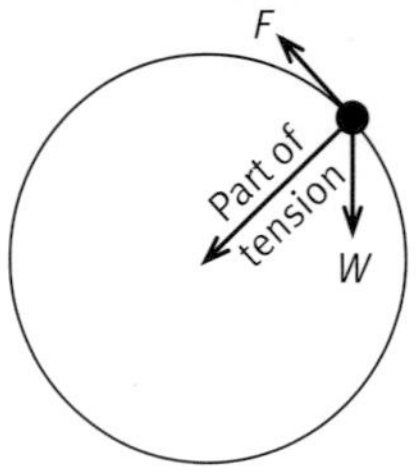

(a) View from above

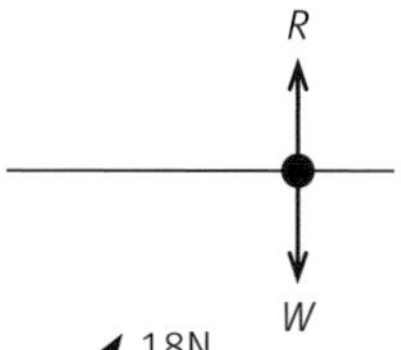

(b) Eye-level view

2 Three coplanar forces act on a particle P as shown. The resultant of these forces acts in the direction of the force of 15 N. Find

a the value of θ

b the magnitude of the resultant force.

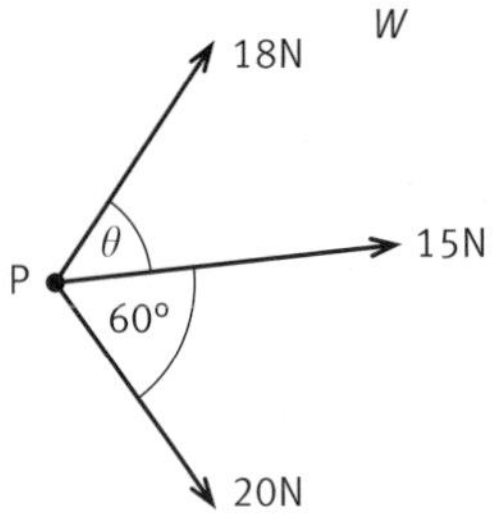

3 A woman of mass 60 kg enters a lift and presses the Down button. The lift goes from rest to 3 ms^{-1} in 6 seconds with constant acceleration.

a Find the acceleration and the reaction between the woman's feet and the floor of the lift.

The lift decelerates to rest at the next floor at the same rate as it accelerated.

b What is the reaction between the woman and the floor?

Answers

1a F is wrong – no force acts in direction of motion. W is wrong – weight acts ⊥ to horizontal plane and cannot be seen, part of tension is correct – tension acts at an angle to the horizontal so has a horizontal component.
b R is wrong – there is no contact, W is right, component of tension is missing.
2a 74.2° **b** 29.9 N. **3a** 0.5 ms^{-2}, 570 N **b** 630 N

PREVIEW

At the end of the topic you will have revised:

- ✔ **what work, mechanical energy and power are, and the units they are measured in,**
- ✔ **the relationship between work and energy,**
- ✔ **the principle of conservation of mechanical energy and when to use it in problems,**
- ✔ **the relationship between the power of a moving vehicle and its speed.**

Before you start you should:

- know that a vector quantity has direction as well as magnitude,
- know that force, velocity and acceleration are all vector quantities,
- know that displacement also is a vector but its value depends, in addition, on the chosen position from which it is measured.

Work

Work is done by a force acting on an object when that object moves in any direction except perpendicular to the force.

When the force is constant the work done, W, is given by $W = Fs$ where s is the displacement of the object and F is the component of the force *in the direction of the displacement*.

The unit of work is the joule (J) where 1 joule is the amount of work done when a force of 1 Newton moves an object 1 metre in its own direction, e.g. the work done by the tension in this rope when the block moves 3 m along the plane is given by $(2\cos 30°)\ \text{N} \times 3\ \text{m} \Rightarrow 3\sqrt{3}\ \text{J}$.

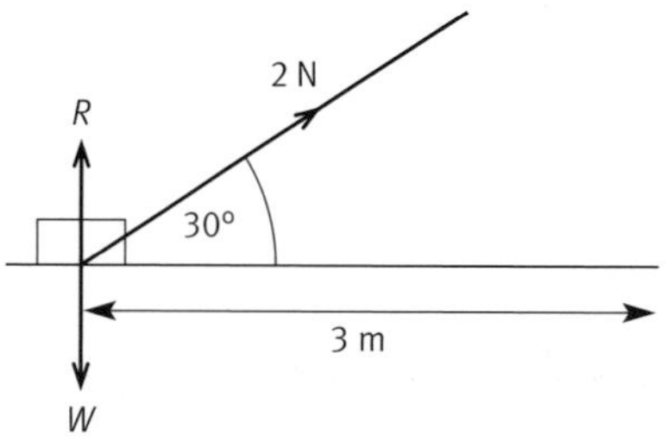

Note that the block moves at right angles to both the normal reaction R and the weight W, so R and W do no work.

Energy

When work is done, the energy of an object changes.

The amount of work done is equal to the change in energy.

As work and energy are interchangeable they are measured in the same unit, i.e. the unit of energy is the joule.

Mechanical energy

A moving object possesses *kinetic energy* given by $\text{KE} = \frac{1}{2}mv^2$ where m is the mass and v the speed of the object. KE is always positive, as v^2 is positive.

An object that is at a height h above a specified level possesses *potential energy* which is given by $\text{PE} = mgh$. PE is positive when the object is above the specified level and negative when below it.

Note that the PE of an object is equal to the amount of work that would be done by gravity in moving the object from its height h down to the specified level.

Kinetic energy and potential energy are both forms of mechanical energy (ME).

Solving problems

Whenever potential energy is used in solving a problem it is vital to mark the level from which PE is measured, i.e. where the PE is zero. In problems involving more than one object, where heights and speeds both change, it can be risky to try to work out, and collect, individual increases and decreases in energy. Instead you can avoid getting signs wrong, by using the total mechanical energy in the initial and final positions separately and then finding the difference between them, i.e.

$$(\text{KE} + \text{PE})_1 \sim (\text{KE} + \text{PE})_2 = \text{Work done}$$

Remember that $\sim$ means 'the difference between'.

When solving most practical problems a mathematical model is formed using some assumptions that were listed in Mechanics 3 (page 103).

Be careful when choosing the value you take for g. Unless the assumptions made are reasonably near to the real situation, 10 is a good enough approximation for the value of g but

remember to check the instructions given and if in doubt take $g = 9.8\ \text{ms}^{-2}$.

Example

A vertical force lifts a load of 8 kg vertically upwards from rest at ground level to a platform 3.2 m high. When the load reaches the platform it has a speed of 1.7 ms^{-1}. Find the work done by the force and the average value of the force. Take g as 10 ms^{-2} and give answers correct to 2 sf.

Solution

Initial ME = 0 (PE and KE both zero)

Final ME $= mgh + \frac{1}{2}mv^2$

$= (8)(10)(3.2) + \frac{1}{2}(8)(1.7)^2)$ J

$= 267.56$ J

$\therefore$ change in ME = 270 J (2 sf)

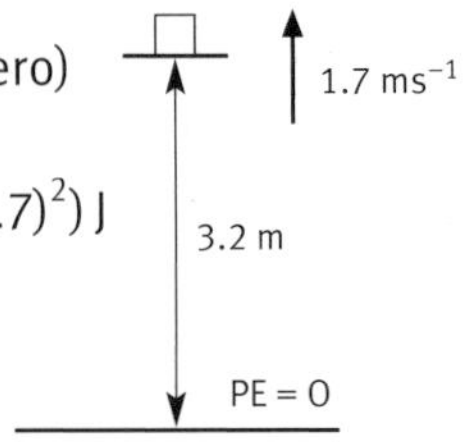

Work done by force = Change in ME = 270 J

Also

work done = average force in direction load moves $\times$ distance it moves.

Average force $= 267.5 \div 3.2$ N = 84 N (2 sf).

This problem can be done by the method in Mechanics 3, i.e. using tension, $F = ma$ and motion with constant acceleration, but work/energy gives a shorter solution, and can be used whenever only position and speed are involved.

Another type of problem deals with the work done by a stationary engine such as a pump.

You can find this by calculating the total mechanical energy it produces in a certain time.

Example

Water is pumped at a rate of 0.6 cubic metres per second from a storage tank 4 metres underground and delivered at ground level through a pipe with cross sectional area 0.05 square metres. Find, correct to 2 sf, the work done by the pump per second. (1 m^3 of water has a mass of 1000 kg.)

Solution

To find the kinetic energy you need the speed at which the water is delivered. To find this you divide the volume of water delivered per second by the area of cross-section.

Mass of water per sec $= 0.6 \times 1000$ kg = 600 kg

Speed of water $= 0.6/0.05\ ms^{-1} = 12\ ms^{-1}$

Initial ME = 0 and

Final ME $= (600 \times 10 \times 4)$ J $+ (\frac{1}{2} \times 600 \times 144)$ J

Work done by pump per second is equal to the increase in the ME of the water = 67 200 J i.e. 67 kJ (2 sf).

Questions

1 A boy walks steadily, pushing his bike, 180 m up a hill inclined at an average angle α to the horizontal where $\sin\alpha = 1/12$. There is an average resistance to motion of 25 N and the total mass of the boy and his bike is 80 kg. Find

a the work the boy does against gravity

b the total work he does.

2 A tank contains thick oil to a depth of 0.9 m. A spark plug, mass 0.5 kg, is inadvertently dropped into the tank. It enters the oil at 1 ms^{-1} and sinks to the bottom where its speed is 1.8 ms^{-1}. Find the resistance that the oil exerts on the plug.

3 Decide whether each statement is *always* true (T). If it isn't, regard it as false (F).

a If the KE of a system is constant, no external forces can be acting on the system.

b If a particle is accelerating in a horizontal straight line its PE is constant.

c Every force that acts on a moving body does some work.

Answers

1a 12 kJ **b** 16.5 kJ **2** 4.38 N **3a** F **b** T **c** F

Take a break

Conservation of mechanical energy

Mechanical energy remains constant if gravity is the only force that does any work on a system of masses and no mechanical energy is converted into other forms of energy such as sound. If speeds and heights change, energy is converted between KE and PE but there is no overall change in ME, i.e.

$$(KE + PE)_{\text{first position}} = (KE + PE)_{\text{second position}}$$

Other forces can be acting but not doing work, e.g. when a block slides a distance s down a smooth slope the normal reaction is perpendicular to the direction of motion, so does no work and ME is conserved.

Example

Two particles, A of mass m and B of mass $2m$, are connected by a light inextensible string which passes over a smooth fixed pulley. They are held as shown in diagram (i) and then released from rest. Find, in terms of m and a, the speed of the particles just as B reaches the ground.

Solution

Just before B hits the ground, (ii), A and B have the same speed. The only external forces acting are weights (the tensions are internal forces and hence do no work) so ME is conserved.

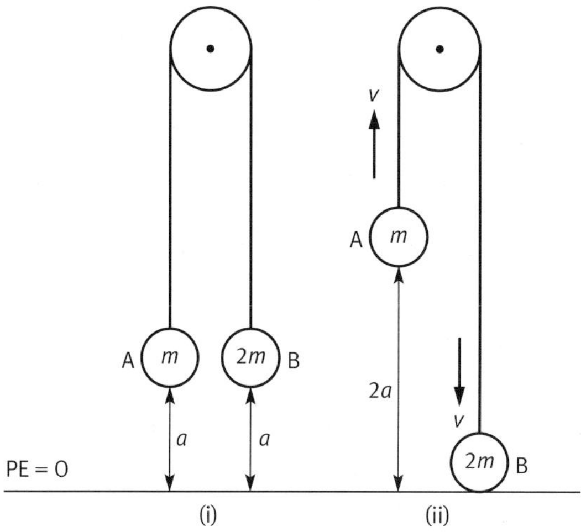

$$(\text{KE} + \text{PE})_{(i)} = 0 + mga + 2mga$$
$$(\text{KE} + \text{PE})_{(ii)} = \tfrac{1}{2}mv^2 + \tfrac{1}{2}(2m)v^2 + mg(2a)$$

Using conservation of ME gives

$$3mga = \tfrac{3}{2}mv^2 + 2mga \Rightarrow v = \sqrt{\frac{2ga}{3}}$$

Again the $F = ma$ method can be used but it is longer than conservation of ME when only speeds and positions are involved. To find tension and/or acceleration however, $F = ma$ **must** be used.

Questions

1

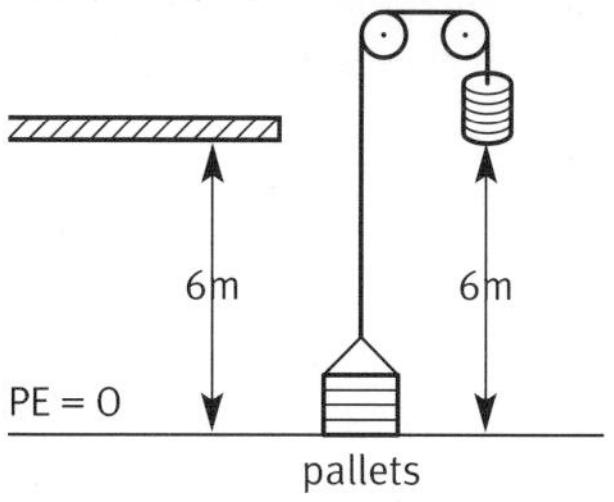

The diagram shows how a construction company raises roof tiles, in pallets of total mass 32 kg, from ground level to a platform 6 m high by using a system of pulleys and a counter-balance with adjustable mass.
The speed of the pallets when they reach the platform must not be greater than 2 ms^{-1}. Taking g as 10, find, correct to 2 sf, the maximum mass of the counter-balance.

2

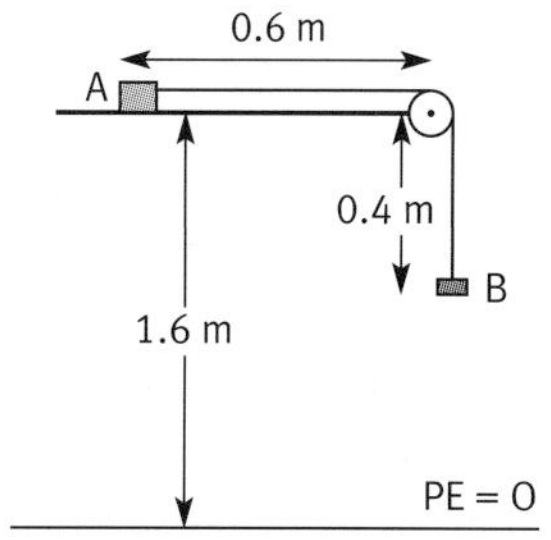

Two particles, A of mass $2m$ and B of mass m, are connected by a light string that passes over a smooth pulley at the edge of a smooth shelf 1.6 m high. A is held at rest on the shelf and B hangs freely over the pulley as shown in the diagram. A is then released from rest.
Find the speed of each particle when A reaches the pulley.

Answers

1 34.2 kg **2** 2 ms^{-1}.

Power

Power is the rate at which work is being done. The unit of power is the watt, W, which is 1 joule per second.

The power of a moving vehicle is the rate at which the driving force (i.e. the force produced by the engine) is doing work.

When the driving force is D and the speed of the vehicle is v, the engine is working at the rate of Dv joules per second, so the power, H, of the vehicle is Dv watts.

Note that using $H = Dv$ gives an *instantaneous* value for the power; the value changes with any alteration in either the driving force or the speed, or both.

Problem solving

Most problems involving power are about vehicles, so the solutions usually include dealing also with the motion of the vehicle.

The force that causes the motion of the vehicle is the resultant of the driving force and any other forces.

If the driving force is greater than the opposing forces the vehicle has an acceleration. You can find the acceleration by using Newton's Law, $F = ma$. If the power is given, mark the driving force as H/v. To drive the vehicle at its maximum speed requires the use of maximum power.

At constant speed, maximum or otherwise, there is no acceleration so the resultant force is zero.

Example

A train of mass 50 000 kg, with its engine working at 1800 kW, is climbing up an incline of gradient 1 in n (i.e. $\sin \alpha = \frac{1}{n}$ where α is the angle of inclination of the slope). There is a constant resistive force of 10 kN.

a Find n if the maximum speed up the incline is $50\ \text{ms}^{-1}$.

b What is the acceleration of the train at the instant when the speed reaches $30\ \text{ms}^{-1}$?

Solution

a

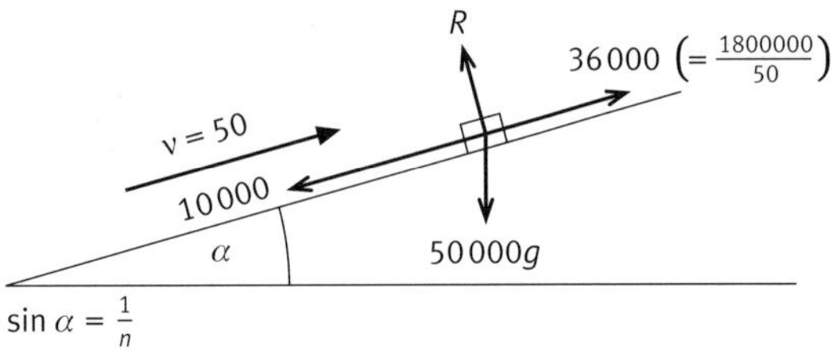

Driving force $= H/v = 1\,800\,000/50$
$= 36\,000$

Speed is max $\Rightarrow$ zero acceleration

$\Rightarrow$ resultant force up incline $= 0$

$\therefore$ $36\,000 - 10\,000 - 50\,000\,g\,(1/n) = 0$

$\Rightarrow$ $n = 19.2$ (3 sf, taking $g = 10$).

b

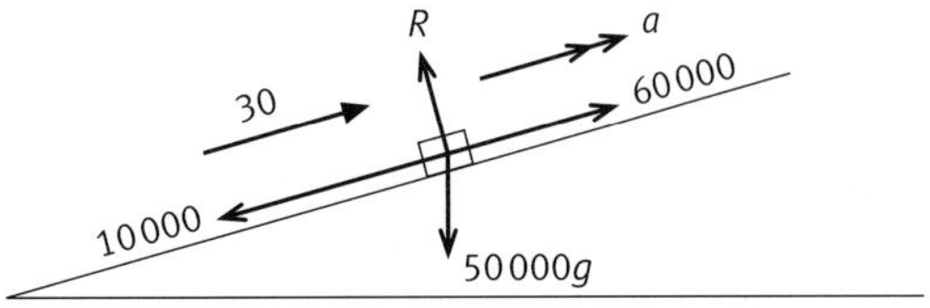

Driving force $= 1\,800\,000/30 = 60\,000$

Resultant force up incline is

$60\,000 - 10\,000 - 50\,000g(1/n) = 24\,000$

Newton's Law, $F = ma$, gives $24\,000 = 50\,000a$

The acceleration at $30\ \text{ms}^{-1}$ is $0.48\ \text{ms}^{-2}$.

Questions

In this exercise use $g = 10\ \text{ms}^{-2}$ and give answers correct to 2 sf.

1 A van of mass 600 kg is being driven at a constant rate of 30 kW along a horizontal road, against an average resistance of 1300 N. At the instant that the speed of the van is $20\ \text{ms}^{-1}$ find

a the tractive force (driving force) of the van

b the acceleration of the van.

2 A pump raises water from a depth of 4 m and ejects it, at $7\ \text{ms}^{-1}$, through a pipe with a cross-sectional area $0.06\ \text{m}^2$. Given that $1\ \text{m}^3$ of water has a mass of 1000 kg, find the rate at which the pump is working.

3 A girl, whose mass is 56 kg, is jogging at a constant speed of $3\ \text{ms}^{-1}$ along a horizontal road. She has to work at rate of 100 W to overcome the air resistance she encounters. Find the value of this air resistance. She comes to a hill inclined to the horizontal at an angle α where $\sin \alpha = 1/20$. Estimate the power she needs to exert in order to jog up the hill at a steady speed of $2\ \text{ms}^{-1}$, assuming that the resistance is unchanged.

4 The power output (i.e. the maximum power it can exert) of a car of mass 480 kg is 16 kW. The car is travelling up a slope inclined at an angle α to the horizontal, where $\sin \alpha = \frac{1}{24}$. The resisting forces are modelled as being of magnitude $20v$ when the speed of the car is v.
Find the maximum speed possible when going

a uphill **b** down the slope.

Answers

1a 1500 N **b** $\frac{1}{3}\ \text{ms}^{-2}$ **2** 27 kW

3 33 N, 120 W **4a** $24\ \text{ms}^{-1}$ **b** $34\ \text{ms}^{-1}$.

Take a break

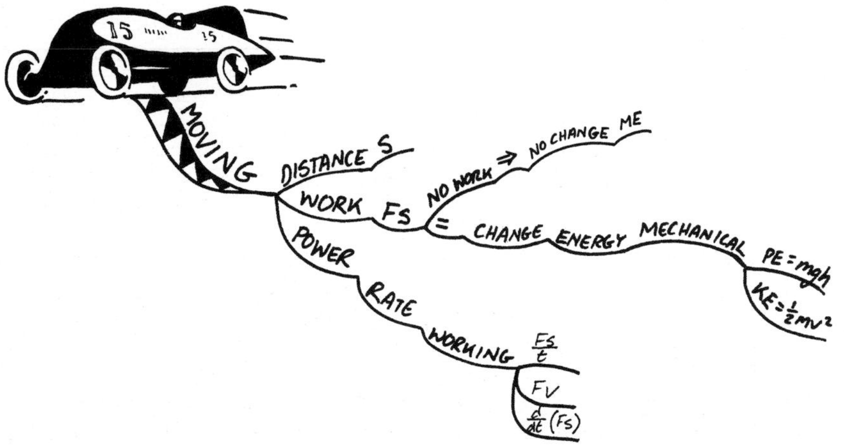

Review

1 A crate, mass m, is being transported in a lift of mass M, supported by a cable.
Draw two diagrams, one showing all the forces that act on the crate, and its acceleration; the other showing all the forces that act on the lift, and its acceleration, when the lift is

a going up with acceleration f **b** going down with acceleration f.

Write down Newton's Law, $F = ma$, for the crate in each case.

2

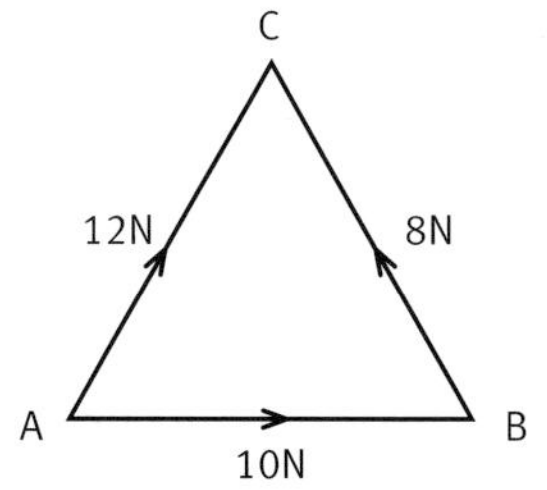

ABC is an equilateral triangle and forces of magnitudes 10 N, 8 N and 12 N act along the sides AB, BC and AC as shown. Find, correct to 3 sf, the magnitude of the resultant force and the angle it makes with AB.

3 A bead P of mass m is threaded onto a smooth wire in the shape of a circle of radius a.
It moves under gravity from rest in position (i) towards position (ii).

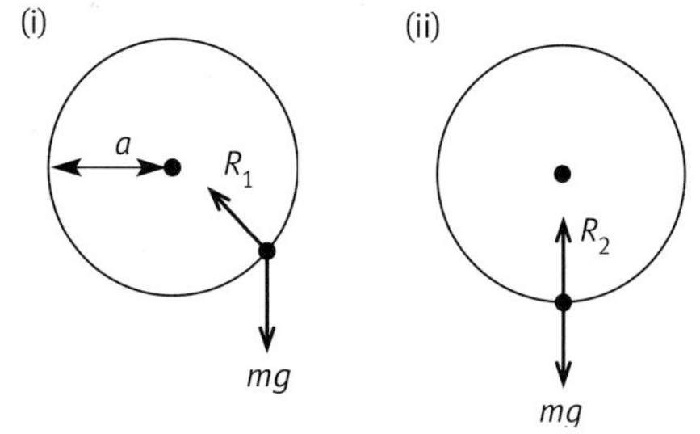

Decide whether each of the following statements is true or false.

a Mechanical energy is conserved. **b** Work is done by the reaction R_1.

c R_1 is marked in the wrong direction. It should be drawn away from the centre.

d The bead comes to rest in position (ii).

4 The engine of a truck travelling up an incline is working at a steady 36 kW against resistive forces of magnitude 560 N. The mass of the truck is 4000 kg and the angle of inclination of the slope is α where $\sin\alpha = \frac{1}{180}$. Find the acceleration of the truck at the instant when its speed is 16 ms^{-1}.
Use $g = 10$ and give answers correct to 2 sf.

Answers

1a and b

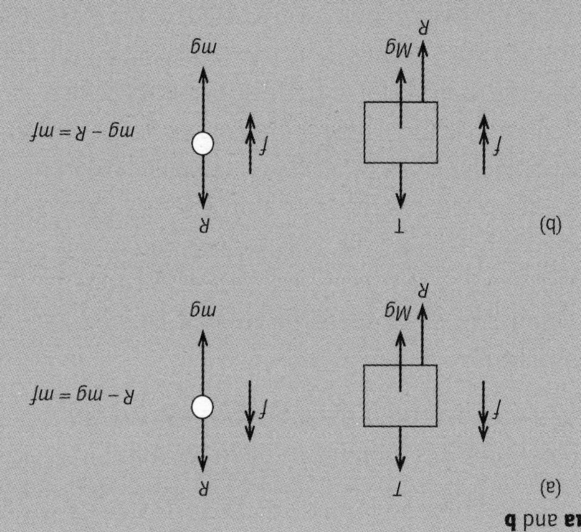

2 21.1 N at 55.3° to AB.

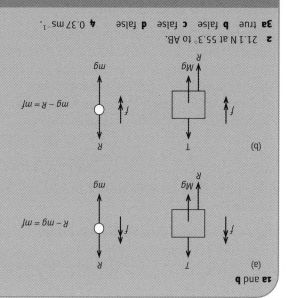

3a true **b** false **c** false **d** false **4** 0.37 ms^{-1}.

PREVIEW

At the end of this topic you will have revised:

- ✔ **what momentum and impulse are, and what units they are measured in,**
- ✔ **the relationship between momentum and impulse,**
- ✔ **the principle of conservation of momentum,**
- ✔ **what an instantaneous impulse is.**

Impulse and momentum

The impulse of a force depends on the magnitude of the force and its time of action.

For a constant force F acting for a measurable time t the impulse I is given by $I = Ft$. The unit of impulse is the Newton second (Ns).

The momentum of a body of mass m, moving with velocity v, is mv.

When an impulse acts on the body, the impulse is equal to the change in momentum produced, i.e. for a constant force F acting for a time t, $Ft = mv_2 - mv_1$ where $v_1$and v_2 are the velocities before and after impact.

If a force acts only for an instant, the force and time are not known separately but there is an instantaneous impulse, I, which can be evaluated only from the change in momentum produced.

$I = mv_2 - mv_1$

The unit used for momentum is the same as that for impulse, i.e. the Newton second (Ns).

Conservation of momentum

If a moving object collides with a fixed surface (i.e. external impact) this surface exerts an impulse on the body and changes its momentum. (The impulse the body exerts on the surface cannot cause movement.) But when there is a collision between two objects, both of which can move (internal impact), each exerts an instantaneous impulse on the other. These impulses, being equal and opposite, cause equal and opposite changes in momentum, so there is no overall change in momentum.

When you use the principle of conservation of momentum in problems, remember that:

- momentum and impulse are vectors so a positive direction must be chosen
- before and after diagrams are essential
- the initial and final total momentum in the same direction is equated
- the impulse is found by considering the change in momentum of one only of the colliding bodies
- if the objects coalesce (become joined) at impact, they then have a common speed
- if there is more than one collision, each impact is an individual case needing its own diagrams and its own choice of positive direction.

Although momentum may be conserved, nearly all collisions result in a loss of kinetic energy (converted into sound energy, etc.).

Example

A truck of mass 500 kg travelling at 5 ms^{-1} collides directly with a stationary truck of mass 240 kg. On impact the trucks are coupled together.
Find, to 3 sf,

a the speed of the linked trucks immediately afterwards,
b the impulse exerted on the stationary truck,
c the loss in kinetic energy due to the collision.

The coupled trucks continue until they reach a buffer and are then brought to rest in 0.6 s.

d Find the force exerted on the trucks by the buffer.

Solution

Just before impact

At impact

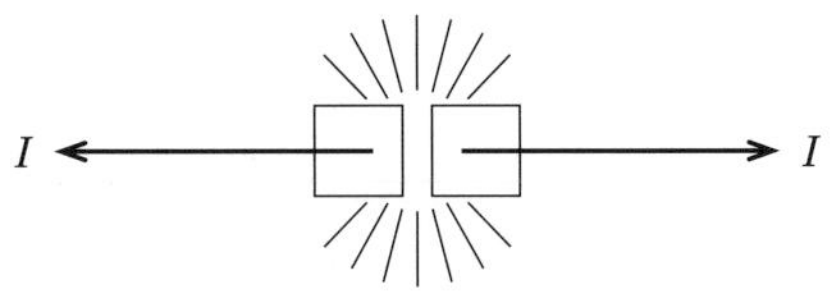

Just after impact

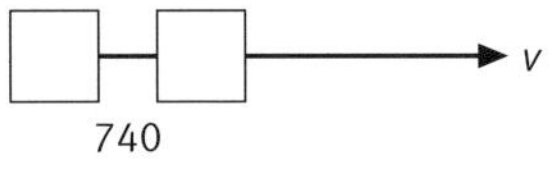

a Initial total momentum (→) $= 500 \times 5 + 0$
Final total momentum (→) $= 740v$
Momentum is conserved ⇒ $740v = 2500$
∴ speed of combined trucks is 3.38 ms^{-1} (3 sf)

b For the stationary truck
$I = 240 \times 3.378\ldots - 0$
$\Rightarrow$ impulse is 811 Ns (3 sf)

c Loss in KE = initial KE − final KE
$= (\frac{1}{2} \times 500 \times 5^2 + 0) - (\frac{1}{2} \times 740 \times 3.378\ldots)$ J
$= 2030$ J (3 sf)

d If F is the force exerted by the buffer, using
$Ft = mv_2 - mv_1$ gives $F \times 0.6 = 740 \times 3.378 - 0$
$\therefore$ buffer exerts a force of 4.17 kN (3 sf).

Example

Two particles, A of mass km and B of mass m, collide head on (i.e. when moving directly towards each other). Their speeds just before impact are $2u$ and $3u$ respectively.

a If $k = 5$ and the collision halves A's speed without a change in direction, find B's speed after impact.
b Find k if the collision brings A to rest and reverses the direction of B without changing its speed.
c Without considering another impact in detail, deduce the range of values of k for which A's direction of motion would be reversed.

Solution

a Just before impact

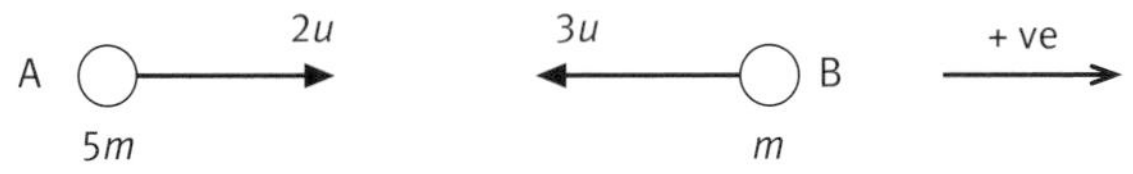

Just after impact

Conservation of momentum (→) gives

$$5m \times 2u - m \times 3u = 5mu + mv \quad \Rightarrow \quad v = 2u$$

b Just before impact

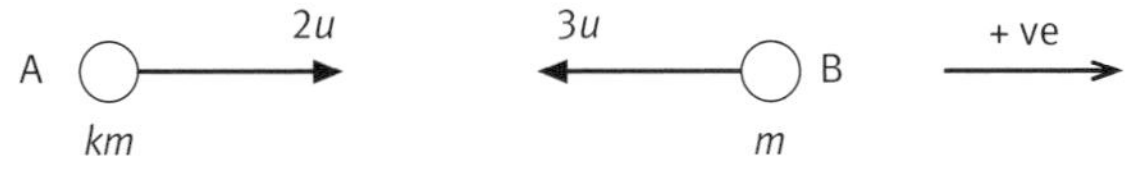

Just after impact

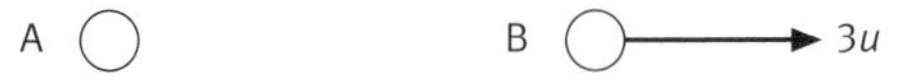

Conservation of momentum (→) gives

$$km \times 2u - m \times 3u = 0 + m \times 3u \quad \Rightarrow \quad k = 3$$

c A's direction is unchanged when $k = 5$ and A is brought to rest when $k = 3$, so A's direction will be reversed if $k < 3$.

Questions

1 A small block P of mass 0.4 kg is moving in a straight line on a horizontal table with speed 2 ms^{-1} when it collides with another block Q of mass 0.3 kg moving directly towards P at a speed of 1 ms^{-1}. The balls coalesce on impact forming a single block R. Find

a the speed of R immediately after the collision,

b the magnitude of the impulses exerted between the blocks when they collide.

2 Just before a tennis racquet strikes a ball of mass 0.04 kg, the ball is travelling at 36 ms^{-1} at right angles to the racquet. The impact reverses the direction of motion of the ball and increases its speed to 42 ms^{-1}.

a Find the magnitude of the impulse exerted on the ball by the racquet.

b If the racquet is in contact with the ball for 0.012 seconds, find the average force that the racquet exerts on the ball.

3 Two particles, A and B, collide when travelling in the same straight line, A following B. The mass of A is $4m$ and its speed is $3u$; B is of mass $3m$. Immediately after they collide A and B have speeds u and $3u$ respectively and both are travelling in A's original direction of motion. Find

a the speed of B before the collision,

b the kinetic energy lost because of the collision,

c the impulse exerted on A.

Answers

1a 0.714 ms^{-1} **b** 0.514 Ns.
2a 3.12 Ns **b** 260 N.
3a $\frac{1}{3}u$ **b** $\frac{8}{3}mu^2$ **c** $8mu$

Impulse in a jerking string

Suppose that a slack inextensible string has a particle attached to each end and one particle is set moving away from the other. When the string reaches its full length it jerks tight. At each end of the string an impulsive tension acts on the particle there. The impulses are equal and opposite, momentum is conserved and the situation is dealt with in the same way as for collisions except that the two particles have the same speed just after the string becomes tight.

Example

Two particles A, of mass km and B, of mass m, lie close together on a smooth horizontal surface. The particles are attached one to each end of a light inextensible string. A is set moving directly away from B with speed $3u$. When the string jerks tight the particles move on with speed u. Find the value of k and the impulsive tension in the string when it jerks.

Just before string jerks

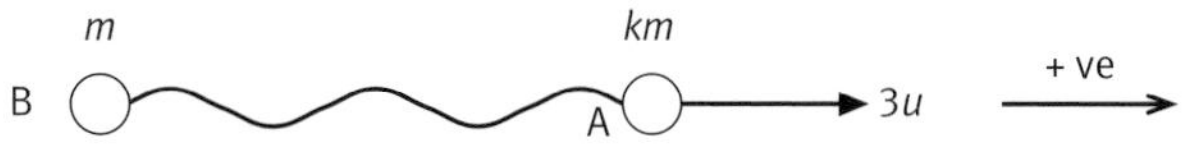

When string jerks

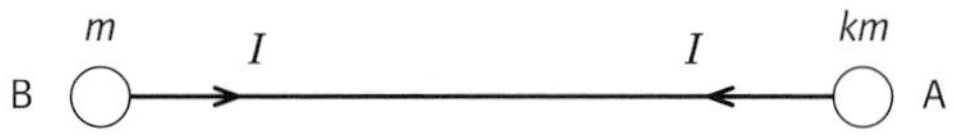

Just after string jerks

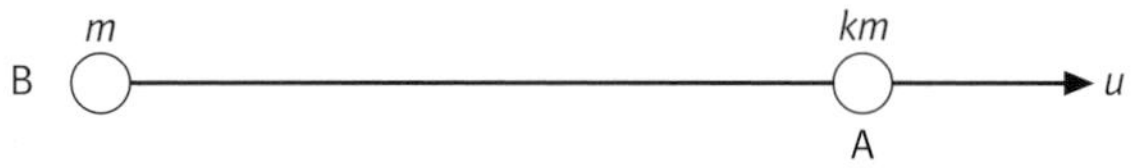

A & B have the same speed.

Using conservation of momentum (→) gives

$km \times 3u + 0 = (km + m) \times u \quad \Rightarrow \quad k = \frac{1}{2}$

For B alone $\qquad I = m(u - 0)$

$\Rightarrow$ Impulsive tension $= mu$

(You could consider A alone but that involves more terms.)

Question

1 A small ball A, of mass m is connected, by a light inextensible string of length a, to a similar ball B, of mass $2m$. They lie together at the edge of a table (height $> a$) and A is gently pushed over the edge.

a Use conservation of energy to find the velocity of A when the string is about to tighten.

When B is jerked off the table find

b the speed of both balls immediately afterwards,

c the impulsive tension in the string when it jerks tight.

Answers

1a $\sqrt{2ga}$ **b** $\frac{1}{3}\sqrt{2ga}$ **c** $\frac{2}{3}m\sqrt{2ga}$

Take a break

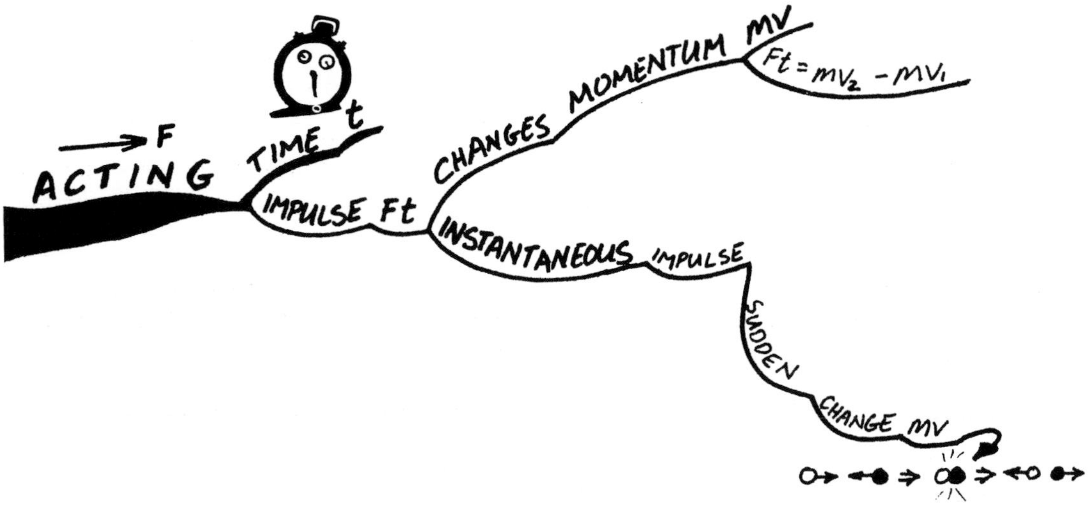

Review

1 A package P of weight 24 N is lying on a rough inclined plane, supported by a force X newtons acting directly up the plane.

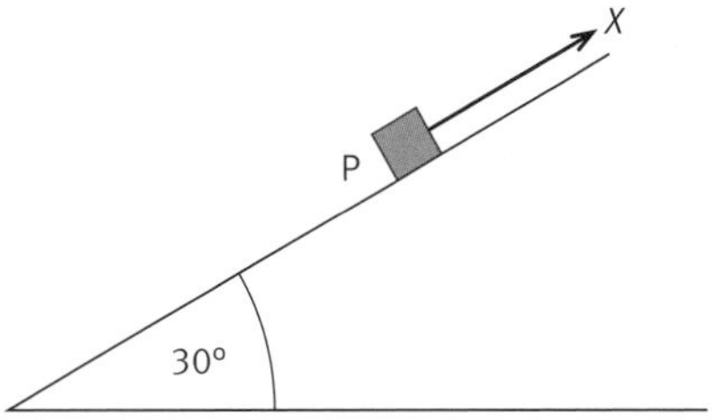

Given that the coefficient of friction between the package and the plane is 0.2 and that the plane is inclined to the horizontal at 30°, find the value of X when P is just about to move

a up the plane **b** down the plane.

Questions 2 and 3 are both based on the same diagram. A and B are two particles joined by a light inextensible string passing over a smooth fixed pulley. Initially each particle is at a height h above a fixed surface. Consider the best method for dealing with each question individually. State your choice and give a reason for it. Then solve each problem.

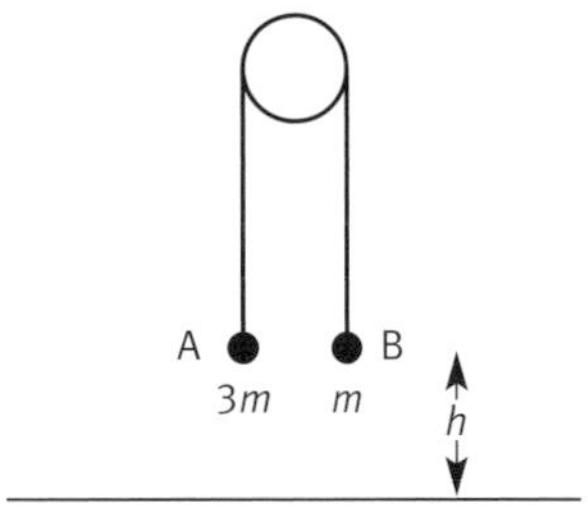

2 The particles are released from rest. Find the tension in the string and the acceleration of the particles while they are both in motion.

3 The particles are released from rest. Find the speed of each particle when A is about to hit the surface.

4 A uniform plank of weight 11 kg hangs in a horizontal position supported by a vertical chain at each end. A load of 20 kg is placed on the plank one third of the way from one end. Draw and mark up separate diagrams to show the forces acting on the plank and on the load.

5 A particle A of mass m is moving on a smooth horizontal table with speed u when it collides with a second particle B, mass km, which is at rest. A is brought to rest by the collision and B moves off with speed $\frac{1}{2}u$.

a Find the value of k.

B then collides with the vertical rim of the table and rebounds with speed $\frac{1}{4}u$ in the opposite direction.

b Find the impulse exerted by the rim on the particle B.

c What is the total loss in kinetic energy caused by both collisions?

Answers

1a 16.2 N **b** 7.8 N

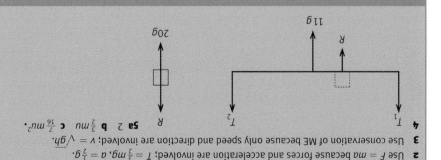

2 Use $F = ma$ because forces and acceleration are involved; $T = \frac{3}{2}mg$, $a = \frac{1}{2}g$.

3 Use conservation of ME because only speed and direction are involved; $v = \sqrt{gh}$.

4

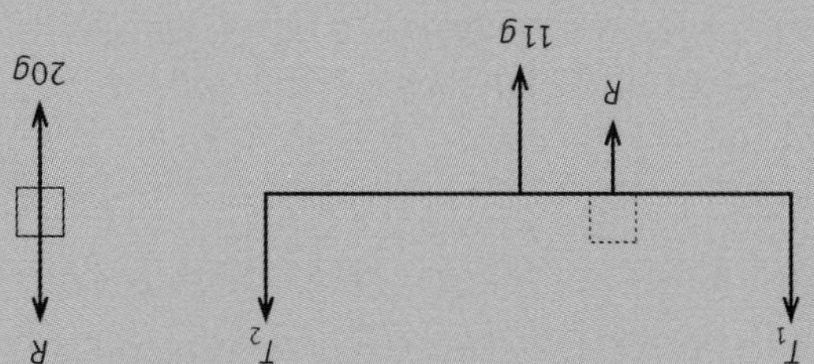

5a 2 **b** $\frac{3}{2}mu$ **c** $\frac{7}{16}mu^2$.

> **PREVIEW**
>
> **At the end of this topic you will have revised:**
>
> ✔ **how a projectile moves horizontally with constant velocity and vertically with constant acceleration under gravity,**
>
> ✔ **how to find the time of flight, the greatest height, the range and the equation of the path of a projectile.**

The motion of a projectile

A stone thrown into the air is an example of a projectile; it travels in a curved path called a trajectory. It is assumed throughout this topic that air resistance can be ignored.

The horizontal and vertical components of the motion must be dealt with separately because:

- horizontally no force acts so the horizontal component of velocity is constant,
- vertically the force of gravity is acting causing a constant downward acceleration of g ms^{-2}.

Basic equations of motion of a projectile

Taking the velocity of projection of a projectile P as V, at an angle α to the horizontal, the initial horizontal and vertical components are $V\cos\alpha \rightarrow$ and $V\sin\alpha \uparrow$.

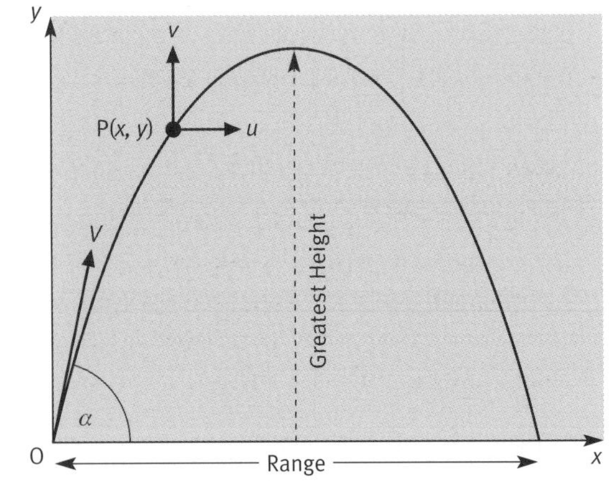

After P has been travelling for a time t, its velocity components are denoted by u and v, and the coordinates of its position by (x, y). Then

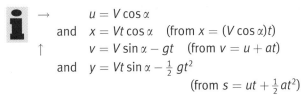

$\rightarrow$ $u = V\cos\alpha$

and $x = Vt\cos\alpha$ (from $x = (V\cos\alpha)t$)

$\uparrow$ $v = V\sin\alpha - gt$ (from $v = u + at$)

and $y = Vt\sin\alpha - \frac{1}{2}gt^2$ (from $s = ut + \frac{1}{2}at^2$)

These are not given in the examination formula book.

Time of flight and range of the projectile

The following formulae also are not provided in your examination, so learn them.

Taking $y = 0$ gives the time of flight and using this value of t in the equation for x gives the range.

$$\text{Time of flight} = \frac{2V\sin\alpha}{g}$$

$$\text{Range} = \frac{2V^2\sin\alpha\cos\alpha}{g} = \frac{V^2\sin 2\alpha}{g}$$

This expression shows that the range is greatest when $\sin 2\alpha = 1$, i.e. the greatest range for a given initial speed is V^2/g and it occurs when $\alpha = 45°$.

Taking $v = 0$ gives the time to the greatest height and using this value of t in the equation for y gives the greatest height reached.

$$\text{Greatest height} = \frac{V^2\sin^2\alpha}{2g}$$

The path of a projectile

Eliminating t from the equations for x and y gives the equation of the path followed (the trajectory).

$$\text{Equation of path is} \quad y = x\tan\alpha - \frac{gx^2}{2V^2\cos^2\alpha}$$

The equations for x and y in terms of t are parametric equations of the path. If you learn and remember the results above you can quote them unless you are asked to prove them.

It is important for you to learn how they are obtained as you may be asked to derive them, and in any case you can easily forget a formula!

Solving problems

As there are so many formulae available it is important to have some guide-lines to help choose the best approach. Here are a few ideas.

- First check whether you need one of the quotable results and, if so, are you asked to prove it.
- If time is mentioned use the separate component equations.
- If only the position of P is involved, and there is no mention of time in the problem, use the equation of the path.
- Be prepared to rearrange the equation of the path as either

$$y = x\tan\alpha - \frac{gx^2\sec^2\alpha}{2V^2}$$

or $$y = x\tan\alpha - \frac{gx^2(1+\tan^2\alpha)}{2V^2}$$

This form is a quadratic equation in $\tan\alpha$, so is particularly useful for finding α.

- If an object A is projected and another object B is projected 2 seconds later say, measure t from the moment of projection of B. Then after t seconds A has been travelling for $(t+2)$ seconds. This avoids the minus sign introduced if t is measured from the moment of projection of A. (It is easier to make mistakes with a minus sign!)
- If an object is projected from a height above the ground (or other base level) take the origin at the point of projection; then the y-coordinate of any point on the ground is negative.

In all the examples and questions that follow, the object projected is modelled as a particle, air resistance is ignored and g is taken as $10\,\text{ms}^{-2}$.

Example

A stone S is thrown from a point O at the top of a cliff 20 m high. S is projected with speed $12\,\text{ms}^{-1}$ at an angle of 30° above the horizontal.

a Find the horizontal and vertical displacements of S from O, t seconds after projection.
b Hence find how long S takes to reach the ground at a point A, level with the foot of the cliff.
c Find the distance OA.

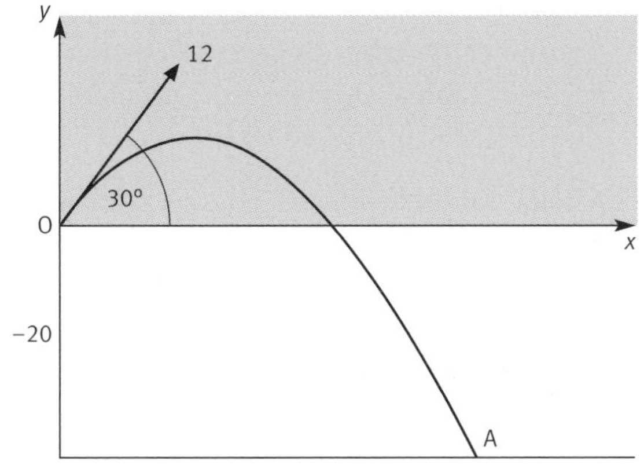

Solution

a If S is at the point P(x, y) after t s, then
$x = 12t\cos 30^\circ$ and $y = 12t\sin 30^\circ - \frac{1}{2}gt^2$.

b At A, $y = -20$
$\therefore\ -20 = 6t - 5t^2 \Rightarrow 5t^2 - 6t - 20 = 0$
Solving this quadratic equation by formula gives
$t = \frac{1}{10}\{6 \pm \sqrt{36+400}\} = 2.68\ldots$ (t is not −ve)
S reaches A after 2.7 s (2 sf).

c When $t = 2.68$,
$x = 12(2.68\ldots)\cos 30^\circ = 27.93\ldots$
$OA^2 = (27.93\ldots)^2 + (-20)^2 = 1180.3\ldots$
OA = 34 m (2 sf).

Example

A cricketer who is fielding, stops the ball and throws it with speed $24\,\text{ms}^{-1}$, from a height of 2 m, towards the wicket-keeper 40 m away.
The wicket-keeper just catches it at ground level.
Taking $g = 10\,\text{ms}^{-2}$ find, to the nearest degree, the possible angles of projection.

Solution

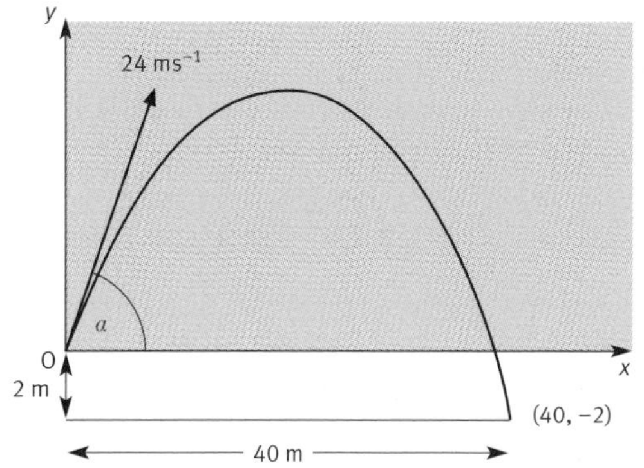

The ball is caught where $y = -2$ and $x = 40$.
Using the equation of the path in the form

$$y = x\tan\alpha - \frac{gx^2(1+\tan^2\alpha)}{2V^2} \quad \text{gives}$$

$$-2 = 40T - \frac{(10)(40)^2(1+T^2)}{(2)(24^2)} \quad (T = \tan\alpha)$$

Simplifying gives $125T^2 - 360T + 107 = 0$
$\Rightarrow$ there are two possible angles of projection, 69° and 19°.
(A good fielder would throw in at 19°!)

Example

A stone A is thrown from a point P with speed $5\,\text{ms}^{-1}$ at an angle of 60° and 1 second later another stone B is thrown from P with the same speed at an angle of 30°. Find, in surd form, the time when A and B are at the same horizontal distance from P.

Solution

When B has been travelling for t seconds, A has been travelling for $(t+1)$ seconds.

For A, $x_A = 5(t+1)\cos 60^\circ = 5(t+1)(\frac{1}{2})$
For B, $x_B = 5(t)\cos 30^\circ = 5t(\frac{\sqrt{3}}{2})$
When
$x_A = x_B$, $\frac{5}{2}(t+1) = \frac{5}{2}t\sqrt{3} \Rightarrow t(\sqrt{3}-1) = 1$

$$\therefore\ t = \frac{1}{\sqrt{3}-1} = \frac{(\sqrt{3}+1)}{2}.$$

The time when A and B are equidistant from P is $\frac{1}{2}(\sqrt{3}+1)$ s after B is thrown.

Example

Two girls are standing one on either side of a wall 2.8 metres high. Laura is 3.2 m from the wall and attempts to throw a ball over the wall to Sara. Assume that the girls throw and catch the ball 1.2 m above the ground.

a Laura throws the ball towards the wall with speed $7\,\text{ms}^{-1}$ at 60° to the horizontal. Write down the horizontal and vertical components of the initial speed and use them to show that the ball does not clear the wall.

b Find the least speed needed to clear the wall with an angle of projection of 60°.

Solution

a

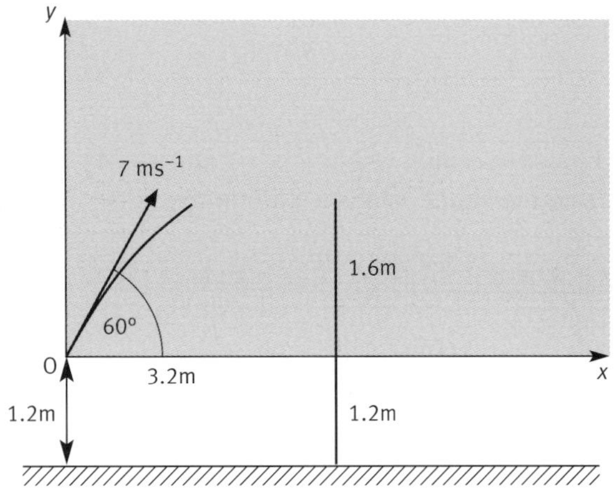

Initial components: $\rightarrow 7\cos 60^\circ = 3.5$

and $\uparrow 7\sin 60^\circ = 6.062$

Time taken to reach wall is $\dfrac{3.2}{3.5} = 0.9143\,\text{s}$

Substituting this time in $y = (V\sin\theta)t - \frac{1}{2}gt^2$ gives $y = 1.363$.

At the top of the wall $y = 1.6$ so the ball does not clear the wall.

b To just clear the wall the ball must pass through the point (3.2, 1.6).

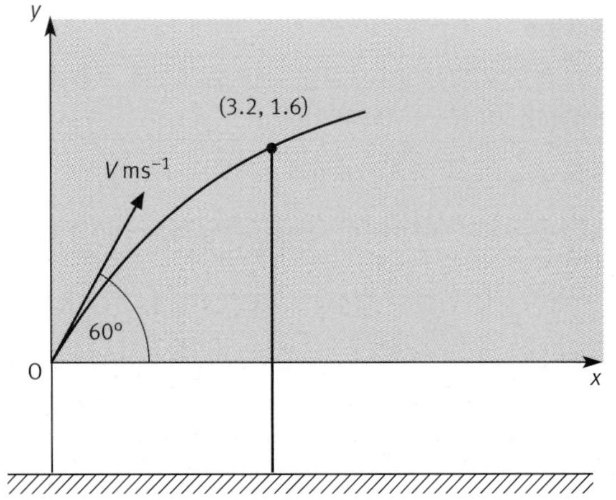

Using the equation of the path gives

$$1.6 = 3.2\tan 60^\circ - \frac{g(3.2)^2(1 + \tan^2 60^\circ)}{2V^2}$$

$$\tan 60^\circ = \sqrt{3} \quad \Rightarrow \quad \frac{5(10.24)(4)}{V^2} = 5.542\ldots - 1.6$$

$$\Rightarrow \quad \frac{204.8}{V^2} = 3.942\ldots \quad \Rightarrow \quad V = 7.2\ldots$$

The speed of projection must be at least $7.2\,\text{ms}^{-1}$.

Questions

In questions **1** and **2**, take g as 10 and give answers to 2 sf.

1 A girl standing on the edge of a harbour wall throws a package to her father who is in a small boat 15 m from the base of the wall. The water level is 24 m below the top of the wall. The package is thrown with speed $5\,\text{ms}^{-1}$ at an angle of elevation α where $\tan\alpha = \frac{3}{4}$.

a How long does it take for the package to reach the water level?

b How far short of the boat does it fall?

2 An athlete throws the discus for a personal best distance of 65 m. The discus is thrown from a height of 1.6 m at an angle of projection of 20°. Find the speed of projection.

3 A golfer tees-off with speed $46\,\text{ms}^{-1}$ at an angle of 30° to the fairway which is horizontal for most of its length. The ball just clears a tree which stands on the fairway 15 m from the tee. Find, using $g = 9.8$ and giving answers to 3 sf,

a the time taken for the ball to reach the tree,

b the height of the tree,

c for how long the ball is more than 15 m above the height of the tree.

Answers

1a 2.5 s

b 5.0 m short of the boat

2 $31\,\text{ms}^{-1}$

3a 0.377 s

b 7.97 m

c 3.02 s.

Take a break

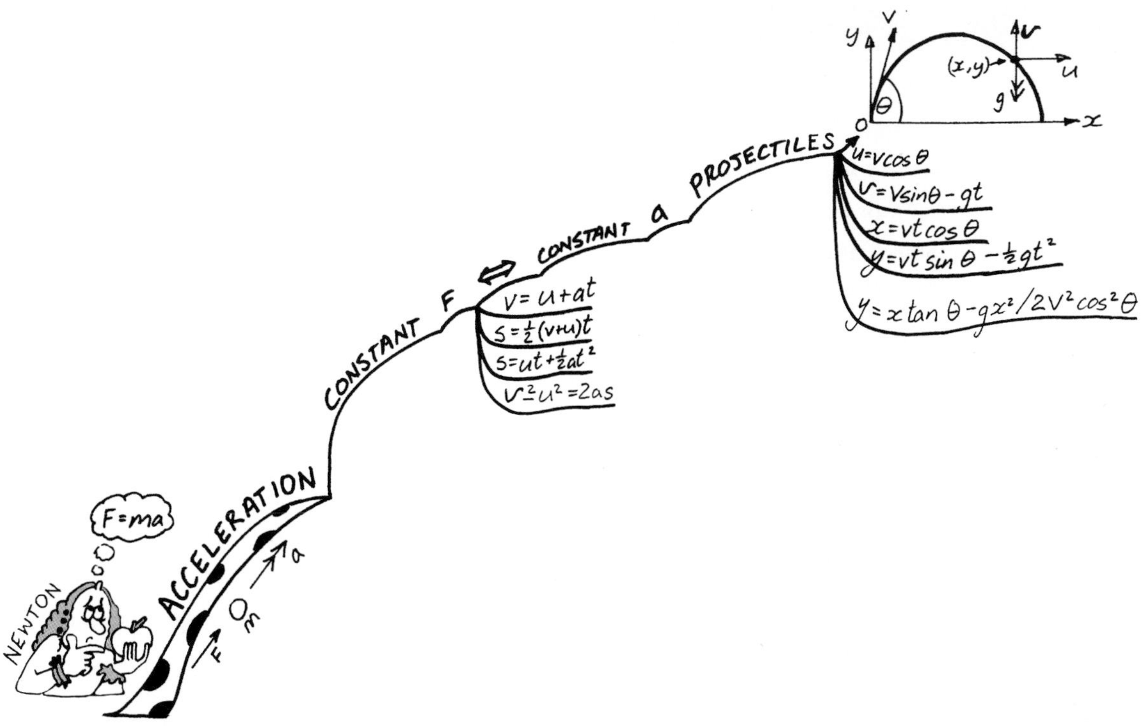

Review

1 Three forces each of magnitude 10 N, act along the sides AB, CB and AC of the equilateral triangle ABC. The order of the letters gives the direction of each force. Find, to 3 sf, magnitude of the resultant, and its direction relative to AC.

2 Forces $\boldsymbol{F}_1 = \mathbf{i} - 4\mathbf{j}$, $\boldsymbol{F}_2 = -6\mathbf{i} + 2\mathbf{j}$, $\boldsymbol{F}_3 = a\mathbf{i} + b\mathbf{j}$ act on a particle which is in equilibrium.
Find, the values of a and b.
Find the resultant, $\boldsymbol{R}$, of $\boldsymbol{F}_1$ and $\boldsymbol{F}_2$ giving the angle between $\boldsymbol{R}$ and the vector $\mathbf{i}$.

3 A slide is 4 m long and is inclined at 40° to the horizontal. Nikki starts from rest at the top. The coefficient of friction between Nikki and the slide is $\frac{1}{4}$. Take g as 10 and find, to 2 sf,

a her acceleration, **b** her speed when she reaches the bottom.

State any assumptions you have made and say whether you think they are reasonable.

4 A girl of mass 40 kg is jogging on the level at a steady speed of $3\,\text{ms}^{-1}$. If she is working at a constant rate of 100 W find the magnitude of the forces of resistance. When she comes to an incline of 5° she increases her rate of working to 110 W. If the resistance is unchanged, find her initial acceleration up the incline.

5 A particle A, of mass m, is moving in a straight line on a horizontal plane when it collides, head-on at speed u, with another particle B of mass km also travelling with speed u. The particles become joined at impact and move on, as a single mass, in the direction of A's initial motion with speed $\frac{1}{2}u$. Find k.

6 A shell from a mortar is fired with speed $50\,\text{ms}^{-1}$ aimed at hitting a rebel hideout 160 m away on an outcrop 30 m high. Take g as 9.8 and give answers to 3 sf.

a Find the two possible angles of projection.

b Find the time taken to hit the target at each of the angles found in part **a**.

Answers

1 20 N at 60° to AC i.e. along AB. **2** $a = 5$, $b = 2$; $\boldsymbol{R} = -5\mathbf{i} - 2\mathbf{j}$, $-158.2°$

3a $4.5\,\text{ms}^{-2}$ **b** $6.00\,\text{ms}^{-1}$, Nikki can be treated as a particle – not a good model as Nikki is quite large compared with the length of the slide; also air resistance can be ignored – quite reasonable.

4 100/3 N, $-0.788\,\text{ms}^{-2}$ (i.e. deceleration) **5** $k = \frac{1}{3}$

6a 68.7° or 31.9° **b** 8.58 s or 3.79 s.

PREVIEW

At the end of this topic you will have revised:

- ✔ **how to find the resultant of two like parallel forces and of two unlike parallel forces,**
- ✔ **the turning effect of non-concurrent forces,**
- ✔ **the meaning of moment and how to calculate the moment of a force about a given axis,**
- ✔ **how to find the resultant moment of a set of coplanar forces,**
- ✔ **problems involving parallel forces in equilibrium.**

The moment of a force

The moment of a force is the measure of its turning effect about a specified axis. The magnitude of the moment of a force F N about an axis through a point A, in the plane of the force, is Fd Nm (newton metres), where d m is the perpendicular distance from A to the *line of action* of the force

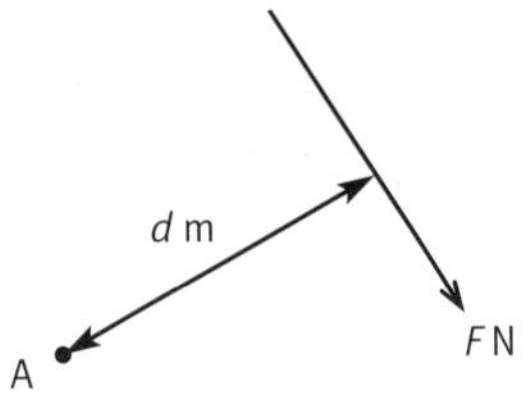

Turning effect has no linear direction but its sense can be either clockwise or anticlockwise.

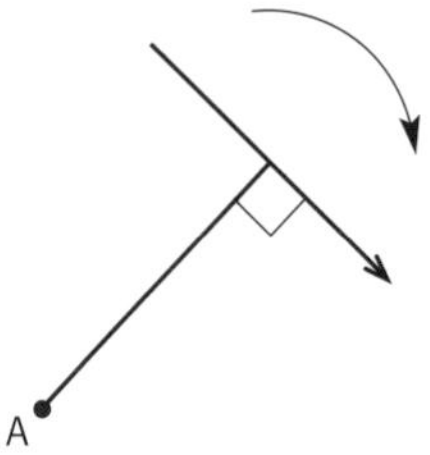

clockwise

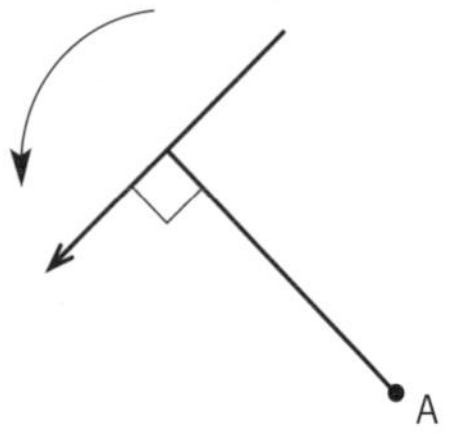

anticlockwise

One of these can be chosen as the positive sense, the other being negative.

Resultant moment

The resultant moment, M, of a set of coplanar forces about a given axis is the algebraic sum (i.e. taking the sign into account) of the individual moments about that axis. We say we are *taking moments about* the axis. This is indicated by a curved arrow whose arrowhead shows the positive sense of the moments.

For example, the resultant moment of the given forces about an axis through A is given by

$$\text{A}\circlearrowright \quad M = 4F \times a - 2F \times a\sqrt{2} - 3F \times 2a + F \times 2a$$
$$= -2Fa\sqrt{2}$$

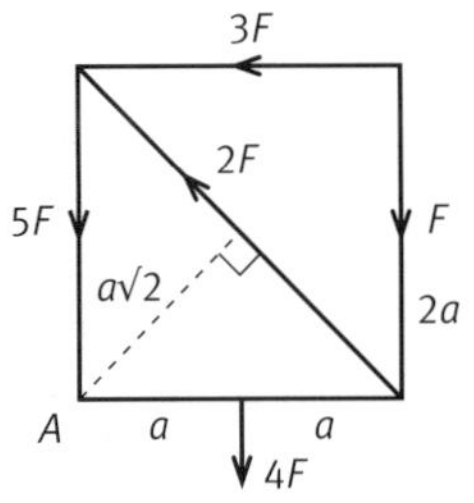

The negative result shows that the resultant moment is $2Fa\sqrt{2}$ units anticlockwise.

i The moment of any force that passes through the axis ($5F$ in this case) is zero.

Questions

1 Find the magnitude and sense of the resultant moment of the given set of forces about an axis through B.

a

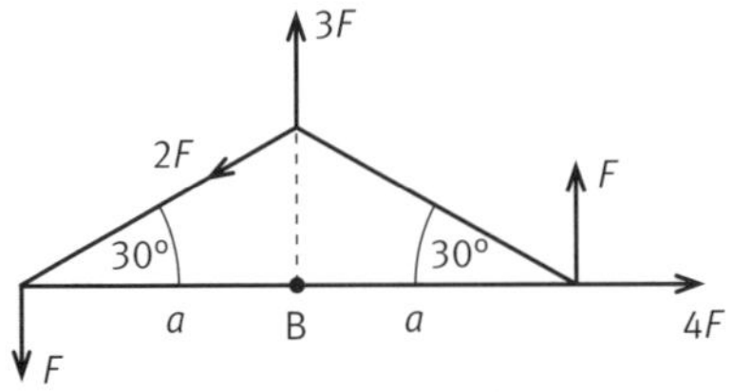

b

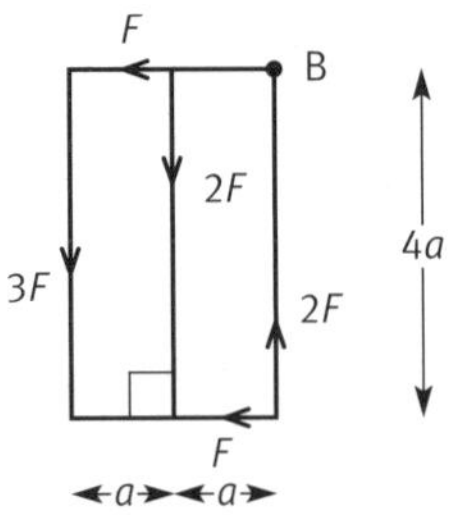

2

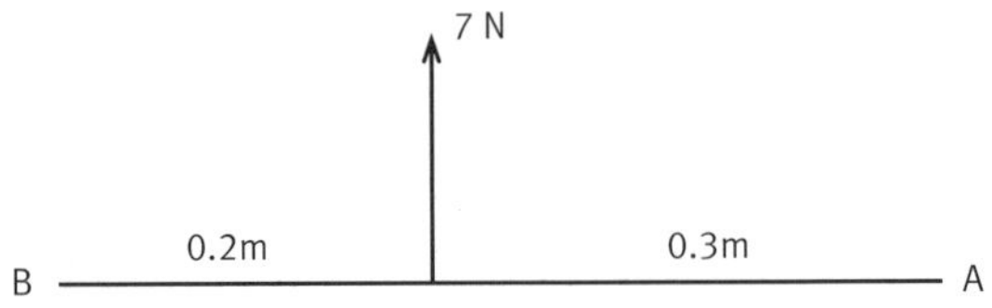

In addition to the force of 7 N shown in the diagram, a force of F N acts vertically through B. Find the value of F if the resultant moment of the two forces about A is 9.5 Nm

a clockwise **b** anticlockwise.

Answers

1a $3Fa$ anticlockwise **b** $4Fa$ anticlockwise.
2a 14.8 N in direction of 7 N
b 23.2 N in direction opposite to 7 N.

The resultant of two parallel forces

When the forces are *like,* i.e. they are in the same direction, the resultant:

- is parallel to the forces and in the same direction
- has a magnitude that is the sum of the forces
- divides the distance between them internally in the ratio of the forces
- is closer to the larger force.

For example, the resultant of the parallel forces $2F$ and $3F$ is of magnitude $5F$; it lies between the forces, dividing the distance between them internally in the ratio 3 : 2 (i.e. it is nearer to $3F$).

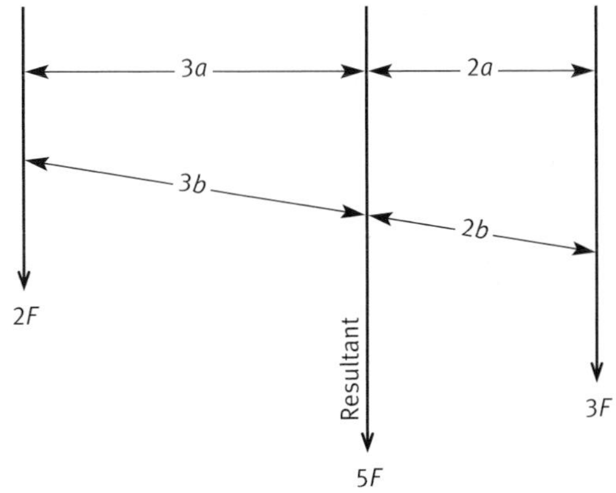

When the forces are *unlike*, i.e. in opposite directions, the resultant:

- is parallel to the forces and in the direction of the larger force
- has a magnitude that is the difference of the forces
- divides the distance between them externally in the ratio of the forces
- is closer to the larger force but is *outside* it.

For example, for two forces $2F$ and $3F$ the resultant is of magnitude F, i.e. $3F - 2F$; it is parallel to the force $3F$ and divides the distance between them *externally* in the ratio 3 : 2, i.e. it lies outside $3F$.

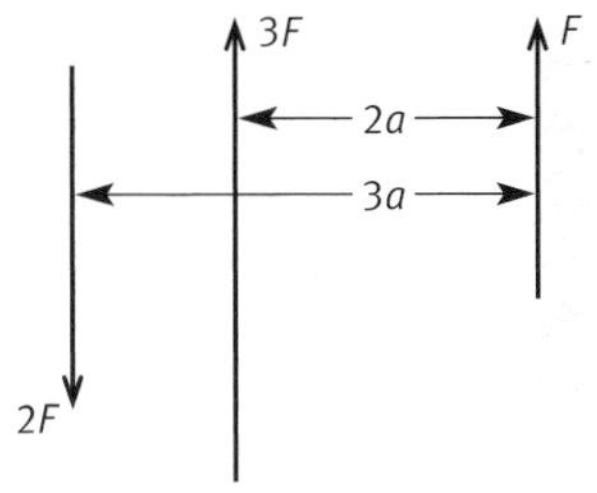

Questions

1 State the magnitude, direction and position of the resultant of each pair of parallel forces.

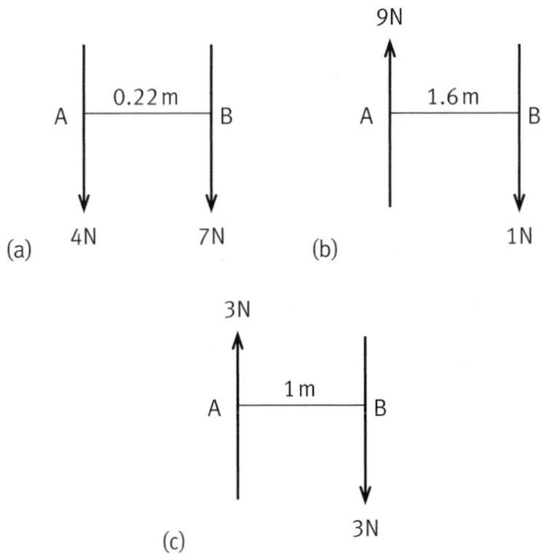

2 A rod AB of length 0.8 m is lying on a smooth horizontal table.

a The rod is pivoted at B. Find the magnitude of the moment about B of a force of 14 N applied at A **i** at right angles to AB **ii** at 30° to AB.

b The rod is not pivoted to the table and forces, each of 6 N, are applied at A and B at right angles to AB and in opposite directions as shown.

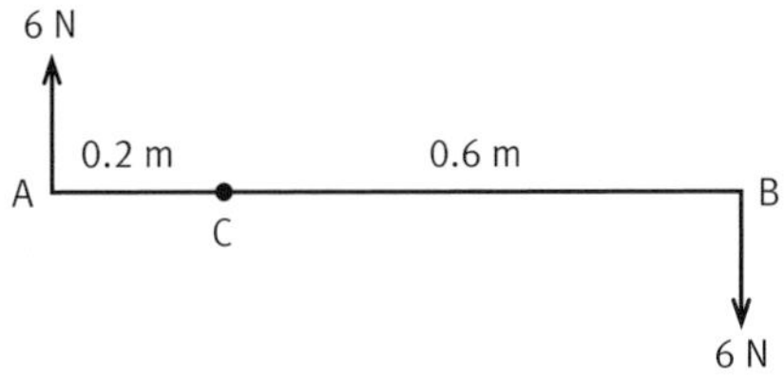

Find the magnitude of the resultant moment exerted on the rod by these forces, about an axis
i midway between A and B,
ii through C.

Answers

1a 11 N, // to given forces, 0.08 m from B, between A and B
b 8 N, in direction of 9 N, 1.8 m from B, outside A.
c zero; exerts turning effect only.
2a i 11.2 Nm **ii** 5.6 Nm
b i 4.8 Nm **ii** 4.8 Nm.

Coplanar parallel forces in equilibrium

i When a set of parallel forces is in equilibrium the resultant of the forces is zero and the resultant moment about any axis is zero.

Solving problems

The aim in any problem is to form equations from which unknown quantities can be found. You need two equations to find two unknown quantities, three equations to find three unknowns and so on.

For a problem about parallel forces you can find two independent equations *either* by collecting the forces and taking moments about one axis *or* by taking moments about two different axes. (In this case the equation given by also summing the forces is not *independent* but it gives a *check* on the values found.).

Remember that if an unknown force passes through the axis you have chosen to take moments about, that force does not appear in the equation.

When an object has parallel forces acting on it, model the object as a uniform rod.

Example

A seesaw, 4 m long, pivots at its midpoint, P. Rachel, whose weight is 26 kg, sits at one end and Jenny, who is 3.5 kg heavier, sits at the other end. The girls want to make the seesaw balance perfectly.

a How far from her end of the see-saw should Jenny sit in order to achieve this?

b If, instead, Jenny sits at the end and Rachel lifts her young sister Claire, weight 13 kg, onto the seesaw, where should Claire be placed? Take g as 10 and work correct to 2 sf.

Solution

a Let the seesaw be in equilibrium (perfectly balanced) when Jenny sits x m from the pivot P.

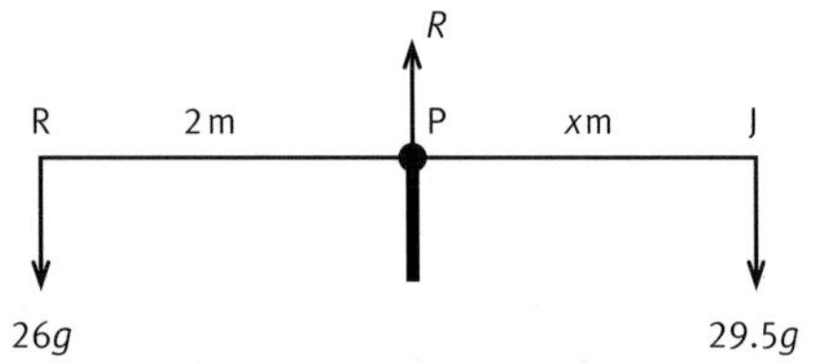

Taking moments about P avoids bringing in the reaction at the pivot.

P↻ $29.5g \times x - 26g \times 2 = 0 \Rightarrow x = 1.76$

Jenny sits 0.24 m from her end (2 sf).

b Let Claire be placed y m from P.

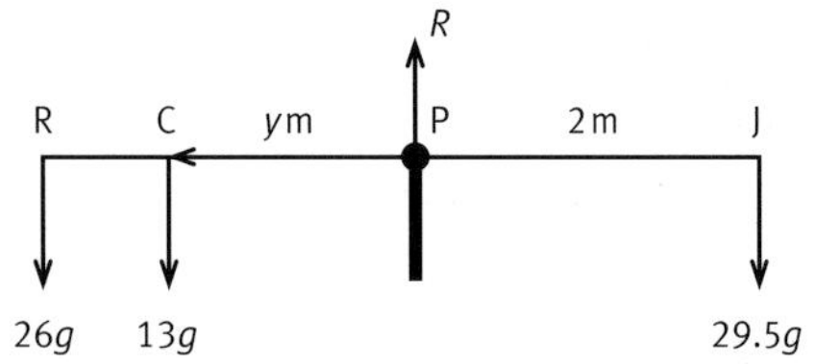

P↺ $26g \times 2 + 13g \times y - 29.5g \times 2 = 0$

$\Rightarrow y = 0.538\ldots$

Claire is placed 0.54 m from P (2 sf).

If you collect the forces, the upward force exerted by the pivot can be found. In **a** it is $(26g + 29.5g)$ N and in **b** it is $(26g + 29.5g + 13g)$ N.

Questions

Use $g = 10$ and give answers correct to 2 sf.

1 The diagram shows a simple scale for weighing vegetables consisting of a rod pivoted at P and carrying a scale pan of mass 1 kg at one end.

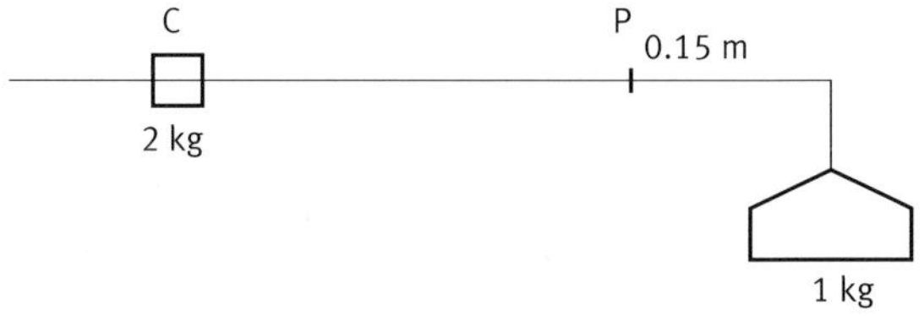

Vegetables are weighed by moving a counter-weight, C, of mass 2 kg along the graduated length of the rod until it is horizontal. Ignoring the weight of the rod, find the distance of C from P when 8 kg of potatoes are placed in the pan.

2 A painter places a uniform plank AD, of mass 24 kg and length 2.4 m, so that it rests on two walls at B and C as shown.

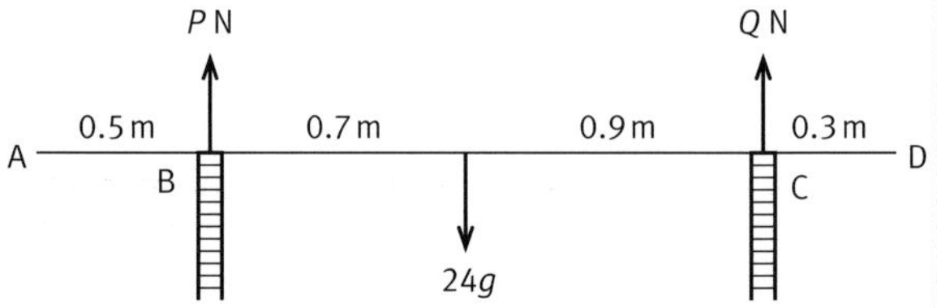

a The painter, of mass 50 kg, stands on the plank between the walls and 0.2 m from B. Find the supporting forces exerted by the walls on the plank.

b Determine how near to the end A the painter can stand without tilting the plank.

3 In a children's playground, one section in the assault course is a uniform bar, length 2.2 m and mass 8 kg, hanging suspended from two vertical ropes, one at each end. Find the tension in each rope when a girl of mass 36 kg is hanging from a point on the bar distant 0.6 m from one end. Describe the model you have used and what assumptions it requires.

4 A uniform rod AD, of mass 2 kg, carries masses of 1.8 kg at A and x kg at D. The rod is supported at two points B and C where AB = CD = 0.4 m and BC = 0.3 m. Find the value of x when the rod is on the point of tilting about **a** B **b** C.

Answers

$Q = 0 \Rightarrow x = 0.336 \Rightarrow 0.5 - x = 0.164$
To be safe he should be at least 0.17 m from A.

3 300 N in rope nearer to girl, 140 N in other rope. Model girl as particle and bar as a uniform rod; assume girl small compared with bar, also bar to be uniform and small in cross-section.

4 When the rod is about to tilt about B the reaction at C is zero.

a 0.6 **b** 3.9.

1 0.675 m

2a $57.25g$ N at B, $16.75g$ N at C (note that $\{57.25g + 16.75g\}$ N $= \{50g + 24g\}$ N – use as a check)

b B↻ $\Rightarrow 1.6Q = 168 - 500x$
When the plank is about to tilt about B it is about to lose contact with the wall at C, i.e. the force Q is zero.

Take a break

Review

1 A small block of mass 3 kg is being pulled at constant speed along a horizontal plane, by a force of 20 N inclined at an angle α to the plane.

a When the block has moved a distance of 2 m along the plane find, in terms of α, the work done by
i the force **ii** the reaction between the block and the plane.

b State, with a reason, whether the plane is rough or smooth.

In questions 2 to 6 take g as 9.8 ms^{-2} and give answers correct to 3 sf.

2 Amy has been told that she can lose weight just by going down in a lift so, to find out whether this is true she takes her scale into the lift at the top floor of a department store and stands on it. Amy's mass is 39 kg and the lift begins its descent with an acceleration of 2 ms^{-2}.

a What is the reading on the scale?

Amy then decides to try going up.

b Explain, with a diagram, what she discovers.

3 A particle, weight w, rests on the rough upper surface of a rectangular block, weight W, which is lying on a rough plane inclined at 30° to the horizontal. On separate diagrams mark all the forces that act on the particle and on the block.

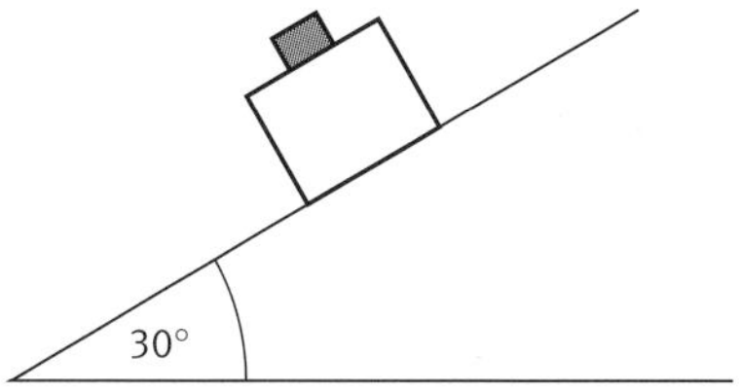

4 Two particles, A and B, lie side by side on a smooth table. The masses of A and B are m and $2m$ respectively and the particles are joined by a string. B is given a velocity $6u$ across the table.

a Find the velocity of A when the string jerks tight.

What assumptions have you made about

b the table **c** the string?

5 Two particles, A of mass $3m$ and B of mass $2m$, are connected by a light inextensible string. The string passes over a smooth pulley at the top of a smooth plane inclined at 30° to the horizontal. B is held at rest just over the pulley, which is 1 m above the ground and A rests on the inclined plane as shown.

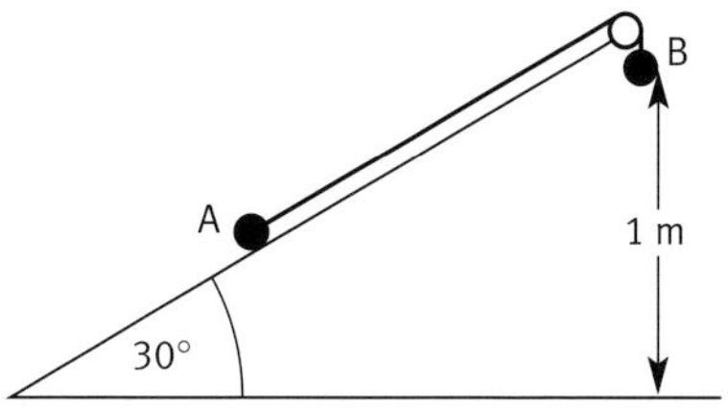

The particles are released from rest. Use conservation of mechanical energy to find

a the speed of the particles just as B reaches the ground,

b how much further up the plane A then moves before coming to rest.

6 A batsman, at the wicket P, hits a cricket ball at a speed of $19\,\text{ms}^{-1}$ and a 28° angle of elevation. The ball, which he strikes at a height of 1.2 m, hits the ground at a point Q. Find

a how long the ball is in the air,

b the horizontal distance between P and Q.

7 Some children playing pirates have constructed a 'walk-the-plank'. This consists of a wooden board, 3.6 m long and weighing 5 kg, resting over a low wall at A and loaded with a concrete block at B as shown.

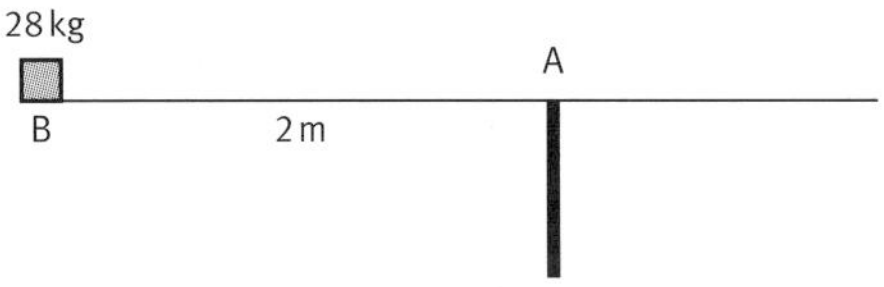

Use $g = 10$ and give answers correct to 2 sf.

a Find the weight of the heaviest child who can walk right to the end of the board without the board tipping.

b Find the force exerted by the board on the wall when this child is at the end.

c Describe any assumptions you have made and say whether you think they are reasonable, giving reasons.

Answers

1a i $40\cos\alpha$ J **ii** 0

b Rough – constant speed means zero resultant in direction of motion therefore there must be a frictional force to balance the pulling force.

2a 31.0 kg **b**

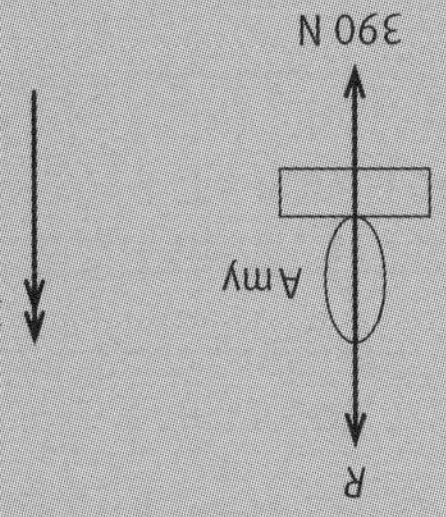

$R - 39g = 39a \Rightarrow R = 39g + 39a \Rightarrow$ scale reading > 39 kg

3

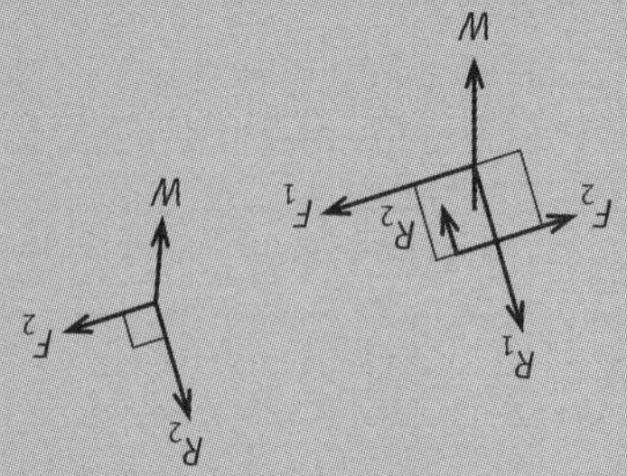

4a $4u$

b smooth and horizontal and > length of string

c light and inextensible.

5a $\sqrt{g/5}\,\text{ms}^{-1}$, $(=\sqrt{2}$ if $g = 10)$ **b** $\frac{1}{5}$ m

6a 1.91 s **b** 32.0 m

7a 360 N **b** 690 N

c child modelled as a particle – reasonable as the weight of a small child does pass through a small area (point) where the feet are; plank uniform and strong enough not to break – reasonable (if optimistic!).

PREVIEW

At the end of this topic you will have revised:

- ✔ **the meaning of centre of mass (C of M) and centre of gravity (C of G) and the relationship between them,**
- ✔ **how to calculate the C of M of a set of particles in a plane,**
- ✔ **how to find the C of G of simple plane figures including simple compound figures,**
- ✔ **the centres of gravity of common plane figures,**
- ✔ **how to deal with the equilibrium of a lamina in a vertical plane, resting on a horizontal plane, or on an inclined plane,**
- ✔ **solving problems where a plane lamina is hanging freely from a point.**

Before you start you should:

- be able to find the moment of a force about a perpendicular axis through a given point
- know how to calculate the resultant moment of a set of forces about a specified axis.

Centre of mass of a set of particles in a plane

If each particle has a mass m_n and is located at a point in the plane with coordinates (x_n, y_n) where $n = 1, 2, 3, \ldots$ the coordinates of the centre of mass are

$$\bar{x} = \frac{\sum m_n x_n}{\sum m_n} \text{ and } \bar{y} = \frac{\sum m_n y_n}{\sum m_n}$$

For example, the coordinates of the C of M of the particles shown are given by

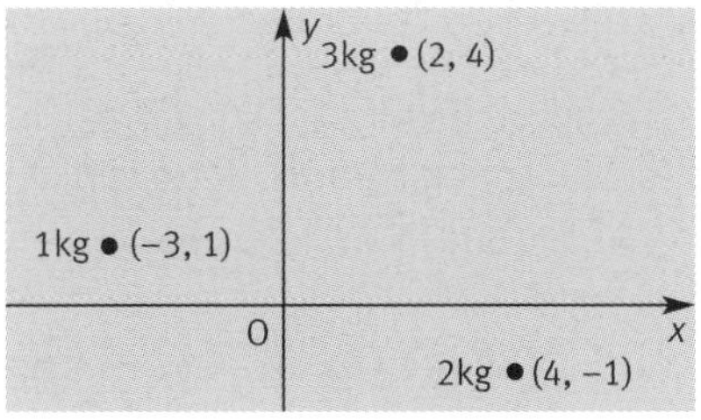

$$\bar{x} = \frac{3 \times 2 + 2 \times 4 - 1 \times 3}{3 + 2 + 1} = \frac{11}{6}$$

$$\bar{y} = \frac{3 \times 4 - 2 \times 1 + 1 \times 1}{3 + 2 + 1} = \frac{11}{6}$$

Centre of mass of a uniform plane lamina

The C of M can be thought of as the point about which the mass is evenly distributed. For some laminas the centre of mass is obvious from the symmetry of its shape, e.g. the C of M of a square or a rectangle is at the midpoint of a diagonal.

The C of M of a triangle is not obvious but is quotable and should be remembered.

For any triangle it lies at the centroid (the point of intersection of the medians) which is $\frac{1}{3}$ of the way from base to vertex on each median. It follows that, for an isosceles triangle, the C of M is on the axis of symmetry and $\frac{1}{3}$ of the way up from the base. It also follows that, for a right-angled triangle the C of M is $\frac{1}{3}a$ and $\frac{1}{3}b$ from the right angle, as shown.

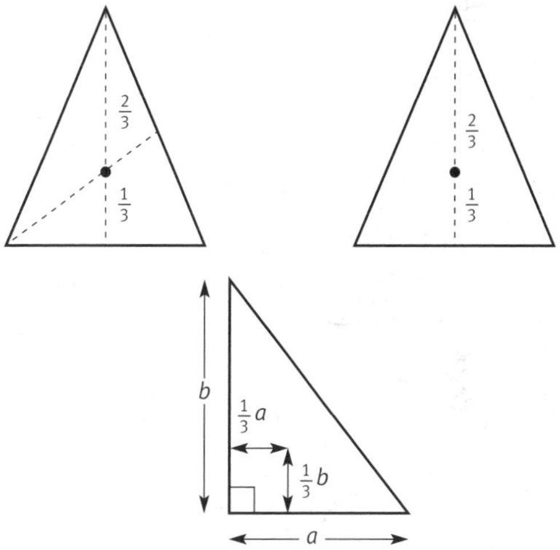

Centre of gravity

The centre of gravity of a lamina is the point at which, if the total *weight* were concentrated, the lamina would balance perfectly. It follows that the sum of the moments of the weights of the parts is equal to the moment of the total weight placed at the centre of gravity. The centre of gravity is usually represented by $G(\bar{x}, \bar{y})$

In normal circumstances the total weight acts through the centre of mass, so the centres of gravity and mass coincide. But if an object is so large that the value of g varies over its extent, the two centres are not the same (mass is independent of g but weight is not).

Centre of gravity of a compound lamina.

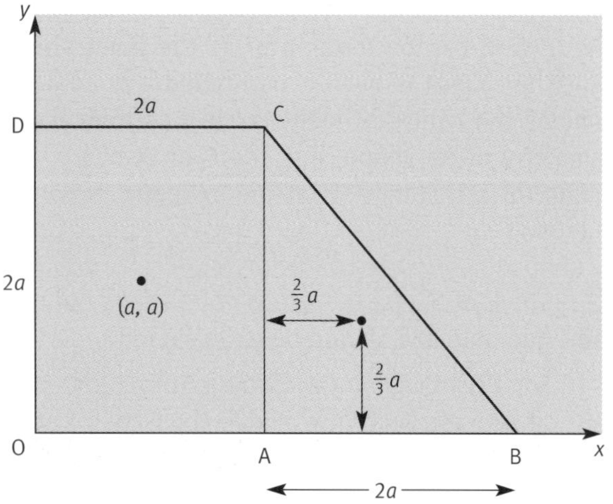

The lamina shown has uniform density. The centres of gravity of the parts are known and the weights of the parts are proportional to their areas (area × density per unit area, ρ). To find both coordinates of G we take moments about both the x-axis and the y-axis, so think of the lamina as being in a horizontal plane with the weights acting into your page.

You need to be organised in this type of problem, so list the coordinates of the centres of gravity of the parts and their weights in a table.

	OACD	ABC	Whole
Weight	$4a^2\rho$	$2a^2\rho$	$6a^2\rho$
C of G	(a, a)	$(\frac{8}{3}a, \frac{2}{3}a,)$	$(\bar{x}, \bar{y})$

Ox↺ $4a^2\rho \times a + 2a^2\rho \times \frac{2}{3}a = 6a^2\rho \times \bar{y}$

$\Rightarrow \quad \bar{y} = \frac{8}{9}a$

Oy↺ $4a^2\rho \times a + 2a^2\rho \times \frac{8}{3}a = 6a^2\rho \times \bar{x}$

$\Rightarrow \quad \bar{x} = \frac{14}{9}a$

$\therefore$ G is $(\frac{14}{9}a, \frac{8}{9}a)$.

The terms can be simplified by cancelling ρ which occurs in every term.

A compound lamina with 'holes' can be dealt with in the same way; the moment of the 'hole' is subtracted from the moment of the whole lamina. A 'hole' can be inside the lamina or it may be a part that has been removed, e.g.

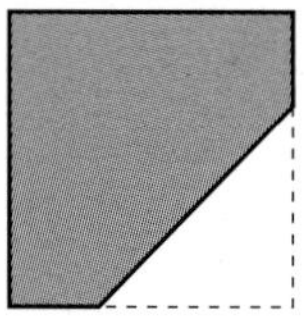

Example

Find the coordinates of the centre of gravity of the lamina shown in the diagram.

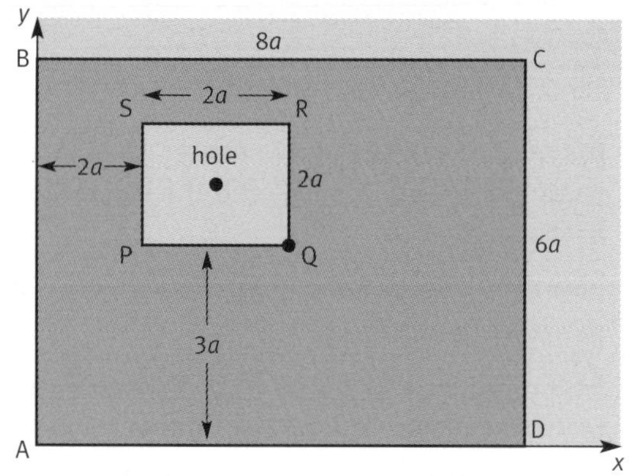

	ABCD	– PQRS	Remainder
Weight	$48a^2\rho$	$4a^2\rho$	$44a^2\rho$
C of G	$(4a, 3a)$	$(3a, 4a)$	$(\bar{x}, \bar{y})$

The minus sign with PQRS reminds you to subtract the items in that column.

AD↺ $48a^2 \times 4a - 4a^2 \times 3a = 44a^2 \times \bar{y} \quad \Rightarrow \quad \bar{y} = \frac{32}{11}a$

AB↺ $48a^2 \times 3a - 4a^2 \times 4a = 44a^2 \times \bar{x} \quad \Rightarrow \quad \bar{x} = \frac{45}{11}a$

$\Rightarrow$ G is $(\frac{45}{11}a, \frac{32}{11}a)$.

⚠ Always look at the diagram to see whether the coordinates of G look reasonable. In this case (just over $4a$, just under $3a$) seem about right.

Using symmetry

ℹ When a lamina has an axis of symmetry, G lies on that axis. For example if, in the example above, PQRS were moved down one unit so that its centre was $(3a, 3a)$, then $\bar{y}$ is obviously $3a$, from symmetry.

When there is an axis of symmetry, but the coordinates of G are not obvious, you only need to calculate one coordinate of G because G is on the axis of symmetry (i.e. taking moments about one axis is sufficient).

Questions

In questions 1 to 3, find distances of the centre of gravity of the given uniform lamina from Ox and Oy. Insert letters on your diagram if necessary, to identify the parts you use and always look for symmetry.

1

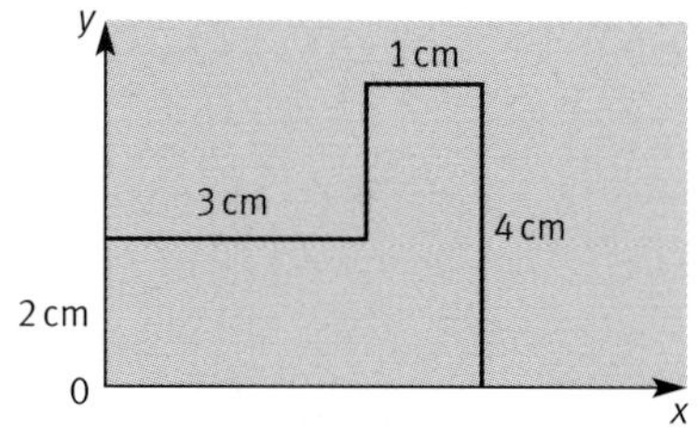

2

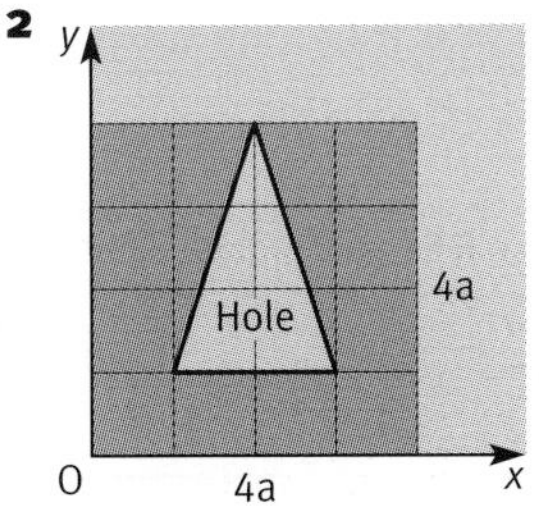

3

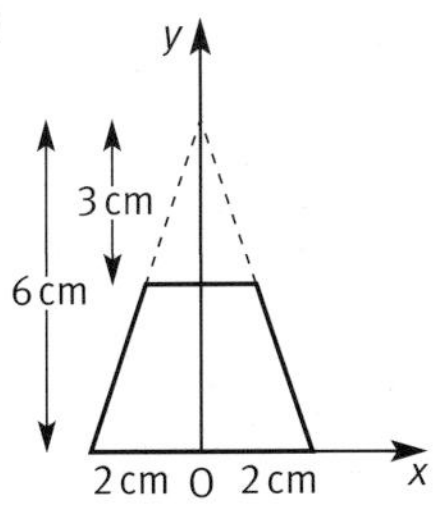

4 A square lamina ABCD of side $6a$ and weight $2W$ has a load of weight W attached to the corner C. Find the coordinates of the centre of gravity of the loaded lamina, taking AB and AD as x- and y-axes. (This is a compound body in which one 'part' is the load – treated as a particle.)

5 Find the centre of gravity of the lamina ACDF in which the density per unit area of BCDE is twice that of ABEF. (In this case use ρ as the density of ABEF and 2ρ for BCDE.)

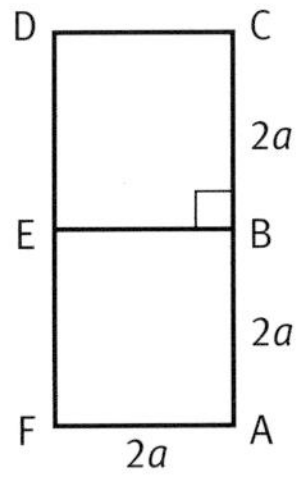

Answers

1 2.3 m, 1.4 m. **2** $(2a, 2a)$. **3** $0, \frac{4}{3}$ cm.
4 $(4a, 4a)$
5 $\frac{7}{3}a$ above AF on vertical line of symmetry.

Take a break

A lamina suspended from a point

When a lamina is freely suspended from a fixed point the centre of gravity is vertically below the point of suspension. You can use this fact to find the position in which the lamina will hang if you know where the centre of gravity is.

Example

At one stage in the construction of a garage, a wall panel, in the shape of the trapezium shown, is being lowered into position by a chain attached at A. Find the angle α between the side AB and the vertical.

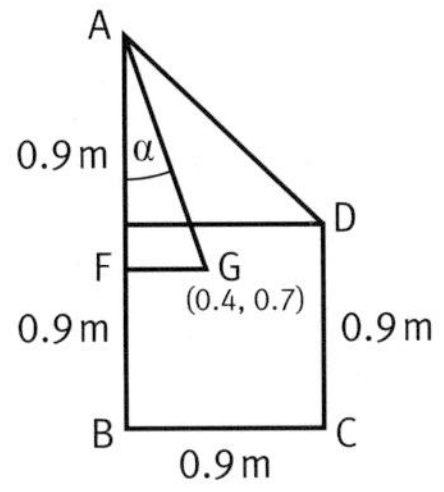

Solution

First find the centre of gravity of the lamina. Taking BC and BA as x- and y-axes gives G as (0.4, 0.7) and G is vertically below A.

i.e. AG is vertical and $\tan\alpha = \text{FG}/\text{FA}$

i.e. $\tan\alpha = 0.4 \div (1.8 - 0.7)$

$\Rightarrow \quad \alpha = 20°$ (to the nearest degree).

It is better to use the diagram in the position used to find G, and draw a 'false vertical', than to redraw the lamina in the hanging position.

Questions

1 Find the angle between AB and the vertical when this lamina is freely suspended from A.

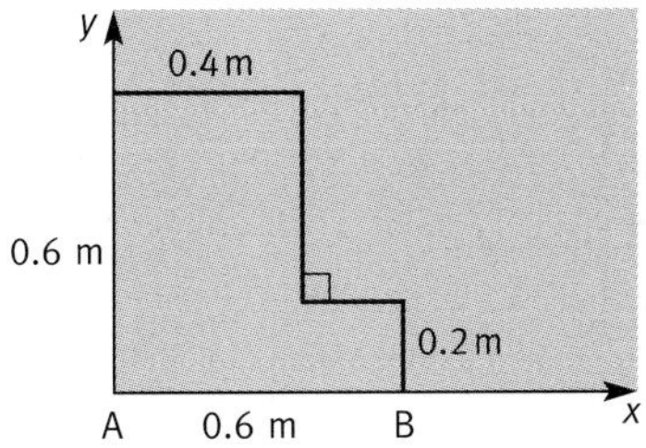

2 Find the angle between DC and the vertical when the lamina given in question 5 on the left is freely suspended from D.

3 A swinging sign is in the shape of a triangle ABC; B is a right angle and the length of BC is 0.6 m. It hangs from the corner A and AB rests at 30° to the vertical. Find the length of AB. (Take x m as the length of AB.)

4 The L-shaped lamina shown is of weight W and has a particle of weight kW attached at A so that it hangs with AB horizontal when suspended from E. Find the value of k.

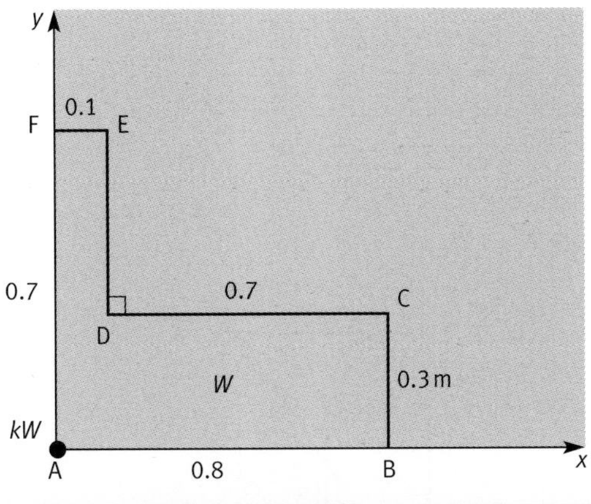

Answers

1 48°. **2** 59°. **3** 0.52 m **4** 2.5.

Stability of a lamina on a horizontal plane

A lamina placed in a vertical plane on a horizontal surface is in a similar situation to the suspended lamina. The only two forces acting, the weight and the contact force from the base, are parallel, so for equilibrium they must be in the same straight line. As the contact force always acts through a point on the base, the stability of the lamina depends on whether the weight also passes through a point within the base, i.e. on whether G lies over a point on the base.

Clearly there is a critical situation where the lamina is just on the point of overturning.

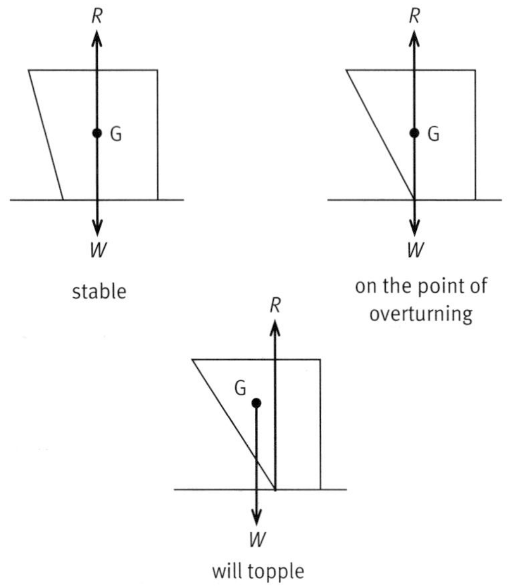

Example

ABCD is a square lamina of side $2a$ and E is a point on AB, distant $\frac{1}{2}a$ from A. The portion EBC is cut off and the remaining trapezium AECD is placed with AE on a horizontal plane. Will the lamina rest in equilibrium or will it overturn?

Solution

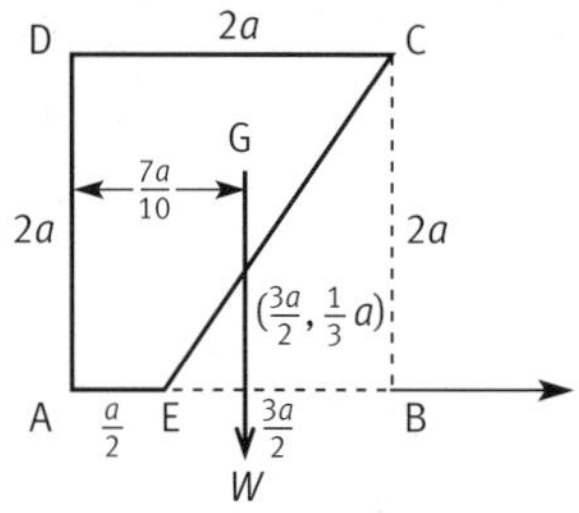

Only the value of $\bar{x}$ is needed and it can be found by taking moments about AD.

	ABCD	−BEC	AECD
Weight	$4a^2$	$\frac{3}{2}a^2$	$\frac{5}{2}a^2$
x-coord	a	$\frac{3}{2}a$	$\bar{x}$

AD↻ gives $\bar{x} = \frac{7}{10}a$, which is $>$ AE. The weight-line meets the plane outside the base AE so the lamina will overturn.

Question

A desk name-card is made in the shape of a 6 cm square with one corner removed as shown.

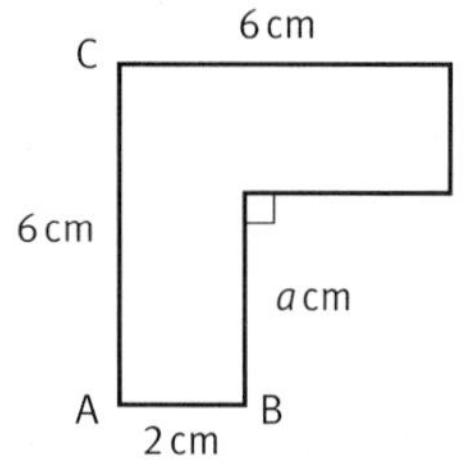

a Show that G, the centre of gravity of the L-shaped card, is $\dfrac{27 - 4a}{9 - a}$ cm from AC. The card is placed in a vertical plane with AB resting on a horizontal desk.

b If $a = 3$, determine whether the card will rest in equilibrium.

c Find the least possible value of a for which the card will not overturn.

Answer

b lamina will overturn (G is 2.5 cm from AC)

c 4.5.

Take a break

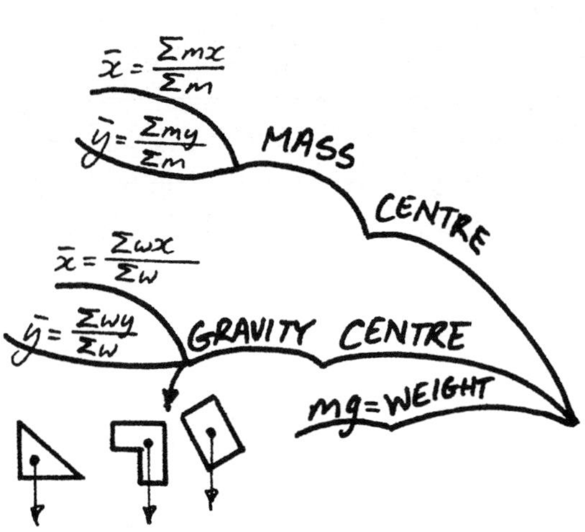

Review

1 Two forces, $\mathbf{F}_1 = (3\mathbf{i} + 5\mathbf{j})$ and $\mathbf{F}_2 = (p\mathbf{i} + q\mathbf{j})$ act on a particle.

a Find the angle between $\mathbf{F}_1$ and the vector $\mathbf{i}$.

b If the resultant of $\mathbf{F}_1$ and $\mathbf{F}_2$ is parallel to the vector $\mathbf{i} + 2\mathbf{j}$ show that $q - 2p = 1$.

2 The diagram shows a rough plane inclined at an angle θ to the horizontal. A block of weight W is placed on the plane, the coefficient of friction between block and plane being $\frac{1}{2}$. A force P is applied as shown.

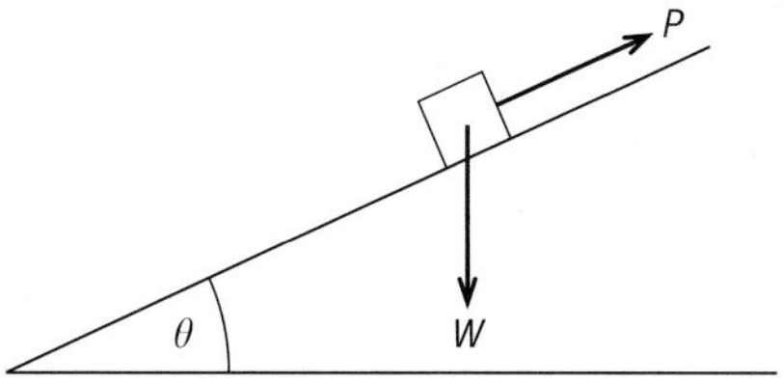

a Find the value of P in terms of W,

i if $\tan\theta = \frac{5}{12}$ and the block is on the point of slipping up the plane,

ii if $\tan\theta = \frac{3}{4}$ and the block is on the point of slipping down the plane.

3 A brick of mass 0.8 kg falls from a balcony onto a lawn 5 m below and makes a dent 0.04 m deep in the grass. Find

a the speed of the brick when it lands on the lawn,

b the time taken to fall,

c the magnitude of the resistance of the ground.

4 A rugby player takes a penalty kick from a position 20 m from the bar which is 4 m high. (The ball has to go *over* the bar in rugby.) The player projects the ball at 18 ms^{-1}. Assuming that the direction of the kick is correct, show that he will score if the angle of projection is between 33° and 69°. Describe the model you have used and say whether you think it will give reliable results.

5 AB is a uniform beam of length 4 m and mass 10 kg, resting on a fulcrum at a point C on the beam. When a load of mass 6 kg is attached at B the beam is horizontal and in equilibrium. Find the length of AC.

6 Find, using AB and AE as x- and y-axes, the position of the centre of gravity of the lamina shown in the diagram. If the lamina is suspended freely from E, what is the angle between AE and the vertical?

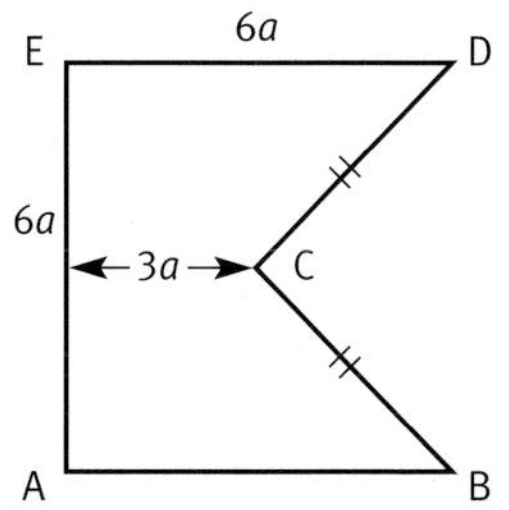

Answers

1a 59.0° **2a i** $\frac{11}{13}W$ **ii** $\frac{1}{5}W$

3a 10 ms^{-1} **b** 1 s **c** 1008 N

4 Modelling a rugby ball, with its unusual shape, as a particle in still air with no resistance, will not give reliable results.

5 2.75 m **6** $(7a/3, 3a)$ 38° (nearest degree).

PREVIEW

At the end of this topic you will have revised:

- ✔ **further methods for solving problems about objects in equilibrium under the action of three coplanar forces,**
- ✔ **equilibrium of a body under the action of any number of coplanar forces,**
- ✔ **the stability of a lamina resting in a vertical plane with one side on an inclined plane.**

Before you start you should:

- be fluent in resolving forces in any direction (If you are not, you need more practice – refer to Mechanics 2),
- be *completely familiar* with using the exact trig ratios of 30°, 45° and 60°,
- know and use the fact that the angle between a line and the horizontal is equal to the angle between a perpendicular line and the vertical.

TEST YOURSELF

This test is not just to make sure that you know what to do, but to find out whether you have the skill to carry out these operations quickly and confidently.

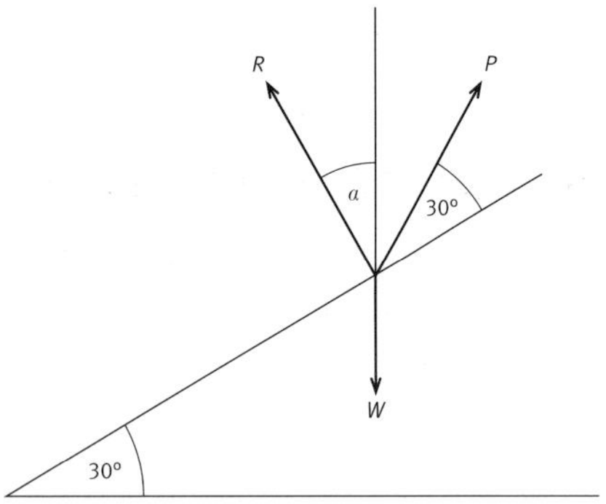

Give exact values whenever possible.

a) Resolve *W* parallel and perpendicular to the inclined plane.

b) Resolve *P*

i) horizontally and vertically

ii) parallel and perpendicular to the plane,

If this takes you longer than 2 minutes you need more practise.

Answers

a) $\parallel W\sin 30° = \frac{1}{2}W$, $\perp W\cos 30° = W\frac{\sqrt{3}}{2}$

b) i) $\rightarrow \frac{1}{2}P$, $\uparrow P\frac{\sqrt{3}}{2}$ **ii)** $\parallel P\frac{\sqrt{3}}{2}$, $\perp \frac{1}{2}P$

Equilibrium in a plane

When an object is in equilibrium under the action of a set of coplanar forces then:

- the resultant force acting on it is zero, i.e. in each of two directions the collected components are zero,

and

- the resultant moment is zero.

But if only three forces are acting , *equilibrium is possible only when the forces are concurrent.* (If two of the forces pass through P and the third force doesn't, it exerts a turning effect about P and equilibrium is impossible.) So it is sufficient that the resultant *force* is zero. Hence only two equations are needed (Mechanics 2).

Stability of a lamina on an inclined plane

A lamina can rest vertically in equilibrium, without support, on an inclined plane *only if the plane is sufficiently rough.* Then the three forces that are acting (friction, normal reaction and weight), must be concurrent. As the normal reaction and the frictional force both act through some point within the base of contact, for equilibrium the centre of gravity, G, must be vertically above the same point. The critical position, when the lamina is about to overturn, is when the weight passes through A, the lowest point of the base.

The diagrams below show a lamina placed on a plane of inclination α, where α has three different values. You know that the angle between the weight and a normal to the plane is equal to the angle of inclination of the plane. You can also find the angle θ, between AG and the normal to the plane.

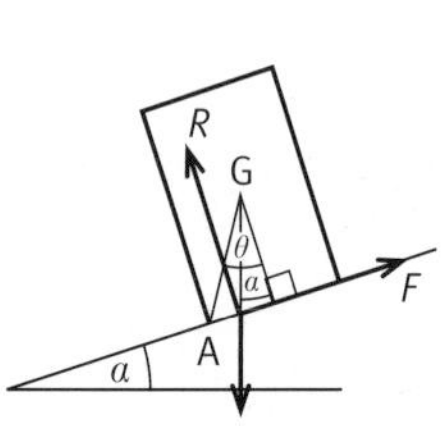

Will not overturn
$\theta > \alpha$

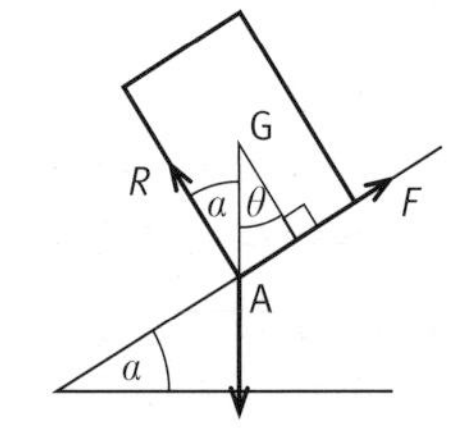

On the point of overturning
$\theta = \alpha$

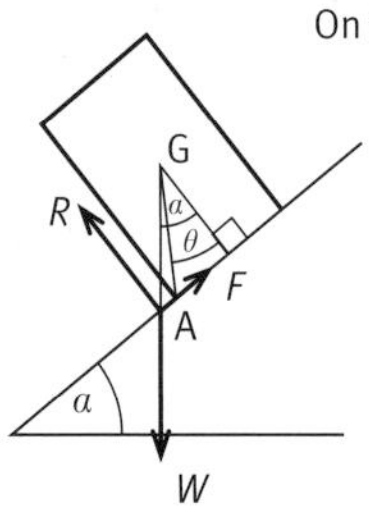

Will overturn
$\theta < \alpha$

Example

The right-angled triangular lamina ABC is placed as shown on a plane inclined to the horizontal at an angle α and is just on the point of overturning about A. Find

a the value of α

b the least possible value of the coefficient of friction between the lamina and the plane.

Solution

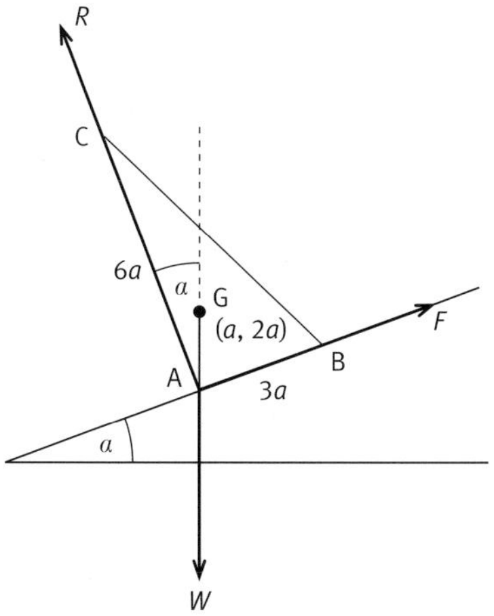

a Taking AB and AC as axes, the centre of gravity of ABC is $(a, 2a)$ and $\angle CAG = \alpha$

$\therefore \quad \tan\alpha = \frac{1}{2} \Rightarrow \alpha = 27^\circ$ (nearest whole number).

b The triangle can rest in this position only if the plane is rough enough to prevent slipping. You should know (Mechanics 2) that the lamina is about to slip when $\tan\alpha = \mu$. So the coefficient of friction must be at least $\frac{1}{2}$.

Questions

In questions 1 to 3, a uniform triangular lamina ABC, right-angled at B, is placed on a plane inclined at 30° to the horizontal, with AB on a line of greatest slope and A uppermost.

1 If $AB = 3a$, $BC = 5a$ and the plane is sufficiently rough to prevent sliding, determine whether the triangle will overturn about B.

2 If $AB = 3a$ and the lamina is on the point of sliding down and overturning simultaneously, find the length of BC and the coefficient of friction between the lamina and the plane.

3 If the lamina does overturn about B so that BC meets the plane, do you think that it would then slide down the plane? Give reasons.

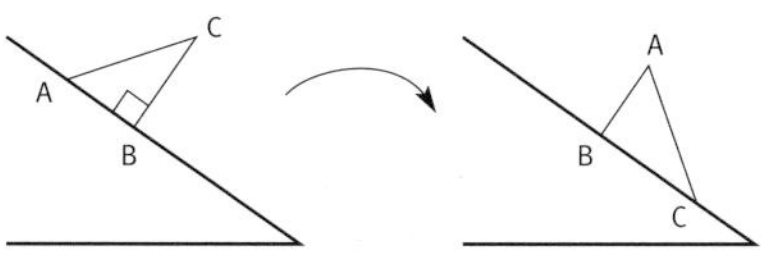

4 Show that G, the centre of gravity of the lamina shown in the diagram, is the point where

$$\bar{x} = \frac{a^2 + 2}{2a + 2}, \quad \bar{y} = \frac{2a + 5}{2a + 2}.$$

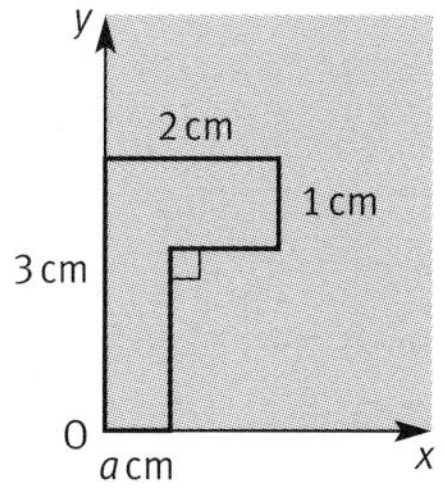

The lamina is placed with Ox on a plane inclined to the horizontal at an angle α and is on the point of overturning about O. If $\tan\alpha = \frac{3}{7}$

a find the value of a,

b what is the minimum coefficient of friction between the lamina and the plane?

Answers

1 No, GB is at 31° to normal, which is $> 30^\circ$.

2 $3a\sqrt{3}$; $\mu = \frac{1}{3}\sqrt{3}$.

3 No, μ is sufficiently large to prevent sliding before overturning so it is also large enough to prevent sliding when BC is in contact with the plane – the normal reaction is the same in both cases.

4a 1 **b** $\frac{3}{7}$.

Take a break

General equilibrium in a plane

When an object is in equilibrium under the action of a set of coplanar forces the resultant force acting on it is zero *and* the resultant moment is zero.

In practice there are three main ways in which the equilibrium of the object can be used to find unknown quantities:

- Resolve the forces in each of two different directions (often, but not always, perpendicular) and equate to zero. Then take moments about a suitable axis and equate to zero.
- Resolve in one direction and take moments about two different axes, equating each to zero.
- Take moments, and equate to zero, about three different axes that do not lie in a straight line, i.e.

A↻ C↻ not A↻ B↻ C↻
B↻

Solving problems

- Check that there are not more than three unknown quantities (forces, angles etc.), because only three independent equations can be formed using equilibrium in a plane. Any extra unknown should be found first from trigonometry, symmetry, etc.
- When choosing an axis to take moments about, it helps if at least one of the forces passes through the chosen point.
- When you have to find an angle, try isolating $\sin\theta$ in one equation and $\cos\theta$ in another to give $\tan\theta$.

Example

A ladder, of mass 35 kg and length 5 m, rests with its foot A on rough horizontal ground and the top B against a smooth vertical wall.
Find the angle θ between the ladder and the wall when the ladder is just about to slip given that the coefficient of friction between the ladder and the ground is $\frac{1}{4}$. State any assumptions you have made.

Solution

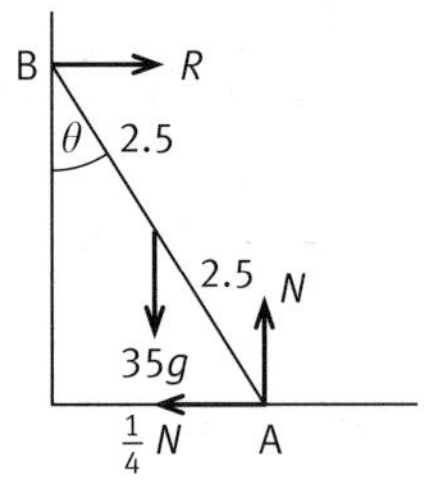

The horizontal reaction is the only force acting at B as there is no friction. The frictional force at A is limiting, i.e. equal to $\frac{1}{4}N$. Resolve horizontally and vertically and take moments about an axis through A (two forces pass through A).

Resolving $\rightarrow$ $\quad \frac{1}{4}N - R = 0$ and $\uparrow N - 350 = 0$
A↻ $\quad R \times 5\cos\theta - 350 \times 2.5\sin\theta = 0$
From the first two equations, $N = 350$ and $R = 87.5$, then from the third,
$\tan\theta = 5R/(350 \times 2.5) = 0.5 \quad \Rightarrow \quad \theta = 26.6°$

The following assumptions have been made:
The weight of the ladder acts at the midpoint. Taking $g = 10$ is accurate enough.

Example

A beam AB, mass 16 kg and length 1.4 m, is hinged to a wall at A and is supported at 60° to the upward vertical by a rope fastened to B. The other end of the rope is attached to the wall at C where angle ABC = 90°. Take g as 10 ms^{-2}.

a Find the tension in the rope and the magnitude of the force at the hinge.

b Without further calculation deduce whether the tension would increase or decrease if the rope were horizontal.

Solution

a There must be both a vertical and a horizontal component of force at the hinge in order to balance the tension and the weight. Taking moments about two axes is useful, as each equation isolates unknown forces.

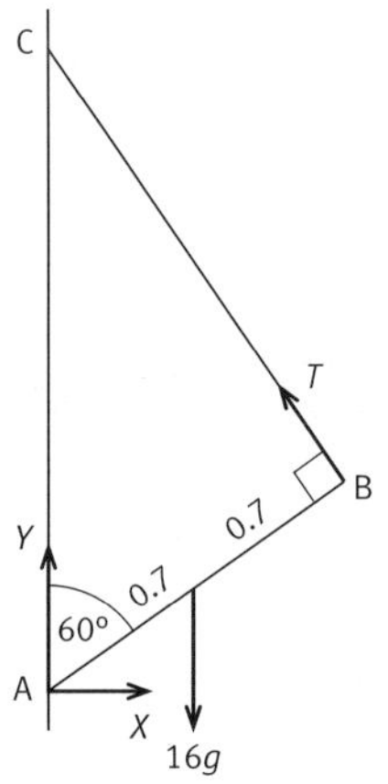

(Take moments about A as X and Y pass through A)
A↻ $16g \times 0.7\sin 60° - T \times 1.4 = 0 \Rightarrow T = 69$ N (2 sf)

(Take moments about C as T and Y pass through C)
C↻ $16g \times 0.7\sin 60° - X \times 1.4 \div \cos 60° = 0$
$\Rightarrow \quad X = 35$ N (2 sf)

We now have values for T and X so resolve ↑ to find Y.
$\uparrow Y + T\sin 60° - 16g = 0 \quad \Rightarrow \quad Y = 100$ N (2 sf)
The force at the hinge is the resultant of X and Y i.e. its magnitude is $\sqrt{(X^2 + Y^2)} = 110$ N (2 sf)

b The perpendicular distance from A to the rope would be reduced so, to give the same moment about A, the tension would increase.

Questions

In questions 1 to 3, a uniform ladder of weight W and length $2a$ rests with one end A on horizontal ground and the other, B, against a vertical wall. The angle between the ladder and the wall is θ.

1 Find the value of θ when the ladder is on the point of slipping

a if the wall is smooth, the ground is rough and the coefficient of friction is $\frac{1}{2}$,

b if both the wall and the ground are rough with a coefficient of friction of $\frac{1}{4}$.

2 When $\theta = 30°$, a man of weight $4W$ climbs the ladder described in question **1a**. How far up the ladder can he go before the ladder is about to slip?

3 Explain briefly why the ladder can never rest in equilibrium if the ground is smooth.

4 A beam AB of weight 40 kg and length 2 m is held with A in contact with a rough vertical wall. The beam is perpendicular to the wall and is supported in this position by a rope fastened to the end B and to a point C on the wall above A such that angle ACB is 20°. If the beam is in limiting equilibrium (about to slip), find

a the tension in the rope,

b the coefficient of friction between the beam and the wall.

Answers

1a 45° **b** 28° **2** $1.9a$ from A.

3 There must be a horizontal force to balance the normal reaction from the wall at the top of the ladder; therefore friction must act at the foot.

4a 213 N **b** 2.75.

Take a break

Review

Questions 1 to 6 each make a statement; it may be fundamentally true (T), occasionally but not always true (OT), or quite false (F). In each case say which category you think the statement belongs in. If is false, comment on how the misconception might have arisen.

1 You can lose weight by standing in a lift that is accelerating downwards. If its acceleration is great enough you become weightless.

2 When an object hits a rigid barrier at speed and does not rebound, its energy is absorbed by the barrier.

3 If a car is towing a caravan, it is the driving force of the car's engine that pulls the caravan.

4 Any set of coplanar forces is in equilibrium if the resultant force is zero.

5 For a given speed of projection you can throw a ball the greatest distance if you throw it at an angle of 60° to the horizontal.

6 When two objects collide with a bang, the sound of the bang comes from some of the kinetic energy the objects had before impact.

7 The diagram shows a collar, of mass 1 kg, that can slide on a rough horizontal rod, the coefficient of friction being $\frac{1}{3}$.
A light string is attached to the collar and is held at 25° to the rod as shown. The string is pulled so that it exerts a gradually increasing force on the collar. Find the value of the force T N when the collar is just about to slip on the rod.

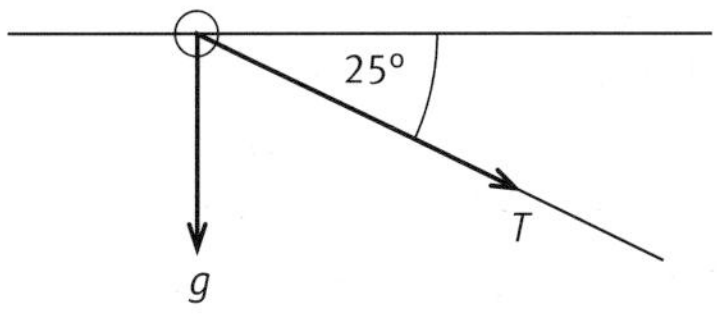

8 The diagram represents a car of mass 1000 kg standing on level ground.
G_1 is the centre of gravity of the vehicle and G_2 is the centre of gravity of a load of 200 kg in the boot.
Find the force exerted by the loaded car on the front axle, A, and on the rear axle, B.

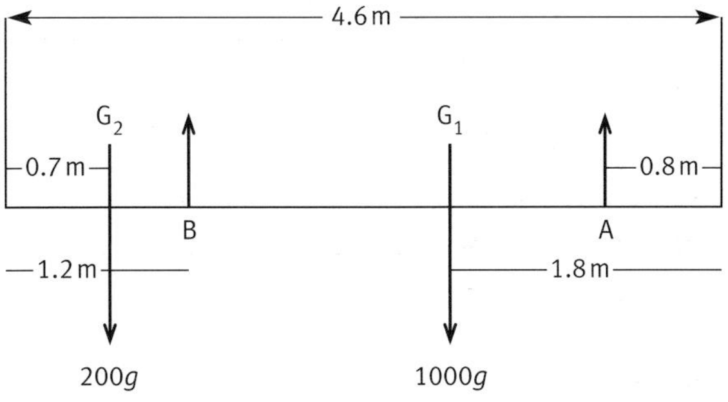

9 A car is moving on a straight stretch of road between two points A and B, 300 m apart. The road is inclined at 6° to the horizontal. The car, whose mass is 600 kg, passes through A at a speed of 12 ms^{-1} and travels down the slope to B where its speed is 36 ms^{-1}.

a Find the driving force of the car, assumed to be constant, if the resistance to motion can be ignored.

b If, instead, there is a constant resistance to motion of 1000 N, find the power of the engine at B given that the car's acceleration at B is zero.

c The power of the car's engine found in **b** is constant from A to B. Find the acceleration of the car at A.

Answers

1. F – scales measure the normal reaction, not the weight; this reaction is reduced in the given circumstances ($mg - R = mf$) and could reach zero if $f = g$.
2. OT – some energy may be converted into sound or heat energy.
3. F – it is the tension in the towbar that pulls the caravan.
4. OT – true if the forces are concurrent; if not concurrent the condition of zero turning effect must also apply.
5. F – angle should be 45° so that $V^2 \sin 2\theta$ is greatest.
6. T.

[Answers are given to 3 sf in the next questions]

7 4.35 N **8** 6230 N; 5770 N **9a** 530 N **b** 13 kW **c** 1.2 ms^{-2}.

PREVIEW

At the end of this topic you will have revised:

- ✔ **what the law of restitution means,**
- ✔ **how to solve problems about colliding objects that bounce,**
- ✔ **the meaning of *e*, the coefficient of restitution,**
- ✔ **the range of possible values of *e*.**

Before you start you should remember that:

- when two objects collide their momentum is unchanged,
- momentum is a vector so diagrams need a chosen positive direction,
- at impact the objects exert equal and opposite impulses on each other; to find the magnitude of each impulse you have to find the change in the momentum of *one* of the objects,
- there is usually a loss in mechanical energy due to a collision.

Collision with a fixed surface

When an object collides with a fixed surface and bounces, e.g. a ball falling to the ground and bouncing, there is a relationship between its speed immediately before impact and its speed immediately after impact, which is

speed just after $= e \times$ speed just before, where e is a constant for a given object and surface.

The fixed surface exerts an external impulse on the object so the momentum of the object changes.

Two colliding objects

When two objects collide and bounce, there is a similar relationship between their speed of approach (the relative speed just before impact) and the speed of separation (the relative speed immediately after impact), i.e.

separation speed $= e \times$ approach speed where e is a constant for two colliding objects and is called the **coefficient of restitution** or, sometimes, the coefficient of elasticity.

This is Newton's Law of Restitution and it applies to a collision between two objects or a collision with a fixed surface.

The law involves only the *instantaneous* speeds at impact and has no bearing on the motion of either object in the time intervals before and after the moment of impact.

The possible values of e are limited to the range

$$0 \leqslant e \leqslant 1.$$

If $e = 0$ there is no bounce and the objects become joined together. This is called *inelastic* impact.
If $e = 1$ there is a 'perfect' bounce and in this case there is no loss in mechanical energy.

Solving problems

For the actual collision between one object and a fixed surface you need only the law of restitution but you will probably have to deal with the motion leading up to, and following, the collision.

For a collision between two objects the laws of restitution and conservation of momentum are both used. It is essential to draw clear 'just before' and 'just after' diagrams and to choose a positive direction for applying conservation of momentum.

If more than one collision takes place, remember that each collision is complete in itself and independent of any subsequent bounce. So you are free to choose a different positive direction for each impact.

Example

A ball of mass m is dropped from a height h on to horizontal ground. The coefficient of restitution between the ball and the ground is e. Find, in terms of h and e, the height to which the ball rises after the second bounce.

Solution

Use conservation of mechanical energy each time while the ball is moving in the air, to find the speed at impact.

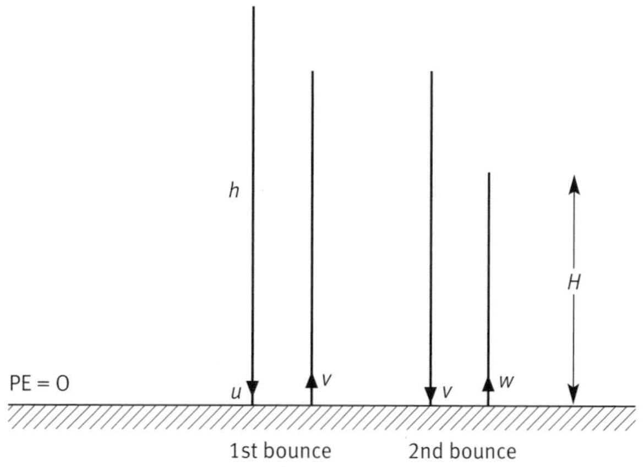

Speed just before 1st bounce

$$\tfrac{1}{2}mu^2 = mgh \quad \Rightarrow \quad u = \sqrt{2gh}$$

1st bounce
At impact the law of restitution gives $v = eu$

$$\Rightarrow \quad v = e\sqrt{2gh}$$

The ball then rises with initial speed eu and falls, hitting the ground with the same speed eu.

2nd bounce
The law of restitution gives $w = e(eu) = e^2u$

$$\Rightarrow \quad w = e^2\sqrt{2gh}.$$

The ball now rises to a height H.
Conservation of ME gives $\tfrac{1}{2}mw^2 = mgH$

$$\Rightarrow \quad mgH = \tfrac{1}{2}m(2ghe^4) \quad \Rightarrow \quad H = he^4.$$

Example

Two small spheres, A and B, are moving in the same straight line and in the same direction. Just before they collide, A, whose mass is m kg, is moving with speed $4\,\text{ms}^{-1}$; the mass of B is 2 kg and its speed is $1\,\text{ms}^{-1}$. If the speeds of A and B after impact are $3\,\text{ms}^{-1}$ and $4\,\text{ms}^{-1}$ respectively, both in the same direction as before impact, find
a the value of m and the coefficient of restitution between A and B,
b the impulse exerted by each sphere on the other.

Solution

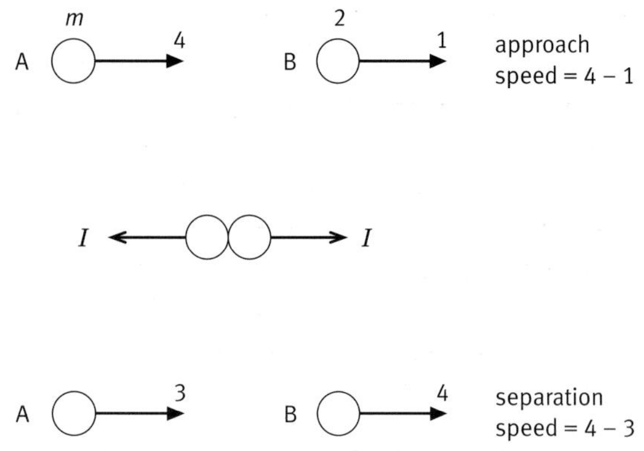

a Conservation of momentum ($\rightarrow +$ve) gives

$$4m + 2 = 3m + 8 \quad \Rightarrow \quad m = 6.$$

Law of restitution gives

$$e(4-1) = 4-3 \quad \Rightarrow \quad e = \tfrac{1}{3}.$$

b For B alone

$\rightarrow +$ve $\qquad I = 2(4-1) = 6$

Impulse exerted is 6 Ns.

Problem solving

Here are some useful tips:

- you should deal with each impact, one at a time, simplifying the results as far as possible before going on to the next
- before and after diagrams for *each* impact are *essential*
- it helps to keep a similar layout for each impact
- you can abbreviate the principles you are using, e.g. Cons. of mom.
- you can use a different letter to represent each different velocity but this can get complicated (especially as solutions are sometimes quite long). A neat way to organise your solution is to use the same symbol throughout for the speed of one object, another symbol throughout for a second object and so on. Then use a suffix to indicate the number of an impact, e,g. if, in a problem, objects A and B collide more than once, the speed of A after the second impact could be denoted by u_2 and the speed of B after the third impact by v_3. This system can be extended to problems with more objects and more impacts.

Example

A small bead A of mass m is moving on a smooth horizontal surface towards an identical bead B that is stationary. A collides with B with speed $2u$. The coefficient of restitution between A and B is 0.8.

a Find the speeds of A and B just after the impact in terms of u.

B then goes on to collide with a vertical barrier perpendicular to the direction of motion. The coefficient of restitution between B and the barrier is $\tfrac{1}{2}$. B rebounds and then collides again with A.

b Find the speeds of A and B just after this collision, in terms of u.

Solution

a 1st impact (A with B)

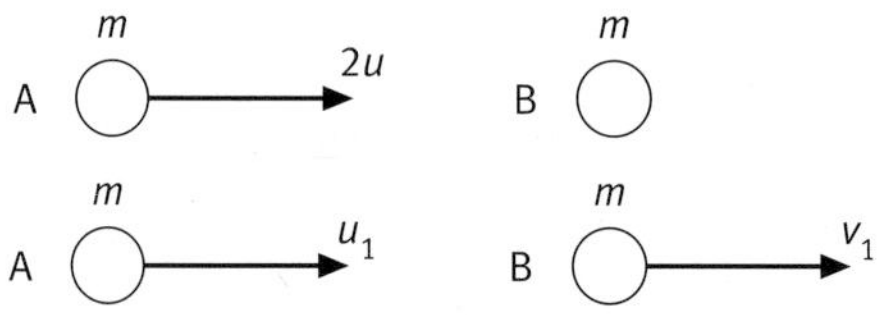

Conservation of momentum ($\rightarrow +$ve)

$$2mu + 0 = mu_1 + mv_1$$

Law of restitution

$$0.8(2u) = v_1 - u_1 = 1.6u$$

Solving these simultaneous equations gives

$$2v_1 = 3.6u \quad \text{and} \quad 2u_1 = 0.4u$$

$\therefore$ $\boxed{v_1 = 1.8u}$ and $\boxed{u_1 = 0.2u}$

Because answers tend to be found at stages throughout the whole solution, it helps in an exam to put boxes round the answers as they arise.

2nd impact (B with barrier).

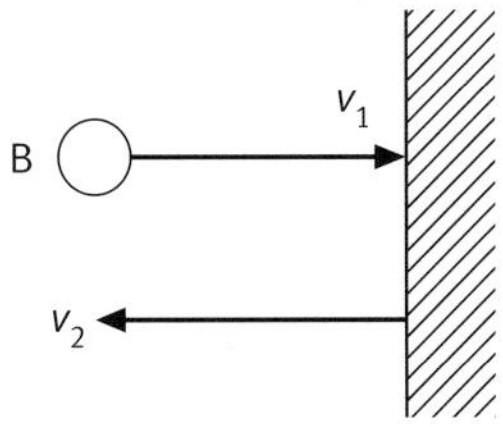

B's speed is constant until it hits the barrier, because the surface is smooth.

B's speed away from the barrier = $e \times$ approach speed, i.e. $v_2 = \frac{1}{2} \times 1.8u \quad \Rightarrow \quad \boxed{v_2 = 0.9u}$
(this is denoted by v_2 as it is B's second impact, but A is not involved so there is no u_2.)

b 3rd impact (B with A)

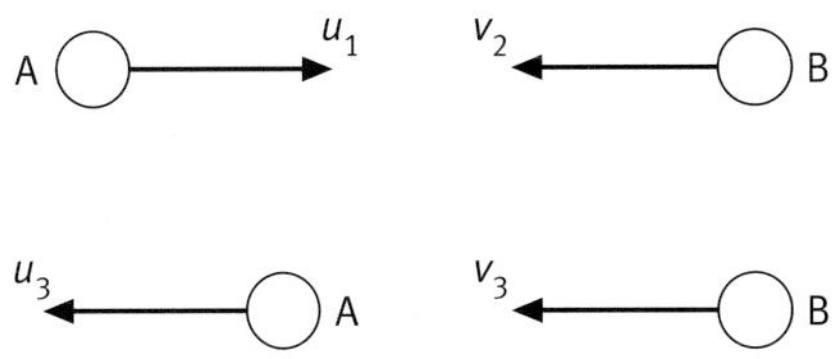

Conservation of momentum $\leftarrow$ +ve

$$-mu_1 + mv_2 = mu_3 + mv_3$$

$$\Rightarrow \quad u_3 + v_3 = -0.2u + 0.9u = 0.7u$$

Law of restitution

$$u_3 - v_3 = 0.8(u_1 + v_2) = 0.8(1.1u) = 0.88u$$

Solving the two equations gives

$$2u_3 = 1.58u \quad \text{and} \quad 2v_3 = -0.18u$$

$\therefore$ A's speed is $0.79u$ away from the barrier and B's speed is $0.09u$ *towards* the barrier.

You cannot always tell which way an object will move after an impact. In this example B's direction of motion was marked away from the barrier but the minus sign given shows that B moves in the opposite direction. You can see from this case that it doesn't matter if you choose the wrong direction – the sign of the answer will put you right.

⚠ You can use the speeds you have already calculated at successive stages instead of the recommended symbols. But if you do this, and make a mistake, you may not notice and it is not easy to trace.

Questions

1 A ball is projected vertically upwards from a point on a horizontal pavement with speed $7\,\text{ms}^{-1}$. The coefficient of restitution between the ball and the pavement is e.

a Find, in terms of g and e, the speed at which the ball begins to rise after the first bounce, and the height it reaches.

b Find, in terms of g and e, the total distance that the ball travels up to moment of the second impact with the ground.

c Show that the total distance that the ball travels before it comes to rest is $\dfrac{49}{g(1-e^2)}$ m.

d If $e = \frac{1}{2}$ and the mass of the ball is 0.4 kg, find the impulse exerted on the ball at the first impact.

2 The diagram shows two particles moving towards each other in the same straight line.

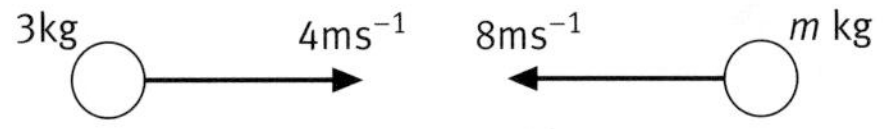

Their masses and speeds just before they collide are as shown.

a Find m if both particles are brought to rest by the impact.

If, instead, $m = 2$ and the particles move away from each other with equal speeds just after impact, find

b the coefficient of restitution between the particles,

c the loss in kinetic energy caused by the collision.

3 A disc A, of mass 0.5 kg, lying on a smooth tray, is projected with speed $3\,\text{ms}^{-1}$ towards the vertical rim of the tray where coefficient of restitution is 0.7. After rebounding, disc A collides directly with a stationary disc B, of mass 0.9 kg, the coefficient of restitution between A and B being 0.6. Determine whether disc A next collides with the rim again.

4 Three particles, A, B and C of masses $3m$, m and $2m$ respectively, lie in order in a straight line on a smooth table. B and C are initially stationary and A is projected towards B with speed $6u$.

a If the coefficient of restitution between A and B is $\frac{1}{2}$, find the speeds of A and B after their first collision.

b Find the speeds of B and C after they collide given that the coefficient of restitution is $\frac{1}{3}$.

c Show that A and B collide for a second time.

Answers

1a $7e$, $\frac{49e^2}{2g}$ **b** $\frac{49(1+e^2)}{g}$

c (this is the sum of a GP) **d** 4.2 N

2a $\frac{2}{3}$ **b** $\frac{3}{2}$ **c** 48 units

3 Yes; A's direction is reversed by the impact with B

4a A: $\frac{15u}{4}$ B: $\frac{27u}{4}$ **b** B: $\frac{3}{4}u$ C: $3u$

c A's speed ← > B's speed ←, so A will collide again with B.

Take a break

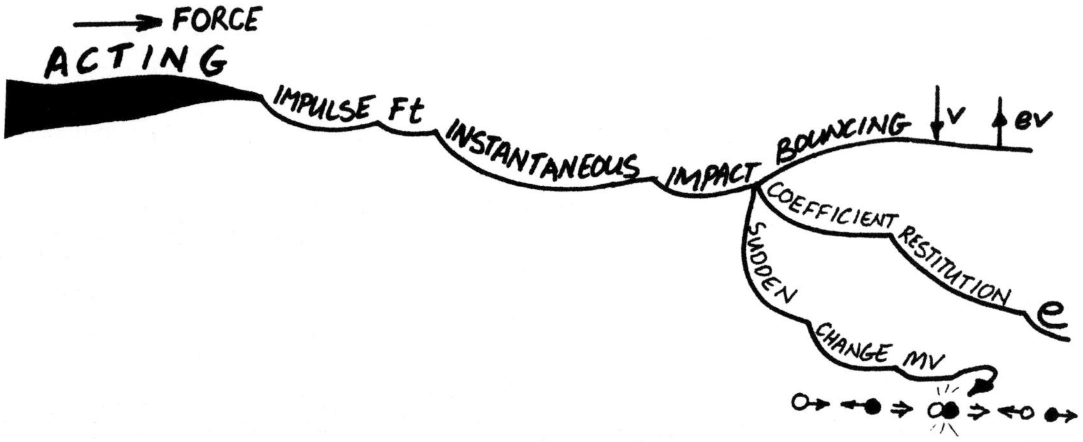

Review

1 The diagram shows a trolley A, of mass 4 kg, connected by an inextensible rope to a counterweight B of mass 3.4 kg. The rope passes over a smooth pulley at the top of the slope which is inclined at an angle θ to the horizontal where $\tan\theta = \frac{3}{4}$.

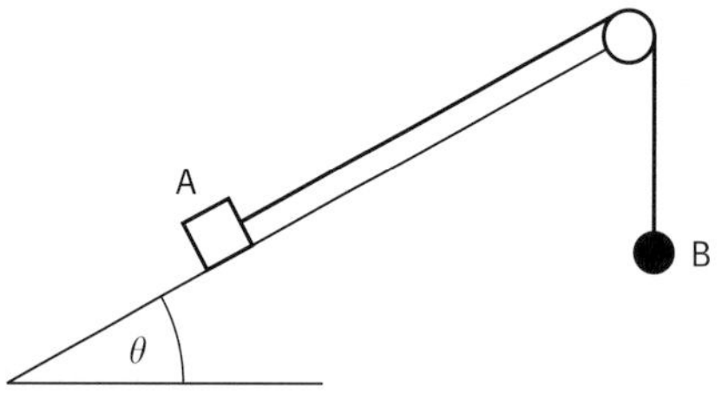

a If the trolley is in limiting equilibrium find the coefficient of friction between the trolley and the plane.

b If, instead, the coefficient of friction is $\frac{1}{4}$, find the acceleration with which the trolley begins to move, giving the direction of motion.

2 The end A of a uniform metal pole AB, of weight W and length $2a$, is hinged to a wall and is held at an angle α to the upward vertical by a chain joining the end B to a point C on the wall. The angle ABC is 90°.

a Find the tension in the chain in terms of W and α.

b Without further calculation deduce whether the tension would be greater or less if AB were held in the same position but the chain were horizontal.

3 An athlete throws a javelin at 50° to the horizontal, from a point A at a height of 2 m above ground level. It hits the ground at a point B where the horizontal distance from A is 80 m. Find

a the speed of projection,

b the time taken for the javelin to reach the ground.

State what assumptions you have made and comment on how reasonable they are.

4 Three small blocks, A of mass m, B of mass $2m$ and C of mass $3m$, lie in a straight line on a smooth table top, in that order. A is connected to B and B to C each by a light inextensible string that is initially slack. A is projected along the table, directly away from B, with speed $6u$.

a Find the speed of A and B when B is jerked into motion, and the impulsive tension in the string joining A and B.

b Find the speed of all three blocks when C is jerked into motion, and the impulsive tension in each string.

c Verify that the final momentum of the three blocks is equal to the initial momentum of A.

5

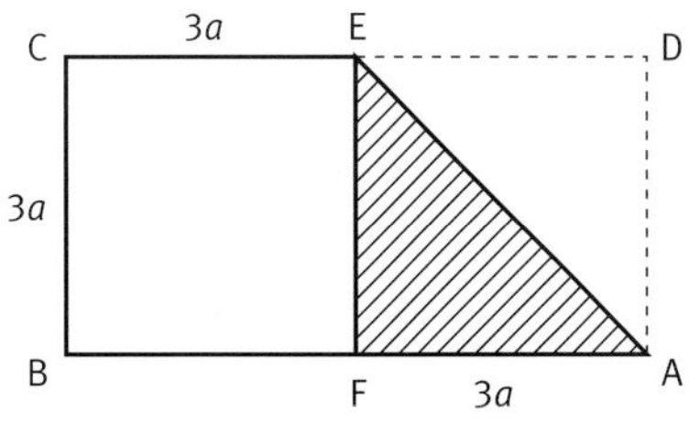

The diagram shows a rectangular card ABCD in which AB $= 6a$ and BC $= 3a$. E is the midpoint of CD and F is the midpoint of AB. A fold is made along AE and the triangle ADE is folded over so that DE lies along FE. Find the distances from BA and BC of the centre of gravity of the folded card.

Answers

1a $\frac{5}{16}$ **b** $\frac{g}{37}$ ms^{-2} towards the pulley

2a $\frac{1}{2}W \sin \alpha$ **b** A would be nearer to the chain so, to give the same moment about A, the tension would be greater.

3a $28.2\ ms^{-1}$

b 4.41 s: Model the javelin as a particle moving with no resistance. Not very reasonable as the javelin is very different from a particle and its twisting flight would encounter air resistance.

4a $2u$; $4mu$ **b** u; mu in AB, $3mu$ in BC **5** $\frac{5a}{4}$, $\frac{11a}{4}$

PREVIEW

At the end of this topic you will have revised:

- ✔ **how an object moving in a circle has an acceleration towards the centre so a force acts in this direction,**
- ✔ **the magnitude of the acceleration for a given radius and speed round the circumference,**
- ✔ **solving problems when a particle moves in a circle on a smooth horizontal plane,**
- ✔ **motion of a particle describing a horizontal circle at the end of a string,**
- ✔ **motion of a vehicle on a banked track.**

Before you start you should know:

- if ω is the angular speed of a particle round a circle of radius r, the speed round the circumference is $r\omega$.

Acceleration of a body describing a circle

As the direction of a particle P travelling in a circular path is continually changing from the tangent to the circumference, there is an acceleration towards O.

The magnitude of this acceleration is $\frac{v^2}{r}$ where v is the speed round the circumference and r is the radius of the circle. Alternatively, if the angular speed is ω, the acceleration is $r\omega^2$ towards O (as $v = r\omega$).

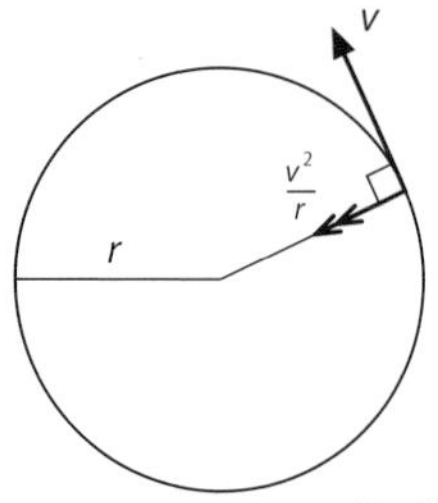

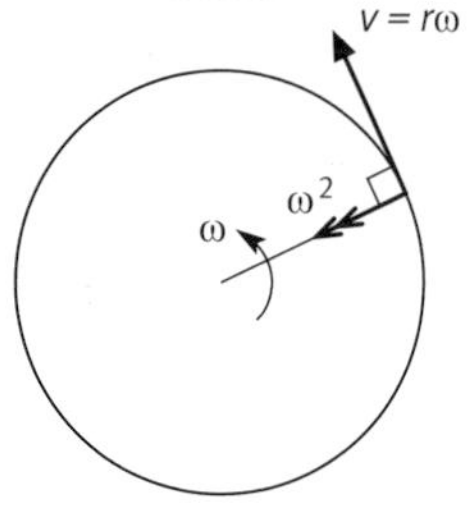

These expressions are valid whether or not the speed is constant. If the speed *is* constant, the acceleration and the force producing it are also constant in magnitude.

Motion in a circle on a horizontal plane

A particle P, mass m, can move in a circle on a smooth horizontal plane at constant speed. There is a force F towards the centre O where $F = mv^2/r$ or $mr\omega^2$ (Newton's Law $F = ma$). This force might be provided by:

- the tension in a string
- pressure from a surrounding circular rim
- friction between P and the surface it is in contact with, etc.

Example

A light inextensible string, of length 0.6 m, is fixed at one end to a point A on a smooth table and has a particle P, of mass 2 kg, attached to the other end. P is set moving in a circle on the table, with the string taut.

a If P is moving at a speed of $4\,\text{ms}^{-1}$, find the tension in the string.

b The string breaks when the tension exceeds 60 N. Find the greatest speed that P can have without breaking the string.

c If the string does break, in what direction will P move immediately afterwards?

Solution

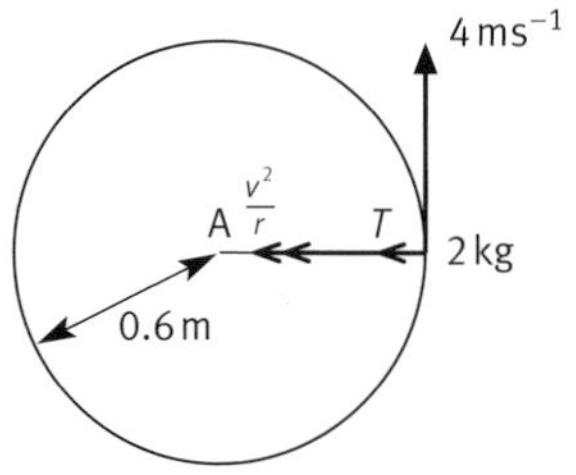

The weight of P and the normal reaction are both vertical, so do not affect the horizontal motion of P.

a Using Newton's Law towards O gives

$$T = \frac{mv^2}{r} = 2 \times \frac{16}{0.6} = 53.33\ldots$$

$\Rightarrow$ the tension is 53.3 N (3 sf)

b $T = \frac{mv^2}{r}$ and $T \leqslant 6‘0$

$\Rightarrow \quad 2 \times \frac{v^2}{0.6} \leqslant 60 \quad \Rightarrow \quad v^2 \leqslant 18$

the greatest speed is $\sqrt{18}\,\text{ms}^{-1} = 4.24\,\text{ms}^{-1}$ (3 sf).

c If the string snaps when P is at a point A on the circle, there is no longer a horizontal force acting on P, so P moves with constant speed along the tangent at A.

When tackling problems about motion in a horizontal circle where you need to know about forces perpendicular to the plane of the circle, draw two diagrams:

a looking along the plane of the circle at eye level; on this one you can mark the acceleration and all the forces that act on the rotating particle,

b looking down on the circle, where you can mark the acceleration and the force towards the centre of the circle.

Example

A turntable is rotating at 2.3 rad s^{-1} and a box A is resting on it at a distance r m from the centre O. If the coefficient of friction between the box and the turntable is 0.6, find the greatest value that r can have without the box slipping.

Solution

(i)

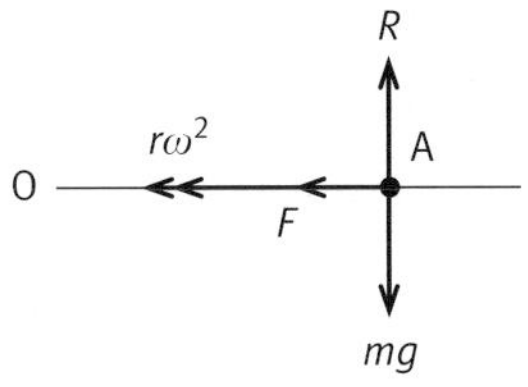

(ii)

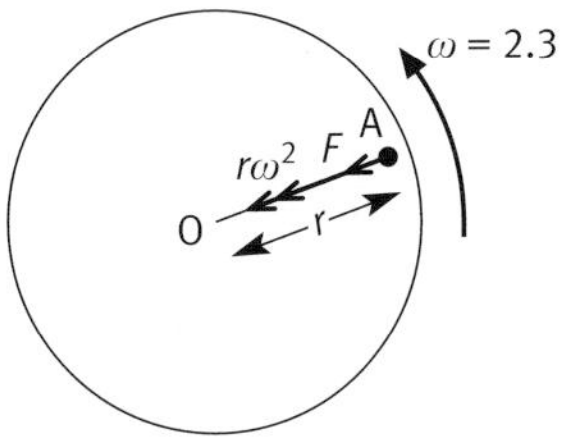

A has a tendency to slip from the circumference to the tangent, i.e. outwards from O. A frictional force opposes this tendency, i.e. acts towards O.

From diagram **i** $\quad F = mr\omega^2 = mr(2.3)^2$

From diagram **ii**, $\quad$ resolving ↑ gives $\quad R = mg$

When r has its greatest value, $F = \mu R = 0.6mg$

$\Rightarrow \quad mr(2.3)^2 = 0.6 \times mg \Rightarrow r = 1.11\ldots (g = 9.8)$

The greatest value of r is 1.11 m (3 sf).

Questions

Take $g = 10$ and give answers to 2 or 3 sf as appropriate.

1 A truck of mass 900 kg is driving round a circular bend with a radius 60 m.

a If the truck's speed is a constant 12 ms^{-1}, find the frictional force acting on the tyres.

b What is the least value of the coefficient of friction between the tyres and the ground?

c If $\mu = 0.32$ what is the greatest speed at which the truck can take the bend without skidding?

2 A girl training her pony is holding a light rope and the pony is trotting in a circle round her. The mass of the pony is 120 kg, the rope has a breaking tension of 2116 N.

a If the tension in the rope is 1024 N when the pony is trotting at 16 ms^{-1}, find the length of the rope.

b Suddenly taking fright, the pony starts to gallop and the rope breaks. At what speed did the pony take off?

Answers

1a 2160 N **b** 0.24 **c** 13.9 ms^{-1}

2a 30 m **b** at least 23 ms^{-1}

Take a break

The conical pendulum

When a light inextensible string, fixed at one end A, has a small mass P attached to the free end, P can be set moving in a horizontal circle below the level of A. If air resistance is ignored, P moves with constant speed. The string is inclined at an angle to the vertical so, as P rotates, the string traces out the surface of a cone and the system is called a conical pendulum.

Example

One end of a light inextensible string is fixed to a point A. A particle P, of mass 2 kg, is fixed to the other end and is moving in a horizontal circle of radius 1.2 m, with its centre O vertically below A. The string is inclined to the vertical at an angle θ. If P is rotating at 5 rads^{-1}, find the value of θ to the nearest degree.

Solution

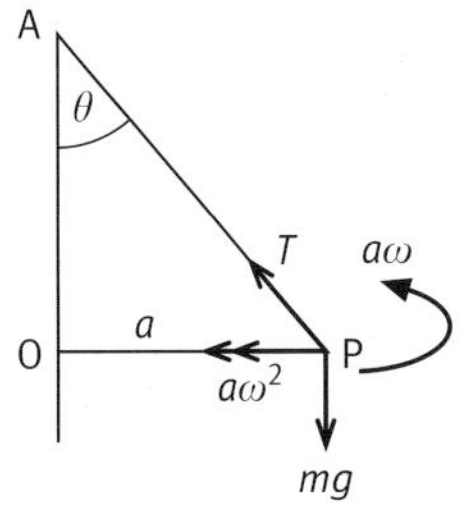

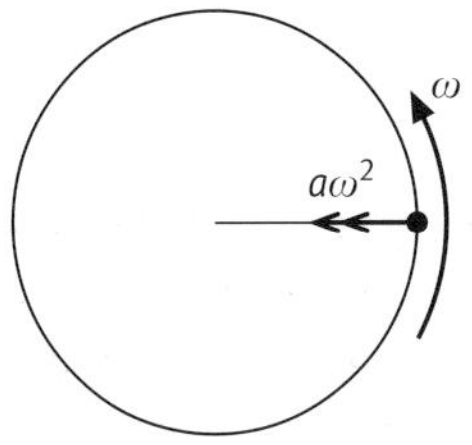

The only forces acting on P are its weight and the tension in the string.

Newton's Law towards O gives

$$T\sin\theta = ma\omega^2 \quad\Rightarrow\quad T\sin\theta = (2)(1.2)(25)$$

Resolving forces vertically gives

$$T\cos\theta = mg \quad\Rightarrow\quad T\cos\theta = (2)(9.8)$$

$$\therefore\quad \tan\theta = \frac{1.2(25)}{(9.8)} \quad\Rightarrow\quad \theta = 72^\circ.$$

Example

The ends of a light inextensible string, of length 1.75 m, are fixed to two points A and B that are in a vertical line, where AB = 1.25 m, with A above B. A particle P of mass 2.5 kg is attached to the string at a point 1 m from A. P is moving in a horizontal circle, centre O, with both strings taut, at an angular velocity of ω rad s^{-1}. Find the tension in each portion of string in terms of ω and g. Hence find the least possible value of ω.

Solution

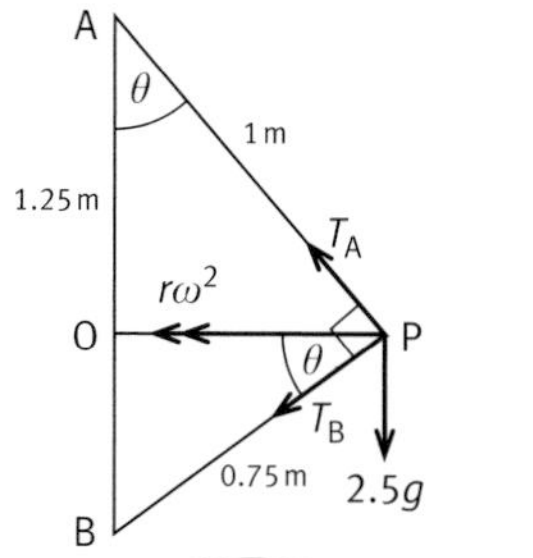

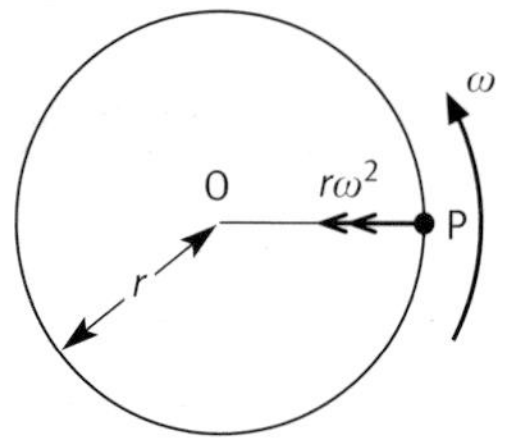

ABP is a 3 : 4 : 5 triangle

$$\Rightarrow\quad \text{APB} = 90^\circ \quad\Rightarrow\quad \text{OP} = 1(\sin\theta).$$

Newton's Law towards O gives

$$T_A\sin\theta + T_B\cos\theta = 2.5(\sin\theta)(\omega^2)$$
$$\Rightarrow\quad T_A + T_B\cot\theta = 2.5\omega^2$$
$$\Rightarrow\quad T_A + \tfrac{4}{3}T_B = 2.5\omega^2 \qquad [1]$$

Resolving vertically gives

$$T_A\cos\theta - T_B\sin\theta = 2.5g$$
$$\Rightarrow\quad \tfrac{4}{5}T_A - \tfrac{3}{5}T_B = 2.5g \qquad [2]$$

Solving [1] and [2] simultaneously gives

$$T_A = 0.9\omega^2 + 2g$$

and $T_B = 1.2\omega^2 - 1.5g$.

Both strings are taut so each tension is $\geqslant 0$.
The string AP can never be slack but, at lower speeds, the string BP may go slack.
So the critical condition is

$$T_B \geqslant 0 \quad\Rightarrow\quad 1.2\omega^2 \geqslant 1.5g \quad\Rightarrow\quad \omega^2 \geqslant 5g/4$$

$\therefore$ the minimum value of ω is $\frac{1}{2}\sqrt{5g}$.

⚠ *Fastening* a particle to a point on the string divides the string into two separate parts with different tensions. If, instead, a smooth bead is *threaded* on to the string, the tensions on both sides of the bead are the same.

Questions

1 A child is holding one end A of a light string which has a conker at the other end. The conker is being swung in a horizontal circle at ω rad s^{-1}. The string is 0.9 m long and the weight of the conker is 0.04 kg.

a Find the tension in the string when $\omega = 10$.

b If the centre of the circle is 0.6 m below A, find ω. Use $g = 10$ ms^{-2}

2

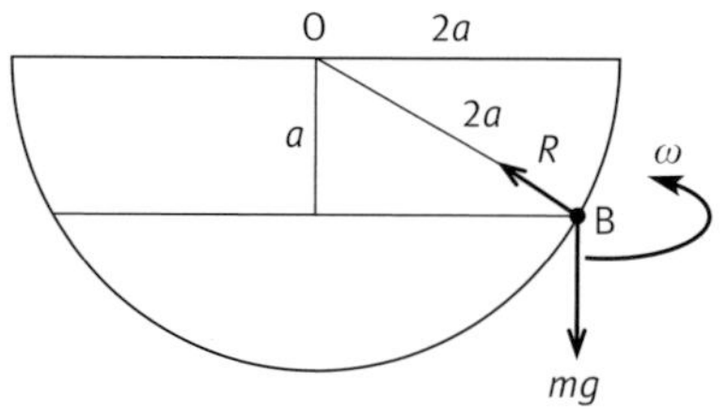

The diagram shows a small bead B travelling in a horizontal circle on the inside of a smooth hollow hemispherical bowl of radius $2a$. The plane of the circle is at a depth a below the centre O of the hemisphere. Find the angular velocity ω of the bead in terms of g and a.

Answers

1a 3.6 N **b** 4.1 rad s^{-1} **2** $\omega = \sqrt{g/a}$

Banked tracks

When vehicles travel round curved tracks at high speed, banking the track tilts the normal reaction R away from the vertical so that its horizontal component helps to provide the force towards the centre.

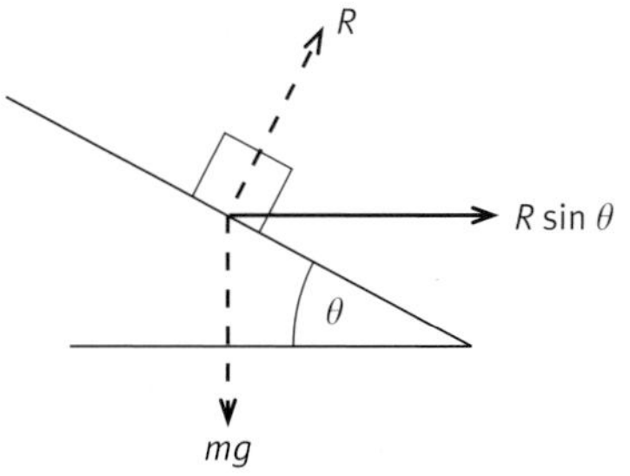

Example

A racing car drives at $36\,\text{ms}^{-1}$ round a circular bend of radius 130 m on a race track banked at an angle θ. Find the value of θ such that there is no tendency for the car to slip on the track. Take g as $10\,\text{ms}^{-2}$ and give the answer to 2 sf.

Solution

Model the car as a particle and ignore air resistance. As there is no tendency to slip there is no friction.

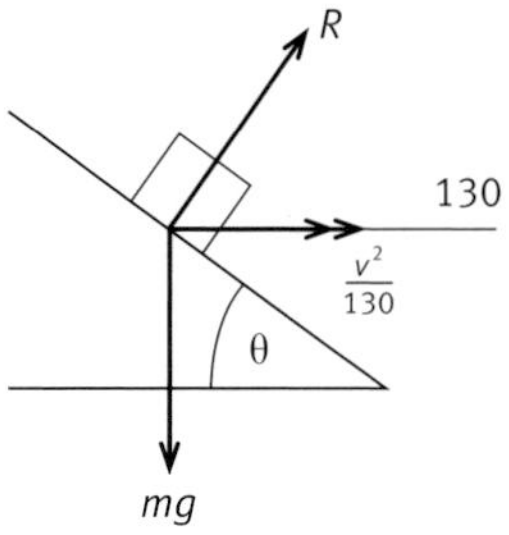

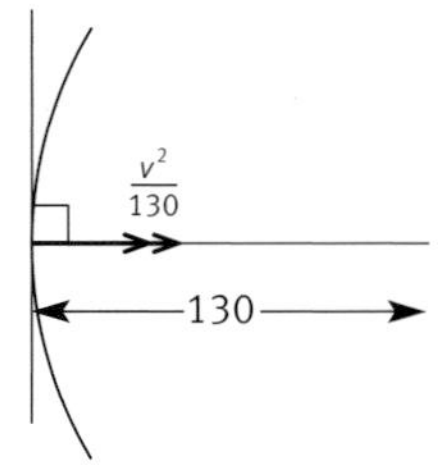

Resolving ↑ $R\cos\theta - mg = 0$

$\Rightarrow \quad R\cos\theta = mg$ [1]

Newton's Law → $\quad R\sin\theta = \dfrac{m(36)^2}{130}$ [2]

[2] ÷ [1] gives $\quad \tan\theta = \dfrac{m(36)^2}{130mg} = 0.996\ldots$

$\Rightarrow \quad \theta = 45^\circ$ (2 sf).

Design speed

The speed for which there is no tendency to slip at a given angle of banking is the design speed for that angle (and the angle is the design angle for that speed). When the actual speed exceeds the design speed there is a tendency for the car to slip up the track opposed by a frictional force down the track. When the friction becomes limiting, the speed has reached the maximum value. But if the actual speed is less than the design speed, the car tends to slip down the track and a frictional force acts up the track.

Example

The racing car specified in the example above drives round the same bend at $40\,\text{ms}^{-1}$. Taking θ to be 45° exactly, find the least coefficient of friction needed to prevent the car from slipping up the track.

Solution

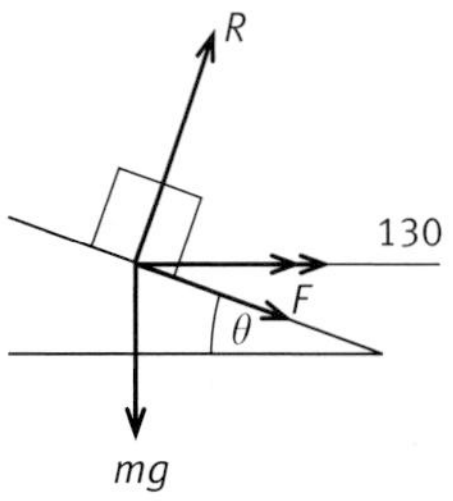

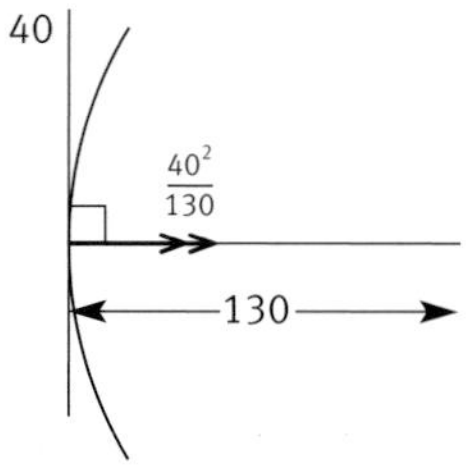

If the car is just on the point of slipping, $F = \mu R$. Resolving vertically (zero resultant force) gives

$$R\cos 45^\circ - F\sin 45^\circ - mg = 0$$

$\Rightarrow \quad \dfrac{1}{\sqrt{2}}(R - \mu R) = mg$

$\Rightarrow \quad R(1-\mu) = \sqrt{2}mg$ [1]

Newton's Law towards the centre gives

$$R\sin 45^\circ + F\cos 45^\circ = \frac{mv^2}{130}$$

$\therefore \quad \dfrac{1}{\sqrt{2}}(R + \mu R) = \dfrac{m40^2}{130} = \dfrac{160m}{13}$

$\therefore \quad R(1+\mu) = \dfrac{160m\sqrt{2}}{13}$ [2]

[2] ÷ [1] gives $\quad \dfrac{1+\mu}{1-\mu} = \dfrac{160}{13g} = \dfrac{16}{13}$

$\therefore \quad 13(1+\mu) = 16(1-\mu)$

$\Rightarrow \quad 29\mu = 3 \quad \Rightarrow \quad \mu = 0.10$ (2 sf).

Question

A car of mass 800 kg is driving round a circular bend of radius 150 m at speed $v\,\text{ms}^{-1}$. The track is flat and the coefficient of friction is 0.8.

a Find the greatest speed that can be used without the car slipping outwards.

If, instead, the track is banked at 36° to the horizontal, find, taking g as 10,

b the design speed,

c the greatest possible speed round the curve.

Answers

a $35\,\text{ms}^{-1}$ **b** $33\,\text{ms}^{-1}$ **c** $74\,\text{ms}^{-1}$

Take a break

Review

1

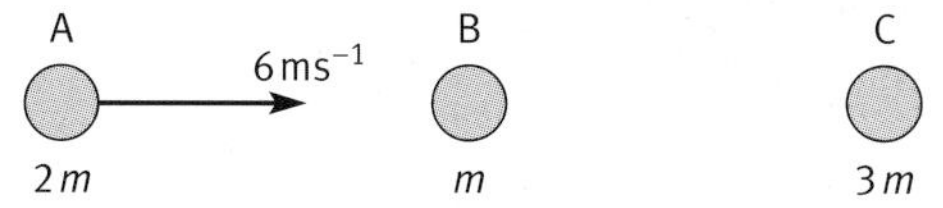

Three marbles are lying in a straight line on a smooth plane. Their masses are shown in the diagram. The coefficient of restitution between each pair of marbles is $\frac{1}{2}$. A is moving with speed 6 ms^{-1} directly towards B, which is stationary.

a Find the speeds of A and B after the collision.

B goes on to collide with the stationary C.

b Show that B's direction of motion is reversed and find its speed.

c Find the impulse exerted on B at each collision.

2 A car of mass 1800 kg is travelling up a straight road inclined at an angle α to the horizontal, where $\sin\alpha = \frac{1}{10}$. With the engine working at 70 kW, the car has a maximum speed of 14 ms^{-1}.

a Find the resistance to motion.

b Assuming that the resistance does not alter, find the greatest speed at which the car can travel down the incline with the engine working at 60% of the previous rate.

3 Two small blocks A and B, of equal mass m, lie close together on a table. The coefficient of friction between A and the table is $\frac{1}{4}$ and that between B and the table is $\frac{1}{3}$. At the same instant each block is given a velocity of 7 ms^{-1} in the same direction towards the edge of the table, 2 m away. Find

a the speed when the table edge is reached and the time taken to reach it for **i** A **ii** B,

b the total work done by friction on both blocks.

4

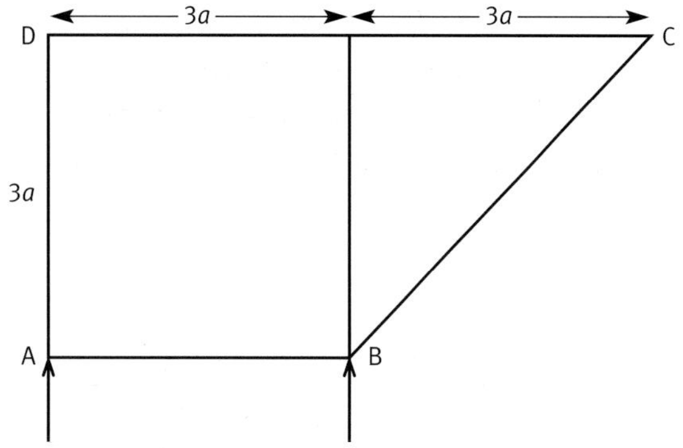

The diagram shows a uniform lamina ABCD, in the shape of a trapezium, resting in equilibrium in a vertical plane supported at A and B. Find

a the horizontal distance from A of the centre of gravity of the lamina,

b the force acting at each support, in terms of W, the weight of the lamina.

Answers

1a A: 3 ms^{-1} →; B: 6 ms^{-1} → **b** B: $\frac{3}{4}$ ms^{-1} ← (i.e. towards A); **c** 6m Ns; $\frac{27}{4}m$ Ns. **2a** 3200 N **b** 30 ms^{-1}.
3a i 6.26 ms^{-1}, 0.302 s **ii** 5.99 ms^{-1}, 0.308 s **b** 11.4J (7mg/6) **4a** 7a/3 **b** A: 2W/9, B: 7W/9

PREVIEW

At the end of this topic you will have revised:

- ✔ **the motion of a particle travelling in a vertical circle with two components of acceleration, one towards the centre and one along the tangent,**
- ✔ **how to solve problems where the motion of a particle P is restricted to a vertical circular path,**
- ✔ **how to solve problems where P moves partly in a vertical circle but can leave the circular path,**
- ✔ **the condition for complete circles to be described in each of the cases above.**

Motion in a circle with non-constant speed

The motion is circular so there is an acceleration towards the centre, of magnitude v^2/r

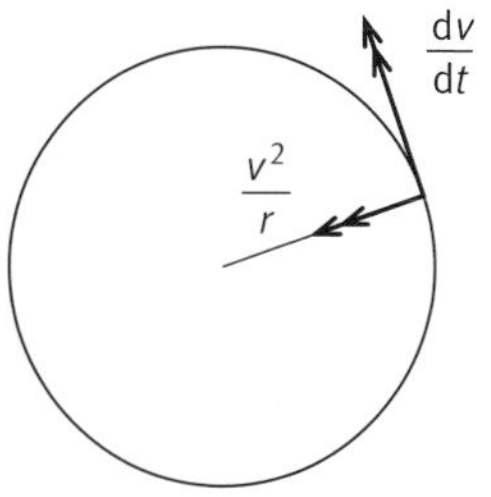

As the speed is not constant there is also a tangential acceleration, of magnitude $\mathrm{d}v/\mathrm{d}t$, (or $\dot{v}$).

The resultant force producing the motion also has variable radial and tangential components.
(The tangential component can also be called the transverse component.)

Motion restricted to a vertical circle

Examples of this type of motion are:

- a bead threaded onto a circular wire
- a particle attached to one end of a light rod which is free to rotate about the other end.

A particle P moving in this way cannot leave the circular path so it either

a moves in complete circles, in which case P reaches the highest point of the circle and *passes through* that point, i.e. the speed of P is greater than zero at the top,

or

b it oscillates on an arc, in which case P comes to instantaneous rest at each end of the arc.

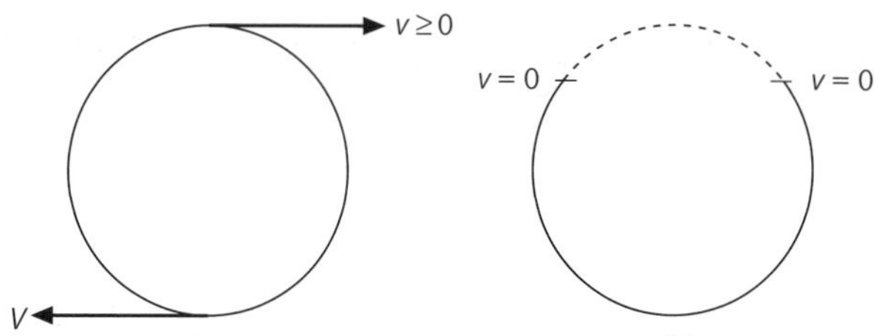

(a) (b)

Solving problems

You can solve almost every question on motion in a vertical circle by using two basic equations.

- The first one is the equation for conservation of ME, from the initial position to a general position. This can be used provided that no forces (other than the weight) do any work; this is likely to be the case in all the questions that you meet in A-level examinations.
- The second is Newton's Law towards the centre of the circle, at a general point.

In this type of question in an examination, some credit is usually given for writing down one or both of these two equations; they are the same whatever the detail of the question is.

If you use m and a for the mass of P and the radius of the circle, you can simplify the equations. The numbers in an actual question can then be put in very easily.

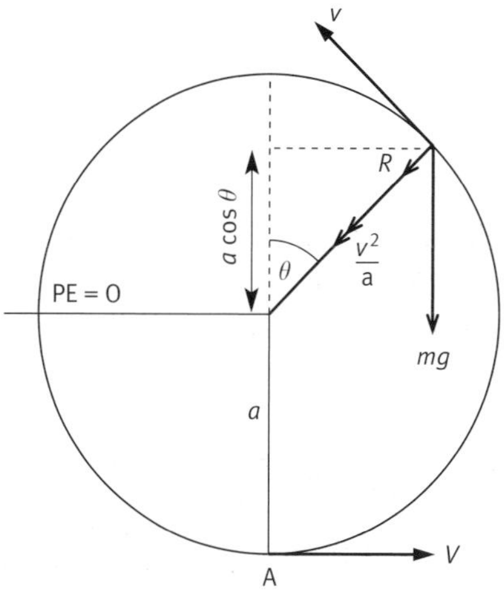

Conservation of ME from position A to a general position gives

$$\tfrac{1}{2}mV^2 - mga = \tfrac{1}{2}mv^2 + mga\cos\theta$$

$$\Rightarrow \quad V^2 = v^2 + 2ga(1 + \cos\theta) \qquad [1]$$

Newton's Law towards O in (ii) gives

$$R + mg\cos\theta = \frac{mv^2}{a}. \qquad [2]$$

⚠ Remember that, when relationships between velocities and positions are required, you can use conservation of ME provided that no forces do any work.
There is no need to work with forces or accelerations, (i.e no need for equation [2]), unless they are asked for.

Example

A bead P, of mass 2 kg, is threaded onto a smooth circular wire, centre O and radius $\frac{1}{2}$ m, fixed in a vertical plane. P is projected from A, the lowest point on the wire, with speed V ms^{-1}. At any instant OP is inclined to the upward vertical at an angle θ.

a Find the range of values of V for which P travels in complete circles.

b Find V if P comes to rest when $\theta = 30^\circ$.

c If $V = 4$ and $\theta = 60^\circ$ find the speed of P, the reaction R exerted by the wire on the bead and the tangential acceleration.
Take $g = 9.8$ and give answers to 3 sf.

Solution

Start by writing down the two standard equations:

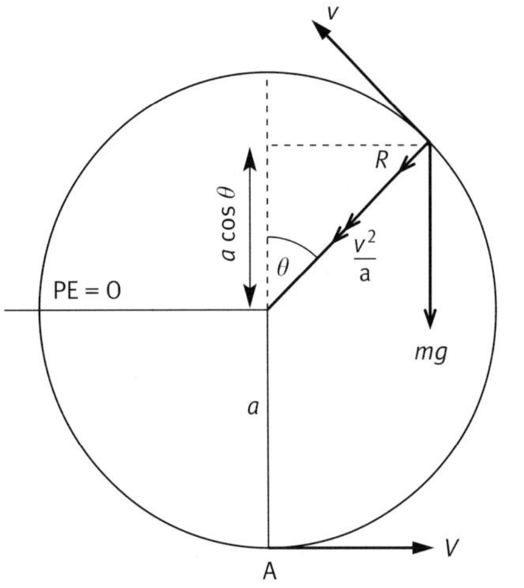

Conservation of ME from A to the general position gives

$$\tfrac{1}{2}mV^2 - mga = \tfrac{1}{2}mv^2 + mga\cos\theta$$
$$\Rightarrow \quad V^2 = v^2 + 2ga(1 + \cos\theta) \qquad [1]$$

Newton's Law towards O gives

$$R + mg\cos\theta = \frac{mv^2}{a} \qquad [2]$$

Parts **a** and **b** involve only speed and position so the equation for conservation of ME is sufficient.

a For complete circles $v > 0$ when $\theta = 0$, so isolate v and take $\theta = 0$ giving
$v^2 = V^2 - 2ag(1 + 1) > 0 \quad \Rightarrow \quad V^2 > 4ag$
Now substitute $g = 9.8$ and $a = \frac{1}{2}$.
$V^2 > 4(9.8)(\frac{1}{2}) \quad \Rightarrow \quad V^2 > 19.6$
$\therefore \quad V > 4.43$ (3 sf)

b Use [1] again with $\theta = 30^\circ$ and $v = 0$, also substitute $g = 9.8$ and $a = \frac{1}{2}$.

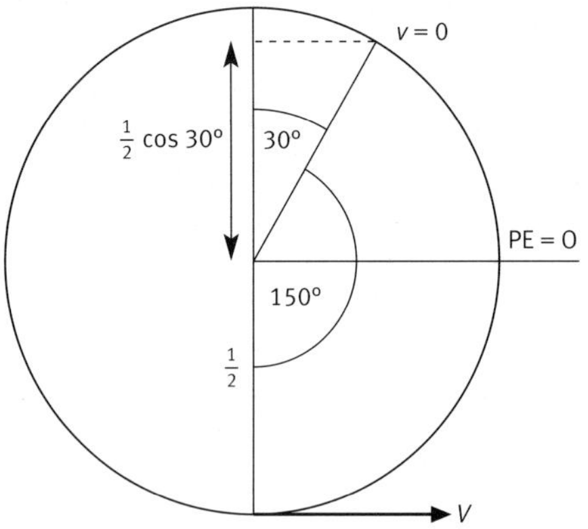

$V^2 = 0 + (2)(9.8)(\frac{1}{2})(1 + \cos 30^\circ)$
$\Rightarrow \quad V = \sqrt{18.28\ldots} = 4.28$ (3 sf).

c

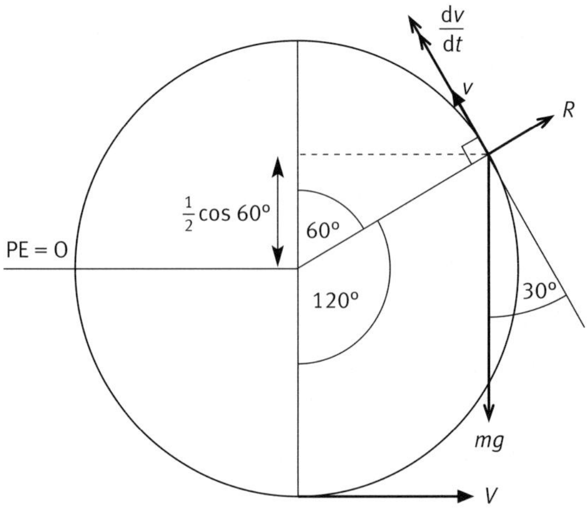

Force is now involved so you need equation [2].

$$R + mg\cos\theta = \frac{mv^2}{a}$$

This contains v, which you get from [1]
i.e. $\quad v^2 = V^2 - 2ga(1 + \cos\theta)$
Taking $V = 4$, $\theta = 60^\circ$, $g = 9.8$ and $a = \frac{1}{2}$ in [1]
$\Rightarrow \quad v^2 = 16 - 9.8(1 + \frac{1}{2}) = 1.3$

Then [2] gives

$$R = \frac{(2)(1.3)}{\frac{1}{2}} - (2)(9.8)(\tfrac{1}{2}) = -4.6$$

ℹ As R was drawn towards O the negative value you get for R shows that R acts outwards.
$\therefore$ the reaction is 4.6 N *away* from O.

To find the tangential acceleration you use Newton's Law along the tangent giving

$$-2g\cos 30^\circ = 3\frac{dv}{dt} \quad\Rightarrow\quad \frac{dv}{dt} = -8.49.$$

The tangential acceleration is $-8.49\,\text{ms}^{-2}$. The negative sign shows that P is decelerating (i.e. v is decreasing).

This example demonstrates most of the questions likely to be asked, and is therefore longer than typical exam questions.

⚠ The level chosen in the example for zero PE, was through the centre of the circle. This is easy to use whatever angle is involved, although other levels can be chosen *and marked.*

Some questions may give θ as the angle with the downward vertical. In this case remember that $\cos(180^\circ - \theta) = -\cos\theta$.

Questions

Take g as 9.8 and give answers to 3 sf.

1 A light straight rigid wire, 0.8 m long is free to rotate in a vertical plane about the end O. A particle P, of mass 1.2 kg, is attached to the other end. When P is hanging at rest at A, it is given a blow that sets it rotating so that it just reaches the position where P is vertically above O. Find

a the initial velocity of P

b the impulse of the blow given to P

c the velocity and the tension in the wire when $\angle$POA is **i** 90° **ii** 120° **iii** 180°.

2 A bead P, of mass m, is disturbed from rest at the highest point A on a smooth circular wire of radius a and centre O. When $\angle$AOP is 60° find, in terms of m, a and g,

a the velocity of the bead and the reaction with the wire,

b the tangential acceleration of the bead.

Without doing any calculation, state with a brief explanation what the tangential acceleration is when $\angle$AOP is 180°.

Answers

1a $5.6\,\text{ms}^{-1}$ **b** 6.72 N

c **i** $3.96\,\text{ms}^{-1}$; 23.5 N towards O **ii** $2.8\,\text{ms}^{-1}$; 5.88 N towards O

iii $v = 0$; 11.8 N away from O

2a $\sqrt{ga}$; $\frac{1}{2}mg$ towards O **b** $\frac{1}{2}g\sqrt{3}$.

Zero; there is no horizontal force as the weight and the reaction are both vertical.

Motion not restricted to a vertical circle

ℹ If a particle P, attached to one end of a light string whose other end is fixed at a point O, is projected horizontally from the position vertically below O, P can:

either

a perform complete circles in a vertical plane about O as centre; in this case the string always taut;

⚠ do not assume that $T = 0$ at the top.

or

b oscillate on a minor arc; in this case the string is always taut, but P comes to momentary rest at each end of the arc;

⚠ do not assume that $T = 0$ when $v = 0$.

or

c P can follow the circle to a level above O where the string goes slack; P does not come to rest but 'falls inside' the circle and continues to move under the action of its weight alone, i.e. it moves as a projectile with initial velocity v along the tangent at B.

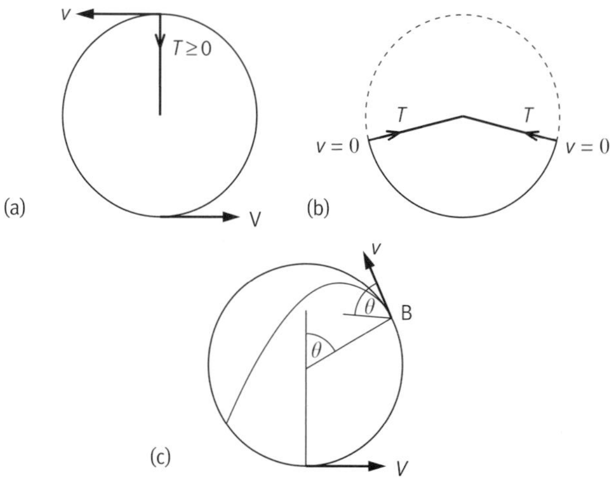

A similar situation arises when a particle is projected from the lowest point on the inside of a smooth circular surface, e.g. the inside of a smooth hollow sphere.
The pressure (i.e. the normal reaction) from the surface is equivalent to the tension in a string.

⚠ The essential difference between these problems and those where the particle is 'tied' to the circular path, is that *if the force directed towards the centre becomes zero, the nature of the motion changes.*

Be very careful when using conservation of ME.

Example

An inextensible string of length a is fixed at one end to a point A and at the other end carries a particle P of mass m. When P is hanging vertically below A, it is projected horizontally with speed V.

a Given that $V^2 = 5ga$, show that P just reaches the point B distant a vertically above A.

b When $V^2 = 4ga$, show that the string will go slack at some stage and find the position of P when this happens.

Solution

Start with a general position of P when the string makes an angle θ with the upward vertical and write down the equations for conservation of ME and Newton's Law towards the centre.

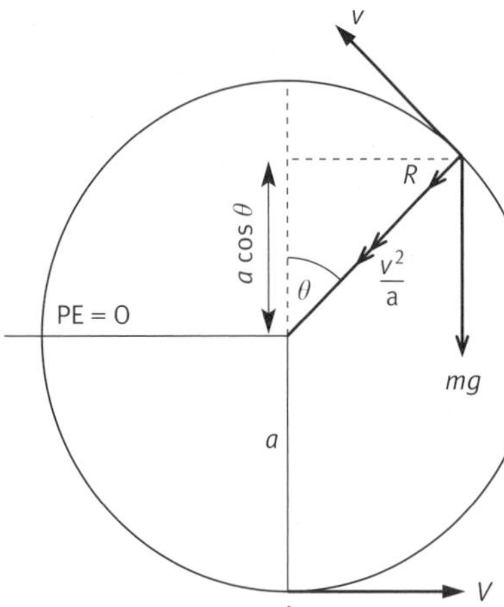

$$\tfrac{1}{2}mV^2 - mga = \tfrac{1}{2}mv^2 + mga\cos\theta$$
$$\Rightarrow \quad V^2 - 2ga = v^2 + 2ga\cos\theta \qquad [1]$$
$$\swarrow \; T + mg\cos\theta = \frac{mv^2}{a}. \qquad [2]$$

a When $V^2 = 5ga$,
$[1] \Rightarrow \quad v^2 = 3ga - 2ga\cos\theta$
then $[2] \Rightarrow \quad T = 3mg - 3mg\cos\theta.$
The string becomes slack when $T = 0$,
i.e. when $\cos\theta = 1 \quad \Rightarrow \quad \theta = 0$
So P just reaches B.

b When $V^2 = 4ga$,
$[1] \Rightarrow \quad v^2 = 2ga - 2ga\cos\theta$
then $[2] \Rightarrow \quad T = 2mg - 3mg\cos\theta$
$\therefore$ the string becomes slack when $T = 0$,
i.e. when $\cos\theta = \frac{2}{3}$.
P is then $(a + \frac{2}{3}a) = \frac{5}{3}a$ above A.

Example

A particle P of mass m is projected horizontally with speed V from the lowest point A of the inner smooth surface of a hollow cylinder with centre O and radius a. When P has rotated until it is at point B, level with O, it collides and coalesces with a stationary particle also of mass m. Given that $V^2 = 16ga$,

a find the initial velocity of the combined mass.

b determine whether the combined mass carries on to perform complete circles.

Solution

a No forces are needed in this part so just use cons. of ME to find the speed of P just before impact at B.

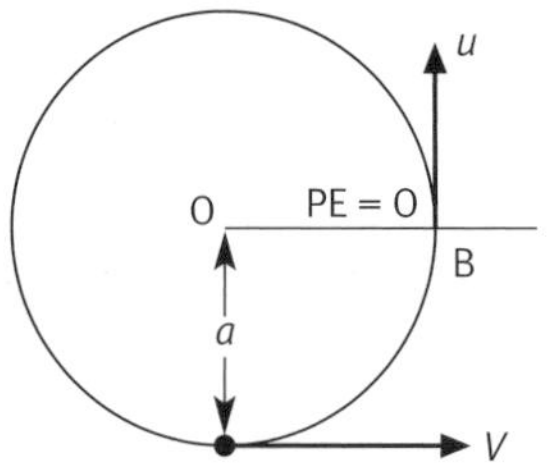

$$\tfrac{1}{2}m(16ga) - mga = \tfrac{1}{2}mu^2 \quad \Rightarrow \quad u^2 = 14ga$$

At impact, conservation of momentum ↑ gives

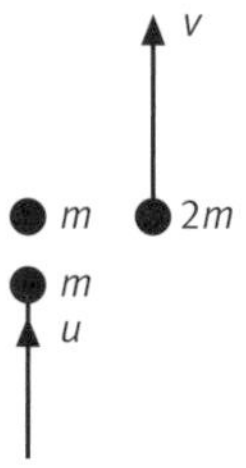

$$mu + 0 = 2mv \quad \Rightarrow \quad v = \tfrac{1}{2}u = \tfrac{1}{2}\sqrt{14ga}$$
$$\Rightarrow \quad v = \sqrt{7ga/2}.$$

b Now write down the two standard equations, i.e. cons. of ME and Newton's Law towards O.

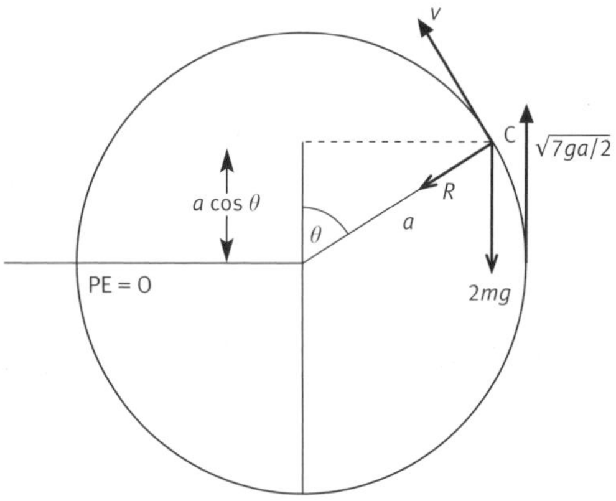

$$\tfrac{1}{2}(2m)(7ga/2) = (\tfrac{1}{2})(2m)v^2 + 2mga\cos\theta$$
$$\Rightarrow \quad v^2 = 7ga/2 - 2ga\cos\theta \qquad [1]$$
$$\swarrow \; R + 2mg\cos\theta = \frac{2mv^2}{a} \qquad [2]$$
$$\Rightarrow \quad R = 2m(7g/2 - 2g\cos\theta) - 2mg\cos\theta$$
$$= 7mg - 6mg\cos\theta$$

When $\theta = 0$, $R = mg$
i.e. the reaction between the combined mass and the cylinder is positive at the highest point, so the mass is in contact with the cylinder there.

$\therefore$ the combined mass describes complete circles.

Questions

1 A light inextensible string of length 1 m is fixed at one end to a point A and at the other end carries a stone S of mass 2 kg.
The stone hangs at rest vertically below A and is then projected horizontally with speed V. Find in terms of g and v

a the least value of V for which S moves in complete circles,

b the tension in the string when it is at 60° to the downward vertical,

c the tangential acceleration when the string is first horizontal.

2

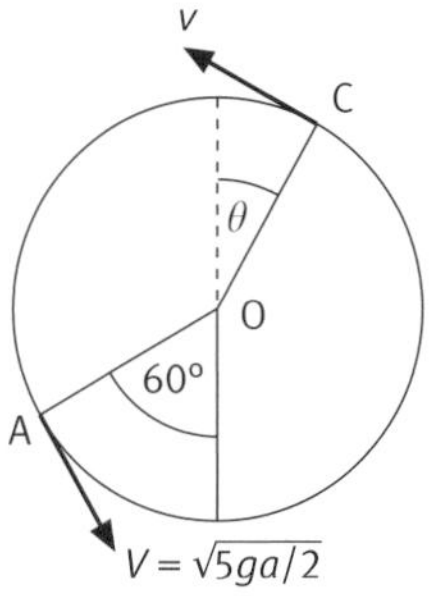

A bead B of mass m is inside the smooth inner surface of a hollow cylinder of radius a and centre O.

B is projected, with speed $\sqrt{5ga/2}$, from a point A on the surface of the cylinder, where AO is at 60° to the downward vertical through O. The bead loses contact with the surface of the cylinder at a point C, where CO is at an angle θ to the upward vertical through O and the speed of the bead is v.

a Find θ and v in terms of g and a.

b Describe how the bead then moves and find the greatest height that it reaches above C

Answers

1a $\sqrt{5g}$ **b** $2V^2 - 7g$ **c** $-g$ (i.e. g downwards)

2a $v = \sqrt{ga/2}$; $\theta = 60°$

b S now moves as a projectile with initial speed v at 30° to the horizontal. This will continue until S hits the inside surface of the sphere; $3a/16$.

Take a break

Review

1 Jan is a member of the school netball team and is making a practice shot. She is standing 3 m from the post and the net is 2.8 m high. When she projects the ball, Jan's hands are 1.6 m high. With an angle of projection of 70° the ball lands in the net. Taking $g = 10$, find

a the speed of projection

b how long the ball is in the air.

2

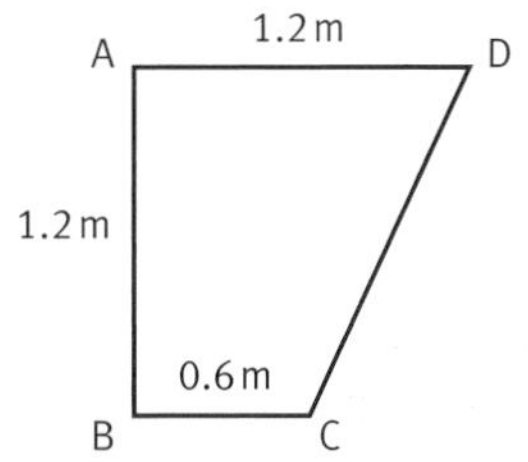

The diagram shows a hanging sign made of uniform material.

a Find the distances of its centre of mass from AB and AD.

It is hung from hooks at A and D.

b Use $g = 10$ to find the forces exerted on each of the hooks given that the mass of the sign is 12 kg.

The hook at D falls out and the sign hangs freely from A in equilibrium.

c Find the angle between AB and the vertical.

3 A particle P of mass 0.4 kg is placed on a turntable, 0.16 m from the centre O. The coefficient of friction between P and the turntable is 0.4. When the turntable rotates in a horizontal plane with constant angular speed ω rad s^{-1}, P goes round with the turntable without slipping.

a Show that the largest possible value of ω is 5.

b If $\omega = 4$, find the frictional force acting on P towards O.

4 A uniform ladder, of length 2.8 m and mass 24 kg, rests with the end B against a smooth wall and the other end A on rough horizontal ground where the coefficient of friction is $\frac{1}{3}$.
The ladder is at an angle θ to the wall.

a Find the greatest value that θ can have without the ladder slipping.

For a particular job the ladder has to be placed at 45° to the wall. To prevent the ladder from slipping a heavy block of mass m is attached to the bottom of the ladder.

b find the least mass that is suitable.

5

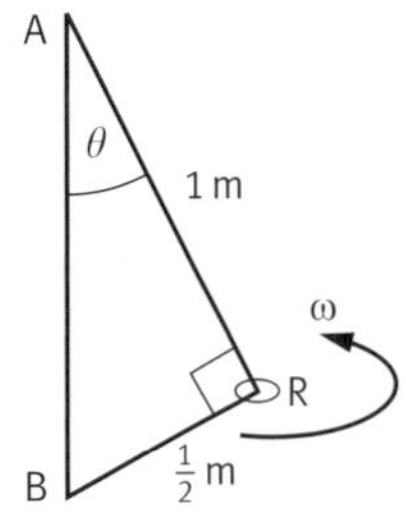

A smooth ring R of mass m is threaded onto a light inextensible string. The ends of the string are fastened to two points A and B where AB is vertical. When the ring is set moving in a horizontal circle with constant angular speed ω, $\angle$ARB is a right angle, the length of AR is 1 m and the length of BR is $\frac{1}{2}$ m.

Show that $\omega^2 = 3g\sqrt{5}$.

Answers

1a 7.39 ms^{-1} **b** 1.19 s **2a** 0.467 m from AB, 0.533 m from AD **b** 73.3 N at A, 46.7 N at D **c** 41.2°
3b 1.02 N **4a** 33.7° **b** 12 kg.

PREVIEW

At the end of this topic you will have revised:

- ✔ **the properties of elastic strings and springs,**
- ✔ **Hooke's Law,**
- ✔ **the energy in a stretched elastic string or spring.**

Elastic strings and springs

When a light elastic string is stretched and then released, it returns to its original unstretched length, called its *natural length,* unless it is stretched so far that the *elastic limit* is exceeded. In this case the string loses its elasticity and remains stretched.

Hooke's Law

Provided that the elastic limit is not exceeded, the tension in an elastic string is proportional to the extension. If a string of natural length a m is extended by an amount x m, the tension T N is given by

$$T = \lambda \frac{x}{a}$$

where λ is a constant called the *modulus of elasticity* of the string and is *measured in newtons.*

The tension is equal and opposite to the force producing the extension.

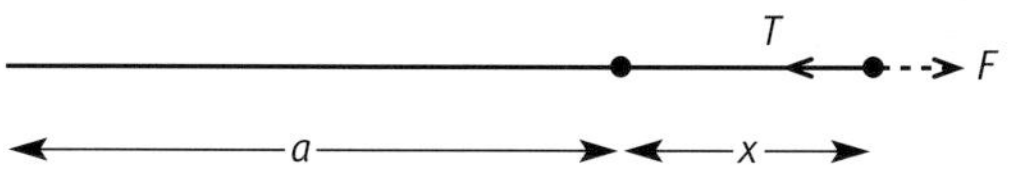

When the extension is equal to the natural length of the string, i.e. when $x = a$, then $T = \lambda$ showing that λ is equal to the force needed to double the length of a string.

Springs

A light spring, when stretched, behaves in the same way as an elastic string, but it can also be compressed, when it exerts a *thrust*, i.e. an *outward* force T at each end. The spring obeys Hooke's Law when in compression, i.e. $T = \lambda \frac{x}{a}$ where x is the reduction in length.

Example

One end of a light elastic string of natural length 0.8 m is fixed at a point A on a smooth table. A particle P of mass 2 kg is attached to the other end and lies on the table. P is pulled away from A by a force of 5 N and P is then at rest distant 1.8 m from A.

a Find the modulus of elasticity of the string.

The force is suddenly removed.

b Find P's acceleration at that instant.

c Does P then move with constant acceleration? Give a reason for your answer.

Solution

a

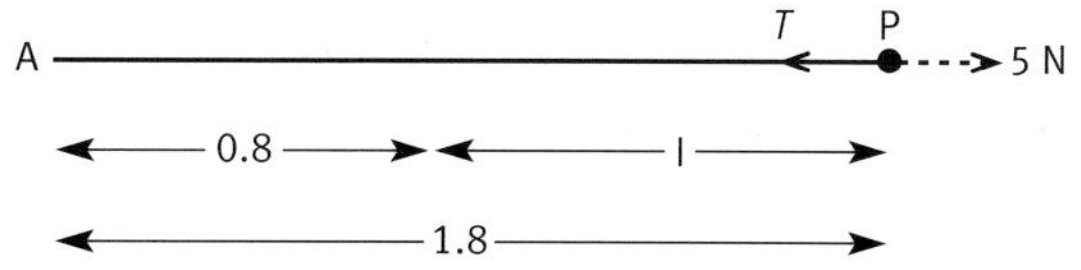

P is in equilibrium $\Rightarrow \quad T = 5$

Hooke's Law gives $\quad T = \dfrac{\lambda(1)}{0.8}$

$\therefore \quad \lambda = 5(0.8) = 4$

The modulus of elasticity is 4 N.

b The only horizontal force acting on P is the tension, with value 5 N.

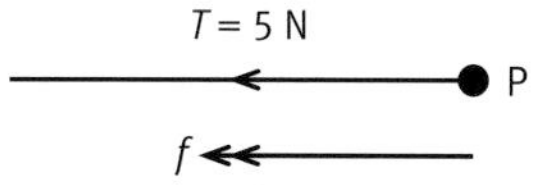

Newton's Law gives $\quad 5 = 2f$

P's acceleration is $2.5\,\text{ms}^{-2}$.

c As P moves towards A the extension in the string reduces, so the tension also reduces, i.e. the force acting on P is not constant. Therefore P does not move with constant acceleration.

Example

One end of an elastic string of natural length a is fixed to a point A and a particle P, of mass m, is attached to the other end B. P is held in equilibrium by a force F acting at right-angles to the string which is at 30° to the vertical and the length of the string is $3a/2$.

a Express F in terms of m and g.

b Show that $\lambda = mg\sqrt{3}$.

Solution

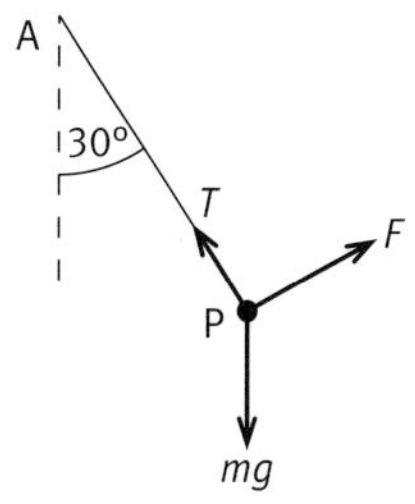

a Resolving the forces acting on P ↗ gives
$F - mg\sin 30° = 0 \quad \Rightarrow \quad F = \frac{1}{2}mg$

b Resolving ↖ gives
$T - mg\cos 30° = 0 \quad \Rightarrow \quad T = \frac{1}{2}mg\sqrt{3}$

From Hooke's Law, $T = \lambda \frac{(\frac{1}{2}a)}{a}$

$\therefore \quad \frac{1}{2}mg\sqrt{3} = \lambda \frac{(\frac{1}{2}a)}{a} \quad \Rightarrow \quad \lambda = mg\sqrt{3}.$

Questions

Take g as 9.8 ms^{-2} and give answers to 3 sf.

1 The diagram shows a mass of 1.2 kg suspended by two identical light elastic strings, each of natural length 10 cm, from two fixed points on the same level and 20 cm apart. When the mass hangs in equilibrium, the length of each string is 15 cm. Find the modulus of elasticity of the string.

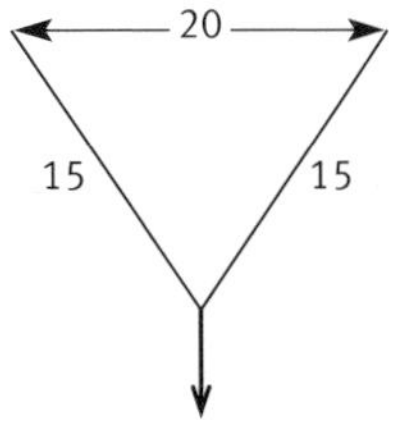

2 A particle P of mass 1.6 kg, attached to one end of a light elastic string, lies on a smooth horizontal table. The other end of the string is fixed to a point O on the table and P is made to rotate, at 5 rad s^{-1}, in a horizontal circle of radius 1.1 m, about O as centre. If the natural length of the string is 0.7 m, find the modulus of elasticity of the string.

3 A light spring, whose modulus of elasticity is 14.7 N, hangs vertically from one fixed end and a particle P of mass 1.7 kg is attached to the other end. When P is at rest the length of the spring is 2.8 m. If P is removed and replaced by another particle Q, the length of the spring is 2.4 m. Find the mass of Q.
(Take a m as the natural length and $(2.8 - a)$ m as the extension produced by P)

Answers

1 15.8 N
2 77 N
3 1.24 kg (3 sf) ($a = 1.31$)

Take a break

The energy in a stretched elastic string

When an elastic string (or spring), of natural length a m and modulus of elasticity λ N, is given an extension of x m, the string has elastic potential energy (EPE) which is equal to the amount of work needed to produce the extension.

i The value of the EPE is given by $\frac{\lambda x^2}{2a}$ joules.

You can now use conservation of mechanical energy, including elastic potential energy, to solve problems on elastic strings and springs.

Example

The end A of a light elastic string is fixed and a particle P of mass 6 kg is attached to the other end. The natural length, AB, of the string is 1.1 m and when P is hanging in equilibrium at E, the extension is 0.7 m. Taking g as 9.8 ms^{-2} and giving answers to 3 sf,

a find the modulus of elasticity of the string.

P is pulled down by a further 0.3 m to C and then released.

b Find P's speed when it passes through E.

Solution

a P is in equilibrium
so $T = 6g$
Hooke's Law gives

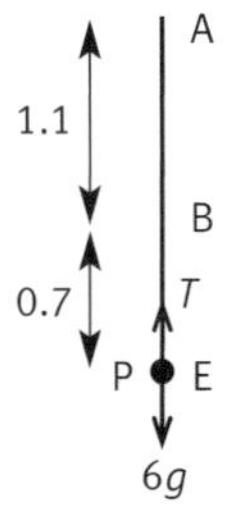

$$T = \lambda \frac{0.7}{1.1}$$

$$\therefore \quad \lambda = \frac{6.6g}{0.7} = 92.4$$

The modulus of elasticity is 92.4 N.

b At C, extension = 1

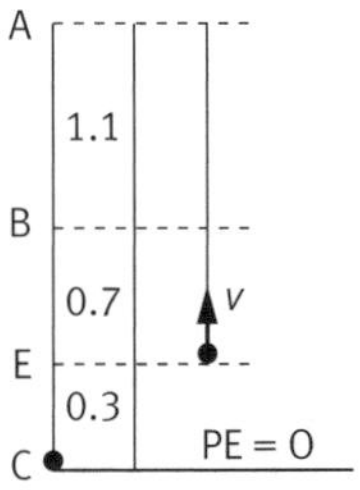

$$\Rightarrow \quad \text{EPE} = \lambda \frac{(1)^2}{2(1.1)}$$

At E, extension = 0.7

$$\Rightarrow \quad \text{EPE} = \lambda \frac{(0.7)^2}{2(1.1)}$$

Conservation of ME, considering PE, KE and EPE from C to E gives

$$0 + 0 + \lambda \frac{(1)^2}{2(1.1)} = 6g(0.3) + \tfrac{1}{2}(6)v^2 + \lambda \frac{(0.7)^2}{2(1.1)}$$

$\Rightarrow \quad 3v^2 = 3.78 \Rightarrow v = 1.12$ (3 sf)
The speed at E is 1.12 ms^{-1}.

Example

To keep it vertical, an elastic spring is supported in a glass cylinder. At the top, A, of the spring is a small light tray. The spring has a natural length of 0.8 m and its modulus of elasticity is 164 N.

A small metal block B, of mass 2.3 kg, is dropped from a height of 1.2 m above A and falls onto the tray without bouncing. Taking g as 10 ms^{-2}, find the compression in the spring when the block first comes to instantaneous rest.

Solution

The tray is not fixed so when B hits the tray there is no loss in momentum. Also, as the tray is light, it moves on together with the block without loss of speed.

Therefore no ME is lost when B hits the tray and you can use conservation of ME from the original position of B (i), to the first position of instantaneous rest (ii).

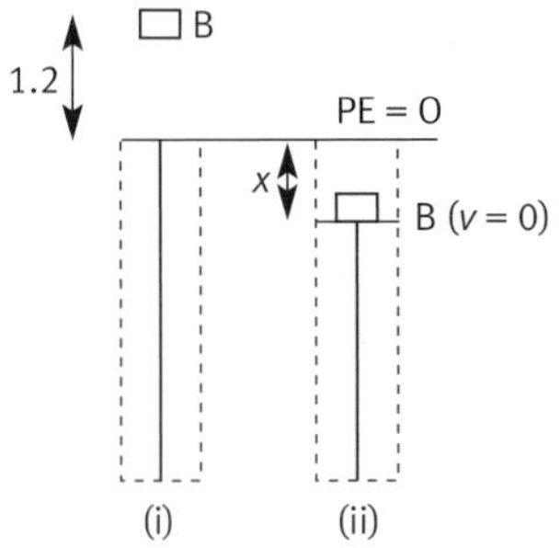

Cons of ME gives

$$mg(1.2) = -mgx + \frac{\lambda x^2}{2a}$$

$$\Rightarrow \quad 23(1.2) = -23x + \frac{164}{1.6}x^2$$

$$\Rightarrow \quad x^2 - 0.224x - 0.269 = 0$$

Use the formula to solve this quadratic,

$$\Rightarrow \quad x = 0.643$$

The compression in the spring is 0.64 m (2 sf)

Questions

Take g as 9.8 ms^{-2} and give answers to 3 sf.

1 A particle P, of mass 0.6 kg, is attached to one end of a light elastic string of natural length 1.2 m and modulus of elasticity 82 N. The other end of the string is fixed to a point A on a smooth horizontal table, on which P lies. P is pulled away from A until the string is 1.5 m long and then released.

a Find the speed of P when the string reaches its natural length, AB.

b State briefly in what way P then moves.

c If the string is replaced by a spring, all quantities being unchanged, what answer would you give to part (b).

2 A light spring, of natural length 1 m, is fixed at one end to a point A and at the other end carries a particle P of mass 2 kg. Given that the modulus of elasticity of the spring is 66 N,

a find the depth below A of the point E where P will rest in equilibrium.

P is lifted up to A and then released from rest.

b Find the length of the spring when P first comes to instantaneous rest.

3 The ends of a light elastic string of natural length 1 m are fixed to two points A and B on the same horizontal level and 1 m apart. A particle P of mass 1.4 kg, is attached to the midpoint of the string.
P is held at the midpoint of AB and is then released from rest. When P first comes to instantaneous rest, each portion of the string is inclined to the vertical at 30°. Find

a the modulus of elasticity of the string

b the speed of P when the strings are each inclined at 60° to the vertical.
(Start by finding the length of the strings and the depth of P below AB.)

Answers

1a 3.20 ms^{-1} **b** $T = 0$ so P moves with constant velocity
c P begins to compress the spring which exerts an opposing force that is proportional to the compression. So P moves with a variable deceleration
2a 1.30 m **b** 2.12 m **3a** 23.8 N **b** 2.29 ms^{-1}.

Take a break

Review

1 One end of an elastic string, natural length a and modulus of elasticity $3mg$, is fixed to a point A. The other end is attached to a particle P of mass m. P travels with constant angular speed ω in a horizontal circle whose centre O is vertically below A. The string is inclined to the vertical at 60°.

a Find the extension in the string in terms of a.

b Express ω in terms of g and a.

2 Two parallel barriers stand 2 m apart on a smooth horizontal table. A ball P is projected from a point on barrier A with speed $4\,\text{ms}^{-1}$ and collides at right angles with barrier B, bounces, and continues to oscillate between A and B. The coefficient of restitution between P and each barrier is $\frac{3}{4}$.

a Starting from when P is first projected, find the times taken for each of the first four crossings (from one side to the other) between the barriers.

b Show that P's speed during the tenth crossing is $\frac{3^9}{4^8}\,\text{ms}^{-1}$.

3 A bead P, of mass m, is projected horizontally, with speed V, from the lowest point A on the inside of a smooth hollow cylinder with centre O and radius a. P moves at right angles to the axis of the cylinder which is horizontal. When the angle between PO and the upward vertical is θ, the speed of the bead is v. Find

a expressions, in terms of m, g, V and θ, for v^2 and for R, the reaction exerted by the cylinder on the bead,

b the least value of V for which P describes complete circles,

c the value of θ when the bead loses contact with the cylinder if $V = \sqrt{5ga/2}$.

4 A van of mass 800 kg is moving down a straight road inclined at θ to the horizontal where $\sin\theta = \frac{1}{15}$. The van's speed at a point A is $16\,\text{ms}^{-1}$. B is another point, 360 m down the slope from A.

a Resistance to the motion of the van can be ignored and the speed of the van at B is $32\,\text{ms}^{-1}$. Find the constant driving force of the van's engine and the power output at A.

b If, instead, there is a constant resistance of 600 N, find the speed of the van and the power output of its engine at B, assuming the same constant driving force as in part **a**. (Take g as $10\,\text{ms}^{-2}$.)

5 The diagram shows an earring, made from uniform material, that hangs from a hook at P. The centre of the circular hole is 8 mm from RS and 15 mm from QR and its area is $18\,\text{mm}^2$.
Find, to the nearest degree, the angle that PQ makes with the vertical when the earring hangs freely.

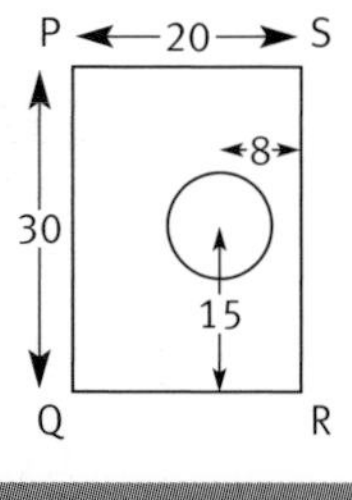

Answers

1a $2a/3$ **b** $\sqrt{6g/5a}$ **2a** $\frac{1}{2}$ s, $\frac{2}{3}$ s, $\frac{8}{9}$ s, $\frac{32}{27}$ s **3a** $v^2 = V^2 - 2ga(1+\cos\theta)$; $R = mg\left(\frac{V^2}{a} - 2g - 3g\cos\theta\right)$ **b** $\sqrt{5ga}$ **c** $\cos^{-1}\frac{1}{6}$

4a 320 N; 5.12 kW **b** $22\,\text{ms}^{-2}$; 7.04 kW **5** 33.5°.

PREVIEW

At the end of this topic you will have revised:

- ✔ **the motion of a particle whose acceleration is a function of time or velocity,**
- ✔ **Newton's Law applied to a variable force,**
- ✔ **variable motion in two and three dimensions.**

Before you start you should know:

- there is no set of formulae that can be used for problems in which the motion is variable,
- you must *never* use the equations that apply to *constant* acceleration.

Acceleration as a function of time

If the acceleration a varies with time t (so that the velocity v and the displacement s also vary with time), problems are solved by using:

$v = ds/dt$
$a = dv/dt$ or d^2s/dt^2

An alternative notation uses a dot to indicate differentiation with respect to time, i.e.

$v = \dot{s}$ (i.e. ds/dt)
$a = \dot{v}$ or $\ddot{s}$ (i.e. d^2s/dt^2)

Conversely, velocity $= \int a\,dt$
and displacement $= \int v\,dt$.
These integrals give the velocity and the displacement as functions of t.

Do not forget to add the constant of integration.

You need extra information, such as initial conditions, to find the numerical value of this constant.

Example

The velocity, $v\,\text{ms}^{-1}$, of a particle P moving on a straight line Ox, is given by $v = t^2 - 14t + 40$. Find

a an expression for the acceleration, $a\,\text{ms}^{-2}$, of P at time t, and find t when the acceleration is zero,
b the times when P is instantaneously at rest.

Using your answers to **a** and **b**, sketch the v/t graph for positive values of t.

Solution

a $v = t^2 - 14t + 40 \quad \Rightarrow \quad a = dv/dt = 2t - 14$
$\Rightarrow \quad a = 0$ when $t = 7$.
b $v = t^2 - 14t + 40 = (t - 4)(t - 10)$
$\therefore \quad v = 0$ when $t = 4$ or $t = 10$.

v is a quadratic function of t, crossing the t-axis at 4 and 10, and with a minimum when $t = 7$.

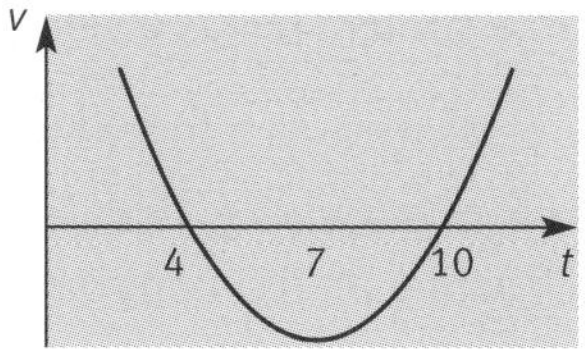

Example

A particle P is travelling on the x-axis and its acceleration at time t seconds is given by

$$a = 12t + 10t^3.$$

When $t = 0$, P has speed $3\,\text{ms}^{-1}$ as it passes through the point where $x = 5$. Find

a the velocity of P in terms of t
b the displacement of P from O when $t = 2$.

Solution

a $a = 12t + 10t^3 \quad \Rightarrow \quad v = 6t^2 + \frac{5}{2}t^4 + K_1$
$v = 3$ when $t = 0 \quad \Rightarrow \quad K_1 = 3$
$\therefore \quad v = 6t^2 + \frac{5}{2}t^4 + 3$
b $x = \int (6t^2 + \frac{5}{2}t^4 + 3)\,dt = 2t^3 + \frac{1}{2}t^5 + 3t + K_2$
$x = 5$ when $t = 0 \quad \Rightarrow \quad K_2 = 5$
$\therefore \quad x = 2t^3 + \frac{1}{2}t^5 + 3t + 5$.
When $t = 2$, $x = 16 + 16 + 6 + 5$, so the displacement of P from O is 43 m.

Using Newton's Law

When the acceleration of a particle P of mass m is a function of t, i.e. $a = f(t)$, Newton's Law gives $F = m\,f(t)$,
e.g. $m = 3$ and $a = 5t - 2t^2 \quad \Rightarrow \quad F = 3(5t - 2t^2)$

Conversely, if F is a function of t, i.e. $F = g(t)$, then using $g(t) = ma$ gives a as a function of t.
e.g. $F = t^3 - 2t$ and $m = 4 \quad \Rightarrow \quad a = \frac{1}{4}(t^3 - 2t)$.

Questions

1 A particle P, travelling on the x-axis, passes through O when $t = 0$. The velocity, $v\,\text{ms}^{-1}$, t seconds later is given by $v = 4 + 3t - t^2$. Find

a the initial velocity of P (i.e. the velocity when $t = 0$),
b the values of t when $v = 0$,
c the displacement of P from O at time t,
d the value of t when the acceleration is zero and the displacement from O at this time.

2 A particle P is travelling in a straight line with an acceleration a. At time t seconds, a is given by $t^4 - 6t^2$. If P passes through the point O with velocity $4\,\text{ms}^{-1}$ when $t = 0$, find

a the velocity of P when $t = 5$,

b the displacement of P when $t = 2$.

3 The displacement from O, s metres, of a body travelling in a straight line is given by $s = t^2 + \dfrac{2}{t}$.

a Find the acceleration as a function of t.

b If the body is of mass 4 kg, find the magnitude of the force acting on the body when $t = 2$.

Answers

1a $4\,\text{ms}^{-1}$ **b** -1 and 4 **c** $4t + \frac{3}{2}t^2 - \frac{1}{3}t^3$ **d** $\frac{3}{2}$; $8\frac{1}{4}$ m.

2a $379\,\text{ms}^{-1}$ **b** $2\frac{2}{15}$ m

3a $2 + \dfrac{4}{t^3}$ **b** 10 N

Variable motion in two dimensions

If a particle P is moving with variable acceleration in the xy plane, the position vector **r** can be expressed in terms of the coordinates of P in **ij** form (s is used for the displacement in linear motion but, in two dimensions, the displacement vector is usually **r**.

i When **r** is a function of time, each coordinate is differentiated separately with respect to time to give the velocity and then the acceleration.

For example,

if $\quad \mathbf{r} = 3t^2\mathbf{i} + (t^3 - 2t)\,\mathbf{j}$

$\quad \mathbf{v} = \dot{\mathbf{r}} = 6t\mathbf{i} + (3t^2 - 2)\,\mathbf{j}$

and $\quad \mathbf{a} = \dot{\mathbf{v}} = 6\mathbf{i} + 6t\mathbf{j}$.

Conversely, if the acceleration is a given function of time, the components of **a** are integrated separately to give **v** and **r** as functions of time.

The constants of integration in this case are *vectors*, i.e. they are of the form $p\mathbf{i} + q\mathbf{j}$.

As force and acceleration are vectors, Newton's Law can be used in the form $\mathbf{F} = m\mathbf{a}$ where both **F** and **a** are given in **ij** form.

Example

The position vector **r** of a mass of 4 kg, is given, in metres, by $\mathbf{r} = 3t^2\mathbf{i} - 2t^3\mathbf{j}$. Find

a the velocity vector **v** of the mass as a function of t,

b the speed and the kinetic energy when $t = 2$,

c the magnitude of the force **F** acting on the mass when $t = 1$.

Solution

a $\mathbf{v} = \dfrac{d\mathbf{r}}{dt} = 6t\mathbf{i} - 6t^2\mathbf{j}$

b Speed $= v = |\mathbf{v}|$

When $t = 2$, $\quad v = \sqrt{12^2 + (-24)^2} = \sqrt{720}$

$\therefore$ the speed is $26.8\,\text{ms}^{-1}$ (3 sf).

$\text{KE} = \frac{1}{2}mv^2 = 2(720)\,\text{J} = 1440\,\text{J}$.

c $\mathbf{F} = m\mathbf{a}$ and $\mathbf{a} = \dfrac{d\mathbf{v}}{dt} = 6\mathbf{i} - 12t\mathbf{j}$

$\therefore \quad \mathbf{F} = 4(6\mathbf{i} - 12t\mathbf{j})$.

When $t = 1$, $\mathbf{F} = 24\mathbf{i} - 48\mathbf{j} \quad \Rightarrow \quad |\mathbf{F}| = 24\sqrt{5}$

$\therefore$ the magnitude of the force is $24\sqrt{5}$ N.

Example

The velocity **v**, of a particle P moving in the xy plane, is given by $4t\mathbf{i} + 6t\mathbf{j}$ at any time t seconds. Initially P is at the point $-3\mathbf{i} + 7\mathbf{j}$. Find

a the magnitude of the acceleration,

b the position vector **r** of P when $t = 2$.

Solution

a $\mathbf{v} = 4t\mathbf{i} + 6t\mathbf{j}$

$\mathbf{a} = \dfrac{d\mathbf{v}}{dt} = 4\mathbf{i} + 6\mathbf{j} \quad \Rightarrow \quad |\mathbf{a}| = \sqrt{16 + 36}$

$\therefore$ the magnitude of **a** is $7.21\,\text{ms}^{-2}$ (3 sf)

b $\mathbf{r} = \int \mathbf{v}\,dt = \int (4t\mathbf{i} + 6t\mathbf{j})\,dt = 2t^2\mathbf{i} + 3t^2\mathbf{j} + p\mathbf{i} + q\mathbf{j}$

$\mathbf{r} = -3\mathbf{i} + 7\mathbf{j}$ when $t = 0 \quad \Rightarrow \quad -3\mathbf{i} + 7\mathbf{j} = p\mathbf{i} + q\mathbf{j}$

$\therefore \quad p = -3$ and $q = 7$.

$\Rightarrow \quad \mathbf{r} = (2t^2 - 3)\mathbf{i} + (3t^2 + 7)\mathbf{j}$

$\therefore$ when $t = 2$, $\quad \mathbf{r} = (8 - 3)\mathbf{i} + (12 + 7)\mathbf{j}$

$\qquad = 5\mathbf{i} + 19\mathbf{j}$.

Variable motion in 3 dimensions

This is dealt with in exactly the same way as for two dimensions (i.e. **i,j**) but with an extra term in **k**, for the third dimension,

e.g. the velocity, **v**, might be $6t\mathbf{i} - 2t\mathbf{j} - 4t^3\mathbf{k}$

$\Rightarrow \quad \mathbf{a} = 6\mathbf{i} - 2\mathbf{j} - 12t^2\mathbf{k}$

and $\quad \mathbf{r} = \int (6t\mathbf{i} - 2t\mathbf{j} - 4t^3\mathbf{k})\,dt$

$\qquad = 3t^2\mathbf{i} - t^2\mathbf{j} - t^4\mathbf{k} + (l\mathbf{i} + m\mathbf{j} + n\mathbf{k})$.

Questions

1 At any time t seconds, the velocity of a particle P travelling in the xy plane is given by $3t^2\mathbf{i} - (2t + 1)\,\mathbf{j}$. If the initial position vector of P is $8\mathbf{i} + 5\mathbf{j}$ find

a the acceleration of P at time t,

b the displacement, **r**, of P at time t,

c the value of t when the direction of motion of P is parallel to the vector **i**. (Remember that the direction of motion is the direction of the *velocity*.)

2 A particle P, of mass 2 kg, is moving in the xy plane, which is horizontal. A force $\mathbf{F}$ acts on P, where $\mathbf{F} = 2\mathbf{i} + 6t\mathbf{j}$. When $t = 0$, P passes through O with velocity $4\mathbf{i}$. Find, at time t, the velocity $\mathbf{v}$ and the displacement $\mathbf{r}$ of P.

3 At any time t seconds, a particle P moving in the horizontal xy plane has a position vector $\mathbf{r}$ where $\mathbf{r} = \mathbf{i}\cos t + \mathbf{j}\sin t$. (Write $\mathbf{i}\cos t$ rather than $\cos t\,\mathbf{i}$.)

a Show that $\mathbf{a} = -\mathbf{r}$.

b If P is of mass 0.5 kg find the force $\mathbf{F}$ acting on P at time t.

c Write down the x and y coordinates of P and hence find the cartesian equation of the path traced out by P.

4 Given that the position vector of a particle at time t is $\mathbf{r} = 2t^2\mathbf{i} + t\mathbf{j} - t^3\mathbf{k}$, find the velocity and acceleration vectors at time t. Find also the *speed* of the particle when $t = 2$.
$(|l\mathbf{i} + m\mathbf{j} + n\mathbf{k}| = \sqrt{l^2 + m^2 + n^2})$

Answers

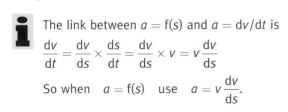

1a $\mathbf{a} = 6t\mathbf{i} - 2\mathbf{j}$
b $\mathbf{r} = (t^3 + 8)\mathbf{i} - (t^2 + t - 5)\mathbf{j}$
c $t = -\frac{1}{2}$ (so that the coefficient of $\mathbf{j}$ is zero)
2 $\mathbf{v} = (t + 4)\mathbf{i} + \frac{3}{2}t^2\mathbf{j}$; $\mathbf{r} = (4t + \frac{1}{2}t^2)\mathbf{i} + \frac{1}{2}t^3\mathbf{j}$
3b $\mathbf{F} = -0.5(\mathbf{i}\cos t + \mathbf{j}\sin t)$
c $x = \cos t,\ y = \sin t;\ x^2 + y^2 = 1$
4 $\mathbf{v} = 4t\mathbf{i} + \mathbf{j} - 3t^2\mathbf{k}$; $a = 4\mathbf{i} - 6t\mathbf{k}$; speed $= \sqrt{209}\ \mathrm{ms^{-1}}$.

Acceleration as a function of displacement

The link between $a = f(s)$ and $a = dv/dt$ is

$$\frac{dv}{dt} = \frac{dv}{ds} \times \frac{ds}{dt} = \frac{dv}{ds} \times v = v\frac{dv}{ds}$$

So when $a = f(s)$ use $a = v\dfrac{dv}{ds}$.

Example

A particle P moves on a straight line and its displacement from O at a time t seconds is s. The acceleration is given by $3s - 2$ and $v = 4$ when $s = 0$. Find

a v^2 as a function of s,
b the speed when $s = 4$,

Solution

a $a = 3s - 2$ gives $v\dfrac{dv}{ds} = 3s - 2$

This is a differential equation with separable variables.

$\therefore\ \int v\,dv = \int (3s - 2)\,ds$
$\Rightarrow\ \frac{1}{2}v^2 = \frac{3}{2}s^2 - 2s + K$
$v = 4$ when $s = 0 \Rightarrow K = 8$
$\therefore\ v^2 = 3s^2 - 4s + 16$

b When $s = 4$, $v = \sqrt{48} = 4\sqrt{3}$.

Example

A particle P is moving on a straight line with an acceleration equal to $-4s$, where s is the *displacement* from a fixed point O on the line. P is initially at rest at a point whose displacement from O is a. Find

a an expression for v^2 in terms of a and s,
b the values of s for which v is zero,
c the point at which v is maximum.
Describe the motion of P.

Solution

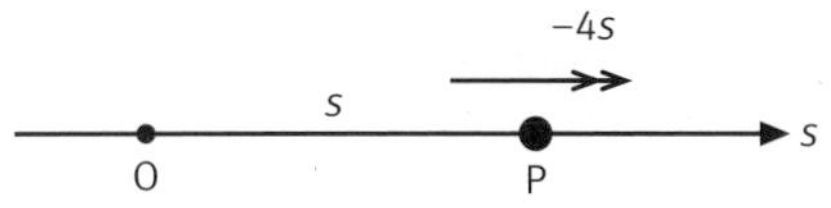

a Using $v\dfrac{dv}{ds}$ for acceleration gives

$v\dfrac{dv}{ds} = -4s \Rightarrow \int v\,dv = -4\int s\,ds$
$\Rightarrow\ \frac{1}{2}v^2 = -2s^2 + K$
$v = 0$ when $s = a \Rightarrow K = 2a^2$
$\therefore\ v^2 = 4(a^2 - s^2)$.

b $v = 0 \Rightarrow a^2 - s^2 = 0 \Rightarrow s = \pm a$.

c When v is maximum, $\dfrac{dv}{ds} = 0 \Rightarrow s = 0$
i.e. P is at O.

$v^2 = 4(a^2 - s^2)$, shows that $s^2 \leqslant a^2$ $(v^2 \geqslant 0)$ and that $v = 0$ when $s = \pm a$, i.e. $-a \leqslant s \leqslant a$.
So P oscillates between $-a$ and $+a$, with centre O where v has its maximum value.

Questions

1 At any time t seconds the acceleration of a particle P moving on a straight line is given by $24/s^2\ \mathrm{ms^{-2}}$, where s metres is the displacement of P from a fixed point A on the line. The speed of P is zero when the displacement from A is 4 m. Find the speed of the particle as it passes through a point distant 8 m from A.

2 A particle P is travelling on the positive x-axis with an acceleration that is inversely proportional to x^2 where x is the displacement of P from O. (Use $a = k/x^2$.)
When $x = 1$, $v = 2$ and when $x = 4$, $v = \sqrt{5}$.

a Express v^2 in terms of x.

b Find x when the velocity is zero.

c Define the section of the x-axis on which P can move.

Answers

1 $\sqrt{3}\,\text{ms}^{-1}$ $(v^2 = 6 - 24/s)$

2a $v^2 = \frac{4}{3}\left(4 - \frac{1}{x}\right)$ $(k = \frac{3}{2})$ **b** $x = \frac{1}{4}$ **c** $x \geqslant \frac{1}{4}$ $(v^2 \geqslant 0)$.

Take a break

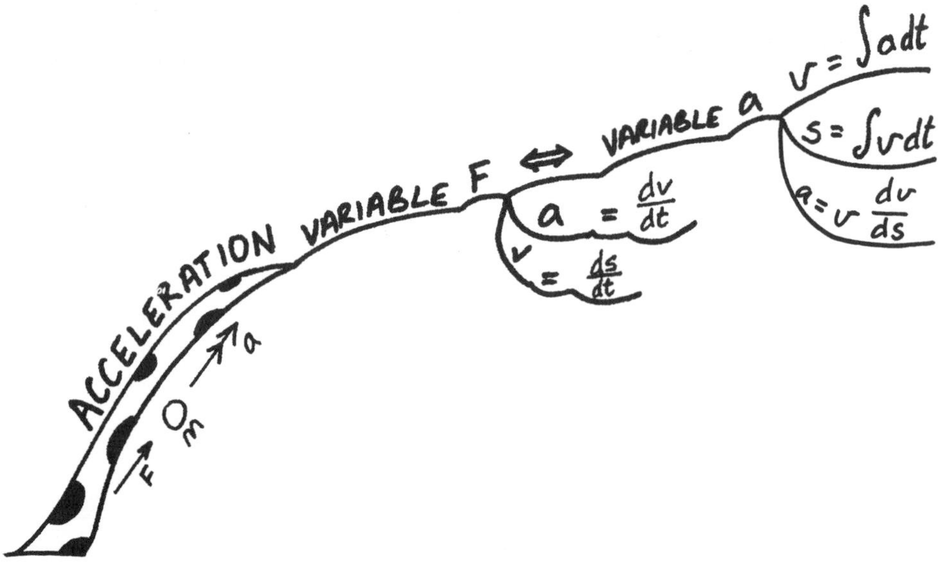

Review

Use $g = 10\,\text{ms}^{-2}$.

1 A light elastic string is fixed at one end A. When a horizontal force of 8 N is applied to the other end B, the string extends by 0.5 cm. If, instead, the string is allowed to hang vertically, supporting a particle of mass 2 kg at B, the length of the string is then 2.4 cm. Find the modulus of elasticity and the natural length of the string.

2 Two metal balls, A of mass $2m$ and B of mass m are lying on a smooth horizontal surface. B is stationary and A is projected directly towards B with speed $4u$. The coefficient of restitution between A and B is $\frac{1}{2}$.

a Show that the speed of B just after the collision is $4u$.

B goes on to hit a barrier perpendicular to its direction of motion where the coefficient of restitution is $\frac{1}{3}$. B rebounds from the barrier and collides with A again.

b Show that after this impact, B moves with speed $2u$ towards the barrier.

3 A car drives round a banked section of a race track that is a circular bend of radius 50 m. The coefficient of friction between the car and the track is 0.6. Take g as $10\,\text{ms}^{-2}$.

a If the greatest speed at which the car can travel round the bend without slipping is $38\,\text{ms}^{-1}$ find the angle of banking to the nearest degree.

b Find the design speed for that angle of banking.

4 A particle P, of mass M, is attached to one end of a light inextensible string of length a. The other end of the string is fixed to a point O. When P is hanging vertically below O it is given a horizontal blow that sets it moving with velocity $\sqrt{3ga}$.

a If θ is the angle made by OP with the upward vertical when the string is about to go slack, find $\cos\theta$.

b Describe briefly how P moves after the string goes slack.

c Find the greatest height above O that P reaches.

5 The position **r** of a particle P of mass 1 kg at time t is given by $\mathbf{r} = 2t^2\,\mathbf{i} + t^3\,\mathbf{j}$.
Working in metres and seconds find,

a the velocity of P at time t,

b the speed of P when $t = 2$,

c the kinetic energy of P when $t = 2$,

d the magnitude of the force acting on P, and the rate at which this force is working when $t = 1$.

Answers

1 $T = 18.4$ N, $a = 1.15$ **3a** 40° **b** 20.5 ms^{-1}

4a $\frac{1}{3}$ **b** as a projectile until the string is taut again. **c** $13a/27$

5a $4t\mathbf{i} + 3t^2\mathbf{j}$ **b** $4\sqrt{13}$ ms^{-1} (14.4) **c** 104 J **d** $2\sqrt{13}$ N (7.21); $10\sqrt{13}$ W (36.1)

PREVIEW

At the end of this topic you will have revised:

- ✔ **the definition and basic equation of simple harmonic motion, SHM,**
- ✔ **the notation and terms used,**
- ✔ **the formulae for velocity and displacement, and the period of oscillations,**
- ✔ **the relationship between SHM and motion in a circle with constant angular velocity,**
- ✔ **solving problems about particles suspended on a stretched elastic string, oscillating with SHM.**

Simple harmonic motion

If a particle P is moving in a straight line Ox, with an acceleration proportional to P's distance from O and directed towards O, the particle is moving with simple harmonic motion.

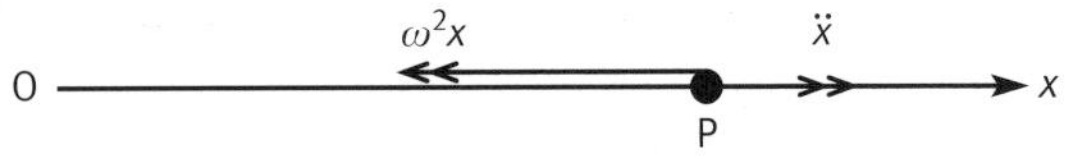

Using $\ddot{x}$ for the acceleration gives the basic equation for simple harmonic motion as $\ddot{x} = -\omega^2 x$ where ω^2 is a constant of proportion.

ω^2 is used because this constant must be positive to ensure that the sign of $-\omega^2$ is always opposite to the sign of $\ddot{x}$.

When you have to show that a particle moves with SHM, you *must* show that $\ddot{x} = -\omega^2 x$.

Solving this differential equation by using $\ddot{x} = v\dfrac{dv}{dx}$ and integrating both sides wrt x gives $\frac{1}{2}v^2 = -\frac{1}{2}\omega^2 x^2 + k$.

If $v = 0$ when $x = a$, then $k = \frac{1}{2}\omega^2 a^2$

$\Rightarrow \quad v^2 = \omega^2(a^2 - x^2)$
$\therefore \quad v = 0$ when $x = \pm a$.

This shows that P oscillates between two points, A and A′ say, distant $2a$ apart.

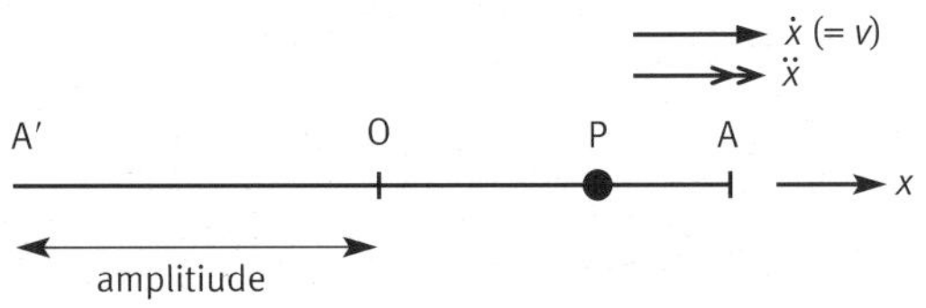

- a is the amplitude of the motion
- AA′ is the path
- the journey from A to A′ and back to A is one oscillation
- $-a \leqslant x \leqslant a$
- $\ddot{x}$ is greatest when $x = \pm a$
- v is greatest when $x = 0$
- the time taken for one oscillation is the *period*.

Example

A particle is moving with SHM and the length of the path (i.e. from A to A′) is 2.4 m. When it is 0.8 m from O, the centre of the path, its speed is 2 m s^{-1}. Find the basic equation of the SHM. Hence find

a the maximum speed,

b the maximum acceleration,

c the speed when the particle is 1 m from the centre.

Solution

AA′ $= 2.4$, so $a = 1.2$
Using $v^2 = \omega^2(a^2 - x^2)$ with $v = 2$ and $x = 0.8$
gives $4 = \omega^2(1.2^2 - 0.8^2) \quad \Rightarrow \quad \omega^2 = 4/0.8 = 5$
The basic equation of the SHM is $\ddot{x} = -\omega^2 x$
i.e. $\ddot{x} = -5x$.

a v is maximum when $x = 0 \quad \Rightarrow \quad v_{max} = \omega a$
Maximum speed is $1.2(\sqrt{5})$ m s^{-1},
i.e. 2.68 m s^{-1} (3 sf).

b the acceleration is maximum when $x = \pm a$
Maximum acceleration is 6 m s^{-2} towards O.

c When $x = 1$, $v^2 = \omega^2(a^2 - x^2)$
$= 5(1.2^2 - 1^2) = 2.2$
$\therefore \quad v = 1.48$ m s^{-1} (3 sf).

The associated circular motion

AA′ is the diameter of a circle with radius a and centre O. If Q travels round the circle with constant angular speed ω, the point P (where PQ is perpendicular to AA′) travels with SHM with amplitude OA.

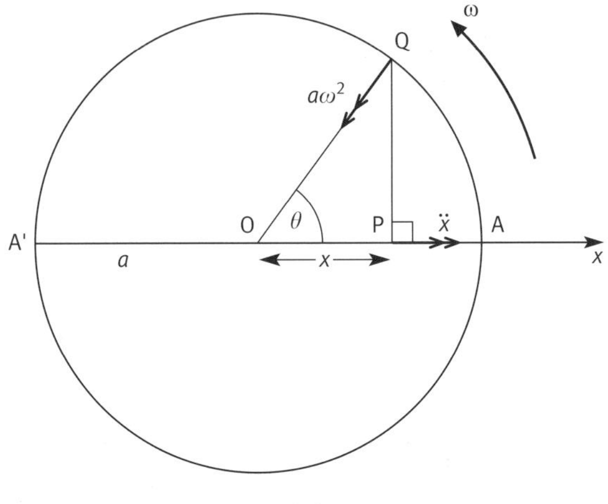

If you are asked to prove this, remember that Q has an acceleration $a\omega^2$ towards O. So P has an acceleration $a\omega^2 \cos\theta$, i.e. $a\omega^2(x/a)$, towards O.
$\therefore$ for P, in the direction OA, $\ddot{x} = -\omega^2 x$, and this is the basic equation of SHM.

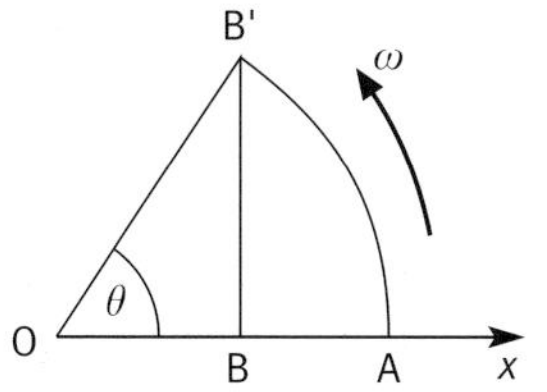

Now if you want to find the time it takes P to move from A to another point B, you can use the time that Q takes to move round the arc AB′ that subtends ∠B′OA (θ rad). This time is given by θ/ω.

i.e. $t = \dfrac{\theta}{\omega} \quad \Rightarrow \quad \theta = \omega t$

$\text{OB} = x = a\cos\theta \quad \Rightarrow \quad x = a\cos\omega t$

In particular, the period T of the SHM, (i.e. the time P takes to travel from A to A′ and back to A)
is given by $T = \dfrac{2\pi}{\omega}$

The period, or periodic time, is independent of the amplitude.

Example

A particle P, of mass 2.1 kg, is moving between A and A′ with SHM. O is the centre of the path and the greatest acceleration is 32 ms^{-2}. If the period of the motion is $\frac{1}{2}\pi$, find

a the amplitude of the motion,

b how long it takes P to travel from B, the midpoint of OA, to B′, the midpoint of OA′,

c the magnitude of the force F acting on P as P passes through B and the rate at which F is working at that instant.

Solution

a The period is given by $\dfrac{2\pi}{\omega}$,

$\therefore \quad \dfrac{2\pi}{\omega} = \dfrac{\pi}{2} \quad \Rightarrow \quad \omega = 4$

Max acceleration $= a\omega^2$,

$\therefore \quad a\omega^2 = 32 \quad \Rightarrow \quad a = 2.$

b

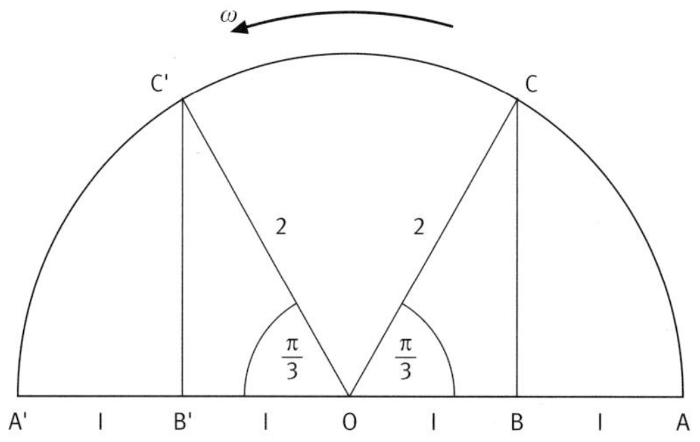

Time taken to cover BB′ with SHM
= time taken to cover arc CC′ at ω rad s^{-1}
= ∠COC′ ÷ ω

$\cos \text{BOC} = \cos \text{B'OC'} = \frac{1}{2}$

$\Rightarrow \quad \angle\text{COC'} = \dfrac{\pi}{3}\text{rad}$

$\therefore \quad$ time from B to B′ $= \left(\dfrac{\pi}{3}\right) \div 4 = \dfrac{\pi}{12}$ s.

c

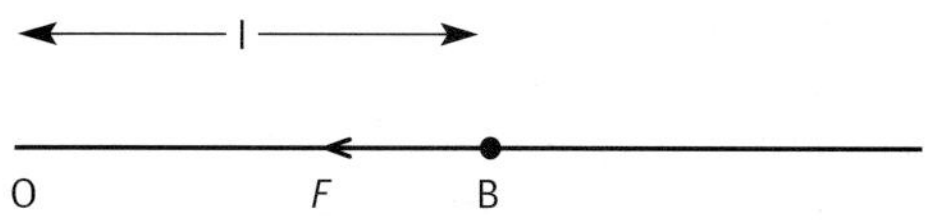

Acceleration of P at B $= (1)\omega^2$

Newton's Law $\Rightarrow \quad F = 2.1\omega^2$
$= 33.6$ N.

At B, $v^2 = \omega^2(a^2 - x^2) = 16(4 - 1)$

$\Rightarrow \quad v = 4\sqrt{3}$.

The rate at which F is working is Fv

$\therefore \quad$ at B, F is working at 233 W (3 sf).

Questions

(Give answers to 3 sf.)

1 P is a particle of mass m, describing SHM with centre O and period 8 s. If it takes P 1.2 s to travel a distance of 0.6 m from O, find the amplitude of the motion.

2 A particle P of mass 1.5 kg is performing SHM with centre O. When P is 0.3 m from O, its speed is half the maximum speed. If P performs three oscillations per second find,

a the amplitude of the motion,

b the maximum acceleration,

c the magnitude and direction of the force F acting on P when P is 0.2 m from O.

3 A particle P is moving in a straight line Ox so that $x = 3\cos 2t$ at any time t.

a Find an expression for $\dot{x}$ in terms of t; hence express $\ddot{x}$ in terms of x and show that P describes SHM.

b Find the period and amplitude of the motion.

Answers

1 0.742 m

2a 0.346 m **b** 123 ms^{-2} **c** 107 N towards O

3a $\dot{x} = -6\sin 2t$; $\ddot{x} = -12\cos 2t$; $\ddot{x} = -4x$ (SHM with $\omega = 2$)

b period $= \pi$, $a = 3(-3 \leqslant x \leqslant 3)$.

Take a break

Oscillations of a particle on a spring

When a particle P, attached to one end of a spring, is given a displacement x from the natural length, the spring exerts a force T on the particle. This force is proportional to x $\left(T = \frac{\lambda x}{a}\right)$ and acts to restore the spring to its equilibrium position, i.e. when x is positive, T is negative.

So $\ddot{x} = \frac{-\lambda x}{a}$.

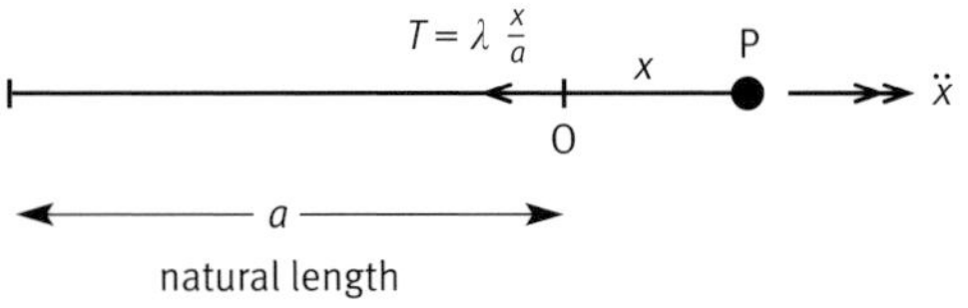

This is equally true when the spring is compressed, where the displacement is negative but T is positive.

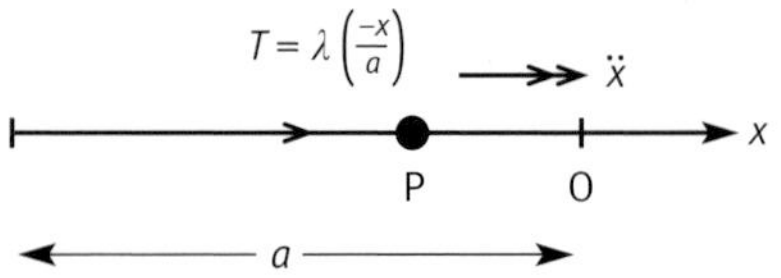

So the acceleration produced by the force exerted on P by the stretched or compressed spring always satisfies the definition of SHM.

Solving problems

The main aim in any problem about a particle oscillating at the end of a spring is to form the basic equation of the SHM being performed. The problems you may meet are of two types. In one type the spring rests on a smooth horizontal surface and, in the other, the spring hangs freely from a fixed point.

Horizontal oscillations

When the spring is resting on a smooth horizontal surface, the only force acting on the particle in the direction of motion is the tension (or thrust) in the spring; these questions are straightforward as the first example shows.

Example

One end A of a light elastic spring, of natural length 1.6 m and modulus of elasticity 40 N, is fixed to a point on a smooth horizontal table. A particle P of mass 3 kg is attached to the other end B. P is pulled away from A until AP is 2.8 m long and is then released.

a Show that P moves with SHM and state the period and amplitude of the oscillations.

b Find the rate at which the tension in the spring is working when AP = 2.6 m.

Solution

a

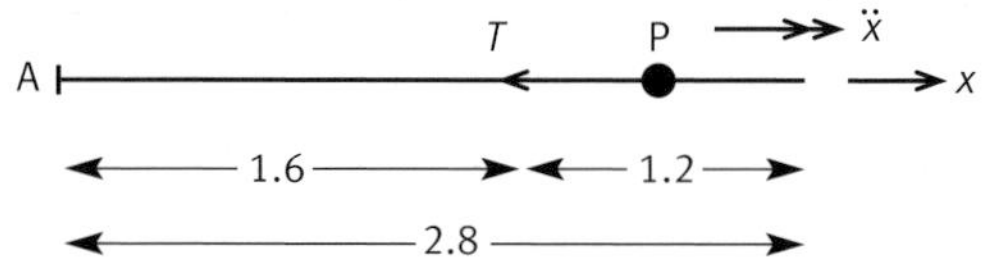

a When P is at a general displacement x from B,

Hooke's Law gives $T = \frac{\lambda x}{a} = \frac{40x}{1.6} = 25x$

Newton's Law gives $T = m(-\ddot{x}) = -3\ddot{x}$

$\therefore\ \ddot{x} = -\frac{25x}{3}$.

Comparing with $\ddot{x} = -\omega^2 x$ shows that P moves with SHM in which $\omega = \sqrt{\frac{25}{3}} = \frac{5}{\sqrt{3}}$

The period of oscillation is $\frac{2\pi}{\omega} = 2\pi\left(\frac{\sqrt{3}}{5}\right)$

$= 2.18$ s (3 sf).

The amplitude is the greatest distance of P from A, the centre of oscillation,

i.e. the amplitude is (2.8 − 1.6) m, i.e. 1.2 m.

b The rate at which the tension is working is given by tension × speed.

When $x = 1$, $v^2 = \omega^2(a^2 - 1)$

$\therefore\ v^2 = 8.33..(1.44 - 1) \Rightarrow v = 1.91..\ \text{ms}^{-1}$

Tension $= 25x = 25$ N when $x = 1$

$\therefore$ the rate of working is $25 \times 1.91..$ W

$= 47.9$ W (3 sf).

Questions

1 A light spring, with natural length 1 m and modulus of elasticity 10 N, is lying on a smooth horizontal surface. One end of the spring is fastened to a fixed point A on the surface and a particle P of mass 0.8 kg is attached to the other end and lies at a point B, distant 1 m from A. If P is projected directly away from A with speed 2 ms^{-2},

a show that P oscillates with SHM,

b find the period of the oscillations,

c find the amplitude of the oscillations.

2 A particle P of mass 1 kg is attached to one end of a light spring whose other end is fixed at a point A on a smooth table. The particle lies on the table, 1.5 m away from A, where 1.5 m is the natural length of the spring. P is struck by a blow of magnitude 12 Ns towards A and P first comes to rest when the length of the spring is 0.7 m.

a Find the modulus of elasticity of the spring.

b Show that P moves with SHM and find the period of the oscillations.

Answers

1a $\ddot{x} = -12.5x$ **b** $\frac{2\pi\sqrt{2}}{5}$ **c** $\frac{2\sqrt{2}}{5}$

2a 337.5 N **b** $(\ddot{x} = -225x)$; $\frac{2\pi}{15}$

Vertical oscillations

If a spring hangs vertically from a fixed point, the oscillations are in a vertical line and depend on the weight of the particle as well as the force in the spring.

Questions are not difficult if you tackle them systematically. It helps if you adopt a standard notation – the one used here is:

- Equilibrium position, E
- Extension (or compression) in equilibrium, e
- General extension, measured from E, is x

⚠ You should also understand that E is the *centre of the oscillations* and not the position where the spring is unstretched.

Start by drawing a diagram and marking clearly the position of the natural end of the spring and the equilibrium position E.

- First find the extension e when P is in equilibrium – mark e on the diagram.
- Then consider P in a general position distant x *from* E and write down the resultant force acting on P towards E.
  The extension in the spring is now $e + x$.
- Use Newton's Law to equate this force to $m\ddot{x}$. Remember that the direction of $\ddot{x}$ is in *the direction of x increasing.*
- Compare with $\ddot{x} = -\omega^2 x$ (i.e. the basic equation of SHM) and hence find ω.
- The amplitude is the greatest distance of P from E and depends on other given information. Be prepared to spot this information when it is given in 'coded' form, e.g. 'P is pulled down a distance a from E and then released.'

Example

Symbols are used for all the quantities in this example, so that you can easily follow the steps in the solution (which are basically the same in all problems where the spring hangs vertically).

A particle P of mass m is attached to one end of a light spring of natural length a and modulus of elasticity λ. The other end is fixed to a point A and P hangs freely.

a Find the extension e in the spring when P hangs in equilibrium at E.

b If P is pulled vertically downwards from E, through a distance b and then released, show that P describes simple harmonic motion oscillations and find the periodic time.

Solution

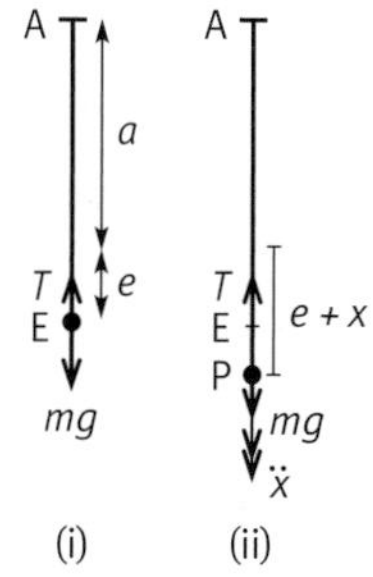

a In diagram (i):

Hooke's Law gives $T = \frac{\lambda e}{a}$

P is in equilibrium

$\therefore \quad T = mg \quad \Rightarrow \quad e = \frac{amg}{\lambda}$

b In diagram (ii):
Measure x from E and take the downward direction as positive. When P is below E the extension is $(e + x)$.

Hooke's Law gives $T = \frac{\lambda(e + x)}{a}$

But $\frac{\lambda e}{a} = mg \quad \Rightarrow \quad T = mg + \frac{\lambda x}{a}$

Newton's Law gives $\quad mg - T = m\ddot{x}$

$$\Rightarrow \quad mg - \left(mg + \frac{\lambda x}{a}\right) = m\ddot{x}$$

$$\Rightarrow \quad \ddot{x} = -\frac{\lambda x}{ma}$$

Comparing with $\ddot{x} = -\omega^2 x$ shows that P performs SHM where $\omega = \sqrt{\frac{\lambda}{ma}}$

and the periodic time is $\frac{2\pi}{\omega}$, i.e. $2\pi\sqrt{\frac{ma}{\lambda}}$.

(P moves with the same SHM when it is above E because the extension here is $e - (-x) = e + x$ and Newton's Law gives the same equation as before.)

All problems involving a particle oscillating on a light spring can be solved using the method described above.

If the amplitude of the oscillations is required, look for extra information in the question that gives the greatest distance of P from E (the amplitude is b in the example above). Or you might be told that P is dropped from a height above E, in which case use conservation of mechanical energy (including elastic potential energy) to find the depth below E of the lowest point reached.

Do not try to use the amplitude before deriving the equation of SHM.

The motion of a particle oscillating on the end of an elastic *string* is identical to that for a spring *as long as the string is taut*. If the string goes slack be careful, because in this case the tension disappears and so does simple harmonic motion.

Questions

Take g as $9.8\,\text{m s}^{-2}$ and give answers to 3 sf.

1 A particle P of mass 2 kg is attached to one end of a light spring of natural length 1.2 m and modulus of elasticity 39.2 N. The other end is fixed to a point A and P hangs freely at E.

a Find the extension in the spring when P hangs in equilibrium.

P is then pulled vertically down from E through a distance of 0.3 m and is released from rest.

b Show that P describes simple harmonic motion; state the amplitude and find the period of the oscillations.

2 A factory producing springs has a contract to supply a spring 0.4 m long that will carry a small block of mass 0.6 kg and make it oscillate vertically at 3 oscillations per second.

a Using e for the equilibrium extension, show that $\lambda e = 0.24g$.

b Find and simplify the equation of motion for an extension $(e + x)$ and show that the motion is SHM for which $\omega^2 = \lambda/0.24$.

c Find the modulus of elasticity required to satisfy the specification.

A prototype spring is made but, when tested, it produces 3.05 oscillations per second.

d Find the modulus of elasticity of the prototype spring.

3 A particle P of mass m is attached to one end of a light string of natural length a and modulus of elasticity λ. The other end is fixed to a point A and P hangs freely.

a When P hangs in equilibrium, at E, show that the extension e in the string is mga/λ.

P is then pulled down to a point distant $2e$ below E and released from rest.

b Show that initially P performs SHM and state the amplitude.

c Explain why P ceases to move with SHM at some point and define this point.

Answers

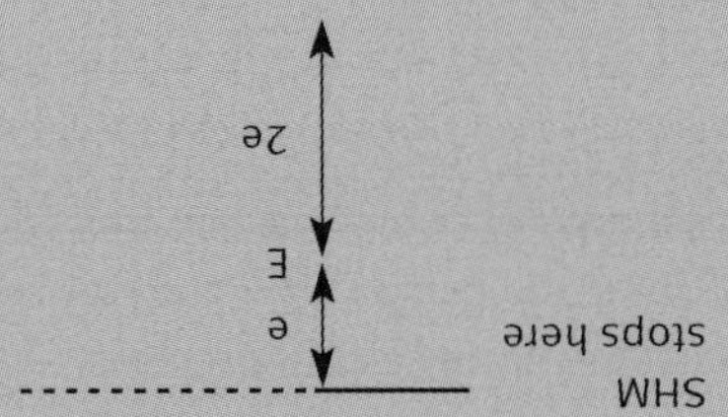

1a 0.6 m **b** $\ddot{x} = -16.33x \Rightarrow$ SHM; amplitude = 0.3; period = 1.55 s.

2c 85.3 N **d** 88.1 N **3b** $\left(\ddot{x} = -\frac{\lambda x}{ma} \Rightarrow \text{SHM}\right)$; $2e$

c As P rises above E, (the centre of the SHM), it reaches the point distant e above E, where the string reaches its natural length. Then the string goes slack and SHM ceases.

Take a break

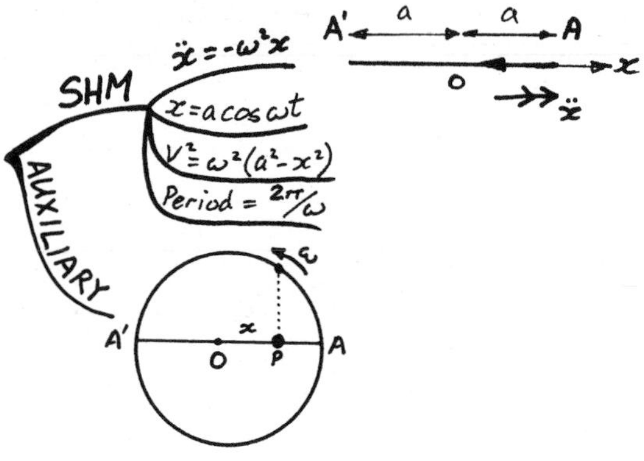

Review

1 A particle P, of mass 3 kg, is fastened to the midpoint of an elastic string of natural length 2 m. The ends of the string are attached to two fixed points A and B, on the same level and 1 m apart. C is the midpoint of AB. When P hangs in equilibrium at D, CD is of length 1.2 m.

a Find the modulus of elasticity of the string.

b If the particle is now raised to C and released from rest there, show that P's speed as it passes through D is 4.51 ms^{-1} (3 sf).

2 The acceleration of a particle P, travelling in a straight line, is given by $(3t - 5)\ \text{ms}^{-2}$ where t is the time. When $t = 0$, the displacement of P from O, a fixed point on the line, is -2 m and P's velocity is 4 ms^{-1}.

a Find expressions for the velocity and displacement from O of the particle at time t.

b Find the values of t when P is at instantaneous rest, and P's displacement from O at these times. Sketch the vt graph marking the coordinates of axes crossing points and any turning points.

c Find the total distance that P travels in the first two seconds.

3 A light elastic string, lying on a smooth horizontal surface, has a mass 2 kg attached at one end. The other end is fixed to a point A on the surface. The natural length of the string is 1 m, the modulus of elasticity is 36 N and the string breaks if the tension exceeds 36 N. The mass is set moving in a horizontal circle with constant speed v.

a If $v = 4\ \text{ms}^{-1}$ find the tension in the string and its length.

b Find the greatest value that v can have without breaking the string.

4 Two beads each of mass m are threaded on to a smooth circular wire with centre O and radius a. One bead, L, is at rest at the lowest point A of the wire. The other bead, M, is disturbed from rest at the highest point B so that it moves round the wire and collides with L. The beads coalesce at impact. Find

a the initial speed of the combined beads,

b the magnitude of the impulses that act at impact,

c the height above A of the combined beads when they first come to instantaneous rest.

5 One end A of a light spring, of natural length a, is attached to a fixed point. The spring hangs freely, carrying a particle P of mass m at the other end. When P is in equilibrium the length of the spring is $3a/2$.

a Find the modulus of elasticity of the spring in terms of m and g.

The spring with the mass attached is now placed on a smooth horizontal table with A fixed. The mass is pulled away from A, to a point B where the spring is of length $7a/4$, and then released.

b Show that the spring describes SHM and find the period.

c Find how long it takes for the mass to move from B through a distance $\frac{1}{2}a$.

Answers

1a 53.1 N

2a $v = \frac{3}{2}t^2 - 5t + 4$; $s = \frac{1}{2}t^3 - \frac{5}{2}t^2 + 4t - 2$

b $t = \frac{4}{3}$ s, $s = \frac{2}{27}$ m; $t = 2$ s, $s = 0$

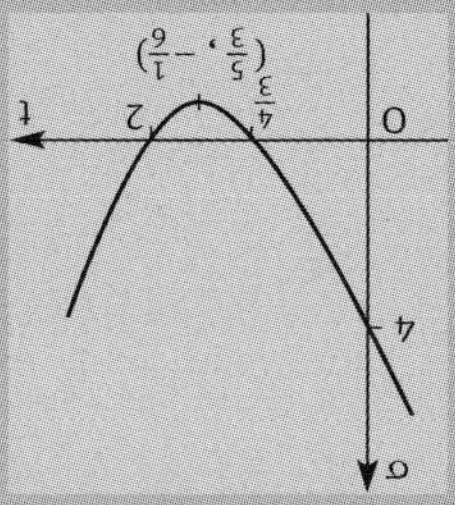

c $\frac{58}{27}$ m (2.15 m)

3a 20.4 N; 1.57 m **b** 6 ms^{-1} **4a** $\sqrt{ga}$ **b** $m\sqrt{ga}$ **c** $\frac{1}{2}a$ **5a** $2mg$ **b** $\ddot{x} = -\frac{2g}{a}x$; $2\pi\sqrt{\frac{a}{2g}}$ **c** $1.23\sqrt{\frac{a}{2g}}$.

PREVIEW

By the end of this topic you will have revised:

- ✔ **how to use integration to find the centre of mass of a rigid body,**
- ✔ **the equilibrium of a rigid body.**

Before you start you should:

- know how to find a volume of revolution by integration,
- understand the work on centres of mass in Mechanics 8 and know the centre of mass of a uniform triangular lamina,
- understand the work on equilibrium of a lamina in Mechanics 8 and 9,
- know the formulae for volumes of cones and spheres.

TEST YOURSELF

You should be able to do these questions without looking anything up. If you cannot, you need to revise earlier work.

1 Write down, in terms of π, the volume of
 a) a sphere of radius 3 mm,
 b) a cone of height 6 cm and base radius 2 cm.

2 Find the volume generated when the area between the part of the curve $y = x^2$ and the line $y = 4$ is rotated by 360° about the y-axis.

3 The diagram shows a uniform lamina whose shape is a square surmounted by an isosceles triangle. Find the distance of the centre of mass of this lamina from the line AB.

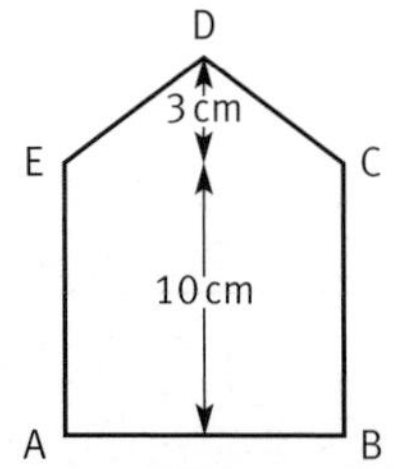

Answers

1 a) 36π mm³ **b)** 8π cm³
2 8π **3** $\frac{133}{23}$ cm (= 5.78 cm (3 sf)).

Centre of mass of a rigid body

When a rigid body is made from uniform material, its centre of mass lies on any axis of symmetry that the body possesses.

So, the centre of mass of a uniform cylinder is half way along its axis of symmetry, the centre of mass of a uniform cuboid is at the midpoint of its axes of symmetry and so on.

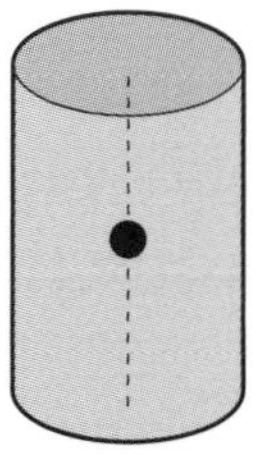

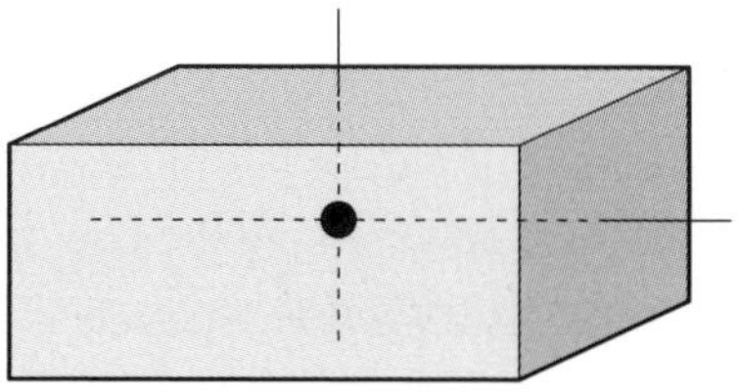

Centre of mass of a compound body

You can find the centre of mass of a compound body when you know the centres of mass of its constituent parts. You do this by using the fact that the sum of the moments of the weights of the constituent parts about an axis is equal to the moment of the weight of the compound body about the same axis.

For example, this solid, made from uniform material, is a cube with a cylindrical hole drilled through the centre of one face to a depth of 6 cm.

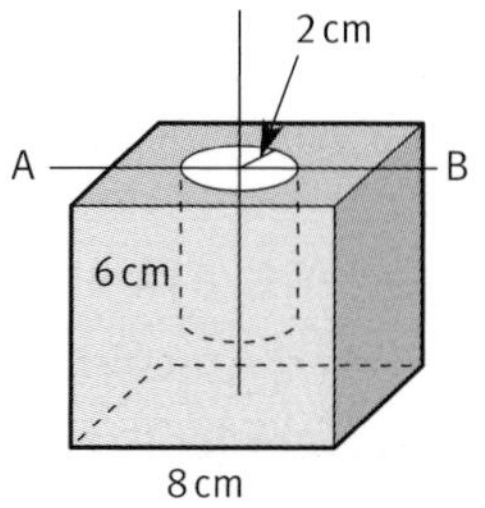

Its centre of gravity, G, lies on the axis of symmetry through the centre of the hole. You need to take moments to find where G lies on this axis. It is easier to work with a 'flat' diagram, so draw the section through the line AB.

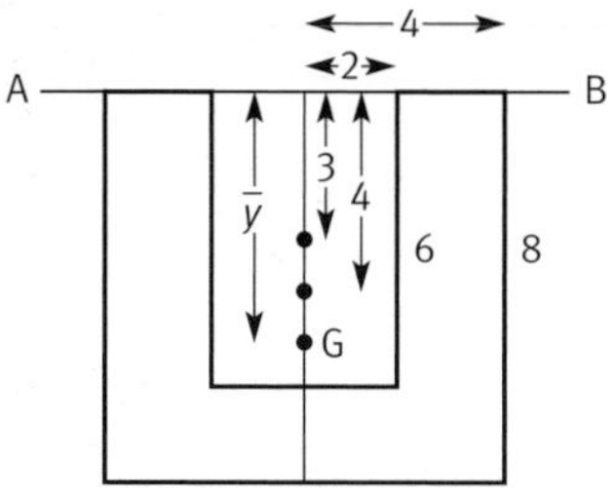

Next, make a table similar to those in Mechanics 8 remembering that, for solid bodies, the weight of each part is ρ times its *volume* where ρ is the density.

	cube	– cylinder	remainder
weight	512ρ	$24\pi\rho$	$(512 - 24\pi)\rho$
distance of C of G from AB	4	3	$\bar{y}$

A↻B $512 \times 4 - 24\pi \times 3 = (512 - 24\pi)\bar{y}$

$$\Rightarrow \quad \bar{y} = \frac{256 - 9\pi}{64 - 3\pi}$$

$\therefore$ G is $\dfrac{256 - 9\pi}{64 - 3\pi}$ cm below the cut face on the axis of symmetry.

The centre of mass of a prism

A uniform prism can be cut into a series of identical laminas equal in shape to its cross-section. It follows that the centre of mass is halfway along its length on the line through the centres of mass of the cross-sections.

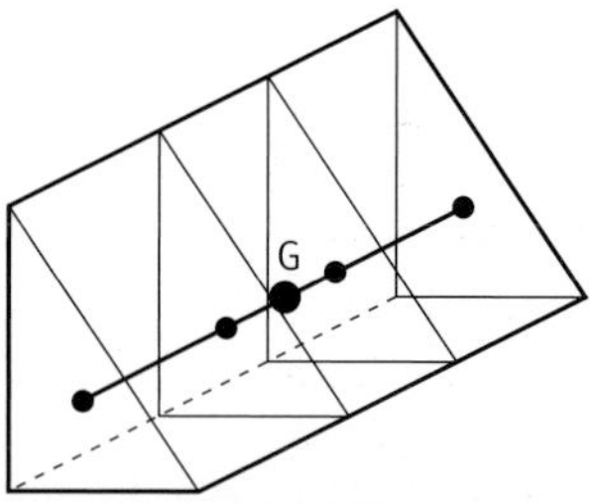

Question

The solid shown is a uniform cube of edge 12 units with a part removed by slicing perpendicular to a face through the midpoints of two adjacent edges. Find the coordinates of the centre of mass.

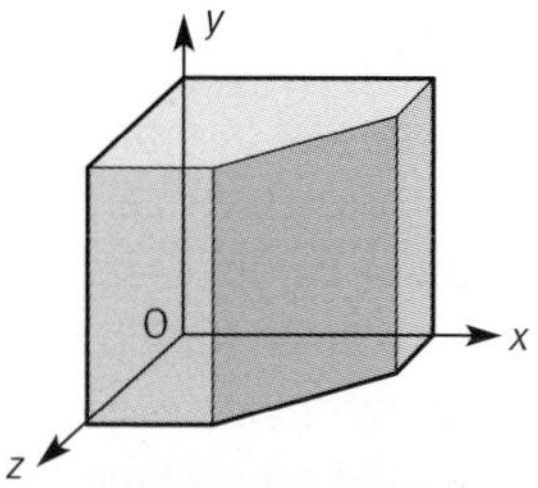

Answer

$(5\frac{3}{7}, 6, 5\frac{3}{7})$.

Finding the centre of mass by integration

A solid of revolution is formed by rotating an area through one revolution about an axis. The centre of mass of the solid lies on the axis of revolution.

You can find where it is on the axis by dividing the solid into thin discs by cuts perpendicular to the axis of symmetry.

Using Ox as the axis of symmetry, take a general disc, i.e. one that has a face at the point $P(x, y)$ on the curve and treat it as a cylinder, of radius y and thickness δx.

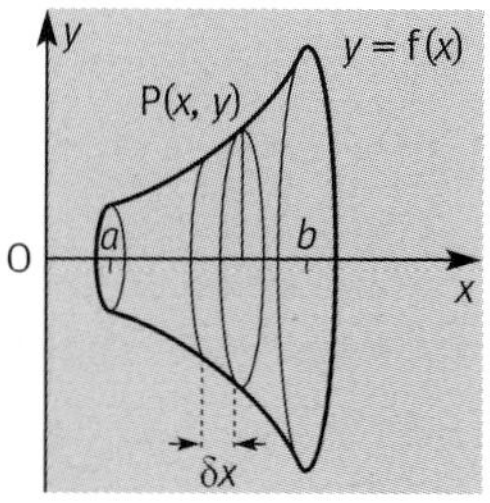

Then you say that the weight of the disc is approximately $\rho\pi y^2 \delta x$;
its C of M is at the point $(x, 0)$;
$\therefore$ the moment of its weight about $Oy \approx x(\rho\pi y^2 \delta x)$.
Summing these moments for the whole solid

$$\Rightarrow \quad \sum_{x=a}^{x=b} \rho\pi y^2 x\, \delta x \approx \rho(\text{volume}) \times \bar{x}$$

where $\bar{x}$ is the distance of the C of M from O.
(ρ cancels, so it can be left out.)

$$\therefore \quad \int_a^b \pi y^2 x\, dx = \bar{x} \times \text{volume}$$

If you do not know the volume of the solid, you can calculate it by integration.

Example

The area between the x-axis and the part of the curve $y = x^2$ from $x = 0$ to $x = 2$, is rotated through one revolution about Ox. Find the centre of mass of the uniform solid formed.

Solution

The mass of a general disc, treated as a cylinder, is approximately $\pi y^2\, \delta x$.

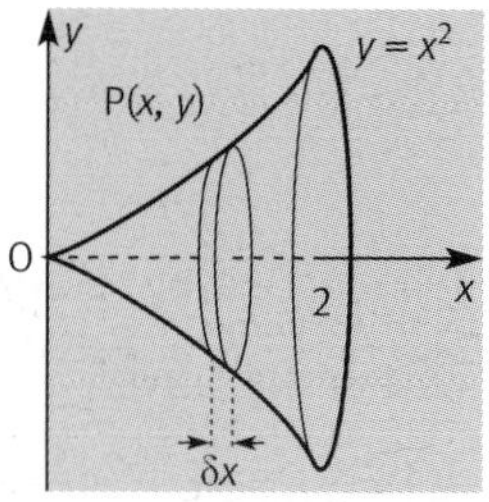

Taking moments about Oy for all such discs gives

$$\sum_{x=0}^{x=2} \pi y^2 x\, \delta x \approx \bar{x} \times \text{volume} = \bar{x} \times \pi \int_0^2 y^2 dx$$

$$\Rightarrow \int_0^2 x^5 dx = \bar{x} \times \int_0^2 x^4 dx \quad (\pi \text{ cancels and } y = x^2)$$

$$\Rightarrow \quad \bar{x} = \tfrac{5}{3}$$

$\therefore$ the centre of mass is at the point $(\frac{5}{3}, 0)$.

Example

Prove that the centre of mass of a hemisphere of radius a is $\frac{3}{8}a$ from the plane face along the axis of symmetry.

Solution

A hemisphere is formed when a quadrant of the circle $x^2 + y^2 = a^2$ is rotated by 360° about the x-axis.

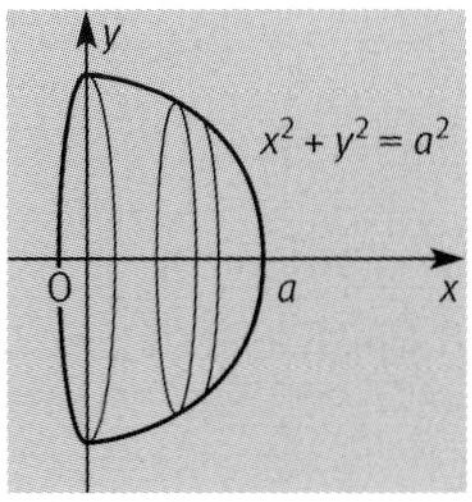

The centre of mass lies on Ox, distant $\bar{x}$ from O

where $\sum_{x=0}^{a} \pi y^2 x\, \delta x \approx \bar{x}V$

and V is the volume of the hemisphere.

Now $\quad y^2 = a^2 - x^2 \quad$ and $\quad V = \frac{1}{2}(\frac{4}{3}\pi a^3)$

$$\therefore \quad \pi \int_0^a x(a^2 - x^2)\mathrm{d}x = (\tfrac{2}{3}\pi a^3) \times \bar{x}$$

$$\Rightarrow \quad \tfrac{2}{3}a^3\bar{x} = \left[\tfrac{1}{2}a^2x^2 - \tfrac{1}{4}x^4\right]_0^a \Rightarrow \bar{x} = \tfrac{3}{8}a$$

Questions

1 A uniform cone is of height h and base radius r. Find the distance of its centre of mass of from the plane face. (A cone, height h and base radius r, is formed when the area between the line $y = \frac{r}{h}x$, the x-axis and the line $x = h$ is rotated by 360° about Ox.)

2 A uniform solid is formed by rotating the area between the part of the curve $y = \frac{1}{x}$ from $x = 1$ to $x = 3$, through 360° about the x-axis. Find the distance of the centre of mass from the smaller plane face of the solid.

Answer

1 $\frac{1}{4}h$

2 $3 - \frac{2}{3}\ln 3 \; [\bar{x} = \frac{2}{3}\ln 3]$.

Take a break

Equilibrium of a rigid body

A hemisphere often occurs in problems on equilibrium and it is worth remembering where its centre of mass is.

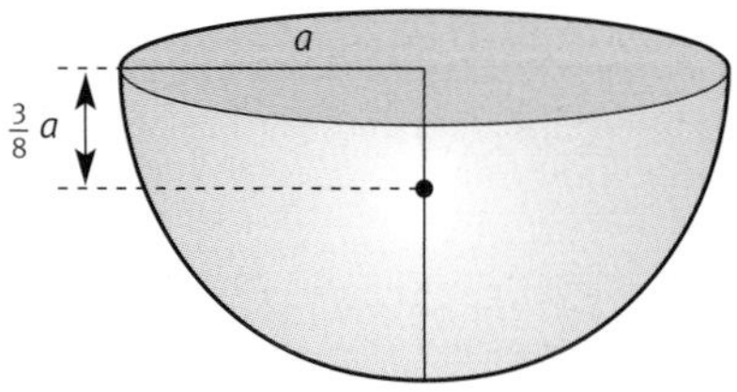

It is also worth remembering the position of the centre of mass of a right cone, which is $\frac{1}{4}$ of its height from the base. The centre of mass of a right pyramid is also $\frac{1}{4}$ of its height from the base.

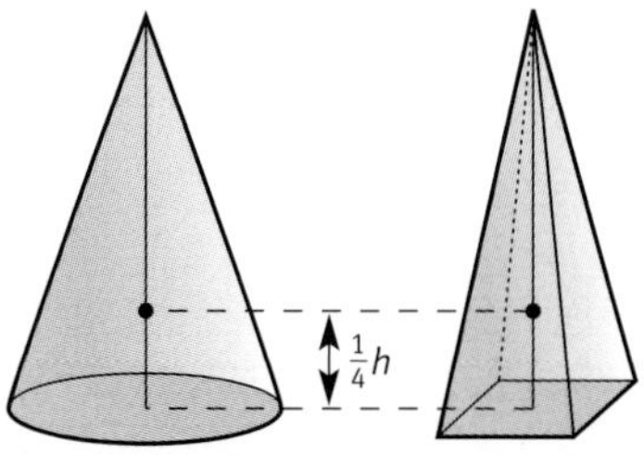

The principles that apply to the equilibrium of a lamina, apply also to the equilibrium of a rigid body.

- A rigid body hanging freely from a fixed point has only two forces acting on it; the tension in the string and its weight. For the body to be in equilibrium, the centre of gravity must be vertically below the point of suspension.
- For a rigid body to rest in equilibrium on a plane, the vertical line through its centre of mass must pass through the area of contact.
- A rigid body can rest in equilibrium on a sloping plane only when the plane is rough.
- A rigid body, resting on a plane (horizontal or sloping), is on the point of toppling when the vertical line through its centre of mass passes through the edge of the contact area.
- When a rigid body is in equilibrium under the action of a set of *coplanar* forces,
  i) the sum of their resolved components in any direction is zero,
  ii) the resultant moment about any axis is zero.
  In particular, when there are only three forces acting, those forces are concurrent.

⚠ The normal reaction between the curved surface of a sphere (or part of a sphere) and a plane goes through the centre of the sphere.

Problem solving

Problems often involve a compound body, e.g. a hemisphere surmounted by a cone. If you are not given the position of the centre of mass, you need to find this first.

When a body is in contact with a plane, you must identify the shape of the contact; it may be a plane, a line, a point or several points.

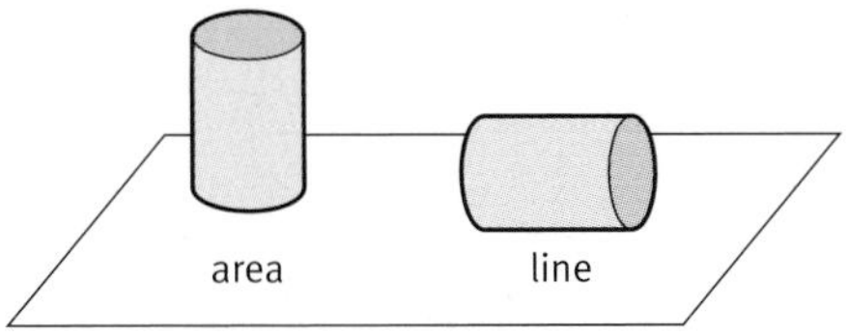

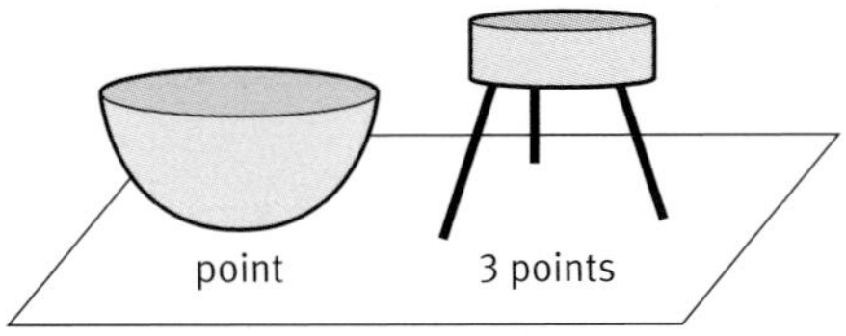

Example

A uniform solid brass knob is a frustum of a cone with the dimensions shown in the diagram.

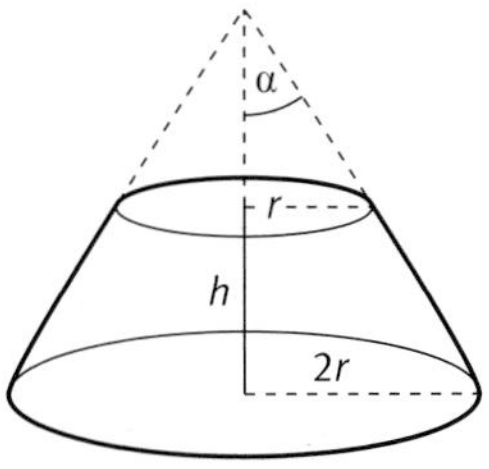

a Find the height of the centre of mass above the larger face.

When the knob is placed with its curved surface in contact with a horizontal plane, it is on the point of toppling.

b Find α.

Solution

a Start by drawing a section through the axis of symmetry.
From similar triangles, AF $= 2h$, so the height of the smaller cone is h.

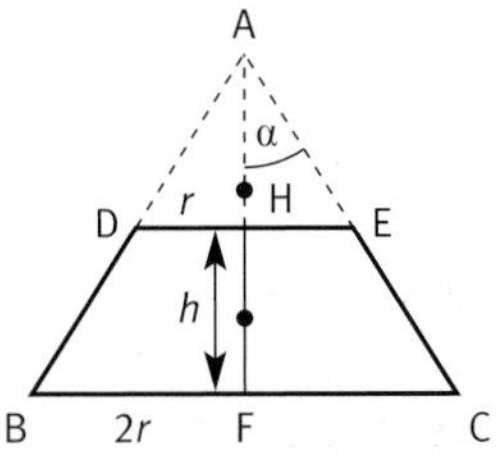

Consider the frustum as a complete cone ABC with the cone ADE removed:
C of M of cone ABC is $\frac{1}{4}$FA from BC,
C of M of cone ADE is $\frac{1}{4}$HA from DE.

	cone ABC	cone ADE	frustum
mass	$\frac{1}{3}\pi(2r)^2(2h)\rho$	$\frac{1}{3}\pi r^2 h\rho$	$\frac{7}{3}\pi r^2 h\rho$
distance of C of M from BC	$\frac{1}{2}h$	$\frac{5}{4}h$	$\bar{x}$

Taking moments about BC gives

$$\left[\tfrac{8}{3}\pi r^2 h\right] \times \tfrac{1}{2}h - \left[\tfrac{1}{3}\pi r^2 h\right] \times \tfrac{5}{4}h = \left[\tfrac{7}{3}\pi r^2 h\right] \times \bar{x}$$

$$\Rightarrow \quad \tfrac{4}{3}h - \tfrac{5}{12}h = \tfrac{7}{3}\bar{x} \quad \Rightarrow \quad \bar{x} = \tfrac{11}{28}h$$

$\therefore$ the centre of mass of the frustum is $\frac{11}{28}h$ above the larger flat face.

b When the knob is resting with its curved surface on a flat plane, there is a line of contact; this is BD in the diagram. The knob is on the point of toppling when the line of action of the weight passes through D, i.e. MD is vertical where M is the centre of mass of the knob.

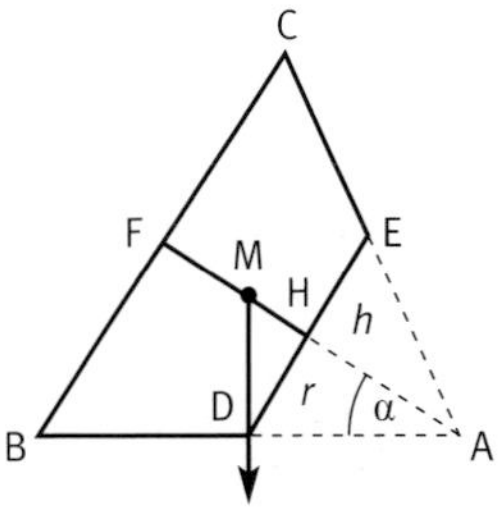

As $\angle$MDH $= \alpha$, you can get two expressions for $\tan\alpha$, one from $\triangle$ADH and one from $\triangle$DMH.

$\triangle$ADH: $\tan\alpha = \dfrac{r}{h}$ and $\triangle$DMH: $\tan\alpha = \dfrac{\frac{17}{28}h}{r}$

Equating these gives $r = h\sqrt{\frac{17}{28}}$

$\Rightarrow \tan\alpha = \sqrt{\frac{17}{28}} \quad \Rightarrow \quad \alpha = 37.9°$ (1 d.p.)

Questions

1 The diagram shows a uniform hemisphere of radius a resting on a rough horizontal floor and against a smooth vertical wall. The flat face is inclined at 30° to the horizontal.

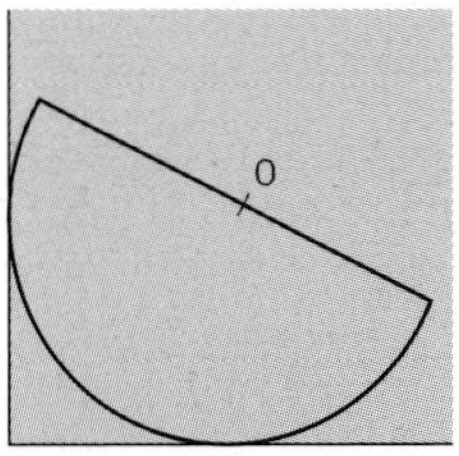

Find the minimum value of the coefficient of friction between the hemisphere and the floor.

2 The diagram shows a child's toy made from a uniform hemisphere of radius 6 cm surmounted by a uniform cone of height 6 cm.

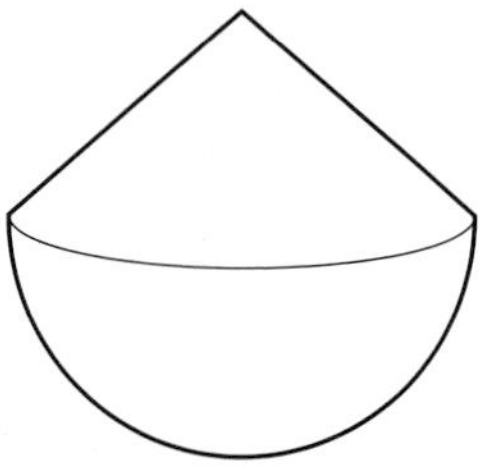

The cone is made from material that is half the density of the hemisphere.
Explain why, when the toy is placed with any part of the surface of the hemisphere on a flat horizontal surface, it will right itself.

Answers

1 $\frac{3}{16}$ (Take moments about O.)

2 The C of M of the toy is within the hemisphere, $1\frac{1}{2}$ cm below the join of the flat faces.

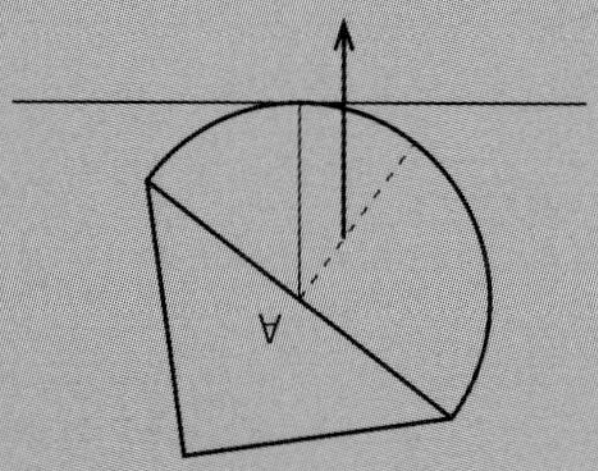

The toy can rest in equilibrium with the surface of the hemisphere in contact with a horizontal plane only when the weight and the normal reaction are collinear, i.e. when the axis is vertical. In any other position, the weight has a moment about the point of contact so the toy will rock until it comes to rest in the equilibrium position, i.e. with its axis vertical.

Take a break

Review

(Take $g = 10$)

1 A uniform smooth sphere, A, of mass m is moving with speed 3 ms^{-1} when it collides with a stationary uniform smooth sphere, B, of equal radius of mass $2m$. The coefficient of restitution between the spheres is $\frac{1}{3}$. Calculate the impulse of the impact on B.

2 A light elastic string of length 2 m and modulus 40 N has a particle of mass 2 kg attached to one end A. The other end of the string is attached to a fixed point B.

a Find the distance below B of the point C at which the particle hangs in equilibrium.
The particle is held at B and then released.

b Find the speed of the particle as it passes through C.

c Show that, while the string is taut, the motion of the particle is simple harmonic.

3 A bowl is made by removing a hemisphere of radius 10 cm from a uniform wooden cuboid with a square section and dimensions shown. Find, to 3 sf, the height of the centre of mass of the bowl above the base.

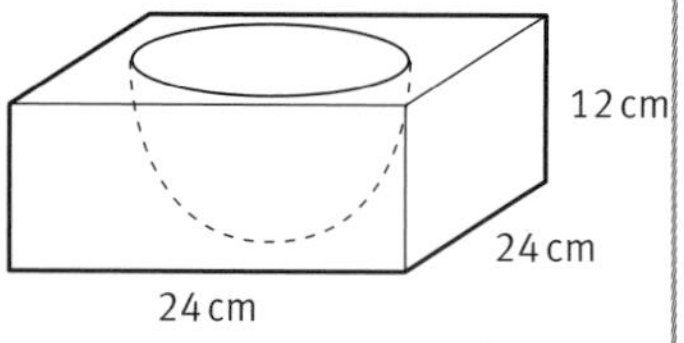

4 A particle of mass 1 kg is attached to one end of a light inelastic string of length l. The other end of the string is attached to a fixed point O. The particle is released from rest when it is level with O and the string is taut. When the string becomes vertical it meets a small fixed peg P, a distance kl below O.
Find the least value of k for which the particle describes a complete circle about P.

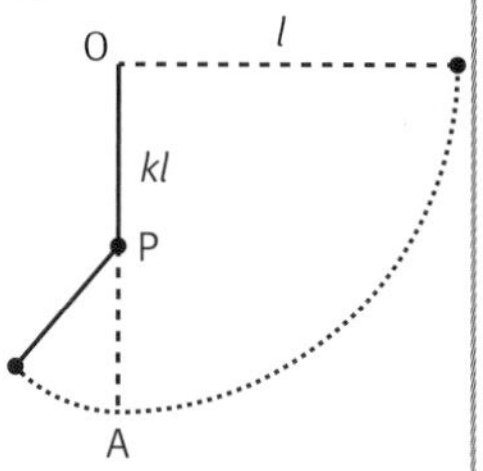

5 A small smooth pebble of mass 0.1kg is dropped from above the surface of some liquid in a tank. The resistance to the motion of the pebble in the liquid is proportional to the square of the speed of the pebble and is such that the speed of the pebble is reduced to a steady 0.5 ms^{-1}. Show that, while it is slowing down, the equation of motion of the pebble in the liquid is given by $\frac{dv}{dt} = 10 - 40v^2$.

Answers

1 $\frac{8}{3}m$ **2a** 3 m **b** $\sqrt{50}$ ms^{-1} **c** when the particle is x m from C, $F = ma \Rightarrow \ddot{x} = -10x \Rightarrow$ SHM **3** 5.02 cm **4** $k \geqslant \frac{3}{5}$.

Statistics

1 **Collecting and defining data**.

2 **Representing data**. Stem and leaf diagrams. Cumulative frequency polygons. Histograms.

3 **Methods for summarising sample data**. Measures of central tendency. Measures of dispersion. Box and whisker plots. Skew. Outliers. Interpolation. Mean. Variance. Linear coding.

4 **Probability**. Venn diagrams. Conditional probability. Independent events. Mutually exclusive events. Tree diagrams. Permutations. Combinations.

5 **Random variables**. Discrete random variables. Continuous random variables. Cumulative distributive function. Expectation and variance of a linear function of a random variable. Continuous uniform distribution.

6 **Correlation and regression**. Correlation. Product-moment correlation coefficient. Hypothesis testing. One- and two-tailed tests. Critical value and critical region. Spearman's rank correlation coefficient. Regression.

7 **The binomial and Poisson distributions**. The binomial distribution. The Poisson distribution. How do you know whether to use the Poisson distribution or the binomial distribution? Using the Poisson distribution as an approximation to the binomial distribution. The distribution of the sum of two independent Poisson distributions.

8 **The normal distribution**. Calculating probabilities with the normal distribution. Finding μ and σ using given probabilities. Linear combinations of independent random variables. Approximations using the normal distribution.

9 **Estimation and confidence intervals**. Unbiased estimates for population parameters. The distribution of the sample mean and the central limit theorem. Confidence intervals of the mean when μ is known. Interpreting the confidence interval. Finding the confidence interval when the width of the confidence interval is known. Confidence intervals for a small sample from a normal distribution when μ is unknown. The t-distribution.

10 **Hypothesis testing**. Hypothesis testing. One- and two-tailed tests. Critical value and critical region. Hypothesis test for the mean of a normal distribution when σ is known. Hypothesis test for the mean of a normal distribution when σ is unknown. Testing for the difference between the means of two independent normal distributions. Type I and Type II errors. Hypothesis test for the proportion of a binomial distribution, p. Hypothesis test for the mean of a Poisson distribution, λ.

11 **The χ^2 significance test**. Procedure for testing the goodness-of-fit. Critical region of the χ^2 distribution. Using the χ^2 test for goodness-of-fit for different distributions. Summary of the degrees of freedom for different distributions. The χ^2 test for independence in a contingency table. Yates' continuity correction.

PREVIEW

By the end of this topic, you will have revised:

- ✔ **different terms used in statistics,**
- ✔ **methods of classifying data.**

LEARN all the definitions below.

A **variate** is a measure of data in terms of quantity or quality.

A **statistical model** is a statistical process devised to describe or make predictions about the expected behaviour of real-life variates.

Continuous variates may take any value within a given range.

Discrete variates can only take particular values.

Example

State whether each of the following variates is discrete or continuous:

a number of cars in a family,
b height of a man,
c a woman's salary in pounds and pence,
d a child's weight at birth.

Solution

a and **c** are discrete; **b** and **d** are continuous.

Quantitative variates describe numerical data.

Qualitative variates describe non-numerical information.

Example

Upon the birth of a newborn baby, midwives take the following information:

a name,
b height,
c weight,
d gender.

Which of these items of information are qualitative and which are quantitative?

Solution

a and **d** are qualitative; **b** and **c** are quantitative.

A **population** is the entire group of individuals or items that is being studied.

Populations may be **finite** or **infinite**. In a **finite population** it may be possible to count and number each member. In an **infinite population** it is impossible to measure the exact size of the population.

A **census** is a survey in which measures or observations are taken from every member of the population.

In statistics, it is often expensive and time-consuming and sometimes impossible to take observations or measurements from the entire population. A group of individual members of the population is taken: this is a **sample**. The members of the sample are the **sampling units**.

If each sampling unit contains several individuals, then each individual is known as a **sampling element**.

When each sampling unit within a population is given a unique name, number or reference code, then the list of sampling units is known as a **sampling frame**.

Example

A survey is taken of the number of travellers to Spain during the first week in August. Suggest a possible sampling frame.

Solution

The most obvious answer is passport numbers of all the travellers.

Example

An angler wants to find the average length of trout in a river. Give two reasons why he would choose to take a sample rather than a census.

Solution

It is quicker; it is generally cheaper; it is difficult to catch all the fish and measure them.

Questions

1 A study was undertaken of salaries of employees in U.K. industry by examining the employees of some companies based in the U.K. What was the

a sampling unit,
b sampling frame,
c population.

2 One thousand lawyers attended a training course. The personnel departments of the lawyers' employers wanted to find out what the lawyers thought of the course. Would you recommend them to use a census or a sample survey? Give a reason for your answer. Give one disadvantage of using the method you chose.

3 State whether the following variates are discrete or continuous:

a the length of a rug,

b the number of lamps sold in a week,

c the weight of a table,

d the number of pages in a book.

Answers

1a An employee.

b All the employees in the companies.

c All the employees in U.K. industry.

2 A sample survey would be better to take as it is less time-consuming and cheaper; however there is some loss of accuracy.

3a and **c** are continuous, **b** and **d** are discrete.

Take a break

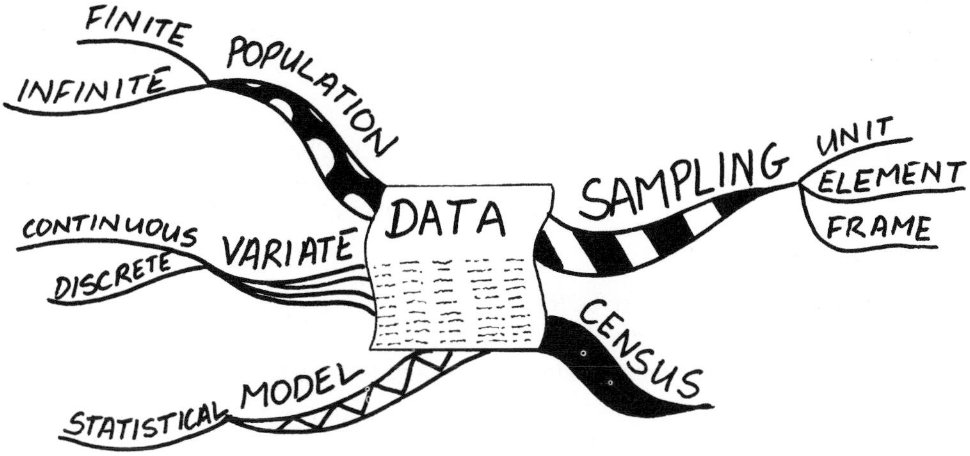

PREVIEW

By the end of this topic you will have revised:

- ✔ **how to draw stem and leaf diagrams,**
- ✔ **lower and upper class limits of grouped data,**
- ✔ **how to draw cumulative frequency polygons,**
- ✔ **how to draw histograms.**

Before you start you should know:

- how to group data,
- the meaning of frequency and cumulative frequency,
- how to draw a cumulative frequency curve,
- the difference between a cumulative frequency curve and a cumulative frequency polygon.

Stem and leaf diagrams

This is a method of grouping, ordering and showing data. Stem and leaf diagrams may be used to represent data with integer or non-integer values.

Example

Construct a stem and leaf diagram to represent these data:

5.5 4.3 6.2 4.1 4.7 3.8 3.3
3.6 4.0 5.8 5.9 6.1 4.5 5.5
3.9 3.9 5.8 6.1 6.2 5.3 4.3
3.7 6.7 4.6 4.8 5.1 3.2 4.4
4.8 4.8

Solution

Usually the last digit of each number is taken as the leaf, and the other digit(s) as the stem. Write the stems on the left, with each leaf by the appropriate stem, but do not worry about getting the leaves in the correct order to start with. Redraw the diagram with the leaves in the correct order. A key should be included in the diagram to ensure that the diagram is read correctly. For example, if 2.1 is written as 2|1, write '2|1 means 2.1' at the top of your diagram.

Stems	*leaves*	*3|8 means 3.8*
3	8 3 6 9 9 7 2	(7)
4	3 1 7 0 5 3 6 8 4 8 8	(11)
5	5 8 9 5 8 3 1	(7)
6	2 1 1 2 7	(5)

The numbers in brackets show the number of leaves in each stem. Use these to check that the total number of leaves matches the number of items in the data given, and to check that you have used all the leaves in the reordered diagram.

		3|2 means 3.2
3	2 3 6 7 8 9 9	(7)
4	0 1 3 3 4 5 6 7 8 8 8	(11)
5	1 3 5 5 8 8 9	(7)
6	1 1 2 2 7	(5)

Back-to-back stem and leaf diagrams

Stem and leaf diagrams may be used to compare two sets of data by representing them both on the same diagram.

Example

A survey was conducted from a random sample of news articles from *The Daily Tabloid* and *The Daily Broadsheet*. The numbers of words in each article were counted and the results are shown below.

The Daily Tabloid

305 458 260 320 580 182 222 347 405
506 377 287 365 480 450 541 555 343
357 516 435 289 499 521 604 680 328
358 333 610

The Daily Broadsheet

648 657 540 488 380 420 580 628 387
480 521 602 710 555 543 476 729 676
707 405 440 390 579 290 378 777 720
844 690 652

Construct a 'back-to-back' stem and leaf diagram to represent these data. Comment on your results.

Solution

The ordered stem and leaf diagrams are as follows:

The Daily Tabloid

Length of article		1|82 means 182
1	82	(1)
2	22 60 87 89	(4)
3	05 20 28 33 43 47 57 58 65 77	(10)
4	05 35 50 58 80 99	(6)
5	06 16 21 41 55 80	(6)
6	04 10 80	(3)

The Daily Broadsheet

Length of article		2|90 means 290
2	90	(1)
3	78 80 87 90	(4)
4	05 20 40 76 80 88	(6)
5	21 40 43 55 79 80	(6)
6	02 28 48 52 57 76 90	(7)
7	07 10 20 29 77	(5)
8	44	(1)

Put the two diagrams together on one 'back-to-back' diagram (i.e. with common stems):

Length of article

The Daily Tabloid			*The Daily Broadsheet*	2|90 means 290
(1)	82	1		
(4)	89 87 60 22	2	90	(1)
(10)	77 65 58 57 47 43 33 28 20 05	3	78 80 87 90	(4)
(6)	99 80 58 50 35 05	4	05 20 40 76 80 88	(6)
(6)	80 55 41 21 16 06	5	21 40 43 55 79 80	(6)
(3)	80 10 04	6	02 28 48 52 57 76 90	(7)
		7	07 10 20 29 77	(5)
		8	44	(1)

'Back-to-back' diagrams make for easy comparison between data: in this case, articles from *The Daily Broadsheet* were, in general, longer than those from *The Daily Tabloid*.

Questions

1 The numbers of pages in 30 randomly selected novels are given below.

321 418 303 409 280 210 180 472 135 358
367 209 389 286 177 144 490 222 338 279
299 302 317 255 196 200 286 348 402 526

Construct a stem and leaf diagram to represent these data.

2 There are 20 pupils in Class A and 26 in Class B. Each pupil is given a model to build. The time taken by each pupil to complete it is recorded to the nearest minute:

Class A
21 33 42 30 15 19 37 34 23 38
32 20 37 25 26 39 44 40 28 36

Class B
13 21 17 27 30 26 25 14 14 24 37
25 27 30 19 29 21 11 18 26 32 34
21 28 16 40

Represent these data using a single stem and leaf diagram.

Answers

1

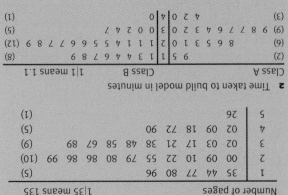

Number of pages — 1|35 means 135

1	35 44 77 80 96	(5)
2	00 09 10 22 55 79 80 86 86 99	(10)
3	02 03 17 21 38 48 58 67 89	(9)
4	02 09 18 72 90	(5)
5	26	(1)

2 Time taken to build model in minutes

Class A			Class B	1|1 means 1.1
(2)	9 5	1	1 3 4 4 6 7 8 9	(8)
(6)	8 6 5 3 1 0	2	1 1 1 4 5 5 6 6 7 7 8 9	(12)
(9)	9 8 7 7 6 4 3 2 0	3	0 0 2 4 7	(5)
(3)	4 2 0	4	0	(1)

Grouped data and class boundaries

Data are often represented by groups in tables. When data are continuous, the variates are rounded. For example, this table shows weight rounded to the nearest kilogram.

Weight in kilograms	Frequency
...	...
70–74	13
75–79	17
80–85	20
...	...

The 75–79 group has a lower class boundary of 74.5 and an upper class boundary of 79.5. The class mid-point is the average of the upper and lower class boundaries: i.e. 77 in this case. The class width is the difference between the upper and lower class boundaries: 5 in this example.

However in a survey of a people's ages (x years), 45–49 years of age may be written as $45 \leqslant x < 50$, since ages are always rounded down (for example, if someone is 45 years and 10 months they are taken as 45 years old). The lower class boundary is 45 and the upper class boundary is 50. The class width is 5 and the mid-point is 47.5.

Cumulative frequency polygons

The cumulative frequencies are always plotted against the upper class boundaries. Cumulative frequency polygons must be drawn using a ruler.

Example

In a survey, 200 fourteen-year-olds were asked to estimate, to the nearest hour, the average number of hours they spend watching television per school night. The results are summarised in the table on p. 176.

Time (hours)	No. of people
0–1	36
2–3	62
4–5	58
6–7	30
8–9	14

Represent the data using a cumulative frequency polygon.

Solution

Complete a column for cumulative frequency. The figures are 36, 98, 156, 186, 200. Check that the final figure is the same as the size of the sample given in the first line of the question.

Plot the cumulative frequencies against the upper class boundaries. The upper class boundary for the first group is 1.5, for the 2–3 group, 3.5, etc. So plot the points (1.5, 36), (3.5, 98), (5.5, 156), (7.5, 186), (9.5, 200). As the data starts at 0 hours with 0 people, join the origin to the first plotted point with a ruler, then connect the points using a ruler. This gives the cumulative frequency polygon shown below:

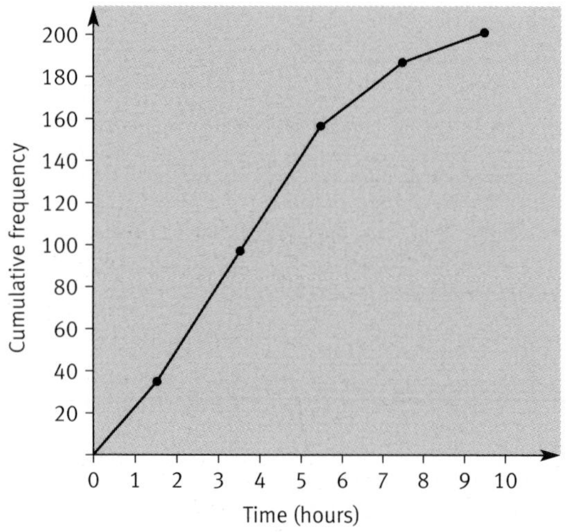

Question

A random sample of 40 CDs was taken. Their playing times to the nearest minute are given below. Construct a grouped frequency distribution for these data. Draw a cumulative frequency polygon to represent your distribution.

45 55 39 49 42 58 43 46 47 40
50 53 51 37 39 49 52 55 58 59
35 55 58 44 46 45 42 39 50 52
42 41 47 48 52 47 38 49 50 53

Answer

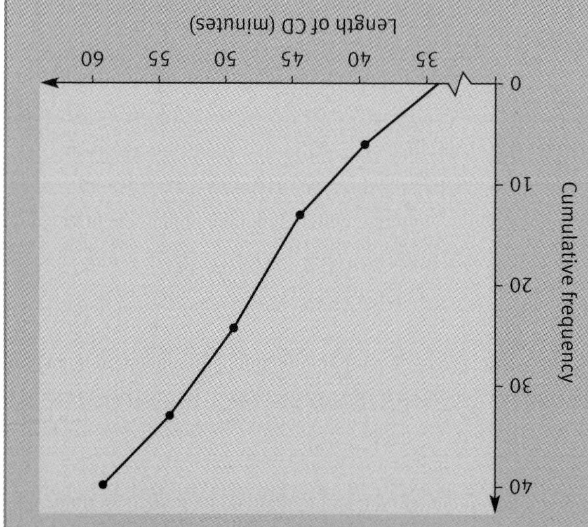

Length (minutes)	35–39	40–44	45–49	50–54	55–59
Frequency	6	7	11	9	7

Histograms

Histograms look similar to bar charts but there are two differences.

- They are used to represent continuous data, so there are no gaps between bars.
- The frequency is represented by the area of each bar.

You can use Frank FeeDs CoWs to draw histograms:

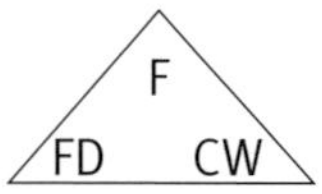

where F = frequency, FD = frequency density, CW = class width.

Frequency density is the frequency per 1 unit interval along the *x*-axis.
For example, if a histogram representing the weight of adults has a bar that represents a frequency of 20 people between 74.5 and 79.5 kg, the frequency density is 4 (= frequency ÷ class width = 20/5), i.e., for each 1 kilogram width of the bar, there is a frequency of 4. The frequency density in this case may also be written as 'frequency per 1 kilogram interval'.

Example

The length of time, to the nearest minute, that 80 people spent waiting for a vet in her surgery is summarised in the table on p. 177:

Time (minutes)	No. of people
2–3	4
4–5	9
6–8	15
9–12	22
13–16	16
17–19	6
20–29	8

Draw a histogram to illustrate the information.

Estimate the number of people who waited for 11 to 18 minutes, inclusive.

Solution

Add extra columns for class width and for frequency density.

The lower class boundary for the 2–3 class is 1.5 and the upper class boundary is 3.5.
So the class width is $3.5 - 1.5 = 2$.

Time (minutes)	No. of people	Class width	Frequency density
2–3	4	2	2
4–5	9	2	4.5
6–8	15	3	5
9–12	22	4	5.5
13–16	16	4	4
17–19	6	3	2
20–29	8	10	0.8

Now represent these on a histogram. The height of each bar is the frequency density and the base of each bar spans the class width, i.e. 1.5–3.5 for the group 2–3 minutes, and so on.

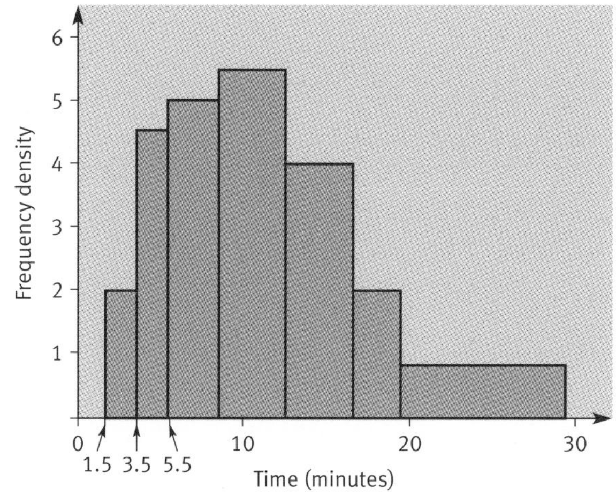

First find the lower and upper limits of this range of values: i.e. 10.5 and 18.5. This includes half of the 9–12 group, all of the people in the 13–16 group, and two thirds of the 17–19 group:
i.e. $11 + 16 + 4 = 31$ people.

Questions

1 A student recorded the heights, to the nearest centimetre, of all the plants in a conservatory. The heights were summarised in a grouped frequency distribution and represented by a histogram. The first group in the distribution was 40–49 centimetres and its frequency was 10 plants. This was represented by a rectangle of width 1.6 cm and height 5 cm. If the total area under the histogram was 184 cm^2, find the total number of plants in the conservatory.

2 A teacher recorded the time, to the nearest minute, that each child of a school year took to solve a particular problem. Represent these data by a histogram. Estimate the number of children who took from 16 to 20 minutes inclusive to complete the task.

Time (to the nearest minute)	Number of children
5–9	2
10–13	6
14–17	10
18–19	8
20–21	10
22–23	9
24–27	12
28–32	5

Answer

1 Area represented by 10 plants $= 1.6 \times 5 = 8\ \text{cm}^2$
Number of plants per cm^2 $= 1.25$
Total frequency $= 1.25 \times 184 = 230$.

2

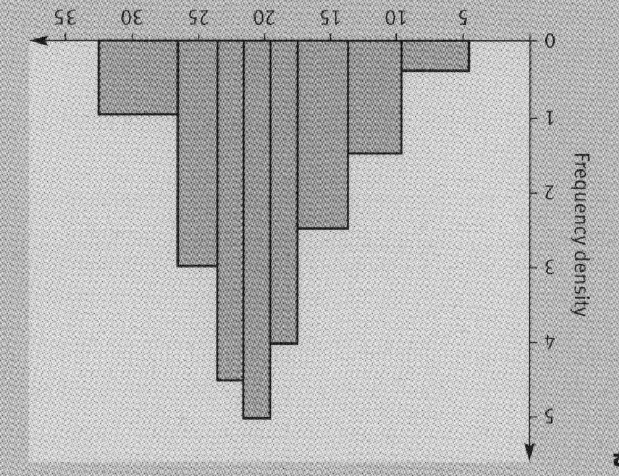

Estimated number who took from 16 to 20 minutes to complete the task $= \frac{2}{4} \times 10 + 8 + \frac{1}{2} \times 10 = 18$ children.

Take a break

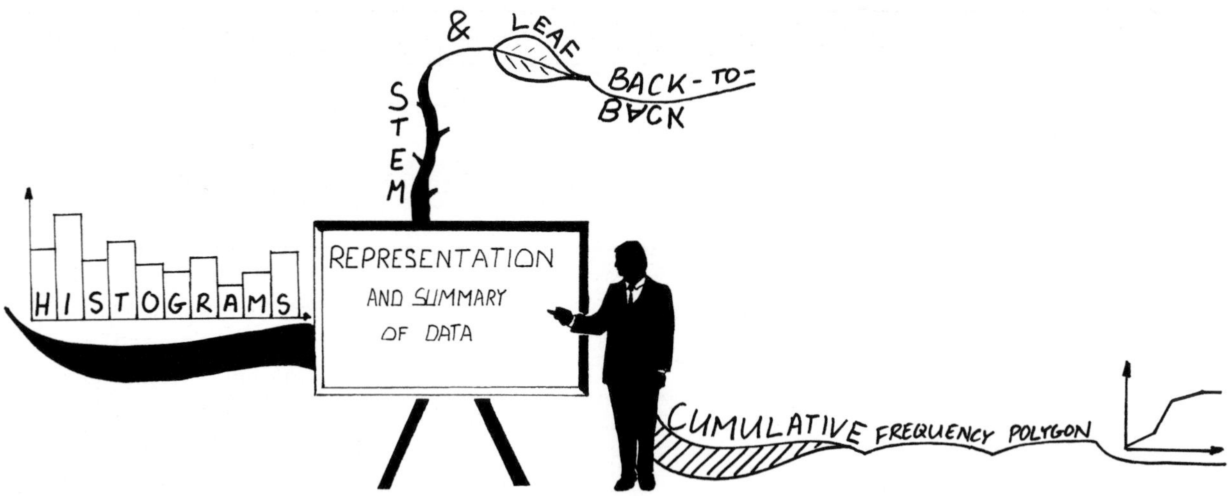

Review

1 For a survey on the weight of hand-made chocolates, suggest:

a a suitable sampling unit **b** a suitable sampling frame.

2 The following table gives a grouped frequency distribution of the length of time, in minutes, that 100 people spent eating in a fast food restaurant.

Time, t minutes	Number of people
$0 < t \leqslant 5$	6
$5 < t \leqslant 10$	10
$10 < t \leqslant 15$	15
$15 < t \leqslant 20$	35
$20 < t \leqslant 30$	22
$30 < t \leqslant 60$	12

Draw a histogram to illustrate these data.

3 Thirty boys estimate the length of a piece of string, in cm, to the nearest mm:

5.4 4.3 4.4 5.6 5.0 5.1 6.2 6.7 7.4 6.0
3.9 4.2 4.3 4.7 5.3 7.8 3.3 5.7 6.6 4.5
4.9 3.2 3.6 5.4 6.2 6.4 5.8 5.9 6.2 5.5

Draw a stem and leaf diagram to represent the data.

4 The table below shows the frequency distribution of the heights, in cm, of 200 children in a particular school.

Height, h cm	Frequency
$100 < h \leqslant 110$	12
$110 < h \leqslant 120$	32
$120 < h \leqslant 130$	62
$130 < h \leqslant 140$	48
$140 < h \leqslant 150$	30
$150 < h \leqslant 160$	12
$160 < h \leqslant 170$	4

Draw a cumulative frequency polygon to represent these data.

Answers

1a A single chocolate, **b** the chocolates in one batch in the order in which they are made.

2

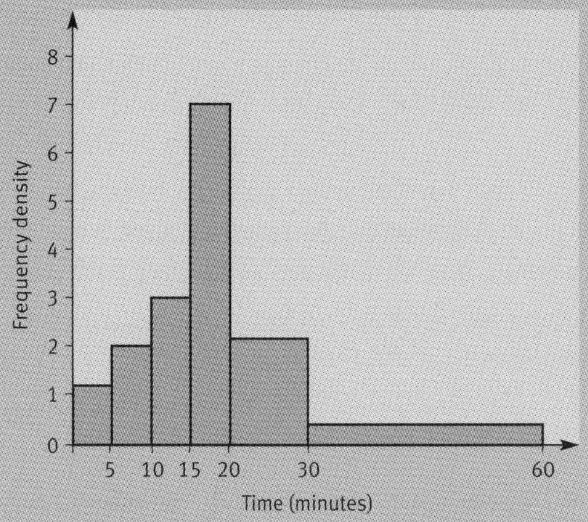

3 Estimated lengths 3|2 means 3.2

3	2 3 6 9	(4)
4	2 3 3 4 5 7 9	(7)
5	0 1 3 4 4 5 6 7 8 9	(10)
6	0 2 2 2 4 6 7	(7)
7	4 8	(2)

4

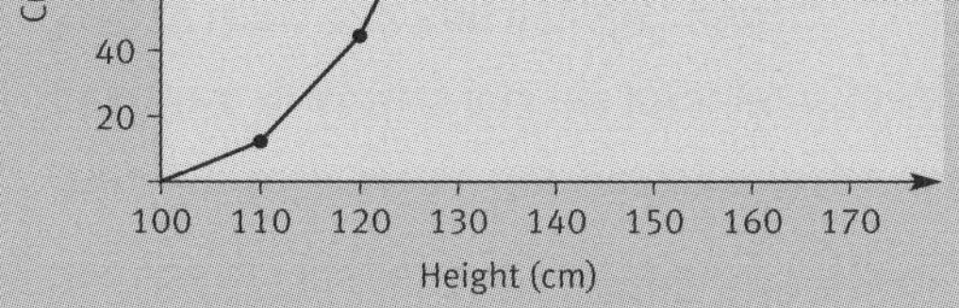

PREVIEW

By the end of this topic you will have revised:

- ✔ **the arithmetic mean, the median and the mode,**
- ✔ **quartiles, quantiles and the interquartile range,**
- ✔ **how to draw box and whisker plots,**
- ✔ **how to determine the skewness of data,**
- ✔ **how to calculate variance and standard deviation of discrete and grouped data.**

Before you start you should:

- know how to calculate the mean and median of raw data and of grouped data.

Measures of central tendency

Measures of central tendency are also called **averages** and there are three you need to know: the **arithmetic mean**, the **median** and the **mode**.

Mode

The mode is the most common value (remember that the first two letters of **mo**de and **mo**st are the same). In a grouped frequency distribution, the modal class is the class with the highest frequency.
The advantages of using the mode are that

- it is easy to calculate
- it is not affected by 'outliers' (extreme values in the data set).

Disadvantages of the mode are that

- there may be more than one mode
- it is a fairly simplistic measure of the average
- it cannot be used to calculate other statistical measures.

Calculating the mode from a histogram

The mode lies in the class with the highest frequency density. Draw a cross as shown on the diagram below.

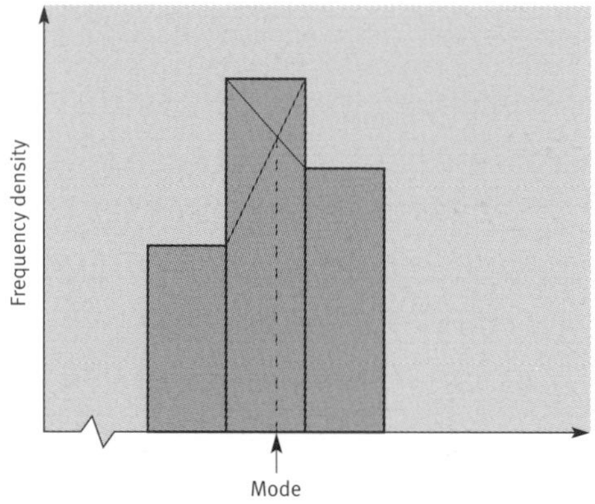

Draw a line from the centre of the cross down to the horizontal axis to find an estimate of the mode.

Median

The median is the middle value when the data is arranged in order from smallest to largest. (Remember me**d**ian and mi**d**dle have the same number of letters and they both have d as the third letter.)

The middle value of n items is the $\left(\frac{n+1}{2}\right)^{\text{th}}$ value.
If n is even, take the average of the $\left(\frac{n}{2}\right)^{\text{th}}$ and the $\left(\frac{n}{2}+1\right)^{\text{th}}$ values.

Advantages of the median are that

- it is easy to calculate
- it is not affected by 'outliers'.

A disadvantage is

- it cannot be used to calculate other statistical measures.

Quartiles

Quartiles of an ordered set of data are such that

- 25% of the data is less than or equal to Q_1, the first or lower quartile
- 50% is less than or equal to Q_2, the second quartile or median, and
- 75% is less than or equal to Q_3, the third or upper quartile.

Strictly, the median is the $\frac{1}{2}(n+1)^{\text{th}}$ value, but for large values of n and for grouped frequency distributions, this is approximated to the $\frac{1}{2}n^{\text{th}}$ value.

Similarly the upper quartile is the $\frac{3}{4}(n+1)^{\text{th}}$ value, but for large values of n and for grouped frequency distributions this is approximated to the $\frac{3}{4}n^{\text{th}}$ value. The lower quartile is the $\frac{1}{4}(n+1)^{\text{th}}$ value, but for large values of n and for grouped frequency distributions this is approximated to the $\frac{1}{4}n^{\text{th}}$ value.

When finding the lower or upper quartiles of discrete data, if $\frac{1}{4}(n+1)$ or $\frac{3}{4}(n+1)$ are not integers (whole numbers), it is usually acceptable to round these to the nearest whole number. e.g. If $n = 74$, the lower quartile is the 18.75th value, so take the 19th value.

Quantiles

Data can be divided into any number of equal parts. These are called **quantiles**. Quartiles are most commonly used, but if the data are split into ten equal parts the divisions are called **deciles** and if they are split into a hundred equal parts, they are called **percentiles**.

Measures of dispersion

The **interquartile range** is the range of the middle 50% of the data, where

interquartile range = upper quartile (Q_3) – lower quartile (Q_1)

The **semi-interquartile range** = $\frac{1}{2}$interquartile range

The **variance** is the mean value of the squares of the differences between each value and the mean.
The **standard deviation** is the positive square root of the variance. The formulae for finding the variance and the standard deviation are given on page 183.

Box and whisker plots, or box plots

The box is used to represent the central 50% of the data and the whiskers show the range of values.

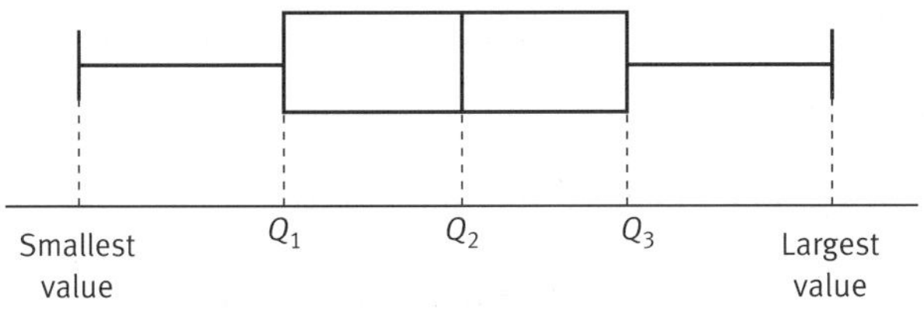

A scale must be drawn below a box plot.

Skew

When the data are symmetrical, $Q_2 - Q_1 = Q_3 - Q_2$.

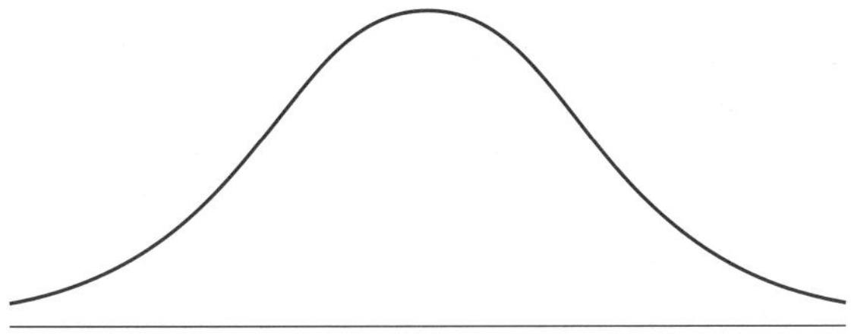

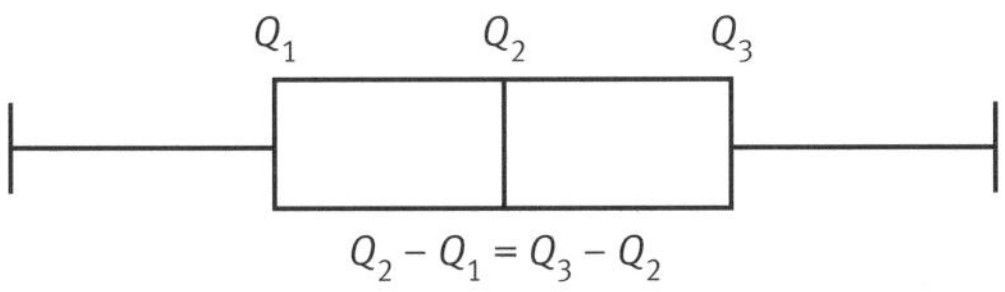

If data are not symmetrical, then the distribution is skewed.

The data below have **positive skew** as the tail is on the positive side of the mode.

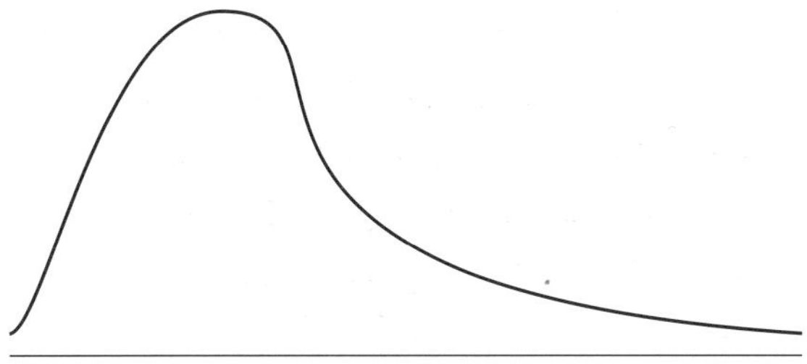

Using box plots, when $Q_2 - Q_1 < Q_3 - Q_2$, the data has positive skew.

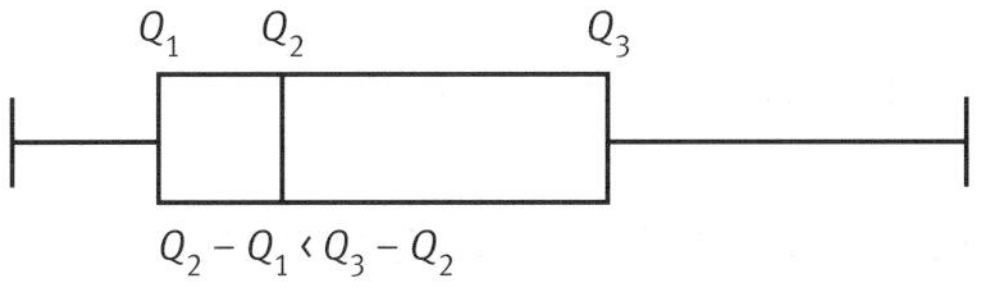

The data below have **negative skew** as the tail is on the negative side of the mode.

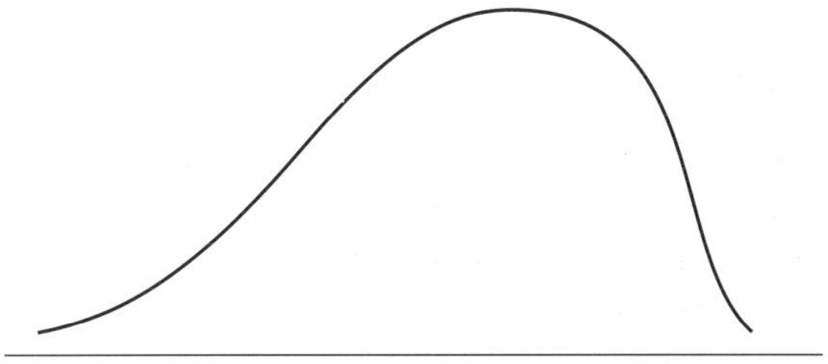

When $Q_2 - Q_1 > Q_3 - Q_2$, then the data has negative skew.

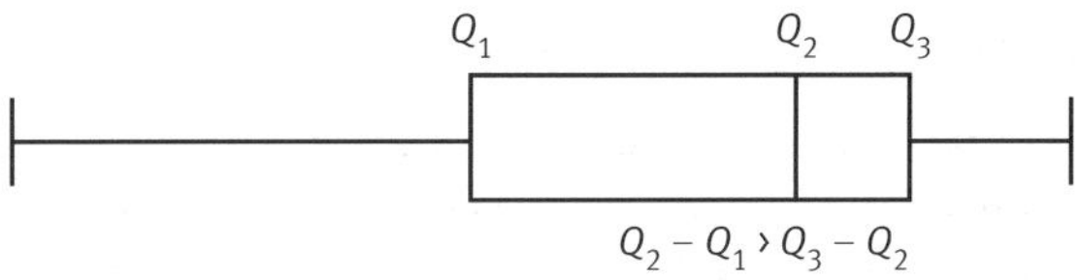

If the data are very skewed, the median and interquartile range are better measures of the average and dispersion than the mean and variance (or standard deviation) respectively, as the latter are distorted by the values causing the skew.

Outliers

Outliers are unusually small or large observations. If an outlier is identified, exclude it from the whiskers of the box-and-whisker plot and mark it with an asterisk.

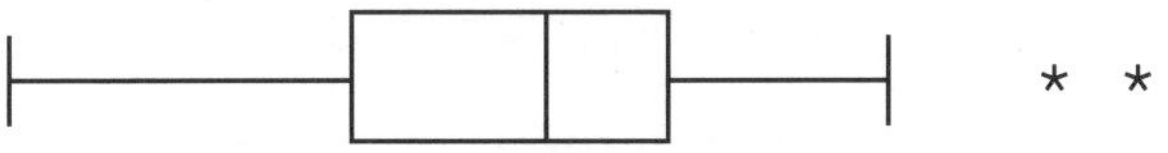

Example

This stem and leaf diagram shows the marks scored by a class on a mathematics test.

2|9 means 29

2	9								
3	4	7	8	9					
4	0	0	1	2	3	4	8	8	9
5	1	1	3	5	6	6	9		
6	2	4	4	5					
7	5	7	7						
8	2	3							
9	1								

a Find
  i the median mark,
  ii the interquartile range.

b Represent the data by a box plot.

c Comment on the skewness of the distribution.

Solution

a There are 31 items of data.
  i The median is the $\frac{1}{2}(31+1)^{\text{th}}$ value, or the 16th value. i.e. 51.
  ii The lower quartile is the 8th value (the $\frac{1}{4}(31+1)^{\text{th}}$ value), i.e. 41, and the upper quartile is the 24th value (the $\frac{3}{4}(31+1)^{\text{th}}$ value), i.e. 64. So the interquartile range $= 64 - 41 = 23$.

b

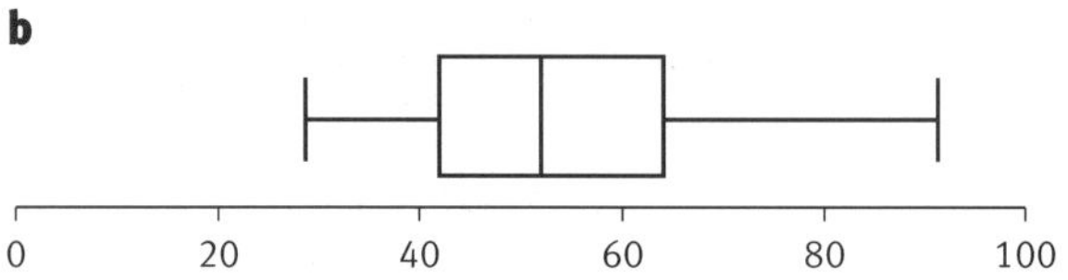

c The data has positive skew because $Q_2 - Q_1 < Q_3 - Q_2$ (i.e. $51 - 41 < 64 - 51$).

Interpolation

This method can be used to find an estimate for the median, quartiles or quantiles from a grouped frequency distribution. First find the position of the observation you want to estimate: for the median take the $\frac{1}{2}n^{\text{th}}$ value, for the lower quartile take the $\frac{1}{4}n^{\text{th}}$ value, etc. If this is the xth value, locate the class in which it lies: $b < x^{\text{th}}$ value $\leqslant b + w$.

Measured values	**Frequency**	**Cumulative frequency**
...	...	...
...	...	f_c
$b < x^{\text{th}}$ value $\leqslant b + w$	f	...
...	...	...
...	...	...

Estimate the xth value using interpolation
i.e. x^{th} value $\approx b + \frac{(x - f_c)}{f} \times w$

where b is the lower class boundary,
w is the class width,
f is the frequency of the class,
f_c is the cumulative frequency up to and including the previous class.

Example

The table below shows, to the nearest minute, the average amount of time it takes 60 people to get to work in the morning.

Journeys	0–9	10–19	20–29	30–39	40–49	50–59
Frequency	4	8	12	19	10	7

From the data above, calculate an estimate for

a the median,
b the first quartile,
c the third quartile,
d the interquartile range,
e the 68th percentile.

Solution

a Add an extra row for the cumulative frequency.

Cumulative frequency	4	12	24	43	53	60

The median is the 30th value. From the cumulative frequency row, you can see that it lies in the 30–39 interval. This interval has a lower class boundary of 29.5 and an upper class boundary of 39.5. Hence it has a class width of 10. Up to and including the previous interval, the cumulative frequency is 24. So an estimate of the median is

$$29.5 + \frac{(30 - 24)}{19} \times 10 = 32.7 \text{ to 1 decimal place.}$$

b The first quartile is the $\frac{1}{4}n^{\text{th}}$ value, or the 15th value. This lies in the 20–29 interval.

Using linear interpolation,

$$Q_1 = 19.5 + \frac{(15 - 12)}{12} \times 10 = 22$$

c The third quartile is the $\frac{3}{4}n^{\text{th}}$ value, or the 45th value. This lies in the 40–49 interval.

$$Q_3 = 39.5 + \frac{(45 - 43)}{10} \times 10 = 41.5$$

d Interquartile range $= 41.5 - 22 = 19.5$

e The 68th percentile is the $\left(\frac{68}{100} \times 60\right)^{\text{th}}$ value $= 40.8^{\text{th}}$ value.

$$29.5 + \left(\frac{\frac{68}{100}(60) - 24}{19}\right) \times 10 = 38.3 \text{ (1 d.p.)}$$

Mean

The mean, $\bar{x}$, is also called the expected value of the data.

mean, $\bar{x} = \dfrac{\sum x}{n}$

or, $\bar{x} = \dfrac{\sum fx}{\sum f}$. for frequency distributions

Variance

The variance of a population $x_1, x_2, \ldots x_n$, is the mean of the sum of the squares of the deviations from the mean, $\bar{x}$.

Variance $= s_x^2 = \dfrac{\sum (x - \bar{x})^2}{n}$

This formula may also be written as

Variance $= s_x^2 = \dfrac{\sum x^2}{n} - \bar{x}^2$

The second formula is more commonly used than the first.

For frequency distributions,

variance $= s_x^2 = \dfrac{\sum f(x - \bar{x})^2}{\sum f} = \dfrac{\sum fx^2}{\sum f} - \bar{x}^2$

The standard deviation, s_x, is the positive square root of the variance and is written as follows:

$$s_x = \sqrt{\frac{\sum (x - \bar{x})^2}{n}} = \sqrt{\frac{\sum x^2}{n} - \bar{x}^2}$$

For frequency distributions,

$$s_x = \sqrt{\frac{\sum f(x - \bar{x})^2}{\sum f}} = \sqrt{\frac{\sum fx^2}{\sum f} - \bar{x}^2}$$

when data are grouped, take x as the mid-class value.

Example

Six months after planting, 60 plants from a certain species had their heights measured, to the nearest 0.1 metres. From the table below, estimate the mean and standard deviation of the heights of the sample.

Height (m)	0.2–0.3	0.4–0.5	0.6–0.7	0.8–0.9	1.0–1.1	1.2–1.3
Frequency	4	8	12	19	10	7

Use the mid-interval values, 0.25, 0.45, 0.65, 0.85, 1.05, 1.25, and the formulae for grouped frequency:

$$\bar{x} = \frac{\sum fx}{\sum f} = 0.797 = 0.80 \text{ to 2 dp}$$

$$s_x = \sqrt{\frac{\sum fx^2}{\sum f} - \bar{x}^2} = 0.28 \text{ to 2 dp}$$

Using the statistical functions on your calculator to find the mean, variance and standard deviation could save time in the examination.

Example

The mean mark of 10 boys in a class was 54 and the variance was 22. If the mean mark of the 20 girls in the class was 50 and the variance was 34, find the mean and variance of the marks of the whole class.

Solution

Let x represent the boys' marks and y represent the girls' marks.

Mean of the boys' marks $= \dfrac{\sum x}{10} = 54 \Rightarrow \sum x = 540$

Mean of the girls' marks $= \dfrac{\sum y}{20} = 50 \Rightarrow \sum y = 1000$

Variance of the boys' marks $= \dfrac{\sum x^2}{10} - 54^2 = 22$

$\Rightarrow \quad \sum x^2 = 29380$

Variance of the girls' marks $= \dfrac{\sum y^2}{20} - 50^2 = 34$

$\Rightarrow \quad \sum y^2 = 50680$

Mean of the whole class $= \dfrac{\sum x + \sum y}{30} = 51.3$ (3 sf)

Variance of whole class $= \dfrac{\sum x^2 + \sum y^2}{30} - 51.3\ldots^2$

$= 33.6$ (3 sf).

Linear coding

This is a method of changing the values of x_i to y_i, where $i = 1, 2, \ldots n$, by using the coding formula

$$y = \frac{x - b}{a}.$$

Rearranging this gives $x = ay + b$.

The mean of x is calculated by using $\bar{x} = a\bar{y} + b$.

The variance of x (s_x^2) is found by transforming the variance of y (s_y^2) using the formula

$$s_x^2 = a^2 s_y^2$$

(Compare these formulae with $E(aX + b) = aE(X) + b$ and $Var(aX + b) = a^2 Var(X)$ found in Statistics 5.)

As the standard deviation is the square root of the variance,

$$s_x = as_y$$

Coding can be used to find the new mean, variance and standard deviation after the scaling of data, such as marks, or to make calculations easier.

Example

The following table summarises the results of a survey taken on the amount spent by customers in a D.I.Y. store during the month.

£	Number of orders
0–	20
20–	46
40–	92
80–	140
160–	223
300–	161
500–	52
1000–	0

a Let x represent the mid-point of each group. Using the coding $y = \dfrac{x - 20}{10}$, show that $\sum fy = 16391$, where f represents the frequency in each group.

b Estimate the mean and the variance of the value of the orders, given that $\sum fy^2 = 623473$.

Solution

a For a grouped frequency distribution, the values to change are the mid-class values.

£	Number of orders	Mid-point, x	y
0–	20	10	−1
20–	46	30	1
40–	92	60	4
80–	140	120	10
160–	223	230	21
300–	161	400	38
500–	52	750	73
1000–	0	–	

$$\sum fy = 20 \times -1 + 46 \times 1 + 92 \times 4 + \ldots + 52 \times 73$$
$$= 16391$$

b $$\bar{y} = \frac{\sum fy}{\sum f} = \frac{16391}{734} = 22.33 \text{ (4 s.f.)}$$

$$s_y^2 = \frac{\sum fy^2}{\sum f} - \bar{y}^2 = \frac{623473}{734} - \left(\frac{16391}{734}\right)^2$$
$$= 350.74 \text{ (5 s.f.)}$$

Rearranging $y = \dfrac{x - 20}{10}$ gives $x = 10y + 20$

$\therefore\ \bar{x} = 10\bar{y} + 20 = 10 \times 22.33 + 20$
$= 243.3$ (1 d.p.)

and $s_x^2 = 10^2 s_y^2 = 100 \times 350.74 = 35074$ (5 s.f.)

Questions

1 A motoring magazine is investigating the number of miles, x, driven by 500 people over the previous year. In order to simplify the numbers used, the data were coded such that $u = \dfrac{x - 5000}{1000}$, giving $\sum u = 4230$ and $\sum u^2 = 35815$. Find the mean and the variance of the number of miles driven in a year by the people in the sample.

2 The stem and leaf diagram below represents the number of cars passing a point on a motorway each minute for 27 minutes.

0|6 means 6

0	6	7	8								(3)
1	0	1	2	2	4	5	6	7	9	9	(10)
2	2	2	2	5	6	6	8	8			(8)
3	0	0	4	8							(4)
4	1	4									(2)

a Draw a box and whisker plot for the data.

b Comment on the skewness of the distribution, giving a reason for your answer.

3 The frequency distribution below shows the time taken by 80 pupils to revise for their French test. Times have been measured to the nearest minute.

Times	Frequency
0–5	5
6–10	9
11–15	15
16–20	26
21–25	10
26–30	8
31–35	5
36–40	2

Estimate:

a the median and the quartiles,

b the eighth decile,

c the sixty-third percentile,

d the mean number of items sold per day,

e the standard deviation.

4 The acceleration times, from rest to sixty-two miles per hour, of ten cars are shown below:
8.9 9.0 12.1 10.6 6.8 7.7 11.6 8.3 13.2 9.4

a Find the mean and standard deviation of the data.

b The mean and standard deviation of another 15 cars was 10.23 and 2.02 respectively. Find the mean and standard deviation of the twenty-five cars combined.

Answers

1 $\bar{u} = 8.46 \Rightarrow \bar{x} = 1000\bar{u} + 5000 = 13460$
$s_u^2 = 0.0584 \Rightarrow s_x^2 = 58\,400.$

2a

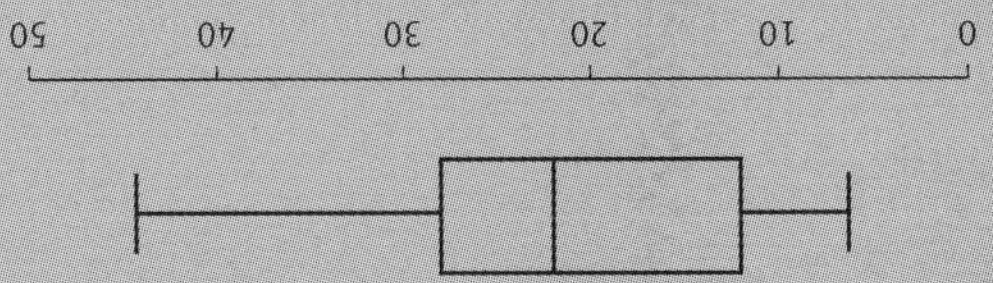

b There is positive skew because $Q_2 - Q_1 > Q_3 - Q_2$ (i.e. $22 - 12 > 28 - 22$).

3a median = 17.6, lower quartile = 12.5, upper quartile = 23

b 25 **c** 19.6 **d** 18.0 **e** 8.3.

4a mean = 9.76, s.d. = 1.95 (2 d.p.)

b mean = 10.04, s.d. = 2.02 (2 d.p.).

Take a break

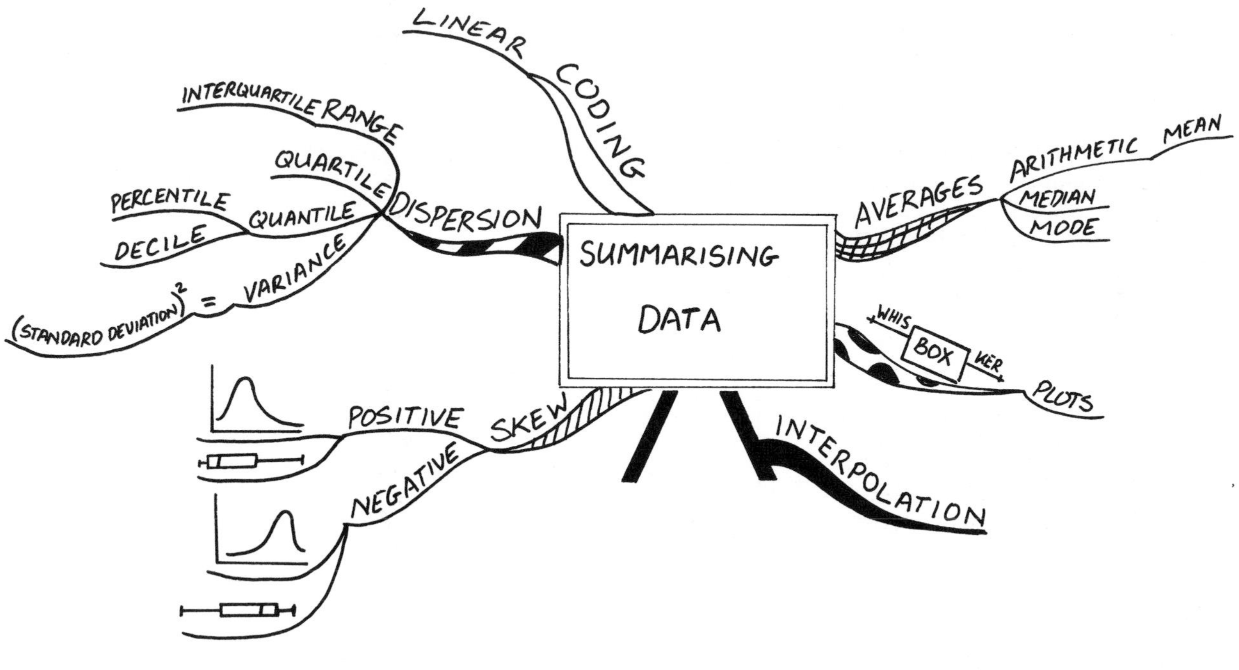

Review

1 Suggest suitable sampling frames for the following:

a the number of cars over 5 years old in Leicestershire,

b the number of times books are borrowed from a library during the course of a year.

2 The mark obtained by each of 43 students, randomly selected from a group who sat an entrance examination, was recorded. The stem and leaf diagram below summarises the marks.

Mark	(3|2 means 32)								Totals
3	2	3	4	6	7				(5)
3	3	4	5	6	7	9			(6)
4	0	1	1	2	3	4	7	7	(8)
4	2	3	6	8	9	9	9		(7)
5	0	1	1	1	2	3	7		(7)
5	2	4	5	8					(4)
6	1	2	9						(3)
6	4	6							(2)
7	5								(1)

a Using graph paper and showing your scale clearly, construct a box plot to represent these data.

b Comment on the skewness of this distribution.

3 The mean and standard deviation of the marks of a group of 80 people who sat an examination, were 72 and 15.5 respectively. After moderation, it was found that the scripts had been marked wrongly and hence each paper had 5 marks deducted and then the mark was further reduced by 20%.
For the adjusted marks, find

a the mean, **b** the standard deviation.

4 The time spent by an accountant with a random sample of 110 clients was recorded. The times, to the nearest minute, are summarised in the following table.

Time	Number of clients
10–19	3
20–29	7
30–39	10
40–49	15
50–59	22
60–69	33
70–89	15
90–119	5

a Using interpolation, obtain estimates for the median and quartiles for the data.

b Comment on the skewness of the data.

c Calculate estimates of the mean and variance of the data.

Answers

1a Records of the registration numbers of cars registered in Leicestershire.

b Dewey decimal numbers of books (i.e. the numbers on the spines of books in a library).

2a

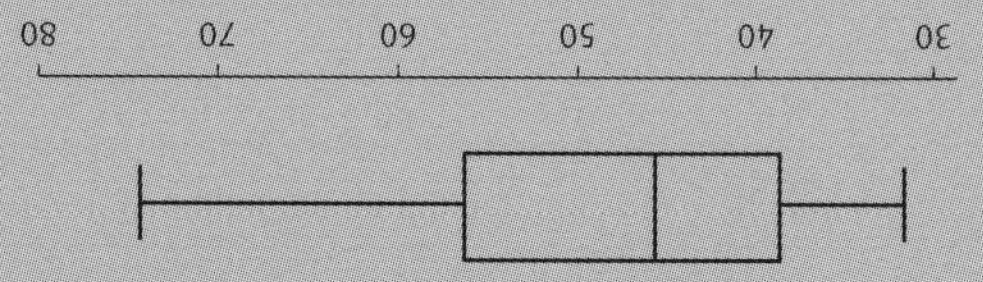

b There is positive skew.

3 If x was the mark before moderation, and y the mark after, then $y = 0.8(x - 5)$.

a mean $= 0.8(72 - 5) = 53.6$ **b** standard deviation $= 0.8 \times 15.5 = 12.4$.

4a $Q_2 = 58.6$ $Q_1 = 44.5$ $Q_3 = 67.2$ **b** positive skew **c** mean $= 57.2$, variance $= 396.0$ (1 d.p.).

PREVIEW

By the end of this topic you will have revised:

- ✔ **Venn diagrams,**
- ✔ **conditional probability,**
- ✔ **independent events,**
- ✔ **mutually exclusive events,**
- ✔ **using tree diagrams,**
- ✔ **permutations and combinations.**

Before you start you should know:

- basic probability,
- how to draw tree diagrams.

TEST YOURSELF

1 One letter is chosen at random from the word CHAPTER. What is the probability that it will
   a) be the letter A,
   b) not be the letter A,
   c) be the letter N,
   d) be one of the letters C, H, A, P, T, E or R?

2 Draw a tree diagram showing all the possible outcomes when a 10p coin and a 50p coin are tossed.

Answers

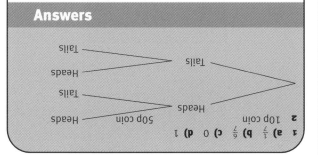

1 a) $\frac{1}{7}$ **b)** $\frac{6}{7}$ **c)** 0 **d)** 1

2

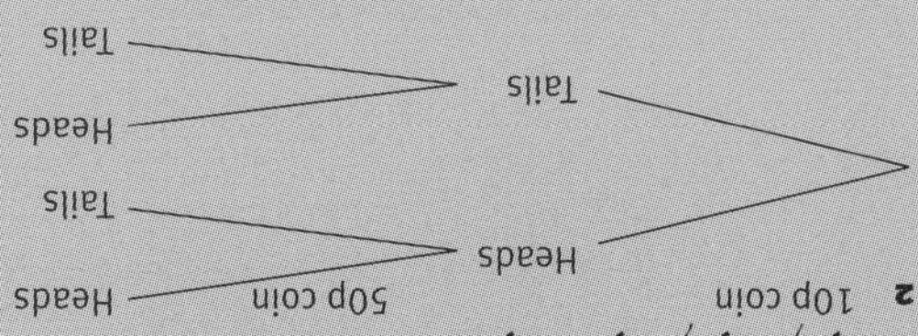

Venn diagrams

When, in an experiment, you are interested in two events, A and B, you can use Venn diagrams to illustrate the set of possible outcomes.

There are several possible outcomes in an experiment; the entire possibility space is the set of all possible outcomes; e.g. when a coin is tossed, the entire possibility space is heads, tails. In the diagram below, the box indicates the entire possibility space, which has a probability of 1.

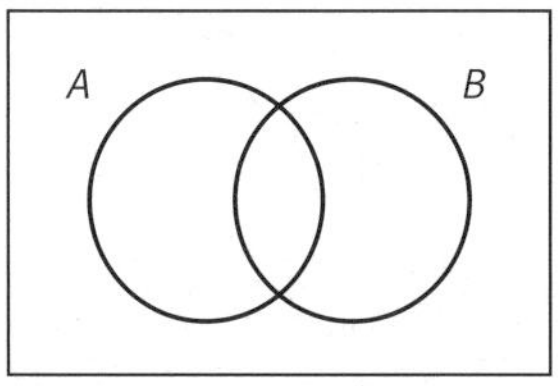

The notation P(A) means the probability of A occurring.

P(A)

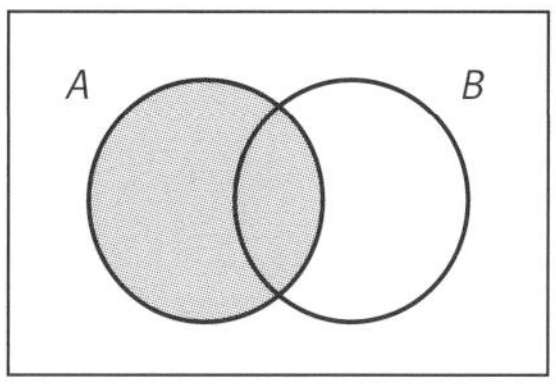

P(B)

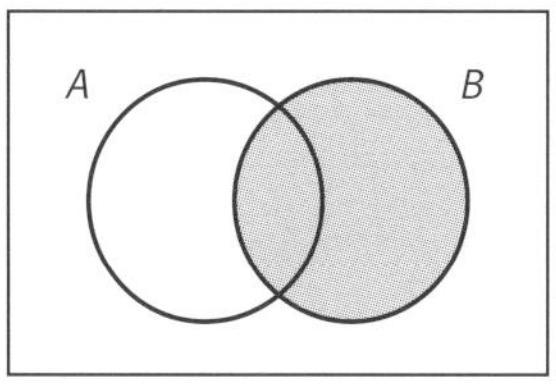

A' or $\bar{A}$ called **not *A*** is shaded below.
$P(A') = 1 - P(A)$.

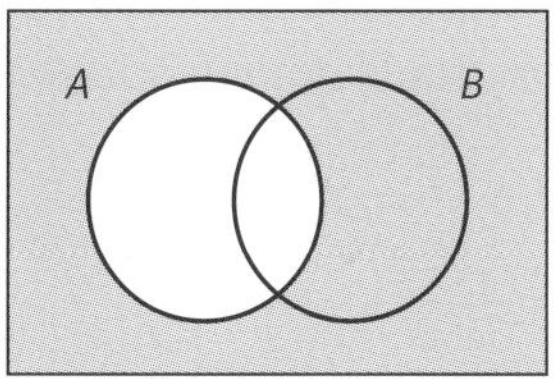

$A \cap B$ or **A intersection *B*** is the space where both A and B occur. This is the same as $B \cap A$.

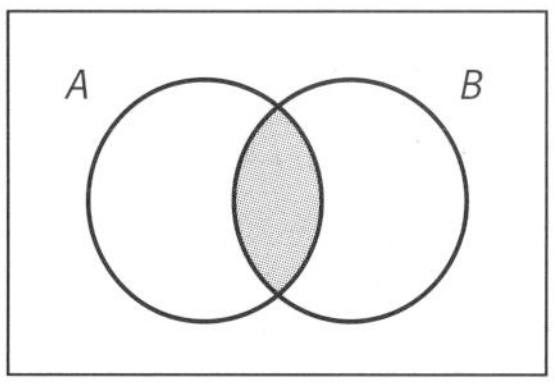

$A \cup B$ or **A union *B*** is the space where either A or B occur. This is the same as $B \cup A$.

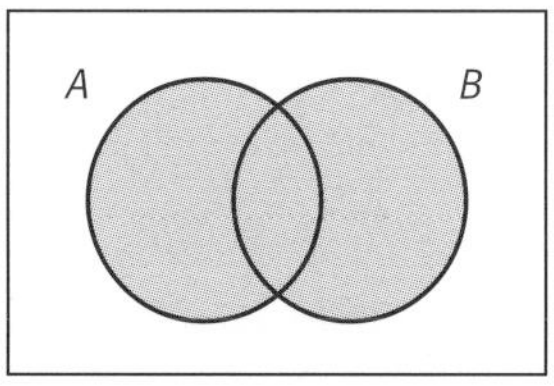

Examining the Venn diagrams shows that

$$P(A \cup B) = P(A) + P(B) - P(A \cap B)$$

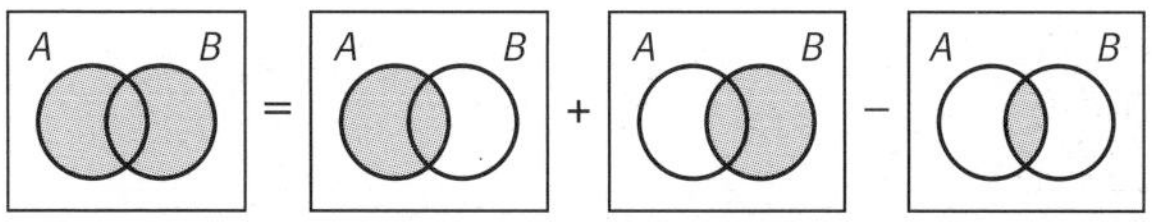

To find the probability space $A' \cup B'$, shade possibility spaces A' and B': $A' \cup B'$ is the combined shaded space:

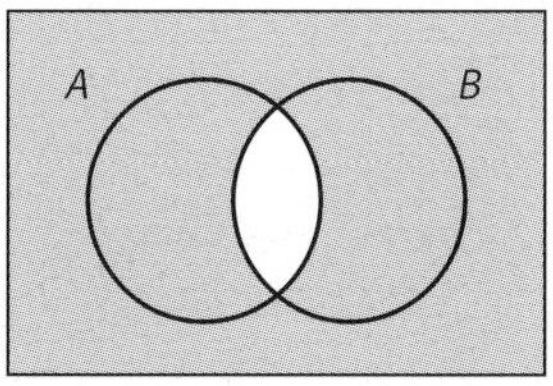

$A' \cap B'$ is the space where A' and B' overlap:

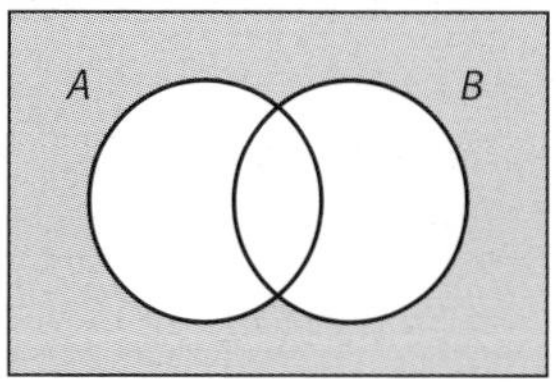

$A' \cap B$ is the space outside A but inside B:

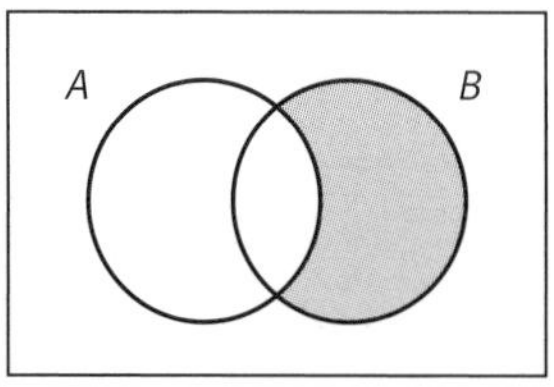

Probabilities are usually rounded to 3 or 4 decimal places.

Example

The events A and B are such that $P(A \cup B) = 0.5$, $P(A) = 0.4$, $P(B) = 0.3$. Find

i $P(A \cap B)$ **ii** $P(A \cap B')$
iii $P(A' \cap B')$ **iv** $P(A' \cup B')$

Solution

First sketch the given information on Venn diagrams:

$P(A \cup B) = 0.5$

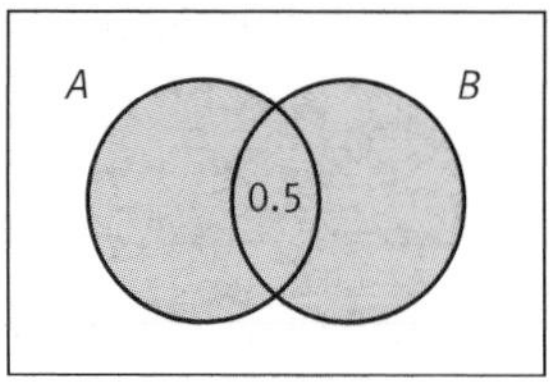

$P(A) = 0.4$

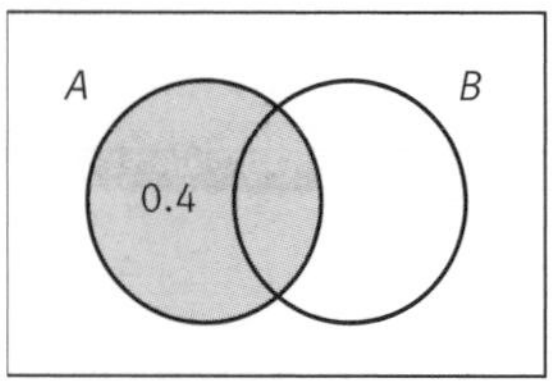

$P(B) = 0.3$

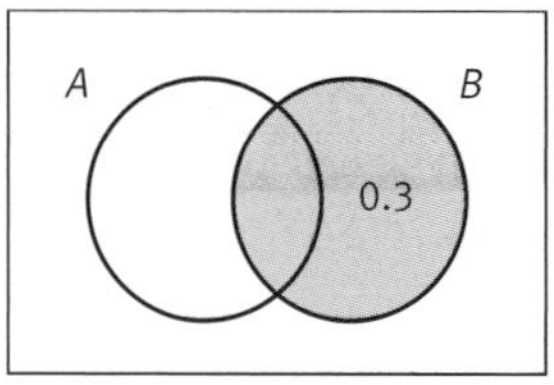

i Using the formula:

$$P(A \cap B) = P(A) + P(B) - P(A \cup B)$$
$$= 0.4 + 0.3 - 0.5 = 0.2$$

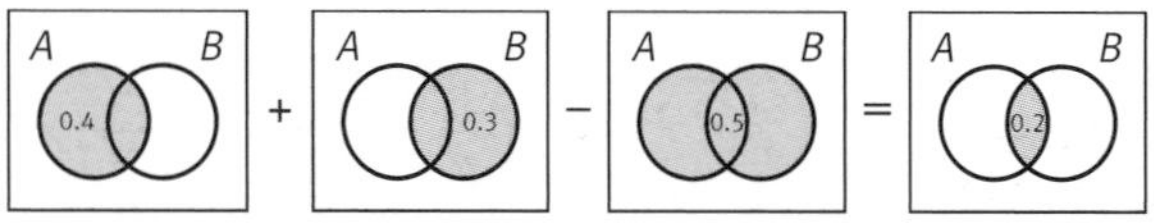

ii $P(A \cap B')$ denotes the probability space that is both inside A and outside B:

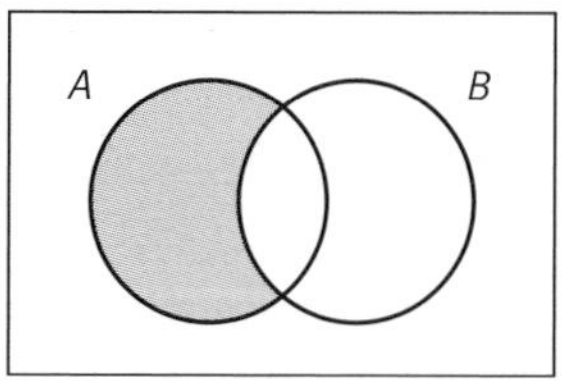

$P(A \cap B') = P(A \cup B) - P(B)$,

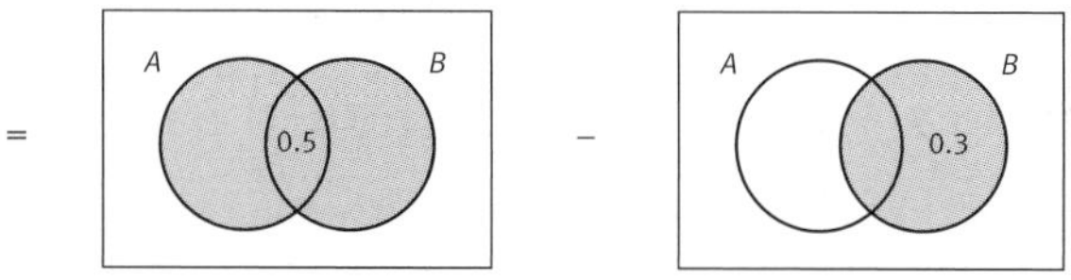

or $P(A \cap B') = P(A) - P(A \cap B)$

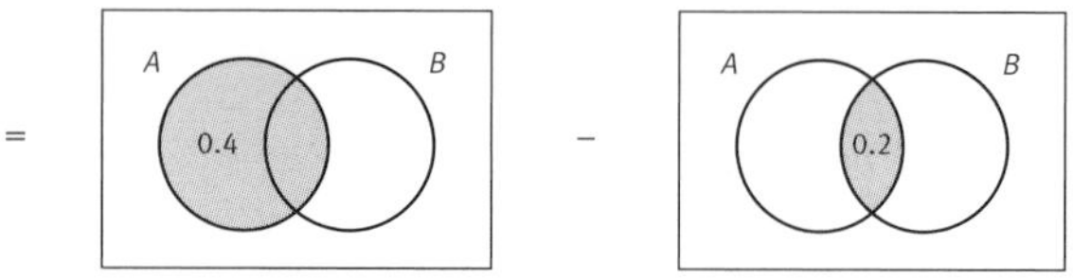

$P(A \cap B') = 0.2$

iii

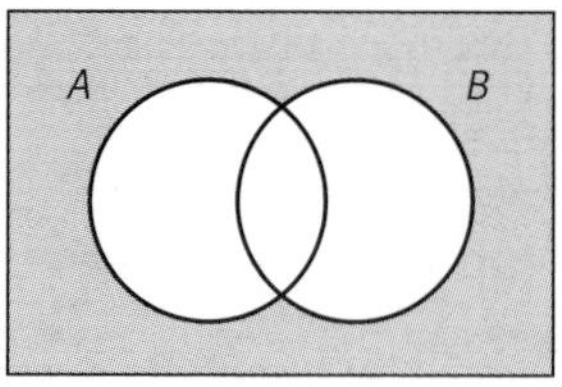

$P(A' \cap B') = 1 - P(A \cup B) = 0.5$

iv

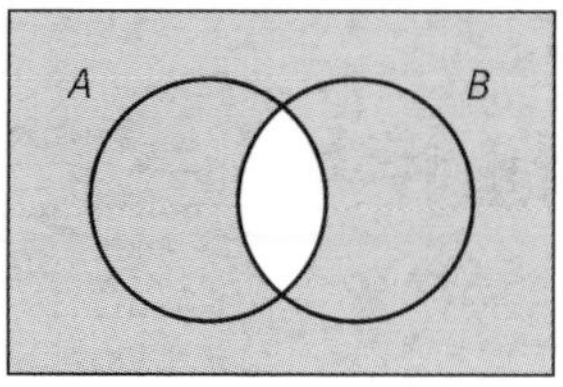

$P(A' \cup B') = 1 - P(A \cap B) = 0.8$

Conditional probability

Conditional probability is the probability that an event will occur when another event has already occurred. You can often recognise conditional probability by the words 'given that'.

The probability of A given B

$$= P(A|B) = \frac{P(A \cap B)}{P(B)}$$

Conditional probabilities are difficult to show on Venn diagrams.

Independent events

If A and B are independent events, then

- the occurrence of A does not effect that of B and vice-versa
- $P(A \cap B) = P(A) \times P(B)$
- $P(A|B) = P(A)$ and $P(B|A) = P(B)$.

Mutually exclusive events

If A and B are mutually exclusive events, then they cannot occur simultaneously, i.e.

$$P(A \cap B) = 0$$

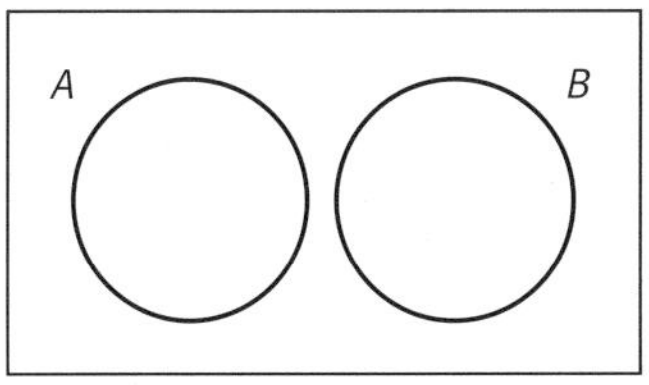

Tree diagrams

The sum of the probabilities on all branches from a common point is 1. The probabilities associated with each part of the tree diagram are shown below, with a first event A and a second event B:

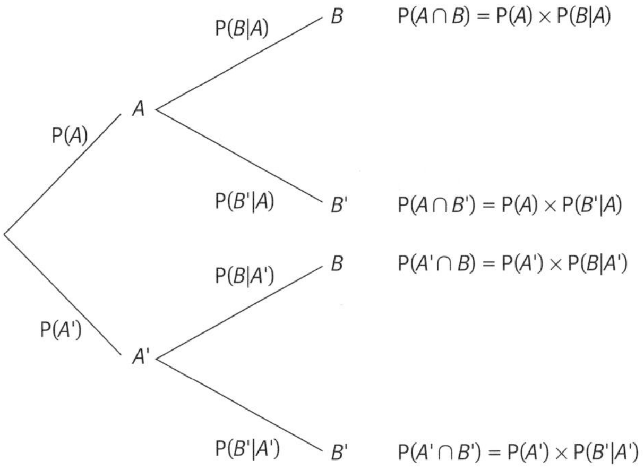

How to solve problems on probability

In general, use algebra with tree diagrams when the question involves conditional probabilities. If the probabilities are difficult to show on a tree diagram, use Venn diagrams and/or algebra.

Example

A company manufactures widgets on production lines X, Y and Z. Line X produces 35% of total output, line Y, 45% and line Z, 20%. Of the widgets produced on lines X, Y and Z, 5%, 3% and 6% respectively are faulty.

a Find the probability that a randomly chosen widget is from line Y and is faulty.

b Find the probability that a part is faulty.

c Given that the part is faulty, find the probability that it is from line X.

d Find the probability that the part is from line Z if it is not faulty.

Solution

Let X, Y and Z represent the events that the widget is manufactured on line X, Y and Z respectively and let F denote the event that the widget is faulty.

Convert the probabilities into decimals, as percentages are slightly more difficult to work with.

As this question involves conditional probability, show the information on a tree diagram as follows:

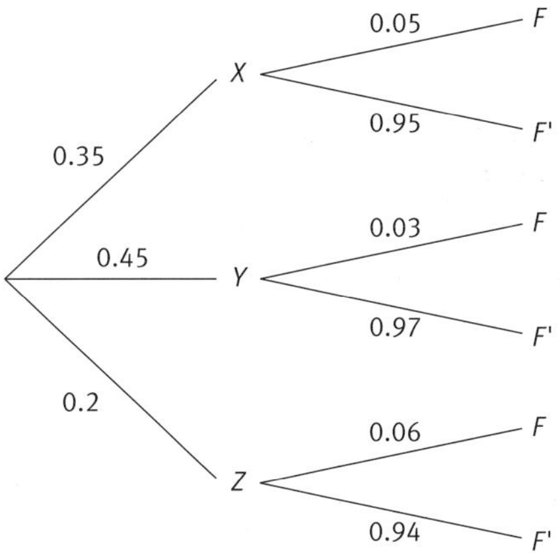

It is important to write the problem algebraically, as this will help to use the probabilities if they are required later in the question.

a $P(Y \cap F) = 0.45 \times 0.03 = 0.0135$

b $P(F) = P(X \cap F) + P(Y \cap F) + P(Z \cap F)$
$= 0.35 \times 0.05 + 0.45 \times 0.03 + 0.2 \times 0.06$
$= 0.043$

c $P(X|F) = \dfrac{P(X \cap F)}{P(F)} = \dfrac{0.35 \times 0.05}{0.043} = 0.407$ (3 d.p.)

d $P(Z|F') = \dfrac{P(Z \cap F')}{P(F')} = \dfrac{0.2 \times 0.94}{1 - 0.043} = 0.196$ (3 d.p.)

Example

Given that $P(A) = 0.8$, $P(B) = 0.6$ and $P(A|B) = 0.9$, find:

a $P(A \cap B)$
b $P(A \cup B)$
c $P(B|A)$
d $P(B|A')$.

Solution

You can solve this problem just using algebra.

a $P(A|B) = \dfrac{P(A \cap B)}{P(B)} \Rightarrow P(A \cap B) = P(A|B) \times P(B)$

$= 0.54$

b $P(A \cup B) = P(A) + P(B) - P(A \cap B) = 0.86$

Note that $P(A \cup B)$ is the same as $P(B \cup A)$.

c $P(B|A) = \dfrac{P(A \cap B)}{P(A)} = \dfrac{0.54}{0.8} = 0.675$

d $P(B|A') = \dfrac{P(A' \cap B)}{P(A')}$

where $P(A' \cap B) = P(A \cup B) - P(A)$
or $P(A' \cap B) = P(B) - P(A \cap B)$
$= 0.06$

$\therefore \quad P(B|A') = \dfrac{0.06}{1 - 0.8} = 0.3$

Example

The events Q and R are such that $P(Q) = 0.6$, $P(R|Q) = 0.7$ and $P(R|Q') = 0.2$. Find

a $P(Q \cap R)$,
b $P(Q' \cap R)$,
c $P(R)$,
d $P(Q|R)$.

Solution

Show the information on a tree diagram:

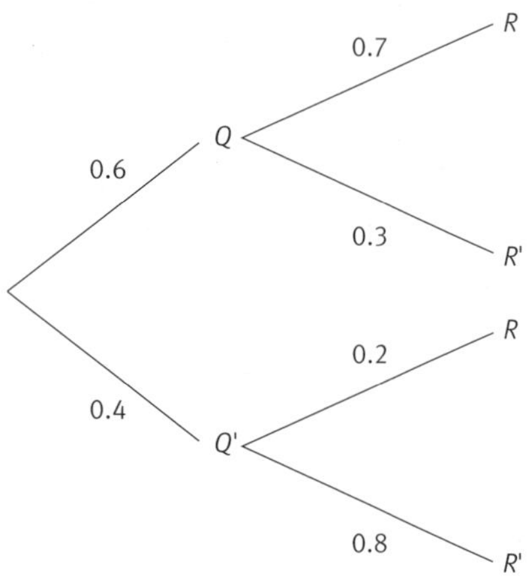

a $P(Q \cap R) = 0.42$

b $P(Q' \cap R) = 0.08$

c $P(R) = P(Q \cap R) + P(Q' \cap R) = 0.5$

d $P(Q|R) = \dfrac{P(Q \cap R)}{P(R)} = 0.84.$

Questions

1 M and N are independent events such that $P(M) = 0.6$ and $P(M \cup N) = 0.95$. Find

a $P(M|N)$ **b** $P(N)$.

2 The events A and B are such that $P(A) = 0.4$, $P(A \cup B) = 0.85$ and $P(B'|A) = 0.6$. Calculate

a $P(B)$

b $P(A \cap B)$

c $P(A' \cap B')$.

3 Define the following terms, using words or symbols:

a mutually exclusive

b independent.

4 Two per cent of people in a population have a disease. A new test has been developed for the disease. If a person has the disease, then the test has a likelihood of 90% of showing a positive result; if a person does not have the disease then it is has an 85% chance of showing a negative result. Find the probability that

a a person does not have the disease but shows a positive result,

b a person shows a positive result,

c a person does not have the disease, if the test is positive.

5 A college contains 80 students. Physics is studied by 26 of them, chemistry by 35 of them and 15 study chemistry but not physics. Find the probability that a randomly selected student

a studies both physics and chemistry,

b studies neither physics nor chemistry.

6 Nikki and Anita play 3 games of tennis. Games are either won or lost. If the Nikki wins a game, the probability her winning the next game is 0.6. If Anita wins a game, the probability that Nikki wins the next game is 0.3.
Given that Nikki has a 60% chance of winning the first game, find

a the probability that Anita wins both the first and the third game,

b the probability that Anita wins the third game,

c the probability that Nikki wins the first game, given that Anita wins the third game.

Answers

1a $P(M|N) = P(M)$ if M and N are independent
$= 0.6$

b If M and N are independent events, then
$P(M \cap N) = P(M) \times P(N) = 0.6P(N)$
Using $P(M \cup N) = P(M) + P(N) - P(M \cap N)$
$0.95 = 0.6 + P(N) - 0.6P(N)$
$P(N) = 0.875.$

2a $P(B'|A) = \dfrac{P(B' \cap A)}{P(A)}$
As $P(B' \cap A) = P(A \cup B) - P(B)$, $P(B) = 0.61$

b 0.16

c 0.15.

3a They cannot occur simultaneously; or $P(A \cap B) = 0$

b The outcome of one event does not affect the outcome of the other event; or $P(A \cap B) = P(A) \times P(B)$.

4 Let D be the event that the person has the disease, and let T be the event that the test is positive.

a $P(D' \cap T) = 0.147$

b $P(T) = P(D \cap T) + P(D' \cap T) = 0.165$

c $P(D'/T) = 0.891$ (3 d.p.).

5 Let P be the event that a person studies physics and let C be the event that a person studies chemistry

a $P(P \cap C) = \frac{20}{80} = \frac{1}{4}$

b $P(P' \cap C') = \frac{39}{80}$.

6 1st game 2nd game 3rd game

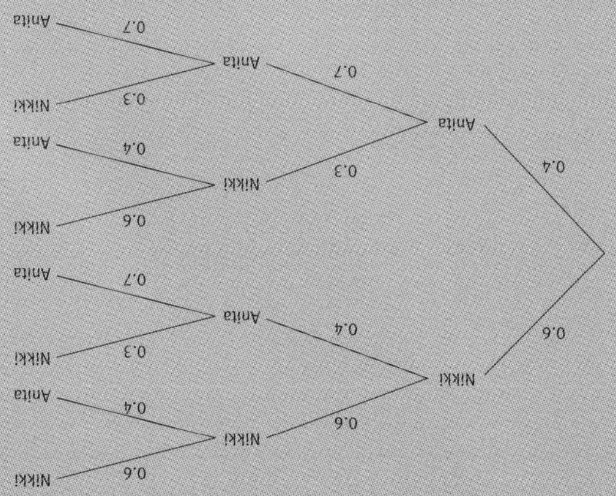

a $0.4 \times 0.3 \times 0.4 + 0.4 \times 0.7 \times 0.7 = 0.244$

b $0.244 + 0.6 \times 0.6 \times 0.4 + 0.6 \times 0.4 \times 0.7 = 0.556$

c $\dfrac{0.6 \times 0.6 \times 0.4 + 0.6 \times 0.4 \times 0.7}{0.556} = 0.561$ (3 d.p.).

Permutations and combinations

Permutations

A permutation is an arrangement of a set of items.

The number of permutations of n different items is $n!$

The number of permutations of n different items with one of the items repeated i times is $\dfrac{n!}{i!}$.

The number of permutations of n different items with one of the items repeated i times and another repeated j times is $\dfrac{n!}{i!\,j!}$.

Example

The letters of the word OSTENTATIOUS are jumbled and then rearranged in a straight line.

a How many different arrangements are there?

b How many of these arrangements begin and end with the letter T?

c In how many arrangements are no two vowels and no two consonants together?

d In how many of these arrangements are all the vowels together?

e Calculate the probability that all the vowels are together and all the consonants are together.

Solution

a There are 12 letters, with the letters O and S each occurring twice and T occurring 3 times.
So the number of arrangements is

$$\frac{12!}{2!2!3!} = 19\,958\,400.$$

b Simply take two Ts out of the word, stick one at each end of the word and arrange the remaining 10 letters.
This leaves T OSENATIOUS T.
Number of arrangements of

$$\text{OSENATIOUS} = \frac{10!}{2!2!} = 907\,200.$$

c In this case, each 2 vowels must be separated by a consonant and each 2 consonants must be separated by a vowel. If V and C represent a vowel and consonant respectively, then the arrangement must be in the form VCVCVCVCVCVC or CVCVCVCVCVCV. In either arrangement, there are 6 specific places for the vowels and 6 places for the consonants to be positioned.
The number of ways of arranging vowels OEAIOU is $\dfrac{6!}{2!} = 360.$

The number of ways of arranging the consonants STNTTS is $\dfrac{6!}{2!3!} = 60.$

To find the number of permutations, multiply the product of 360 and 60 by 2, because the arrangement may begin with a vowel or a consonant.

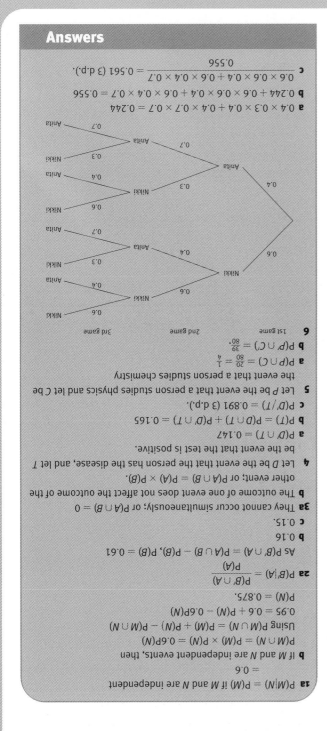

$360 \times 60 \times 2 = 43\,200.$

d Imagine that the letters are written on the spines of different books, which are placed on a shelf. The books with vowels on are then placed in a box as a boxed set of books.
Write the letters as OEAIOU STNTTS. Now consider the boxed set as just another consonant. These consonants can be arranged in

$\frac{7!}{2!3!} = 420$ ways.

For each of these arrangements, the vowels inside the box can be arranged in $\frac{6!}{2!} = 360$ ways.

The number of permutations
$= 420 \times 360 = 151\,200$.

e Firstly find the number of permutations in which all vowels are together and all consonants are together. Box the vowels and box the consonants:
OEAIOU STNTTS
The number of ways of arranging vowels OEAIOU is $\frac{6!}{2!} = 360$.

The number of arrangements of STNTTS
$= \frac{6!}{2!3!} = 60$.

The number of arrangements required
$= 360 \times 60 \times 2! = 43\,200$.
The 2! is included as the boxes may be arranged in 2! ways.
Probability of all vowels being together and all consonants being together is

$$\frac{\begin{pmatrix}\text{number of permutations in which all vowels are} \\ \text{together and all consonants are together}\end{pmatrix}}{\text{total number of permutations}}$$

$$= \frac{43\,200}{19\,958\,400} = \frac{1}{462} \text{ or } 0.00216 \text{ (3 s.f.)}.$$

This example covers most variations on permutations and so is longer than any question you are likely to be asked in an examination.

Questions

1 The letters of the word BINOMIAL are jumbled up then rearranged in a straight line.

a Find the total number of permutations.

b Find the number of arrangements in which all vowels are together.

c Find the number of arrangements in which the letters I are not consecutive.

d Calculate the probability that no two vowels and no two consonants are next to each other.

2 Nine different CDs are placed on top of each other. If 4 CDs are classical and the rest are folk music,

a Find the number of different arrangements.

b Find the probability that all the classical CDs are together.

Answers

1a $\frac{8!}{2!} = 20160$ **b** $\frac{5! \times 4!}{2!} = 1440$

c total number of permutations – number of permutations in which the letters I are together = 15120

d Number of ways in which no two vowels and no two consonants are next to each other $= \frac{2 \times 4! \times 4!}{2!} = 576$

Probability $= \frac{576}{20160} = 0.0286$ (3 s.f.) or $\frac{1}{35}$

2a $9! = 362880$

b Classical CDs are together in $6! \times 4! = 17280$ ways.

Probability $= \frac{17280}{362880} = 0.0476$ (3 s.f.) or $\frac{1}{21}$.

Combinations

A combination is a choice of items from a larger set of items, regardless of order. The number of combinations of r items from n items is

$$^nC_r = \frac{n!}{r!(n-r)!}$$

Example

A delegation of 5 people is to be selected from a group of 3 men and 8 women.

a Calculate the total number of different delegations that could be chosen.

b Find the number of these delegations in which
i two specific people must be chosen
ii there must be people of both sexes.

c Calculate the probability that, if the members of the delegation are selected at random, the delegation contains only women.

Solution

a The number of combinations of 5 people chosen from 11 is $^{11}C_5 = 462$

i If two specific people are chosen, there are 3 places to fill from the remaining 9 people, so the number of delegations is $^9C_3 = 84$.

ii There must be either 1 man and 4 women, 2 men and 3 women or 3 men and 2 women, so the number is
$^3C_1 \times {}^8C_4 + {}^3C_2 \times {}^8C_3 + {}^3C_3 \times {}^8C_2 = 406$.
Alternatively, this may be calculated as the total number of combinations minus the combinations which are all men (although this is impossible as there are not enough men) or all women $= 462 - {}^8C_5 = 406$.

c Probability =

$$\frac{\text{no. of ways of choosing 5 members from 8 women}}{\text{total number of combinations}}$$

$= \dfrac{^8C_5}{462} = 0.121$ (3 d.p.) or $\frac{4}{33}$.

Example

Four letters are chosen from the word CLASSES. Find

a the number of selections

b the number of arrangements of the four letters.

Solution

S occurs three times: so use a table:

a If no S is chosen, then pick four letters from the remaining 4 of CLAE: $^4C_4 = 1$
If 1 S is chosen, pick 3 from CLAE: $^4C_3 = 4$, etc.

Number of Ss	Number of selections
0	$^4C_4 = 1$
1	$^4C_3 = 4$
2	$^4C_2 = 6$
3	$^4C_1 = 4$
	Total = 15

b

Number of Ss	Number of selections	No. of arrangements per selection	Total no. of arrangements
0	1	$4! = 24$	24
1	4	$4! = 24$	96
2	6	$\frac{4!}{2!} = 12$	72
3	4	$\frac{4!}{3!} = 4$	16
			Total = 208

Example

Each of the letters of the word BREEDER is written on a separate card. The cards are then shuffled and rearranged in a line.

a Find the number of different permutations.

b Find the probability that the cards spell the word BREEDER.

c Four cards are picked at random from the pack. Find the probability that the cards are all different.

Solution

a $\dfrac{7!}{3!2!} = 420$

b Only one of the arrangements spells the word, so the probability is $\dfrac{1}{420}$.
This may also be calculated using probabilities: the probability of the first letter being a B is $\frac{1}{7}$, the second being an R is $\frac{2}{6}$ (or $\frac{1}{3}$), the third being an E is $\frac{3}{5}$, etc.
So the probability is
$\frac{1}{7} \times \frac{2}{6} \times \frac{3}{5} \times \frac{2}{4} \times \frac{1}{3} \times \frac{1}{2} \times 1 = \frac{1}{420}$.

c The letters must be B, R, E and D.
If chosen in this order the probability is
$\frac{1}{7} \times \frac{2}{6} \times \frac{3}{5} \times \frac{1}{4}$.
However, these 4 different letters may be chosen in 4! ways:
Probability $= \frac{1}{7} \times \frac{2}{6} \times \frac{3}{5} \times \frac{1}{4} \times 4! = \frac{6}{35}$.

Questions

1 Eight people take part in a race. Medals are awarded to the first 3 people who finish.

a Find the number of combinations of the medal-winners.

b If gold, silver and bronze medals are awarded respectively to the first, second and third to finish, find the number of permutations of the medal-winners.

2 A committee of either 3, 4 or 5 people is to be selected from 4 staff and 3 parents.

a **i** Find the total number of possible committees.
ii Find the probability that there is an equal number of members of staff and parents on the committee.

b Find the number of ways in which the committee may be formed if there must be at least one parent, and there must more members of staff than parents.

Answers

1a $^8C_3 = 56$

b The three medal winners may be arranged in 3! ways:

$^8C_3 \times 3! = 336$

2a i $^7C_3 + {}^7C_4 + {}^7C_5 = 91$ **ii** $\frac{^4C_2 \times {}^3C_2}{91} = \frac{18}{91}$

b $^4C_2 \times {}^3C_1 + {}^4C_3 \times {}^3C_1 + {}^4C_3 \times {}^3C_2 + {}^4C_4 \times {}^3C_1 = 45.$

Take a break

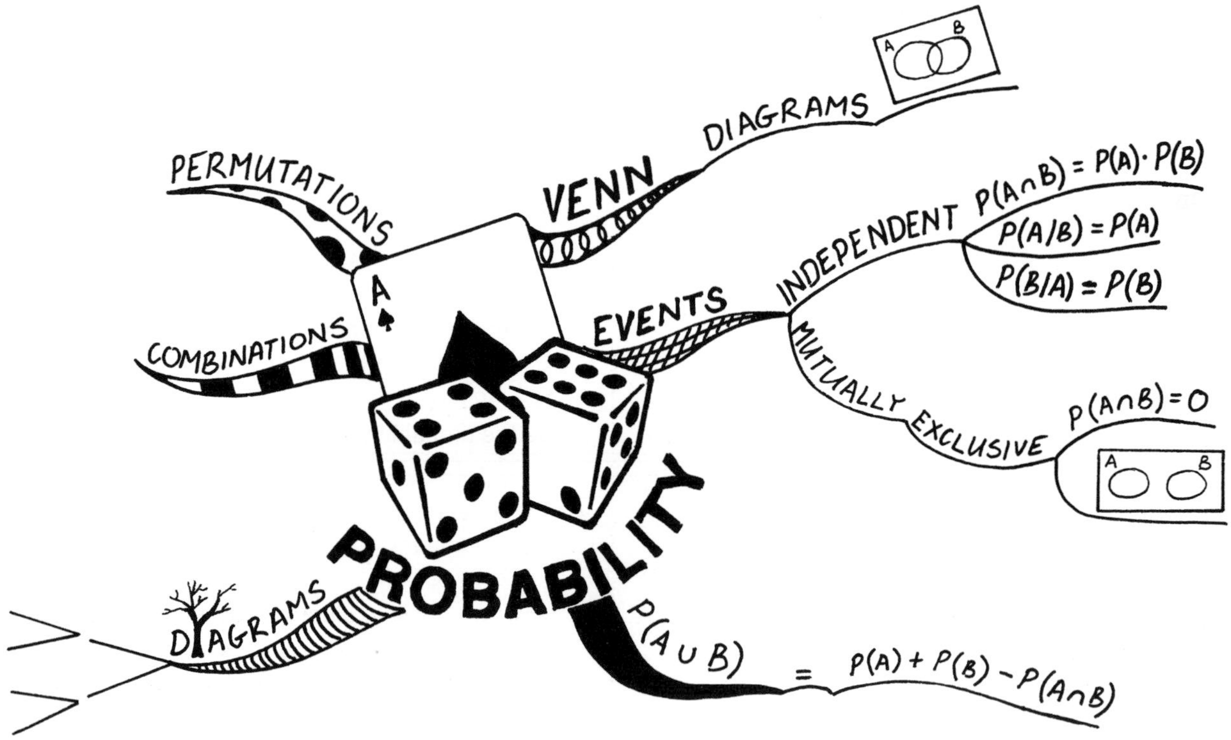

Review

1 Write down **i** an advantage and **ii** a disadvantage of taking

a a census, **b** a sample.

2 The data below gives the number of seconds, to the nearest tenth of a second, that a random sample of 51 cars took to accelerate from 0 to 60 miles per hour.

Seconds 7|1 means 7.1

7	1	( )
8	0 1 1 3 4 8	( )
9	0 2 2 3 6 8 9 9	(8)
10	1 1 2 2 2 5 5 6 7 7 8 8 9	(13)
11	3 3 5 5 6 9 9	(7)
12	2 6 6 7 9 9	(6)
13	0 1 3	(3)
14	2 6 8	(3)
15	2 3	(2)
16	7	(1)
17	4	(1)

a Write down the values needed to complete the stem and leaf diagram.

b Find the median and the quartiles of these times.

c On graph paper, construct a box plot for these data, showing your scale clearly.

d Comment on the skewness of the distribution.

3 A and B are two events such that $P(A) = \frac{2}{5}$, $P(B) = \frac{3}{4}$ and $P(B'|A) = \frac{1}{2}$. Find

a $P(A \cap B')$ **b** $P(A \cup B)$ **c** $P(A' \cup B)$ **d** $P(A' \cap B')$.

State, giving reasons for your answer, whether A and B are

e mutually exclusive events, **f** independent events.

4 A contestant on a game show has three envelopes to pick from: A, B and C. The probability of her picking envelopes A, B and C are 0.3, 0.5 and 0.2 respectively. In each envelope there is a task that she has to complete within a minute. The probability of her completing the task inside envelopes A, B and C are 0.7, 0.5 and 0.4 respectively. Find the probability of her

a picking envelope C and completing the task,

b completing the task,

c choosing envelope A given that she did not complete the task.

5 A committee of 4 people is to be chosen from a group of 3 men and 8 women. Find the number of different ways in which the committee can be selected if

a all the 11 members are available, **b** people of both sexes have to be represented.

Answers

1a **i** It is accurate. **ii** It may be expensive; it may take a long time.

b **i** It is quick; it is inexpensive. **ii** It may not be very accurate.

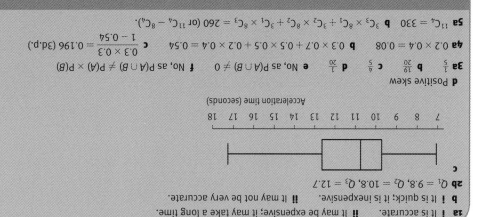

2b $Q_1 = 9.8$, $Q_2 = 10.8$, $Q_3 = 12.7$

c

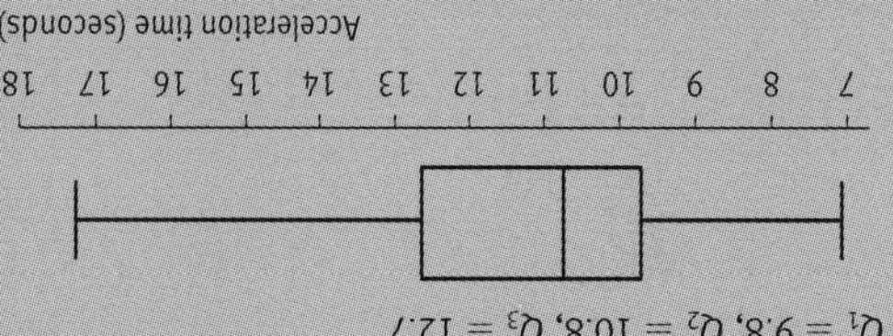

d Positive skew

3a $\frac{1}{5}$ **b** $\frac{19}{20}$ **c** $\frac{4}{5}$ **d** $\frac{1}{20}$ **e** No, as $P(A \cap B) \neq 0$ **f** No, as $P(A \cap B) \neq P(A) \times P(B)$

4a $0.2 \times 0.4 = 0.08$ **b** $0.3 \times 0.7 + 0.5 \times 0.5 + 0.2 \times 0.4 = 0.54$ **c** $\frac{0.3 \times 0.3}{1 - 0.54} = 0.196$ (3d.p.)

5a ${}^{11}C_4 = 330$ **b** ${}^{3}C_3 \times {}^{8}C_1 + {}^{3}C_2 \times {}^{8}C_2 + {}^{3}C_1 \times {}^{8}C_3 = 260$ (or ${}^{11}C_4 - {}^{8}C_4$).

PREVIEW

By the end of this topic you will have revised:

- ✔ **discrete random variables,**
- ✔ **continuous random variables,**
- ✔ **the continuous uniform (rectangular) distribution.**

Before you start you should:

- know how to find a definite integral of a polynomial.

TEST YOURSELF

If wrong, see Pure 10 or an A level text book for information and practice.

Find $\int_1^3 (3x^2 - x^3)\,dx$.

Answer

6.

A random variable, such as X, is a numerical quantity that can take any range of values with specified probabilities. Lower case letters, such as x, are used to represent a particular value of the random variable.

E(X) means the expected value of X or the mean of X, and Var(X) is the variance of X.

Note the similarities between the formulae for the discrete and continuous random variables: replace p(x) with f(x) and the sigma sign with 'integrate with respect to x'.

The cumulative distribution function, F(*x*), for discrete random variables

F(x) is the sum of the probabilities up to and including x, i.e. $F(x) = P(X \leqslant x)$.

The cumulative distribution function for continuous random variables

This function shows the probability that the random variable X is less than or equal to x. The cumulative distribution function is written as F(x).

$$F(x) = P(X \leqslant x) = \int_{-\infty}^{x} f(x)\,dx$$

If $f(x) = \begin{cases} f(x) & a \leqslant x \leqslant b \\ 0 & \text{otherwise} \end{cases}$

then $F(x) = \begin{cases} 0 & x < a \\ \int_a^x f(x)\,dx & a \leqslant x \leqslant b \\ 1 & x > b \end{cases}$

If $x < a$, there is zero probability that $X < x$.
If $x > b$, then the probability that $X < x$ is 1.

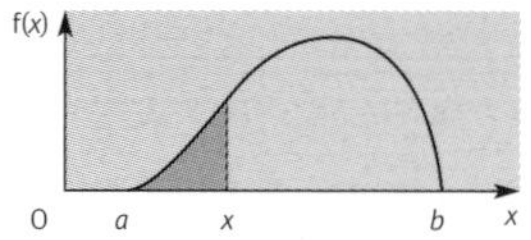

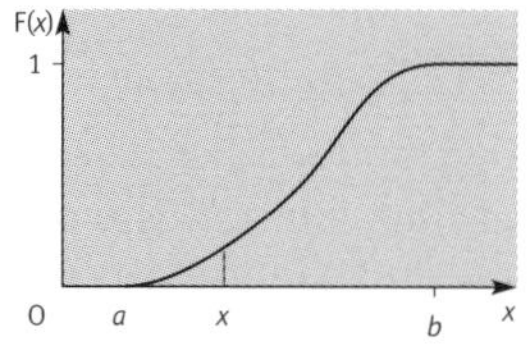

The area under the curve of f(x) between a and x is the same as the height of F(x) at x.

Discrete Random Variables

p(x) is called the probability function, where $P(X = x) = p(x)$.

$$\sum_{x=a}^{b} p(x) = 1$$

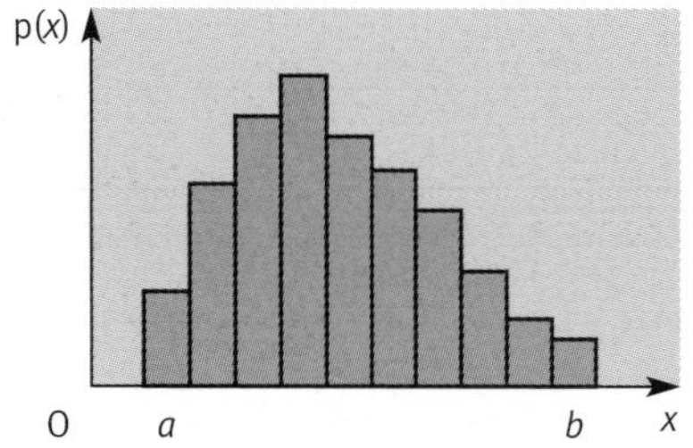

$$E(X) = \sum_{x=a}^{b} x p(x)$$

$$E(X^2) = \sum_{x=a}^{b} x^2 p(x)$$

Continuous Random Variables

f(x) is called the probability density function and is such that $P(x_1 \leqslant X \leqslant x_2) = \int_{x_1}^{x_2} f(x)\,dx$

$$\int_a^b f(x)\,dx = 1$$

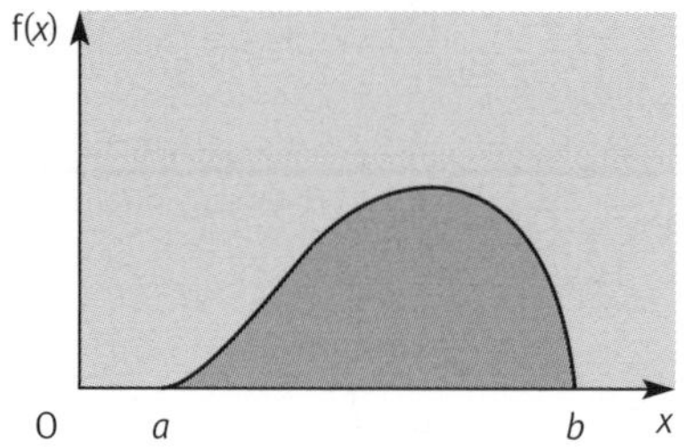

$$E(X) = \int_a^b x f(x)\,dx$$

$$E(X^2) = \int_a^b x^2 f(x)\,dx$$

$\text{Var}(X) = E(X^2) - [E(X)]^2$ where

Mode and median

The mode of f(x) is x at the greatest value of f(x). This is often where $f'(x) = 0$.

The median, m, is the value of x where $P(X < m) = 0.5$.

This is where $\int_a^m f(x)\,dx = \frac{1}{2}$

i.e. where $F(m) = \frac{1}{2}$.

You can use either of these forms to find m.

Expectation and variance of a linear function of a random variable

If X is a random variable and a and b are constants then

$$E(aX + b) = aE(X) + b$$
$$Var(aX + b) = a^2 Var(X).$$

Discrete random variables

Example

The random variable X has the probability function

$$p(x) = \begin{cases} \frac{k}{x} & x = 1, 2, 3, 4 \\ 0 & \text{otherwise} \end{cases}$$

a Show that $k = \frac{12}{25}$

Find the value of

b E(X)
c Var (X)

Solution

Lay the information out in a table:

x	1	2	3	4
$P(X = x)$	$\frac{k}{1}$	$\frac{k}{2}$	$\frac{k}{3}$	$\frac{k}{4}$

a $\sum_{x=1}^{4} p(x) = 1 \Rightarrow \frac{k}{1} + \frac{k}{2} + \frac{k}{3} + \frac{k}{4} = 1$

$$\Rightarrow k\left(1 + \frac{1}{2} + \frac{1}{3} + \frac{1}{4}\right) = \frac{25k}{12} = 1$$

$$\Rightarrow k = \frac{12}{25}$$

b $E(X) = \sum_{x=1}^{4} xp(x) = 1 \times \frac{k}{1} + 2 \times \frac{k}{2} + 3 \times \frac{k}{3} + 4 \times \frac{k}{4}$
$= 4k = 1\frac{23}{25}$

c $E(X^2) = \sum_{x=1}^{4} x^2 p(x)$
$= 1^2 \times \frac{k}{1} + 2^2 \times \frac{k}{2} + 3^2 \times \frac{k}{3} + 4^2 \times \frac{k}{4}$
$= 10k = 4\frac{4}{5}$

$var(X) = E(X^2) - [E(X)]^2 = 4\frac{4}{5} - \left(1\frac{23}{25}\right)^2$
$= 1.11$ to 2 d.p.

Example

A discrete random variable X has the probability function shown in the table below:

x	0	1	2	3	4
$P(X = x)$	0.4	0.2	0.2	0.15	0.05

Find

a $P(0 < X \leqslant 3)$ **b** E(X) **c** var(X)
d F(2.5) **e** $E(4X - 3)$ **f** $var(2X - 1)$

Solution

a $P(0 < X \leqslant 3) = P(X = 1) + P(X = 2) + P(X = 3)$
$= 0.2 + 0.2 + 0.15 = 0.55$

b E(X)
$= 0 \times 0.4 + 1 \times 0.2 + 2 \times 0.2 + 3 \times 0.15 + 4 \times 0.05$
$= 1.25$

c $E(X^2)$
$= 0^2 \times 0.4 + 1^2 \times 0.2 + 2^2 \times 0.2 + 3^2 \times 0.15 + 4^2 \times 0.05$
$= 3.15$
$var(X) = 3.15 - 1.25^2 = 1.5875$

d $F(2.5) = P(X \leqslant 2.5) = P(X = 0) + P(X = 1)$
$+ P(X = 2) = 0.4 + 0.2 + 0.2 = 0.8$

e $E(4X - 3) = 4E(X) - 3 = 2$

f $var(2X - 1) = 2^2 var(X) = 6.35.$

Continuous random variables

Example

The length of time, in minutes, that people spend in a shop is modelled by a continuous random variable T, having probability density function f(t) where

$$f(t) = \begin{cases} k(6t - t^2) & 0 \leqslant t \leqslant 6 \\ 0 & \text{otherwise} \end{cases}$$

a Find the value of k.
b Find E(T).
c Find Var(T).
d Find the cumulative distribution function of T, specifying it for all values of t.
e Find the probability that somebody spent more than 5 minutes in the shop.

Solution

a $\int_0^6 \mathrm{f}(t)\,\mathrm{d}t = 1$

$\Rightarrow k\int_0^6 (6t - t^2)\,\mathrm{d}t = k\left[3t^2 - \frac{1}{3}t^3\right]_0^6 = 36k$

$\therefore \quad 36k = 1 \quad \Rightarrow \quad k = \frac{1}{36}$

b $\mathrm{E}(T) = \int_0^6 t\mathrm{f}(t)\,\mathrm{d}t = \frac{1}{36}\int_0^6 (6t^2 - t^3)\,\mathrm{d}t$

$= \frac{1}{36}\left[2t^3 - \frac{1}{4}t^4\right]_0^6 = 3$

c $\mathrm{E}(T^2) = \int_0^6 t^2\mathrm{f}(t)\,\mathrm{d}t = \frac{1}{36}\int_0^6 (6t^3 - t^4)\,\mathrm{d}t$

$= \frac{1}{36}\left[\frac{3}{2}t^4 - \frac{1}{5}t^5\right]_0^6 = 10.8$

$\mathrm{var}(T) = \mathrm{E}(T^2) - \mathrm{E}(T)^2 = 10.8 - 9 = 1.8$

d For $0 \leqslant t \leqslant 6$, $\mathrm{F}(t) = k\int_0^t (6t - t^2)\,\mathrm{d}t$

$\mathrm{F}(t) = \frac{1}{36}\left[3t^2 - \frac{1}{3}t^3\right]_0^t = \frac{1}{36}\left(3t^2 - \frac{1}{3}t^3\right)$

$= \frac{1}{12}t^2 - \frac{1}{108}t^3$

⚠ Remember to write F(t) for all values of t, as shown below.

$$\therefore \quad \mathrm{F}(t) = \begin{cases} 0 & t < 0 \\ \frac{1}{12}t^2 - \frac{1}{108}t^3 & 0 \leqslant t \leqslant 6 \\ 1 & t > 6 \end{cases}$$

e $\mathrm{P}(T > 5) = 1 - \mathrm{P}(T \leqslant 5) = 1 - \mathrm{F}(5)$

$= 1 - 0.9259\ldots = 0.074$ (2 s.f.).

Example

The cumulative distribution function of a random variable X is given by:

$$\mathrm{F}(x) = \begin{cases} 0 & x < 0 \\ k(x^3 - \frac{1}{4}x^4) & 0 \leqslant x \leqslant 3 \\ 1 & x > 3 \end{cases}$$

a Find k.

b Find f(x), specifying it for all values of x.

c Find the mode of X.

d Verify that the median lies in the interval (1.84, 1.85).

Solution

a As you can see from the graph, F(x) must be 1 at the point where $x = 3$.

$\mathrm{F}(3) = 1 \quad \Rightarrow \quad \frac{27}{4}k = 1 \quad \Rightarrow \quad k = \frac{4}{27}$

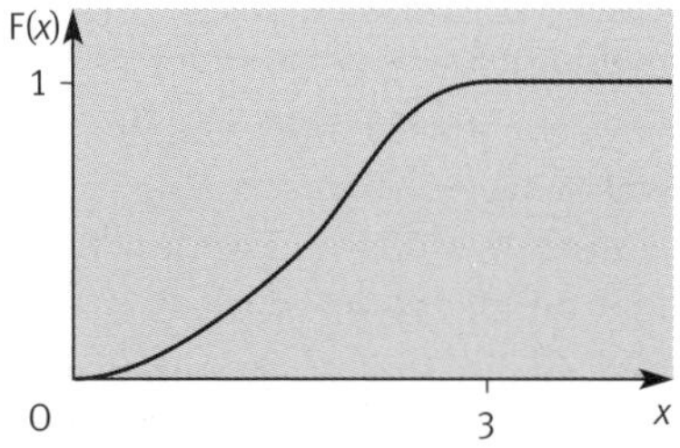

b $\mathrm{f}(x) = \mathrm{F}'(x)$

For $0 \leqslant x \leqslant 3$, $\mathrm{f}(x) = k(3x^2 - x^3)$

$$\mathrm{f}(x) = \begin{cases} \frac{4}{27}(3x^2 - x^3) & 0 \leqslant x \leqslant 3 \\ 0 & \text{otherwise} \end{cases}$$

c The mode is the value if x where f(x) is a maximum.

$\mathrm{f}'(x) = \frac{4}{27}(6x - 3x^2) = 0 \quad \Rightarrow \quad 6x - 3x^2 = 0$

$\Rightarrow \quad x = 0 \quad \text{or} \quad x = 2$

$x = 2$ gives a maximum value (this can be seen by sketching the graph of f(x) as shown below).

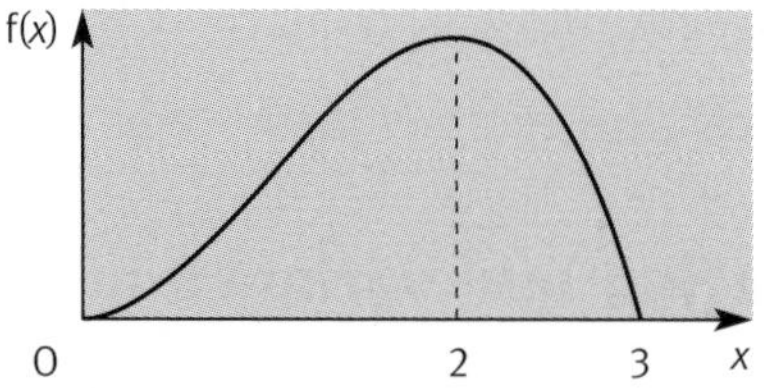

$\therefore$ the mode is 2.

d $\mathrm{F}(1.84) = 0.498$ (3 sf)

$\mathrm{F}(1.85) = 0.504$ (3 sf)

Since 0.5 lies between these two cumulative probabilities, the median must lie in the interval (1.84, 1.85).

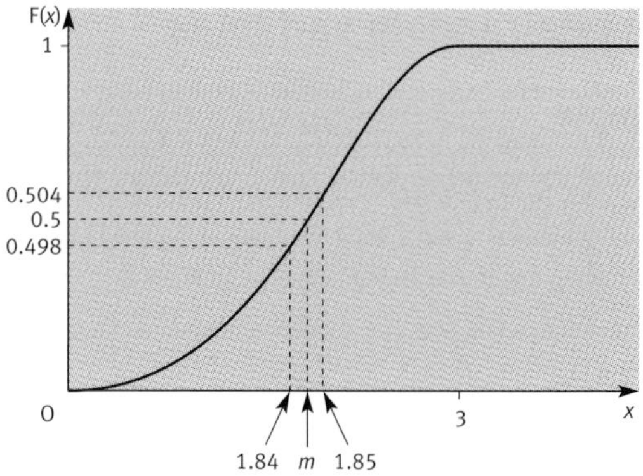

Questions

1 The random variable X has probability function given by

$$\mathrm{p}(x) = \begin{cases} k(x+1) & x = 1, 2, 3, 4 \\ \frac{1}{15} & x = 5 \\ 0 & \text{otherwise} \end{cases}$$

where k is a constant.

a Determine the value of k.

b Find **i** E(X), **ii** Var(X).

2 A student has two twenty pence coins and three £1 coins in his pocket. He keeps taking coins out of his pocket, one at a time, until he is holding both twenty pence coins.

a Find the probability that he takes

i four coins from his pocket,

ii less than three coins from his pocket.

b If X is the number of coins he has to take out of his pocket, write down the probability function of X.

c Find the expected number of coins he has to take from his pocket.

3 The amount of time, X minutes, that a train arrives late, is modelled by a random variable with probability density function f(x) where

$$f(x) = \begin{cases} c(12 - x) & 0 \leqslant x \leqslant 12 \\ 0 & \text{otherwise} \end{cases}$$

where c is a constant.

a Find c.

b Calculate **i** E(X), **ii** Var(X).

c Find the probability that the train is less than 5 minutes late.

d Sketch f(x).

e Specify the cumulative distribution function for all values of x.

f Write down a limitation of this model.

g Sketch a possible alternative probability density function for X.

4 The cumulative distribution function of a random variable X is given by:

$$F(x) = \begin{cases} 0 & x < 1 \\ k(6x^2 - x^3 + 3x - 8) & 1 \leqslant x \leqslant 4 \\ 1 & x > 4 \end{cases}$$

where k is a constant.

a Find the value of k.

b Find the probability density function, f(x), specifying it for all values of x.

c Calculate

i E(X),

ii Var(X),

iii $P(2 < X < 3)$,

iv the mode of X.

d Verify that the median of X lies between 2.26 and 2.27.

5 The discrete random variable X has the probability function shown below.

x	2	3	4	5	6
P(X = x)	0.1	a	a	a	b

Given that E(X) = 4.4, find

a find the values of a and b,

b Var(X).

Answers

1a $\frac{1}{15}$

b 3

c $1\frac{1}{3}$

2a i $\frac{3}{10}$

ii $\frac{1}{10}$

b

x	2	3	4	5
$P(X = x)$	$\frac{1}{10}$	$\frac{1}{5}$	$\frac{3}{10}$	$\frac{2}{5}$

c 4

3a $\frac{1}{72}$

b i 4 **ii** 8

c 0.660 (3 d.p.)

d

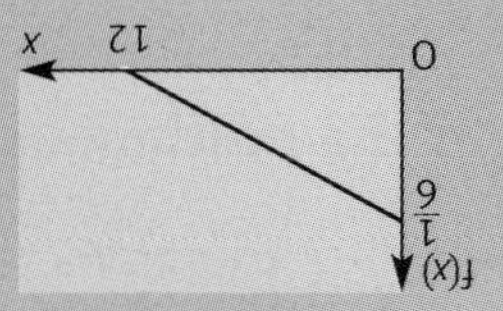

e $F(x) = \begin{cases} 0 & x < 0 \\ \frac{1}{144}(24x - x^2) & 0 \leqslant x \leqslant 12 \\ 1 & x > 12 \end{cases}$

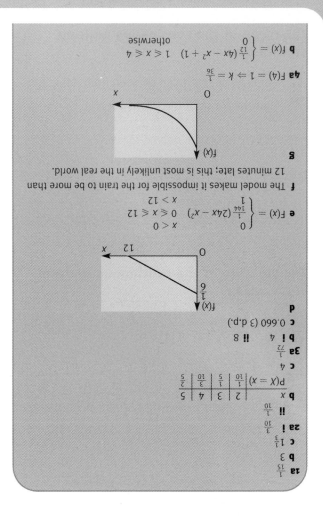

f The model makes it impossible for the train to be more than 12 minutes late; this is most unlikely in the real world.

g

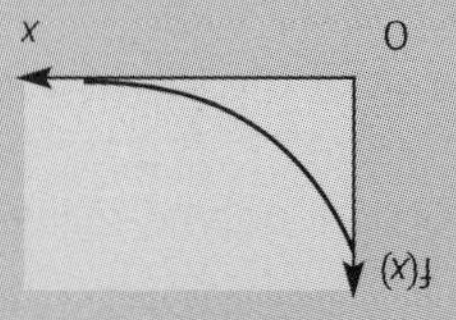

4a $F(4) = 1 \Rightarrow k = \frac{1}{36}$

b $f(x) = \begin{cases} \frac{1}{12}(4x - x^2 + 1) & 1 \leqslant x \leqslant 4 \\ 0 & \text{otherwise} \end{cases}$

c i 2.3125

ii $Var(X) = E(X^2) - E(X)^2 = 5.95 - 2.3125^2 = 0.602$ (3 d.p.)

iii $F(3) - F(2) = 0.389$ (3 d.p.)

iv 2

d $F(2.26) = 0.497$ (3 d.p.)

$F(2.27) = 0.501$ (3 d.p.)

Since $F(m) = 0.5$ when m is the median, the median must lie between 2.26 and 2.27.

5a $a = 0.2$, $b = 0.3$ **b** 1.84.

Continuous uniform distribution

The continuous uniform distribution of a random variable X is such that $P(X = x)$ has a constant value in the range (α, β) and zero outside this range.

It is also known as the rectangular distribution because of the shape of its probability density function.

The area under the graph is 1 and, as the width of the rectangle is $\beta - \alpha$, its height must be $\frac{1}{\beta - \alpha}$.

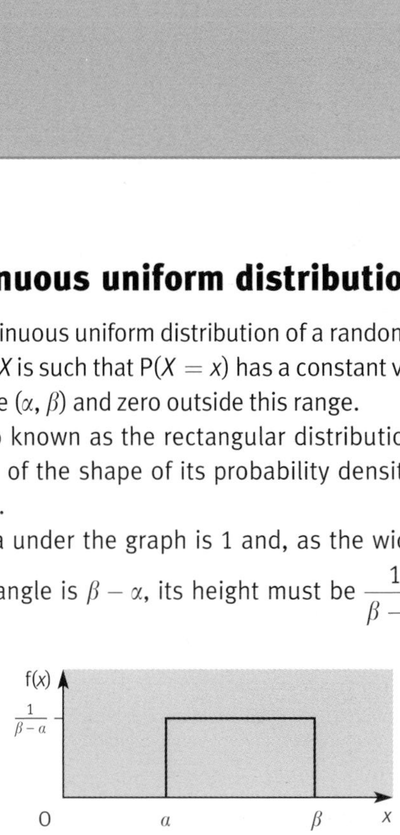

If the continuous random variable X has this distribution, then it is written as $X \sim R(\alpha, \beta)$.

For a random variable X having a uniform distribution over the interval (α, β) then

$$f(x) = \begin{cases} \frac{1}{\beta - \alpha} & \alpha < x < \beta \\ 0 & \text{otherwise} \end{cases}$$

The mean of the continuous uniform distribution

From symmetry it can be seen from the graph that the mean of the distribution is $\frac{\alpha + \beta}{2}$.

Alternatively it may be proved using

$$E(X) = \int_\alpha^\beta x f(x)\,dx = \int_\alpha^\beta x \frac{1}{\beta - \alpha}\,dx = \frac{1}{\beta - \alpha}\left[\frac{1}{2}x^2\right]_\alpha^\beta$$

$$= \frac{\beta^2 - \alpha^2}{2(\beta - \alpha)} = \frac{(\beta - \alpha)(\beta + \alpha)}{2(\beta - \alpha)} = \frac{\beta + \alpha}{2}.$$

The variance of the continuous uniform distribution

The variance may be found using
$\mathrm{Var}(X) = E(X^2) - E(X)^2$

$$E(X^2) = \int_\alpha^\beta x^2 f(x)\,dx = \frac{1}{\beta - \alpha}\int_\alpha^\beta x^2\,dx = \frac{1}{\beta - \alpha}\left[\frac{1}{3}x^3\right]_\alpha^\beta$$

$$= \frac{\beta^3 - \alpha^3}{3(\beta - \alpha)} = \frac{(\beta - \alpha)(\beta^2 + \alpha\beta + \alpha^2)}{3(\beta - \alpha)} = \frac{\beta^2 + \alpha\beta + \alpha^2}{3}$$

$$\mathrm{Var}(X) = \tfrac{1}{3}(\beta^2 + \alpha\beta + \alpha^2) - \left(\tfrac{1}{2}(\alpha + \beta)\right)^2$$

$$= \tfrac{1}{3}(\beta^2 + \alpha\beta + \alpha^2) - \tfrac{1}{4}(\alpha^2 + 2\alpha\beta + \beta^2)$$

$$= \tfrac{1}{12}(4\beta^2 + 4\alpha\beta + 4\alpha^2 - 3\alpha^2 - 6\alpha\beta - 3\beta^2)$$

$$= \tfrac{1}{12}(\beta^2 - 2\alpha\beta + \alpha^2) = \tfrac{1}{12}(\beta - \alpha)^2$$

Learn these proofs as you may be asked to produce them in the examination.

Example

The continuous variable X is uniformly distributed over the interval (3, 7). Find:

a $E(X)$ **b** $\mathrm{Var}(X)$ **c** $P(X > 4.5)$.

Solution

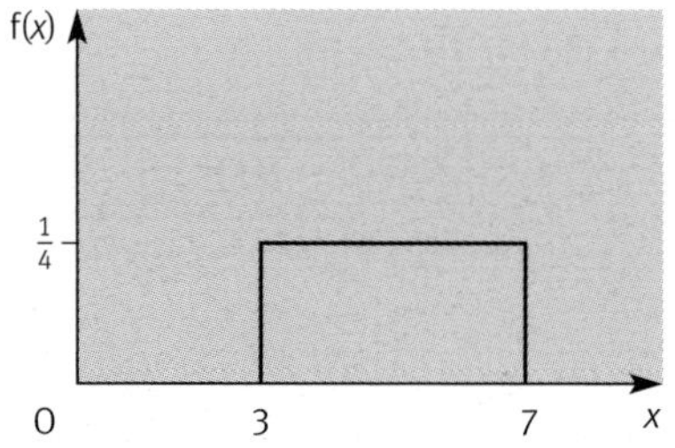

a $E(X) = \frac{3 + 7}{2} = 5$

b $\mathrm{Var}(X) = \frac{1}{12}(\beta - \alpha)^2 = \frac{1}{12}(7 - 3)^2$

$= \frac{16}{12} = 1.33$ (2 d.p.)

c

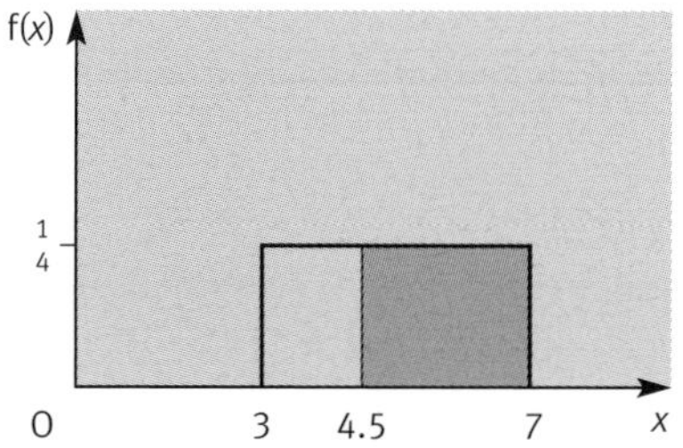

$P(X > 4.5) = \frac{7 - 4.5}{4} = 0.625.$

Questions

1 The probability density function of a random variable X is given by

$$f(x) = \begin{cases} \frac{1}{8} & 2 \leqslant x \leqslant 10 \\ 0 & \text{otherwise} \end{cases}$$

Find

a $E(X)$

b $\mathrm{Var}(X)$

2 A random variable X is distributed such that $E(X) = 5$ and $\mathrm{Var}(X) = 3$.

Given that $X \sim R(\alpha, \beta)$,

a find the values of α and β,

b find $P(X > 6)$.

3 The continuous random variable X has a uniform distribution over the interval (3, 9).

a Find

i $E(X)$

ii $\mathrm{Var}(X)$.

b Write down the cumulative distribution function for X, specifying it for all values of X.

Answers

1a 6

b $5\frac{1}{3}$

2a $\alpha = 2, \beta = 8$

b $\frac{2}{6} = \frac{1}{3}$

3a i 6 **ii** 3

b $F(x) = \int_3^x \frac{1}{6}\,dx = \left[\frac{1}{6}x\right]_3^x = \frac{1}{6}x - \frac{1}{2}$ for $3 \leqslant x \leqslant 9$

$$F(x) = \begin{cases} 0 & x < 3 \\ \frac{1}{6}x - \frac{1}{2} & 3 \leqslant x \leqslant 9 \\ 1 & x > 9 \end{cases}$$

Take a break

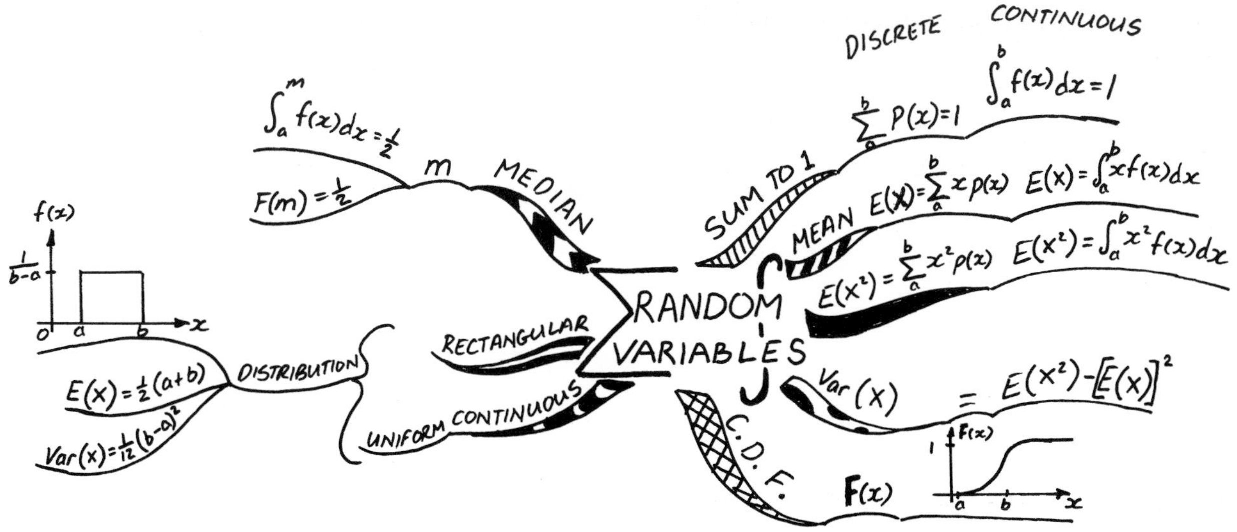

Review

1 Explain briefly the following terms:

a a sampling unit, **b** a sampling frame, **c** a census.

2 The discrete random variable Y has the probability function shown in the table below.

y	0	1	2	3	4
$P(Y = y)$	0.18	0.39	0.27	0.11	0.05

Find

a $P(1 < Y \leqslant 3)$, **b** $F(1.7)$, **c** $E(Y)$, **d** $Var(Y)$.

3 Each of the letters of the word VARIABLE is written on a tile. These tiles are jumbled up and laid out in a line.

a Calculate the number of different arrangements.

b Find the number of arrangements in which all the vowels are together.

c Determine the probability that no two vowels are together and no two consonants are together.

4 A football team is to be selected from a team of 22 players. One goalkeeper is to be chosen from 2 men, 4 defenders from 7, 4 midfielders from 8 and 2 attackers from 5. Determine the number of different teams that can be chosen.

5 A commuter travels to work by car, train or bus. The probabilities of her taking the car, train and bus are 0.2, 0.5 and 0.3 respectively. The probabilities of her being late to work if she takes the car, train or bus are 0.35, 0.15 and 0.2 respectively. Calculate the probability that

a she takes the car and she is late,

b she is late,

c she takes the train, given that she is late.

Answers

1a An individual member of a population **b** A list of sampling units
c In a census, measures or observations are taken from every member of the population.

2a 0.38 **b** 0.57 **c** 1.46 **d** 1.13.

3a 20 160 **b** 1440 **c** $\frac{1}{35}$.

4 ${}^2C_1 \times {}^7C_4 \times {}^8C_4 \times {}^5C_2 = 49\,000$.

5a 0.07 **b** 0.205 **c** 0.366 (3 d.p.)

PREVIEW

By the end of this topic you will have revised:

- ✔ **the product moment correlation coefficient, r,**
- ✔ **Spearman's rank correlation coefficient, r_s,**
- ✔ **hypothesis testing for r and r_s,**
- ✔ **the method of least squares regression of y on x.**

Correlation

When one random variable is measured against another, such as weight against time taken to run 100 metres, the pairs of observations are called a **bi-variate distribution**.

There are two methods of measuring correlation: the product moment correlation coefficient (PMCC), which gives the variable r, and Spearman's rank correlation coefficient, denoted by r_s.

Both give broadly similar figures for linear correlation:

- if all points of the data lie in straight line with positive gradient (there is perfect positive linear correlation), then $r = +1$ and $r_s = +1$

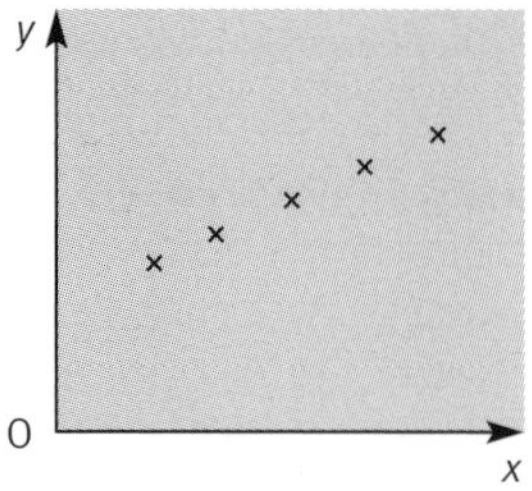

- if all points lie in a straight line with negative gradient (perfect negative linear correlation) then $r = -1$ and $r_s = -1$

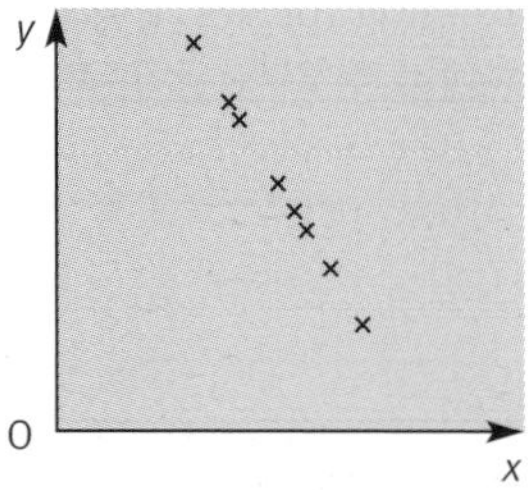

- if there is no or little linear correlation then r and r_s will be close to zero

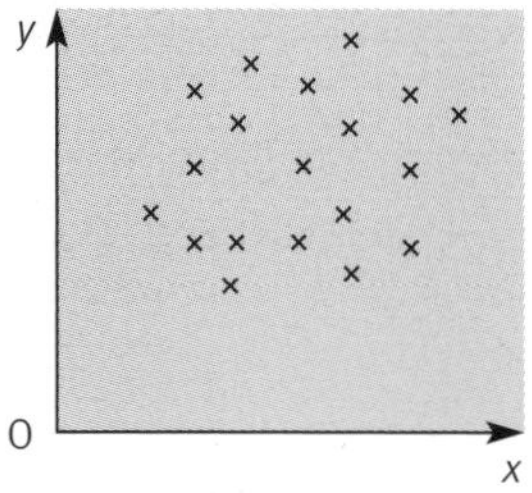

Product moment correlation coefficient (PMCC)

You may calculate the PMCC by using this method:

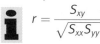

$$r = \frac{S_{xy}}{\sqrt{S_{xx}S_{yy}}}$$

where $S_{xx} = \frac{1}{n}\sum x^2 - \frac{(\sum x)^2}{n^2}$

and $S_{yy} = \frac{1}{n}\sum y^2 - \frac{(\sum y)^2}{n^2}$

and $S_{xy} = \frac{1}{n}\sum xy - \frac{(\sum x \sum y)}{n^2}$

This is just one of a number of methods for calculating the product moment correlation coefficient. If you know another method and are comfortable with using it, stick with it.

Example

For the following data, find the value of the product-moment correlation coefficient, r, to 3 decimal places.

x	1	2	3	4	5	6	7	8
y	4	7	8	10	10	13	16	18

Solution

$n = 8$, $\sum x = 36$, $\sum y = 86$

$\sum x^2 = 204$, $\sum y^2 = 1078$, $\sum xy = 466$

$$S_{xx} = \frac{204}{8} - \frac{36^2}{8^2} = 5.25$$

$$S_{yy} = \frac{1078}{8} - \frac{86^2}{8^2} = 19.1875$$

$$S_{xy} = \frac{466}{8} - \frac{(36)(86)}{8^2} = 9.875$$

$$r = \frac{S_{xy}}{\sqrt{S_{xx}S_{yy}}} = \frac{9.875}{\sqrt{5.25 \times 19.1875}} = 0.984 \text{ (3 d.p.)}$$

Using calculators to calculate r

1. Set to your calculator to linear regression mode.
2. Clear any statistical data already in the calculator.
3. Enter the data.
4. Once all data has been entered, check it. The question will often give you various pieces of data, such as n, $\sum x$, $\sum y^2$ or $\sum xy$. Check as many as these as you can with your calculator.
5. Now you are ready to access the product-moment correlation coefficient, r.
6. Return to the normal calculator mode.

Read your calculator's instruction book to find more details about entering the data.

Hypothesis testing

Two hypotheses are proposed: the null hypothesis, H_0, and the alternative hypothesis, H_1. The null hypothesis is assumed to be true, while the alternative hypothesis has to be shown 'beyond reasonable doubt' to be true. You can never be 100% sure that either the null or alternative hypothesis is true: a significance level should be used to show the level of certainty that your choice of hypotheses is correct. For example, if a 5% significance level is chosen and the alternative hypothesis is chosen, then you are 95% sure that you are right in rejecting the null hypothesis.

The letter ρ (rho) is used for the true correlation coefficient for the entire population.

One-tailed and two-tailed tests, critical value and critical region

The null hypothesis, H_0, is $\rho = 0$.

A one-tailed test tests either that the PMCC is positively correlated ($H_1{:}\rho > 0$ against $H_0{:}\rho = 0$), or that it is negatively correlated ($H_1{:}\rho < 0$ against $H_0{:}\rho = 0$).

A two-tailed test tests $H_1{:}\rho \neq 0$ against $H_0{:}\rho = 0$ (it is called a two-tailed test as it tests for both $\rho > 0$ and $\rho < 0$).

⚠ Divide the significance level by two when performing a two-tailed test.

The range of values of r for which the null hypothesis, H_0, is rejected give the critical region. The boundary of the critical region is the critical value.
When comparing the values of r with the critical value found from the tables, reject H_0 if $|r| >$ critical value.

Testing whether the population product-moment correlation coefficient is zero

Example

a Compute the product-moment correlation coefficient for the following data.

x	35	40	42	43	50	52	60	61
y	72	66	68	59	54	58	48	49

b Use a 5% significance level and a suitable test to check the assertion that there is negative correlation between the readings.

Solution

a Using a calculator, $r = -0.9487$ to 4 d.p.

b $H_0{:}\rho = 0$; there is zero correlation between the data.
$H_1{:}\rho < 0$; there is negative correlation.

For a one-tailed test at 5%, in the PMCC tables, look up the value where the level is 0.05 (or 5%) and $n = 8$: the critical value of r is 0.6215.

Since $|r| > 0.6215$, reject H_0 and accept $H_1{:}\rho < 0$.

Example

A group of pupils scored the following marks in their Biology and French examinations.

Student	A	B	C	D	E	F	G
Biology	56	30	53	64	43	22	70
French	72	41	20	85	60	45	48

a Find the value of the product-moment correlation coefficient between the marks of these students.

b Stating your hypotheses and using a 5% level of significance, interpret your value.

Solution

a Using a calculator, $r = 0.3442$ (4 d.p.)

b $H_0{:}\rho = 0$; there is zero correlation between the data,
$H_1{:}\rho \neq 0$; there is correlation.

For a two-tailed test at 5%, look up the value where the level is 0.025 (or 2.5%) and $n = 7$: the critical value is 0.7545.

Since $|r| < 0.7545$, accept $H_0{:}\rho = 0$.

Question

The examination marks for a group of ten students in a pure mathematics and a statistics paper are as shown.

a Find the product moment correlation coefficient.

b Test, at the 5% level, whether there is positive correlation between the results.

Pure mathematics	**Statistics**
34	52
46	50
48	59
79	75
88	66
90	78
62	47
24	16
38	46
70	58

Answers

a $r = 0.8374$

b $H_0:\rho = 0$. There is zero correlation between the data.
$H_1:\rho > 0$. There is positive correlation.
The critical value for $n = 10$ at the 5% significance level is 0.5494.
Reject H_0 at the 5% level as $|r| > 0.5494$.

Spearman's rank correlation coefficient

To calculate Spearman's rank correlation coefficient, r_s, rank the order of both x and y using the numbers 1, 2, 3 . . ., n. It does not matter whether you rank them in ascending or descending order, as long as you do the same for both sets of values. Then, for each pair of rankings of (x, y), calculate d, the difference between the two rankings.

Spearman's coefficient of rank correlation, r_s, is given by

$$r_s = 1 - \frac{6\sum d^2}{n(n^2 - 1)}$$

As with the product moment correlation coefficient, r_s takes values between -1 and $+1$ inclusive. However, unlike the PMCC, the data does not have to be linear for there to be a coefficient of $+1$.

If $r_s = +1$, the values of y increase as the values of x increase.

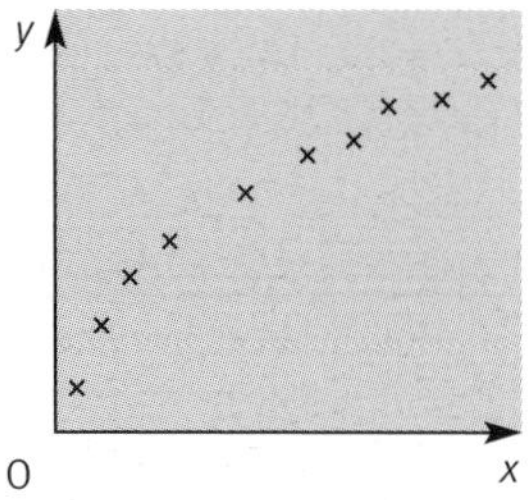

For $r_s = -1$, the values of y decrease as the values of x increase.

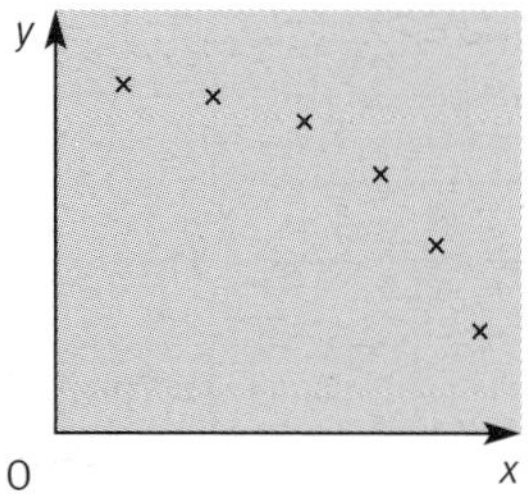

Example

Two wine judges are asked to rank 8 wines in order of quality, with the best wine having a score of 1.

Wine	Judge 1	Judge 2
A	2	1
B	7	8
C	5	3
D	3	6
E	4	4
F	8	7
G	1	2
H	6	5

Find Spearman's rank correlation coefficient between the two judges. Use a suitable test at the 5% level to test whether the judges agree.

Wine	Judge 1	Judge 2	d	d^2
A	2	1	1	1
B	7	8	−1	1
C	5	3	2	4
D	3	6	−3	9
E	4	4	0	0
F	8	7	1	1
G	1	2	−1	1
H	6	5	1	1
				$\sum d^2 = 18$

$$r_s = 1 - \frac{6 \times 18}{8(64 - 1)} = 0.7857$$

$H_0:\rho = 0$: There is no correlation.
$H_1:\rho > 0$: The rankings are positively correlated.

Using a one-tailed test at 5% and tables for Spearman's rank correlation coefficient, the critical value for $n = 8$ is 0.6429.

As $0.7857 > 0.6429$, the result is significant at the 5% level.

Reject H_0 and accept H_1: the rankings are positively correlated.

Example

A child is asked to estimate the ranking in weight of 10 objects and gives the ordering as

C D B G H A E J I F

The correct order is

A B C D E F G H I J

a Find Spearman's rank correlation coefficient between the child's ordering and the correct ordering.

b Use a 5% significance level and a suitable test to test the assertion that the child has some ability in ordering the weights of objects.

Solution

If the A, B, C, D, . . . are given the ranks 1, 2, 3, 4, . . . then this gives the table below.

Objects	Child's rank order	Correct rank order	d	d^2
A	6	1	5	25
B	3	2	1	1
C	1	3	−2	4
D	2	4	−2	4
E	7	5	2	4
F	10	6	4	16
G	4	7	−3	9
H	5	8	−3	9
I	9	9	0	0
J	8	10	−2	4
				$\sum d^2 = 76$

a $r_s = 1 - \dfrac{6\sum d^2}{n(n^2-1)} = 1 - \dfrac{6 \times 76}{10(100-1)} = 0.5394.$

b $H_0{:}\rho = 0$. There is no correlation.
$H_1{:}\rho > 0$. The rankings are positively correlated.

The critical value at 5% for $n = 10$ is 0.5636. As $0.5394 < 0.5636$, accept $H_0{:}\rho = 0$: there is no correlation between the rankings.

Question

Nine women who regularly attended a gym were asked to keep a record of their average running time for 5 miles over the period of a month. The table shows the average times T, to the nearest minute, set alongside the number of years, N, that each woman had been attending the gym.

N (years)	T (mins)
1	55
1.5	59
2.5	52
3	46
4	48
4.5	44
5	42
6	43
7	38

a Calculate Spearman's rank correlation coefficient for the data.

b Stating your hypotheses clearly, test at the 1% level whether there is negative rank correlation between N and T.

Answers

a $r_s = -0.95$

b $H_0{:}\rho = 0$. There is no correlation.
$H_1{:}\rho < 0$. The rankings are negatively correlated.
When $n = 9$, critical value at 1% is 0.7833.
As $|-0.95| > 0.7833$, reject H_0 and accept H_1 at 1% significance level.

Regression

Linear regression is a method of finding the line of best fit to a set of data of the form (x_i, y_i), where $n = 1, 2, \ldots, n$.

If the line of best fit is found to be $y = \alpha + \beta x$, then $y_i = \alpha + \beta x_i + \varepsilon_i$, where ε_i is the vertical difference between the line and the point (x_i, y_i). The method of least squares for finding the regression line of y on x minimises $\sum \varepsilon_i^2$.

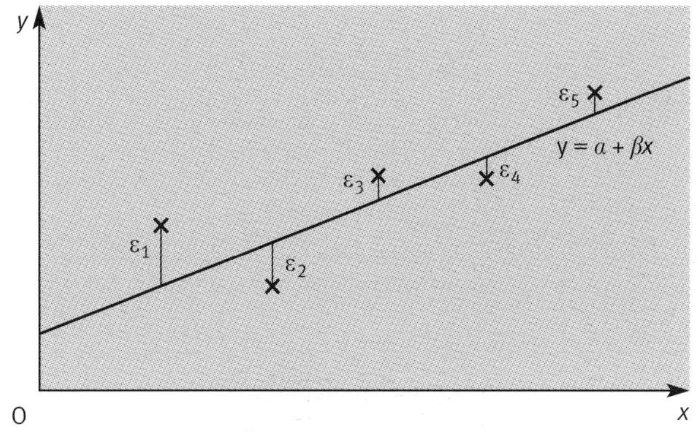

The regression line always passes through $(\bar{x}, \bar{y})$.

The variable x is the independent variable as it may be altered by the person conducting the investigation; y is called the dependent variable as it depends upon the value of x.

The equation of the regression line of y on x is: $y = \alpha + \beta x$ which is found from

$$y - \bar{y} = \frac{S_{xy}}{S_{xx}}(x - \bar{x}) \text{ where}$$

$$S_{xx} = \frac{\sum x^2}{n} - \frac{(\sum x)^2}{n^2} \text{ and}$$

$$S_{xy} = \frac{\sum xy}{n} - \frac{(\sum x)(\sum y)}{n^2}$$

Example

For the following data, find

i the equation of the regression line y on x in the form $y = \alpha + \beta x$,

ii an estimated value of y when $x = 10.2$

x	4.7	5.3	6.2	6.9	8.0	9.8	11.3	12.7
y	10.4	11.8	12.3	13.6	14.8	16.2	18.3	20.4

You may use $\sum x = 64.9$ $\sum y = 117.8$
$\sum x^2 = 585.25$ $\sum y^2 = 1816.18$ $\sum xy = 1024.55$

Solution

i Start by calculating $\bar{x}$ and $\bar{y}$.

$$\bar{x} = \frac{\sum x}{n} = \frac{64.9}{8} = 8.1125$$

$$\bar{y} = \frac{\sum y}{n} = \frac{117.8}{8} = 14.725$$

$$S_{xx} = \frac{585.25}{8} - \frac{64.9^2}{8^2} = 7.34 \text{ (2d.p)}$$

$$S_{xy} = \frac{1024.55}{8} - \frac{64.9 \times 117.8}{8^2} = 8.61 \text{ (2d.p)}$$

Using $y - \bar{y} = \frac{S_{xy}}{S_{xx}}(x - \bar{x})$,

$$y - 14.725 = \frac{8.61}{7.34}(x - 8.1125)$$

Rearranging, this becomes $y = 5.21 + 1.17x$ (both α and β are given to 2 d.p.)

ii When $x = 10.2$, $y = 5.21 + 1.17 \times 10.2$
$= 17$ (2 s.f.)

The regression line may only be used to estimate y for values of x within the range of the data (i.e. between 4.7 and 12.8 in the above example) as the relationship between x and y is assumed to be linear over this range of values. The behaviour of the relationship is not known outside these values.

You can use the statistical functions on a calculator to find a regression line. Follow the steps given for correlation.

Questions

1 The turnover, £x million, and profit, £y million, for a manufacturing company for six successive years are shown in the table.

Turnover (£m)	Profit (£m)
120.4	10.3
103.8	8.6
138.2	15.5
149.5	22.4
159.6	39.4
98.7	0.6

a Calculate the equation of the regression line of profit on turnover.

b If the regression equation is denoted by $y = a + bx$, give an interpretation to each of a and b.

c Using the equation for the regression line, find an estimate of the break-even level of turnover.

2a Calculate the regression line of y upon x for the data below.

x	9.4	8.2	4.5	6.7	7.8	6.0	5.3	5.9	7.1	8.8
y	1.2	3.3	10.6	6.2	4.3	6.4	7.6	6.9	5.0	5.0

$\sum x = 69.7$ $\sum y = 56.5$ $\sum x^2 = 508.33$
$\sum y^2 = 377.95$ $\sum xy = 360.01$

b Use your line to calculate an estimate for y when $x = 7.5$.

c Do you think your line could be used to find an estimate for y when $x = 11.8$? Give a reason for your answer.

Answers

1a $y = -48.6 + 0.5x$

b -48.6 refers to the loss, £48.6m, when turnover is zero (this is also known as a firm's fixed costs); as 0.5 is the gradient of the line it is the amount of profit earned from each extra unit of turnover: as both are in £million, £0.5m profit is earned from each extra £1m of turnover.

c £97.2m (using values from 1a, substitute $y = 0$ and rearrange to find x.)

2a $y = 16.1 - 1.5x$ **b** 4.85

c No, as it lies outside the range of x.

Take a break

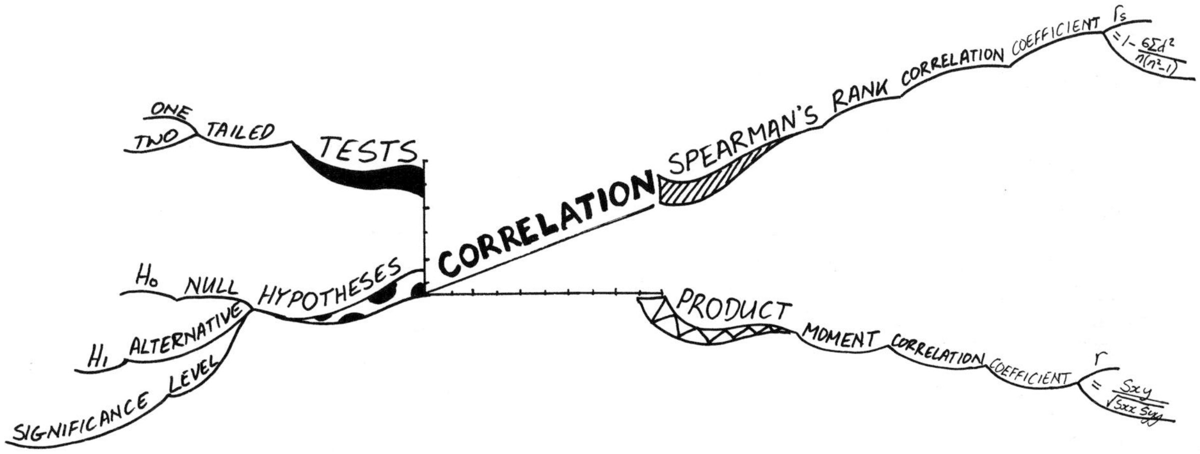
ONE
TWO
TAILED
TESTS
H₀ NULL
HYPOTHESES
H₁ ALTERNATIVE
SIGNIFICANCE LEVEL
CORRELATION
SPEARMAN'S RANK CORRELATION COEFFICIENT
$r_s = 1 - \frac{6\Sigma d^2}{n(n^2-1)}$
PRODUCT MOMENT CORRELATION COEFFICIENT
$r = \frac{S_{xy}}{\sqrt{S_{xx}S_{yy}}}$

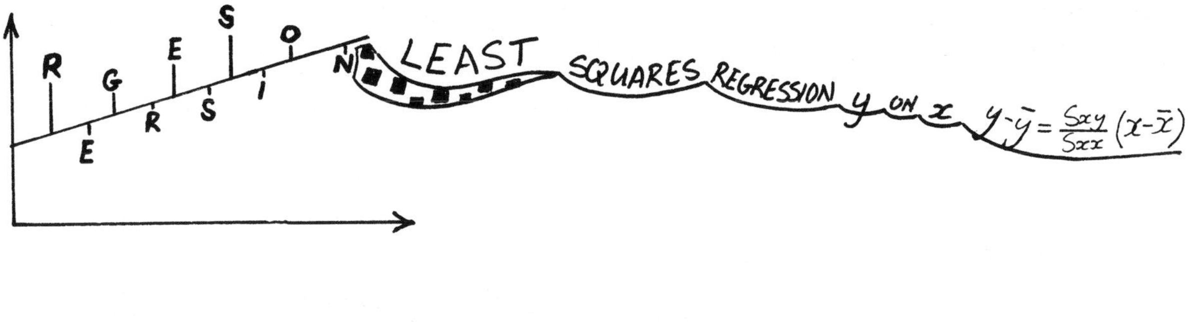
REGRESSION
LEAST SQUARES REGRESSION
y ON x
$y - \bar{y} = \frac{S_{xy}}{S_{xx}}(x - \bar{x})$

Review

1 A party of either 4, 5 or 6 people is to be sent to a conference from a group of 9.

a Calculate the total number of possible parties.

b If it is decided that two of the 9 people must be members of the party, find the total number of possible parties.

2 The events A and B are such that $P(A) = \frac{3}{4}$, $P(A \cap B) = \frac{2}{5}$ and $P(A|B') = \frac{7}{10}$. Find

a $P(B)$ **b** $P(A \cup B)$ **c** $P(A|B)$ **d** $P(A'|B)$.

3 A random variable X has probability density function f, defined by

$$f(x) = \begin{cases} kx(2-x) & 0 \leqslant x \leqslant 2 \\ 0 & \text{otherwise} \end{cases}$$

Find

a the value of k, **b** $E(X)$, **c** $\text{var}(X)$.

4 The amount of time, x minutes, spent waiting for a doctor by a random sample of 200 patients was coded such that $y = \dfrac{x - 35}{20}$, giving

$\sum fy = -40$ and $\sum fy^2 = 248$.

Find the mean and variance of the length of time spent waiting for the doctor.

5 A man has 5 notes screwed up in his pocket: one \$5 bill, two \$10 bills and two \$20 bills. He takes two bills out of his pocket at random. The random variable, X dollars, represents the sum of the value of the two bills.

a Write down the probability distribution function of X.

b Find $E(X)$.

c Calculate $\text{Var}(X)$.

Answers

1a ${}^9C_4 + {}^9C_5 + {}^9C_6 = 336$ **b** ${}^7C_2 + {}^7C_3 + {}^7C_4 = 91$.

2a $P(A|B') = \frac{7}{10} \Rightarrow \dfrac{P(A \cap B')}{P(B')} = \frac{7}{10}$. $P(A \cap B') = P(A) - P(A \cap B) = \frac{7}{20} \Rightarrow P(B) = \frac{1}{2}$ **b** $\frac{17}{20}$ **c** $\frac{4}{5}$ **d** $\frac{1}{5}$.

3a $\frac{3}{4}$ **b** 1 **c** 0.2. **4a** 31 **b** 480.

5a

x	15	20	25	30	40
$P(X = x)$	$\frac{1}{5}$	$\frac{1}{10}$	$\frac{1}{5}$	$\frac{2}{5}$	$\frac{1}{10}$

b 26 **c** 54

PREVIEW

By the end of this chapter, you will have revised:

- ✔ **the mean and variance of the binomial distribution,**
- ✔ **how to calculate the probability of individual events in the binomial distribution,**
- ✔ **how to calculate cumulative probabilities in the binomial distribution,**
- ✔ **the mean and variance of the Poisson distribution,**
- ✔ **how to calculate the probability of discrete events using the formula for the Poisson distribution,**
- ✔ **how to calculate the cumulative probabilities from the Poisson distribution,**
- ✔ **how and when to use the Poisson distribution as an approximation to the binomial distribution.**

The binomial distribution

If a random variable follows a binomial distribution, then

- there must be **fixed number of trials, *n***
- the outcomes of the trials are **independent**
- there are only **two outcomes** for each trial: success or failure
- the **probability of success, *p*, is constant** for each trial.

The important variables in the binomial distribution are

- the number of trials, n
- the probability of success in any single trial, p
- the probability of failure in any single trial, q, where $q = 1 - p$

The quantities n and p are called parameters because when they are given particular values, the distribution is determined.

A variable, such as X, is chosen to represent the number of successes. If X is distributed binomially with n trials and a probability of success of p, the distribution may be written as $X \sim \mathrm{B}(n, p)$.

The mean of this distribution is $\mathrm{E}(X) = np$, and the variance is $\mathrm{Var}(X) = npq$.

For example, a survey involved selecting three people at random and asking if they voted at the last election. If 60% of the population voted at the last election, then p, the probability of success (i.e. picking someone who voted in the last election), is 0.6. Therefore the probability of failure (i.e. of picking someone who did not vote at the last election) is $q = 1 - p = 0.4$. As three people are interviewed in the survey, $n = 3$.

For all three people to have voted, there is only one possible combination, VVV. So the probability that all three people voted, $\mathrm{P}(X = 3)$, is given by $\mathrm{P}(X = 3) = 0.6 \times 0.6 \times 0.6 = 0.6^3$.

There are three possible ways in which two out of the three people chosen voted at the last election: $\mathrm{VV\bar{V}}$, $\mathrm{V\bar{V}V}$, $\mathrm{\bar{V}VV}$. The probability of each of these is $0.6^2 \times 0.4$. So $\mathrm{P}(X = 2) = 3 \times 0.6^2 \times 0.4$.

The possible combinations in which only one out of three people voted are $\mathrm{\bar{V}\bar{V}V}$, $\mathrm{\bar{V}V\bar{V}}$ and $\mathrm{V\bar{V}\bar{V}}$. The probability of each of these is 0.6×0.4^2.
So $\mathrm{P}(X = 1) = 3 \times 0.6 \times 0.4^2$.

There is only one way of choosing three non-voters: $\mathrm{\bar{V}\bar{V}\bar{V}}$. So $\mathrm{P}(X = 0) = 0.4^3$

In general, the probability of r successes from n trials is $\mathrm{P}(X = r) = {}^n\mathrm{C}_r\, p^r q^{n-r}$

${}^n\mathrm{C}_r$ represents the number of different combinations of r successes from n trials, such as 2 voters out of 3 in the above example.
There are r successes so that p, the probability of success, is to the power of r.
There are $n - r$ failures and so q, the probability of failure, is to the power of $n - r$.

Example

Ninety five per cent of seeds from a certain manufacturer germinate when planted. If ten seeds are planted, find the probability that eight seeds germinate.

Solution

Let X be the number of seeds that germinate.
Write down as much of the information in mathematical symbols as soon as you can:-
The number, n, of seeds planted is 10.
The probability of any one seed germinating is p so $p = 0.95$.
The probability of any one seed not germinating is q: $q = 1 - p = 0.05$.
$\mathrm{P}(X = 8) = {}^{10}\mathrm{C}_8 0.95^8 0.05^2 = 0.0746$ (4 d.p.)

The binomial distribution and cumulative probabilities

You use cumulative probabilities when the question asks you to find the probability of the occurrence of a range of outcomes. In the previous example this could be where the question asks for the probability that at least 6 seeds germinate, or less than 2 seeds germinate, or at most 5 seeds germinate. These questions usually require the use of the binomial cumulative distribution function tables. You may find these either in your statistics text book or in your exam board's formula book. The tables vary between exam boards. In some tables, the given values of p are multiples of 0.05 and up to and including 0.5. Therefore, in questions of this type, if you are not sure which probability to take as p, choose the smaller probability. Probabilities are only tabulated for $P(X \leqslant x)$.

Example

There are three times as many red balls in a bag as blue balls. Twenty balls are chosen at random, each ball being replaced after it is chosen. Find the probability that

a no more than six blue balls were chosen
b at least 12 red balls were chosen
c at least 10 blue balls were chosen
d less than 4 blue balls were chosen
e at most 15 red balls were chosen
f between 3 and 7 blue balls were chosen, inclusive.

Solution

There is a twist at the start of this question: the probability is not given as a figure, but as a ratio. If it is written as a ratio, then it is much easier to find p and q. The ratio of red balls to blue balls is 3 : 1, so the probability of picking a red ball is $\frac{3}{4}$ and of picking a blue ball is $\frac{1}{4}$. As the tables only give values of p less than or equal to 0.5, use $p = \frac{1}{4}$, which is the probability that a blue ball is chosen. Let X be the number of blue balls chosen. (The answers below have been given to 4 decimal places.)

a This question may be thought of as 'Less than or equal to six blue balls were chosen'. Go to the tables, find the section where $n = 20$, the column where $p = 0.25$ and the row where $r = 6$.
$P(X \leqslant 6) = 0.7858$.
b If at least 12 red balls are taken, this means that 8 or less blue balls were taken.
$P(X \leqslant 8) = 0.9591$.
c $P(X \geqslant 10) = 1 - P(X \leqslant 9) = 1 - 0.9861 = 0.0139$ (4 d.p.)

If you have problems with this, write down a few possible values of X: $X \geqslant 10$ gives the values 10, 11, 12, ... which is not 9, 8, 7, ... i.e. $P(X \geqslant 10) = 1 - P(X \leqslant 9)$

d $P(X < 4) = P(X \leqslant 3) = 0.2252$.
e If at most 15 red balls were chosen, then there were at least 5 blue balls, or $P(X \geqslant 5)$.
$P(X \geqslant 5) = 1 - P(X \leqslant 4) = 1 - 0.4148 = 0.5852$.
f $P(3 \leqslant X \leqslant 7) = P(X \leqslant 7) - P(X \leqslant 2)$
$= 0.8982 - 0.0913 = 0.8069$.
Be careful not to subtract $P(X \leqslant 3)$ from $P(X \leqslant 7)$: if you do you are subtracting away $P(X = 3)$.

Occasionally you will not be able to look up probabilities of this type using the tables. This will usually be because the given value of n or p is not in the tables. To calculate these probabilities you must work out each discrete probability individually. The question is only likely to ask you to do this for a maximum of three separate discrete probabilities.

Example

A pub quiz team has a 30% probability of winning top prize on any one night. In 12 quizzes, what is the probability that it

a wins less than 3 times
b wins between 6 and 8 contests inclusive?

Solution

Let X be the number of games won by the team.
$X \sim B(12, 0.3)$

a $P(X < 3) = P(X \leqslant 2)$
$= P(X = 0) + P(X = 1) + P(X = 2)$
$= {}^{12}C_0\, 0.3^0 0.7^{12} + {}^{12}C_1 0.3^1 0.7^{11} + {}^{12}C_2 0.3^2 0.7^{10}$
$= 0.2528$ (4 d.p.).
b $P(6 \leqslant X \leqslant 8) = P(X = 6) + P(X = 7) + P(X = 8)$
$= {}^{12}C_6 0.3^6 0.7^6 + {}^{12}C_7 0.3^7 0.7^5 + {}^{12}C_8 0.3^8 0.7^4$
$= 0.1162$ (4 d.p.).

More complicated questions on the binomial distribution

Some questions start as one binomial distribution and change to another binomial distribution.

Example

Chickens in a farm lay 4 times as many brown eggs as white eggs. Eggs are packed into trays containing 20 eggs. The eggs are randomly distributed within the trays.

a Find the probability that in a tray containing 20 eggs there are
i exactly 5 white eggs
ii less than 16 brown eggs.
b Trays are then packed into boxes containing 6 trays. Find the probability that exactly 2 of the 6 trays contain exactly 5 white eggs.

Solution

The probabilities are given as a ratio: the ratio of brown to white eggs is 4 to 1. So the probability of choosing a brown egg at random is 0.8, and of choosing a white egg is 0.2. Take p to be the lower of these two probabilities, as this makes the cumulative binomial probability tables easier to use.

a Let X be the number of white eggs in a tray.

i $P(X = 5) = {}^{20}C_5 0.2^5 0.8^{15} = 0.17455\ldots$
$= 0.1746$ (4 d.p.).

ii If there are less than 16 brown eggs, then there are at least 5 white eggs.
$P(X \geqslant 5) = 1 - P(X \leqslant 4) = 1 - 0.6296$
$= 0.3704$ (4 d.p.).

b Let Y be the number of trays containing exactly 5 white eggs.

The problem has changed from the number of white eggs in a tray to the number of trays containing exactly 5 white eggs: the probability that a tray contains exactly 5 white eggs is 0.1746 (from part **a**), so $p = 0.1746$ and, as there are 6 trays, $Y \sim B, (0.1746)$

$$P(Y = 2) = {}^6C_2(0.17455\ldots)^2(1 - 0.17455\ldots)^4 = 0.2122 \text{ to 4 d.p.}$$

Questions

1 A football team takes 5 penalty shots at goal. If they have a probability of 0.2 of scoring a goal with any penalty shot, find the probability that

a they score 1 goal

b they score less than 3 goals.

2 The random variable X has the binomial distribution B(20, 0.45). Find

a $P(X \leqslant 9)$

b $P(5 \leqslant X \leqslant 10)$.

3a State the conditions under which a binomial distribution may be used as a model for a variate.

b When playing tennis in a county league, the local favourite is three times more likely to win than to lose. If she plays 10 games, find the probability that she wins

i exactly 8 games

ii less than 5 games.

c Find the mean and variance of the number of wins in 10 games.

4 One word puzzle is published in *The Daily News* every weekday from Monday to Friday. A woman attempts to complete it every day. On average, she can complete 6 out of 10 puzzles.

a Find the expected value and the variance of the number of completed puzzles in any given week.

b Find the probability that she completes at least four puzzles in a week.

c Calculate the probability that, over a period of four weeks, she completes at least four puzzles in exactly 2 weeks.

Answers

1a 0.4096

b 0.9421 (4 d.p.).

2a 0.5914 (4 d.p.)

b $P(X \leqslant 10) - P(X \leqslant 4) = 0.7318$ (4 d.p.).

3a There are a fixed number of events, the events occur independently with constant probability of success or failure.

b i 0.282 (3 d.p.)

ii 0.0197 (3 s.f.)

c Mean = 7.5, Variance = 1.875.

4a Mean = 3, variance = 1.2

b 0.337 (3 d.p.)

c Let Y be the number of weeks in which she completes at least 4 puzzles.
$Y \sim B(4, 0.337)$.
$P(Y = 2) = 0.2995$ (4 d.p)

The Poisson distribution

The Poisson distribution is a discrete distribution as it can only take whole number values.

Only one parameter is required for this distribution: this is the mean and it is called λ or μ.

If a random variable follows a Poisson distribution then the events occur

- **randomly**
- **independently**
- with a **constant mean**
- **singly**.

If X has a Poisson distribution with mean (or parameter) λ, then the distribution may be written as $X \sim Po(\lambda)$. The variance of the Poisson distribution is also λ.

To calculate the probability of r events occurring in a Poisson distribution with mean λ, use $P(X = r) = \dfrac{e^{-\lambda}\lambda^r}{r!}$

For discrete probabilities use the formula, and for cumulative probabilities use the Poisson cumulative distribution function tables or the sum of the discrete probabilities using the formula.

How do you know whether to use the Poisson distribution or the binomial distribution?

The simplest way is to ask yourself whether there is a fixed maximum or an unlimited possible number of events. If it is fixed, then the distribution is binomial. If there is no limit to the number of events, then the distribution is Poisson.

For example, for the number of car accidents at a junction in a year, use the Poisson distribution (there is no maximum number of accidents). If there are ten penalty shots at goal, use the binomial distribution as there is a maximum of 10 for the possible number of goals scored. For the number of flaws in a length of material, use the Poisson distribution. If a fair die is thrown ten times, the possible number of sixes scored is at most 10, so use a binomial distribution.

Example

A shop sells a particular T-shirt at a rate of 7 per week on average. The number sold in a week has a Poisson distribution.

a Find the probability that, in a given week,
  i the shop sells 8 T-shirts
  ii less than 6 T-shirts are sold
  iii sales exceed 9 T-shirts.
b Find the probability that 15 T-shirts are sold in a fortnight.
c Find the minimum number of T-shirts that the firm should hold in stock in order to have at least a 95% chance of being able to meet all orders during that week.

Solution

Let X be the number of T-shirts sold in a week.
$\lambda = 7$
$X \sim \text{Po}(7)$

a i $P(X = 8) = \dfrac{e^{-7}7^8}{8!} = 0.1304.$
You may also use the cumulative Poisson probabilities table:
$P(X = 8) = P(X \leqslant 8) - P(X \leqslant 7)$
$= 0.7291 - 0.5987 = 0.1304.$
ii $P(X < 6) = P(X \leqslant 5) = 0.3007.$
iii $P(X > 9) = 1 - P(X \leqslant 9) = 1 - 0.8305 = 0.1695.$
b The average number of T-shirts sold in a fortnight is twice that sold in a week, so $\lambda = 14$.
Let Y be the number of T-shirts sold in a fortnight.
$Y \sim \text{Po}(14)$
$P(Y = 15) = \dfrac{e^{-14}14^{15}}{15!} = 0.0989.$
c Think of this question as 'The probability that the number sold, X, is less than or equal to the level of stock. When the no. of T-shirts in stock is n, $P(X \leqslant n)$ should be at least 0.95.'

Refer to the column in the Poisson cumulative probability tables where $\lambda = 7$ and find the first probability which is greater than 0.95. As $P(X \leqslant 11) = 0.9467$ and $P(X \leqslant 12) = 0.9730$, the minimum stock level is 12.

More complicated questions using the Poisson distribution

Questions on exam papers often mix distributions – they may ask you to find probabilities using the Poisson distribution and then use one of these probabilities in calculating another probability using the binomial distribution.

Example

The number of telephone calls made on a weekday by a particular person has a Poisson distribution with parameter 6.

a State any assumptions required about the distribution of telephone calls for this model to be valid.
b Show that in any randomly selected day the probability that she makes 5 telephone calls is 0.161 to 3 d.p.
c Find the probability that she makes 11 calls in 2 days.
d Find the probability that on exactly 2 days of a 5 day week she makes exactly 5 calls.

Solution

a The calls made are independent of each other, they occur singly and with a constant mean in a given interval of time or space.
b This is best shown by using the formula:
$P(X = 5) = \dfrac{e^{-6}6^5}{5!} = 0.161$ to 3 d.p.
c In a two day period, $\lambda = 2 \times 6 = 12$
$P(X = 11) = \dfrac{e^{-12}12^{11}}{11!} = 0.114$ (3 d.p.)
d Let Y be the number of days on which she makes exactly 5 calls. There is a maximum of 5 days on which she can make exactly 5 calls, so $n = 5$, and Y has a binomial distribution. p is the probability that she makes exactly 5 calls on one day and $p = P(X = 5) = 0.161$.
$\therefore \quad Y \sim B(5, 0.161)$ so
$P(Y = 2) = {}^5C_2 0.161^2 0.839^3 = 0.153$ (3 d.p.)

Using the Poisson distribution as an approximation to the binomial distribution

It can be time-consuming to calculate probabilities for large values of n using the binomial distribution. If n is large (usually $n \geqslant 50$) and p is small (usually $p \leqslant 0.1$ so that $np < 5$), you can use the Poisson distribution as an approximation to the binomial distribution.

If $X \sim \text{Po}(\lambda)$ then the mean and the variance are both λ. If $X \sim \text{B}(n, p)$, then the mean is np and the variance is npq. For the mean and the variance to be close to each other, q must be close to 1, and so p must be close to 0.

If $X \sim \text{B}(n, p)$, then $X \sim \text{Po}(\lambda)$ approximately, where $\lambda = np$.

Example

A factory produces electric motors, two percent of which are faulty. A client orders 100 motors. Using a suitable approximation, find the probability that

a 2 are faulty,
b more than 3 are faulty.

Solution

$n = 100$, $p = 0.02$
Let X be the number of faulty items in the order.
mean $= np = 100 \times 0.02 = 2$
As $np < 5$ and $n \geqslant 50$, use the Poisson distribution as an approximation to the binomial distribution.
$X \sim \text{Po}(2)$ approx.

a $\text{P}(X = 2) = \dfrac{e^{-2}2^2}{2!} = 0.2707$ (4 d.p.).

b $\text{P}(X \geqslant 4) = 1 - \text{P}(X \leqslant 3) = 1 - 0.8571 = 0.1429$ (4 d.p.).

The distribution of the sum of two independent Poisson distributions

If X and Y are two independent Poisson distributions such that $X \sim \text{Po}(\lambda)$ and $Y \sim \text{Po}(\mu)$, then $X + Y \sim \text{Po}(\lambda + \mu)$.

Example

The numbers of children's books written by Mary Childs and by Peter Jung in a year follow Poisson distributions with means 4.5 and 3 respectively. Find the probability that they have a combined output of

a exactly 7 books in a given year
b more than 8 books in a given year.

Solution

Let X be the number of books Mary writes in a year and Y be the number of books Peter writes in a year.
$X + Y \sim \text{Po}(7.5)$

a $\text{P}(X + Y = 7) = \dfrac{e^{-7.5}7.5^7}{7!} = 0.146$ (3 dp).

b $\text{P}(X + Y > 8) = 1 - \text{P}(X + Y \leqslant 8) = 1 - 0.6620$
$= 0.338$ (3 dp).

Questions

1 On average, a newsagent sells 9 copies of *The Morning Bugle* per day.

a Calculate the probability that the shop sells
i eight newspapers in a day
ii between 18 and 20 newspapers, inclusive, over a two day period.

b Find the probability that the shop sells exactly 8 newspapers in exactly two days out of a seven-day week.

c Find the minimum number of newspapers that should be held in stock to ensure that there is insufficient stock to meet demand no more than once in a 30-day month.

2 In the Elchester cricket league, the probability of any game ending in a draw is 0.02. Using a suitable approximation, estimate the probability that, in 200 games, four are drawn.

3a State the conditions under which a Poisson distribution is a suitable model to use in statistics.

b The number of accidents per month at a certain road crossing is a Poisson random variable with parameter 2.
i Find the probability that in any month, more than 3 accidents occur.
ii Calculate the probability that in a year there are 25 accidents.
iii Find the probability that more than 3 accidents occur in exactly two months of a six-month period.

4 Two weaving machines, A and B, produce chintz fabric. The number of flaws per 100 m in each machine follows a Poisson distribution with mean 1.8 and 2.2 respectively. Find the probability that, in a combined output of 200 m (of which 100 m was produced by each machine),

a 1 flaw was found,
b at least 7 flaws were found.

Answers

1a i 0.132 (3 d.p.)

ii 0.262 (3 d.p.) For a two day period, the mean is 18, and this is not on some tables. In this case the probabilities for 18, 19 and 20 newspapers must be calculated separately using the formula.

b Let Y be the number of days in which exactly 8 newspapers are sold.

$Y \sim B(7, 0.132)$

$P(Y = 2) = 0.180$ (3 d.p.)

c Let X be the number of newspapers sold per day, and n be the minimum number of papers held in stock per day.

$P(X > n) < \frac{1}{30}$

$1 - P(X \leqslant n) < \frac{1}{30}$

$P(X \leqslant n) > 0.9667$ (4 d.p.)

From tables, $n = 15$.

2 Approximate to the Poisson distribution as $n \geqslant 50$ and $np < 5$

Let X be the number of draws in 200 games.

$X \sim Po(4)$ approximately

$P(X = 4) = 0.1954$ (4 d.p.)

3a The events must occur singly, independently, randomly and with a constant mean over a given period of time or space.

b i 0.1429 (4 d.p.)

ii 0.0779 (4 d.p.)

c 0.1653 (4 d.p.) This is a binomial distribution where $n = 6$, $p = 0.1429$ and $r = 2$

4 The combined output has a mean of 4.

a 0.0732 (4 d.p.)

b 0.1107 (4 d.p.)

Take a break

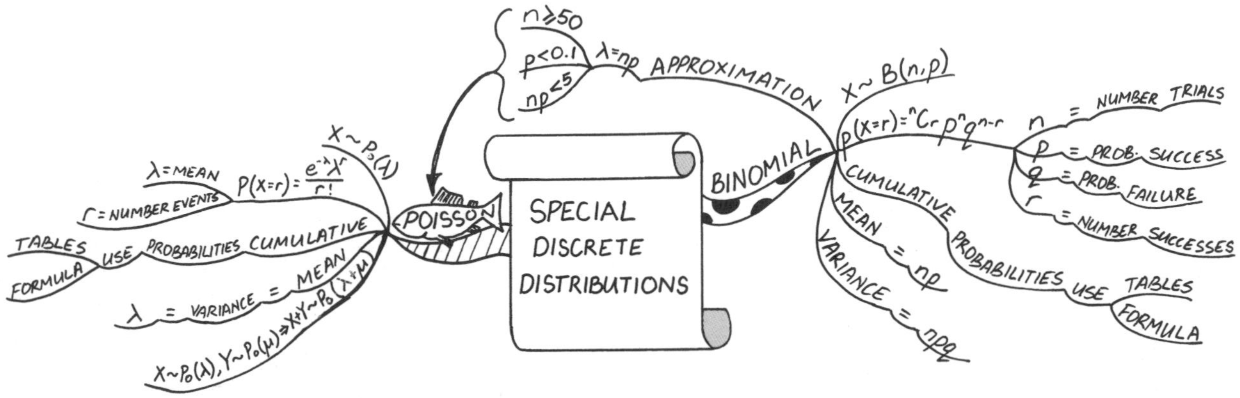

Review

1 The length of time a student takes to complete a problem is the random variable X with cumulative distribution function

$$F(x) = \begin{cases} 0 & x < 5 \\ k(30x - x^2 - 125) & 5 \leqslant x \leqslant 15 \\ 1 & x > 15 \end{cases}$$

Find

a the value of k,

b the probability density function f(x), specifying it for all values of x,

c E(X), **d** Var(X), **e** the median m.

2 A tea manufacturer produces equal quantities of two types of tea bag: Darjeeling and Assam. Assuming that boxes contain a random selection from the output, calculate the probability that in a box containing 20 tea bags there are

a equal numbers of Darjeeling and Assam tea bags,

b more than 12 Darjeeling bags.

It is found that 2% of the bags are underweight. A catering pack contains 100 bags.

c Find the probability that less than 3 bags in a catering pack are underweight.

3 In a store the weekly demand for the game Mutant Monsters follows a Poisson distribution with parameter 8.

a Calculate the probability that the store sells at least 11 in a week.

b Find the minimum number of games the store should hold in stock in order that they have less than a 2% chance of not being able to meet demand.

4 At a gym, the time taken for women running 3 miles was monitored and the results are shown.

Age, x years	18	20	21	25	27	29	30	33
Time, y minutes	32	31	35	38	38	41	44	49

a Find the product moment correlation coefficient between the time and the age of the runner.

b Using a 5% significance level, state whether or not your result leads you to conclude that there is a linear association between the age of the runner and the time it takes to run 3 miles. State your hypotheses clearly.

c Calculate the equation of the regression line of y on x.

d Give an interpretation of the coefficient of x in the equation.

5 The probability density function of a random variable X, is given below.

$$f(x) = \begin{cases} \frac{1}{6} & 4 \leqslant x \leqslant 10 \\ 0 & \text{otherwise} \end{cases}$$

Find

a $E(X)$, **b** $Var(X)$, **c** $P(X > 8)$,

d the distribution function $F(x)$, specifying it for all values of x.

Answers

1a $\frac{1}{100}$ **b** $f(x) = \begin{cases} \frac{1}{50}(15 - x) & 5 \leqslant x \leqslant 15 \\ 0 & \text{otherwise} \end{cases}$ **c** $8\frac{1}{3}$ **d** $5\frac{5}{9}$ **e** 7.93

2 Let X be the number of Darjeeling bags

a $P(X = 10) = 0.176$ (3 d.p.)

b $P(X > 12) = 1 - P(X \leqslant 8) = 0.1316$ (4 d.p.)

c Let Y be the number of underweight bags in a catering pack. As $np = 100 \times 0.02 = 2$ is less than 5 and $n > 50$, approximate to the Poisson distribution.
$Y \sim Po(2)$ approx.
$P(Y < 3) = P(Y \leqslant 2) = 0.6767$ (4 d.p.).

3 Let X be the number of games sold in a week.

a $P(X \geqslant 11) = 1 - P(X \leqslant 10) = 0.1841$ (4 d.p.) **b** $P(X > n) < 0.02 \Rightarrow n = 14$.

4a 0.9626

b H_0: $\rho = 0$. There is zero correlation between the data.
H_1: $\rho \neq 0$. There is linear correlation.
Using a two-tailed test, critical value at 5% is 0.7067
Accept H_1: there is evidence of linear relationship.

c $y = 10.6 + 1.1x$

d It is the estimated increase in the running time (in minutes) per yearly increase in age.

5a 7 **b** 3 **c** $\frac{1}{3}$ **d** $F(x) = \begin{cases} 0 & x < 4 \\ \frac{1}{6}(x - 4) & 4 \leqslant x \leqslant 10 \\ 1 & x > 10 \end{cases}$

PREVIEW

By the end of this topic you will have revised:

- ✔ **the normal distribution,**
- ✔ **the standard normal distribution,**
- ✔ **finding μ and σ using given probabilities,**
- ✔ **linear combinations of independent random variables,**
- ✔ **using the normal distribution as an approximation to the binomial distribution**
- ✔ **using the normal distribution as an approximation to the Poisson distribution.**

A sketch of the normal distribution with mean μ is shown below:

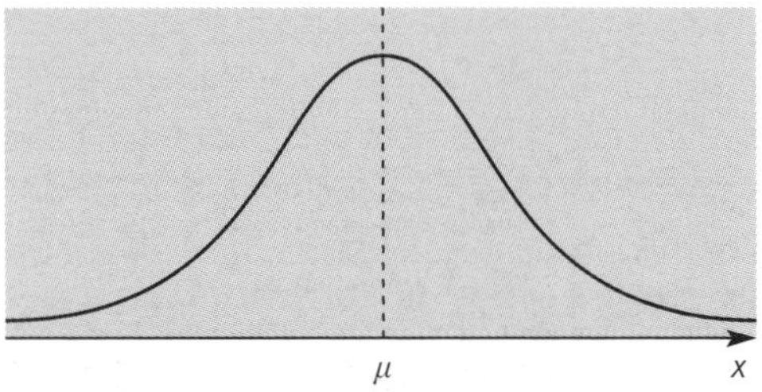

The normal distribution has these properties

- it is symmetrical about the mean, μ
- it has a range of values of X from $-\infty$ to $+\infty$
- as $x \to \pm\infty$, $f(x) \to 0$
- the area under the curve is 1

If X has a normal distribution with mean μ and standard deviation σ, then $X \sim N(\mu, \sigma^2)$. To calculate probabilities using the normal distribution tables, you need to know how to standardise. The standard normal distribution has mean 0 and standard deviation 1. This is written as $Z \sim N(0, 1)$.

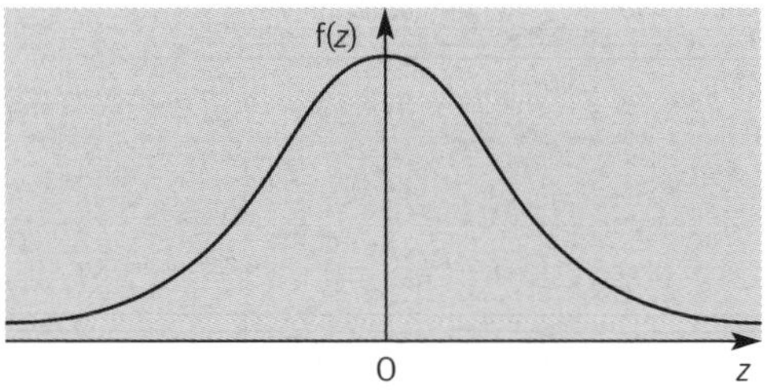

To standardise values of X, use the formula

$$z = \frac{x - \mu}{\sigma}$$

Sketching the normal distribution function often makes it easier to calculate probabilities. The tables give probabilities for $P(Z < z)$ for positive values only of z. The normal distribution is symmetrical, so to find probabilities for negative values of z, reflect the graph in the y-axis.

$P(Z > -a) = P(Z < a)$.

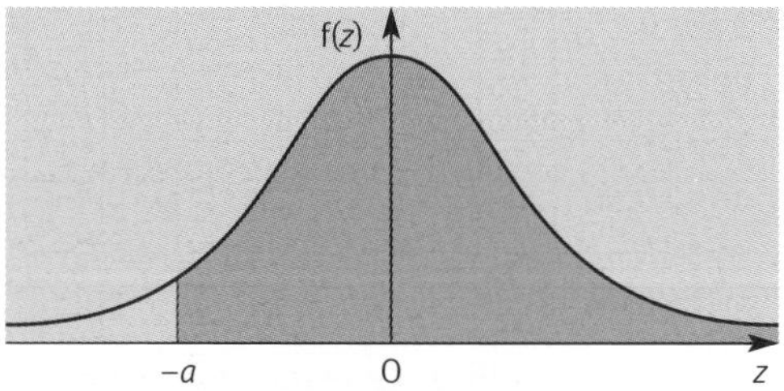

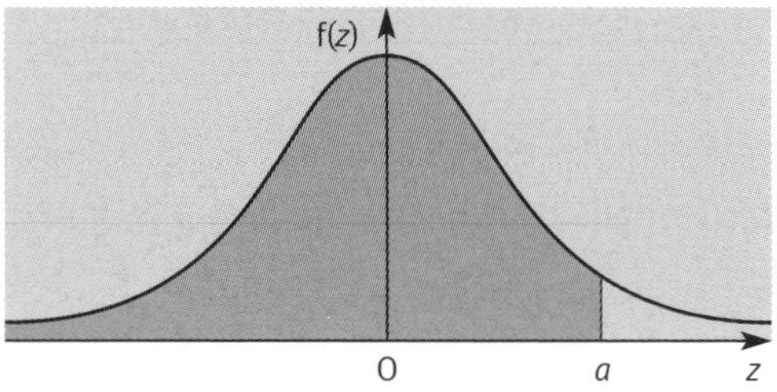

and $P(Z < -b) = P(Z > b) = 1 - P(Z < b)$.

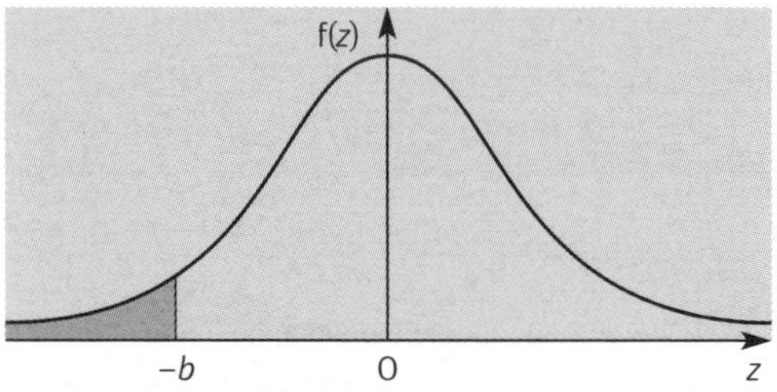

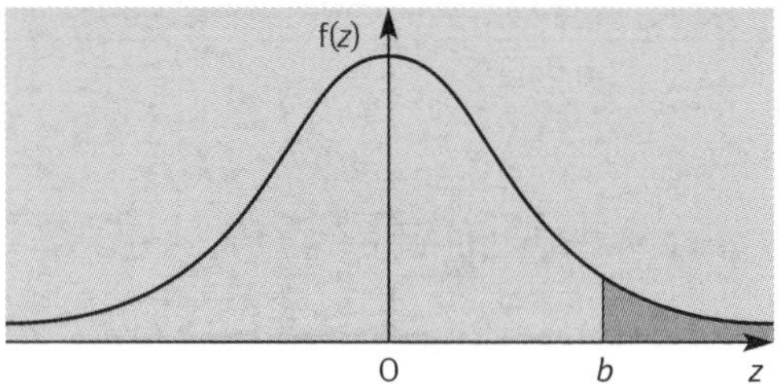

The normal distribution function tables differ between examination boards. Some allow you to find the probability using your z value rounded to 2 decimal places, while others have more complicated tables that give the probability more accurately.

Probabilities in this topic are given accurately. If you find that your answer is very close to the given answer, then the difference is probably due to rounding errors so don't worry. Probabilities are usually given corrected to 3 or 4 decimal places.

Calculating probabilities with the normal distribution

Example

The random variable $X \sim N(16, 25)$. Find:

a $P(X < 22)$ **b** $P(X > 14)$ **c** $P(X > 19.5)$

d $P(X < 13.1)$ **e** $P(18.3 < X < 21.7)$

f $P(10.2 < X < 14.1)$ **g** $P(|X - 15| < 1.1)$

h $P(|X - 16.3| > 0.7)$

Solution

$\mu = 16, \quad \sigma = \sqrt{25} = 5$

a Using $z = \dfrac{x - \mu}{\sigma}$,

$$P(X < 22) = P\left(Z < \frac{22 - 16}{5}\right)$$

$= P(Z < 1.2) = 0.8849$ (4 d.p.) (from tables)

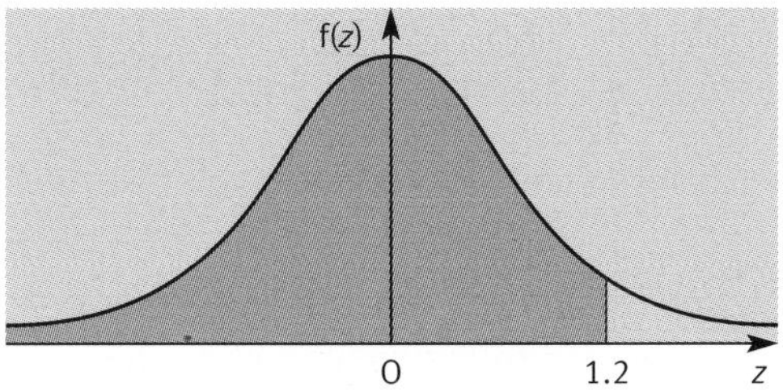

b $P(X > 14) = P\left(Z > \dfrac{14 - 16}{5}\right) = P(Z > -0.4)$

As the diagram is symmetrical,
$P(Z > -0.4) = P(Z < 0.4)$

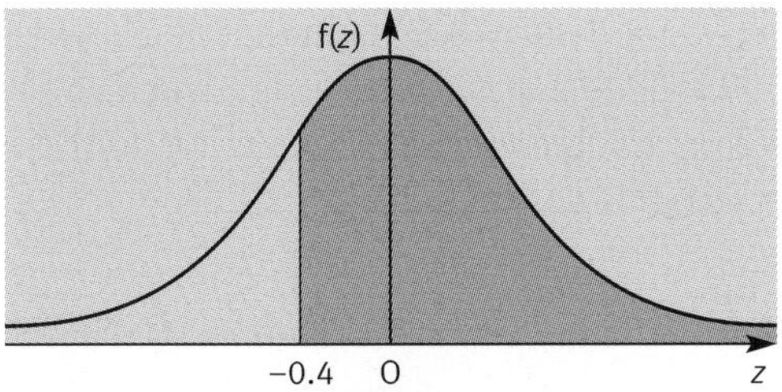

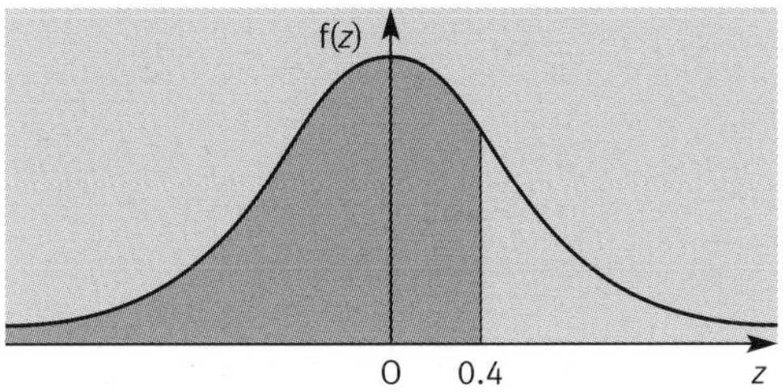

$P(Z > -0.4) = P(Z < 0.4) = 0.6554$ (4 d.p.)

c $P(X > 19.5) = P\left(Z > \dfrac{19.5 - 16}{5}\right) = P(Z > 0.7)$

$= 1 - P(Z < 0.7) = 1 - 0.7580 = 0.2420$ (4 d.p.)

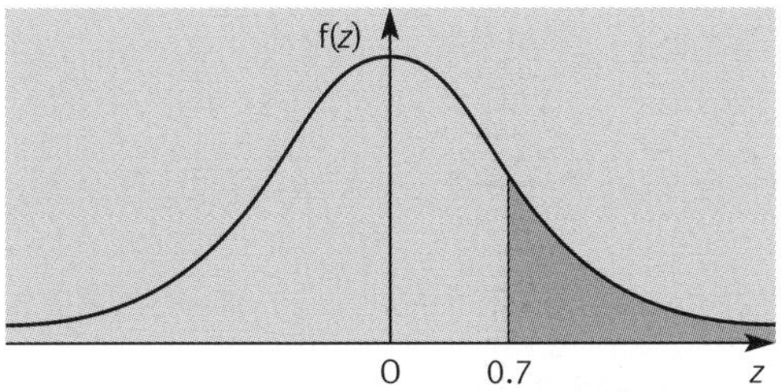

d $P(X < 13.1) = P(Z < -0.58) = 1 - P(Z < 0.58)$

$= 1 - 0.7190 = 0.2810$ (4 d.p.)

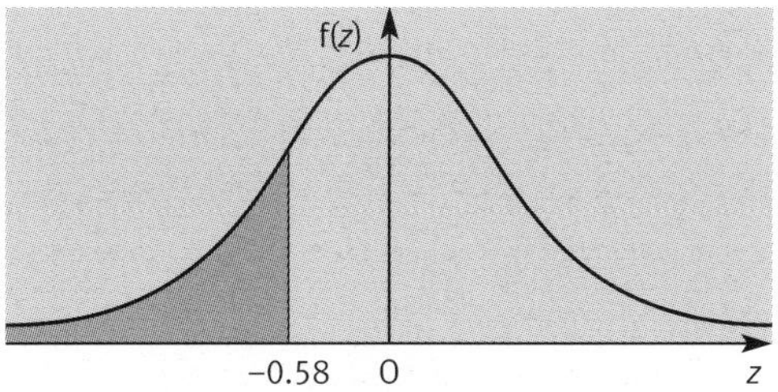

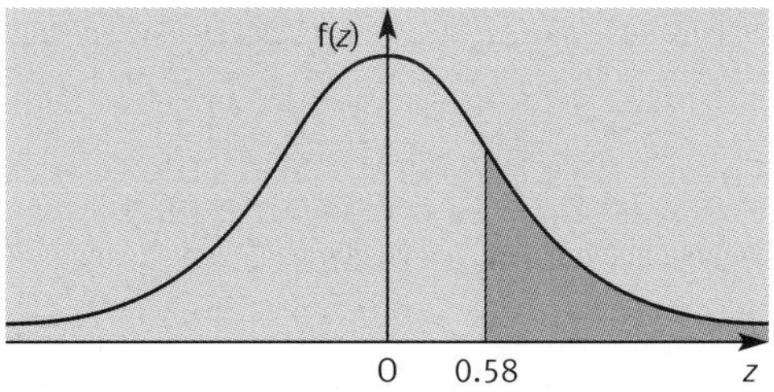

e $P(18.3 < X < 21.7) = P(0.46 < Z < 1.14)$

$= P(Z < 1.14) - P(Z < 0.46) = 0.8729 - 0.6772$

$= 0.1957$ (4 d.p.)

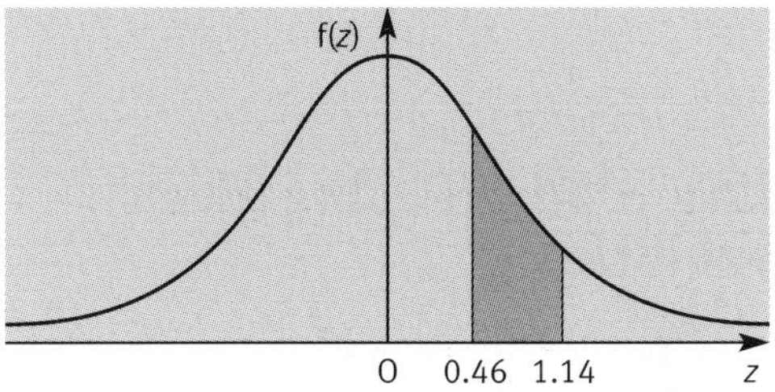

f $P(10.2 < X < 14.1) = P(-1.16 < Z < -0.38)$

$= P(0.38 < Z < 1.16) = 0.8770 - 0.6480$

$= 0.2290$ (4 d.p.)

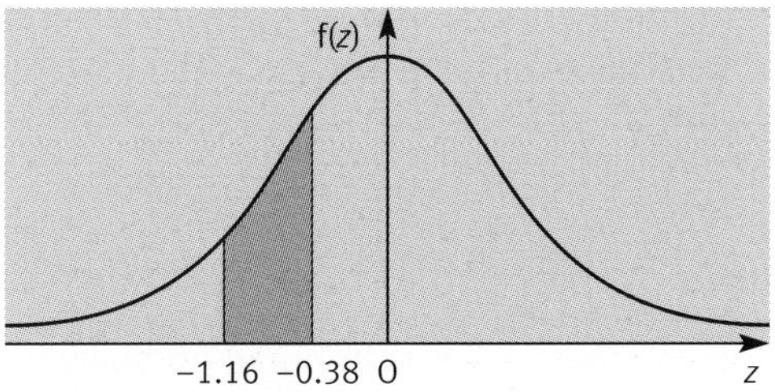

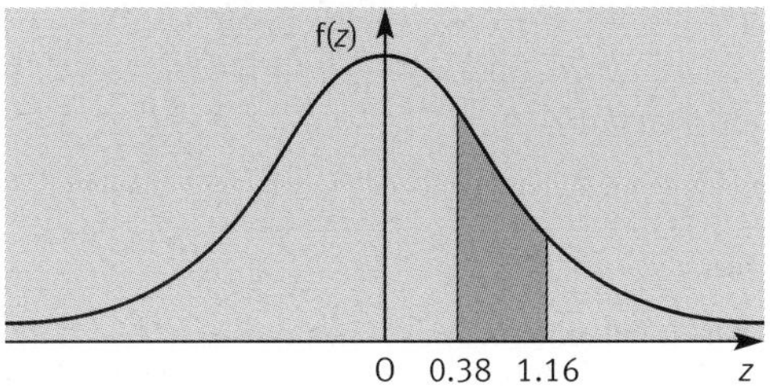

g $P(|X - 15| < 1.1) = P(-1.1 < X - 15 < 1.1)$
$= P(13.9 < X < 16.1) = P(-0.42 < Z < 0.02)$
$= P(Z < 0.02) - P(Z < -0.42)$
$= P(Z < 0.02) - (1 - P(Z < 0.42))$
$= 0.1707$ (4 d.p.)

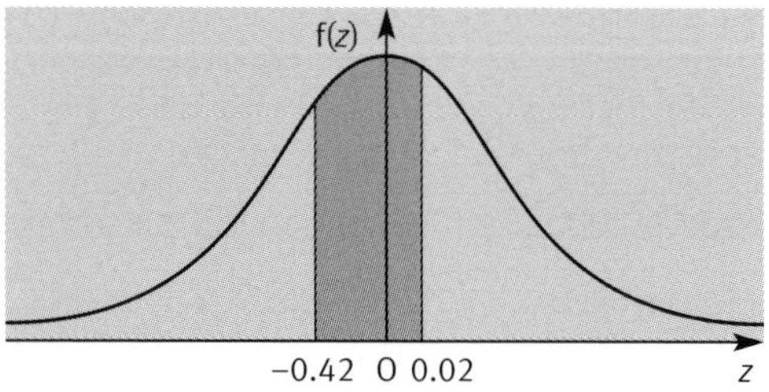

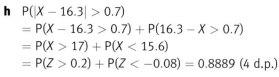

h $P(|X - 16.3| > 0.7)$
$= P(X - 16.3 > 0.7) + P(16.3 - X > 0.7)$
$= P(X > 17) + P(X < 15.6)$
$= P(Z > 0.2) + P(Z < -0.08) = 0.8889$ (4 d.p.)

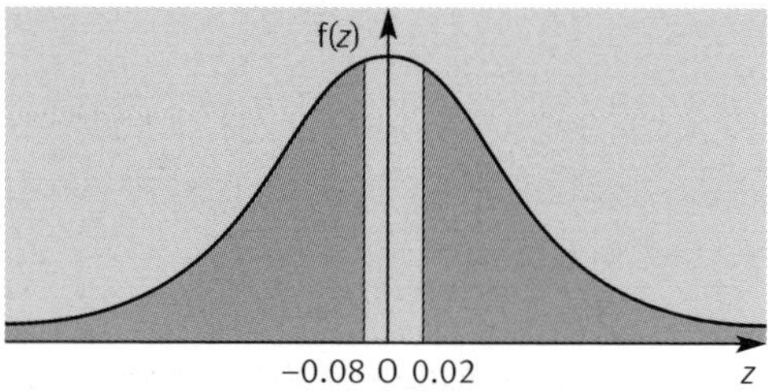

Finding μ and σ using given probabilities

This involves either working back from the normal distribution function tables by finding the given probabilities and then the corresponding z value, or by using the 'percentage points of the normal distribution' table, which gives values of z of the commonly used probabilities such as 10%, 5% and 1%. To find μ and σ from the x values, use the standardisation formula. Always sketch a diagram. Ensure that any z value to the left of the mean (i.e. 0) is negative.

Example

The random variable X is distributed normally with mean μ and standard deviation σ. Given that $P(X > 9.3) = 0.32$ and $P(X < 6.4) = 0.41$, find the value of μ and σ.

Solution

Show the information on a single diagram, as shown below.

The first row of labels shows the values of X. Use the second row to show the Z values writing 0 below the mean.

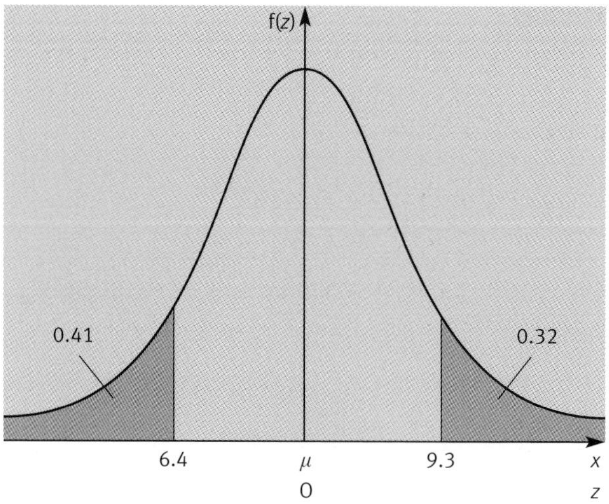

To find the z values you need to work back from the probability column to the column of z values.
A probability of 0.32 is not given in the table, but $1 - 0.32 = 0.68$ is.

$P(X > 9.3) = 1 - P(X < 9.3) = 1 - 0.32 = 0.68$.
When $P(Z < z) = 0.68$, $z \approx 0.47$ (from tables)

A probability of 0.41 is not given in the table and corresponds to a negative value of z, but using symmetry, $1 - 0.41 = 0.59$ is in the tables. When $P(Z < z) = 0.59$, $z \approx 0.23$. However, when you write this second z value on the diagram, it is to the left of 0, so it should be -0.23.

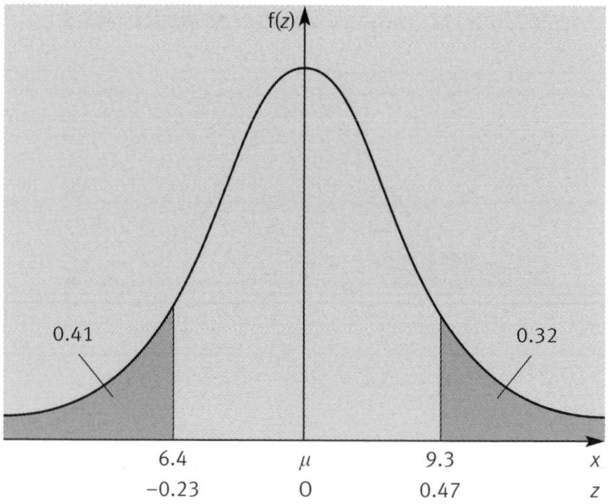

Using the standardisation formula gives

$$\frac{9.3 - \mu}{\sigma} = 0.47 \Rightarrow 9.3 - \mu = 0.47\sigma \qquad (1)$$

$$\frac{6.4 - \mu}{\sigma} = -0.23 \Rightarrow 6.4 - \mu = -0.23\sigma \qquad (2)$$

(1) − (2) gives $0.7\sigma = 2.9 \quad \Rightarrow \quad \sigma = 4.1$ (1 d.p.)

Hence $\mu = 7.4$ (1 d.p.)

⚠ If the probabilities given in the question are recognisable values such as 0.05, 0.01, etc. then use the 'Percentage points of the Normal Distribution' table to find values of z.

Linear combinations of independent random variables

If X and Y are independent and normally distributed then a linear combination of X and Y is also normally distributed where

$$E(X \pm Y) = E(X) \pm E(Y)$$
$$Var(X \pm Y) = Var(X) + Var(Y)$$

⚠ *Remember: don't subtract variances!*

Example

The weights of bags of sand follow a normal distribution with mean 1.2 kg and standard deviation 130 grams. The weights of packing boxes are distributed normally with mean 1.4 kg and standard deviation 200 grams. A box is filled with ten bags of sand. Find the probability that the weight of a full box lies between 13 kg and 14 kg.

Solution

The question has given some of the weights in kilograms and some in grams. Write all weights in one measure, e.g. kilograms.

Let X_i be the weight in kilograms of the ith bag of sand. Let Y be the weight in kilograms of an empty box. Let F be the weight in kilograms of a full box.

$X_i \sim N(1.2, 0.13^2)$
$Y \sim N(1.4, 0.2^2)$
$F = X_1 + X_2 \ldots + X_{10} + Y$
$E(F) = E(X_1) + E(X_2) + \ldots + E(X_{10}) + E(Y)$
$= 10 \times 1.2 + 1.4 = 13.4$
$Var(F) = var(X_1) + var(X_2) + \ldots + var(X_{10}) + var(Y)$
$= 10 \times 0.13^2 + 0.2^2 = 0.209$
$F \sim N(13.4, 0.209)$

$$P(13 < F < 14) = P\left(\frac{13 - 13.4}{\sqrt{0.209}} < Z < \frac{14 - 13.4}{\sqrt{0.209}}\right) = 0.715 \text{ (3 d.p.)}.$$

⚠ *Remember to find the square root of 0.209, as 0.209 is the variance not the standard deviation.*

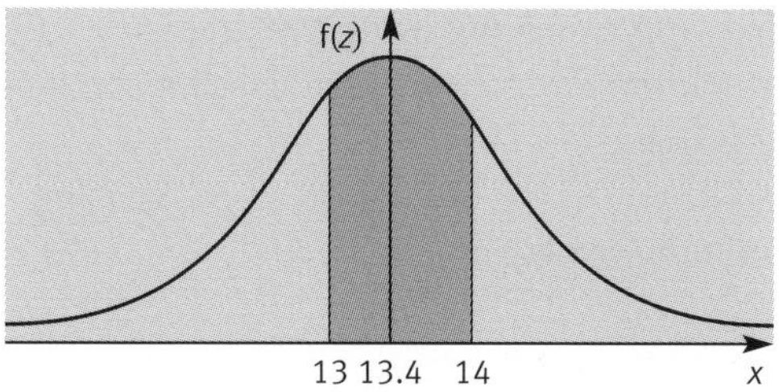

Example

A gardener grows tulips of varieties A and B. The heights of the flowers are normally distributed: those of variety A have a mean of 26.8 cm and a standard deviation of 3.1 cm, those of variety B have a mean of 24.5 cm and a standard deviation of 4.2 cm. Find the probability that

a the heights of two flowers of variety A differ by more than 5 cm

b a flower from variety A is bigger than one from variety B.

Solution

Let X and Y be the heights of flowers from variety A and B respectively.

$X \sim N(26.8, 3.1^2), \quad Y \sim N(24.5, 4.2^2)$

a If the first flower is bigger than the second by more than 5, then $X_1 - X_2 > 5$, but if the second flower is bigger than the first by more than 5, then $X_1 - X_2 < -5$. As a single inequality, this is written as $|X_1 - X_2| > 5$.
$X_1 - X_2$ is normally distributed where
$E(X_1 - X_2) = 0$ and $var(X_1 - X_2) = 19.22$, i.e.
$X_1 - X_2 \sim N(0, 19.22)$
$P(|X_1 - X_2| > 5)$
$= P(X_1 - X_2 > 5) + P(X_1 - X_2 < -5)$
$= P(Z > 1.14) + P(Z < -1.14) = 0.2542$

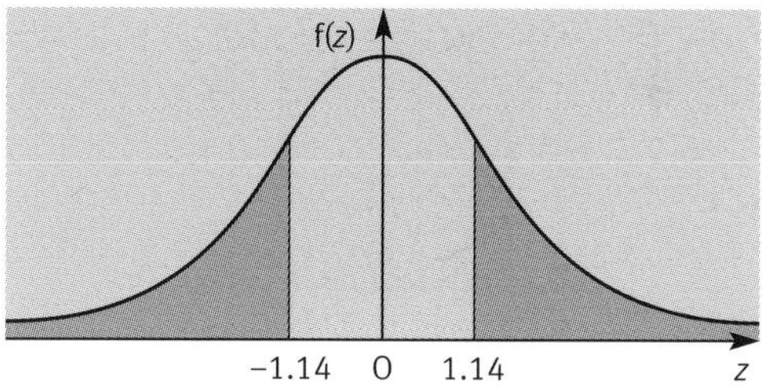

b $X - Y \sim N(2.3, 27.25)$
$P(X > Y) = P(X - Y > 0) = P(Z > -0.44)$
$= 0.670$ (3 d.p.)

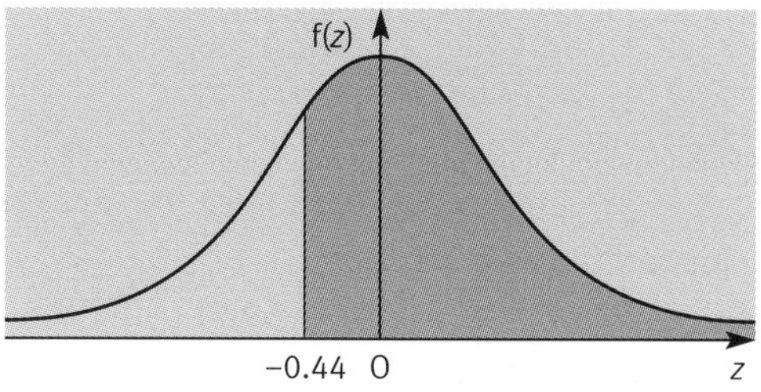

Approximations using the normal distribution and the continuity correction

When using the normal distribution to approximate to a binomial distribution or Poisson distribution, you are using a continuous distribution to approximate to a discrete distribution. In these cases, you must use the continuity correction.

The binomial and Poisson distributions give probabilities for discrete variates e.g. $P(X = 5)$. When using a continuous distribution as an approximation for either of these, you must use the continuity correction to change discrete values to a range of values. You do this by treating discrete values as corrected numbers. So $P(X = 5)$ becomes $P(4.5 < X < 5.5)$.

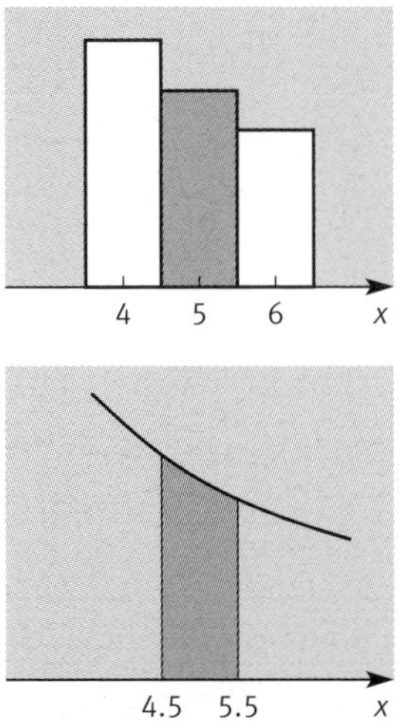

$P(2 \leqslant X \leqslant 6)$ becomes $P(1.5 < X < 6.5)$ using the continuity correction.

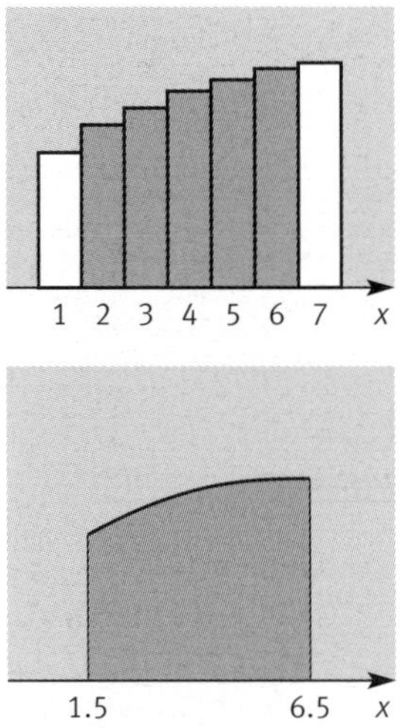

$P(22 < X < 25)$ approximates to $P(22.5 < X < 24.5)$ using the continuity correction.
$P(47 < X \leqslant 50) \approx P(47.5 < X < 50.5)$ using the continuity correction.

Using the normal distribution to approximate to the binomial distributions

If $X \sim B(n, p)$, and if n is large and p is not too large or too small (in practice use $n \geqslant 50$, $np > 5$ and $nq > 5$) then use the normal distribution as an approximation to the binomial distribution.

The mean of the distribution is np and the variance is npq. So $X \sim N(\mu, \sigma^2)$ approx., where $\mu = np$ and $\sigma^2 = npq$.

Using the normal distribution as an approximation to the Poisson distribution

If $X \sim Po(\lambda)$, and λ is large (usually $\lambda > 20$), then use the normal distribution as an approximation to the Poisson distribution. The mean of the distribution is λ and the variance is λ, so $X \sim N(\mu, \sigma^2)$ approx., where $\mu = \lambda$ and $\sigma^2 = \lambda$.

Example

The Choosies Company Ltd. produces sweets of which 48% are chocolate and 3% are sugar-coated. The company packs them at random into bags containing 150 sweets. Using a suitable approximation, calculate the probability that a bag contains

a exactly 5 sugar-coated sweets,

b between 55 and 65 chocolate sweets inclusive.

Solution

a Let X be the number of sugar-coated sweets in a bag.
$X \sim Bin(150, 0.03)$. As $n \geqslant 50$ and $np < 5$, use the Poisson distribution to approximate to the binomial distribution with $\lambda = np = 4.5$.
$X \sim Po(4.5)$ approx.

No continuity correction is needed since the binomial and Poisson distributions are both discrete.

$$P(X = 5) \approx \frac{e^{-4.5}4.5^5}{5!} = 0.1708 \text{ (4 d.p.)}$$

b Let Y be the number of chocolate sweets in a bag.
$Y \sim Bin(150, 0.48)$. As $n \geqslant 50$, $np > 5$ and $nq > 5$, use the normal distribution to approximate to the binomial distribution. The mean $= np = 72$ and the variance $= npq = 37.44$, so $X \sim N(72, 37.44)$ approx.
When approximating using the normal distribution, do not forget to use the continuity correction.
$P(55 \leqslant X \leqslant 65) \approx P(54.5 < X < 65.5)$ using the continuity correction
$= P(-2.86 < Z < -1.06)$
$= 0.142$(3 d.p.).

Questions

1 A tennis player measures the speeds of his first serves. He finds that 10% travel faster than 114 kmh^{-1}, and 5% are slower than 98 kmh^{-1}. Find the mean and the standard deviation of the speed of the serves, giving your answers to 3 significant figures.

2 On the Isle of Ingram locally knitted woollen jumpers are sent to shops in boxes containing 12 jumpers each. The weights of the jumpers are normally distributed with mean 1.5 kg and standard deviation 300g. The weights of the empty boxes are normally distributed with mean 1.8 kg and standard deviation 200g.

a Given that all random variables are independent, find the probability that a full box weighs between 18 kg and 19 kg.

b Two jumpers are selected at random. What is the probability that they differ in weight by more than 200g?

3 Bottles are filled with lemonade of nominal net weight 1.5 litres. The amount of lemonade poured into the bottles by machines is normally distributed about the mean quantity set, with a standard deviation of 0.15 litres.

a Given that the machines are set with mean quantity of 1.53 litres, find the probability that a bottle chosen at random contains less than the nominal weight.

b Find the minimum setting of the filling machine in order that no more than 1% of the bottles contain less than the nominal weight.

4 The number of people calling a breakdown organisation in an hour has a Poisson distribution with parameter 150. Using a suitable approximation, find the probability that more than 155 people call in an hour.

5 Fifty five percent of people attending a doctor's surgery are male. In a week, the doctor sees 200 patients. Using a suitable approximation, find the probability that under half of them are male.

Answers

1 To find the values of z, use the 'Percentage Points of the Normal Distribution' table.

$$\frac{114-\mu}{\sigma} = 1.2816 \Rightarrow 114 - \mu = 1.2816\sigma \qquad (1)$$

$$\frac{98-\mu}{\sigma} = -1.6449 \Rightarrow 98 - \mu = -1.6449\sigma \qquad (2)$$

$(1) - (2) \Rightarrow 2.9265\sigma = 16 \Rightarrow \sigma = 5.47$ (3 s.f.)

$\Rightarrow \quad \mu = 107$ (3 s.f.)

(Remember to give your answers to 3 significant figures.)

2 If W is the weight of a full box in grams, then

$W \sim \mathrm{N}(19800, 1120000)$

a $\mathrm{P}(18000 < W < 19000) = \mathrm{P}(-1.70 < Z < -0.76) = 0.180$ (3 d.p.)

b Let Y_1 and Y_2 represent the weight of jumpers 1 and 2 respectively.

$Y_1 - Y_2 \sim \mathrm{N}(0, 180000)$

$\mathrm{P}(|Y_1 - Y_2| > 200) = \mathrm{P}(Y_1 - Y_2 > 200) + \mathrm{P}(Y_1 - Y_2 < -200)$

$= 0.637$ (3 d.p.)

3 Let X be the amount poured in litres.

a $X \sim \mathrm{N}(1.53, 0.15^2)$

$\mathrm{P}(X < 1.5) = 0.421$ (3 d.p.)

b $\mathrm{P}(X < x) \leqslant 0.01$

$$\frac{1.5-\mu}{0.15} = -2.3263$$

$\mu = 1.85$ (2 d.p.)

4 Let X be the number of people calling the organisation per hour.

$X \sim \mathrm{N}(150, 150)$ approx.

$\mathrm{P}(X > 155) \approx \mathrm{P}(X > 155.5)$ using continuity correction

$= 0.327$ (3 d.p.).

5 Let X be the number of people attending the surgery.

$X \sim \mathrm{N}(110, 49.5)$ approx.

$\mathrm{P}(X < 100) \approx \mathrm{P}(X < 99.5)$ using continuity correction

$= 0.068$ (3 d.p.).

Take a break

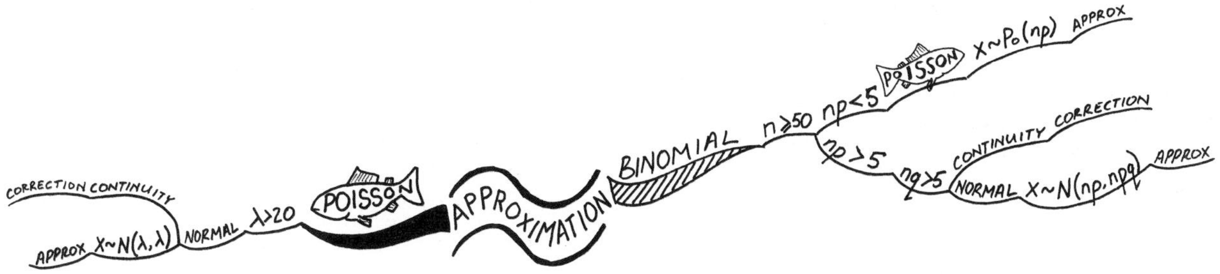

Review

1 The random variable X has probability density function

$$f(x) = \begin{cases} 4x^k & 0 \leqslant x \leqslant 1 \\ 0 & \text{otherwise} \end{cases}$$

where k is a positive integer. Find

a the value of k,

b the mean of X,

c the cumulative distribution function, specifying it for all values of X,

d the median of X.

2 The random variable Y is normally distributed with mean μ and variance σ^2. Given that $P(Y < 36) = 0.0047$ and $P(Y > 72) = 0.0139$, find μ and σ.

3 The random variable X has a normal distribution with a mean of 42 and a standard deviation of 5.2. Find $P(|X - 39| > 3)$.

4 The numbers of people using a certain telephone box in a day have a Poisson distribution with mean 3.5.

a Find the probability that, in any day,

i exactly 6 people use the phone, **ii** more than 4 people use the telephone box.

b Calculate the probability that less than 5 people use it over a two day period.

c Calculate the probability that, on exactly 3 days of a 7 day week, more than 4 people use the phone.

d Using a suitable approximation, find the probability that more than 80 people use the phone over a twenty day period.

5 The corresponding values of eight pairs of the variables x and y are given in the table below:

x	17	14	22	29	25	18	20	24
y	60	65	45	30	42	57	48	38

a Find the equation of the least squares regression line of y on x.

bi Calculate the product moment correlation coefficient between x and y.

ii Using a 5% significance level, interpret your result from **bi**.

6 A committee of 5 people is to be selected at random from a group of 4 men and 5 women.

a Find the total number of ways of choosing the committee.

b Calculate the probability that the committee contains 3 men.

Answers

1a 3 **b** $\frac{4}{5}$ **c** $F(x) = \begin{cases} 0 & x < 0 \\ x^4 & 0 \leqslant x \leqslant 1 \\ 1 & x > 1 \end{cases}$ **d** 0.841 **2** $\mu = 55.5, \sigma = 7.5$

3 $|X - 39| > 3 \Rightarrow X > 42$ or $X < 36$

$P(X < 36) + P(X > 42) = 0.624$ (3 d.p.)

4ai 0.0771 (4 d.p.) **ii** 0.2746 (4 d.p.)

b 0.1730 (4 d.p.)

c Let Y be the number of days in which more than 4 people use the phone.

$n = 7 \quad p = 0.2746 \quad Y \sim B(7, 0.2746)$

$P(Y = 3) = 0.2007$ (4 d.p.)

d Let B be the number of people that use the phone in a twenty day period.

$\lambda = 20 \times 3.5 = 70$

$B \sim N(70, 70)$ approx.

$P(B > 80) \approx P(B > 80.5)$ using the continuity correction

$= 0.1047$ (4 d.p.)

5a $y = 98.8 - 2.4x$

bi -0.9815

ii $H_0: \rho = 0$. There is zero correlation between the data.

$H_1: \rho \neq 0$. There is correlation.

The critical value of r for a two-tailed test is 0.7067. So reject H_0 and accept $H_1: \rho \neq 0$.

6a 126 **b** $\frac{20}{63}$.

PREVIEW

By the end of this topic you will have revised:

- ✔ **unbiased estimates for μ and σ,**
- ✔ **the distribution of the sample mean and the central limit theorem,**
- ✔ **confidence intervals for the mean $\bar{x}$ when σ is known,**
- ✔ **confidence intervals for the mean $\bar{x}$ when σ is unknown using the *t*-distribution.**

Before you start you should:

- know how to calculate the mean and variance of a sample,
- know the mean and variance of the binomial, Poisson and continuous uniform (rectangular) distributions,
- know how to calculate probabilities using the normal distribution.

TEST YOURSELF

If you have trouble with any of the following questions, see the relevant topic in this book or use an A level text book.

1 Find the mean and variance of the sample below.

6.7, 6.9, 7.2, 8.8, 7.7, 7.0, 7.5, 8.2, 8.4, 7.9

2 Write down the mean and variance of the following random variables:

a) $A \sim B(n, p)$,

b) $B \sim Po(\lambda)$,

c) C where C has a continuous uniform distribution over the interval $[a, b]$.

3 The random variable $X \sim N(16, 10)$. Calculate

a) $P(X > 14.7)$

b) $P(16.3 < X < 18.2)$

c) a if $P(X < a) = 0.05$.

Answers

1 mean = 7.63, variance = 0.4361

2a mean = np, variance = npq

b mean = λ, variance = λ

c mean = $\frac{1}{2}(a + b)$, variance = $\frac{1}{12}(b - a)^2$

3a 0.6595 (4 d.p.)

b 0.219 (3 d.p.)

c 10.8 (3 s.f.)

1 wrong? see Statistics 3
2a or **b** wrong? see Statistics 7
2c wrong? see Statistics 9
Trouble with question 3? see Statistics 8.

Unbiased estimates for population parameters

When the mean and variance of a population are unknown, it is often difficult or impossible to calculate them accurately. Therefore a sample is taken from the population and estimates for the mean and variance of the population are calculated from these. A method for finding these gives unbiased estimates if, for a large number of estimates made using the same size samples the expected value, or mean, of these is the actual value.

Method for calculating unbiased estimates

The sample mean is written as $\bar{x}$ and the sample variance is s^2. If the sample is of size n,

- the unbiased estimate of the mean is written as $\hat{\mu}$ and $\hat{\mu} = \bar{x}$
- the unbiased estimate of the population variance is written as $\hat{\sigma}^2$ where

$$\hat{\sigma}^2 = \frac{n}{n-1}s^2$$

Example

Find unbiased estimates of the mean and variance of the population from which the following random sample has been taken.

33.6, 40.2, 38.9, 37.6, 37.7, 39.0, 36.5, 33.8, 36.4, 36.0.

Solution

$$\hat{\mu} = \bar{x} = \frac{\Sigma x}{n} = \frac{33.6 + 40.2 + \ldots + 36.0}{10} = 36.97$$

$$s^2 = \frac{\Sigma x^2}{n} - \bar{x}^2 = \frac{33.6^2 + \ldots + 36.0^2}{10} - 36.97^2$$
$$= 4.21\ldots$$

$$\hat{\sigma}^2 = \frac{n}{n-1}s^2 = \frac{10}{9}(4.21\ldots) = 4.68 \text{ (2 d.p.)}.$$

Example

The table below summarises the number of pens, p, that 25 randomly selected Year 9 schoolchildren take to school.

Number of pens, p	0	1	2	3	4	5
Number of children	2	11	7	3	1	1

Calculate unbiased estimates of the mean and variance of the number of pens that they take to school.

Solution

$$\hat{\mu} = \bar{x} = \frac{\Sigma fx}{\Sigma f} = 1.72$$

$$s^2 = \frac{\Sigma fx^2}{\Sigma f} - \bar{x}^2 = \frac{107}{25} - 1.72^2 = 1.3216$$

$$\hat{\sigma}^2 = \frac{n}{n-1}s^2 = \frac{25}{24}(1.3216) = 1.38 \text{ (2 d.p.)}$$

The distribution of the sample mean and the central limit theorem

The **central limit theorem** states that if $X_1, X_2, \ldots X_n$ are large random samples of the same size from a population with mean μ and variance σ^2 then

$$\bar{X} \sim \mathrm{N}\left(\mu, \frac{\sigma^2}{n}\right) \text{ approximately}$$

i.e. when several samples of the same size are taken from the same population (whatever the distribution of the population), the means of these samples are approximately normally distributed. The larger the value of n, the better the approximation.

The standard deviation of $\bar{X}$ is called the **standard error of the mean** and is $\frac{\sigma}{\sqrt{n}}$.

If $X_1, X_2, \ldots X_n$ are normally distributed then

$$\bar{X} \sim \mathrm{N}\left(\mu, \frac{\sigma^2}{n}\right) \text{ exactly}$$

for any value of n.

Example

The number of sales of Forest Pine wardrobes per week follows a Poisson distribution with parameter 5. Find the probability that over a period of 50 weeks the mean number of sales per week is less than 4.7.

Solution

Let X be the number of sales of wardrobes in a week.

$X \sim \mathrm{Po}(5)$

$\mu = 5$

$\sigma^2 = 5$

Using the central limit theorem,

$\bar{X} \sim \mathrm{N}\left(\mu, \frac{\sigma^2}{n}\right)$ approximately

$\bar{X} \sim \mathrm{N}\left(5, \frac{5^2}{50}\right)$ approximately

$\bar{X} \sim \mathrm{N}(5, 0.5)$ approx.

So $\mathrm{P}(\bar{X} < 4.7) = \mathrm{P}\left(Z < \frac{4.7 - 5}{\sqrt{0.5}}\right)$

$= \mathrm{P}(Z < -0.424)$

$= 0.336$ (3 d.p.).

Questions

1 A random sample of 16 batteries was tested for longevity in a radio. The lifetimes of the batteries, in hours, are shown below.

6.3, 7.2, 6.6, 8.4, 7.5, 6.8, 7.9, 9.0, 8.7, 6.9, 7.0, 7.3, 8.4, 9.4, 6.8, 8.3.

a Find unbiased estimates of

i the mean

ii the variance of the lifetimes of the batteries.

b Find the standard error of the mean.

2 Children's swings produced by a manufacturer are known to have breaking weights that are normally distributed with mean 784 Newtons and standard deviation 84 N. Find the probability that a random sample of 40 swings will have a mean breaking strength of more than 788 N.

3 The random variable X has a continuous uniform distribution over the range [3, 12]. A random sample of size 20 is taken from this distribution.

a Write down the approximate distribution of the sample mean, $\bar{X}$.

b Why is your distribution approximate and not exact?

c Find the probability that the sample mean is between 7.2 and 8.5.

4 A class contains 20 children. Each child rolls a fair die 60 times and records the number of sixes they obtain.

a Write down the mean and variance of the numbers of sixes obtained by each child.

b Find the probability that the mean number of sixes recorded for the class is greater than 9.5. Give your answer to 3 decimal places.

Answers

1a i 7.66 (2 d.p.) **ii** 0.887 (3 d.p.)

b $\frac{\sqrt{0.887}}{\sqrt{16}} = 0.235$ (3 d.p.)

2 Let X be the breaking weights of the swings.

$\bar{X} \sim \mathrm{N}\left(784, \frac{84^2}{40}\right)$

$\mathrm{P}(\bar{X} > 788) = 0.3816$ (4 d.p.)

3 $\mu = 7.5$

$\sigma^2 = 6.75$

a Using the central limit theorem, $\bar{X} \sim \mathrm{N}\left(7.5, \frac{6.75}{20}\right)$

b Because X is not normally distributed

c 0.655 (3 d.p.)

4a mean $= np = 10$

variance $= npq = 8\frac{1}{3}$

b 0.781 (3 d.p.)

[Remember to give your answer to the required number of decimal places.]

Confidence intervals of the mean when σ is known

To determine the range of values over which you are confident that a population mean lies, you may use confidence intervals. In general, a confidence interval is symmetrical about the mean.

For a 90% confidence interval, 5% of the distribution would lie above the upper limit and 5% would lie below the lower limit.

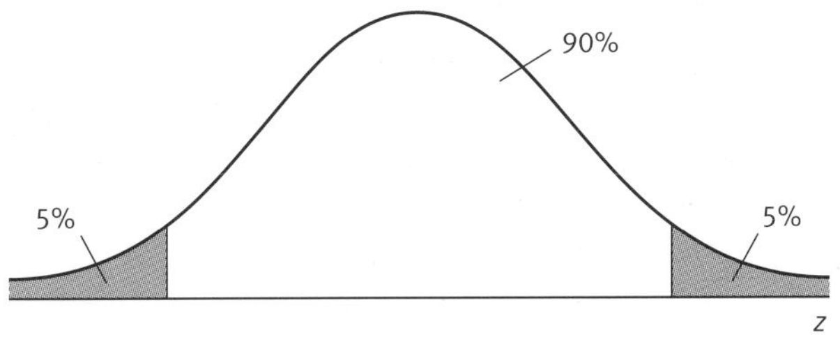

For a 95% confidence interval, 2.5% of the distribution would lie above the upper limit and 2.5% would lie below the lower limit.

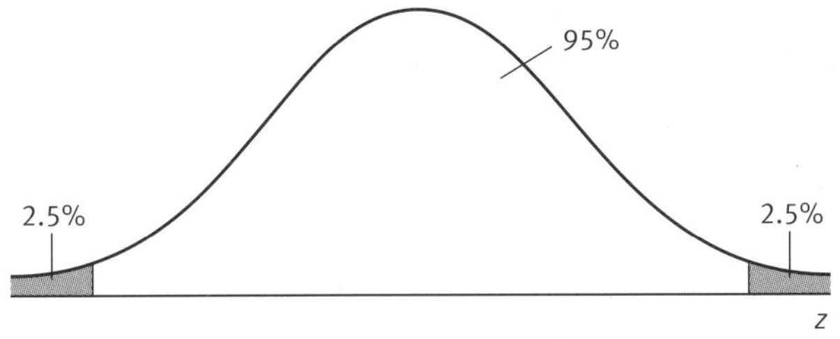

For a 99% confidence interval, 0.5% of the distribution would lie above the upper limit and 0.5% would lie below the lower limit.

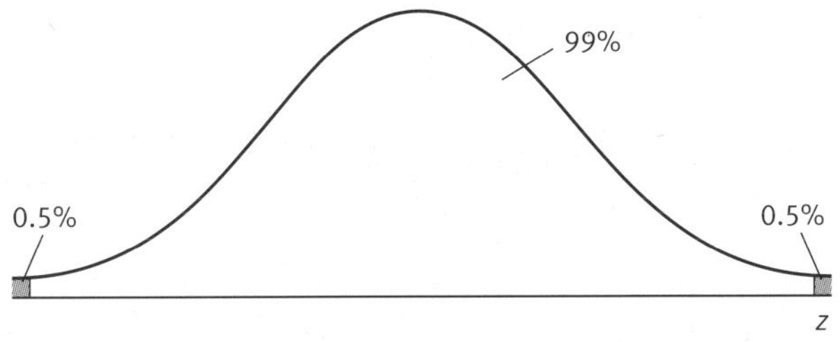

For any distribution of X with mean μ and variance σ^2, then, for samples of size n where n is large, the distribution of the sample mean, $\bar{X}$, is given by the central limit theorem as $\bar{X} \sim \mathrm{N}\left(\mu, \dfrac{\sigma^2}{n}\right)$ approximately.

For a 95% confidence interval, look up $p = 0.0250$ in the 'Percentage points of the normal distribution' table, which gives $z = 1.9600$, i.e.
$\mathrm{P}(Z > 1.9600) = 0.0250$
Therefore Z lies between -1.96 and 1.96 or, written mathematically, $-1.96 < Z < 1.96$.

The formula for standardising values of $\bar{X}$ is

$$Z = \frac{\bar{X} - \mu}{\sigma/\sqrt{n}}$$

$$\Rightarrow \quad -1.96 < \frac{\bar{X} - \mu}{\sigma/\sqrt{n}} < 1.96$$

Rearranging gives the 95% confidence interval for μ:

$$\bar{X} - 1.96\frac{\sigma}{\sqrt{n}} < \mu < \bar{X} + 1.96\frac{\sigma}{\sqrt{n}}$$

The width of a 95% confidence interval for μ is $2 \times 1.96\dfrac{\sigma}{\sqrt{n}}$

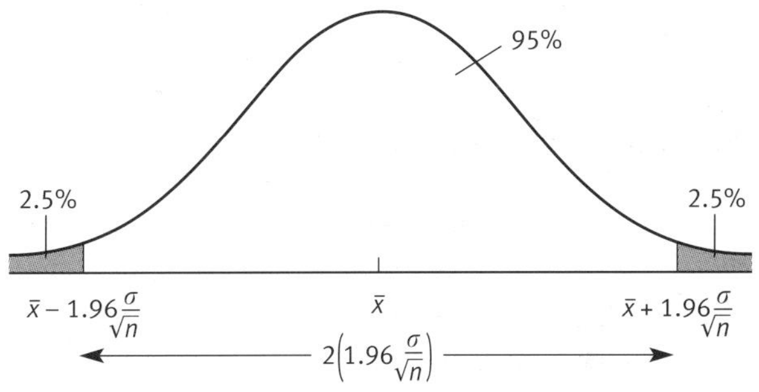

The 99% confidence interval for μ is:

$$\bar{X} - 2.5758\frac{\sigma}{\sqrt{n}} < \mu < \bar{X} + 2.5758\frac{\sigma}{\sqrt{n}}$$

The width of a 99% confidence interval is $2 \times 2.5758\dfrac{\sigma}{\sqrt{n}}$

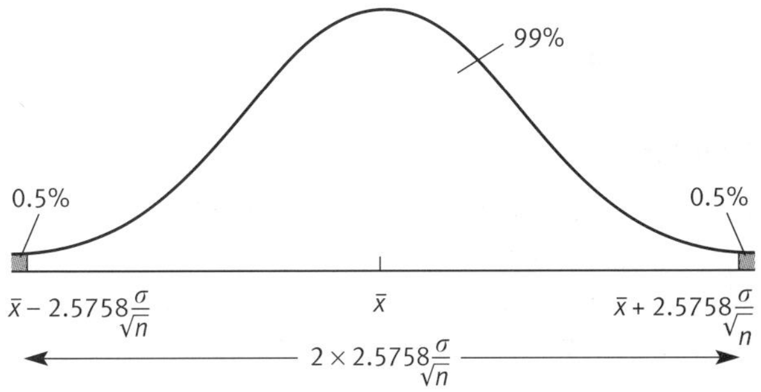

The 90% confidence interval for μ is:

$$\bar{X} - 1.645\frac{\sigma}{\sqrt{n}} < \mu < \bar{X} + 1.645\frac{\sigma}{\sqrt{n}}$$

The width of a 90% confidence interval is $2 \times 1.645\dfrac{\sigma}{\sqrt{n}}$

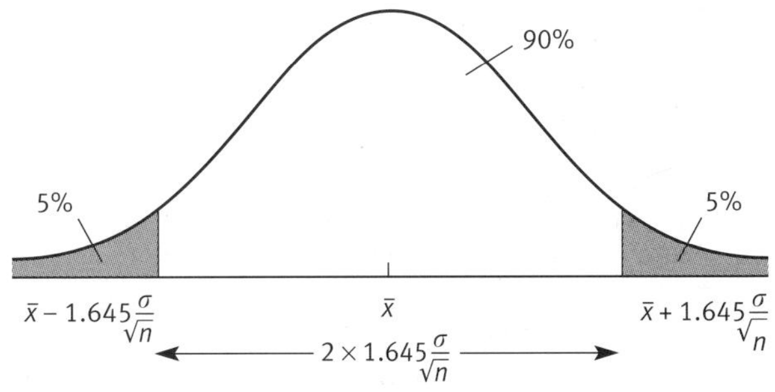

Interpreting the confidence interval

The mean, μ, is a fixed, but unknown, number. A 95% confidence interval means that there is a 95% probability that μ lies in this interval.

Finding the confidence level when the width of the confidence interval is known

When the width, w, is known, but the confidence level is not, $w = 2 \times z \times \dfrac{\sigma}{\sqrt{n}}$ from which you can find z and hence the confidence level.

Example

A random sample of size 36 is taken from a normal population with standard deviation of 2.4. The sample mean is 26.4.

a Find a 99% confidence interval for the population mean μ.
b What size sample is required to obtain a 99% confidence interval of width at most 2?

Solution

a Using $\bar{X} - 2.5758\dfrac{\sigma}{\sqrt{n}} < \mu < \bar{X} + 2.5758\dfrac{\sigma}{\sqrt{n}}$

$\Rightarrow \quad 25.37 < \mu < 27.43$

b The width of the confidence interval is

$2 \times 2.5758\dfrac{\sigma}{\sqrt{n}} \quad \Rightarrow \quad 2 \times 2.5758 \times \dfrac{2.4}{\sqrt{n}} \leqslant 2$

$\therefore \sqrt{n} \geqslant 6.18\ldots \quad \Rightarrow \quad n \geqslant 38.21\ldots \quad \Rightarrow \quad n = 39.$

Example

A sample of size 16 is taken from a normal distribution with standard deviation 15. The sample mean is 77.3. What confidence level would be associated with a symmetrical interval of width 8.1?

Solution

The width of the confidence interval is $2 \times z \times \dfrac{\sigma}{\sqrt{n}}$

$= 2 \times z \times \dfrac{15}{\sqrt{16}} = 8.1$

$z = 1.08$

$P(Z < 1.08) = 0.8599$

$P(-1.08 < Z < 1.08) = 0.8599 - (1 - 0.8599)$

$= 0.7198$

The confidence level is 72%. (2 sf)

Questions

1 It is known that the net contents of a tin of molasses from a certain production line have standard deviation 3.62 g.
A sample of size 150 is taken from the production line, and the net contents of the tins in the sample are found to have a mean weight of 456 g.

a Calculate a 99% confidence interval for the mean weight of the net contents of the tins.

b i Was it necessary for you to assume that the net weights of the tins are normally distributed?
Give a reason for answer.

ii What difference does it make if the net weights of the tins are normally distributed?

2 A normal population has variance 20.
Find the size of the smallest sample that could be taken from the population so that the symmetrical 95% confidence interval for the population mean has width of, at most, 4 units.

3 A sample of size 8 is taken from a normal population with standard deviation 2.8. The sample is shown below.

10.2, 12.6, 11.8, 12.0, 13.1, 11.3, 11.8, 10.9.

a Calculate a 90% confidence interval for the sample mean.

b What confidence level would be associated with a confidence interval of width 2.6?

Answers

1a (455.2, 456.8)

b i No because the central limit theorem can be used for large values of n and does not require the distribution to be normally distributed.

ii The distribution used in calculating the confidence interval is exact rather than approximate.

2 $2 \times 1.96 \times \dfrac{\sqrt{20}}{\sqrt{n}} \leqslant 4$

$n \geqslant 19.2\ldots$

$n = 20$

3a (10.08, 13.34)

b 81%

Confidence intervals for a small sample from a normal population when σ is unknown

When small samples of size n are taken from a normal population and the standard deviation of the population is not known, the distribution of the mean follows the t-distribution.

For large values of n, the t-distribution approximates to the normal distribution, but as n decreases, the distribution remains bell-shaped but becomes flatter and more spread out.

The shape of the curve depends upon the number of degrees of freedom, v, where $v = n - 1$.

The t-value is calculated using the formula

$$t_{n-1} = \frac{\bar{x} - \mu}{\hat{\sigma}/\sqrt{n}}$$

But as

$$\hat{\sigma} = s\sqrt{\left(\frac{n}{n-1}\right)}$$

where s is the standard deviation of the sample and $\hat{\sigma}$ is the unbiased estimator of the standard deviation of the population, the formula may be written as

$$t_{n-1} = \frac{\bar{x} - \mu}{s/\sqrt{n-1}}$$

Make sure that you know whether your tables for the t-distribution are for one- or two-tailed tests:

- if they are for one-tailed tests, halve the percentage of the distribution outside the confidence interval. e.g. for a 95% confidence interval, refer to the 2.5% probability column,
- if they are tabulated for two-tailed tests, look up the percentage of the distribution outside the confidence interval. e.g. for a 95% confidence interval, refer to the 5% column.

Example

Eight eggs are taken at random from a large batch from a poultry farm. Their masses, in grams, are found to be 50.6, 51.2, 52.6, 53.0, 54.0, 54.1, 54.8, 55.2. Assuming that the weights of the eggs form a normal distribution, find a 95% confidence interval for the mean mass of the eggs from the batch.

Solution

$x = 53.188$ (3 d.p.)

$s^2 = 2.396$ (3 d.p.)

$s = 1.548$ (3 d.p.)

The degrees of freedom $= v = n - 1 = 7$.

The tables for the t-distribution are usually given as the percentages *outside* the confidence intervals. In this example, for a 95% confidence interval with 7 degrees of freedom, look up the values corresponding to $v = 7$ under $P = 2.5$ for a one-tailed set of tables, giving $t_7 = 2.365$.

Using $t_{n-1} = \dfrac{\bar{x} - \mu}{s/\sqrt{n-1}}$,

$$-2.365 < \frac{53.188 - \mu}{1.548/\sqrt{7}} < 2.365$$

$-1.3837 < 53.188 - \mu < 1.3837$
$53.188 - 1.3837 < \mu < 53.188 + 1.3837$
$51.80 < \mu < 54.57$.

Exercise

The weights, in kilograms, of 5 male students aged 19 taken from a large normal population of male students of the same age are

65, 72, 77, 80, 69.

Find 95% confidence limits for the mean of the population. Give your answers to 3 significant figures.

Answers

As n is small and the standard deviation is unknown, use the t-distribution.

The confidence limits are $72.6 \pm 2.776 \times \dfrac{5.39}{\sqrt{4}} = (65.1, 80.1)$.

Take a break

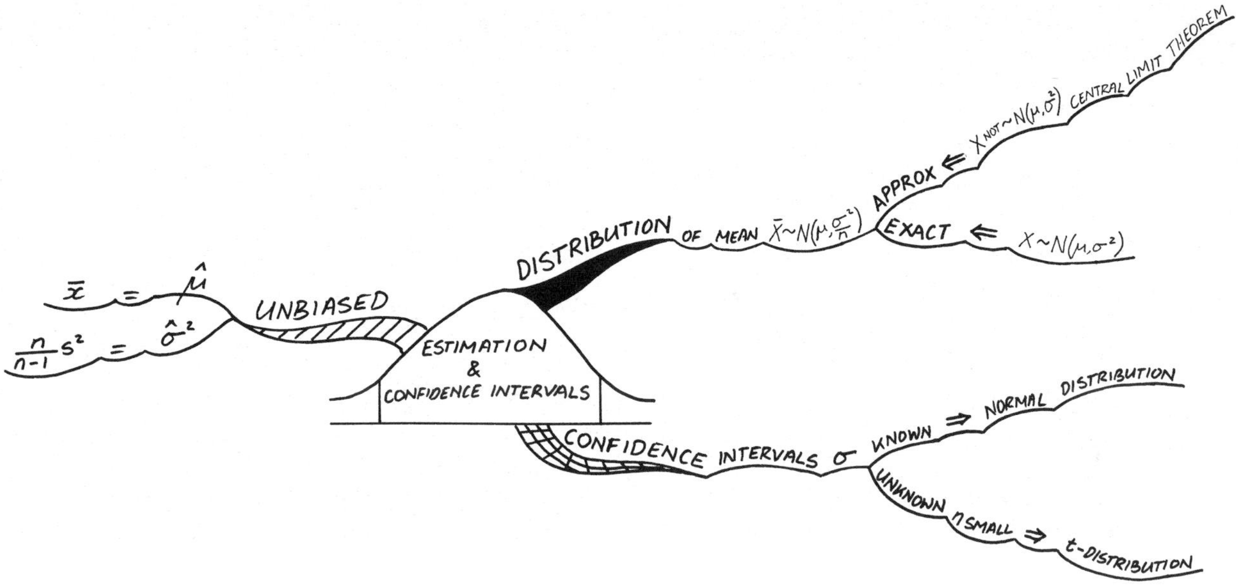

Review

1 A hamper contains 3 blocks of cheese and 10 baguettes. The weights of the empty hampers are normally distributed with mean 3000 g and standard deviation 120 g. The weights of the blocks of cheese are normally distributed with mean 500 g and standard deviation 80 g. The weight of the baguettes is a normal random variable with mean 600 g and standard deviation 60 g.

a Find the mean and standard deviation, in grams, of the weight of a full hamper.

b Find, to 3 decimal places, the probability that the total weight of the full hamper lies between 10 kg and 11 kg.

2 It is known that 4% of a population suffer from a certain genetic disorder. Using a suitable approximation, find the probability that less than 6 people out of a sample of 100 have the disorder.

3 The random variable x is normally distributed with mean μ and standard deviation σ. Given that $P(X < 2.5) = 0.0869$ and $P(X > 6.8) = 0.0301$. Find μ and σ.

4 The weight of bags of Tweazers sweets is normally distributed with a mean of 155 g and standard deviation 10 g. Find the probability that the mean weight of a random sample of 25 bags exceeds 156 g.

5 Calculate unbiased estimates for
i the mean
ii the variance of the population from which the following sample was taken:
28.8, 29.6, 30.2, 30.4, 27.6, 29.3, 28.6.

6 A random sample of size 36 is taken from a population that is normally distributed with standard deviation 4.2. The mean of the sample is 28.6.

a i Find a symmetric 95% confidence interval for the population mean μ.
ii What confidence level would be associated with the interval (26.7, 30.5)?

b What size sample is required to obtain a 95% confidence interval of width no greater than 2.2?

7 In order to investigate the weights of apples from a large orchard, ten apples were selected at random. Their weights, in grams, were 134, 150, 155, 144, 168, 129, 140, 151, 170 and 167.

a Use this sample to find a symmetrical 95% confidence interval for the mean length of components in the batch.

b State one assumption that you need to make.

Answers

1a mean $= 10\,500$, standard deviation $= \sqrt{69\,600}$

b 0.942

2 Let X be the number of people that suffer from the disorder. As $np < 5$ and $n \geqslant 50$, approximate using the Poisson distribution.
$X \sim \text{Po}(4)$ approx.
$\text{P}(X < 6) = 0.7851$.

3 $\mu = 4.30$ $\sigma = 1.33$.

4 0.3085 (4 d.p.)

5 **i** 29.2 (3 s.f.)
ii 0.948 (3 s.f.)

6a **i** (27.23, 29.97)
ii 99.3%

b 57

7a $150.8 \pm 2.262 \times \dfrac{13.659}{\sqrt{9}} = (140.5, 161.1)$

b As the t-distribution has been used, the weights of the apples are assumed to be normally distributed.

PREVIEW

By the end of this topic you will have revised:

- ✔ **the null and alternative hypotheses,**
- ✔ **hypothesis testing for the mean of a normal distribution both when σ is known and when σ is unknown,**
- ✔ **hypothesis testing for the difference between means of two independent normal distributions,**
- ✔ **hypothesis testing for the proportion of a binomial distribution, p,**
- ✔ **hypothesis testing for the mean of a Poisson distribution, λ.**

Before you start you should:

- know how to calculate cumulative probabilities using the binomial and Poisson distributions,
- know how to calculate probabilities using the normal distribution,
- know the meaning of the null and alternative hypotheses,
- know what one- and two-tailed tests are,
- know what the critical region is,
- understand and know how to use the central limit theorem,
- know how and when to use the *t*-distribution.

TEST YOURSELF

Any wrong answers, see Statistics 6, 7 or 8 or an A level text book for information and practice

1 The random variable $X \sim B(20, 0.4)$. Find
  a) $P(X \geqslant 8)$,
  b) $P(X < 4)$.

2 The random variable $Y \sim \text{Po}(6)$ Find
  a) $P(Y > 8)$,
  b) $P(Y \leqslant 5)$.

3 The random variable $C \sim N(35.5, 2.5^2)$. Find
  a) $P(C > 34.3)$,
  b) $P(33.6 < C < 35.1)$.

4 The random variable X has mean 25.6 and variance 16. A random sample of size 25 is taken from the distribution.
  a) Write down the distribution of the sample mean $\bar{X}$.
  b) What difference does it make to $\bar{X}$ if X has a normal distribution?

5 The diameters of 8 wooden poles are measured and found to have a mean of 4.15 cm and a standard deviation of 0.12 cm. Calculate a 99% confidence interval for the mean diameter of the population from which these poles are drawn, given that the distribution is normal.

6 An athlete claims that her average running time to complete the marathon is 3 hours. Her trainer claims that her mean time is longer than this.
  a) Write down null and alternative hypotheses for her mean running time, μ hours.
  b) Is the hypothesis test one- or two-tailed?

Answers

1a 0.5841 **b** 0.0160
2a 0.1528 **b** 0.4457
3a 0.6844 **b** 0.2128
4a $\bar{X} \sim N(25.6, 0.64)$ approximately
b $\bar{X} \sim N(25.6, 0.64)$ exactly
5 (4.04, 4.26)
6a $H_0: \mu = 3$ $H_1: \mu > 3$ **b** One-tailed.

Hypothesis testing

Two hypotheses are proposed: the null hypothesis, H_0, and the alternative hypothesis, H_1. The null hypothesis is assumed to be true, while the alternative hypothesis has to be shown to be true 'beyond reasonable doubt'. You can never be 100% sure that either the null or alternative hypothesis is true: a significance level should be used to show the level of certainty that your choice of hypothesis is correct. For example, if a 5% significance level is chosen and the alternative hypothesis is chosen, then you are 95% sure that you are right in rejecting the null hypothesis.

One- and two-tailed tests, critical value and critical region

If you take the hypothesis that the mean of a normal distribution is 100 and are asked to test whether it is in fact greater than 100, then the test is a one-tailed test. The null and alternative hypotheses are;

$$H_0: \mu = 100, \ H_1: \mu > 100$$

The test is only examining values of μ in one direction, so it is called a **one-tailed test**. The region of values of X or Z for which the null hypothesis, H_0 is rejected is known as the **critical region**. The boundary of the critical region is the **critical value**.

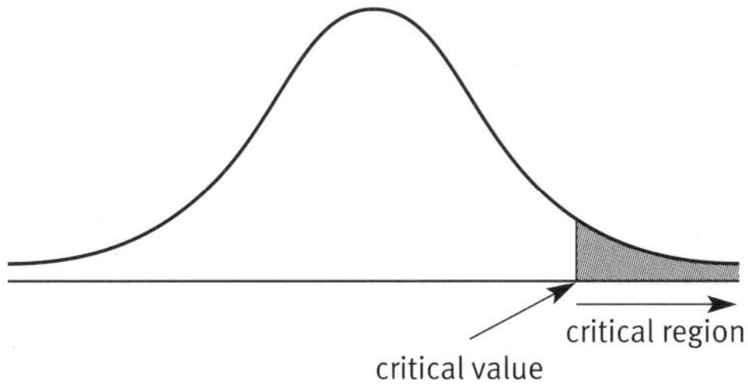

If the significance level is 5%, then the shaded area under the graph represents a probability of 0.05.

The test of the null and alternative hypotheses H_0: $\mu = 100$, H_1: $\mu < 100$ is also a one-tailed test.

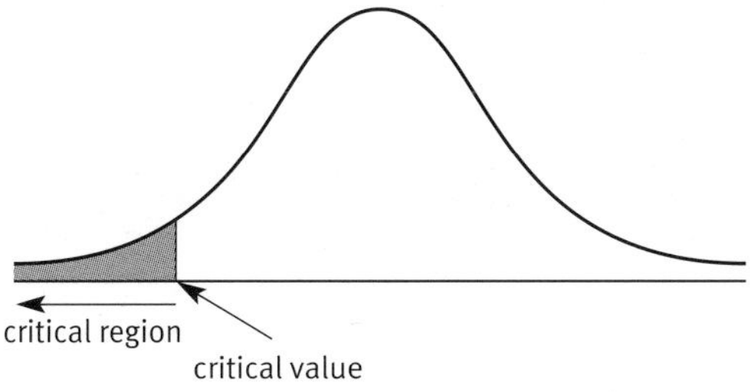

A **two-tailed test** is one where the alternative hypothesis specifies neither greater than nor less than a given value, e.g. H_0: $\mu = 100$, H_1: $\mu \neq 100$
For a two-tailed test, the level of significance is usually split equally over both tails. For example, for a 5% significance level, the area under each tail is 2.5%:

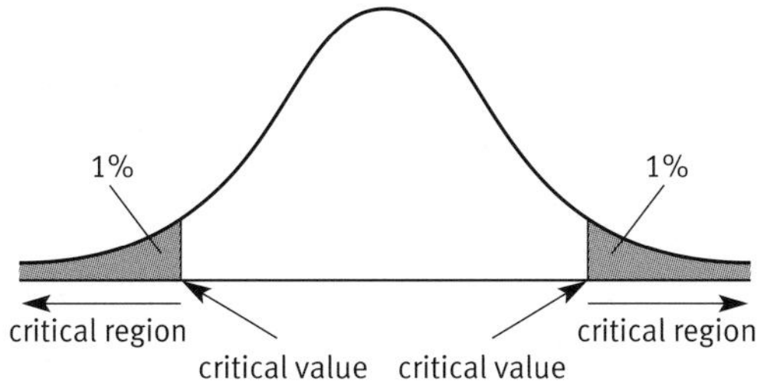

Hypothesis test for the mean of a normal distribution when σ is known

The mean of X is distributed normally, i.e.
$\bar{X} \sim N\left(\mu, \dfrac{\sigma^2}{n}\right)$

Example

The distribution of the net weight of a can of baked beans by a certain manufacturer is normal, with a mean of 400 g and a standard deviation of 5 g. A random sample of 60 cans from a new batch was weighed and the mean net weight was found to be 401.3 g. Assuming that the standard deviation has not changed and that the net weights of the new batch were also normally distributed, test, at the 5% level, whether there is evidence that the mean net weight of the new batch is more than 400 g.

Solution

H_0: $\mu = 400$
H_1: $\mu > 400$

The diagram below shows the one-tailed test for a 5% significance level.

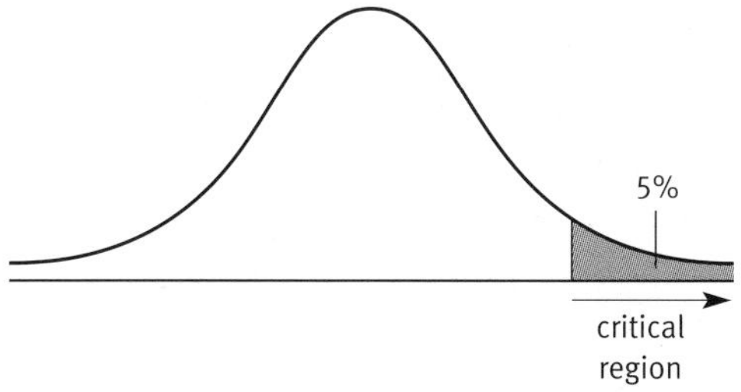

Let $\bar{X}$ be the mean weight of a can of baked beans.
$\bar{X} \sim N\left(400, \dfrac{5^2}{60}\right)$
From the 'Percentage points of a normal distribution' table, the critical region is $Z > 1.6449$. There are various methods in which to perform this significance test: three are shown below.

Method 1: comparing the values of *z*

The z value for the sample mean is

$$z = \frac{401.3 - 400}{5/\sqrt{60}} = 2.01 \text{ (2 dp)}$$

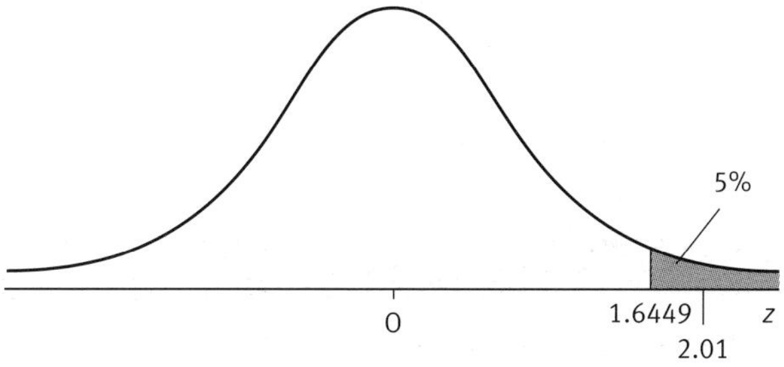

As this is bigger than the critical value of 1.6449, reject H_0 and accept H_1: there is evidence to show that the mean has risen.

Method 2: comparing probabilities

An alternative method is to find the probability that the mean is greater than 401.3 g. If this probability is less than the significance level, reject H_0, if it is greater, then accept H_0.

$$P(\bar{X} > 401.3) = P(Z > 2.01) = 1 - 0.978 = 0.022$$

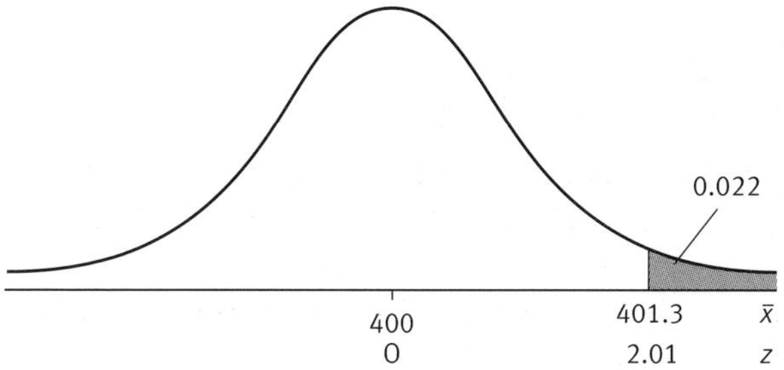

As this is less than the significance level, 5%, reject H_0.

Method 3: comparing the critical values of $\bar{X}$

The critical region for Z is $Z > 1.6449$

$$\frac{\bar{X} - 400}{5/\sqrt{60}} > 1.6449$$

$$\bar{X} > 401.06$$

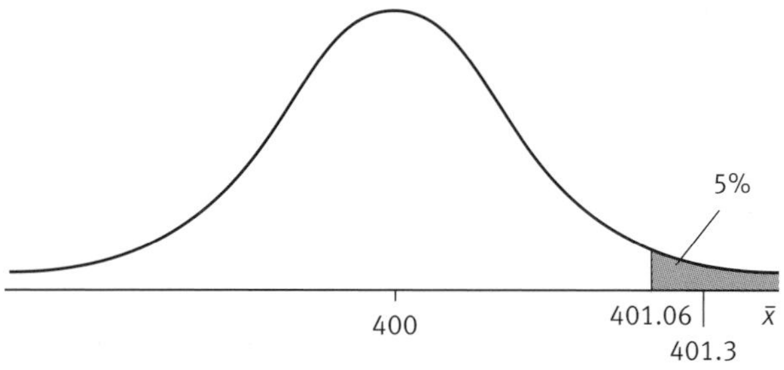

As the mean weight of the new batch is greater than 401.06, reject the null hypothesis, H_0.

Example

The maximum tension, in Newtons, that a certain make of elastic band can take, follows a normal distribution of mean 60 and standard deviation 5.8. A random sample of 90 elastic bands from a new batch is taken, to test whether the mean of the new batch has changed from 60 N. The mean maximum tension of the 90 elastic bands is 61.3 N. Test, at the 2% level, whether or not there is evidence that the mean has changed. (Assume that the standard deviation is unchanged.)

Solution

This is a two-tailed test as the question asks for a test of whether the mean has changed.

H_0: $\mu = 60$

H_1: $\mu \neq 60$

Since the critical region is split into two equal parts, each part should have a probability of 1%.

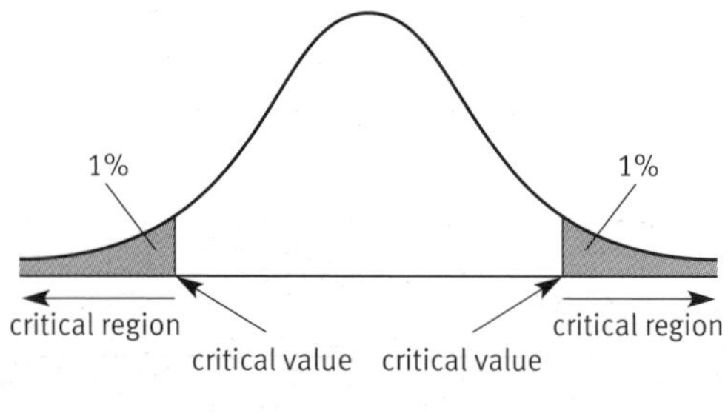

Method 1: Comparing values of z

From the 'Percentage points of the normal distribution' table, the critical region of Z is $Z < -2.3263$ or $Z > 2.3263$.

Standardising the mean of the sample,

$$z = \frac{61.3 - 60}{5.8/\sqrt{90}} = 2.126$$

This is not in the critical region and therefore there is not sufficient evidence to reject H_0.

Method 2: Comparing probabilities

Let X be the maximum tension, in Newtons, of the elastic bands.

$P(\bar{X} > 61.3) = P(Z > 2.13) = 1 - 0.9834 = 0.0166$

As this probability is greater that 1%, accept H_0.

Method 3: Comparing the critical values of $\bar{X}$

The upper tail of the critical region is $Z > 2.326$

$$\frac{\bar{X} - 60}{5.8/\sqrt{90}} > 2.326$$

$$\bar{X} > 61.42$$

As 61.42 is not in the critical region, accept H_0.

Questions

1 A certain brand of jam is sold in jars. The net weight of the jam, in grams, follows a normal distribution of mean μ and standard deviation 5. The manufacturer claims that the population mean, μ, is 355 g. In order to test his claim, a sample of 20 jars was taken and the mean net weight of jam was found to be 353.3 g. Stating your hypotheses clearly, test at the 5% level whether or not there is evidence to show that the value of μ is lower than 355 g.

2 The times taken for a car to accelerate from 0 to 100 kmh^{-1} are normally distributed with mean 8.6 seconds and a standard deviation of 0.6 seconds. An oil company claims to have developed an additive for petrol that will increase the car's performance. The car was then tested 20 times and the mean acceleration time was 8.35 seconds. Test at the 10% level whether or not there is evidence of a change in the car's performance.

Answers

1 H_0: $\mu = 355$

H_1: $\mu < 355$

If X is the weight of jam in a jar in grams,

$P(\bar{X} < 353.3) = 0.0642$ (4 d.p.)

Accept H_0 at the 5% significance level.

Any one of the given methods may be used in the hypothesis test, but only one has been shown.

2 H_0: $\mu = 8.6$

H_1: $\mu \neq 8.6$

Let X be the acceleration time of the car.

$P(\bar{X} < 8.35) = 0.031$ (3 d.p.)

As this is a two-tailed test, and $0.03 < 0.05$, reject H_0 at the 10% level.

Hypothesis test for the mean of a normal distribution when σ is unknown

When σ is unknown and a small sample is taken from a large normal population, use the t-distribution to perform the hypothesis test.

Example

The owner of Crusties Bakery describes their cottage loaves as having a mean weight of 550 g. After employing a new head baker, a sample of 10 loaves were found to have the following weights, in grams: 560, 552, 549, 555, 559, 557, 562, 563, 557, 560. Assuming the population distribution to be normal, test whether the sample mean is significantly different from the claimed mean of 550 g. Use a 5% significance level.

Solution

H_0: $\mu = 550$
H_1: $\mu \neq 550$
First find the sample mean and variance:

$\bar{x} = 557.4$
$s^2 = 17.44$
$s = \sqrt{17.44} = 4.176$ (3 d.p)

As $n = 10$, the degrees of freedom, v, is 9.

Method 1: Comparing the calculated value of t with the critical value

Find the value of t using the formula

$$t_{n-1} = \frac{\bar{x} - \mu}{s/\sqrt{n-1}} \Rightarrow t_9 = \frac{557.4 - 550}{4.176/\sqrt{9}} \Rightarrow t_9 = 5.32$$

Compare this value with the critical value for a two-tailed test at 5% significance level with 9 degrees of freedom which is 2.26.
As 5.32 is in the critical region, reject H_0 at the 5% significance level.

Method 2: Comparing with the confidence interval

Using

$$t_{n-1} = \frac{\bar{x} - \mu}{s/\sqrt{n-1}}$$

$$-2.26 < \frac{557.4 - \mu}{4.176/\sqrt{9}} < 2.26$$

$$557.4 - \frac{2.26 \times 4.176}{\sqrt{9}} < \mu < 557.4 + \frac{2.26 \times 4.176}{\sqrt{9}}$$

$$554.3 < \mu < 560.5$$

$\mu = 550$ and is outside the confidence interval, so reject H_0.

Example

The number of nails in a sample of 7 bags of nails from the output of a filling machine is found to have a mean of 64 and a standard deviation of 2. Given that the number of nails in a bag is normally distributed, test whether the sample mean is significantly greater than 60, at which the mean is meant to be set. Use a 5% level of significance.

Solution

H_0: $\mu = 60$
H_1: $\mu > 60$
$v = n - 1 = 6 \Rightarrow$ critical value of t is 1.943 for a one-tailed test.

$$t_{n-1} = \frac{\bar{x} - \mu}{s/\sqrt{n-1}} \quad \Rightarrow \quad t_6 = \frac{64 - 60}{2/\sqrt{6}} = 4.90 \text{ (2 d.p.)}$$

Therefore reject H_0 at the 5% level.

Questions

1 A saleswoman claims that the rulers she is selling have a mean breaking force of 100 N. The manager of a large stationery store tests the claim using a random sample of 8 rulers. The breaking forces, in Newtons, are shown below.

98.3, 102.4, 104.4, 96.7, 95.2, 88.6, 89.3, 91.5.

Using a two-tailed test, test the saleswoman's claim at the 5% level of significance.

2 It is known that the length of adult males of a certain species of snake is normally distributed with mean of 1.4 m. A colony of the species of snake was discovered on an island. A sample of 10 of the snakes from the island was found to have a mean length of 1.55 m and a sample variance of 1.2 m^2. Use a 5% significance level to test whether the population mean is greater than 1.4 m.

Answers

1 H_0: $\mu = 100$
H_1: $\mu \neq 100$
$t_7 = \frac{95.8 - 100}{5.449/\sqrt{7}} = -2.039$ (3 d.p.)
The critical value of $t_7 = 2.365$.
As $2.039 < 2.365$, accept the saleswoman's claim at the 5% level.

2 H_0: $\mu = 1.4$
H_1: $\mu > 1.4$
$t_9 = \frac{1.55 - 1.4}{\sqrt{1.2/9}} = 0.411$ (3 d.p.)
Critical value of $t_9 = 1.833$ for a one-tailed test at 5%, so accept H_0.

Testing for difference between the means of two independent normal distributions

From the earlier section on linear combinations of independent random variables, if $X_1 \sim N(\mu_1, \sigma_1^2)$, and $X_2 \sim N(\mu_2, \sigma_2^2)$, then $X_1 - X_2 \sim N(\mu_1 - \mu_2, \sigma_1^2 + \sigma_2^2)$.

Similarly if $\bar{X}_1 \sim N\left(\mu_1, \frac{\sigma_1^2}{n_1}\right)$, and

$$\bar{X}_2 \sim N\left(\mu_2, \frac{\sigma_2^2}{n_2}\right), \text{ then}$$

$$\bar{X}_1 - \bar{X}_2 \sim N\left(\mu_1 - \mu_2, \frac{\sigma_1^2}{n_1} + \frac{\sigma_2^2}{n_2}\right)$$

To test for the difference between the means, the null hypothesis is that $\mu_1 - \mu_2 = 0$, i.e. there is no difference, so $\bar{X}_1 - \bar{X}_2 \sim N\left(0, \frac{\sigma_1^2}{n_1} + \frac{\sigma_2^2}{n_2}\right)$

To use the test, first standardise using the formula

$$z = \frac{\bar{x}_1 - \bar{x}_2}{\sqrt{\frac{\sigma_1^2}{n_1} + \frac{\sigma_2^2}{n_2}}}$$

then compare this value of z with the critical value and accept or reject H_0 accordingly.

Example

The times taken by children to complete an egg-and-spoon race are normally distributed with standard deviation of 12 s. A random sample of 30 children from school A took part in the race and their mean time was 56.3 s. The mean time from a random sample of 35 children from school B was 60.4 s. The P.E. teacher from school B claimed that the children from her school must have a higher mean than that of school A. Given that the two samples were independent, test the P.E. teacher's claim at the 5% level.

Solution

Let X_1 and X_2 be the time, in seconds, for children from school A and school B to complete the task.

$\bar{X}_1 \sim N\left(\mu_1, \frac{12^2}{30}\right)$, and $\bar{X}_2 \sim N\left(\mu_2, \frac{12^2}{35}\right)$, then

$\bar{X}_2 - \bar{X}_1 \sim N\left(\mu_2 - \mu_1, \frac{12^2}{30} + \frac{12^2}{35}\right)$.

If H_0: $\mu_2 = \mu_1$ then $\bar{X}_2 - \bar{X}_1 \sim N(0, 8.91)$

H_1: $\mu_2 > \mu_1$

Using a one tailed test and comparing values of z: the critical region is $Z > 1.6449$ (at 5%).

$$z = \frac{60.4 - 56.3}{\sqrt{\frac{12^2}{30} + \frac{12^2}{35}}} = 1.37$$

Accept H_0 as the test value of z is not significant.

Question

An experiment was conducted to test whether or not a new variety of carrot was longer than the current variety grown by a farmer.

In the experiment, 120 carrots were tested from each of the two varieties. It was found that the new variety had a mean length of 22.1 cm with a standard deviation of 3.6, while the other variety had a mean length of 20.6 cm and a standard deviation of 2.9 cm.

The lengths of the carrots of the two varieties were both normally distributed and independent.

Using a 5% significance level, test whether or not the mean length for the new variety of carrot is greater than that for the currently grown variety. State your hypotheses clearly.

Answer

H_0: the means are equal

H_1: the mean for the new variety is greater than the mean for the current variety

$$z = \frac{22.1 - 20.6}{\sqrt{\frac{3.6^2}{120} + \frac{2.9^2}{120}}} = 3.55$$

The 5% critical region for Z is $Z > 1.6449$, so reject H_0.

Type I and type II errors

When performing hypothesis tests, H_0 may be rejected when it is true, or accepted when it is not true.

A Type I error occurs if H_0 is rejected when it is true,
i.e. P(Type I error) = P(reject $H_0 | H_0$ is true).

A Type II error occurs if H_0 is accepted when H_1 is true,
i.e. P(Type II error) = P(accept $H_0 | H_1$ is true).

Example

The lifetime, in hours, of Eternal batteries when used in a personal stereo is distributed normally with a mean of 10.7 hours and a standard deviation of 1.2 hours. Twenty-five batteries are sampled from a new batch to test whether there has been any improvement in the mean lifetime of the batteries.

a i Find the critical region for the test statistic $\bar{X}$, the mean lifetime of the batteries in the personal stereo, using a 1% level of significance.

ii Write down the probability of making a Type I error using this critical value.

b Given that the true value for μ for the new batch is 11.1 hours, find the probability of a Type II error.

Solution

a i H_0: $\mu = 10.7$

H_1: $\mu > 10.7$

The 1% critical region for Z is $Z > 2.3263$, so to find the critical region for $\bar{X}$, use

$$\frac{\bar{X} - 10.7}{1.2/\sqrt{25}} > 2.3263$$

$\bar{X} > 11.258$

ii Start by writing the definition of a Type I error:

$$\begin{aligned} \text{P(Type I error)} &= \text{P(reject } H_0 | H_0 \text{ is true)} \\ &= \text{P}(\bar{X} > 11.258 | \mu = 10.5) \\ &= 0.01 \end{aligned}$$

b The true mean is actually 11.1, so

$$\bar{X} \sim \text{N}\left(11.1, \frac{1.2^2}{\sqrt{25}}\right)$$

Start by writing the definition of a Type II error:

$$\begin{aligned} \text{P(Type II error)} &= \text{P(accept } H_0 | H_1 \text{ is true)} \\ &= \text{P}(\bar{X} < 11.258 | \mu = 11.1) \\ &= \text{P}\left(Z < \frac{11.258 - 11.1}{1.2/\sqrt{25}}\right) \\ &= \text{P}(Z < 0.66) = 0.745. \end{aligned}$$

Hypothesis test for the proportion of a binomial distribution, p

The parameter p is the proportion of the binomial distribution.

Example

When a person contracts a certain type of rash, the probability that it clears up without treatment is 0.45. A new cream is developed, and, when 20 people with the disease are treated with it, the rash clears up on 14 people. The producer of the cream claims that it is an improvement over no treatment.

a Investigate the claim at the 5% level.

b Write down the probability of a Type I error occurring.

Solution

a H_0: $p = 0.45$

H_1: $p > 0.45$

Let X be the number of patients who are cured from the rash.

$X \sim \text{B}(20, 0.45)$

$\text{P}(X \geqslant 14) = 1 - \text{P}(X \leqslant 13) = 1 - 0.9786 = 0.0214$

As this is less than 5%, reject H_0 and conclude that the producer's claim is true at the 5% level of significance.

b As $X \geqslant 14$ is the critical region ($\text{P}(X \geqslant 13) = 0.0580$ so this is not in the critical region),

$$\begin{aligned} \text{P(Type I error)} &= \text{P(reject } H_0 | H_1 \text{ is true)} \\ &= \text{P}(X \geqslant 14 | p = 0.45) \\ &= 0.0214. \end{aligned}$$

The probability of a Type I error occurring is $\text{P}(X \geqslant 14) = 0.0214$.

For large values of n, the distribution of X can be approximated as $X \sim \text{N}\left(p, \frac{pq}{n}\right)$

Hypothesis test for the mean of a Poisson distribution, λ

Example

The number of people buying a luxury car from one franchise was found to average 9 per month. In the month following an advertising campaign, the sales rose to 14 cars. Using a 5% level of significance, investigate whether there has been a change in the mean number of sales.

Solution

H_0: $\lambda = 9$

H_1: $\lambda \neq 9$ (a two-tailed test)

Let X be the number of sales in a month.

$X \sim \text{Po}(9)$

$\text{P}(X \geqslant 14) = 1 - \text{P}(X \leqslant 13) = 1 - 0.9261 = 0.0739$

Since the test is two-tailed, the probability should be compared to 2.5%. As it is greater than 2.5%, accept H_0 at the 5% level of significance.

Questions

1 The transport department of Chalkham Council observed that, during weekday lunchtimes, the average number of vehicles travelling down a side street, X, was 9.5 per 5 minutes. After a traffic-calming scheme was introduced, the average number per 5 minutes had reduced to 4. Test, at the 5% level, whether or not the number of vehicles using the side street over weekday lunchtimes had decreased.

2 A student was studying the number X, of telephone calls she received per day. She modelled the number of calls as a Poisson distribution. She tested the null hypothesis that the mean was 6 against the alternative hypothesis that the mean was greater than 6. Using the observation of just one day, she decided that the critical region was 11 or more.

a Calculate the probability of a Type I error.

b Given that the mean was 9 telephone calls per day, find the probability of a Type II error.

3 Every morning, a pupil is given 20 mental arithmetic questions. Over a long period of time, it is found that the probability of him getting a question correct is 0.35. After a weeklong holiday, he is given 20 mental arithmetic questions to test whether there has been a change in his performance.

a Find the critical values for a two-tailed test using a 5% significance level, with each 'tail' being less than 2.5%.

b Determine the actual significance level of this critical region.

4 A manufacturer claims that the burning times of candles produced by his factory is 6.6 hours. The burning time of a candle has a normal distribution with standard deviation 0.4 hours. He takes a random sample of 25 candles from each batch produced. Using a 5% significance level, find the critical values of the mean of the sample that would determine whether or not he rejects the batch. Give your answer to 2 decimal places.

Answers

1 $P(X \leqslant 4) = 0.0403$

This is significant (i.e. less than 5%), so there is evidence of a decrease.

2a P(Type I error) = P(reject H_0/H_0 is true)

$= P(X \geqslant 11/\mu = 6)$

$= 0.0426$

b P(Type II error) = P(accept H_0/H_1 is true)

$= P(X \leqslant 10/\mu = 9)$

$= 0.7060$

3a $X \leqslant 2, X \geqslant 12$

b $P(X \leqslant 2) + P(X \geqslant 12) = 0.0121 + 0.0196$

$= 0.0317$ (4 d.p.)

The significance level is approximately 3.2%

4 (6.44, 6.76) (2 d.p.)

Take a break

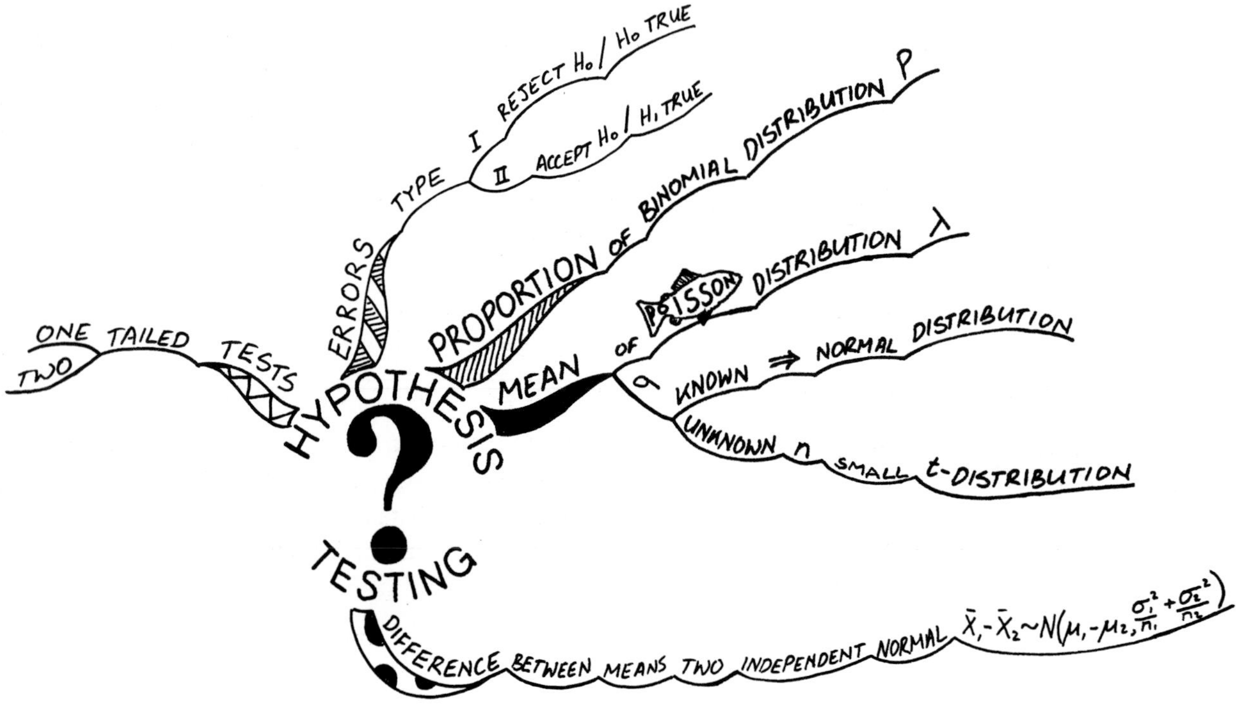

Review

1 The random variable M is defined as

$$M = \sum_{i=1}^{3} B_i + 2C$$

where B_1, B_2, B_3 and C are independent and $B_i \sim \text{N}(8, 6^2)$ and $C \sim \text{N}(10, 4^2)$. Find

a $\text{E}(M)$, **b** $\text{Var}(M)$, **c** $\text{P}(M > 48)$.

2 The number of mistakes made by a data-entry temp per page follows a Poisson distribution with parameter 5.

a Find the probability that she makes less than 5 mistakes on a page.

b Find the probability that, on a ten page letter, exactly four pages contain less than 5 mistakes.

c Using a suitable approximation, find the probability that she makes more than 34 mistakes on an eight page document.

3 A quality controller for a large sandwich-making company weighs the cheese in one ploughman's sandwich each day for a total of 25 days. He recorded the weight, x grams. His results are summarised as follows:

$n = 25 \quad \Sigma x = 1950 \qquad \Sigma x^2 = 153\,700.$

Calculate unbiased estimates of

i the mean and

ii the variance of the weight of the sandwiches.

4 The lengths, in cm, of the petals of a flower are known to be normally distributed with standard deviation 0.74 cm. A sample of 30 flowers is found to have a mean of 5.5 cm.

a Estimate the standard error of the mean.

b Find a 95% confidence interval for the mean length of the population of flower petals.

c Find the minimum size of the sample of leaves which must be taken if the width of the symmetrical 99% confidence interval for the population mean is at most 0.34.

5 A computer school runs Saturday classes that contain a maximum of 10 people. Over a long period of time, it is found that the ratio of women to men is 9 to 11. On one Saturday a full class contains only 2 men. Carry out a significance test to determine whether the proportion of women attending is greater than usual. State clearly your null and alternative hypotheses, and use a 5% significance level.

6 The number of purchases of an expensive sports car at a dealership has a Poisson distribution with mean 3.5 per month. In the month following an advertising campaign the mean number of sales was found to be 7 per month.

a Test, at the 5% level, whether or not the mean number of sales has risen.

b Find the probability of a Type I error.

c Given that the mean after the campaign is in fact 8.5, find the probability of a Type II error.

7 A company manufactures tyres at two plants. The standard deviation of the durability of the tyres is known to be 1255 and 1745 miles from plants A and B respectively. A random sample of 15 tyres from plant A has a mean life of 32,300 miles and a random sample of 18 tyres from plant B has a mean life of 30,200 miles. Assuming that the lives of the tyres follow a normal distribution, test, at the 5% level, whether or not the plants are producing tyres of the same mean life.

Answers

1a 44

b $3\ \text{Var}(B) + 2^2\text{Var}(C) = 172$ (see page 197)

c 0.380 (3 d.p.).

2a 0.4405 (4 d.p.)

b ${}^{10}C_4(0.4405)^4(1 - 0.4405)^6 = 0.2426$ (4 d.p.)

c In an eight page document, $\lambda = 40$.

If X is the number of mistakes in an eight page document, then $X \sim N(40, 40)$ approx.

$P(X > 34) \approx P(X > 34.5)$ using continuity correction

$= 0.808$ (3 d.p.).

3i 78

ii 64

4a 0.135 (3 d.p.)

b $5.24 < \mu < 5.76$

c 126.

5 $H_0: p = \frac{9}{20} = 0.45$

$H_1: p > 0.45$

Let X be the number of women in the class.

$P(X \geqslant 8) = 0.0274$ (4 d.p.), so reject H_0

6 Let X be the number of sales per month.

a $H_0: \lambda = 3.5$

$H_1: \lambda > 3.5$

$P(X \geqslant 7) = 0.0653$ (4 d.p.)

Accept H_0.

b The smallest value of n for which $P(X \geqslant n)$ is less than 0.05 is 8.

So the critical region (when H_0 is rejected) is $X \geqslant 8$.

$P(X \geqslant 8/\lambda = 3.5) = 0.0267$ (4 d.p.)

c $P(X \leqslant 7/\lambda = 8.5) = 0.3856$ (4 d.p.).

7 $$z = \frac{32\,300 - 30\,200}{\sqrt{\frac{1255^2}{15} + \frac{1745^2}{18}}} = 4.01 \text{ (2 d.p.)}$$

As the critical region for a two-tailed 5% significance test is $Z > 1.96$, there is evidence to show a difference between means.

PREVIEW

By the end of this topic you will have revised:

- ✔ **how to use the χ^2 test to test for goodness-of-fit of a given table of data to a theoretical model,**
- ✔ **how the number of degrees of freedom is affected if the mean and/or variance are estimated from the data,**
- ✔ **using the χ^2 test to test for independence of factors in a contingency table,**
- ✔ **Yates' continuity correction.**

Before you start you should:

- be able to calculate probabilities using the binomial distribution,
- be able to calculate probabilities using the Poisson distribution,
- be able to calculate probabilities using the normal distribution.

TEST YOURSELF

For wrong answers on question 1, 2, 3 or 4 see Statistics 3, 7, 8 or 9 respectively; alternatively refer to an A level text book for further information and practice.

1 a) The random variable $X \sim B(10, 0.4)$.
i) Calculate $P(X = 3)$.
ii) Find the mean and variance of X.
b) The random variable $Y \sim Po(5)$.
i) Calculate $P(Y = 6)$.
ii) Write down the mean and variance of Y.

2 The random variable $C \sim N(45, 16)$. Find $P(42 < C < 47.5)$

Answers

1 a) i) 0.215 (3 d.p.) **ii)** mean = 4; variance = 2.4
b) i) 0.146 (3 d.p.) **ii)** mean = variance = 5
2 0.5074 (4 d.p.)

The χ^2 distribution (called kye-squared) is used to test

- how well a given distribution fits a theoretical distribution
- whether two factors are independent of each other.

Testing for the goodness-of-fit

1 Determine the most appropriate distribution to use with the given data.

2 If necessary, calculate parameters.

3 Null and alternative hypotheses are then written down. In general, the null hypothesis is that the observed values follow the theoretical distribution; the alternative hypothesis is that the observed values do not follow the theoretical distribution.

4 Calculate expected frequencies, combining classes if frequencies are less than 5.

5 Find v, the number of degrees of freedom.
- for n classes, $v = n - 1$
- for each parameter that is estimated from the given data, subtract 1 further from v.

6 The critical value of χ^2 is then found from tables and compared to the value of X^2 found by comparing the observed data with the expected data. To do this use the formula for the test statistic

$$X^2 = \sum \frac{(O_i - E_i)^2}{E_i},$$

where O_i are the observed frequencies and E_i are the expected frequencies. The distribution of X^2 is approximated by the χ^2 distribution.

7 Reject or accept the null hypothesis accordingly.

The critical region of the χ^2 distribution

The graph for the χ^2 distribution varies with the number of degrees of freedom, v.

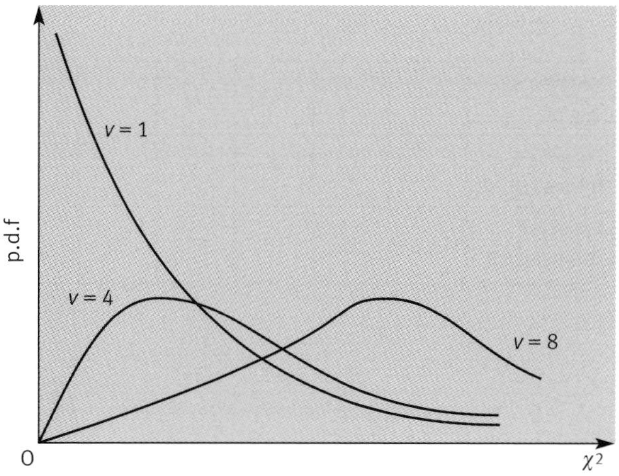

As the test statistic, $X^2 = \sum \frac{(O_i - E_i)^2}{E_i}$, increases as the differences between O_i and E_i increase, accept H_0 when the test statistic is less than the critical value and reject H_0 when it is greater.

The critical region for a 5% significance level is shown below on the χ^2 distribution for $v = 8$.

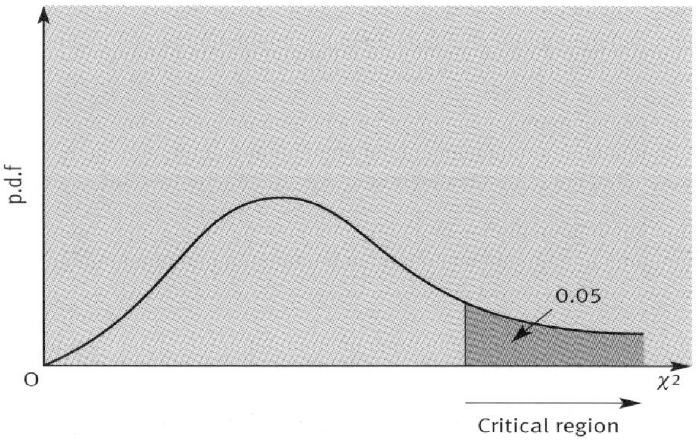

The χ^2 distribution and the discrete uniform distribution

Example

A die is rolled ninety times. The frequency of each score is shown in the table below.

Number on die, *n*	1	2	3	4	5	6
Observed frequency, O_i	22	12	18	9	17	12

Conduct a χ^2 test at a 5% significance level to test whether the die is fair. State your conclusions.

Solution

Firstly write down the null and alternative hypotheses:
H_0: The die is not biased.
H_1: The die is biased.
Use a discrete uniform distribution to find the expected frequencies for a fair die.

Number on die, *n*	1	2	3	4	5	6
Observed frequency, O_i	22	12	18	9	17	12
Expected frequency, E_i	15	15	15	15	15	15

Now use the formula

$$\sum\frac{(O_i - E_i)^2}{E_i} = \frac{(22-15)^2}{15} + \frac{(12-15)^2}{15} + \frac{(18-15)^2}{15} + \frac{(9-15)^2}{15} + \frac{(17-15)^2}{15} + \frac{(12-15)^2}{15}$$

$$= 7.733 \text{ (3 d.p.)}$$

The number of degrees of freedom, v, $=$ number of classes $-1 = 5$.
For $v = 5$, the χ^2 value at 5% is 11.070.
As $7.733 < 11.070$, accept H_0.

The χ^2 distribution and the binomial theorem

To calculate probabilities using the binomial distribution you need n and p. p may be given in the question or it may be estimated from the information given.
If p is not estimated, the number of degrees of freedom is $v =$ (number of classes after combining) $- 1$
If p is estimated from the given data, the number of degrees of freedom is v where
$v =$ (number of classes after combining) $- 2$.

Example

A botanist grows plants from seed. She plants them in trays of 6 to sell to shops. She expects that 30% will have purple flowers. Eighty trays are examined, and the number of purple flowers in each tray is shown below.

Number of purple flowers	0	1	2	3	4	5	6
Number of trays	8	16	25	20	6	4	1

A possible model is thought to be B(6, 0.3). Conduct a goodness of fit test at the 5% significance level.

Solution

Let X be the number of plants with purple flowers in a tray.
H_0: $X \sim B(6, 0.3)$
H_1: X does not have the distribution B(6, 0.3)
$P(X = 0) = {}^6C_0 0.3^0\, 0.7^6 = 0.1176$ (4 d.p.)
$P(X = 1) = {}^6C_1 0.3^1\, 0.7^5 = 0.3025$ (4 d.p.)
$P(X = 2) = {}^6C_2 0.3^2\, 0.7^4 = 0.3241$ (4 d.p.) etc.
Use these to calculate the table for expected values:

Number of purple flowers	**Observed frequencies, O_i**	**Probability (4 d.p.)**	**Expected frequencies, E_i = Probability × 80 (1 d.p.)**
0	8	0.1176	9.4
1	16	0.3025	24.2
2	25	0.3241	25.9
3	20	0.1852	14.8
4	6	0.0595	4.8
5	4	0.0102	0.8
6	1	0.0007	0.1

Check that your probabilities total 1. (The column in the table sums to 0.9998, but this is acceptable because of rounding errors.) Also confirm that your expected values have the same sum as the observed values, in this case 80.

Combine the last 3 classes to make the expected frequency greater than 5.

Number of purple flowers	Observed frequency, O_i	Expected frequency, E_i
0	8	9.4
1	16	24.2
2	25	25.9
3	20	14.8
4 or more	11	5.7

To calculate χ^2, use a table to help.

O_i	E_i	$\frac{(O_i - E_i)^2}{E_i}$
8	9.4	0.208...
16	24.2	2.778...
25	25.9	0.031...
20	14.8	1.827...
11	5.7	4.928...
$\sum O_i = 80$	$\sum E_i = 80$	$\sum \frac{(O_i - E_i)^2}{E_i} = 9.773$ (3 d.p.)

As there are 5 classes, the number of degrees of freedom, v, is $5 - 1 = 4$
The critical value of χ^2 at 5% is 9.488, so reject H_0 at the 5% level.

The χ^2 distribution and the Poisson distribution

If the mean is given, the number of degrees of freedom, v, is
(number of classes after combining) -1.
If the mean is estimated using the data, the number of degrees of freedom is (number of classes after combining) -2.

Example

The number of hurricanes hitting a certain stretch of coastline per year is said to be modelled by a Poisson distribution with parameter 1. The results of the last 50 years are summarised in the table.

Number of hurricanes	0	1	2	> 2
Frequency	14	22	10	4

Using a 5% level of significance test whether the Poisson distribution is a suitable model.

Solution

Let X be the number of hurricanes per year.
H_0: X follows a Poisson distribution with $\lambda = 1$.
H_1: X does not follow this Poisson distribution.
Under $H_0, X \sim Po(1)$

$$P(X = 0) = \frac{e^{-1}1^0}{0!} = 0.3679 \text{ (4 d.p.)}$$

Expected frequency $= 50 \times 0.3679 = 18.4$ (1 d.p.)

$$P(X = 1) = \frac{e^{-1}1^1}{1!} = 0.3679$$

Expected frequency $= 50 \times 0.3679 = 18.4$ (1 d.p.)

$$P(X = 2) = \frac{e^{-1}1^2}{2!} = 0.1839$$

Expected frequency $= 50 \times 0.1839 = 9.2$ (1 d.p.)

$P(X > 2)$
$= 1 - (P(X = 0) + P(X = 1) + P(X = 2))$
$= 1 - 0.9197 = 0.0803$
Expected frequency $= 50 \times 0.0803 = 4.0$ (1 d.p.)

As the expected frequency for $X > 2$ is less than 5, combine it with $X = 2$. The expected frequency for $X \geqslant 2$ is $9.2 + 4.0 = 13.2$.

Number of hurricanes	0	1	$\geqslant 2$
Frequency, O_i	14	22	14
Expected frequency, E_i	18.4	18.4	13.2

O_i	E_i	$\frac{(O_i - E_i)^2}{E_i}$
14	18.4	1.052...
22	18.4	0.704...
14	13.2	0.048...
$\sum O_i = 50$	$\sum E_i = 50$	$\sum \frac{(O_i - E_i)^2}{E_i} = 1.805$ (3 d.p.)

Number of degrees of freedom,
$v =$ number of classes $- 1 = 2$.
The critical value of χ^2 at the 5% level of significance is 5.991.

As $1.801 < 5.991$, accept H_0.

The χ^2 distribution and the normal distribution

Example

The weights of 150 bananas were taken and the results are summarised in the table below.

Weight (grams)	Frequency
75–99	15
100–124	17
125–149	60
150–174	37
175–199	10
200–224	11

a Test at the 5% significance level whether or not the weights of bananas could be modelled by a normal distribution with mean 150 and standard deviation 35.

b Describe how you would modify this test if the mean and variance were unknown.

Solution

a Let X be the weight of a banana.
H_0: The distribution $N(150, 35^2)$ is a suitable model.
H_1: The distribution $N(150, 35^2)$ is not a suitable model.
To ensure that all frequencies sum to 1, make the lower bound of the first group $-\infty$, even though there are no values of X less than 74.5, and make the upper bound of the last class ∞ even though there are no values greater than 224.5. As the weight has been rounded to the nearest gram, take the first class as $X < 99.5$,
the second as $99.5 < X < 124.5$,
the third as $124.5 < X < 149.5$, etc.
The final interval should be $X > 199.5$.

Weight (X)	Probability	Expected frequency = Probability × n
$X < 99.5$	0.0746	11.2
$99.5 < X < 124.5$	0.1586	23.8
$124.5 < X < 149.5$	0.2612	39.2
$149.5 < X < 174.5$	0.2637	39.6
$174.5 < X < 199.5$	0.1633	24.5
$X > 199.5$	0.0786	11.8

As none of the expected frequencies is less than 5, there is no need to combine adjacent classes.
$v =$ (number of classes) $- 1$ since μ and σ are given.

Weight (X)	O_i	E_i	$\frac{(O_i - E_i)^2}{E_i}$
75–99	15	11.2	1.2893
100–124	17	23.8	1.9429
125–149	60	39.2	11.0367
150–174	37	39.6	0.1707
175–199	10	24.5	8.5816
200–224	11	11.8	0.0542
	$\sum O_i = 150$	$\sum E_i = 150$	$\sum \frac{(O_i - E_i)^2}{E_i} = 23.075$ (3 d.p.)

As the critical value of χ^2 at 5% for 5 degrees of freedom is 11.070, reject H_0 and accept H_1: there is no evidence of the distribution N(150.35) being a suitable model for the data.

b If μ and σ were not given, then
$v =$ (number of classes) $- 3$
Find estimates for the mean and standard deviation from the data.
For the mean, use $E(X) = \frac{\sum fx}{\sum f} = 144.2$.
For the standard deviation, use

$$\sqrt{\frac{\sum x^2 - nx^2}{n - 1}} = 31.77$$

Summary of the degrees of freedom for different distributions

Distribution	Classes*	Conditions	v
Binomial	n	p known p estimated from data	$n-1$ $n-2$
Poisson	n	λ known λ unknown	$n-1$ $n-2$
Normal	n	μ, σ known μ known, σ unknown μ unknown, σ unknown	$n-1$ $n-2$ $n-3$

*Classes after merging.

Questions

1 A group of 100 students each threw five slices of buttered toast to test whether they landed on the buttered side. They each recorded the number of times the toast landed on its buttered side. It is suggested that the data can be modelled by the binomial distribution.

Number landing buttered side down	0	1	2	3	4	5
Frequency	0	6	25	38	25	6

a i Find the mean from the data.

ii Find an estimate for the probability of a slice of toast landing buttered side down.

b Carry out a χ^2 test at the 5% level to determine whether the proposed model should be accepted.

2 The numbers of birds visiting a feeder were counted in 5-minute intervals. The results are shown in the table below.

Number of birds	0	1	2	3	4	5	more than 5
Frequency	8	15	19	11	5	2	0

a It is thought that these data follow a Poisson distribution with parameter 2. Use a χ^2 test at the 5% level to test this hypothesis.

b Describe how you would modify this test if the mean were unknown.

3 A child psychologist undertook a study to examine the age at which a child says its first recognisable words. The results, in months are shown below:

Age (months)	11–	13–	15–	16–	17–	18–	20–22
Frequency	2	11	18	26	21	10	2

The psychologist believes that the data follow a normal distribution with mean 16.5 months and standard deviation 1.67 months. Use a χ^2 test at 5% level to test this assertion.

Answers

1a i 3 **ii** $np = 3 \Rightarrow 5p = 3 \Rightarrow p = 0.6$

b

Number	0–1	2	3	4	5
O_i	6	25	38	25	6
Probability	0.087	0.230	0.346	0.259	0.078
E_i	8.68	23.0	34.6	25.9	7.8

$\sum \frac{(O_i - E_i)^2}{E_i} = 1.79$ (2 d.p.)

Number of degrees of freedom, $v = n - 2 = 3$

The critical value of χ^2 at 3 degrees of freedom = 7.815.

Accept H_0: the binomial distribution may be used to model these data.

2 Combine the last 3 classes to ensure that the expected value of each class is at least 5:

O_i	8	15	19	11	7
E_i	8.12	16.24	16.24	10.82	8.58

a $\sum \frac{(O_i - E_i)^2}{E_i} = 0.859$

Critical value of $\chi^2 = 9.488$, so accept H_0: there is evidence to show that the data can be modelled by $P_o(2)$.

b The mean would be calculated from the data, and the number of degrees of freedom would be one less ($n - 2 = 3$).

3

x	O_i	E_i
$x < 15$	13	16.61
$15 < x < 16$	18	17.80
$16 < x < 17$	26	21.18
$17 < x < 18$	21	17.80
$x > 18$	12	16.61

$\sum \frac{(O_i - E_i)^2}{E_i} = 3.739$ (3 d.p.)

The critical value at 5% for 4 degrees of freedom is 9.488, so accept H_0: the data can be modelled by $N(16.5, 1.67^2)$.

The χ^2 test for independence in a contingency table

Procedure for performing a χ^2 test for independence in a contingency table

1 Write the null and alternative hypotheses as follows:

H_0: the two factors are independent

H_1: they are not independent

2 Calculate row totals, column totals and the grand total using the observed data.

3 Calculate the expected frequency E for each cell using

$$E = \frac{(\text{row total}) \times (\text{column total})}{\text{grand total}}$$

Construct a separate table for the expected frequencies.

If any cells have an expected frequency of less than 5, then combine any adjacent cells in both the expected and observed tables.

4 Calculate the degrees of freedom, v, using the formula $v = (h - 1)(k - 1)$ for an h by k contingency table.

5 Calculate χ^2 using $\chi^2 = \sum \frac{(O_i - E_i)^2}{E_i}$

For a 2×2 contingency table, use Yates' continuity correction where

$$\chi^2 = \sum \frac{(|O_i - E_i| - 0.5)^2}{E_i}$$

6 Look up the critical value of χ^2 in the tables and accept or reject H_0 accordingly.

Example

A cafe records the number of sales of ice creams sold to men, women and children on Saturdays and Sundays over a four week month. The results are shown in the table below.

	Saturday	Sunday
Males	124	147
Females	89	141
Children	266	355

Use the χ^2 test to assess whether or not there is significant difference between the ice creams sold on Saturdays and Sundays and the type of customer. Use a 5% significance level.

Solution

H_0: The numbers of ice creams sold are independent of the day and the type of customer.
H_1: the numbers of ice creams sold are not independent of the day and the type of customer.
Calculate row and column totals and the grand total.

	Saturday	Sunday	Total
Males	124	147	271
Females	89	141	230
Children	266	355	621
Total	479	643	1122

Calculate the table for expected values: for example, the expected number of ice creams sold to males on Sunday $= \dfrac{271 \times 643}{1122} = 155.3$ (1 d.p.)

	Saturday	Sunday	Total
Males	115.7	155.3	271
Females	98.2	131.8	230
Children	265.1	355.9	621
Total	479	643	1122

The number of degrees of freedom
$=$ (no. of rows $- 1) \times$ (no. of columns $- 1) = 2$

O_i	E_i	$\dfrac{(O_i - E_i)^2}{E_i}$
124	115.7	0.595...
147	155.3	0.443...
89	98.2	0.861...
141	131.8	0.642...
266	265.1	0.003...
355	355.9	0.002...
$\sum O_i = 1122$	$\sum E_i = 1122$	$\sum \dfrac{(O_i - E_i)^2}{E_i} = 2.548$ (3 d.p.)

As this is smaller than the critical value of 5.991, accept H_0 at the 5% significance level.

Example

A survey was taken to investigate whether or not there was any association between people being left-handed and passing a literacy test.

	Pass	Fail
Right-handed	46	33
Left-handed	72	35

Stating your hypotheses, test whether or not there is any association between left-handedness and literacy. Use a 5% level of significance.

Solution

H_0: There is no connection between left-handedness and literacy
H_1: There is a connection between left-handedness and literacy

	Pass	Fail	Total
Right-handed	46	33	79
Left-handed	72	35	107
Total	118	68	186

The expected table is shown below.

	Pass	Fail	Total
Right-handed	50.1	28.9	79
Left-handed	67.9	39.1	107
Total	118	68	186

This is a 2 by 2 table, so Yates' continuity correction should be used.

The number of degrees of freedom for a 2 by 2 table is $(2 - 1) \times (2 - 1) = 1$.
The critical value of χ_1^2 (5%) is 3.841.

O_i	E_i	$\dfrac{(\lvert O_i - E_i\rvert - 0.5)^2}{E_i}$
46	50.1	0.258...
33	28.9	0.448...
72	67.9	0.190...
35	39.1	0.331...
$\sum O_i = 186$	$\sum E_i = 186$	$\sum \dfrac{(\lvert O_i - E_i\rvert - 0.5)^2}{E_i} = 1.229$ (3 d.p.)

As $\sum \dfrac{(\lvert O_i - E_i\rvert - 0.5)^2}{E_i} < 3.841$, accept H_0:
there is no reason to believe that there is an association between left-handedness and literacy.

Questions

1 A χ^2 test for independence was performed on a 4×5 contingency table. No cells were combined and the result of $\sum \frac{(O_i - E_i)^2}{E_i} = 16.2$ was obtained. Test, at the 5% significance level, whether or not there is any evidence that the two factors of the contingency table are independent.

2 After an advertising campaign about the dangers of smoking, 200 smokers were asked whether they were going to attempt to 'kick the habit.' The results are summarised in the contingency table below.

	Yes	**No**
Male	67	23
Female	48	62

Stating clearly your hypotheses, test whether or not there is any association between gender and the inclination to give up smoking. Use a 10% level of significance.

3 Samples of trees were taken from two forests. The species of each tree was noted and classified into the following groups: oak, elm and other. The results are summarised in the table below.

		Forest	
		Shelby	Turford
Species	Oak	39	27
	Elm	18	21
	Other	13	7

Use a 5% significance level to see whether or not there is any association between the forests and the composition of species of trees within them.

Answers

1 Critical value = 21.026, so accept the hull hypothesis that there is no correlation between the two factors on the contingency table.

2 H_0: there is no correlation between gender and the desire to give up smoking

H_1: there is correlation between gender and the desire to give up smoking

Expected values	**Yes**	**No**	**Total**
Male	51.75	38.25	90
Female	63.25	46.75	110
Total	115	85	200

O_i	E_i	$\frac{(\lvert O_i - E_i \rvert - 0.5)^2}{E_i}$
67	51.75	4.204…
23	38.25	5.687…
48	63.25	3.439…
62	46.75	4.653…
$\sum O_i = 200$	$\sum E_i = 200$	$\sum \frac{(\lvert O_i - E_i \rvert - 0.5)^2}{E_i} = 17.985$ (3 d.p.)

$\sum \frac{(\lvert O_i - E_i \rvert - 0.5)^2}{E_i} = 17.985$, the critical value for 1 degree of freedom = 2.71, so reject H_0 at 5% level.

3

O_i	E_i	$\frac{(O_i - E_i)^2}{E_i}$
39	36.96	0.112…
27	29.04	0.143…
18	21.84	0.675…
21	17.16	0.859…
13	11.2	0.289…
7	8.8	0.368…
$\sum O_i = 125$	$\sum E_i = 125$	$\sum \frac{(O_i - E_i)^2}{E_i} = 2.448$ (3 d.p.)

$\sum \frac{(O_i - E_i)^2}{E_i} = 2.448$, critical value for $\chi_2^2 = 5.991$, so accept the null hypothesis that there is no correlation between the forests and the composition of trees.

Take a break

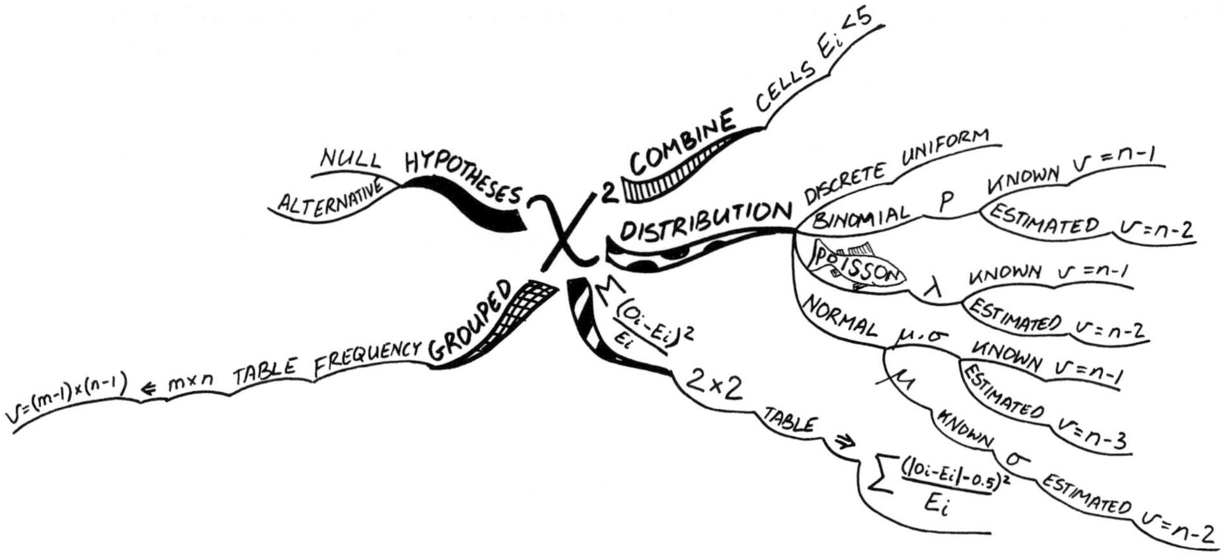

Review

1 Each year on the 30th July, the number of hours of sunlight on that day, S, is measured. The records for a random selection of 10 years are given below.

5.3, 2.1, 8.8, 9.0, 7.0, 10.2, 7.7, 9.3, 3.2, 10.3

a Find unbiased estimates of the mean and variance of S.

b Assuming the number of sunlight hours has a normal distribution, find a 90% confidence interval for the mean of S.

2 The random variable X has a normal distribution with mean μ and standard deviation 3.
The mean of X is thought to be 11. A random sample of 36 observations is taken and the sample mean $\bar{X}$ is calculated in order to test whether the mean is greater than 11.

a Using a 5% level of significance, find the critical region for $\bar{X}$.

b Given that $\mu = 12.3$, find the probability of a type II error occurring.

3 The manager of a factory that makes teddy bears takes a random sample of five from the production line. The sample had the following weights, in grams:

550, 561, 572, 543, 566

a Find an unbiased estimate for
i the mean **ii** the variance of the weights of the bears.

b Over a long period of time, the manager knew that the standard deviation of the weights of the bears was 15 grams. Using this value for the standard deviation of the population, find a 95% confidence interval for the mean of the sample.

4 The number of accidents at a road junction per month has a Poisson distribution with parameter 8. In the first month after a speed camera was installed, there were 3 accidents.

a State the appropriate null and alternative hypotheses to test whether the camera has reduced the number of accidents.

b Find the critical region at the 5% level to test the null hypothesis.

c Find the probability of a Type I error using your critical region.

d Given that, after the camera was installed, the mean number of accidents was in fact 2 accidents per month, find the probability of a Type II error.

5 Pipes are cut by two machines. The lengths of the components produced by both machines are normally distributed. The lengths of the pipes cut by machine A are known to have a standard deviation of 0.12 cm while for machine B the standard deviation is 0.15 cm, but they should both produce pipes with the same mean length.

A random sample of eight components from machine A were found to have the following lengths (in cm):

5.62, 5.83, 5.77, 5.74, 5.66, 5.80, 5.69, 5.71.

A random sample of six components from machine B were found to have the following lengths (in cm):

5.67, 5.55, 5.60, 5.54, 5.72, 5.68.

a State your null and alternative hypotheses clearly.

b Estimate, using a 5% significance level, whether the difference between the means is significant.

6 A coin is tossed 20 times and shows a head 14 times.

a Using a 5% significance level, test the null hypothesis that the coin is unbiased against the alternative hypothesis that the coin is biased towards throwing a head.

b Find the probability of a Type I error.

c Given that the coin is biased with the probability of scoring a head on any throw being 0.7, find the probability of a Type II error.

7 Perform a χ^2 test to investigate whether or not the following data is drawn from a binomial distribution with $n = 5$. Use a 5% level of significance.

x	0	1	2	3	4	5
Frequency	0	6	15	31	33	15

8 One hundred drivers were asked how many accidents they had had over the last three years. The results are summarised in the table below.

Number of accidents	0	1	2	3	4	5 or more
Frequency	34	40	18	6	2	0

Use a χ^2 test at the 5% level to test whether the data can be modelled by a Poisson distribution.

9 The marks awarded for Art A-level by 3 different examiners were assessed. The grades awarded by the different examiners were as shown in the table.

		Examiner X	**Examiner Y**	**Examiner Z**
Grades awarded	C or above	64	41	52
	D or below	48	61	34

Test the hypothesis that the proportion of grades (in the two bands) awarded by the examiners is the same. Use a 10% level of significance.

Answer

1a mean = 7.29, variance = 8.294 (3 d.p.)

b As the unbiased estimator of the variance has been calculated, use the formula

$$t_{n-1} = \frac{\bar{x} - \mu}{\hat{\sigma}/\sqrt{n}}$$

$5.62 < \mu < 8.96$.

2a $\bar{X} > 11.82$ (2 d.p.)

b P(Type II error) = P(accept H_0/H_1 is true)

$= P(\bar{X} < 11.82 / \bar{X} \sim N(12.3, 0.25))$

$= 0.1685$ (4 d.p.).

3ai 558.4 **ii** 139.3 **b** (545.3, 571.5).

4a $H_0: \lambda = 8, H_1: \lambda < 8$ **b** If X is the number of accidents per month, $X \leqslant 3$. **c** 0.0424 **d** $P(X \geqslant 4/\lambda = 2) = 0.1429$.

5a Let μ_A and μ_B be the population means of machines A and B respectively.

$H_0: \mu_A = \mu_B$

$H_1: \mu_A \neq \mu_B$

$$z = \frac{5.7275 - 5.6267}{\sqrt{\frac{0.12^2}{8} + \frac{0.15^2}{6}}} = 1.35$$

The critical value of z is 1.96.

As $1.35 < 1.96$, the difference between the means is not significant, so accept H_0.

6a Let X be the number of heads thrown.

$P(X \geqslant 14) = 0.0577$.

Accept H_0 at the 5% level.

b The critical region is $X \geqslant 15$

$P(X \geqslant 15) = 0.0207$

c Let Y be the probability of a tail.

$p = 0.3$

$P(X \leqslant 14) = P(Y \geqslant 6) = 0.6836$ (4 d.p.)

7 $\sum \frac{(O_i - E_i)^2}{E_i} = 0.24$

$\chi_2^2 = 5.991$, so accept H_0: the distribution is binomial.

8 From the data, the estimated mean = 1.02

Number of accidents	0	1	2	3 or more
O_i	34	40	18	8
Probability	0.361	0.368	0.188	0.083
E_i	36.1	36.8	18.8	8.3

$\sum \frac{(O_i - E_i)^2}{E_i} = 0.45$

The degrees of freedom $= n - 2 = 2$

${\chi_2}^2 = 5.991$, so accept H_0: the distribution is Poisson.

9 $\sum \frac{(O_i - E_i)^2}{E_i} = 9.34$

Critical value of ${\chi_2}^2 = 4.605$, so reject H_0: there is evidence of correlation between the grades awarded and the different examiners.

PURE MATHEMATICS
Algebraic division 47
Algebraic fractions 5
Angle between two vectors 82
Approximate solution of equations 79
Approximations using series 77
Arc length 25
Area bounded by a curve 42
Area by integration 42
Area of sector 25
Arithmetic progression 22
Asymptote 5

Base of a logarithm 14
Binomial theorem 76

Chain rule 61
Circle, equation of 51
Coefficient 5
Common difference 22
Common ratio 22
Comparing coefficients 12
Complementary angle 5
Completing the square 12
Compound angle identities 57
Compound transformations 19
Constant of integration 41, 66
Cosecant 56
Cotangent 56
Counter example 46
Coverup method 49
Cubic expression 5
Cubic graphs 6

Decreasing function 37
Definite integral 42
Demonstration 45
Derivative 37
Derivatives of trig functions 61
Differential equations 73
Differentiating a function of a function 61
Differentiating a product 61
Differentiating a quotient 61
Differentiating exponential functions 37, 61
Differentiating a log function 37, 61
Differentiating implicit functions 63
Differentiating parametric equations 62
Direct proof 45
Discriminant 5, 6
Distinct roots 6
Dividend 5
Divisor 5
Domain 17
Double angle identities 57

Ellipse 53
Equation of a circle 51
Equation of a line 9, 82
Equations 5, 30, 79
Expansion of brackets 13
Exponent 5
Exponential decay 74
Exponential function 28
Exponential growth 74

Factor theorem 13, 48
First order derivative 37
Formula for solving a quadratic equation 5
Function 17
Function of a function 17

Geometric progression 22
Gradient of a line 9
Gradient of a curve 37, 38

Hyperbola 53

Identity 5
Implicit function 63
Increasing function 37
Indefinite integral 42
Inequalities 30
Inflexion 38
Integer 5
Integration 41
Integration by parts 67
Integration by substitution 67
Integration of fractions 68
Integration of products 67
Integration of trig functions 69
Intersection of lines in 3-D 83
Inverse function 18
Inverse trig functions 56
Irrational number 5
Iteration 79

Laws of logarithms 14
Linear approximation 77
Linear expression 5
Location of a root of an equation 79
Logarithmic function 28
Logarithms 14

Maximum value 38
Minimum value 38
Modulus function 28

Natural number, e 14
Normal to a curve 38

One-way stretch 19
Ordinate 5

Parabola 6
Parallel lines 9
Parametric equations 53
Parametric equations of a circle 53
Parametric equations of a hyperbola 53
Parametric equations of an ellipse 53
Partial fractions 48
Pascal's triangle 13
Perpendicular lines 9
Point of inflexion 38
Polynomial 5
Proof 45
Proof by contradiction 45
Proper fraction 47

Quadratic equations 6
Quadratic expression 5
Quadratic graph 6
Quotient 5

Radian 25
Range of a function 17
Rational function 47
Rational number 5
Rationalising a denominator 14
Reciprocal trig functions 56
Reflection 19
Remainder theorem 48
Repeated factor 7
Repeated roots 6
Roots 5

Scalar product 82
Secant 56
Second order derivative 37
Separating the variables 74
Sequence 22
Series 22
Simultaneous equations 6
Skew lines 83
Stationary value 38
Subject of a formula 5
Subtend 5
Sum of an AP 22
Sum of a GP 22
Sum of the first n natural numbers 22
Sum to infinity 22
Supplementary angles 5
Surds 12, 14

Tangent to a curve 38
Tangents to circles 52
Transforming curves 19
Translation 19
Trapezium rule 70
Trig equations 33, 59
Trig functions 33
Trig identities 33, 57
Trig ratios 5

Variables separable 74
Vector equation of a line 82
Vectors 81
Volumes of revolution 69

MECHANICS
Acceleration as a function of displacement 157
Acceleration as a function of time 155
Acceleration due to gravity 101
Acceleration of a body describing a circle 140, 145
Air resistance 90
Amplitude of SHM 160
Angle of friction 97
Angular speed 140
Associated circular motion 160

Banked tracks 143

Centre of gravity 125, 126
Centre of mass 125
Centre of mass by integration 167
Centre of mass of a hemisphere 168
Centre of mass of a prism 167
Centre of mass of a right cone 168
Centre of mass of a triangle 125
Centre of mass of rigid body 166
Circular motion 140, 145
Coefficient of friction 97
Coefficient of restitution 135
Collision 112, 135
Components 94
Conditions for equilibrium 131
Conical pendulum 141
Connected particles 104
Conservation of mechanical energy 108, 145, 152
Conservation of momentum 112
Constant acceleration 100
Contact force 90

Design speed 143
Displacement 100
Displacement 100, 155
Distance 100
Driving force 90, 109

Elastic limit 151
Elastic potential energy 152
Elastic springs 151
Energy 107
Energy in a stretched elastic string 152
Equation of motion 102
Equations for simple harmonic motion 160
Equations of motion for constant acceleration 101
Equations of motion of a projectile 116
Eqilibrium of an object 130, 131
Equilibrium of concurrent forces 96

Fixed object 90, 112
Force 90
Forces of attachment 90
Friction 96

Gravity 101
Greatest height of a projectile 116

Hooke's law 151

Impact 112, 135
Impulse 112
Impulse in a jerking string 113

Joule 107

Kinetic energy 107, 112

Lamina suspended from a point 127
Like forces 121
Limiting friction 97

Mass 102, 125
Mechanical energy 107, 108
Modelling 90, 91, 103
Modulus of elasticity 151
Moment of a force 120
Momentum 112
Motion in a horizontal circle 140
Motion in a straight line 100
Motion in a vertical circle 145

Natural Length 151
Newton 102
Newton's law of restitution 135
Newton's law 102, 155

Oscillation 160, 162, 163

Parallel forces 121
Path of a projectile 116
Period of SHM 160
Perpendicular components 94
Potential energy 107
Power 109
Projectile 116
Pumps 108

Radial component of acceleration 145
Range of a projectile 116
Resolving forces 95
Resultant force 94, 95
Resultant moment 120

Simple harmonic motion 160
Springs 151
Stability of a lamina 128, 130
Suspended laminas 127
Suspended bodies 168

Tangential component of acceleration 145
Tension in a string 90, 104, 151
Time of flight of a projectile 116
Turning effect 120

Unlike forces 121

Variable acceleration in 2-D 156
Variable acceleration in 3-D 156
Vector 81, 94
Velocity 100, 155

Watt 109
Weight 90
Work 107

STATISTICS
Alternative hypothesis 203, 230
Approximations 213, 219, 220
Arithmetic mean 180
Averages 180

Back-to-back stem and leaf diagrams 174
Binomial distribution 209
Bi-variate distribution 202
Box and whisker plots 181

Census 172
Central limit theorem 224
Central tendency 180
Chi-squared test for goodness-of-fit 239, 240, 241, 242
Chi-squared test for contingency tables 243
Class boundaries 175
Class width 175
Coding 183
Combinations 192
Conditional probability 188
Confidence intervals 225
Contingency tables 243
Continuity correction 216
Continuous random variable 196
Continuous uniform distribution 199
Continuous variate 172
Correlation 202
Critical region 203, 230, 239
Critical value 203, 230
Cumulative binomial probabilities 209
Cumulative distribution function 196
Cumulative frequencies 175
Cumulative frequency polygon 175
Cumulative Poisson probabilities 209

Deciles 181
Degrees of freedom 239, 242
Discrete random variable 196
Discrete variate 172

Estimation of unbiased population parameters 223
Expected value 183, 196

Frequency density 176

Goodness-of-fit tests 239, 240, 241, 242
Grouped data 175

Histograms 176
Hypothesis testing 203, 230, 231, 233, 234, 235

Independent events 189
Interpolation 182
Interquartile range 181

Linear coding 183
Linear function of a random variable 197
Linear regression 205
Lower quartile 180

Mean 183
Mean of the binomial distribution 209
Mean of the continuous uniform distribution 200
Mean of the Poisson distribution 209

Median 180, 197
Mode 180, 197
Mutually exclusive events 189

Negative skew 181
Normal approximation to a binomial distribution 220
Normal approximation to a Poisson distribution 220
Normal distribution 216
Null hypothesis 203, 230

One-tailed test 203, 230
Outliers 181

Parameter of the Poisson distribution 209
Parameters of binomial distribution 209
Percentiles 181
Permutations 191
Poison approximation to a binomial distribution 213
Poisson distribution 211
Population 172
Positive skew 181
Probability function 196
Probability density function 196
Product moment correlation coefficient 202
Proportion of the binomial distribution 235

Qualitative variate 172
Quantitative variate 172
Quantiles 181
Quartiles 180

Random variable 196
Rectangular distribution 199
Regression 205
Regression line of y on x 206

Sample 172
Sampling element 172
Sampling frame 172
Sampling units 172
Semi-interquartile range 181
Significance level 203, 230
Skew 181
Spearman's rank correlation coefficient 202, 204
Standard deviation 181, 183
Standard error of the mean 224
Standard normal distribution 216
Standardising values 216
Statistical model 172
Stem and leaf diagrams 174
Sum of normal random variables 219
Sum of two independent Poisson distributions 213

t-distribution 227
Tree diagrams 189
Two-tailed test 203, 230
Type I error 234
Type II error 234

Unbiased estimate of population mean 223
Unbiased estimate of population variance 223
Upper quartile 180

Variance 181, 183, 196
Variance of the binomial distribution 209
Variance of the continuous uniform distribution 200
Variance of the Poisson distribution 209
Variate 172
Venn diagrams 187

Width of a confidence interval 225

Yates' continuity correction 243